Sandy Diz

Congratulations

You have just purchased a book that was developed by hospitality industry experts.

Keep this book — you will use it throughout your career.

HOSPITALITY INDUSTRY MANAGERIAL ACCOUNTING

Educational Institute Books

CONVENTION MANAGEMENT & SERVICE
Frank W. Berkman/David C. Dorf/Leonard R. Oakes

HOSPITALITY FOR SALE
C. DeWitt Coffman

UNIFORM SYSTEM OF ACCOUNTS AND EXPENSE DICTIONARY FOR SMALL HOTELS,
MOTELS, AND MOTOR HOTELS
Revised Edition

RESORT DEVELOPMENT AND MANAGEMENT
Chuck Y. Gee

PLANNING AND CONTROL FOR FOOD AND BEVERAGE OPERATIONS, Second Edition
Jack D. Ninemeier

STRATEGIC MARKETING PLANNING IN THE HOSPITALITY INDUSTRY: A BOOK OF READINGS
Edited by Robert L. Blomstrom

TRAINING FOR THE HOSPITALITY INDUSTRY
Lewis C. Forrest, Jr.

UNDERSTANDING HOTEL/MOTEL LAW
Jack P. Jefferies

SUPERVISION IN THE HOSPITALITY INDUSTRY
John P. Daschler/Jack D. Ninemeier

SANITATION MANAGEMENT: STRATEGIES FOR SUCCESS
Ronald F. Cichy

ENERGY MANAGEMENT
Robert E. Aulbach

PRINCIPLES OF FOOD AND BEVERAGE OPERATIONS
Jack D. Ninemeier

MANAGING FRONT OFFICE OPERATIONS
Charles E. Steadmon

STRATEGIC HOTEL/MOTEL MARKETING, Revised Edition
Christopher W.L. Hart/David A. Troy

MANAGING SERVICE IN FOOD AND BEVERAGE OPERATIONS
Anthony M. Rey/Ferdinand Wieland

THE LODGING AND FOOD SERVICE INDUSTRY
Gerald W. Lattin

SECURITY AND LOSS PREVENTION MANAGEMENT
Raymond C. Ellis, Jr. & the Security Committee of AH&MA

HOSPITALITY INDUSTRY MANAGERIAL ACCOUNTING
Raymond S. Schmidgall

PURCHASING FOR HOSPITALITY OPERATIONS
William B. Virts

UNDERSTANDING HOSPITALITY ACCOUNTING I
Raymond Cote

THE ART AND SCIENCE OF HOSPITALITY MANAGEMENT
Jerome J. Vallen/James R. Abbey

MANAGING COMPUTERS IN THE HOSPITALITY INDUSTRY
Michael L. Kasavana/John J. Cahill

MANAGING HOSPITALITY ENGINEERING SYSTEMS
Michael H. Redlin/David M. Stipanuk

HOSPITALITY INDUSTRY MANAGERIAL ACCOUNTING

Raymond S. Schmidgall, Ph.D., CPA

the EDUCATIONAL INSTITUTE
OF THE AMERICAN HOTEL & MOTEL ASSOCIATION

Disclaimer

The author, Raymond S. Schmidgall, is responsible for the contents of this publication. All views expressed herein are solely his and do not necessarily reflect the views of the Educational Institute of the American Hotel & Motel Association (the Institute) or the American Hotel & Motel Association (AH&MA). Nothing contained in this publication shall constitute an endorsement by the Institute or AH&MA of any information, opinion, procedure, or product mentioned, and the Institute and AH&MA disclaim any liability with respect to the use of any such information, procedure, or product, or reliance thereon.

Neither AH&MA nor the Institute make or recommend industry standards. Nothing in this publication shall be construed as a recommendation by the Institute or AH&MA to be adopted by, or binding upon, any member of the hospitality industry.

Library of Congress Cataloging-in-Publication Data
Schmidgall, Raymond S., 1945)
   Hospitality industry managerial accounting.

   Includes index.
   1. Hotels, taverns, etc.—Accounting. 2. Restaurants, lunch
rooms, etc.—Accounting. 3. Motels—Accounting. 4. Managerial
accounting. I. Title.
HF5686.H75S34 1986 647'.94'0681 86-19622
ISBN 0-86612-032-7

Editor: John Glazer
            George Glazer

Accredited by the Accrediting
Commission of the National
Home Study Council

Contents

Chapter 7   Food and Beverage Control.. **219**

Chapter 8   Basic Cost Concepts.. **251**

Preface

Hospitality Industry Managerial Accounting presents managerial accounting concepts and explains how they apply to specific operations within the hospitality industry. This book is written not only for managers in the hospitality industry, but also for hospitality students at both the two-year and four-year college levels. Readers of this textbook should already be familiar with basic accounting concepts and procedures, or have taken an introductory course in basic accounting.

Each chapter begins by posing a number of questions that managers in the hospitality industry may have regarding accounting concepts which will be developed within the chapter. At the close of each chapter there are a number of discussion questions and problems designed to challenge the reader's understanding of the accounting concepts covered within that chapter. Some chapters are followed by supplemental readings which present more detailed approaches to advanced managerial accounting concepts mentioned in the text.

In addition, computer applications of managerial accounting concepts appear throughout the text in sections prior to the chapter summaries. Readers who are unfamiliar with fundamental computer terminology may find it helpful to read Appendix B, "Essentials of Computer Systems."

The text consists of 16 chapters and begins with an overview of accounting in Chapter 1. Chapters 2 through 4 cover the three basic financial statements—the balance sheet, the income statement, and the statement of changes in financial position, respectively. While the presentations of the balance sheet and the statement of changes in financial position are similar to the coverage found in most financial accounting texts, the presentation of the income statement is based on various schedules from the *Uniform System of Accounts for Small Hotels, Motels, and Motor Hotels*.

Chapter 5 focuses on ratio analysis as a means of interpreting information reported on financial statements. For each ratio presented, the chapter outlines its purpose, the sources of data needed for the ratio's calculation, the formula by which it is calculated, and the interpretation of the ratio results from the varying viewpoints of owners, creditors, and managers.

Internal control and food and beverage control are the topics of Chapters 6 and 7, respectively. Chapter 6 presents basic requirements of internal accounting control for various accounting functions including cash receipts, cash disbursements, accounts receivable, accounts payable, payroll, inventories, fixed assets, and marketable securities. Chapter 7 focuses on characteristics of food and beverage control systems that help to maximize the profitability of hospitality operations.

Chapters 8, 9, and 10 cover basic cost concepts, cost-volume-profit analysis, and cost approaches to pricing. Chapter 8 presents the various types of costs and how managers can identify the relevant costs in particular decision-making situations. Chapter 9's discussion of cost-volume-profit analysis is presented in both equation and graphic form. In addition, this chapter discusses and illustrates the determination of a cash breakeven point. Chapter 10 takes a cost approach to pricing and includes pricing examples for food, beverages, and rooms.

Operations budgeting and forecasting sales are the subjects of Chapters 11 and 12, respectively. The operations budgeting chapter discusses how budgets are prepared, how budgets are used for controlling operations, and how the operations budgeting process may take different forms at multi-unit hospitality enterprises as compared with single properties. Chapter 12 focuses on basic mathematical models for forecasting sales. This chapter also presents hospitality industry examples of sales forecasting procedures at Stouffers Hotels, Canteen Corporation, and Pizza Hut.

Chapter 13 covers cash management and includes sections on cash budgeting and managing working capital. Capital budgeting is the subject of Chapter 14, and the capital budgeting models presented include payback, accounting rate of return, net present value, and internal rate of return.

The final two chapters deal with lease accounting and income taxes. Although both of these topics are generally found in financial accounting texts, they are addressed here because managers of hospitality operations should have some knowledge in each of these areas. The chapter on lease accounting includes illustrations of accounting for various types of leases, and the appendix to the chapter provides a sample lease document. The chapter on income taxes does not dwell on tax details. Instead, the chapter provides an overview of the elements of taxes, discusses tax avoidance, and presents the advantages and disadvantages of various forms of business organization from a tax point of view.

Writing this textbook has been a most challenging experience, and could not have been completed without the assistance of many industry personnel and several of my colleagues at the School of Hotel, Restaurant, and Institutional Management at Michigan State University.

I am most indebted to Joseph F. Cotter, Vice President of Development of The Sheraton Corporation, for his assistance in reviewing the manuscript, submitting outlines for several chapters, and supplying several exhibits. Other Sheraton personnel who assisted in the development of this book are: Brian Baker, Joseph Beatty, Peter Johnson, William Dewhurst, Jose Fardullia, Edward Gremlich, John Pignataro, and Ronald Sawyer.

Richard Brooks of Stouffers Hotels provided the primary input for the computerization sections of most chapters. Michael Kasavana provided Appendix B, "Essentials of Computer Systems." Julie Smith, my former graduate assistant and now a management consultant with Arthur Andersen & Co., was most helpful with reviewing the entire manuscript and providing several of the computerization illustrations.

Special thanks is in order for A. Paul Matteucci, Director of Internal Audits for Westin Hotel & Resorts, who supplied the internal questionnaire forms appended to Chapter 6.

The industry examples of sales forecasting were provided by Raymond Holmes, John Kuntz, and Alex Wilson of Stouffers Hotels;

Brian Cohen and Donald Finger of Canteen Corporation; and Donald Myer and Mark Willoughby of Pizza Hut, Inc.

My colleague, John Tarras, critically reviewed the chapter on taxes; and, another colleague, Jack Ninemeier, provided essential input for the food and beverage control chapter.

Wesley Byloff, while financial controller of Metro Hotels Corporation, reviewed the entire manuscript and provided several useful suggestions for improvement.

My wife, Barbara, spent hundreds of hours typing, editing, and retyping the manuscript. Her patience and dedication to this project are largely responsible for its completion.

Special Acknowledgments

The Educational Institute extends special appreciation to the International Association of Hospitality Accountants (IAHA) for encouraging and financially supporting the publication of this text.

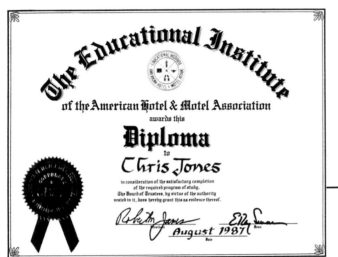

This text, used in conjunction with the corresponding student manual, is one in a series of courses available through the Educational Institute of the American Hotel & Motel Association leading to completion of a certification program. To date, nearly half a million individuals have benefited from Educational Institute programs, distinguishing the Institute as the world's largest educational center for the hospitality industry. For information regarding the available programs, please contact:

The Educational Institute of AH&MA
1407 South Harrison Road
P.O. Box 1240
East Lansing, Michigan 48826
(517) 353-5500

1 Introduction to Managerial Accounting

The hospitality industry is big and getting bigger! The knowledge required of a property manager is greater today than ever before, and it will be even greater tomorrow. Managerial accounting focuses upon those aspects of accounting over which hospitality managers are most concerned, such as internal financial statements, budgeting, internal control, and costs in decision-making. This introductory chapter will provide answers to many questions, including the following:

1. How does the hospitality industry differ from many other industries?

2. Why are food and beverage inventories relatively low in hospitality operations?

3. What are three aspects of seasonality in lodging properties?

4. What is the scope of the accounting function in hotels?

5. What are the major principles of accounting?

6. What are the various branches of accounting?

7. What are the steps in the accounting cycle?

8. Why are rooms, in essence, perishable inventory?

In this chapter, we will first present an overview of the hospitality industry and then focus on the accounting function within the industry. We will briefly review the principles, branches, and mechanics of accounting and discuss the accounting cycle.

Overview of the Hospitality Industry

Hospitality operations are part of the travel and tourism industry. Exhibit 1.1 shows travel and tourism as an umbrella industry covering five segments—lodging operations, transportation services, food and beverage operations, retail stores, and activities—all of which provide products and services for travelers. Most of these businesses also serve the residents of their own communities. In fact, whether any particular business in any one of these five segments considers itself part of the travel and tourism industry may depend on how much of its income is

Exhibit 1.1 Overview of Travel and Tourism Industry

Travel and Tourism Industry				
Lodging Operations	**Transportation Services**	**Food and Beverage Operations**	**Retail Stores**	**Activities**
Hotels	Ships	Restaurants	Gift Shops	Recreation
Motels	Airplanes	Lodging Properties	Souvenir Shops	Business
Motor Hotels	Autos	Retail Stores	Arts Crafts Shops	Entertainment
Resorts	Buses	Vending	Shopping Malls	Meetings
Camps	Trains	Catering	Markets	Study Trips
Parks	Bikes	Snack Bars	Miscellaneous Stores	Sporting Events
	Limousines	Cruise Ships		Ethnic Festivals
		Bars Taverns		Art Festivals
				Cultural Events
				Seasonal Festivals

derived from travelers, compared with how much is derived from local residents.

The hospitality industry comprises the lodging and food and beverage operations highlighted in Exhibit 1.1. In addition, there is another segment of food and beverage service typically classified as part of the hospitality industry which does not cater to the traveling public. Institutional (non-profit) food service operations are offered in health care and educational facilities, in business offices and industrial plants, and in the military; food service in correctional facilities, seminaries, and charitable organizations operate under the same basic principles of accounting and management as do their commercial counterparts.

The hospitality industry consists of several different types of service operations providing both products and services to its clients or guests. It includes hotels, motels, motor hotels, inns, quick service restaurants, fine dining restaurants, cafeterias, resorts, country clubs, and city clubs, to mention a few. Again, both the traveling public and local residents are served by these hospitality operations. This is particularly true of food and beverage operations, but many lodging properties market their room accommodations to local residents by promoting weekend "escape" packages.

Properties in the lodging segment of the hospitality industry range from the single-unit operation of fewer than 10 rooms to Holiday Inns, Inc., the largest chain operation in the United States with over 1,700 hotels totaling over 300,000 rooms. In 1986, there were over 50 mega-hotels in the United States, that is, hotels with more than 1,000 rooms each. Laventhol & Horwath (L&H) reports that there were 2.7 million rooms in 54,000 establishments in 1985, and they predict that in 1995 there will be 3 million rooms.[1] The differences among lodging operations are vast. At one extreme, there are budget hotels and motels providing only rooms, and at the other, luxury properties providing nearly every imaginable service a guest might desire.

There are also many different types of food service operations. Properties in the food and beverage segment of the hospitality industry range from the single-unit operation with only window service to the McDonald's Corporation, with over 9,000 restaurants in the McDonald's system throughout the world. In the club segment of the hospitality industry, there are clubs with fewer than 200 members and others with in excess of 12,500 members.

The dimension of the lodging and food service segments of the industry is reflected by the $41 billion spent at U.S. lodging facilities in a recent year, while approximately $178 billion was spent in food service establishments.[2] The total spending of these two segments of the hospitality industry approximated 5% of the total gross national product of the United States.

Exhibits 1.2 and 1.3 provide further insights into financial aspects of the hospitality industry. Exhibit 1.2 graphically illustrates what happens to the average revenue dollar in the lodging industry—where it came from and where it went. Exhibit 1.3 shows the same for the average revenue dollar in the food service industry. Notice that in the lodging industry, next to room rentals, food sales provide the second largest source of total revenue. Also, notice that the largest category of expense for lodging operations is payroll and related expenses, while for the restaurant industry, payroll costs are second only to the cost of food. Finally, note that for both lodging and food service operations, net income before taxes represents a relatively small percentage of total revenue.

Seasonality of Business

Although both manufacturing firms and hospitality operations frequently experience "seasonal" fluctuations in sales volume, hospitality operations also deal with variations in levels of activity throughout the day. Check-in time may vary, but many hotels are busiest between 3:00 and 5:00 p.m., while check-out at many hotels is extremely busy between 7:00 and 9:00 a.m., and between 11:00 a.m. and 1:00 p.m. Similarly, some food service operations may be full from 7:30 to 8:30 a.m., 11:30 a.m. to 1:30 p.m., and 6:00 to 8:00 p.m., and nearly empty during other hours of the day. Not only is the business seasonal throughout a day, but many hospitality operations also experience seasonality during a week and throughout the year.

A prime measure of activity for lodging operations is occupancy percentage. Although we will discuss this measure more fully in Chapter 5, it simply expresses what percent of the rooms available for sale are actually sold, and it is calculated by dividing the number of rooms sold by the number of rooms available. A hotel catering primarily to business-people (transient hotels) may experience 100% occupancy Monday through Thursday and only 30% for Friday through Saturday, to average 70% for the week. Weekly seasonality for many resort hotels is the

Exhibit 1.2   U.S. Lodging Industry Dollar

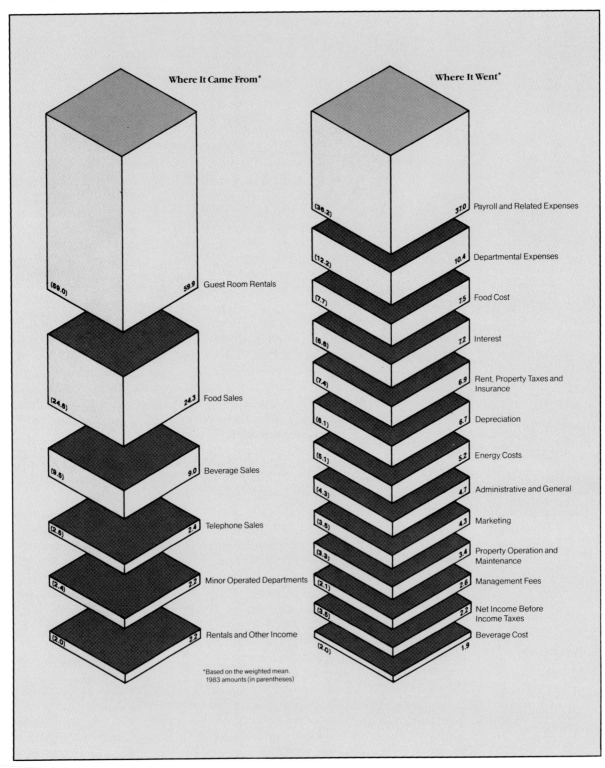

Source: Laventhol & Horwath, *U.S. Lodging Industry Digest*, 1985, p. 8.

Exhibit 1.3   The Restaurant Industry Dollar

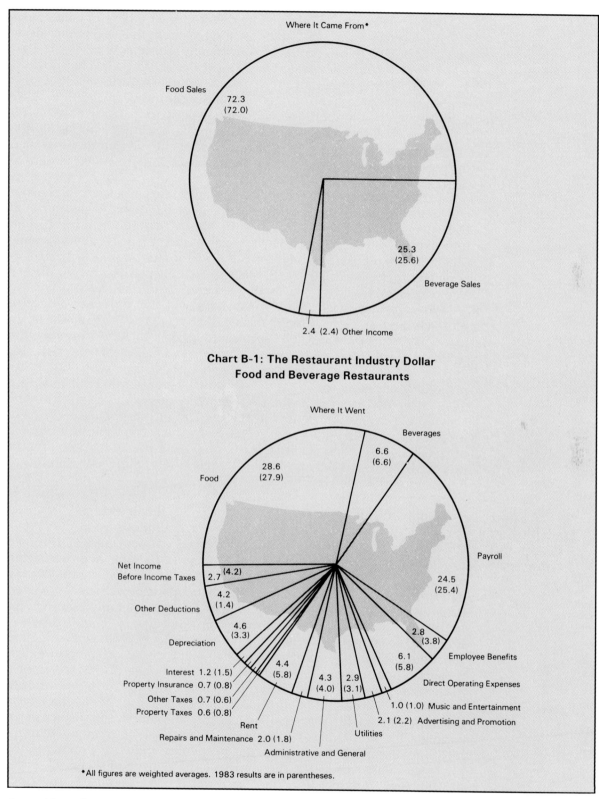

Where It Came From*

Food Sales
72.3
(72.0)

25.3
(25.6)

Beverage Sales

2.4 (2.4) Other Income

Chart B-1: The Restaurant Industry Dollar
Food and Beverage Restaurants

Where It Went

Beverages
6.6
(6.6)

Food
28.6
(27.9)

Payroll
24.5
(25.4)

Net Income
Before Income Taxes   2.7   (4.2)

Other Deductions   4.2 (1.4)

Depreciation   4.6 (3.3)

Interest 1.2 (1.5)
Property Insurance 0.7 (0.8)
Other Taxes 0.7 (0.6)
Property Taxes 0.6 (0.8)

4.4 (5.8)

4.3 (4.0)

2.9 (3.1)

2.8 (3.8)

6.1 (5.8)   Employee Benefits

Direct Operating Expenses

1.0 (1.0) Music and Entertainment

2.1 (2.2) Advertising and Promotion

Utilities

Administrative and General

Rent
Repairs and Maintenance 2.0 (1.8)

*All figures are weighted averages. 1983 results are in parentheses.

Source: National Restaurant Association and Laventhol & Horwath, *Restaurant Industry Operation, Report '85 for the United States*, p. 53.

opposite of that experienced by transient hotels. Their busiest periods are usually weekends rather than week days. In addition, their average occupancy per room, determined by dividing the number of paid guests by the number of rooms sold, is higher than that experienced by transient hotels. In a recent year, the average occupancy per room sold was 1.36 and 1.71 for transient and resort hotels, respectively.[3]

Seasonality throughout the year is a serious factor for many hotels. Several resorts are open for only one season of the year. Other lodging establishments, although open all year, experience considerably higher activity during certain times of the year. For example, many Florida hotels experience higher occupancy during the winter months than during the summer, as vacationers from the north descend on Florida to enjoy its warmth and sunshine.

Exhibit 1.4 shows the monthly occupancy rates in selected U.S. cities and states for 1984. The occupancy percentage nationwide was lowest in December (49%) and highest in both March and June (71%). Boston hotels registered 92% occupancy in October and 48% in December, while Miami hotels registered a high of 74% in February and a low of 51% in September. Thus, Exhibit 1.4 reveals seasonal fluctuations by month and also considerable differences among selected cities and states.

The seasonality of business throughout a day and the variety of products and services offered dictate that adequate safeguards be in place. At a major hotel, the services available include not only the obvious room, food, beverages, and recreational facilities, but also in-room movies, video games, and gift shops. The cash and other physical assets of a property must not only be safeguarded but also used in an efficient manner to maximize the quality of services to guests while providing a reasonable return to the owners of the operation. A daily report for management's use is prepared by the accounting staff of most hospitality properties. Exhibit 1.5 is an example of a daily report prepared for the Midway Motor Lodge. Note the vast amount of information provided by this report.

Short Distribution Chain and Time Span

Another consideration that underscores the importance of safeguarding cash and assets of food service operations is the very fast conversion of raw materials into a finished product and of the sold product into cash. The food service at most lodging and restaurant operations is similar to the products offered by manufacturing enterprises in that it must meet the consumer's expectations. However, the distribution chain and time span is considerably shorter for hospitality "products" than for most consumer goods. The distribution chain is considerably shorter because the product is produced, sold, and consumed at the same location. These three processes often occur in less than two hours. By comparison, a new automobile purchased from a dealer may have been built seven days to six months (or more) prior to the sale, at a location up to 12,000 miles (or more) away, and by a different firm. The parts making up the automobile may have been supplied by 50 (or more) companies. In contrast, the "manufacturer" in the food service segment of the hospitality industry purchases the raw ingredients, prepares them to suit the consumer's tastes, serves the finished "product" on the "manufacturer's" premises, and does all this within minutes. The food service operator will, in many cases,

Exhibit 1.4 Monthly Occupancy Rates

	1st Quarter 1985	Average for Year 1984	Dec.	Nov.	Oct.	Sept.	Aug.	July	June	May	April	Mar.	Feb.	Jan.
									1984					
Albuquerque	70%	67%	46%	57%	77%	75%	73%	68%	79%	75%	69%	73%	66%	58%
Atlanta	67	66	47	63	72	65	71	67	71	68	67	73	69	64
Austin	71	73	49	70	76	70	77	77	84	81	77	83	78	69
Baton Rouge	48	57	39	49	62	46	56	58	68	69	64	61	61	66
Boston	N/A	70	48	69	92	81	76	71	80	78	75	62	52	51
Chattanooga	57	66	48	54	72	60	77	75	77	70	69	72	59	49
Chicago	58	66	49	65	81	77	74	63	77	74	61	65	55	50
Colorado Springs	48	67	39	47	62	77	92	91	84	76	62	62	60	44
Corpus Christi	50	57	35	45	50	55	70	70	75	63	50	53	47	43
Dallas/Fort Worth	67	62	46	55	68	63	71	66	67	72	65	72	67	64
Denver	62	59	42	41	56	60	77	66	74	66	64	64	60	51
Fort Lauderdale	N/A	65	60	69	58	50	54	51	54	67	72	90	82	68
Houston	50	53	39	45	52	44	53	55	55	51	51	57	52	52
Knoxville	53	58	44	57	70	62	67	61	65	59	63	56	49	41
Los Angeles	71	68	53	63	67	77	77	66	77	70	66	74	68	62
Memphis	62	69	51	66	73	68	80	76	79	74	69	69	58	52
Miami	79	62	59	64	57	51	62	58	52	57	62	66	74	68
Nashville	59	70	47	61	79	76	80	82	86	74	70	70	58	47
New Orleans	54	67	36	56	84	73	75	69	82	77	62	69	61	52
New York City	65	75	68	81	90	81	72	67	81	80	74	73	67	59
Orlando Area:														
Disney/Kissimmee	69	75	49	60	61	48	86	91	87	82	91	94	79	59
International Drive	75	72	52	59	69	57	74	83	76	74	84	88	79	67
City of Orlando	69	62	46	42	43	41	67	76	64	61	81	92	77	56
Palm Beach	N/A	73	71	73	71	59	61	56	58	72	70	88	88	74
Philadelphia	53	62	43	62	76	69	70	61	70	68	63	57	52	47
Phoenix	82	68	51	71	73	63	44	46	61	70	75	87	91	72
San Antonio	68	74	55	63	71	69	81	78	81	78	82	76	68	54
San Francisco	67	72	50	70	84	82	79	81	79	79	69	68	62	54
Scottsdale	75	60	47	51	59	51	44	43	61	72	65	87	88	69
Tampa Bay	74	73	54	59	68	56	67	70	68	77	79	90	74	57
Tucson	84	65	60	69	72	53	46	46	53	52	61	77	69	56
Tulsa	46	57	43	44	55	53	59	50	45	49	53	46	48	47
Washington, D.C.	65	70	46	65	82	78	70	67	82	85	83	72	62	50
Alabama	56	66	49	65	71	66	74	72	—	—	—	—	—	—
Arizona	79	66	51	66	69	59	47	46	61	68	70	85	84	69
Colorado	63	61	46	46	61	68	82	72	66	60	61	65	63	58
Hawaii	88	76	72	65	76	70	79	79	78	73	76	88	89	75
Illinois	59	60	41	56	68	66	71	64	68	60	61	62	57	50
Louisiana	52	62	37	53	74	65	70	66	76	72	59	63	59	52
Mississippi	51	61	35	51	63	54	66	72	75	69	68	71	59	52
New Mexico	68	66	49	55	75	72	73	69	73	71	64	70	64	56
New York State	63	74	65	78	88	80	73	67	79	79	72	71	65	58
North Carolina	62	67	46	63	81	70	70	65	70	68	72	66	60	58
Northern California	69	72	52	69	80	78	80	78	80	80	71	70	65	59
Oklahoma	49	57	43	52	61	59	60	59	59	58	59	59	54	53
South Carolina	61	70	48	62	68	68	77	80	77	77	82	73	64	38
Tennessee	57	66	47	60	75	68	77	76	78	69	66	65	56	47
Texas	61	62	45	54	63	58	66	65	67	66	64	67	63	57
Virginia	50	62	43	64	64	66	63	63	62	59	54	67	46	41
Wyoming-Utah-Montana-Nebraska	60	63	44	54	62	71	80	78	74	62	62	65	67	55
Nationwide Averages*	68%	67%	49%	60%	70%	65%	70%	68%	71%	70%	68%	71%	65%	56%

* Estimated occupancies for nation's total hotel-motel industry.

Source: Pannell Kerr Forster & Company, *Trends – USA*, 1985, p. 21.

receive immediate feedback regarding the quality of the food and service product, especially if the consumer's expectations were not met.

As a result of this short distribution chain and time span, there is little advance production, and thus, the stockpiling of the finished product is minimal. This means that, unlike manufacturing firms, the quantity of inventory of the goods provided by hospitality operations is

Exhibit 1.5 Daily Operations Report

DAILY OPERATIONS REPORT

Summary of Revenue and Accounts Receivable

Line	Summary of Revenue and Accounts Receivable		Today	Month To Date	Last Year
1	Room Revenue	+			
2	Meeting Room Rental	+			
3	Sales Tax	+			
4	Local Calls	+			
5	Long Distance	+			
6	Dry Cleaning - Laundry	+			
7	Guest Paid Outs	+			
8	Soda Machines	+			
9	Pool Tables	+			
10	Newspapers & Magazines	+			
11	Restaurant and Bar	+			
12	Commissions Earned	+			
13	Restaurant Rent	+			
14A	Taxable Misc. Sales	+			
14B	Nontaxable Misc. Sales	+			
15	Returned (List name & amount below Cks. in daily comments section)	+			
16A	Midway Money	+			
16B		+			
16C		+			
16D		+			
17	Misc. (List Below)	+			
18	TOTAL REVENUE	=			
19	Front Desk Paid	-			
20	City Ledger Paid	-			
21	Discounts (List Below)	-			
22	Yesterday's Outstanding Balance	+			
23	Today's Outstanding Balance	=			
24	Today's TL Balance	-			
25	Today's CL Balance	=			
26	Today's CL Transfers (Total Line 27 through 34)				
27	American Express				
28	Bank Americard				
29	Carte Blanche				
30	Diners Club				
31	Exxon				
32	Master Charge				
33	Sohio				
33a					
34	Direct Billing				
35	CL Credits Today (Total of Lines 20 & 21)	+			
36	Yesterday's CL Balance	=			
37	Auditor's Signature				
37B	Mgrs. Signature				

Approved as correct to the best of my knowledge & belief

PAID OUTS

Line	Account	Amount
38	Cleaning Supplies	
39	Laundry Supplies	
40	Room Supplies	
41	Office Supplies (including postage)	
42	Advertising	
43	Donations (List Name)	
44	Guest Transportation Including Van Expense	
45	Repair & Maint.	
46	Pool Supplies	
47	Guest DC&L	
48	Guest Paid Outs	
49	Papers & Mags.	
50	Mileage Expense	
51	Rest. & Bar	
52		
53		
54	TOTAL PAID OUTS	

Room Statistics

Line	Room Statistics		Today	Month To Date	Last Year
55	Rooms Sold - 1 Person	+			
56	Rooms Sold - 2 Persons	+			
57	Rooms Sold - 3 or more	+			
58	Total Rooms Sold	=			
59	Complimentary Rooms	+			
60	Total Rooms Occupied	=			
61	Total Rooms Available				
62	PER CENT OCCUPANCY (Line 60 - Line 61)		%	%	%
63	Average Rate Per Room Sold (Line 1 - Line 58)				
64	Av. Rate Per Available Room Line 1 - Line 61				
65	Total Guests				
66	No. Guests Per Occ. Room (Line 65 - Line 60)				
67	List Comp. Rooms (Include Rm. No. & Name)				
68	List Number of Gtd. No Show Rooms Posted on tonights business (included in Line 1)				
69	List Special Groups In Lodge				
69a	Outside Temperature				
69b	General Weather				
69c	General Road Cond.				

DEPOSITS / DEPOSIT PROOF

Line	Cashier	Amount	+ -	Line	Item		Amount
70	Desk - 1st		70a	87	Yesterday's Outs. Bal.	(22) +	
71	Desk - 2nd		71a	88	Today's Revenue	(18) +	
72	Desk - 3rd		72a	89	Today's Outs. Bal.	(23) -	
73	American Express			90	Discounts	(21)	
74	Bank Americard			91	Paid Outs	(54)	
75	Carte Blanche			92	Line 81a	+ -	
76	Diners Club			93		+ -	
77	Exxon			94	TOTAL DEPOSIT	=	
78	Master Charge						
79	Sohio						
79a					Lodge		
80	Direct Charge				Day		
81	TOTAL DEPOSIT		81a		Date		

SUMMARY OF MISC. REVENUE [Line 17]

Line	Description	Amount
82		
83		
84		
85		
86	TOTAL MISC. REVENUE	

Daily Comments

CITY LEDGER PAYMENTS

Company Name	Gross	Credit Card Discounts	OTHER DEDUCTIONS* Amount	Describe	Net

TOTAL (continue on back side if additional space needed)

Home Office Approval:

MML 4 Revised 4/77

* Only credit card charge backs; imprinter fees, tax exempt amount, travel agent commissions or District Mgr. adjustments can be entered here.

Source: Midway Motor Lodge

kept to a minimum. This is reflected by the fact that major operations in the hospitality industry generally have less than 5% of their total assets invested in inventory of goods for resale. In contrast, the inventory of many major manufacturing firms may equal at least 30% of their total assets.

A Labor-Intensive Industry

These differences between hospitality and manufacturing operations help explain yet another contrast between the two industries. Increasingly, automatic manufacturing equipment has reduced the need for intensive labor contribution to production processes. But, as we have already seen, payroll expense is a major factor in the cost of sales for both the lodging and food service segments of the hospitality industry. The greater seasonality affecting sales in hospitality operations also contributes to their labor intensive aspect. The busy check-in and check-out times during daily hotel operations require considerable amounts of labor in the rooms department in order to provide quality service. Similarly, food service operations have increased labor needs for spurts of activity throughout the day. The proper scheduling of personnel to meet the rush of guests is essential in order for hospitality operations to generate profits while being able to meet guests' needs and wants. Another important dimension of food and beverage operations in lodging facilities is the need to provide service even when it may not be profitable. For example, food service must be provided to guests even on low-occupancy days, and room service must always be available in first-class properties.

The short distribution chain and time span characteristic of the delivery and consumption of hospitality products and services also contributes to this labor intensive quality. Personnel are required to prepare, produce, sell, and service the offerings provided at the hospitality facility. Labor must be available to prepare the food when the guest wants it. Advertising by some food service operations promises the finished product within minutes after the guest's order is taken. Such prompt guest-oriented service can only be provided by a large and efficient staff. The total labor cost may range from as low as 20% of the total revenue dollar at a quick service restaurant, to upwards of 50% for a private club. Effective management concerned with controlling the costs of labor, while at the same time satisfying the requirements of the operation to serve the needs and wants of guests, is crucial to the success of any hospitality operation.

Major Investment in Fixed Assets

In addition to being labor-intensive, hospitality properties are also, for the most part, fixed-asset-intensive as well. Lodging facilities provide rooms for guests to relax, rest, entertain, and conduct business. The "room" as a product is carried as a fixed asset, and its cost is written-off (depreciated) over time. However, the basic cost of the room is the same whether it is sold or remains unoccupied for a night. In this sense, a room is the most perishable product a lodging operation has, because an unsold room for a given day can never be sold in the future. The construction cost per room of lodging facilities, including the furniture and fixtures, may vary between $10,000 and $200,000. The cost of rooms represents a major investment by lodging operations, and the fixed assets of major hotels range between 55% and 85% of their total assets.

In contrast, the fixed assets of many manufacturing companies approximate only 30% of their total assets.

This overview of the hospitality industry has shown its relation to the umbrella industry of travel and tourism, described many of the different types of hospitality operations, and indicated the impressive dimensions of the industry. As we have seen, the hospitality industry is greatly affected by seasonal (daily, weekly, monthly, and yearly) fluctuations of sales, by the short distribution chain and quick consumption of its offerings, by the need for a large, efficient work force, and by considerable investment in fixed assets. These characteristics of hospitality operations give shape to the challenges faced by the accounting function within the industry.

Accounting Function in the Hospitality Industry

The accounting function in hospitality industry properties is provided by a group of specialists ranging from bookkeepers to chief accounting executives with such titles as Executive Vice-President and Controller (or Comptroller). Chief accounting executives are responsible for such typical accounting functions as receivables, payables, and payroll, and in some cases, storage and security. Exhibit 1.6 summarizes a recent survey of 278 hotel property controllers (not hotel corporation controllers) and shows a wide range of reported responsibilities.

The size of accounting staffs may vary widely from a part-time bookkeeper in the small 10-room motel to several hundred people in a large hotel or restaurant chain. For example, the accounting staff at a major worldwide hotel firm totals approximately 190 while the corporate accounting staff (A/P, payroll, internal audit, tax, etc.) at Pizza Hut, Inc.'s headquarters totals 138. A large hotel corporation's accounting staff covers many areas as reflected by the organizational chart in Exhibit 1.7.

The size of the accounting staff at an individual property varies in relation to the size and diversity of the hotel's operations. The accounting staff at hotels with greater than 1,000 rooms ranges from 30 to 50 people consisting of personnel ranging from receiving clerks to the hotel controller. Exhibit 1.8 is a sample organizational chart for the accounting function at a large hotel.

The accounting function within a lodging property is information-oriented, that is, the major role is providing information to users. To external parties, such as financial institutions, the communication vehicle is generally financial statements while internally, a wide variety of financial reports are provided including operating statements. Exhibit 3.3 in Chapter 3 lists various management reports generally prepared by accounting department personnel. The operating statements are formatted to reflect revenues and related expenses by areas of responsibility. In addition to the summary income statement relating to the property as a whole, departmental statements are prepared for each department generating revenues and incurring expenses, such as the rooms, food and beverage, telephone, and other similar departments. Further, separate statements are provided by service centers such as marketing, and property operation and maintenance. (These statements are presented in greater detail in Chapter 3.)

Exhibit 1.6   Responsibilities of Hotel Controllers

Area	Percentage Reporting Responsibility
Payroll	89%
Accounts Receivable	95
Accounts Payable	93
Electronic Data Processing	46
Night Auditors	86
Cashiers	65
Food Controls	54
Purchasing	51
Receiving	51
Storage	36
Security	9

Regardless of the size of a hospitality operation's accounting department, the diversity of its responsibilities, and the number and types of reports produced, the accounting staff is responsible to provide *service*. The primary purpose of accounting in any operation, either within or outside the hospitality industry, is service. The accounting staff must work closely with operating management and other service departments in order for the hospitality property to meet its objectives.

Principles of Accounting

Accounting methods, to be properly understood, must be presented in light of their underpinnings—accounting principles. These generally accepted accounting principles provide a uniform basis for preparing financial statements. Although not "etched in stone" by some boards of accountants, accounting principles have become accepted over time due to their common usage and also due to the work of such major accounting bodies as the American Institute of Certified Public Accountants, the American Accounting Association, and Financial Accounting Standards Board (FASB).

Students of hospitality accounting may often wonder why an accounting transaction is recorded in a particular way at a particular time, or why some asset value is not changed at some point. Generally, the reasons relate to accounting principles. For example, a fixed asset may have cost $10,000 in 19X1 but has a market value in 19X5 of $15,000. The *cost principle* dictates that the fixed asset is retained on the books at its cost of $10,000 rather than being increased to its market value of $15,000. A second example is the accrual of payroll at the end of the month. Assume employees have worked the last few days of the month and will be paid the next pay date which falls in the following month. The *matching principle* dictates that the unpaid payroll for the period be recognized both as expense and as a liability.

Exhibit 1.7 Controller Organizational Chart

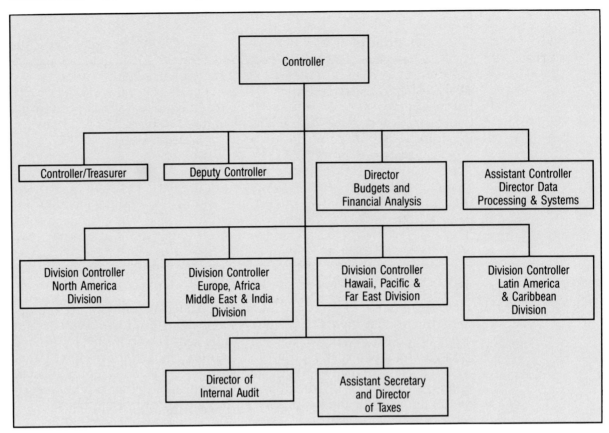

Exhibit 1.8 Controller's Department Organizational Chart

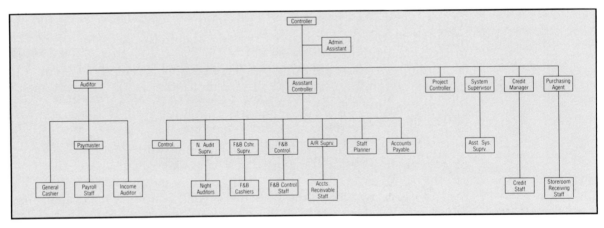

The following sections briefly discuss several generally accepted accounting principles.

The Cost Principle

This principle states that when a transaction is recorded, it is the transaction price (cost) that establishes the accounting value for the product or service purchased. For example, if a restaurateur buys a dishwasher, the agreed-upon price between the restaurant and the supplier determines the amount to be recorded. If the agreed-upon price is $5,000, then the dishwasher is initially valued at $5,000 in the accounting records of the restaurant. The supplier may have acquired the dishwasher from the manufacturer for $4,000; further, the restaurant may receive an offer of $5,500 for it the day it is purchased; however, it is the cost which establishes the amount to be recorded. If amounts other than cost, such as estimates or appraisals, were used in recording transactions, then accounting records would lose their usefulness. When cost is the basis for recording a transaction, the buyer and seller determine the amount to be used in recording the transaction. This amount is generally an objective and fair measure of the value of the goods or services purchased.

When the value of *current* assets is clearly less than cost recorded on the books, it is acceptable to recognize this decline in value. Thus, the conservatism principle (to be discussed later) overrides the cost principle. For example, many properties carry inventory at the *lower* of cost or market. Property and equipment (also frequently called fixed assets) normally are carried at cost less the depreciated amounts and are not reduced to market value so long as management plans to retain them for their useful life. This treatment of property and equipment is based on the going-concern principle discussed more fully below.

Business Entity

Accounting and financial statements are based on the concepts that (1) each business entity maintains its own set of accounts, and (2) there is a separation of these accounts from the other financial interests of the owners. For example, if a hotel owner decides to take some food home from the hotel for personal use, this should be properly charged to the owner's account. Recording activity for a business separately from its owner's personal affairs allows a reasonable determination of the property's profitability. Not only does separate recording provide excellent information for managing the business, but it is also necessary for proper filing of tax returns. Whether the hospitality business is organized as a sole proprietorship, partnership, or corporation, separate tax forms or portions of forms must be filed for the business.

Continuity of the Business Unit (Going Concern)

In preparing the accounting records and reports, it is assumed that the business will continue indefinitely and that liquidation is not in prospect. This assumption is based on the concept that the real value of the hotel or motel is its ability to earn a profit, rather than the value its assets would bring in liquidation. Under this concept, the market value of the property and equipment need not appear on the financial statements, and prepaid expenses are considered assets. If there is a reasonable chance the hospitality property may be unable to continue operations in the near future, allowance for this future event should be reflected in the financial statements. This may be best accomplished by reducing asset values to their market value.

Unit of Measurement

The financial statements are based on transactions expressed in monetary terms. The monetary unit is assumed to represent a stable unit of value, so that transactions from past periods and the current period can be included on the same statement. However, there have been significant changes in price levels in the United States in recent years, and the dollar is not as stable as it has been in the past.

In the late 1970s and early 1980s, inflation, as measured by the Consumer Price Index, exceeded 10% for several years. The FASB responded by requiring the larger hospitality firms to show current replacement cost of their property and equipment in footnotes to their financial statements. For some lodging properties, current values of their property and equipment may exceed twice the amount of the fixed assets carried on their books.

Some hospitality businesses, such as Hilton Hotels Corporation, have chosen to provide financial information in addition to that required by the FASB. Hilton not only provides the traditional financial statements based on historical cost as well as certain figures to reflect current replacement cost, but also provides certain figures based on the present value of income streams from their fixed assets.

Objective Evidence

Accounting transactions and the resulting accounting records should be based on objectively determined evidence to the greatest possible extent. Generally, this evidence is an invoice and/or canceled check. However, estimates must be assumed in the absence of such objective evidence. For example, suppose the owner of a restaurant contributes equipment, purchased several years ago for personal use, to a restaurant corporation in exchange for 100 shares of stock. Further, assume there is no known market value for the restaurant corporation's stock. Ambiguity arises as the owner believes the equipment is worth $1,200, while the catalog used by the owner when the equipment was purchased shows the cost several years ago of $1,400, and an appraiser appraises the equipment at $850. In this example, the most objective estimate of its value today would be the appraiser's estimate of $850.

Full Disclosure

The financial statements must provide information on all the significant facts that have a bearing on the interpretation of the financial statements. Full disclosure is accomplished either by reporting the information in the body of the financial statements or in the footnotes to the financial statements. Several types of disclosures normally provided in the footnotes, when appropriate, include the accounting methods used, changes in the accounting methods, contingent liabilities, events occurring subsequent to the financial statement date, and unusual and nonrecurring items. An example of each type of disclosure is found in Exhibit 1.9.

Consistency

Frequently, several accounting methods are available for reporting a specific kind of "activity." From the available choices and the circumstances present, the preferred method is selected by management. For example, there are several methods available for determining inventory

Exhibit 1.9 Types of Disclosure and Examples

Type of Disclosure	Example
Accounting methods used	Straight-line method of depreciation
Change in the accounting methods	A change from depreciating a fixed asset using the straight-line method to using the double declining balance method
Contingent liability	A lawsuit against the company for alleged failure to provide adequate security for a guest who suffered personal injury
Events occurring subsequent to the financial statement date	A fire destroys significant uninsured assets of the hotel company one week after the end of the year
Unusual and nonrecurring items	A hotel firm in Michigan suffers significant losses due to an earthquake

values, and there are several methods for depreciating fixed assets. The consistency principle requires that once an accounting method has been adopted, it should be followed from period to period in the future unless a change is warranted and disclosed. When the consistency principle is adhered to, the user of financial information is able to make reasonable comparisons between periods. Without consistent accounting, trends indicated by supposedly comparable financial statements would be misleading.

When it becomes necessary to change to another method, disclosure of the change must be made and the dollar effect on earnings and/or the balance sheet must be reported. The consistency principle does not dictate that a hospitality operation must use the same accounting methods for preparing tax returns as it uses for preparing financial statements for external users. Further, this principle does not even require that a method selected for one element of a company be used for all similar elements. For example, the straight-line method of depreciation may be used to depreciate one hotel and an accelerated method of depreciation used to depreciate another hotel owned by the same company.

Matching   The matching principle pertains to relating expenses to revenues. For example, a hotel purchases a computerized reservations system which will benefit the hotel for several years. Therefore, the cost is recorded as a fixed asset and the cost of the system is written-off over the computerized reservations system's life. The result is a partial write-off of the fixed asset each year against the revenue generated in part by using the system. This process is referred to as matching and is the basis for adjusting entries prepared by properties at the end of each accounting period.

The matching principle is used when transactions are recorded on an accrual basis rather than on a cash basis. The accrual basis and cash basis of accounting are two methods of determining when to record a transaction. The cash basis recognizes an accounting transaction at the point of cash inflow or outflow. Although this is the simpler of the two methods, it generally is not a fair reflection of the operations of a business and is only used by small motels and food service operations.

The more commonly used accrual basis recognizes revenue when earned and expenses when incurred. Periodically, expense must be recognized, because of the matching principle, even when no transaction has occurred. Examples of non-transaction expense recognition include depreciation of property and equipment, reduction of prepaid insurance, accrual of payroll, and providing an allowance for uncollectible receivables.

Conservatism

The conservatism principle calls for recognizing expenses as soon as possible but delaying the recognition of revenues until they are ensured. The practical result is to be conservative (low) in the recognition of net income in the current year. It is not proper to deliberately understate net income; however, many accountants desire to be cautious in their recognition of revenue and "generous" in their recognition of expense. A good example of this is the accounting treatment of lawsuits. If a hotel is a plaintiff in a lawsuit, and its legal counsel indicates the case will be won and estimates the amount, the amount is not recorded as revenue until a judgment is rendered. On the other hand, if the same hotel is a defendant in a lawsuit, and its legal counsel indicates the hotel will lose the lawsuit and most likely will pay a stated amount, then the "expense" should be recognized immediately.

Other selected accounting areas where conservatism is apparent are the valuation of inventory at the lower of cost or market, and the recognition of nonrefundable deposits for future banquets as a liability until the banquet is catered.

Materiality

A final accounting principle discussed in this book is materiality. An event is considered material if "it makes a difference." Whether an item is material is relative to a standard of comparison. Some accountants have attempted to establish materiality by rules of thumb. For example, an item may be recognized if it exceeds X% or more of total assets or X% of total income. However, this approach fails to resolve the problems of relative unimportance of an item today and relative importance in the future. Also, several immaterial items when viewed collectively may be material.

One general area where the materiality principle is applied is fixed assets. Tangible items used in a business with lives beyond one year are commonly recorded as fixed assets. However, items with a fixed asset nature but with a cost less than a specified limit dictated by the board of directors of the purchasing organization are expensed since the cost is considered immaterial. An example would be a wastebasket. A $39 wastebasket might have a useful life of ten years, but since its cost is less than the $100 cutoff (assumed to be set by the board) for recording expenditures as fixed assets, it is expensed. In this case, the expenditure was immaterial to record as a fixed asset. In addition, when a hospitality property provides footnotes to supplement the body of its financial statement, only material or potentially material items are presented.

Branches of Accounting

Accounting activities are variously classified by accountants; however, most agree that there are distinct but overlapping branches of financial accounting, cost accounting, management accounting, tax accounting, auditing, and accounting systems.

Financial accounting relates to accounting for revenues, expenses, assets, and liabilities, and involves the basic accounting processes of recording, classifying, and summarizing transactions. This area is often limited to accounting concerned with the preparation and distribution of financial reports. Financial accounting is historical in nature; that is, it deals with past events. Managerial accounting, on the other hand, deals with proposed events.

Cost accounting is the branch of accounting dealing with the recording, classification, allocation, and reporting of current and prospective costs. Cost accountants determine costs by departments, functions, responsibilities, and products and/or services. The chief purpose of cost accounting is to aid operations personnel in controlling operations.

Management accounting is the branch of accounting designed to provide information to various management levels in the hospitality operation for the enhancement of controls. Management accountants prepare performance reports including comparisons to the budget. A major purpose of these reports is to provide in-depth information as a basis for management decisions. Although management accounting may vary among segments of the hospitality industry and certainly among different establishments, many management accountants will use various management science techniques.

Tax accounting is the branch of accounting relating to the preparation and filing of tax forms with the various governmental agencies. Tax planning to minimize tax payments is a significant part of the tax accountant's work. The emphasis is usually income tax at the federal, state, and local levels, but also includes sales, excise, payroll, and property taxes. Not only are tax accountants employed by hospitality operations, but services of tax accountants employed by certified public accounting firms are also used by hospitality properties.

Auditing is the branch of accounting that is most often associated with the independent, external audit called a financial audit. The financial auditor reviews the financial statements of the hospitality operation, the underlying internal control system, and accounting records (journals, vouchers, invoices, checks, bank statements, etc.) with the purpose of rendering an opinion of the financial statements. Financial audits may only be conducted by certified public accounting firms who generally also provide recommendations for strengthening internal controls of the properties they audit.

Over the past several years, hospitality operations have increasingly employed internal auditors. The primary purpose of internal auditors is the review and evaluation of internal control systems. Many large hospitality firms have a full staff of internal auditors who conduct audits at individual properties with the purpose of assisting management.

A final branch of accounting is accounting systems. Accounting systems personnel review the information system of hospitality organizations which includes not only the accounting system but other elements of the information system such as reservations of guests at hotels. As more and more hospitality operations are computerized, many accounting systems experts are electronic data processing specialists, such as programmers and systems analysts. The trend toward larger accounting systems staffs by hospitality organizations will continue as the information revolution continues into the twenty-first century.

Review of Accounting Mechanics

Introductory accounting textbooks use several chapters to cover the mechanics of accounting, from the fundamental accounting equation to the preparation of the financial statements. Coverage of these topics in this text are for review purposes only.[4]

The fundamental accounting equation is simply assets equal liabilities plus owners' equity. The equation is a balance to be tested and proven, not a formula to be calculated. This equality is reflected in the balance sheet prepared at the end of each accounting period. Assets, simply defined, are things owned by the hospitality operation which include cash, inventory, accounts receivable, land, buildings, and equipment. Liabilities, simply stated, are obligations to outside parties and include accounts payable, notes payable, income tax payable, long-term debt payable, and accrued payroll. Owners' equity is the residual claims owners have on assets. In other words, assets less liabilities equals owners' equity. After each business transaction is recorded, the total of the assets must equal the total of liabilities and owners' equity.

There are two major subclassifications of owners' equity—permanent accounts and temporary accounts. An account is simply a device for showing increases and/or decreases in an individual asset, liability, or owners' equity item. For example, hospitality operations would have an account for cash in their bank account called "cash in bank." Permanent owners' equity accounts are not closed at the end of an accounting period and include accounts for recording capital stock and retained earnings. On the other hand, temporary owners' equity accounts are closed out at the end of each fiscal year. Temporary owners' equity accounts include all revenue and expense accounts. Revenues result in increases to owners' equity while expenses have the opposite effect, that is, decreasing owners' equity.

The fundamental accounting equation can now be expanded as follows:

Assets (A) = Liabilities (L)
+ Permanent Owners' Equity Accounts (POEA)
+ Temporary Owners' Equity Accounts (TOEA)

By substituting revenues (R) and expenses (E) for the TOEA, the equation is as follows:

$$A = L + POEA + R - E$$

Debit and Credit

The left side of any account is called the "debit" side and the right side is the "credit" side. To debit an account means to record an amount on the left side, while to credit an account means to record an amount on the right side of the account. The difference between the total debits and total credits of an account is called the "balance." The normal balance of an account is the kind of balance, either debit or credit, which an account generally shows. The major classes of accounts have normal balances as follows:

Type of Account	Normal Balance
Asset	Debit
Liability	Credit
Owners' Equity:	
Permanent	Credit
Revenue	Credit
Expense	Debit

Each transaction is recorded with equal dollar amounts of debits and credits in ledger accounts. This equality of debits and credits in ledger accounts is tested by preparing a trial balance which will be discussed later.

Debits (dr) and credits (cr) increase (+) and decrease (−) the various classes of accounts as follows:

Assets	=	Liabilities	+	Owners' Equity
+ | −		− | +		− | +
dr | cr		dr | cr		dr | cr

Revenues	Expenses
− | +	+ | −
dr | cr	dr | cr

Accounting Cycle

In every accounting period of generally one year, an accounting cycle begins, starting with recording transactions and ending with a post-closing trial balance. Each step in the cycle will be briefly defined and discussed.

Preliminary to recording transactions is the occurrence of the transactions. Five common types of transactions which every hospitality operation has are:

1. Sales of products and services

2. Cash receipts

3. Purchases of products and services

Exhibit 1.10   Documents and Transactions

	Documents	
Type of Transaction	**Prepared by Firm**	**Prepared Outside of Firm**
Sales of products and services	Food-guest check Telephone-voucher Laundry-voucher	—
Cash receipts	Cash register tape	Checks
Purchases of products and services	Purchase order	Suppliers' invoices
Payroll	Time cards Payroll checks	—
Cash disbursements	Check	—

4.   Payroll

5.   Cash disbursements

With each transaction, documents are prepared and/or received from which bookkeepers record the transaction. Exhibit 1.10 lists a few key documents for each type of transaction.

Step 1 in the accounting cycle is the recording of transactions in journals. Journals are simply books used for initially recording the individual transactions. For each type of transaction, there is generally a separate journal, generically called a specialized journal. In addition, each establishment maintains a general journal for recording entries not recorded in specialized journals. The process of recording requires that each transaction be analyzed and that a minimum of two accounts be affected. For example, a cash sales transaction results in increases to the cash account and the sales account.

Step 2 in the accounting cycle is transferring the amounts from the journals to the ledger accounts. This process, called posting, results in the tracking of individual accounts. For example, assume cash at the beginning of the period is $1,000, cash receipts for the month total $50,000 (per cash receipts journal), while cash disbursements equal $45,000 (per cash disbursements journal). The cash account after these postings would show the following:

CASH

Date	P/R	Debit	Credit	Balance
Bal.		1,000		1,000
EOM	CR	50,000		51,000
EOM	CD		45,000	6,000

Normally, the columns of each specialized journal are totaled and these totals are posted to the proper accounts at the end of the month

Exhibit 1.11   Manson Motel Trial Balance

Manson Motel
Trial Balance
December 31, 19X1

	Debits	Credits
Cash	$ 5,000	
Marketable Securities	10,000	
Accounts Receivable	8,000	
Cleaning Supplies	2,500	
Prepaid Insurance	4,500	
Furniture	40,000	
Accumulated Depreciation, Furniture		$ 20,000
Equipment	10,000	
Accumulated Depreciation, Equipment		5,000
Building	300,000	
Accumulated Depreciation, Building		100,000
Land	20,000	
Accounts Payable		5,000
Notes Payable		5,000
Mortgage Payable		100,000
Melvin Manson, Capital		103,000
Room Revenue		150,000
Manager's Salary	15,000	
Assistant Manager's Salary	7,500	
Maids' Wages	15,000	
Payroll Taxes	3,000	
Cleaning Supplies Expense	2,000	
Office Supplies	1,000	
Utilities	5,000	
Advertising	500	
Repairs and Maintenance	9,000	
Property Taxes	22,000	
Interest Expense	8,000	
Total	$488,000	$488,000

Source: Clifford T. Fay, Jr., Raymond S. Schmidgall, and Stanley B. Tarr, *Basic Financial Accounting for the Hospitality Industry* (East Lansing, Mich.: Educational Institute of the American Hotel & Motel Association, 1982), p. 55.

(EOM) as reflected in the example above. The exception would be that amounts recorded in the general journal are posted individually. The above cash example shows posting references (P/R) of CR for the cash receipts journal and CD for the cash disbursements journal. The beginning cash of $1,000 increased to $6,000 by the end of the month since $50,000 was received and $45,000 disbursed ($1,000 + $50,000 − $45,000 = $6,000).

Preparing a trial balance is Step 3 in the accounting cycle. The trial balance is simply a listing of all account balances with debit balance accounts and credit balance accounts in separate columns. The total of each column should equal and prove the equality of debits and credits. Exhibit 1.11 contains the trial balance for the Manson Motel for the month ended December 31, 19X1. Notice the debit and credit columns both total $488,000.

Preparing adjusting entries is Step 4 in the accounting cycle.

Exhibit 1.12 Major Categories for Adjusting Entries

		Accounts	
Category	Examples	Debited	Credited
1. Prepaid expense	a. Reduction of prepaid insurance	Insurance Expense	Prepaid Insurance
	b. Reduction of prepaid rent	Rent Expense	Prepaid Rent
2. Accrued expense	a. Accrual of payroll	Payroll Expense	Accrued Payroll
	b. Accrual of interest expense on a note payable	Interest Expense	Interest Payable
3. Unearned revenue	Reduction of unearned rent	Unearned Rent	Rental Revenue
4. Accrued revenue	Accrual of interest earned on note receivable	Interest Receivable	Interest Income
5. Estimated items	Depreciation expense	Depreciation Expense	Accumulated Depreciation, Fixed Assets
6. Inventory adjustment	Recording of ending inventory from physical inventory. (Note: other account balances such as Purchases are also transferred to the Cost of Goods Sold account.	Inventory end of month	Cost of Goods Sold

Adjusting entries are required to adjust accounts to reflect proper balances in the accounts. The adjusting entries are recorded in the general journal at the end of the accounting period. The major categories of adjusting entries along with examples are shown in Exhibit 1.12.

Step 5 is the posting of adjusting entries. All adjusting entries are posted individually from the general journal. All adjustments are different, so that there are no common accounts affected by the adjustments as there are similar entries recorded in specialized journals such as the cash receipts journal.

Preparing an adjusted trial balance is the next step (Step 6) in the accounting cycle. After the adjusting entries are posted to the accounts, an adjusted trial balance is prepared to once again test equality of debit and credit accounts. This process may be facilitated by using a worksheet as shown in Exhibit 1.13.

Step 7 is the preparation of the financial statements. Using a worksheet approach, the accountant simply extends all figures from the adjusted trial balance to the proper income statement and balance sheet columns. Exhibit 1.13 reveals that the difference between the debit and credit columns under the "income statement" results in net income. For the Manson Motel, revenues of $150,000 exceeded expenses of $105,350, resulting in net income of $44,650. Further, net income of $44,650 added to the total credits of $353,150 (balance sheet columns) equals total debits of $397,800 (balance sheet columns).

In addition, the accountant prepares a formal income statement and balance sheet in accordance with generally accepted accounting princi-

Exhibit 1.13 Manson Motel Work Sheet

Manson Motel
Work Sheet
For the year ended December 31, 19X1

Account Title	Trial Balance Debit	Trial Balance Credit	Adjustments Debit	Adjustments Credit	Adjusted Trial Balance Debit	Adjusted Trial Balance Credit	Income Statement Debit	Income Statement Credit	Balance Sheet Debit	Balance Sheet Credit
Cash	5000				5000				5000	
Marketable Securities	10000				10000				10000	
Accounts Receivable	8000				8000				8000	
Cleaning Supplies	2500			(b) 700	1800				1800	
Prepaid Insurance	4500			(a) 1500	3000				3000	
Furniture	40000				40000				40000	
Accumulated Depreciation, Furniture		20000		(c) 4000		24000				24000
Equipment	10000				10000				10000	
Accumulated Depreciation, Equipment		5000		(d) 1000		6000				6000
Building	300000				300000				300000	
Accumulated Depreciation, Building		100000		(e) 10000		110000				110000
Land	20000				20000				20000	
Accounts Payable		5000				5000				5000
Notes Payable		5000				5000				5000
Mortgage Payable		100000				100000				100000
Melvin Manson, Capital		103000				103000				103000
Room Revenue		150000				150000		150000		
Managers Salary	15000				15000		15000			
Assistant Managers Salary	7500				7500		7500			
Maids' Wages	15000		(f) 150		15150		15150			
Payroll Taxes	3000				3000		3000			
Cleaning Supplies Expense	2000		(b) 700		2700		2700			
Office Supplies	1000				1000		1000			
Utilities	5000				5000		5000			
Advertising	500				500		500			
Repairs & Maintenance	9000				9000		9000			
Property Taxes	22000				22000		22000			
Interest Expense	8000				8000		8000			
	488000	488000								
Insurance Expense			(a) 1500		1500		1500			
Depreciation Expense, Furniture			(c) 4000		4000		4000			
Depreciation Expense, Equipment			(d) 1000		1000		1000			
Depreciation Expense, Building			(e) 10000		10000		10000			
Accrued Wages				(f) 150		150				150
			17350	17350	503150	503150	105350	150000	353150	
Net Income							44650			44650
							150000	150000	397800	397800

Source: *Basic Financial Accounting*, pp. 68, 69.

ples, especially the full disclosure principle. This necessitates footnotes to the bodies of the statements and additional financial statements such as the statement of changes in financial position.

After preparation of the financial statements, the revenue and expense accounts are closed (Step 8). These temporary owners' equity accounts are closed into retained earnings. The closing entries increase retained earnings when the hospitality operation earned a profit, or decrease retained earnings if a loss was suffered. In addition, the closing entries result in zero balances in all revenue and expense accounts. The closing entries are recorded in the general journal and posted to the proper accounts.

The final step (Step 9) in the accounting cycle is the preparation of a post-closing trial balance. This post-closing trial balance is prepared to once again prove the equality of debits and credits.

Computer Applications

In most of the chapters which follow, typical computer applications for the chapter subject will be mentioned under the section titled "Computerization." Less than ten years ago, the computer was almost unknown in the hospitality industry. Generally, computers were only located at corporate headquarters. Now, they are becoming common even in the smallest hospitality operations. Originally used to process accounts payable, accounts receivable, and general ledger transactions, computers are now used to process payroll, make reservations, post charges to guest accounts, and even report rooms ready for occupancy. Restaurants are using computers to record reservations, control food cost, and even notify the maitre d' when a table is ready.

In the discussions to follow, two types of computers will be commonly referenced—the minicomputer and the personal computer (PC). Larger computers, or mainframe computers, can also be used in most of these discussions. However, they are expensive to own and operate, and are still not common in most hotel properties. Minicomputers and personal computers generally do not require a data processing staff to operate them. In fact, the personal computer is so sophisticated, it allows the user, without any knowledge of computer programming, to make the machine do what is needed. For example, the user simply instructs the computer in a near English language to add, subtract, or calculate the present value and the machine does the rest.

A word of caution is appropriate, however. If the principles of accounting are not understood, a computer can provide incorrect results. It is critical that management understand the principles of accounting and what the machine should be doing. Without that knowledge, it will be impossible to properly control a business. Financial results can be improperly reported, and management may be allowing fraud by employees who understand what the machine should be doing. The computer must be considered a management tool. If management does not know how to properly use the tool, it will become useless or even harmful.

Summary

The major objectives of this chapter have been to provide a brief overview of the hospitality industry and a review of basic accounting procedures and concepts. Businesses in the hospitality industry, although different in several respects from firms in many other industries, maintain their accounts according to the same basic principles. A hospitality manager must, therefore, be well-versed in accounting and the special considerations necessary for the hospitality operation.

Hotels and restaurants may experience large fluctuations in demand and often maintain very perishable products. Although inventories of manufacturing firms may have a shelf life of several years, restaurants' inventories will perish after a few days, and an unsold hotel room-night can never be recovered. Hospitality operations do not maintain extensive inventories, so labor must be readily available for preparation and service of food and similar products. This labor force must be able to satisfy many ranges of seasonality: different times of the day, days of the week, and seasons of the year will generate different levels of sales.

In order to accurately reflect the operations of these businesses, and to ensure consistent recording between periods and properties, hospitality accountants follow the generally accepted accounting principles. The cost principle stipulates that items be recorded at the amount for which they were purchased. The continuity of the business unit principle assumes that the organization is a going concern which is not threatened by having to liquidate immediately. The property must be treated as an entity separate from its owners according to the business entity principle. Other requirements are that accountants use objective evidence, whenever possible, and fully disclose financial items of significance to the users of the financial statements. If these principles are adhered to, there is greater confidence that the resultant statements will more accurately report the property's operations and financial position.

The final section of this chapter provided a brief overview of basic accounting mechanics. It is important to understand that assets are items owned by the property and have debit balances; liabilities are amounts the property owes and have credit balances. The difference between assets and liabilities is owners' equity—the amount of residual claims owners have on assets. The following chapters will build upon this base.

Notes

1. Laventhol & Horwath, *Economic Trends in the Lodging Industry: A Special Analysis*, 7th Annual National Hospitality Investment Conference, New York, May 20-21, 1985 (Philadelphia: Laventhol & Horwath, 1985).
2. National Restaurant Association and Laventhol & Horwath, *Restaurant Industry Operations Report '85*, (Washington, D.C.: National Restaurant Association, 1985; Philadelphia: Laventhol & Horwath, 1985), p. 6.
3. Laventhol & Horwath, *U.S. Lodging Industry*, (Philadelphia: Laventhol & Horwath, 1983).
4. The authors assume the reader has read an introductory accounting text or has ready access to one. The Educational Institute's text, *Basic Financial Accounting for the Hospitality Industry* contains several chapters which provide detailed coverage of the concepts covered in this section.

Discussion Questions

1. Explain differences between hospitality operations and manufacturing firms.

2. What types of seasonality would a transient hotel most likely be expected to experience?

3. Labor cost in the hospitality industry is approximately what percent of total revenues?

4. What is the matching principle? Illustrate it with an example.

5. What are some problems the unit of measurement principle has experienced in recent years?

6. What accounts are included in the Temporary Owners' Equity Accounts?

7. What is the definition of posting?

8. What are the five types of accounts which are included in the general ledger of all hospitality firms?

9. What is the concept of materiality? Give an example.

10. What are the six branches of accounting and the major responsibilities of each?

Problem 1.1

Complete the following situations with the accounting principle which best applies.

A.   Cost Principle
B.   Business Entity
C   Continuity of the Business Unit
D.   Unit of Measurement
E   Objective Evidence
F.   Full Disclosure
G.   Consistency
H.   Matching
I.   Conservatism

1.   A fire occurred in your hotel during the previous year. The estimated loss due to a pending lawsuit is recorded due to the _____ principle.

2.   You purchased a new dishwasher from Mike's Machines for $1,250, and, because of the _____ principle, it is recorded at $1,250, even though you now could sell it for $1,500.

3.   Although the last biweekly pay period ended December 26, your employees have worked through the end of December. The unpaid salaries and wages are accrued as of December 31, 19X1 because of the _____ principle.

4.   Your firm is the defendant in a major lawsuit. Your attorney believes you may lose. Although he/she is unable to estimate the potential loss, the lawsuit is briefly mentioned in a footnote to the financial statements because of the _____ principle.

5.   You went to a bankruptcy auction yesterday and china, almost identical to that used in your restaurant, was selling for $.20 a piece. Yours is on the books for $1.00 a piece. You do not write down your china because of the _____ principle.

6.   You have historically depreciated furniture in your hospitality firm by the straight-line method. You are going to change to an accelerated method for depreciating the furniture you previously depreciated using the straight-line method. This violates the _____ principle.

Problem 1.2

You have been hired as the accountant by the owner of Holly's Hideaway, Holly Hibble. During your first day on the job, the following transactions occur:

A.   Ms. Hibble purchases a new microcomputer to be used at the front desk. It costs $5,000 and was purchased on account.

B.   The pay period ended, and the motel's employees are paid their salaries/wages of $2,000 (ignore any tax withholdings or deductions for simplicity's sake). They will receive cash today.

C.   This is also the final day of the accounting period (one month), and the depreciation expense must be recorded. The fixed assets total $1,000,000 and should be depreciated over 20 years using the straight-line method. Assume the salvage value is $-0-.

D.   Cash sales for this day totaled $3,000.

E.   Ms. Hibble lends $20,000 to the firm in the form of a two-year note.

Required:

Prepare the necessary journal entries showing the debit and credit entries and provide a brief explanation of each entry.

Problem 1.3

Mr. Gregory Vain is a successful businessperson but does not fully understand the fundamental accounting equation and how various transactions affect it. You have been hired to share your knowledge with him.

Required:

1.   State the basic equation and briefly explain each element of it.

2.   Explain how each type of account could be increased. Illustrate each with an example. Be sure to describe all effects of your examples.

     Example: Asset accounts would increase when a new hotel is purchased. However, in order to remain in equilibrium, another asset account, "cash," would decrease if the hotel is purchased with cash.

3.   State how temporary accounts relate to the fundamental accounting equation.

Problem 1.4

Browny Brad's Beach Motel (BBBM's), a 40-room lodging facility, has operated over the past three years. BBBM's night auditor has kept accurate records during the past year, but has not run any analysis of this data. The following is a summary of the rooms sold by month:

Rooms sold:

January	400
February	600
March	700
April	840
May	960
June	980
July	992
August	973
September	800
October	705
November	650
December	500

Required:

1.   Determine the occupancy percentage for:
   a.   the summer months,
   b.   the off season, and
   c.   the entire year.

Assume there are 365 days in the year, and that summer months include May, June, July and August. Also, assume that the off season includes all months except May, June, July, and August.

Problem 1.5—Principles of Accounting

Robbie Hanson owns a resort located on an excellent fishing lake. Her busy season begins May 15 and extends through mid-fall. During the winter, she engaged a contractor to build a boat house and boat dock for a total price of $25,000. The contract called for completion by May 15, because the resort was completely reserved for the week of May 15 to 22, the opening week of the fishing season. Because the completion date was so important to Hanson, she specified in the contract that if the construction was not completed by May 15, the price would be adjusted downward by a penalty of $100 per day, until completed.

The construction was not completed until June 9, at which time Hanson paid the contract price of $22,500, deducting $100 for each of the 25 days of delay. Hanson is convinced that she lost goodwill because the resort's facilities were inadequate and that several of her clients reduced their stay because the facilities were still under construction.

In the balance sheet prepared on September 30, the end of her fiscal year, Hanson included the boat house and dock as assets valued at $25,000. Included in her revenue was an item "Penalty payments received in lieu of lost revenue, $2,500."

The auditor who examined Hanson's report objected to this treatment and insisted that the facilities be recorded at their actual cost, $22,500. Hanson stated that she could not understand the logic of this position. "Accounting principles are out of tune with reality," she complained. "What if the contract had been 250 days late and the boat house and dock had cost me nothing; would you record on my balance sheet that I had no asset? I lost at least $100 per day in revenue because of the construction delay."

Required:

At what amount should these facilities be reported on the balance sheet on September 30? (You may ignore any questions of depreciation from June 9 to September 30.) Explain your position in terms of accounting principles.

2 Balance Sheet

useful to you

The balance sheet reflects a balance between an organization's assets and claims to its assets called liabilities and owners' equity. This statement is also referred to as a statement of financial position. It is a major financial statement prepared at the end of each accounting period, and contains answers to many questions that managers, owners (investors), and creditors may have, such as:

1. How much cash was on hand at the end of the period?

2. What was the total debt of the hospitality operation?

3. What was the mix of internal and external financing at the end of the period?

4. How much was owed to the hotel by guests?

5. What amount of taxes was owed to the various governmental tax agencies?

6. What was the operation's ability to pay its current debt?

7. What was the financial strength of the operation?

8. How much interest do stockholders have in the operation's assets?

This chapter addresses the purposes and limitations of the balance sheet. We will also consider the formats and contents of balance sheets with special attention to the suggested balance sheet from the *Uniform System of Accounts and Expense Dictionary for Small Hotels, Motels and Motor Hotels* (USASH). In addition, we will discuss the kinds and purposes of footnotes attached to balance sheets. Finally, we will consider techniques for analyzing the financial information contained in a balance sheet. The appendix at the end of this chapter includes the financial statements and the accompanying footnotes for the Hilton Hotels Corporation from its 1985 annual report.

Purposes of the Balance Sheet

The balance sheet reflects the financial position of the hospitality operation at a given date, whereas other major financial statements—the income statement, the statement of retained earnings, and the statement of changes in financial position—pertain to a period of time. The financial position reflected by the balance sheet reveals the assets, liabilities, and owners' equity at a given date.

Management, although generally more interested in operating statements, will find balance sheets useful for conveying financial information to creditors and investors. In addition, management must determine if the balance sheet reflects to the best extent possible the financial position of the hospitality operation. For example, many long-term loans specify a required current ratio (which is current assets divided by current liabilities). Failure to meet the requirement may result in all long-term debt being reclassified as current and thus due immediately. Since few operations could raise large sums of cash quickly, bankruptcy could result. Therefore, management must carefully review the balance sheet to determine that the operation is in compliance. For example, assume at December 31, 19X1 (year-end), a hotel has $500,000 of current assets and $260,000 of current liabilities. Further, assume the current ratio requirement in a bank's loan agreement with the hotel is 2:1. The required current ratio can be attained by simply taking the appropriate action. In this case, the payment of $20,000 of current liabilities with cash of $20,000 results in current assets of $480,000 and current liabilities of $240,000, resulting in a current ratio of 2:1.

Creditors are interested in the hospitality operation's ability to pay its current and future obligations. The ability to pay its current obligations is shown, in part, by a comparison of current assets and current liabilities. The ability to pay future obligations depends, in part, on the extent of long-term financing by owners vis á vis creditors. Everything else being the same, the greater the financing from investors, the higher the probability that long-term creditors will be paid and the lower will be the risk that these creditors take in "investing" in the enterprise.

Investors, most often, are interested in earnings which lead to dividends. However, to maximize earnings, an organization should have financial flexibility, which is the operation's ability to change its cash flows to meet unexpected needs and take advantage of opportunities. Everything else being the same, the greater the financial flexibility of the hospitality operation, the greater its opportunities to take advantage of new profitable investments, thus, increasing net income and, ultimately, cash dividends for investors.

In addition, the balance sheet reveals the liquidity of the hospitality operation. Liquidity measures the operation's ability to convert assets to cash. Even though a property's past earnings have been substantial, this does not in itself guarantee that the operation will be able to meet its obligations as they become due. The hospitality operation should have sufficient liquidity not only to pay its bills, but also to provide its owners with adequate dividends.

Analysis of several balance sheets for several periods will yield trend information which is more valuable than single period figures. In addition, comparison of balance sheet information to projected balance sheet numbers (when available) will reveal management's ability to meet various financial goals.

Limitations of the Balance Sheet

As useful as the balance sheet is, it is generally considered less useful than the operations statement, to both investors and long-term creditors and especially to management. Since the balance sheet is based on the cost principle, it often does not reflect current values of some assets, such as property and equipment. For hospitality operations whose assets are appreciating rather than depreciating, this difference may be significant. Hilton Corporation may be a fair reflection of this difference. In its 1985 annual report, it revealed the current value of its assets (footnote disclosure only) to be $2,936,000,000 while its balance sheet showed the book value of its assets to be $1,225,605,000. The difference between current value and book value was $1,710,395,000. The assets reflected in the balance sheet for Hilton were only 41.74% of their current value.[1] This "understatement," if unknown or ignored by management, investors, and creditors, could lead to less than optimal use of Hilton's assets.

Another limitation of balance sheets is that they fail to reflect many elements of value to hospitality operations. Most important to hotels and motels, restaurants, clubs, and operations in other sectors of the hospitality industry are people. Nowhere in the balance sheet is there a reflection of the human resource investment. Millions of dollars are spent in recruiting and training to achieve an efficient and highly motivated work force, yet this essential ingredient for successful hospitality operations is not shown as an asset. Other valuable elements not directly shown on the balance sheet include such things as goodwill, superior location, loyal customers, and so on.[2] Understandably, it may be difficult to assign an objective value to these elements. Nevertheless, they are not only critical to an operation's success, they are also of significant value.

Balance sheets are limited by their static nature; that is, they reflect the financial position for only a moment. Thereafter, they are less useful because they become outdated. Thus, the user of the balance sheet must be aware that the financial position reflected at year-end may be quite different one month later. For example, a hospitality operation with $1,000,000 of cash may seem financially strong at year-end, but if it invests most of this cash in fixed assets two weeks later, its financial flexibility and liquidity are greatly reduced. This situation would generally only be known to the user of financial documents if a balance sheet and/or other financial statements were available for a date after this investment has occurred.

Finally, the balance sheet, like much of accounting, is based on judgments; that is, it is not exact! Certainly, assets equal liabilities plus owners' equity. However, several balance sheet items are based on estimates.

The amounts shown as accounts receivable (net) reflect the estimated amounts to be collected. The amounts shown as inventory reflect the amount expected to be sold, and the amount shown as property and equipment reflects the cost less estimated depreciation. In each case, accountants use estimates to arrive at "values." To the degree these estimates are in error, the balance sheet items will be wrong.

Balance Sheet Formats

The balance sheet can be arranged in either the account or report formats. The account format lists the asset accounts on the left side of the

Exhibit 2.1   Balance Sheet Account Format

Manson Motel
Balance Sheet
December 31, 19X1

ASSETS		LIABILITIES AND OWNERS' EQUITY	
Current Assets:		Current Liabilities:	
Cash	$ 2,500	Notes Payable	$ 23,700
Accounts Receivable	5,000	Accounts Payable	8,000
Cleaning Supplies	2,500	Wages Payable	300
Total	10,000	Total	32,000
Property & Equipment:		Long-term Liabilities:	
Land	20,000	Mortgage Payable	120,000
Building	300,000	Total Liabilities	152,000
Equipment	10,000		
Furnishings	40,000	Melvin Manson, Capital at	
	370,000	January 1, 19X1	64,500
		Net Income for 19X1	38,500
Less Accumulated		Melvin Manson, Capital at	
Depreciation	125,000	December 31, 19X1	103,000
Net Property &		**Total Liabilities**	
Equipment	245,000	**and Owners' Equity**	$255,000
Total Assets	$255,000		

page and the liability and owners' equity accounts on the right side. Exhibit 2.1 illustrates this arrangement.

Alternatively, the report format shows assets first followed by liabilities and owners' equity. The group totals on the report form can show that either assets equal liabilities and owners' equity or that assets minus liabilities equal owners' equity. Exhibit 2.2 illustrates the report format.

Content of the Balance Sheet

The balance sheet consists of assets, liabilities, and owners' equity. Simply stated, assets are "things owned by the firm," while liabilities are claims of outsiders to assets, and owners' equity is claims of owners to assets. Thus, assets must equal (balance) liabilities and owners' equity. Assets include various accounts such as cash, inventory for resale, buildings, and accounts receivable; while liabilities include accounts such as accounts payable, wages payable, and mortgage payable; and owners' equity includes capital stock and retained earnings. These major elements are generally divided into various classes as shown in Exhibit 2.3.

Exhibit 2.2   Balance Sheet Report Format

Manson Motel
Balance Sheet
December 31, 19X1

ASSETS

Current Assets:

Cash		$ 2,500
Accounts Receivable		5,000
Cleaning Supplies		2,500
Total Current Assets		10,000

Property and Equipment:

Land	$ 20,000	
Building	300,000	
Equipment	10,000	
Furnishings	40,000	
Less Accumulated Depreciation	125,000	
Net Property Equipment		245,000
Total Assets		**$255,000**

LIABILITIES AND OWNERS' EQUITY

Current Liabilities:

Notes Payable	$ 23,700	
Accounts Payable	8,000	
Wages Payable	300	$ 32,000

Long-term Liabilities:

Mortgage Payable		120,000
Total Liabilities		152,000

Owners' Equity:

Melvin Manson, Capital at January 1, 19X1	64,500	
Net Income for 19X1	38,500	
Melvin Manson, Capital at December 31, 19X1		103,000
Total Liabilities and Owners' Equity		**$255,000**

While balance sheets may be organized differently, most hospitality operations follow the order shown in Exhibit 2.3.

Current Accounts   Under both "assets" and "liabilities and owners' equity" is a current classification. Current assets normally refer to items to be converted to cash or used in operations within one year or in a normal operating cycle. Current liabilities are obligations that are expected to be satisfied either by using current assets or by creating other current liabilities within one year or a normal operating cycle.

Exhibit 2.4 reflects a normal operating cycle which includes (1) the

Exhibit 2.3   Major Elements of the Balance Sheet

Assets	**Liabilities and**
Current Assets	**Owners' Equity**
Noncurrent Assets:	Current Liabilities
Noncurrent Receivables	Long-term Liabilities
Investments and Advances	Owners' Equity
Property and Equipment	
Other Assets	

Exhibit 2.4   Normal Operating Cycle

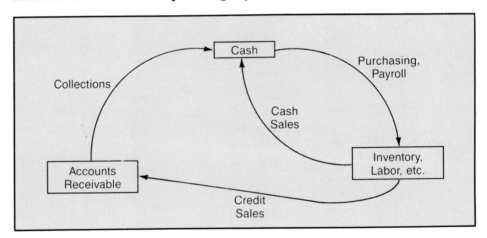

purchase of inventory for resale and labor to produce goods and services, (2) the sale of goods and services, and (3) the collection of accounts receivable from the sale of goods and services.

A normal operating cycle may be as short as a few days, as is common for many quick service restaurants, or it may extend over several months for some hospitality operations. It is more common in the hospitality industry to classify assets as current/noncurrent on the basis of one year rather than on the basis of the normal operating cycle.

Current Assets

Current assets, listed in the order of liquidity, generally consist of cash, marketable securities, receivables, inventories, and prepaid expenses. Cash consists of cash in house banks, cash in checking and savings accounts, and certificates of deposit. The exception is cash restricted for retiring long-term debt which should be shown under other assets. Cash is shown in the balance sheet at its stated value.

Marketable securities are shown as current assets when they are available for conversion to cash. Marketable securities which are not available for conversion to cash are considered as investments. Generally, the critical factor in making this current/noncurrent decision is management's intent. Marketable equity securities, that is, temporary investments in capital stock of other companies, are usually valued at the lower of cost or market, while marketable debt securities, such as temporary investments in bonds of other companies, are carried at cost for balance sheet purposes.

The current asset category of receivables consists of accounts receivable-trade which are open accounts carried by a hotel or motel on the guest, city, or rent ledgers. Receivables also include notes receivable due within one year except for notes from affiliated companies which should be shown under "Investments and Advances." Receivables should be stated at the amount estimated to be collectible. An allowance for doubtful accounts, the amount of receivables estimated to be uncollectible, should be subtracted from receivables to provide a net receivables amount.

Inventories of a hospitality operation consist of merchandise held for resale. Inventories are generally an insignificant percentage of the total assets of a hospitality operation and may be valued at cost. If the amount of inventory is material and the difference between cost and market is significant, then the inventory should be stated at the lower of cost or market.

The final current asset category is prepaid expenses. Prepaid expenses represent purchased goods and services to be used by the hospitality operation within one year. For example, assume a fire insurance premium of $6,000 affords insurance protection for one year after the transaction. At the date of the expenditure, the $6,000 is classified as prepaid insurance and, thereafter, is amortized by a monthly reduction of $500 (1/12 of $6,000) which is shown on the operating statement as insurance expense. Other prepaid expenses include prepaid rent, prepaid property taxes, prepaid interest, and prepaid maintenance and service contracts. Prepaid expenses which will benefit the operation beyond one year from the balance sheet date should be classified as other assets. For example, assume a three-year fire insurance policy costs $18,000. The entry to record the cash disbursement would be to debit prepaid insurance for $6,000 (the cost of coverage for the next 12 months) and to debit deferred charges—insurance for $12,000 (the cost of insurance coverage paid that benefits the operation for periods beyond twelve months from the balance sheet date).

Current Liabilities   Current liabilities are obligations at the balance sheet date which are expected to be paid by converting current assets within one year and generally consist of one of the four following types:

1. Payables resulting from the purchase of goods and services, labor, and the various payroll taxes payable.

2. Amounts received in advance of the delivery of goods and services such as advance deposits on rooms and banquet deposits.

3. Obligations to be paid in the current period relating to fixed asset purchases or to reclassification of long-term debt as current.

4. Other current liabilities include dividends payable and income taxes payable.

Obligations to be paid with restricted cash (sinking fund) should not be classified as current but as long-term.

Current liabilities are often compared to current assets. The difference between the two is commonly called working capital. The current ratio results from dividing current assets by current liabilities. Many hospitality properties operate successfully with a current ratio approximating 1 to 1, compared to a reasonable current ratio for many other industries of 2 to 1. The major reason for this difference lies with the relatively low amount of inventories required and relatively high turnover of receivables by hospitality operations as compared to enterprises in many other industries.

Noncurrent Receivables

Noncurrent receivables include both accounts and notes receivables which are not expected to be collected within one year from the balance sheet date. If any collectibility is uncertain regarding noncurrent receivables, an allowance for doubtful noncurrent receivables should be used, similar to the allowance account for current receivables and subtracted from net noncurrent receivables.

Investments and Advances

Investments and advances consist of long-term investments to be held for more than one year. Included as investments and advances are investments in securities (capital stock and debt instruments), cash advances to affiliated companies, and investments in property not currently used in operations. For example, a hotel company may have invested in center city land with the expectation of constructing a hotel in the future. The land purchase should be shown as an "investment" and not listed under "property and equipment" on the balance sheet. Investments and advances should be stated on the balance sheet at cost or at the lower of cost or market. For example, a hotel corporation invests $10,000 in 100 shares of a large firm ($100 per share) intending to hold the shares for several years. At the balance sheet date, the market value per share is $85. The market for the stock is $8,500 and, based on the principle of conservatism, the investment generally should be reflected at the lower of cost ($10,000) or market ($8,500) on the balance sheet. Alternatively, if the market price exceeds cost of $10,000, the investment would be stated at cost of $10,000.

Property and Equipment

Property and equipment consists of fixed assets including land, buildings, furniture and equipment, construction in progress, leasehold improvements, and finally china, glassware, silver, linens, and uniforms.[3] On the balance sheet, fixed assets are shown at cost and are reduced by the related accumulated depreciation and amortization except for china, glassware, silver, linen, and uniforms, which are simply shown at their net amount.

Other Assets

Other assets consist of all assets not included in the aforementioned categories. The uniform system of accounts for small hotels, motels, and motor hotels (USASH) identifies "other assets" as:

1. Preopening expenses, less accumulated amortization—capitalized expenditures that are incurred prior to the opening of a hotel

property and amortized over a relatively short period of time, generally three to five years.

2. Deferred charges—charges for services received but which should benefit future periods, such as advertising and maintenance. Deferred expenses also include financing costs related to long-term debt.

Other assets also include the costs to organize the hospitality operation (organization costs) and unamortized franchise costs. The initial franchise fee paid by the franchisee should be recorded as an other asset and amortized against revenue over the life of the franchise agreement.

Long-term Liabilities

Long-term liabilities are obligations at the balance sheet date which are expected to be paid beyond the next 12 months, or, if paid in the current year, will be paid from restricted funds. Common long-term liabilities consist of notes payable, mortgages payable, bonds payable, lease obligations, and deferred income taxes payable. Any long-term debt to be paid with current assets within the next year is reclassified as current liabilities.

Lease obligations, when reported as long-term liabilities, generally cover several years while short-term leases are usually expensed when paid. (Chapter 15 is devoted to detailed discussion of lease accounting.) Deferred income taxes result from timing differences in reporting for financial and income tax purposes, that is, the accounting treatment of an item for financial reporting purposes results in a different amount of expense (or revenue) than that taken for tax purposes. Generally, the most significant timing difference for hotels and motels relates to depreciation, since many operations use the straight-line method for financial reporting purposes and an accelerated method for income tax purposes.

For example, suppose a hotel decides to depreciate a fixed asset on a straight-line basis at $15,000 a year for reporting purposes, and depreciate the same asset $25,000 for the year using an accelerated method for tax purposes. If the firm's marginal tax rate is 46%, then the difference in depreciation expense of $10,000 ($25,000 − $15,000) times 46% results in $4,600 cash saved and reported as a noncurrent liability. The book entry to record this savings is as follows:

Income tax expense	$4,600	
Deferred income taxes		$4,600

Owners' Equity

The owners' equity section of the balance sheet reflects the owner's interest in the operation's assets and includes capital stock, additional paid-in capital, retained earnings, and treasury stock. Capital stock for most hospitality operations is common stock; however, a few operations have also issued preferred stock. When more than one type of stock has been issued, each should be reported separately.

The additional paid-in capital category consists of payments for capital stock in excess of the stated and/or par value of the capital stock. For example, cash of $50 received from the sale of common stock with a par value of $10 would be recorded as $10 to the common stock account and the remainder ($40) as "paid-in capital in excess of par."

Retained earnings reflects the past results of operations less dividends declared. Changes in this account during the year are commonly shown on a statement of retained earnings.

Treasury stock represents the property's own capital stock which has been repurchased but not retired. The cost of the treasury shares is shown as a reduction of owners' equity.

Exhibit 2.5 is the prescribed format of the assets section of the balance sheet according to *USASH*. Exhibit 2.6 is the liabilities and owners' equity section of the balance sheet from the *USASH*.

Footnotes

The balance sheets of hospitality operations, although packed with considerable financial information, are not complete without the other financial statements and footnotes. The income statement and statement of changes in financial position are subjects of Chapters 3 and 4 in this text, while footnotes are discussed below.

The full disclosure principle (discussed in Chapter 1) requires that financial information be sufficient to inform the users—creditors, owners, and others. This can only be accomplished by providing footnote disclosure in addition to the financial statements. Thus, footnotes are an integral part of the financial statements of a hospitality operation. They should contain additional information not presented in the body of the financial statements. They should not contradict or soften the disclosure of the financial statements, but rather provide additional explanations. Hilton Hotels Corporation's 1985 financial statements, found in the appendix to this chapter, include the following footnotes:

1. Summary of Significant Accounting Policies
2. Accounts and Notes Receivable
3. Property and Equipment
4. Investments
5. Income Taxes
6. Long-term Debt
7. Capital Stock
8. Employment Benefit Plans
9. Leases
10. Commitments and Contingent Liabilities
11. Segments of Business
12. Supplementary Financial Information
13. Current Cost Information

Exhibit 2.5 Balance Sheet — Assets

BALANCE SHEET

Assets

	Date	
	19	19

CURRENT ASSETS
  Cash
    House Banks $ $
    Demand Deposits
    Temporary Cash Investments
      Total Cash
  Marketable Securities
  Receivables
    Accounts Receivable—Trade
    Notes Receivable
    Other
      Total Receivables
    Less Allowance for Doubtful Accounts
      Net Receivables
  Inventories
  Prepaid Expenses
  Other
    Total Current Assets

NONCURRENT RECEIVABLES
  Owners and Officers
  Other
    Total Noncurrent Receivables

INVESTMENTS

PROPERTY AND EQUIPMENT
  Land
  Buildings
  Leaseholds and Leasehold Improvements
  Construction in Progress
  Furnishings and Equipment
  China, Glassware, Silver, Linen, and Uniforms
  Less Accumulated Depreciation and Amortization
    Net Property and Equipment

OTHER ASSETS
  Security Deposits
  Preopening Expenses
  Deferred Charges
  Other
    Total Other Assets

TOTAL ASSETS $ $

Exhibit 2.5 Balance Sheet — Assets

BALANCE SHEET

Assets

	Date	
	19____	19____
CURRENT ASSETS		
Cash		
House Banks	$	$
Demand Deposits		
Temporary Cash Investments	_____	_____
Total Cash	_____	_____
Marketable Securities		
Receivables		
Accounts Receivable—Trade		
Notes Receivable		
Other		
Total Receivables	_____	_____
Less Allowance for Doubtful Accounts	_____	_____
Net Receivables	_____	_____
Inventories		
Prepaid Expenses		
Other	_____	_____
Total Current Assets	_____	_____
NONCURRENT RECEIVABLES		
Owners and Officers		
Other	_____	_____
Total Noncurrent Receivables	_____	_____
INVESTMENTS		
PROPERTY AND EQUIPMENT		
Land		
Buildings		
Leaseholds and Leasehold Improvements		
Construction in Progress		
Furnishings and Equipment		
China, Glassware, Silver, Linen, and Uniforms	_____	_____
Less Accumulated Depreciation and Amortization	_____	_____
Net Property and Equipment	_____	_____
OTHER ASSETS		
Security Deposits		
Preopening Expenses		
Deferred Charges		
Other	_____	_____
Total Other Assets	_____	_____
TOTAL ASSETS	$ _____	$ _____

Exhibit 2.6 Balance Sheet — Liabilities and Owners' Equity

BALANCE SHEET (continued)

Liabilities and Owners' Equity

CURRENT LIABILITIES
Notes Payable $ $
Current Maturities of Long-Term Debt
Accounts Payable
Federal, State, and City Income Taxes
Deferred Income Taxes
Accrued Expenses
Advance Deposits
Other
    Total Current Liabilities

LONG-TERM DEBT
Notes and Other Similar Liabilities
Obligations Under Capital Leases

Less Current Maturities
    Total Long-Term Debt

OTHER LONG-TERM LIABILITIES

DEFERRED INCOME TAXES

COMMITMENTS AND CONTINGENCIES

***OWNERS' EQUITY**
Preferred Stock, Par Value $_____
    Authorized _____ Shares
    Issued _____ Shares
Common Stock, Par Value $_____
    Authorized _____ Shares
    Issued _____ Shares
Additional Paid-In Capital
Retained Earnings
    Total Owners' Equity

TOTAL LIABILITIES AND OWNERS' EQUITY $ $

See the accompanying notes to financial statements.

*The line items of this section reflect a corporate form of business organization. For line items appropriate to proprietorships and partnerships, see the explanatory notes for this section.

Balance Sheet Analysis

The information shown on the balance sheet is most useful when it is properly analyzed. The analysis of a balance sheet may include the following:

1. Horizontal analysis (comparative statements)

2. Vertical analysis (common-size financial statements)

3. Ratio analysis

In the remainder of this chapter, the first two techniques will be discussed. The third, ratio analysis, will be discussed in considerable detail in Chapter 5.

Horizontal Analysis   Horizontal analysis compares two balance sheets—the current balance sheet and the balance sheet of the previous period. In this analysis, the two balance sheets are often referred to as comparative balance sheets. This represents the simplest approach to analysis and is essential to the fair reporting of the financial information. Often included for management's analysis are the two sets of figures with the changes from one period to the next—both in absolute and relative terms.

Absolute changes show the change in dollars between two periods. For example, assume that cash was $10,000 at the end of year 19X1 and $15,000 at the end of year 19X2. The absolute change is simply the difference of $5,000.

The relative change (also called the percentage change) is found by dividing the absolute change by the amount for the previous period. The relative change, using the cash example above, is 50% ($5,000 divided by $10,000 equals 50%). The $5,000 absolute change may not seem significant by itself, but viewed as a relative change, it is a 50% increase over the previous year.

Examine the comparative balance sheets for the Stratford Hotel found in Exhibit 2.7. Comparative analysis shows that marketable securities increased by $629,222 in absolute terms and 404.7% in relative terms. The increase is substantial. In light of these figures, a manager would desire answers to several questions, including the following:

1. Are the marketable securities readily convertible to cash?

2. Is the amount invested in marketable securities adequate for cash needs in the next few months?

3. Should some of the dollars invested in marketable securities be moved to less liquid, but higher rate-of-return investments?

Significant changes in other accounts should be similarly investigated.

To explain the drastic change in some balance sheet items, a "fluctuation explanation" may be prepared. This explanation provides detail not available on the balance sheet. Exhibit 2.8 illustrates a fluctuation explanation of marketable securities for the Stratford Hotel.

Exhibit 2.7   Comparative Balance Sheet

Comparative Balance Sheets
Stratford Hotel

	Years Ended December 31		Change from 19X1 to 19X2	
ASSETS	19X2	19X1	Amount	Percentage
Current Assets:				
Cash	$ 104,625	$ 85,600	$ 19,025	22.2%
Marketable Securities (Bonds, notes)	784,687	155,465	629,222	404.7
Accounts Receivable (net) (people owe us)	1,615,488	1,336,750	278,738	20.9
Inventories	98,350	92,540	5,810	6.3
Other	12,475	11,300	1,175	10.4
Total	2,615,625	1,681,655	933,970	55.5
Property and Equipment: Fixed assets:				
Land	905,700	905,700	0	0
Buildings	5,434,200	5,434,200	0	0
Furnishings and Equipment	2,617,125	2,650,500	(33,375)	(1.3)
Less: Accumulated Depreciation	1,221,490	749,915	471,575	62.9
Total	7,735,535	8,240,485	(504,950)	(6.1)
Other Assets	58,350	65,360	(7,010)	(10.7)
Total Assets	$10,409,510	$ 9,987,500	$ 422,010	4.2%
LIABILITIES				
Current Liabilities:				
Accounts Payable	$ 1,145,000	$ 838,000	$ 307,000	36.6%
Current maturities of long-term debt (monthly payments)	275,000	275,000	0	0
Income taxes payable	273,750	356,000	(82,250)	(23.1)
Total	1,693,750	1,469,000	224,750	15.3
Long-term Debt				
Notes Payable	50,000	0	50,000	N.M.
Mortgage payable	1,500,000	1,775,000	(275,000)	(15.5)
Less: Current maturities	275,000	275,000	0	0
Total	1,275,000	1,500,000	(225,000)	(15.0)
Total Liabilities	2,968,750	2,969,000	(250)	
OWNERS' EQUITY				
Common stock	1,750,000	1,750,000	0	0
Additional paid-in capital	250,000	250,000	0	0
Retained earnings	5,440,760	5,018,500	422,260	8.4
Total	7,440,760	7,018,500	422,260	6.0
Total Liabilities and Owners' Equity	$10,409,510	$ 9,987,500	$ 422,010	4.2%

N.M. = not meaningful

Exhibit 2.8   Fluctuation Explanation

Fluctuation Explanation – Marketable Securities
Stratford Hotel

| | Balance at Dec. 31 | | Increase |
	19X2	19X1	(Decrease)
Marketable Securities			
Commercial Paper	$240,000	$ 90,000	$150,000
Bank Repurchase Agreements	44,687	15,465	29,222
Treasury Bills	150,000	25,000	125,000
Treasury Bonds	150,000	25,000	125,000
Corporate Stocks & Bonds	200,000	0	200,000
	$784,687	$155,465	$629,222

Vertical Analysis

Another approach to analyzing balance sheets is to reduce them to percentages. This vertical analysis, often referred to as common-size financial statement analysis, is accomplished by having total assets equal 100% and individual asset categories equal percents of the total 100%. Likewise, total liabilities and owners' equity equal 100% and individual categories equal percents of 100%.

Common-size balance sheets permit a comparison of amounts relative to a base within each period. For example, assume cash at the end of year 19X1 is $10,000 and total assets are $100,000. At the end of year 19X2, assume cash is $15,000 and total assets are $150,000. A horizontal analysis shows a $5,000/50% increase. But, cash at the end of each year is 10% of the total assets ($10,000 divided by $100,000 equals 10%; $15,000 divided by $150,000 equals 10%). What first appears to be excessive cash at the end of year 19X2 ($5,000) may not be excessive since cash is 10% of total assets in both cases. However, only a detailed investigation would resolve whether cash equal to 10% of total assets is required in each case.

Examine the Stratford Hotel's comparative common-size balance sheets (Exhibit 2.9). Notable changes include marketable securities (1.6% to 7.5%); total current assets (16.9% to 25.1%); accumulative depreciation (7.5% to 11.7%); and accounts payable (8.4% to 11.0%). Management should investigate significant changes such as these to determine if they are reasonable. If the changes are not found to be reasonable, management should attempt to remedy the situation.

Common-size statement comparisons are not limited strictly to internal use. Comparisons may also be made against other operations' financial statements or against industry averages. Common-size figures are helpful in comparing hospitality operations which differ materially in size. For example, assume a large hospitality operation has current assets of $500,000, while a much smaller operation's current assets are $50,000 and that both figures are for the same period. If total assets equal $1,500,000 for the large operation and $150,000 for the small enterprise, then both operations have current assets to total assets of 33.3%. These percentages provide a more meaningful comparison than the dollar

Exhibit 2.9 Comparative Common-Size Balance Sheet

	Comparative Common-Size Balance Sheets			
	Stratford Hotel			
	Years Ended December 31		Common Size	
ASSETS	19X2	19X1	19X2	19X1
Current Assets:				
Cash	$ 104,625	$ 85,600	1.0%	0.9%
Marketable Securities	784,687	155,465	7.5	1.6
Accounts Receivable (net)	1,615,488	1,336,750	15.5	13.4
Inventories	98,350	92,540	1.0	0.9
Other	12,475	11,300	0.1	0.1
Total	2,615,625	1,681,655	25.1	16.9
Property and Equipment:				
Land	905,700	905,700	8.7	9.1
Buildings	5,434,200	5,434,200	52.2	54.4
Furnishings and Equipment	2,617,125	2,650,500	25.1	26.5
Less: Accumulated Depreciation	1,221,490	749,915	(11.7)	(7.5)
Total	7,735,535	8,240,485	74.3	82.5
Other Assets	58,350	65,360	0.6	0.6
Total Assets	$10,409,510	$ 9,987,500	100.0%	100.0%
LIABILITIES				
Current Liabilities:				
Accounts Payable	$ 1,145,000	$ 838,000	11.0%	8.4%
Current maturities of long-term debt	275,000	275,000	2.6	2.8
Income taxes payable	273,750	356,000	2.6	3.6
Total	1,693,750	1,469,000	16.2	14.8
Long-term Debt				
Notes Payable	50,000	0	0.5	0
Mortgage payable	1,500,000	1,775,000	14.4	17.8
Less: Current maturities	275,000	275,000	(2.6)	(2.8)
Total	1,275,000	1,500,000	12.3	15.0
Total Liabilities	2,968,750	2,969,000	28.5	29.8
OWNERS' EQUITY				
Common stock	1,750,000	1,750,000	16.8	17.5
Additional paid-in capital	250,000	250,000	2.4	2.5
Retained earnings	5,440,760	5,018,500	52.3	50.2
Total	7,440,760	7,018,500	71.5	70.2
Total Liabilities and Owners' Equity	$10,409,510	$ 9,987,500	100.0%	100.0%

Exhibit 2.10 Lincoln Motel's Computerized Depreciation Schedule

	Cost	Year Purchased	Year Life		Year's Depreciation			
				XX XX XX	1987	1988	1989	1990
Building	$1,000,000	1978	40	XX	$25,000	$25,000	$25,000	$25,000
Furniture	200,000	1978	10	XX	20,000	0	0	0
Truck	15,000	1988	3	XX		5,000	5,000	5,000
				XX				
				XX				
				XX				
				XX				
				XX				
				XX				
				XX				
				XX				
Total F/A	$1,215,000			XX				
				XX				
				XX				
TOTAL DEPRECIATION EXPENSE:					**$45,000**	**$30,000**	**$30,000**	**$30,000**

amount of the current assets when comparing financial statements of the two companies.

Computerization

The balance sheet preparation was one of the first activities to be computerized. There are software programs (general ledger packages) available which require that the bookkeeper enter all of the journal entries as they occur, and which use this information to generate the financial statements at the end of the period. Many of these packages require sophisticated hardware to operate; however, in recent years, more packages for minicomputers and personal computers have been developed.

Even if a general ledger package is not used by a hospitality operation, the computer can be used as a tool in the balance sheet preparation. For example, a property's fixed assets can be controlled and the depreciation expense calculated with a spreadsheet program. Exhibit 2.10 is a partial listing of the Lincoln Motel's fixed assets. Using this spreadsheet, an accountant could merely enter the fixed asset's name, cost, purchase date, and expected life, and the computer could then generate the depreciation amounts (straight-line with no salvage value) in the following years. The sum of each individual asset's depreciation is automatically calculated for the income statement's depreciation expense. With a more sophisticated spreadsheet, the user could record accumulated depreciation, make use of salvage values, and even calculate depreciation using different methods such as double declining balance or sum-of-the-years'-digits.

Summary

Although the balance sheet may not play the vital role in management decision-making as other financial statements, it is still an important tool. By examining it, managers, investors, and creditors may determine the financial position of the hospitality operation at a given point in time. It is used to help determine an operation's ability to pay its debts, offer dividends, and to purchase fixed assets.

The balance sheet is divided into three major categories: assets, liabilities, and owners' equity. Assets are the items owned by the operation, while liabilities and owners' equity represent claims to the operation's assets. Liabilities are amounts owed to creditors; owners' equity represents the residual in assets for investors. Both assets and liabilities are divided into current and noncurrent sections. Current assets are cash and other assets which will be converted to cash or used in the property's operations within the next year. Current liabilities represent present obligations which will be paid within one year. The major categories of noncurrent assets include noncurrent receivables, investments and advances, property and equipment, and other assets, while long-term liabilities are present obligations expected to be paid beyond the next 12 months from the date of the balance sheet.

Owners' equity generally includes common stock, paid-in capital in excess of par, and retained earnings. Common stock is the product of the number of shares outstanding and the par value of the shares, while paid-in capital in excess of par is the amount over the par value paid by investors when they purchased the stock from the hospitality property. Retained earnings are the past earnings generated by the operation but not distributed to the stockholders in the form of dividends.

As assets are the items owned by the property, and liabilities and owners' equity are claims to the assets, the relationship involving the three is stated as follows: Assets = Liabilities + Owners' Equity. The balance sheet is prepared with either assets on one side of the page and liabilities and owners' equity on the other (account format), or with the three sections in one column (report format).

In order to gain more information from the balance sheet, it is frequently compared to the balance sheet prepared at the end of the previous period. One tool used is horizontal analysis which presents not only the current year's data, but also the data from the prior period, and calculates absolute and relative differences between the two periods. Significant differences are generally analyzed. Another type of analysis is vertical analysis, which states all accounts as percentages of either total assets or total liabilities and owners' equity. Differences between the end results of two periods can then be examined. A final analysis is the comparison of the balance sheet figures for the particular hospitality operation with data from other properties or with averages for the hospitality industry as a whole. These comparisons can highlight differences and help management identify areas of concern.

Notes

1. Hilton Hotels Corp., *Hilton Hotels Corporation 1985 Annual Report*, (Beverly Hills, Calif.: Hilton Hotels Corp., 1985), pp. 16, 28.
2. The exception is that purchased goodwill is shown on the balance sheet. This goodwill results when a purchaser of a hospitality operation is unable to assign the entire purchase price to the operation's individual assets. The excess of the purchase price over the dollars assigned to the individual assets is labeled goodwill. Self-generated goodwill, which for many hospitality operations is significant, is not shown on the balance sheet.
3. The detailed accounting for these items (capitalization, depreciation, amortization) is covered in the Educational Institute's *Basic Financial Accounting for the Hospitality Industry*.

Discussion Questions

1. How do creditors and investors use the balance sheet?

2. What are some of the limitations of the balance sheet?

3. What are the differences and similarities between the account and report formats of the balance sheet?

4. Define assets, liabilities, and owners' equity. What is the relationship among the three?

5. What is meant by the term "the lower of cost or market"? When is it used?

6. Define "deferred income taxes" and explain where they are recorded on the balance sheet.

7. What are the differences between a comparative balance sheet and a common-size balance sheet?

8. What is the order of liquidity for the following accounts (most liquid first): Marketable Securities, Prepaid Expenses, Cash, Inventories, and Receivables?

9. How do the terms "current" and "long-term" relate to the balance sheet?

10. How is the current ratio determined, and what does it reflect?

Problem 2.1

Listed below are asset, liability, and owners' equity accounts for Sue & Jerry's Sleepy Hollow as of December 31, 19X1.

Common Stock	$ 44,600
Inventories	23,241
Treasury Stock	7,278
Land	111,158
House Banks	11,738
Deferred Income Taxes (noncurrent/credit balance)	190,038
Paid-in Capital in Excess of Par	115,501
Notes Payable	42,611
Retained Earnings	327,137
Demand Deposits	8,803
Dividend Payable	21,246
Accounts Receivable	128,179
Accrued Salaries	78,293
Certificates of Deposit	2,934
Prepaid Expenses	13,499
Notes Receivable	22,420
Building	682,093
Marketable Securities	134,634
Long-Term Debt	262,930
Investments	30,049
Accounts Payable	58,690
Allowance for Doubtful Accounts	16,316
Deferred Expenses	12,794
Advance Deposits—Banquets	14,203
Current Maturities on Long-Term Debt	25,824
Security Deposits	8,569

Required:

1. Prepare the current assets section of the balance sheet for Sue & Jerry's Sleepy Hollow in accordance with the uniform system of accounts for small hotels, motels, and motor hotels (USASH).

2. Prepare the liabilities section of the balance sheet in accordance with the USASH.

3. Determine the current ratio.

Problem 2.2

The following information is KRS, Inc.'s balance sheet account balances as of December 31, 19X1 and 19X2. You have been hired by Kermit Smith, the owner, to prepare a financial package for a bank loan including comparative balance sheets.

Assets	19X1	19X2
Cash	$ 16,634	$ 20,768
Accounts Receivable	16,105	11,618
Marketable Securities	10,396	10,496
Inventories	14,554	18,554
Prepaid Expenses	4,158	3,874
Land	116,435	116,435
Building	1,007,090	1,007,090
China, Glass, etc.	269,255	284,934
Accumulated Depreciation	453,263	537,849

Liabilities & Owners' Equity		
Accounts Payable	13,265	12,945
Accrued Expenses	2,047	1,039
Deferred Income Taxes	8,163	7,927
Current Portion of Long-Term Debt	20,407	20,060
Long-Term Debt	553,429	533,369
Retained Earnings	192,853	149,380
Common Stock	211,200	211,200

Required:

Prepare comparative balance sheets for December 31, 19X1 and 19X2 in accordance with the uniform system of accounts for small hotels, motels, and motor hotels (USASH). Note: the comparative approach is shown in Exhibit 2.7.

Problem 2.3

Noreen Bayley, the manager of Winkie's Motel, has come to you with some accounting questions. As a result of a fire at the motel, many of the records as of December 31, 19X2 were either burned or soaked by the sprinkler system. You are to help her determine the following balances:

1. In one report, the current ratio for the motel is 1.2:1. In addition, you have determined the amount of current liabilities (including $14,736 of current portion of long-term debt) to be $105,380 and long-term debt to be $60,000. What is the amount of current assets for Winkie's Motel?

2. Ms. Bayley has her December 31, 19X2 bank statement which says she has $49,765 in her savings account and $36,072 in her checking account. She has a copy of the inventory sheet which states total inventory on December 31, 19X2 of $15,491. Assuming that the only current assets are cash, inventory, and accounts receivable, what is the total accounts receivable owed to Ms. Bayley?

3. Ms. Bayley has a copy of the balance sheet from November 30, 19X2 which states that current assets were 30% of the total assets. Assuming this relationship is the same at December 31, 19X2, what are the total assets as of December 31, 19X2?

4. Based on the information in parts 1 through 3, what is the Owners' Equity as of December 31, 19X2?

Problem 2.4

Wayne Smith is the new owner of the Noreen Hotel in Wilmington, Delaware. However, he has no experience in the hospitality industry and has hired you to help the hotel's newest employee, Carol Zink, computerize the back office operations. The first job you must tackle is teaching her about the balance sheet. The following is a list of selected account balances in the General Ledger on December 31, 19X1, and also some additional information.

Bank Balance	$ 141,002
Marketable Securities	532,000
Accounts Payable	1,530,761
Land	3,861,725
Retained Earnings	3,462,476
Current Portion Long-Term Debt	392,000
Building	4,768,333
Accounts Receivable	1,843,999
Furniture & Equipment	2,000,741
Paid-in Capital in Excess of Par	1,795,463
Prepaid Insurance	??
Accumulated Depreciation	847,937
Long-Term Debt	??
Capital Stock	??

Other Information:

1. The market value of the marketable securities as of December 31, 19X1 is $575,998.

2. On January 1, 19X1, the previous owner purchased a two-year insurance policy for $40,000 to cover the years of 19X1—19X2.

3. On December 31, 19X1, there were 50,000 shares of stock issued and outstanding with a par value of $10/share. The 50,000 shares were sold for $2,295,463.

4. Long-term debt is the difference between total assets and owners' equity plus other liabilities than long-term debt.

Required:

1. Prepare the balance sheet in accordance with the uniform system of accounts for small hotels, motels, and motor hotels (USASH).

2. Calculate the common-size percentages for the December 31, 19X1 balance sheet.

Problem 2.5

Below is selected information from the comparative and common-size asset portion of balance sheets for Martin's Motel.

| | Martin's Motel | | | |
| | December 31 | | Dollar | Common-Size |
	19X1	19X2	Difference	(Dec. 31, 19X2)
Current Assets				
Cash				
House Bank	$_____	$_____	$ (10)	_____%
Demand Deposit	_____	60	_____	.6
Total Cash			(10)	1.0
Accounts Receivable	1,241	_____	_____	14.0
Inventories	_____			
Total Current Assets		1,620	201	_____
Investments	_____	_____	25	2.0
Property & Equipment (net)				
Land	957	1,030	_____	_____
Building	4,350	_____	_____	_____
Furniture	_____	_____	(75)	25.0
Other Assets	49	_____	_____	.5
Total Assets	$_____	$_____	$_____	_____%

Required:

Fill in the blanks above. Round all amounts to the nearest dollar.

1985 Annual Report

Hilton Hotels Corporation and Subsidiaries

Consolidated Statements of Income
(In thousands, except per share amounts)

Year Ended December 31,		1985	1984	1983
Revenue	Rooms	$237,047	226,772	236,753
	Food and beverage	174,892	167,472	174,237
	Casino	204,649	190,859	182,154
	Casino promotional allowances	(26,637)	(24,258)	(25,189)
	Management and franchise fees	56,402	51,669	43,624
	Other	37,164	34,783	37,701
	Operating income from unconsolidated affiliates	27,057	30,267	33,648
		712,374	686,564	682,028
Expenses	Rooms	78,012	74,288	74,289
	Food and beverage	136,515	134,121	135,728
	Casino	69,633	61,428	60,431
	Other operating expenses	134,873	118,158	120,479
	Property operations	50,015	59,624	59,956
	Lease rentals	7,672	6,162	6,602
	Property taxes	12,621	13,211	14,941
	Depreciation	46,272	42,020	40,859
		545,513	509,012	513,285
		166,861	177,552	169,643
	Gain (loss) from property transactions	3,055	(600)	37,581
Operating Income		169,916	176,952	207,224
	Interest and dividend income	18,080	22,181	20,204
	Interest expense (net of $11,010, $11,326 and $4,965 capitalized)	(20,332)	(15,341)	(19,938)
	Interest expense, net, from unconsolidated affiliates	(9,448)	(10,036)	(8,203)
	Corporate expense	(14,982)	(10,743)	(10,519)
Income before Securities Transaction		143,243	163,013	188,768
	Securities transaction	—	28,482	—
Income before Income Taxes		143,243	191,405	188,768
	Provision for income taxes	43,080	77,512	76,131
Net Income		$100,163	113,983	112,637
Net Income per Share		$ 4.03	4.33	4.20

See notes to consolidated financial statements

Hilton Hotels Corporation
and Subsidiaries

Consolidated Balance Sheets
(In thousands)

Assets	December 31,	1985	1984
Current Assets	Cash and temporary investments		
	(at lower of cost or market)	$ 266,507	150,547
	Accounts and notes receivable	86,250	97,293
	Inventories — at cost (first-in, first-out)	8,718	8,404
	Other current assets	9,062	5,391
	Total current assets	370,537	261,635
Investments and Other Assets	Investments in and notes from unconsolidated affiliates	173,087	156,459
	Other investments	34,110	35,050
	Restricted securities	81,701	—
	Other assets	15,198	15,789
	Total investments and other assets	304,096	207,208
Property and Equipment	Property and equipment	791,548	930,189
	Less accumulated depreciation	241,476	235,370
	Net property and equipment	550,072	694,819
Total Assets		$1,225,605	1,163,752

Liabilities and Stockholders' Equity	December 31,	1985	1984
Current Liabilities	Accounts payable and accrued expenses	$ 104,517	120,287
	Current maturities of long-term debt	4,062	3,654
	Income taxes payable	2,703	11,966
	Total current liabilities	111,282	135,907
Long-term Debt	Secured notes payable	52,677	52,910
	Unsecured notes payable	231,620	222,668
	Total long-term debt	284,297	275,578
Other Liabilities	Deferred income taxes	151,752	132,537
	Insurance reserves and other	26,828	26,904
	Total other liabilities	178,580	159,441
Stockholders' Equity	Common stock, 24,784 and 24,608 shares outstanding, respectively	67,369	67,155
	Additional paid-in capital	13,152	10,358
	Retained earnings	682,416	626,804
		762,937	704,317
	Less treasury shares, at cost	111,491	111,491
	Total stockholders' equity	651,446	592,826
Total Liabilities and Stockholders' Equity		$1,225,605	1,163,752

See notes to consolidated financial statements

Hilton Hotels Corporation and Subsidiaries	*Consolidated Statements of Changes in Financial Position* (In thousands)			
	Year Ended December 31,	1985	1984	1983
Funds from Operations	Net income	$100,163	113,983	112,637
	Non-cash charges and (credits) to operations			
	Depreciation	46,272	42,020	40,859
	Deferred income taxes	9,090	17,943	16,621
	After-tax gain on property and securities transactions	(4,287)	(17,880)	(26,711)
	Undistributed earnings of unconsolidated affiliates	(413)	(7,145)	(5,227)
	Funds from operations	150,825	148,921	138,179
Changes in Working Capital	Accounts and notes receivable	11,043	(41,502)	(1,929)
	Inventories	(314)	445	655
	Other current assets	(3,671)	1,538	(836)
	Accounts payable and accrued expenses	(15,770)	32,872	5,836
	Current maturities of long-term debt	408	(6,748)	(4,750)
	Income taxes payable	(9,263)	7,975	3,991
	Funds before investments	133,258	143,501	141,146
Investments and Capital Expenditures	Capital expenditures	(219,004)	(196,862)	(71,622)
	After-tax proceeds from property and securities transactions	334,430	33,265	38,215
	Additional investments	(20,107)	(20,686)	(19,068)
	Funds before financing activities	228,577	(40,782)	88,671
Financing Activities	Long-term borrowings	85,328	73,103	75,000
	Changes in restricted securities	(81,701)	94,904	(47,224)
	Reduction of long-term debt	(76,609)	(39,742)	(12,330)
	Deferred income taxes — tax leasing transaction	11,295	12,045	12,722
	Cash dividends	(44,551)	(47,146)	(48,068)
	Treasury stock purchases	—	(109,952)	—
	Other, net	(6,379)	12,227	182
Increase (Decrease) in Cash and Temporary Investments		$115,960	(45,343)	68,947

See notes to consolidated financial statements

Hilton Hotels Corporation
and Subsidiaries

*Consolidated Statements
of Stockholders' Equity*
*(In thousands, except shares and
per share amounts)*

	Number of Shares Outstanding	Common Stock	Additional Paid-in Capital	Retained Earnings	Treasury Shares	Total Stockholders' Equity
Balance, December 31, 1982	26,678,076	$66,905	7,737	495,398	(1,539)	568,501
Exercise of stock options	46,611	117	1,110	—	—	1,227
Net income	—	—	—	112,637	—	112,637
Dividends ($1.80 per share)	—	—	—	(48,068)	—	(48,068)
Balance, December 31, 1983	26,724,687	67,022	8,847	559,967	(1,539)	634,297
Exercise of stock options	53,326	133	1,511	—	—	1,644
Treasury stock acquired	(2,080,000)	—	—	—	(109,952)	(109,952)
Net income	—	—	—	113,983	—	113,983
Dividends ($1.80 per share)	—	—	—	(47,146)	—	(47,146)
Balance, December 31, 1984	24,698,013	67,155	10,358	626,804	(111,491)	592,826
Exercise of stock options	85,536	214	2,794	—	—	3,008
Net income	—	—	—	100,163	—	100,163
Dividends ($1.80 per share)	—	—	—	(44,551)	—	(44,551)
Balance, December 31, 1985	24,783,549	$67,369	13,152	682,416	(111,491)	651,446

See notes to consolidated financial statements

Hilton Hotels Corporation
and Subsidiaries

Notes to Consolidated Financial Statements
December 31, 1985

Summary of significant accounting policies

PRINCIPLES OF CONSOLIDATION

The consolidated financial statements include the accounts of Hilton Hotels Corporation and its majority and wholly-owned subsidiaries (the Company). All material inter-company transactions are eliminated. No significant restrictions exist on the transfer of funds from the Company's subsidiaries to Hilton Hotels Corporation.

Investments in unconsolidated affiliates are stated at cost plus equity in undistributed earnings less losses since acquisition.

CASINO REVENUES

Casino revenues are the aggregate of gaming wins and losses. Promotional allowances consist of complimentary food, beverage and accommodations.

PROPERTY, EQUIPMENT AND DEPRECIATION

Property and equipment are stated at cost. Interest incurred during construction of new facilities or major additions to facilities is capitalized and amortized over the life of the asset.

Depreciation has been computed by the straight-line method using the following estimated useful lives: buildings and improvements — average of approximately 44 years; leasehold improvements — the remaining lives of existing leases; furniture and equipment — average of eight years. Expenditures for revisions and alterations to existing facilities are classified with buildings and leasehold improvements and are amortized over varying periods in accordance with the useful lives of the respective assets.

Costs of major improvements are capitalized; costs of normal repairs and maintenance are charged to expense as incurred. Upon the sale or retirement of property and equipment, the cost and related accumulated depreciation are removed from the respective accounts, and the resulting gain or loss, if any, is included in income.

PRE-OPENING COSTS

Operating costs and expenses associated with the opening of hotels or major additions to hotels are deferred and charged to income over a three year period after the opening date.

UNAMORTIZED LOAN COSTS

Debt discount and issuance costs incurred in connection with long-term debt are amortized by charges to expense, principally on the bonds outstanding method.

INCOME TAXES

The provisions for deferred income taxes in the accompanying notes to consolidated financial statements reflect the results of timing differences in recognizing income or deductions for financial reporting and income tax purposes.

Casino revenues are excluded from taxable income until collected. Federal income tax payable upon collection is included in current liabilities.

Investment tax credits are accounted for on the flow-through method as a reduction of Federal income taxes.

EMPLOYEE BENEFIT AND STOCK OPTION PLANS

Retirement plan costs charged to income include normal cost and interest on unfunded supplemental actuarial value.

No charges or credits to income are made with regard to the options granted under the Company's stock option plans.

RESTRICTED SECURITIES

In 1983 and 1984 the Company had restricted the use of certain negotiable securities for funding the construction of a hotel-casino in Atlantic City, New Jersey. These funds were fully expended at December 31, 1984.

In 1985 the Company restricted the proceeds from two issues of industrial development revenue bonds for the redevelopment of two existing hotel properties.

OTHER INVESTMENTS

During 1981 the Company entered into a "safe harbor lease" under the Economic Recovery Tax Act of 1981, which provides for the deferral of income tax payments through the use of accelerated cost recovery system deductions related to the leased assets. The cost totalling $15,502,000 was recorded as a long-term investment in tax benefits and the portion of the cost not directly recovered through tax deductions is being amortized over a ten year period beginning in 1983.

Hilton Hotels Corporation and Subsidiaries

Notes to Consolidated Financial Statements
(continued)

NET INCOME PER SHARE

Net income per share is based on the weighted average number of common shares outstanding plus the common stock equivalents which arise from the assumed exercise of stock options. Earnings per common share assuming full dilution does not differ significantly from primary earnings per share.

RECLASSIFICATIONS

The consolidated financial statements for prior years reflect certain reclassifications to conform with classifications adopted in 1985. These reclassifications have no effect on net income.

Accounts and Notes Receivable

Accounts and notes receivable at December 31, 1985 and 1984 are as follows:

(In thousands)	1985	1984
Hotel accounts and notes receivable	$72,405	55,215
Less allowance for doubtful accounts	1,108	1,283
	71,297	53,932
Casino accounts receivable	13,034	11,770
Less allowance for doubtful accounts	3,330	1,850
	10,508	9,923
Due from sale of securities	—	33,000
Federal tax refund receivable	4,385	438
Total	$86,250	97,293

Based primarily on historical trends, an allowance for estimated uncollectible casino receivables is provided to reduce casino receivables to amounts anticipated to be collected within twelve months of the date credit was granted. Such allowances are included in casino expenses in the amount of $3,471,000, $1,355,000 and $1,040,000 in 1985, 1984 and 1983, respectively.

Property and Equipment

Property and equipment at December 31, 1985 and 1984 are as follows:

(In thousands)	1985	1984
Land	$ 56,107	57,152
Buildings and leasehold improvements	499,125	470,402
Furniture and equipment	204,211	194,134
Property held for sale or development	10,108	8,825
Construction in progress	21,997	190,076
Total	$791,548	930,189

Investments

The composition of the Company's total investments in and notes from unconsolidated affiliates at December 31, 1985 and 1984 is as follows:

(In thousands)	1985	1984
Equity investments		
50% owned unconsolidated affiliates		
Hotel partnership joint ventures (nine in 1985 and in 1984)	$153,029	136,042
Compass Computer Services, Inc.	5,400	5,410
Hilton Reservation Equipment Company	1,955	—
Less than 50% owned unconsolidated affiliates		
Hotel partnership joint ventures (eight in 1985, five in 1984)	9,288	10,625
Total equity investments	170,572	152,077
Notes receivable (net of current maturities of $743 and $697)	3,415	3,482
Total	$173,987	156,459

The changes in the Company's equity investments in such affiliates are as follows:

(In thousands)	1985	1984
Investments, January 1	$152,077	149,475
Earnings	18,500	20,231
Distributions received	(18,996)	(22,086)
Sale of investment in hotel partnership joint venture	—	(2,760)
Additional investments	17,182	8,117
Investments, December 31	$170,572	152,077

Three unconsolidated affiliates have limitations on distributions of earnings under certain circumstances. At December 31, 1985 one property had a restriction on such distributions of $8,850,000. At December 31, 1985 undistributed earnings from unconsolidated affiliates aggregated $31,420,000.

Management fees totalling approximately $13,027,000, $13,585,000 and $10,368,000 were charged by the Company to its unconsolidated affiliates in 1985, 1984 and 1983, respectively. Other group services were provided to unconsolidated affiliates with no significant element of profit.

Summarized balance sheet information of the 50% owned affiliates is as follows:

(In thousands)	1985	1984
Current assets	$ 74,603	67,735
Property and other assets, net	524,047	406,535
Current liabilities	53,810	50,107
Long-term debt and other	150,800	147,080
Equity	394,874	300,087

Summarized balance sheet information of the less than 50% owned affiliates is as follows:

(In thousands)	1985	1984
Current assets	$ 31,816	30,630
Property and other assets, net	400,370	330,147
Current liabilities	41,317	33,000
Long-term debt and other	368,334	200,500
Equity	91,535	123,584

Of total joint venture obligations of $614,000,000 at December 31, 1985, $451,000,000 is secured solely by venture assets or is guaranteed by other venture partners without recourse to the Company.

The Company's proportionate share of equity as reflected in the unconsolidated affiliates' financial statements is $35,766,000 and $37,666,000 in excess of its cost in 1985 and 1984, respectively, and is being amortized over the estimated useful lives of the underlying assets. Such amortization amounted to $1,900,000, $1,936,000 and $1,955,000 in 1985, 1984 and 1983, respectively.

The Company's proportionate shares of capital expenditures and depreciation expense of unconsolidated affiliates were $74,143,000 and $19,087,000, respectively, in 1985, $64,565,000 and $16,865,000, respectively, in 1984 and $27,904,000 and $15,876,000, respectively, in 1983.

Summarized results of operations of these affiliates are as follows:

(In thousands)	1985	1984	1983
Revenue	$516,375	505,828	456,688
Expenses	487,175	454,727	400,903
Operating income	27,473	48,516	45,056

The proportionate taxable income or loss of all partnership joint ventures is included in the taxable income of their respective partners. Therefore, no provisions for income taxes on such entities, except for certain local taxes on income of partnership joint ventures in the District of Columbia and the Federal income tax of a corporate joint venture, are included in the above statements.

Other investments at December 31, 1985 and 1984 consist of:

(In thousands)	1985	1984
Safe harbor tax lease benefits	$13,865	14,718
Other notes and investments	20,245	20,332
Total	$34,110	35,050

The lessee under the safe harbor lease has recently filed a petition for reorganization under Chapter 11 of the United States Bankruptcy Code. Management does not believe such reorganization will have a material adverse effect on the Company's consolidated financial position.

Hilton Hotels Corporation
and Subsidiaries

Notes to Consolidated Financial Statements
(continued)

Income Taxes

The provisions for income taxes for the three years ended December 31, 1985 are as follows:

(In thousands)	1985	1984	1983
Current			
Federal	$44,895	56,132	55,876
Investment and other tax credits	(14,598)	(6,810)	(3,496)
State and local	4,659	11,781	7,174
	34,956	61,103	59,554
Deferred	8,124	16,409	16,577
Total	$43,080	77,512	76,131

Deferred tax expense arises primarily from excess tax over book depreciation of $21,559,000 in 1985, $22,854,000 in 1984 and $23,728,000 in 1983, differences in financial and tax basis reporting of income from joint ventures ($10,663,000 in 1985) and from differences in the reporting of income related to self-insurance and operating equipment. In 1984 deferred tax expense also arose from capitalized interest of $11,080,000. Deferred taxes arising from the safe harbor leasing transaction are credited directly to deferred income tax liabilities.

Reconciliation of the Federal income tax rate and the Company's effective tax rate is as follows:

	1985	1984	1983
Federal income tax rate	46.0%	46.0	46.0
Increase (reduction) in taxes			
State income tax (net of Federal tax benefit)	1.8	3.3	2.1
Investment and other tax credits	(10.0)	(3.6)	(1.9)
Benefit of capital gains rate	(.6)	(2.5)	(3.6)
Benefit of municipal bond income	(2.6)	(2.0)	(1.8)
Charitable contribution	(1.7)	—	—
Other	(2.8)	(.7)	(.5)
Effective tax rate	30.1%	40.5	40.3

Long-term Debt

Long-term debt at December 31, 1985 and 1984 is as follows:

(In thousands)	1985	1984
Mortgage bonds and notes, 4½% to 9%, due 1986 to 2003	$ 43,931	46,794
Collateral trust bonds, 8%, due 1986 to 1993	9,096	9,285
Senior debentures, 11⅜%, due 1992	74,620	74,565
Senior debentures, 10⅝%, due 1994	75,000	75,000
Industrial development revenue bonds at adjustable rates, due 2015	82,000	—
Unsecured notes payable	—	73,103
Other	3,712	485
	288,359	279,232
Less current maturities	4,062	3,654
Net long-term debt	$284,297	275,578

Debt maturities during the next five years will be as follows:

(In thousands)	
1986	$4,062
1987	3,468
1988	2,717
1989	3,203
1990	3,360

Secured notes and bonds payable are collateralized by property with a net book value of $296,678,000 and are payable serially over remaining terms ranging to seventeen years.

The collateral trust bonds, due December 1, 1993, are presented net of $378,000 and $444,000 of unamortized discount and $3,026,000 and $4,021,000 principal amount of treasury bonds in 1985 and 1984, respectively.

The $150 million of senior debentures are redeemable by the Company, in whole or from time to time in part, at 100% of the principal amount plus accrued interest to the date of redemption on or after December 1, 1989 for the 11⅜% issue and January 15, 1991 for the 10⅝% issue. The 11⅜% debentures are presented net of $380,000 and $435,000 unamortized discount at December 31, 1985 and 1984, respectively.

In 1985 the Company filed shelf registration statements whereby it could offer up to $300 million in senior debentures and $300 million in subordinated debentures. There were no borrowings under these facilities in 1985.

In 1985 $82 million in adjustable tender industrial development revenue bonds were issued by certain local authorities in Georgia and Louisiana. The proceeds of these issues will provide for the renovation of airport properties in those jurisdictions.

Lines of credit available include $82.5 million in money-market facilities with interest and maturity terms as quoted by the participating banks at the time of any borrowing thereunder. The money-market facilities carry no commitment fees and may be withdrawn at the discretion of the participating banks. There were no borrowings under these facilities in 1985 and 1984.

During 1985, 1984 and 1983, the Company issued and renewed commercial paper for varying periods with interest at market rates. The Company had no commercial paper outstanding at any year end. In 1985, 1984 and 1983 average amounts of commercial paper outstanding were $89,629,000, $8,800,000 and $3,800,000, respectively, with the largest amounts outstanding at any one time being $104,032,000, $26,000,000 and $25,000,000, respectively. Weighted average interest rates were 8.26%, 11.21% and 9.20%, respectively.

Under the Company's most restrictive indenture the Company is limited on the amount of retained earnings available for payment of cash dividends and acquisition of the Company's stock. At December 31, 1985, approximately $507,345,000 of retained earnings was not restricted.

Capital Stock

Ninety and sixty million shares of common stock with a par value of $2.50 per share were authorized in 1985 and 1984, respectively, of which 26,947,483 and 26,861,947 were issued at December 31, 1985 and 1984, respectively, including treasury shares of 2,163,934 in 1985 and 1984.

Ten million shares of preferred stock with a par value of $1.00 per share were authorized in 1985. No preferred shares were outstanding at December 31, 1985.

At December 31, 1985, 1,060,856 shares of common stock were reserved for the exercise of options under the Company's stock option plans. Options may be granted to salaried officers and other key employees of the Company to purchase common stock at not less than fair market value at the date of grant.

Options may be exercised in installments commencing one year after the date of grant and expire either five or ten years after the date of grant. The plans also permit the granting of Stock Appreciation Rights (SAR's). There were no SAR's outstanding at either December 31, 1985 or 1984.

Changes in stock options during 1985 were as follows:

	Options Price Range (Per Share)	Options Outstanding	Available for Grant
Balance at			
January 1	$ 8.44-62.36	533,849	612,543
Granted	56.75-67.38	118,975	(118,975)
Exercised	27.03-56.69	(85,536)	—
Cancelled	36.06-56.75	(29,968)	29,068
Balance at			
December 31	8.44-67.38	537,320	523,536
Exercisable at			
December 31	$ 8.44-56.69	99,339	

Under provisions of Nevada and New Jersey gaming laws and the Company's certificate of incorporation, certain securities of the Company are subject to restrictions on ownership which may be imposed by specified governmental commissions. Such restrictions may require the holder to dispose of his securities or, if the holder refuses to make such disposition, the Company may be obligated to repurchase the securities.

Hilton Hotels Corporation
and Subsidiaries

Notes to Consolidated Financial Statements
(continued)

Employee Benefit Plans

The Company has a non-contributory retirement plan covering substantially all regular full-time, non-union employees. The retirement plan expense in 1985 was $1,163,000. There was no retirement plan expense in 1984 or 1983. The Company's pension expense and benefits are determined under the entry age actuarial cost method.

Accumulated plan benefits and plan net assets, as of the latest valuation dates, are as follows:

(In thousands, except percentages)	January 1, 1985	January 1, 1984
Actuarial present value of accumulated plan benefits		
Discount rate	8½%	8
Vested	$31,047	31,058
Nonvested	4,682	6,222
Total accumulated plan benefits	$36,629	37,280
Plan net assets available for benefits	$56,305	47,222

During 1985 the Financial Accounting Standards Board (FASB) issued new standards on employers' accounting for pensions. The Company is required to adopt the new expense and disclosure standards by 1987, although earlier adoption is permitted. There is no effect on financial statements issued prior to the year of adoption.

The Company has not determined when it will implement the new standards, but does not believe the new standards will have a material impact on either its results of operations or financial position.

A significant number of the Company's employees are covered by union sponsored, collectively bargained multi-employer pension plans. The Company contributed and charged to expense approximately $6,235,000, $5,983,000 and $5,038,000 in 1985, 1984 and 1983, respectively, for such plans. Information from the plans' administrators is not sufficient to permit the Company to determine its share of unfunded vested benefits, if any.

The Company also has an employee investment plan for certain employees whereby the Company contributes certain percentages of employee contributions, a supplemental retirement plan for senior officers and a retirement benefit plan for non-officer directors. The costs of the plans are not significant.

Leases

The Company operates six properties under non-cancellable operating leases, all of which are for land only, having remaining terms up to 48 years. Upon expiration of two of the leases, the Company has renewal options ranging from 40 to 60 years. Four leases require the payment of additional rentals based upon varying percentages of revenue or income. Additionally, the Company is committed under non-cancellable leases for office space having remaining terms up to 20 years.

Minimum lease rental commitments under non-cancellable operating leases are as follows:

Year Ended December 31,	(In thousands)
1986	$ 6,515
1987	6,118
1988	5,878
1989	5,755
1990	5,653
1991 to 2033	70,395
Total	$100,314

Total lease rental expense for all operating leases is composed of:

(In thousands)	1985	1984	1983
Minimum rentals	$5,850	4,221	4,848
Additional rentals	1,813	1,941	1,754
Total	$7,072	6,162	6,602

Commitments and Contingent Liabilities

At December 31, 1985 the Company had contractual commitments at its wholly-owned or leased properties for major expansion and rehabilitation projects of approximately $37,421,000. There were also entertainer commitments of $1,027,000. Additionally, the Company is committed, under certain conditions, to invest or loan up to $38,703,000 to entities developing hotel properties.

Several lawsuits are pending against the Company. In the opinion of management, disposition of these lawsuits is expected to have no material effect on the consolidated financial statements.

Segments of Business

Revenues and income contribution by business segment are included in the Ten Year Summary (pages 30 and 31). Other financial data of the Company's business segments for the years ended December 31, 1985, 1984 and 1983 are as follows:

(In thousands)	1985	1984	1983
Depreciation			
Hotels (1)	$ 42,247	36,438	35,724
Gaming (1)	23,112	22,447	21,011
Total	$ 65,359	58,885	56,735
Capital Expenditures			
Hotels (1)	$ 137,677	103,784	60,666
Gaming (1)	155,470	157,643	38,860
Total	$ 293,147	261,427	99,526
Assets			
Hotels (2)	$ 577,852	446,202	391,751
Gaming (2)	347,437	530,255	392,168
Corporate	300,316	187,295	315,293
Total	$1,225,605	1,163,752	1,099,212

(1) Includes Hilton's proportionate share of unconsolidated affiliates.
(2) Includes investments in unconsolidated affiliates.

Hilton Hotels Corporation
and Subsidiaries

Notes to Consolidated Financial Statements
(continued)

Supplementary Financial Information (unaudited)

Quarterly Financial Data
(In thousands, except per share amounts and percentages)

1985	Occupancy Hotels (1)	Gaming	Revenue	Income Contribution	Sale of Marketable Securities	Income Before Income Taxes	Net Income	Earnings Per Share	Dividends Per Share	High/Low Stock Price
1st Quarter	65%	80	$173,100	41,767	—	38,171	23,450	.94	.45	63.50/55.75
2nd Quarter	66	85	185,738	49,100	—	43,374	27,508	1.11	.45	73.50/62.50
3rd Quarter	62	87	169,142	34,664	—	28,664	20,365	.82	.45	68.88/57.75
4th Quarter	61	83	184,304	41,330	—	33,034	28,750	1.16	.45	70.38/56.63
Year	64%	86	$712,374	166,861	—	143,243	100,103	4.03	1.80	73.50/55.75
1984										
1st Quarter	61%	85	$164,049	37,375	—	33,036	19,146	.71	.45	58.00/47.63
2nd Quarter	68	82	173,486	46,839	—	43,192	24,530	.02	.45	54.75/47.50
3rd Quarter	65	87	107,991	43,190	—	40,216	24,298	.03	.45	53.38/45.50
4th Quarter	62	83	181,038	50,148	28,482	74,151	46,000	1.70	.45	58.00/50.88
Year	64%	84	$686,564	177,552	28,482	191,495	113,983	4.33	1.80	58.00/45.50

(1) Hotels owned or managed.

As of December 31, 1985 there were approximately 7,000 stockholders of record.

Current Cost Information (unaudited)

The Financial Accounting Standards Board (FASB) prescribes the current cost method for measuring the effect of changing prices on assets and income.

The method attempts to measure inflation using the current replacement cost of Company resources. Current costs of property and equipment are based on replacement cost and, in the case of the Company, are based primarily on appraisals made by professional appraisers. The amounts reported in the historical cost financial statements have been changed only for depreciation expense on Company-owned property and equipment, for the Company's proportionate share of revised depreciation expense of unconsolidated affiliates' property and equipment, and gains on property transactions. No adjustment was required for inventories due to their high turnover rate which results in current costs being reflected in the historical cost financial statements. No adjustment has been made to the provision for income taxes.

The development of this information by necessity requires that various critical assumptions and estimates be made. While they are believed to be reasonable, they still remain the subjective judgements of management and the appraisers relevant only to the current time period. The results should be viewed accordingly.

Consolidated Statement of Income Adjusted for Changing Prices (unaudited)
(In thousands)

For the Year Ended December 31, 1985	Income as Adjusted for Current Costs
Net income as presented in the consolidated statements of income	$100,163
Adjustments to restate costs for the effect of general inflation and changes in specific prices (current costs)	
Depreciation — owned properties	(10,302)
— proportionate share of unconsolidated affiliates	(2,812)
Gains on property transactions	(3,055)
Net income as adjusted	$ 83,994
Increase in general price level of property and equipment held during the year	$ 20,153
Increase in specific prices (current cost)	22
Excess of increase in general prices over increase in specific prices	$ 29,175

At December 31, 1985, current cost of property and equipment, net of accumulated depreciation, was $870,074.
(Historical amount — $550,072)

Five Year Comparison of Selected Supplementary Financial Data
Adjusted for Effects of Changing Prices (unaudited)
(In thousands, except per share and index data)

		1985	1984	1983	1982	1981
Revenues	Historical	$712,374	686,564	682,028	633,324	627,362
	Adjusted for general inflation	712,374	711,518	737,397	705,835	742,056
Net income	Historical	100,163	113,983	112,637	83,373	112,623
	Adjusted for specific price changes	83,994	71,020	60,001	70,864	130,531
Per share data	Historical	4.03	4.33	4.20	3.12	4.22
	Adjusted for specific price changes	3.38	2.90	2.24	2.88	5.23
Net assets at year end	Historical	651,440	592,826	634,207	568,501	532,555
	Current value basis	2,362,000	2,387,741	2,532,459	2,533,191	3,154,730
	Adjusted for specific price changes	1,405,480	1,411,082	1,457,007	1,461,802	1,601,099
Gain on net monetary liabilities due to decline of purchasing power of the dollar		13,211	10,086	7,419	6,710	10,904
Cash dividends per common share	Historical	1.80	1.80	1.80	1.80	1.65
	Adjusted for general inflation	1.80	1.87	1.94	2.01	1.95
Market price per common share at year end	Historical	64.88	57.63	57.00	44.75	38.00
	Adjusted for general inflation	64.88	59.80	61.49	50.11	44.20
Average consumer price index		322.2	310.9	298.4	289.1	272.4

All general inflation and specific price dollar amounts are stated in average 1985 dollars.

Supplementary Information — Current Value

The Company's consolidated financial statements are prepared based on historical prices in effect when the transactions occurred. These statements do not reflect changes in (1) the current replacement costs or (2) the fair market values of the assets. In an attempt to address those shortcomings, the FASB requires that major companies provide information regarding specific cost changes (current cost).

The Company also reports market values in addition to the required FASB information. It is management's opinion that presentation of market values based on industry valuation methods and sound theory is significant information for its stockholders. Other qualitative and quantitative methods and considerations, however, are commonly used in valuing companies, including analyses of the market prices of publicly traded equity securities of the Company and of other companies engaged in similar businesses, the financial consideration offered in recent business combinations of competitive companies, the skill and depth of management and business prospects. In addition, market values can be significantly affected by changes in Federal or other tax laws and competitive conditions affecting specific properties. Each method and consideration can result in widely different valuations, and the reader is therefore cautioned against any simplistic use of the information presented.

Presented below are audited, condensed consolidated balance sheets on the current value basis, accompanied by notes thereto.

Condensed Consolidated
Balance Sheets — Current Value Basis
(In thousands)

	December 31,	1985	1984
Assets	Current assets	$ 371,000	262,000
	Investments in and notes from unconsolidated affiliates	506,000	487,000
	Other investments	116,000	37,000
	Operating properties	1,429,000	1,480,000
	Other property	36,000	206,000
	Management and franchise agreements	465,000	380,000
	Other assets	13,000	14,000
	Total current value of assets	$2,936,000	2,875,000
Liabilities and Stockholders' Equity	Liabilities	$ 574,000	571,000
	Stockholders' equity		
	Historical cost basis	651,000	593,000
	Revaluation equity	1,711,000	1,711,000
	Total stockholders' equity	2,362,000	2,304,000
	Total liabilities and stockholders' equity	$2,936,000	2,875,000

The presentation of current value information does not imply management's intent to dispose of any assets or, if such assets were sold, that the current value could be obtained.

Notes to Condensed Consolidated Balance Sheets—Current Value Basis

Current assets and other assets are stated at historical cost, which is estimated to approximate current value. The value of other investments is based on market prices as of December 31, 1985 and 1984, respectively.

Other property consists primarily of construction in progress and vacant land. Construction in progress is stated at historical cost, which is estimated to approximate current value. Vacant land is stated at management's estimate of current value, which does not differ significantly from cost at December 31, 1985 and 1984.

The value of investments in and notes from unconsolidated affiliates is the estimated present value of future income streams minus debt. Operating properties and management and franchise agreements are valued at the present values of the respective net income streams generated. Discount rates used were comparable between 1985 and 1984 and primarily range from 9% to 12%. Estimates for values of wholly-owned and unconsolidated affiliates' properties were made by the following outside appraisers: Joseph J. Blake & Associates, Inc., Valuation Counselors, Inc., Real Estate Research Corporation, Britton Appraisal Associates, Inc., Harps & Harps, Inc., Peter F. Korpacz & Associates, Inc., and Kenneth E. Peltzer, Ph.D.

Long-term debt is valued at the present value of future cash flows based on existing interest rates. This represents an economic savings compared to current rates for an equivalent amount of conventional debt. Such differences were included in the Company's equity interests in operating properties. Consequently, long-term debt is carried at historical cost. Other liabilities are stated on a historical cost basis.

Income taxes have not been computed on the differences between current value and the historical income tax bases of assets.

Revaluation equity is the aggregate difference between current value and historical accounting bases of the Company's assets and liabilities. The components of the change in revaluation equity are as follows:

(In thousands)	1985	1984
Balance—January 1	$1,711,000	1,617,000
Increase (Decrease)		
Unconsolidated affiliates	3,000	28,000
Marketable securities	(2,000)	14,000
Operating properties and others	(77,000)	6,000
Management and franchise agreements	76,000	74,000
Property transactions*	—	(28,000)
Total	—	94,000
Balance—December 31	$1,711,000	1,711,000

*In 1984 one wholly-owned property and one joint venture property were sold, and certain equity securities were sold. In 1985 one wholly-owned property and one completed but unopened wholly-owned property were sold, and certain undeveloped land was sold. The proceeds did not vary significantly from 1984 appraisal or market values.

In summary, these valuations are based on methods believed by management to be reasonable. However, they require many subjective judgements by both management and the appraisers and should be read with this in mind. The resulting information may vary significantly from future values due to changing competitive conditions or changes in Federal or other tax laws.

Hilton Hotels Corporation and Subsidiaries *Ten Year Summary*

(Dollars in thousands, except per share amounts)	1985	1984	1983
Summary Data for Years Ended December 31			
Revenue			
Hotels [1]	$1,138,836	1,086,281	977,962
Management fees	28,178	25,395	20,536
Franchise fees	28,224	26,274	23,088
Total hotels	1,195,238	1,137,950	1,021,586
Gaming	366,652	340,954	323,811
Total	1,561,890	1,478,904	1,345,397
Less non-consolidated managed	877,473	831,607	696,117
Total revenue from consolidated operations	$ 684,417	647,297	649,280
Income contribution			
Hotels [2]	$ 90,503	107,807	101,004
Gaming	76,358	69,745	68,639
Total	166,861	177,552	169,643
Net interest and dividend income (expense) [2]	(11,691)	(3,196)	(7,937)
Corporate expense	(14,982)	(10,743)	(10,510)
Income before property transactions and income taxes	140,188	163,613	151,187
Property transactions	3,055	27,882	37,581
Provision for income taxes	(43,080)	(77,512)	(76,131)
Net income	$ 100,163	113,983	112,637
Net income per share	$ 4.03	4.33	4.20
Return on average stockholders' equity	16.1%	18.6	18.7
Dividends per share	$ 1.80	1.80	1.80
Market price — high/low	73.50/55.75	58.00/45.50	60.25/40.13
Funds provided from operations	150,825	148,921	138,179
Depreciation [2]	65,350	58,885	50,735
Capital expenditures [2]	293,147	261,427	99,526
Financial Position at Year End			
Working capital	$ 259,255	125,728	165,651
Assets	1,225,605	1,163,752	1,099,212
Long-term debt	284,297	275,578	242,217
Stockholders' equity	651,446	592,826	634,297
Stockholders' equity per share	26.29	24.00	23.73
Ratio of long-term debt to total capital [3]	.26	.27	.24
General Information			
Average common and equivalent shares	24,881,903	26,348,220	26,846,197
Percentage of occupancy			
Hotels owned or managed	64	64	60
Gaming	86	84	80
Number of properties at year end			
Wholly-owned or leased	11	11	13
Partially owned	14	13	13
Managed	23	22	23
Franchised	218	204	104
Gaming	4	3	3
Total	270	253	246
Available rooms at year end			
Wholly-owned or leased	7,399	7,580	10,464
Partially owned	14,123	12,904	13,430
Managed	13,692	13,258	12,031
Franchised	54,285	49,543	46,014
Gaming	6,602	6,025	6,025
Total	96,101	89,310	88,864

(1) Includes revenue of managed hotels.
(2) Includes Hilton's proportionate share of unconsolidated affiliates.
(3) Total capital represents total assets less current liabilities.

*Average annual return

1982	1981	1980	1979	1978	1977	1976	Ten-Year Compound Growth Rate
908,038	801,966	832,644	770,137	682,573	578,106	515,060	9.7%
17,728	17,058	15,924	13,963	11,820	9,473	8,518	15.6
19,506	17,528	14,305	10,894	8,342	6,160	4,086	22.4
946,172	926,552	862,873	794,994	702,741	593,739	528,573	10.0
291,422	269,147	251,622	230,856	182,952	143,457	131,233	11.4
1,237,594	1,195,699	1,114,495	1,025,850	885,693	737,196	659,806	10.3
638,075	610,476	500,168	511,916	441,628	365,371	313,036	13.2
599,519	585,223	554,327	513,934	444,065	371,825	340,770	7.5
92,595	113,813	114,520	105,286	88,001	61,696	51,813	9.6
52,248	70,120	70,983	69,864	51,264	24,603	21,301	16.8
144,843	102,930	104,512	175,150	140,165	86,299	73,114	12.3
3,843	12,600	8,580	(3,154)	(13,061)	(9,434)	(8,045)	
(9,082)	(8,965)	(7,793)	(6,147)	(5,487)	(4,983)	(4,625)	14.1
138,704	106,583	105,308	165,849	121,617	71,882	59,544	13.9
2,764	—	—	14,717	—	—	—	
(58,095)	(83,060)	(80,176)	(81,283)	(54,023)	(31,817)	(28,216)	
83,373	112,623	106,132	99,283	67,594	40,065	31,328	9.0
3.12	4.22	4.00	3.76	2.62	1.42	1.10	10.9
15.1	22.7	25.1	29.3	26.5	17.8	14.2	20.4*
1.80	1.65	1.42	1.09	.7375	.4825	.3775	20.7
52.00/27.63	52.25/33.25	48.63/25.50	35.63/22.00	32.75/11.38	13.00/8.50	11.63/7.50	
132,366	141,914	132,002	112,085	87,868	56,422	47,042	
51,076	40,240	36,101	33,826	31,872	28,346	25,050	
131,854	178,695	92,821	57,083	66,230	100,619	38,389	
99,671	100,072	132,063	98,584	60,350	51,400	27,818	
938,321	816,470	696,824	636,076	588,951	511,468	408,770	
170,553	119,524	120,602	125,442	174,074	202,776	102,835	
568,501	532,555	458,878	386,315	200,589	218,859	231,001	
21.31	19.08	17.40	14.83	11.04	9.66	8.81	
.21	.17	.19	.23	.36	.45	.29	
26,740,344	26,698,553	26,545,225	26,445,125	26,253,585	29,246,584	29,694,724	
61	65	60	71	70	68	65	
72	81	81	86	86	82	83	
14	14	15	15	16	16	16	
14	15	14	14	14	14	13	
19	16	15	17	16	16	15	
188	171	163	145	136	126	123	
3	3	2	2	2	2	2	
238	210	209	193	184	174	169	
10,909	11,072	11,737	11,878	13,558	13,778	13,960	
14,152	13,235	12,887	12,894	13,078	12,993	11,900	
8,852	7,977	7,454	8,052	7,808	7,103	6,712	
44,877	39,630	36,877	31,855	28,968	26,125	25,774	
6,025	5,523	4,539	3,997	3,819	2,874	2,874	
84,815	77,437	73,494	68,676	67,231	62,933	61,310	

Report of Independent Public Accountants

To the Board of Directors and Stockholders of Hilton Hotels Corporation:

We have examined the consolidated balance sheets of Hilton Hotels Corporation (a Delaware Corporation) and subsidiaries as of December 31, 1985 and 1984, and the related consolidated statements of income, stockholders' equity, and changes in financial position for each of the three years in the period ended December 31, 1985. Our examinations were made in accordance with generally accepted auditing standards and, accordingly, included such tests of the accounting records and such other auditing procedures as we considered necessary in the circumstances.

In our opinion, the financial statements referred to above present fairly the financial position of Hilton Hotels Corporation and subsidiaries as of December 31, 1985 and 1984, and the results of their operations and the changes in their financial position for each of the three years in the period ended December 31, 1985, in conformity with generally accepted accounting principles applied on a consistent basis.

We have also examined the accompanying condensed consolidated balance sheets—current value basis of Hilton Hotels Corporation and subsidiaries as of December 31, 1985 and 1984. Such statements are based on the historical cost consolidated financial statements referred to above, adjusted, as described in the notes thereto, to present assets at their estimated current values.

The condensed consolidated balance sheets—current value basis have been prepared by management to provide relevant information about assets of the Company which is not provided by the historical cost consolidated financial statements and which differs significantly from the historical cost amounts required by generally accepted accounting principles. Consequently, these condensed consolidated financial statements are not intended to summarize financial position in conformity with generally accepted accounting principles.

In our opinion, the condensed consolidated balance sheets—current value basis as of December 31, 1985 and 1984, present fairly the assets and liabilities of Hilton Hotels Corporation and subsidiaries as of December 31, 1985 and 1984 on the basis of accounting described in the notes thereto applied on a consistent basis.

ARTHUR ANDERSEN & CO.

Los Angeles, California,
January 31, 1986.

3 Income Statement

The Ultimate Report Card

The income statement, also referred to as the statement of earnings, the profit and loss statement, statement of operations, and various other titles, reports the success of the hospitality property's operations for a period of time. This statement may be prepared on a weekly or monthly basis for management's use and quarterly or annually for outsiders such as owners, creditors, and governmental agencies.

Users of financial statements examine an operation's income statements for answers to many questions, such as:

1. How profitable was the hospitality operation during the period?

2. What were the total sales for the period?

3. How much was paid for labor?

4. What is the relationship between cost of sales and sales?

5. How much have sales increased over last year?

6. What is the utilities expense for the year and how does it compare to the expense of a year ago?

7. How much was spent to market the hospitality operation's services?

8. How does net income compare to total sales for the period?

These and many more questions can be answered by reviewing the income statements that cover several periods of time. Income statements, including statements by individual departments called departmental income statements, are generally considered to be the most useful financial statements for management's review of operations. Owners and creditors, especially long-term creditors, find that the income statement yields significant information for determining investment value and credit worthiness. However, when analyzing the operating results of any entity, an income statement should be considered in conjunction with other financial statements as well as with the footnotes to those financial statements.

In this chapter, we will address the major elements of the income statement and consider its relationship with the balance sheet. We will also note the differences between income statements prepared for internal and external users. The uniform system of accounts and the general approach to income statements in the hospitality industry will also be discussed. We will provide an in-depth discussion of the contents of the income statement and consider the uses of departmental statements and industry operating statistics. Finally, we will discuss guidelines and techniques for analyzing income statements.

Major Elements of the Income Statement

The income statement reflects the revenues, expenses, gains, and losses for a period of time. Revenues represent the inflow of assets, reduction of liabilities, or a combination of both resulting from the sale of goods or services. For a hospitality operation, revenues generally include food sales, beverage sales, room sales, interest and dividends from investments, and rents received from lessees of retail space.

Expenses are defined as the outflow of assets, increase in liabilities, or a combination of both in the production and rendering of goods and services. Expenses of a hospitality operation generally include cost of goods sold (for example, food and beverages), labor, utilities, advertising, depreciation, and taxes, to list a few.

Gains are defined as increases in assets, reductions in liabilities, or a combination of both resulting from a hospitality operation's incidental transactions and from all other transactions and events affecting the operation during the period, except those that count as revenues or investments by owners. For example, there may be a gain on the sale of equipment. Equipment is used by the business to provide goods and services and, when sold, only the excess proceeds over its net book value (purchase price less accumulated depreciation) is recognized as gain.

Finally, losses are defined as decreases in assets, increases in liabilities, or a combination of both resulting from a hospitality operation's incidental transactions and from other transactions and events affecting the operation during a period, except those that count as expenses or distributions to owners. In the equipment example above, if the proceeds were less than the net book value, a loss would occur and would be recorded as "loss on sale of equipment." Another example would be a loss from an "act of nature," such as a tornado or hurricane. The loss reported is the reduction of assets less insurance proceeds received.

In the income statement for hospitality operations, revenues are reported separately from gains, and expenses are distinguished from losses. These distinctions are important in determining management's success in operating the hospitality property. Management is held accountable primarily for operations (revenues and expenses) and only secondarily (if at all) for gains and losses.

Relationship with the Balance Sheet

The income statement covers a period of time while the balance sheet is prepared as of the last day of the accounting period. Thus, the income statement reflects operations of the hospitality property for the period between balance sheet dates as shown below.

12/31/X1	◄─────── Year of 19X2 ───────►	12/31/X2
Balance Sheet	results of	Balance Sheet
	operations	
	(Income Statement)	

The results of operations, net income or loss for the period, is added to the proper equity account and shown on the balance sheet at the end of the accounting period (as discussed in Chapter 1).

Income Statements for Internal and External Users

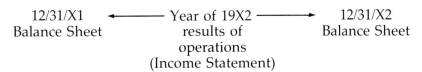

Hospitality properties prepare income statements for both internal users (management) and for external users (creditors, owners, etc.). These statements differ substantially, as the income statements provided to external users are relatively brief, providing only summary detail about the results of operations. Exhibit 3.1 is the income statement presentation of Marriott Corporation and Subsidiaries from its Annual Report for 1985.

Marriott's income statement shows the following:

- Sales by segment

- Operating expenses by segment

- Operating income by segment (sales less operating expenses)

- Interest expense

- Interest income

- Corporate expense

- Income taxes

- Income from discontinued operations

- Net income

- Earnings per share

We have already stressed that footnotes, which generally appear after the financial statements in the financial report (but not included in Exhibit 3.1), are critical to interpreting the numbers reported on the income statement. The Marriott Corporation has notified readers of the integral role footnotes play, as reflected by "the accompanying notes are an integral part of these financial statements" included on the same page as the income statement.

Although the amount of operating information shown in the income statement and accompanying footnotes may be adequate for external users to reflect on the hospitality property's operations, management requires considerably more information. Management also needs this information more frequently than outsiders. In general, the more frequent the need to make decisions, the more frequent the need for financial information. Management's information needs are met, in part, by detailed monthly operating statements which reflect budget numbers

Exhibit 3.1   Income Statement — Marriott 1985 Report

INCOME STATEMENT

Marriott Corporation and Subsidiaries
Fiscal years ended January 3, 1986, December 28, 1984 and December 30, 1983

	1985	1984	1983
	(in millions, except per share amounts)		
Sales			
Lodging	$1,898.4	$1,640.8	$1,320.5
Contract Food Services	1,586.3	1,069.5	923.0
Restaurants	757.0	814.6	707.0
Total sales	4,241.7	3,524.9	2,950.5
Operating Expenses			
Lodging	1,712.6	1,479.6	1,180.8
Contract Food Services	1,467.7	982.7	851.9
Restaurants	678.8	734.9	643.2
Total operating expenses	3,859.1	3,197.2	2,675.9
Operating Income			
Lodging	185.8	161.2	139.7
Contract Food Services	118.6	86.8	71.1
Restaurants	78.2	79.7	63.8
Total operating income	382.6	327.7	274.6
Interest expense	(75.6)	(61.6)	(62.8)
Interest income	42.9	12.9	7.5
Corporate expenses	(54.2)	(42.9)	(34.2)
Income before income taxes	295.7	236.1	185.1
Provision for income taxes	128.3	100.8	76.7
Income from continuing operations	167.4	135.3	108.4
Income from discontinued operations	—	4.5	6.8
Net Income	$ 167.4	$ 139.8	$ 115.2
Earnings per share			
Continuing operations	$ 6.20	$ 5.01	$ 3.90
Net income	$ 6.20	$ 5.18	$ 4.15

The accompanying notes are an integral part of these financial statements.

and report performance for the most recent period, the same period a year ago, and year-to-date numbers for both the current and past year.

If there is expected to be any difference between the year-to-date numbers and the originally budgeted numbers, many operating statements of firms in the hospitality industry also show the latest forecast of results (reforecasting). Management is then able to compare actual results against the most recent forecasts. We will further explore the need for reforecasting when we discuss operations budgeting in Chapter 11. In addition to the monthly operating statement, a more frequent major report prepared for management is the daily report of operations.

Hospitality managers require even more information than is provided by daily reports and monthly statements. Exhibit 3.2 is a list of various management reports including frequency, content, comparisons, who gets the report, and the purpose of each report. Even though 12 reports are included, this list does not include all reports required by the various levels of management in a hospitality operation. For example, two major financial statements included in this text, the balance sheet and the statement of changes in financial position, are absent from the list.

Management's need for financial information on a monthly basis may be met, to a large degree, by using a summary income statement and accompanying departmental income statements that are contained in the various uniform systems of accounts.

Uniform System of Accounts

The uniform systems of accounts are standardized accounting systems prepared by various segments of the hospitality industry. A uniform system of accounts provides a turnkey system for new entrants into the hospitality industry by offering detailed information about accounts, classifications, formats, and the different kinds, contents, and uses of financial statements and reports. For example, the *Uniform System of Accounts for Small Hotels, Motels, and Motor Hotels* (USASH), contains not only the basic financial statements but over fifteen supplementary departmental operating statements and appendices covering budgeting and forecasting, a discussion of compiling revenue by market source, forms of statements, break-even analysis and a uniform account numbering system.[1]

The uniform system of accounts also allows for a more reasonable comparison of the operational results of similar hospitality properties. As various establishments follow a uniform system of accounts, the differences in accounting among these hospitality properties are minimized, thus ensuring comparability.

A uniform system of accounts is a time-tested system. The *Uniform System of Accounts for Hotels* (USAH) was first produced in 1925-26 by a designated group of accountants for the Hotel Association of New York City. Over the past sixty years, the USAH has been revised many times by committees, beginning with New York City accountants and, most recently, by accountants from across the United States. The 8th revised edition of the USAH (1986) was prepared by a select committee of the International Association of Hospitality Accountants. During the work on the 8th revision, consultations on changes were made with various other accounting groups including the British Association of Hospitality Accountants. The *Uniform System of Accounts for Small Hotels, Motels, and Motor Hotels* (USASH) was revised for the second time in 1986.

Finally, the uniform system of accounts can be adapted for use by large and small hospitality operations. The uniform system of accounts illustrated in this chapter is the *Uniform System of Accounts for Small Hotels, Motels, and Motor Hotels* The *Uniform System of Accounts for Hotels* is similar to the USASH and differs primarily by including more profit centers on the Summary Income Statement. The USASH contains many more accounts and classifications than will generally be used by a single hotel or motel. Therefore, each facility simply selects the schedules and accounts that are required for its use and ignores the others.

Exhibit 3.2 Management Reports

Report	Frequency	Content	Comparisons	Who Gets It	Purpose
Daily Report of Operations	Daily, on a cumulative basis for the month, the year to date.	Occupancy, average rate, revenue by outlet, and pertinent statistics.	To operating plan for current period and to prior year results.	Top management and supervisors responsible for day to day operation.	Basis for evaluating the current health of the enterprise.
Weekly Forecasts	Weekly.	Volume in covers, occupancy.	Previous periods.	Top management and supervisory personnel.	Staffing and scheduling; promotion.
Summary Report — Flash	Monthly at end of month (prior to monthly financial statement).	Known elements of revenue and direct costs; estimated departmental indirect costs.	To operating plan; to prior year results.	Top management and supervisory personnel responsible for function reported.	Provides immediate information on financial results for rooms, food and beverages, and other.
Cash Flow Analysis	Monthly (and on a revolving 12-month basis.)	Receipts and disbursements by time periods.	With cash flow plan for month and for year to date.	Top management.	Predicts availability of cash for operating needs. Provides information on interim financing requirements.
Labor Productivity Analysis	Daily Weekly Monthly	Dollar cost; manpower hours expended; hours as related to sales and services (covers, rooms occupied, etc.)	To committed hours in the operating plan (standards for amount of work to prior year statistics).	Top management and supervisory personnel.	Labor cost control through informed staffing and scheduling. Helps refine forecasting.
Departmental Analysis	Monthly (early in following month.)	Details on main categories of income; same on expense.	To operating plan (month and year to date) and to prior year.	Top management and supervisors by function (e.g., rooms, each food and beverage outlet, laundry, telephone, other profit centers.	Knowing where business stands, and immediate corrective actions.
Room Rate Analysis	Daily, monthly, year to date.	Actual rates compared to rack rates by rate category or type of room.	To operating plan and to prior year results.	Top management and supervisors of sales and front office operations.	If goal is not being achieved, analysis of strengths and weaknesses is prompted.
Return on Investment	Actual computation, at least twice a year. Computation based on forecast, immediately prior to plan for year ahead.	Earnings as a percentage rate of return on average investment or equity committed.	To plan for operation and to prior periods.	Top management.	If goal is not being achieved, prompt assessment of strengths and weaknesses.
Long-Range Planning	Annually.	5-year projections of revenue and expenses. Operating plan expressed in financial terms.	Prior years.	Top management.	Involves staff in success or failure of enterprise. Injects more realism into plans for property and service modifications.
Exception Reporting	Concurrent with monthly reports and financial statements.	Summary listing of line item variances from predetermined norm.	With operating budgets.	Top management and supervisors responsible for function reported.	Immediate focusing on problem before more detailed statement analysis can be made.
Guest History Analysis	At least semi-annually; quarterly or monthly is recommended.	Historical records of corporate business, travel agencies, group bookings.	With previous reports.	Top management and sales.	Give direction to marketing efforts.
Future Bookings Report	Monthly.	Analysis of reservations and bookings.	With several prior years.	Top management, sales and marketing, department management.	Provides information on changing guest profile. Exposes strong and weak points of facility. Guides (1) sales planning and (2) expansion plans.

Source: *Lodging,* July 1979, pp. 40–41.

The USASH is designed to be used at the property level rather than at the corporate level. The format of the income statement is based on responsibility accounting, that is, the presentation is organized to focus attention on departmental results such as rooms and the food and beverage departments. The income statements prepared at the corporate level, where more than one lodging property is owned by the lodging corporation, would most likely be considerably different and would include sale of properties, corporate overhead expenses, and so on, not necessarily shown on an individual lodging property's income statement. The focus of our discussion of income statements for management in this text will be the USASH.

Approach to Hospitality Industry Income Statements

In many industries, the income statement format consists of the following:

	Revenue
Less:	Cost of goods sold
Equals:	Gross profit
Less:	Overhead expenses
Equals:	Net income

Revenue less cost of goods sold equals gross profit. The cost of goods sold is the cost of the product sold. For wholesale and retail firms, it is the cost of goods purchased for resale, while for manufacturers, it is a combination of labor, raw materials, and overhead expenses incurred in the manufacturing process. The expenses subtracted from gross profit to equal net income consist of all other expenses such as administration and selling expenses, depreciation, and income taxes.

By contrast, the income statement format in the USASH approach consists of the following:

	Revenue
Less:	Direct operating expenses
Equals:	Departmental operating income
Less:	Overhead expenses
Equals:	Net income

Revenue less direct operating expenses equals departmental operating income. Departmental operating income less overhead expenses equals net income. Direct operating expenses include not only the cost of goods sold, but also the direct labor expense and other direct expenses. Direct labor expense is the expense of personnel working in the profit centers, such as the rooms department and the food and beverage department. Other direct expenses include supplies used by these revenue producing departments. Therefore, everything else being the same, gross profit would exceed departmental operating income, since direct operating expenses include direct labor and other direct expenses in addition to cost of goods sold.

The income statements based on the USASH provide separate line reporting by profit center, that is, sales and direct expenses are shown separately for the rooms department, the food and beverage department, the telephone department, etc. In addition, the overhead expenses are divided between undistributed operating expenses and fixed charges. The undistributed operating expenses are further detailed on the income statement by major service centers such as marketing and data processing. The detail provided by both profit centers and service centers reflects reporting by areas of responsibility and is commonly referred to as responsibility accounting.

Thus, the USASH income statement is useful to managers in the hospitality industry because it is designed to provide the information necessary to evaluate the performance of managers of the lodging facility by area of responsibility.

Contents of the Income Statement

The summary income statement per the USASH (illustrated in Exhibit 3.3) is divided into three major sections—operating departments, undistributed operating expenses, and the final section which includes management fees, fixed charges, gain or loss on sale of property, and income tax.

The first section, operating departments, reports net revenue by department for every major revenue producing department. Net revenue is the result of subtracting allowances from related revenues. Allowances include refunds and overcharges at the time of sale which are subsequently adjusted. For example, hotel guests may have been charged $100 (rack rate) for their rooms when they should have been charged the group rate of $80. The subsequent adjustment of $20 the following day is treated as an allowance. Revenues earned from nonoperating activities such as investments, are shown with rentals. If these amounts are significant, they should be reported separately.

For each department generating revenue, direct expenses are reported. These expenses relate directly to the department incurring them and consist of three major categories: cost of sales, payroll and related expenses, and other expenses. Cost of sales are normally determined as follows:

	Beginning inventory
Plus:	Inventory purchases
Equals:	Goods available for sale
Less:	Ending inventory
Equals:	Cost of goods consumed
Less:	Goods used internally
Equals:	Cost of goods sold

The first major direct expense category of operating departments is "beginning inventory." Inventory purchases include the purchase cost of goods for sale plus the related shipping cost. An important, but relatively small, category of direct expense is "goods used internally" and may best be illustrated by the following example. Food may be provided free of charge to employees (employee meals), to entertainers (entertainers—complimentary food), to guests for promotional purposes (promotion—

Exhibit 3.3   Summary Income Statement

STATEMENT OF INCOME

Current Period

	Schedule	Net Revenue	Cost of Sales	Payroll and Related Expenses	Other Expenses	Income (Loss)
OPERATED DEPARTMENTS						
Rooms	1	$	$	$	$	$
Food and Beverage	2					
Telephone	3					
Gift Shop	4					
Garage and Parking	5					
Other Operated Departments						
Rentals and Other Income	6	____	____	____	____	____
Total Operated Departments		____	____	____	____	____
UNDISTRIBUTED OPERATING EXPENSES						
Administrative and General	7					
Data Processing	8					
Human Resources	9					
Transportation	10					
Marketing	11					
Property Operation and Maintenance	12					
Energy Costs	13			____	____	
Total Undistributed Operating Expenses						
INCOME BEFORE MANAGEMENT FEES AND FIXED CHARGES		$ ____	$	$	$	
Management Fees						
Rent, Property Taxes, and Insurance	14					
Interest Expense	14					
Depreciation and Amortization	14					____
INCOME BEFORE INCOME TAXES AND GAIN OR LOSS ON SALE OF PROPERTY						
Gain or Loss on Sale of Property	14					____
INCOME BEFORE INCOME TAXES						
Income Taxes	15					
NET INCOME						$

food), or to other departments. In each case, the cost of food transferred must be charged to the proper account of the benefiting department and subtracted in the calculation of cost of food sold.

The second major direct expense category of operating departments is "payroll and related expenses." This category includes the salaries and wages of employees working in the designated operating departments, for example, servers in the food and beverage department. Salaries, wages, and related expenses of departments not generating revenue but providing service, such as marketing, are recorded by service departments. The category of "related expenses" includes all payroll taxes and fringe benefits relating to employees of each operated department. For example, in the rooms department, the front office manager's salary and related payroll taxes and fringe benefits would be included in the "payroll and related expenses" of the rooms department.

The final major expense category for the operating departments is "other expenses." This category includes only other direct expenses. For example, the nine major other expense categories for the rooms department (per the USASH) are commissions, contract cleaning, guest transportation, laundry and dry cleaning, linen, operating supplies, reservation expense, uniforms, and other. Expenses such as marketing, administration, and transportation are recorded as expenses of service departments. They benefit the rooms department but only on an indirect basis.

Net revenue less the sum of cost of sales, payroll and related expenses, and other expenses results in departmental income or loss. The departmental income or loss is shown on the summary income statement (Exhibit 3.3) for each operated department.

The second major section of the summary income statement is undistributed operating expenses. This section includes the eight general categories of administrative and general expenses, data processing, human resources, transportation, marketing, property operation and maintenance, and energy costs. These expense categories are related to the various service departments. In the summary income statement, two of the expense elements—payroll and related expenses, and other expenses—are shown for each category. The administrative and general expense category includes service departments such as the general manager's office and the accounting office. In addition to salaries, wages, and related expenses of service department personnel covered by administrative and general, other expenses include, but are not limited to, insurance-general, professional fees, and provision for doubtful accounts. The appendix at the end of this text presents USASH's recommended schedule for administrative and general expenses which details the several expense categories for administrative and general expenses.

The USASH recommends a separate departmental accounting of data processing expenses for those lodging operations with significant investments in data processing. (This recommended schedule is also shown in the appendix at the end of the text.) As with most other service centers, the two major sections of expense are payroll and related expenses, and other expenses. If data processing expenses are not considered significant, then the USASH recommends data processing expenses be included as part of administrative and general expenses.

Another service center for which the USASH recommends separate departmental accounting is the human resources department. This schedule includes labor cost of departmental personnel and other expenses such as employee housing, recruiting expenses, cost of relocating employees, and training costs. The recommended schedule is shown in the appendix.

The fourth service department is transportation. The purpose of this service department is to provide transportation services for lodging guests, such as transportation to and from the airport. The expenses to be included on the transportation department schedule (see the recommended schedule in the appendix) include payroll and related expenses, and other expenses such as fuel, operating supplies, and repairs and maintenance. If guest transportation expenses are not considered significant, then the USASH recommends transportation expenses be included as part of the rooms department expenses.

Marketing expenses include costs relating to personnel working in marketing areas of sales, advertising, and merchandising. In addition, other marketing expenses include advertising and merchandising expenses such as direct mail, in-house graphics, point of sale materials, and print, radio, and television advertising. Agency fees, franchising fees, and other fees and commissions are also included as marketing expenses.

The sixth major category of undistributed operating expenses is property operation and maintenance. Included in property operation and maintenance are salaries and related payroll costs of the property operation and maintenance personnel, and the various supplies used to maintain the buildings, grounds, furniture, fixtures, and equipment.

The final category of undistributed operating expenses is energy costs. The recommended schedule includes separate listings of the various utilities, such as electricity and water. Sales by the hotel to tenants and charges to other departments are subtracted in determining net energy costs.

Subtracting the total undistributed operating expenses from the total operated departments income results in income before management fees and fixed charges. Many industry personnel continue to refer to this difference between operating revenue and expense as gross operating profit, or simply GOP, but this is terminology from an earlier edition of USASH's format for the summary income statement.

Operating management is considered fully responsible for all revenue and expenses reported to this point on the summary income statement, as they generally have the authority to exercise their judgment to affect all these items. However, the management fees and the fixed charges which follow in the next major section of the summary income statement are the responsibility primarily of the hospitality property's board of directors. The expenses listed on this part of the statement generally relate directly to decisions by the board, rather than to management decisions.

Management fees are the cost of using an independent management company to operate the hotel/motel. The fixed expenses are also referred to as capacity costs, as they relate to the physical plant or the capacity to provide goods and services to guests.

The fixed charges include rent, property taxes, insurance, interest, and depreciation and amortization. Rent includes the cost of renting real estate, computer equipment, and other major items that, if they had been purchased, would have been recorded as fixed assets. Rental of miscellaneous equipment for specific functions such as banquets is to be shown as a direct expense of the food and beverage department.

Property taxes include real estate taxes, personal property taxes, taxes assessed by utilities, and other taxes, which cannot be charged to guests, except for income and payroll taxes. Insurance expense is the cost of insuring the facilities including contents for damage caused by fire or some other catastrophe.

Interest expense is the cost of borrowing money and is based on the amounts borrowed, the interest rate, and the length of time for which the funds are borrowed. Generally, loans are approved by the operation's board of directors, as most relate to the physical plant. Thus, interest expense is considered to be a fixed charge.

Depreciation of fixed assets and amortization of other assets are shown on the summary income statement as fixed charges. The depreciation methods and useful lives of fixed assets are normally disclosed in footnotes.[2]

Finally, the summary income statement per the USASH shows gains or losses on the sale of property and equipment and income taxes which are subtracted to determine the bottom line, net income. This item is included on the USASH's Summary Income Statement just prior to income taxes. A gain or loss on sale of property results from a difference between the proceeds from the sale and the carrying value (net book value) of the fixed asset. For example, a 15-unit motel which cost $300,000 and was depreciated by $150,000 was sold for $200,000. The gain in this case is determined as follows:

$$\text{where NBV} = \text{Cost} - \text{Accumulated Depreciation}$$
$$\text{NBV} = \$300,000 - \$150,000$$
$$\text{NBV} = \underline{\$150,000}$$

$$\text{where Gain} = \text{Proceeds} - \text{NBV}$$
$$\text{Gain} = \$200,000 - \$150,000$$
$$\text{Gain} = \underline{\underline{\$50,000}}$$

In the USASH's Summary Income Statement, gains are added while losses are subtracted in determining income before income taxes. Finally, income taxes are subtracted from income before income taxes to determine net income.

Departmental Statements

Departmental statements, supplementary to the summary income statement and referred to as schedules, provide management with detailed information by operating departments and service centers. The classifications listed in the summary income statement suggest up to 15 schedules. Each of these schedules is included in the appendix at the end of this text.

Exhibit 3.4 illustrates an operating department schedule using the rooms department of the Vacation Inn. The operating department schedule reflects both revenue and direct expenses. Totals from the operating department schedules are reflected on the summary income statement. In the rooms department illustration, the following totals are carried from the department statement to the property's summary income statement:

- Net Revenue $1,041,200
- Payroll and Related Expenses $185,334

Exhibit 3.4   Rooms Department Statement

	Schedule B-1
Vacation Inn	
Rooms	
For the year ended December 31, 19X1	
Revenue	
Room Sales	$1,043,900
Allowances	2,700
Net Revenue	1,041,200
Expenses	
Salaries and Wages	159,304
Employee Benefits	26,030
Total Payroll and Related Expenses	185,334
Other Expenses	
Commissions	5,124
Contract Cleaning	3,200
Laundry and Drycleaning	20,706
Linen	9,494
Operating Supplies	21,742
Reservations	9,288
Uniforms	1,400
Other	8,126
Total Other Expenses	79,080
Total Expenses	264,414
Departmental Income	$ 776,786

- Other Expenses $79,080
- Departmental Income $776,786

Exhibit 3.5 is the Vacation Inn's Summary Income Statement. The above figures from the rooms department schedule are reflected in the top row of figures on the summary income statement.

In contrast to the profit center schedules prepared by the revenue producing operating departments of a hospitality operation, a service center schedule reports only expenses by area of responsibility. Although these activity areas do not generate revenue, they do provide service to the operating departments and in some cases, to other service centers. Exhibit 3.6 illustrates a service center departmental schedule by using the property operation and maintenance schedule of the Vacation Inn. The two numbers which are carried over to Vacation Inn's Summary Income Statement (Exhibit 3.5) for this department are total payroll and related expenses of $31,652 and other expenses of $49,312.

The number and nature of the supporting schedules reported in a lodging facility depends on the size and organization of the establish-

Exhibit 3.5   Statement of Income — Vacation Inn

<table>
<tr><td colspan="7" align="center">Vacation Inn
Summary Income Statement
For the year ended December 31, 19X1</td></tr>
<tr><td></td><td>Schedules</td><td>Net
Revenues</td><td>Cost of
Sales</td><td>Payroll
and
Related
Expenses</td><td>Other
Expense</td><td>Income
(Loss)</td></tr>
<tr><td>Operating Departments</td><td></td><td></td><td></td><td></td><td></td><td></td></tr>
<tr><td>Rooms</td><td>B-1</td><td>$1,041,200</td><td>$ 0</td><td>$ 185,334</td><td>$ 79,080</td><td>$ 776,786</td></tr>
<tr><td>Food and Beverage</td><td>B-2</td><td>626,165</td><td>208,448</td><td>218,532</td><td>66,513</td><td>132,672</td></tr>
<tr><td>Telephone</td><td>B-3</td><td>52,028</td><td>46,505</td><td>14,317</td><td>6,816</td><td>(15,610)</td></tr>
<tr><td>   Total Operating Departments</td><td></td><td>1,719,393</td><td>254,953</td><td>418,183</td><td>152,409</td><td>893,848</td></tr>
<tr><td>Undistributed Operating Expenses</td><td></td><td></td><td></td><td></td><td></td><td></td></tr>
<tr><td>Administrative and General</td><td>B-7</td><td></td><td></td><td>47,787</td><td>24,934</td><td>72,721</td></tr>
<tr><td>Data Processing</td><td>B-8</td><td></td><td></td><td>20,421</td><td>11,622</td><td>32,043</td></tr>
<tr><td>Human Resources</td><td>B-9</td><td></td><td></td><td>22,625</td><td>4,193</td><td>26,818</td></tr>
<tr><td>Transportation</td><td>B-10</td><td></td><td></td><td>13,411</td><td>7,460</td><td>20,871</td></tr>
<tr><td>Marketing</td><td>B-11</td><td></td><td></td><td>33,231</td><td>33,585</td><td>66,816</td></tr>
<tr><td>Property Operation and
   Maintenance</td><td>B-12</td><td></td><td></td><td>31,652</td><td>49,312</td><td>80,964</td></tr>
<tr><td>Energy Costs</td><td>B-13</td><td></td><td></td><td>0</td><td>88,752</td><td>88,752</td></tr>
<tr><td>   Total Undistributed Operating Expenses</td><td></td><td></td><td></td><td>169,127</td><td>219,858</td><td>388,985</td></tr>
<tr><td>Income Before Fixed Charges</td><td></td><td>$1,719,393</td><td>$254,953</td><td>$587,310</td><td>$372,267</td><td>504,863</td></tr>
<tr><td>Rent, Property Taxes, and
   Insurance</td><td>B-14</td><td></td><td></td><td></td><td></td><td>200,861</td></tr>
<tr><td>Interest</td><td>B-14</td><td></td><td></td><td></td><td></td><td>52,148</td></tr>
<tr><td>Depreciation and Amortization</td><td>B-14</td><td></td><td></td><td></td><td></td><td>115,860</td></tr>
<tr><td>Income Before Income Taxes</td><td></td><td></td><td></td><td></td><td></td><td>135,994</td></tr>
<tr><td>Income Tax</td><td>B-15</td><td></td><td></td><td></td><td></td><td>48,707</td></tr>
<tr><td>Net Income</td><td></td><td></td><td></td><td></td><td></td><td>$87,287</td></tr>
</table>

ment. For larger hotels, a separate uniform system of accounts very similar to the USASH has been developed.[3]

Industry Operating Statistics

A sale of $X by any operating department increases total revenue by that amount, but the increase in the total operating department income from additional sales of $X depends on the operating department making the sale. The different effects on this bottom line are not caused by income taxes nor by fixed charges, but by the direct expenses of the operating department generating the sale.

Exhibit 3.6 Property Operation and Maintenance

Schedule B-12

Vacation Inn
Property Operation and Maintenance
For the year ended December 31, 19X1

Salaries and Wages	$ 27,790
Employee Benefits	3,862
Total Payroll and Related Expenses	31,652
Other Expenses	
Building	8,251
Curtains and Draperies	649
Electrical and Mechanical Equipment	8,761
Elevators	3,206
Engineering Supplies	1,981
Floor Covering	4,722
Furniture	3,829
Grounds and Landscaping	6,241
Operating Supplies	2,651
Painting and Decorating	2,565
Removal of Waste Matter	2,499
Swimming Pool	2,624
Uniforms	652
Other	681
Total	49,312
Total Property Operation and Maintenance	**$ 80,964**

The difference between an operating department's revenue and direct expenses is referred to as departmental income. The operating department contributing most to the lodging property's ability to pay overhead costs and generate profit is the one which has the greatest departmental income.

Pannell Kerr Forster (PKF), an international accounting firm providing specialized services to establishments in the hospitality industry, recently released figures showing that the average hotel reports rooms departmental income of 74% of total room revenue, while the food and beverage departmental income was only approximately 21% of total food and beverage revenues. Historically, the telephone departments of most hotels have experienced losses from operations. Therefore, all things being the same, a manager would prefer an additional sale of $X to be made in the rooms department versus either the food and beverage department or the telephone department, because the contribution toward overhead costs and profit would be greater than from any other operating department. For example, sales of $100 each in the rooms and food and beverage departments result in departmental incomes approximating $74 and $21, respectively (based on PKF's figures).

Within the food and beverage department, the contribution margin (sales less cost of sales) generally differs substantially between food sales and beverages sales. According to PKF's statistics, the contribution margin of food sales is about 67% compared to about 79% for beverage sales. PKF does not separate payroll and related expenses nor other direct expenses of the food and beverage department between food operations and beverage operations as it does cost of sales. However, if we assume that these expenses relate proportionately to sales, then from a profit perspective, increased beverage sales are more desirable than increased food sales. For example, $100 of food sales and $100 of beverage sales result in a food contribution margin of $67 as compared to a beverage contribution margin of $79—a difference of $12 per $100.

Exhibit 3.7 provides statistics from PKF's 1985 edition of *Trends-USA* revealing the percentage distribution of revenues and expenses for the average hotel/motel. These statistics support the preceeding discussion of the greater desirability of beverage sales compared to food sales, and the increased desirability of rooms sales compared to sales in any other department. However, caution must be taken that these averages not be considered the norm. The operating departments of a particular hotel may produce different percentages. However, of 1,000 hotels and motels in the PKF study, significant numbers noted in Exhibit 3.7 include:

- Rooms revenue approximates 62% of total revenue

- Food revenue approximates 24% of total revenue

- Beverage revenue approximates 9% of total revenue

- Total operated department income approximates 54% of total revenue

- Undistributed operating expenses approximate 27% of total revenue

Hospitality industry statistics for the various segments of the industry are published annually by PKF and Laventhol & Horwath (L&H), another accounting firm specializing in the hospitality industry. Major publications, generally available upon request, are listed in Exhibit 3.8.

Analysis of Income Statements

The analysis of income statements enhances the users' knowledge of the hospitality property's operations. This can be accomplished by horizontal analysis, vertical analysis, and ratio analysis. Since much less financial information is available to owners (stockholders who are not active in the operation) and creditors than is available to management, their analytical approaches will generally differ.

Horizontal analysis compares income statements for two accounting periods in terms of both absolute and relative variances for each line item in a way similar to the analysis of comparative balance sheets discussed

Exhibit 3.7 Comparative Results of Operations

	1984	1983		1984	1983
Revenues:			**Rooms Department:**		
Rooms	61.5 %	60.6 %	Rooms Net Revenue	100.0 %	100.0 %
Food—Including Other Income	23.6	23.7			
Beverages	8.6	9.2	**Departmental Expenses:**		
Telephone	2.3	2.5	Salaries and Wages Including Vacation	13.5 %	13.8 %
Other Operated Departments	2.1	2.0	Payroll Taxes and Employee Benefits	3.9	3.8
Rentals and Other Income	1.9	2.0	Subtotal	17.4 %	17.6 %
Total Revenues	100.0 %	100.0 %	Laundry, Linen and Guest Supplies	3.2	3.1
			Commissions and Reservation Expenses	2.5	2.4
			All Other Expenses	2.9	2.9
Departmental Costs and Expenses:			Total Rooms Expenses	26.0 %	26.0 %
Rooms	15.9 %	15.9 %	Rooms Departmental Income	74.0 %	74.0 %
Food and Beverages	26.5	27.2			
Telephone	2.6	3.0	**Food and Beverage Department:**		
Other Operated Departments	1.5	1.5	Food Net Revenue	100.0 %	100.0 %
Total Costs and Expenses	46.5 %	47.6 %	Cost of Food Consumed	35.2 %	35.8 %
			Less: Cost of Employees' Meals	2.3	2.5
Total Operated Departmental Income	53.5 %	52.4 %	Net Cost of Food Sales	32.9 %	33.3 %
Undistributed Operating Expenses:			Food Gross Profit	67.1 %	66.7 %
Administrative and General	8.3 %	8.4 %	Beverage Net Revenue	100.0 %	100.0 %
Management Fees*	2.1	2.2	Cost of Beverage Sales	21.2	21.5
Marketing and Guest Entertainment*	5.5	5.4	Beverage Gross Profit	78.8 %	78.5 %
Property Operation and Maintenance	5.6	5.6	Food and Beverage Revenue	100.0 %	100.0 %
Energy Costs	5.4	5.5	Net Cost of Food and Beverage Sales	28.6	29.0
Other Unallocated Operated Departments*	.3	.2	Gross Profit on Combined Sales	71.4 %	71.0 %
Total Undistributed Expenses	27.2 %	27.3 %	Public Room Rentals	1.9	1.5
			Other Income	2.0	2.0
Income Before Fixed Charges	26.3 %	25.1 %	Gross Profit and Other Income	75.3 %	74.5 %
Property Taxes and Insurance:			**Departmental Expenses:**		
Property Taxes and Other Municipal Charges	2.8 %	3.0 %	Salaries and Wages Including Vacation	32.4 %	32.3 %
Insurance on Building and Contents	.4	.3	Payroll Taxes and Employee Benefits	9.8	9.4
Total Property Taxes and Insurance	3.2 %	3.3 %	Subtotal	42.2 %	41.7 %
			Laundry and Dry Cleaning	.9	.9
Income Before Other Fixed Charges**	23.1 %	21.8 %	China, Glassware, Silver and Linen	1.9	1.8
			Contract Cleaning	.3	.4
Percentage of Occupancy	67.8 %	64.4 %	All Other Expenses	8.7	9.0
			Total Food and Beverage Expenses	54.0 %	53.8 %
Average Daily Rate per Occupied Room	$58.39	$55.09	Food and Beverage Departmental Income	21.3 %	20.7 %
Average Daily Room Rate per Guest	$41.48	$39.54			
Percentage of Double Occupancy	40.8 %	39.3 %			
Average Size (Rooms)	233	233			

*Averages based on total groups although not all establishments reported data.
**Income before deducting Depreciation, Rent, Interest, Amortization and Income Taxes.
NOTE: Payroll Taxes and Employee Benefits distributed to each department. See Figure No. 6 on Page 37 for Payroll Cost Data.

Source: Pannell Kerr Forster & Company

in Chapter 2. Any significant differences are investigated by the user. Another common comparative analysis approach is to compare the most recent period's operating results with the budget by determining absolute and relative variances. Exhibit 3.9 illustrates the horizontal analysis of operating results of the Vacation Inn for years 19X1 and 19X2.

In this comparative analysis, 19X1 is considered the base. If the

Exhibit 3.8   Major Hospitality Statistical Publications

Publication	Industry Segment	Firm
Trends – Worldwide	Lodging	PKF
Trends – USA	Lodging	PKF
Clubs in Town and Country	Clubs	PKF
Worldwide Lodging Industry	Lodging	L&H
US Lodging Industry	Lodging	L&H
Restaurant Industry Operations Report	Restaurant	NRA/L&H

revenues for 19X2 exceed revenues for 19X1, the difference is shown as positive. On the other hand, if 19X2 revenues are less than 19X1 revenues, the difference is shown as negative. The reverse is true for expenses. Actual 19X2 expenses that have increased compared to 19X1 result in a negative difference, while actual 19X2 expenses that have decreased compared to 19X1 result in a positive difference.

Another approach in analyzing income statements is vertical analysis. The product of this analysis is also referred to as common-size statements. These statements result from reducing all amounts to percentages using total sales as a common denominator. Exhibit 3.10 illustrates comparative common-size income statements for the Vacation Inn.

Vertical analysis allows for more reasonable comparisons of two or more periods when the activity for the two periods was at different levels. For example, assume the following:

	19X1	19X2
Food sales	$500,000	$750,000
Cost of food sales	150,000	225,000

A $75,000 increase in cost of sales may at first appear to be excessive. However, vertical analysis reveals the following:

	19X1	19X2
Food sales	100%	100%
Cost of food sales	30%	30%

In this example, vertical analysis suggests that despite the absolute increase in cost of sales from 19X1 to 19X2, the cost of food sales has remained constant at 30% of sales for both years. The relatively large increase, in terms of absolute dollars, from 19X1 to 19X2 can be attributed to the higher level of activity during the 19X2 period rather than to unreasonable increases in the cost of sales.

Vertical analysis allows more meaningful comparisons among hospitality operations in the same industry segment but differing substantially in size. This common-size analysis also allows comparisons to industry standards, as discussed previously. However, a note of caution

Exhibit 3.9 Comparative Income Statements

	19X1	19X2	Difference $	%
Vacation Inn **Comparative Income Statements**				
Total Revenue	$1,719,393	$1,883,482	$164,089	9.54%
Rooms – Revenue	1,041,200	1,124,300	83,100	7.98
Payroll & Related Expenses	185,334	192,428	7,094	3.83
Other Expense	79,080	84,624	5,544	7.01
Department Income	776,786	847,248	70,462	9.07
Food & Beverage – Revenue	626,165	697,241	71,076	11.35
Cost of Sales	208,448	235,431	26,983	12.94
Payroll & Related Expenses	218,532	249,620	31,088	14.23
Other Expense	66,513	76,675	10,162	15.28
Department Income	132,672	135,515	2,843	2.14
Telephone – Revenue	52,028	61,941	9,913	19.05
Cost of Sales	46,505	50,321	3,816	8.21
Payroll & Related Expenses	14,317	16,289	1,972	13.77
Other Expense	6,816	7,561	745	10.93
Department Income	(15,610)	(12,230)	3,380	21.65
Total Operated Department Income	893,848	970,533	76,685	8.58
Undistributed Operating Expenses				
Administrative and General	72,721	79,421	6,700	9.21
Data Processing	32,043	35,213	3,170	9.89
Human Resources	26,818	28,942	2,124	7.92
Transportation	20,871	21,555	684	3.28
Marketing	66,816	79,760	12,944	19.37
Property Operation and Maintenance	80,964	84,465	3,501	4.32
Energy Costs	88,752	96,911	8,159	9.19
Total Undistributed Operating Expenses	388,985	426,267	37,282	9.58
Income Before Fixed Costs	504,863	544,266	39,403	7.80
Rent, Property Taxes, and Insurance	200,861	210,932	10,071	5.01
Interest	52,148	61,841	9,693	18.59
Depreciation and Amortization	115,860	118,942	3,082	2.66
Income Before Income Taxes	135,994	152,551	16,557	12.17
Income Taxes	48,707	57,969	9,262	19.02
Net Income	$ 87,287	$ 94,582	$ 7,295	8.36%

is offered at this point. Industry averages are simply that—averages. They include firms of all sizes from vastly different locations operating in entirely different markets. The industry averages reflect neither any particular operation nor an average operation, and they certainly do not depict an ideal operation.

Exhibit 3.10 Comparative Common-Size Income Statements

			Percentages	
Vacation Inn				
Comparative Common-Size Income Statements				
	19X1	**19X2**	**19X1**	**19X2**
Total Revenue	$1,719,393	$1,883,482	100.0%	100.0%
Rooms – Revenue	1,041,200	1,124,300	60.6	59.7
Payroll & Related Expenses	185,334	192,428	10.8	10.2
Other Expense	79,080	84,624	4.6	4.5
Department Income	776,786	847,248	45.2	45.0
Food & Beverage – Revenue	626,165	697,241	36.4	37.0
Cost of Sales	208,448	235,431	12.1	12.5
Payroll & Related Expenses	218,532	249,620	12.7	13.3
Other Expense	66,513	76,675	3.9	4.1
Department Income	132,672	135,515	7.7	7.2
Telephone – Revenue	52,028	61,941	3.0	3.3
Cost of Sales	46,505	50,321	2.7	2.7
Payroll & Related Expenses	14,317	16,289	0.8	0.9
Other Expense	6,816	7,561	0.4	0.4
Department Income	(15,610)	(12,230)	(0.9)	(0.7)
Total Operated Department Income	893,848	970,533	52.0	51.5
Undistributed Operating Expenses				
Administrative and General	72,721	79,421	4.2	4.2
Data Processing	32,043	35,213	1.9	1.9
Human Resources	26,818	28,942	1.6	1.5
Transportation	20,871	21,555	1.2	1.1
Marketing	66,816	79,760	3.9	4.2
Property Operation and Maintenance	80,964	84,465	4.7	4.5
Energy Costs	88,752	96,911	5.1	5.1
Total Undistributed Operating Expenses	388,985	426,267	22.6	22.6
Income Before Fixed Costs	504,863	544,266	29.4	28.9
Rent, Property Taxes, and Insurance	200,861	210,932	11.7	11.2
Interest	52,148	61,841	3.0	3.3
Depreciation and Amortization	115,860	118,942	6.7	6.3
Income Before Income Taxes	135,994	152,551	8.0	8.1
Income Taxes	48,707	57,969	2.8	3.1
Net Income	$ 87,287	$ 94,582	5.1%	5.0%

A third approach to analyzing income statements is ratio analysis. Since vertical analysis is a subset of ratio analysis, there is considerable overlap between these two approaches. We will provide an extensive discussion of ratio analysis in Chapter 5 of this text.

Computerization

Like the balance sheet, the income statement is often produced using a general ledger package by the larger hospitality operations, and, as personal computers become more sophisticated, smaller operations will also be able to use these packages.

In the meantime, there are many computer applications for the income statement. For example, Exhibit 3.11 was produced by a spreadsheet program which helps prepare the amounts for common-size statements. The user only had to enter the separate revenue and expense amounts; the computer calculated all totals (such as Department Income) and all percentages.

In addition, many software packages have extensive graphics capabilities. The phrase "a picture is worth a thousand words" applies here. Although graphs do not usually provide detail, managers can more easily track recent performance trends by showing results in line graphs. Exhibit 3.12 is a line graph which highlights a rooms department's revenue over a four-year period; although the revenues are only stated to the tenth of a million, the trend is obvious to anyone looking at the graph. Departmental expenses can be shown using pie charts. Departmental revenues for several years can be shown using bar charts. These charts are easy to understand, and they can be used as management tools to show employees the operation's results more successfully than the traditional financial statements which sometimes seem like a confusing list of numbers.

Summary

The income statement, complete with all departmental statements, is generally considered the most useful financial statement for management. It highlights the important financial aspects of the property's operations over a period of time.

The income statement shows four major elements: revenues, expenses, gains, and losses. Revenues (increases in assets or decreases in liability accounts) and expenses (decreases in assets or increases in liability accounts) are directly related to operations, while gains and losses result from transactions incidental to the property's major operations.

In order to standardize income statements within the hospitality industry, the original *Uniform System of Accounts for Hotels* was written in 1925-26. Since then, there have been changes and revisions, the most recent being the 8th edition published in 1986. By using an accounting system based on a uniform system of accounts the management of a new hotel has a turnkey accounting system for a complete and systematic accounting for their operations. The various uniform systems also facilitate comparison among operations of varying size in the hospitality industry.

In order to enhance the usefulness of the income statement, the format set up by the USASH includes statements of departmental income showing the revenues produced by each profit center and subtracting

Exhibit 3.11   Sample Spreadsheet Printout

```
                              VACATION INN
                      COMMON-SIZE  INCOME STATEMENTS

                          D O L L A R S              P E R C E N T A G E S
                     --------------------------   --------------------------
                        19X1          19X2            19X1         19X2

TOTAL REVENUE         $1,719,393    $1,883,482       100.00%      100.00%
                     ==========================================================

Rooms Revenue         $1,041,200    $1,124,300        60.56%       59.69%
   Payroll & Related     185,334       192,428        10.78        10.22
   Other Expense          79,080        84,624         4.60         4.49
                     --------------------------   --------------------------
Department Income        776,786       847,248        45.18        44.98

Food & Beverage Revenue  626,165       697,241        36.42        37.02
   Cost of Sales         208,448       235,431        12.12        12.50
   Payroll & Related     218,532       249,620        12.71        13.25
   Other Expense          66,513        76,675         3.87         4.07
                     --------------------------   --------------------------
Department Income        132,672       135,515         7.72         7.19

Telephone Revenue         52,028        61,941         3.03         3.29
   Cost of Sales          46,505        50,321         2.70         2.67
   Payroll & Related      14,317        16,289         0.83         0.86
   Other Expense           6,816         7,561         0.40         0.40
                     --------------------------   --------------------------
Department Income        (15,610)      (12,230)       (0.91)       (0.65)

Total Operated Depart-
   ment Income           893,848       970,533        51.99        51.53

Undistributed Operating
   Expenses:
   Administrative &
      General             72,721        79,421         4.23         4.22
   Data Processing        32,043        35,213         1.86         1.87
   Human Resources        26,818        28,942         1.56         1.54
   Transportation         20,871        21,555         1.21         1.14
   Marketing              66,816        79,760         3.89         4.23
   Property Operation &
      Maintenance         80,964        84,465         4.71         4.48
   Energy Costs           88,752        96,911         5.16         5.15
                     --------------------------   --------------------------
Total Undistributed
   Operating Expenses    388,985       426,267        22.62        22.63
Income Before Fixed
   Charges               504,863       544,266        29.36        28.90
Rent, Property Taxes,
   and Insurance         200,861       210,932        11.68        11.20
Interest                  52,148        61,841         3.03         3.28
Depreciation & Amort-
   ization               115,860       118,942         6.74         6.32
                     --------------------------   --------------------------
Income Before In-
   come Taxes            135,994       152,551         7.91         8.10

Income Taxes              48,707        57,969         2.83         3.08
                     --------------------------   --------------------------
Net Income               $87,287       $94,582         5.08%        5.02%
                     ==========================================================
```

Exhibit 3.12   Sample Graphics

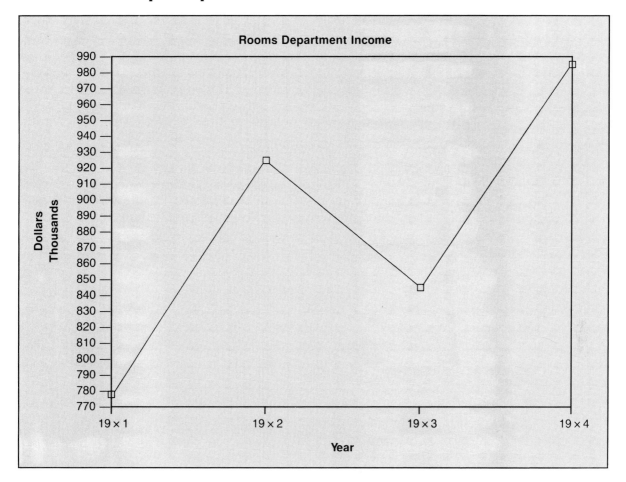

from each the corresponding direct operating expenses. Included in the direct operating expenses is not only the cost of goods sold, but also the direct payroll and other direct expenses. Next, undistributed operating expenses which consist of seven major service center categories—administrative and general expenses, data processing, human resources, transportation, marketing, property operation and maintenance, and energy costs—must be subtracted to determine "income before management fees and fixed charges." This is followed by management fees and fixed charges which include rent, property taxes, fire insurance, interest, depreciation, and amortization. Next, gain (loss) on sale of property and equipment is added (subtracted) to determine income before income taxes. Finally, income taxes are subtracted resulting in net income.

As a supplement to the income statement, several departmental income statements should be presented. These offer management additional insight into the operation of each department. The number of schedules necessary depends on the complexity of the lodging facility; the more cost and profit centers operated, the more supplemental statements should be presented. These departmental statements can be very useful for management. First, they can be used to compare the hotel's operations with industry averages, prior performance, and most important, budgeted standards or goals. Also, the relative profitability of various departments can be compared.

There are three major methods management can use to analyze the income statement. The first method is horizontal analysis which considers both the relative and absolute changes in the income statement between two periods and/or between the budgeted and actual figures. Any major variances, exceeding levels predefined by management, can be further investigated to determine their causes. The next type of analysis is the vertical analysis which reduces all items to a percentage of sales. These percentages, often referred to as common-size statements, can then be used to compare the results of the property's operations to either those of other lodging facilities or to industry standards. Again, any significant differences should be studied. The final method, ratio analysis, will be more thoroughly discussed in Chapter 5.

Notes

1. The *Uniform System of Accounts and Expense Dictionary for Small Hotels, Motels and Motor Hotels*, is published by the Educational Institute of the American Hotel & Motel Association.
2. Clifford T. Fay, Raymond S. Schmidgall, and Stanley B. Tarr, *Basic Financial Accounting for the Hospitality Industry* (East Lansing, Mich.: Educational Institute of the American Hotel & Motel Association, 1982).
3. Uniform systems of accounts are available as follows:
   Uniform System of Accounts for Hotels, 8th rev. ed., (New York, N.Y.: Hotel Association of New York City, 1986).
   Uniform System of Accounts and Expense Dictionary for Small Hotels and Motels, 3rd rev. ed., (East Lansing, Mich.: Educational Institute of the American Hotel & Motel Association, 1986).
   Uniform System of Accounts for Clubs, (Washington, D.C.: Club Managers Association of America, 1982).
   Uniform System of Accounts for Restaurants, 5th rev. ed., (Washington, D.C.: National Restaurant Association, 1983).

Discussion Questions

1. Explain the major differences between the balance sheet and the income statement.

2. Why are creditors interested in the income statement?

3. What are the major differences between a revenue and a gain?

4. Name three examples of direct operating expenses for the rooms department.

5. What is the difference between the income statement used in many nonhospitality industries and one prepared by a lodging facility?

6. Explain how cost of food sold is determined.

7. Explain the advantages of the uniform system of accounts.

8. What detailed expenses are included in the property operation, maintenance, and energy costs of the income statement?

9. Why are supplemental statements valuable to management?

10. What are the different techniques of income statement analysis?

Problem 3.1

As the controller for Kelly's, a hotel with a large restaurant operation, you are responsible for monitoring costs. You have collected the following information concerning the food inventory and need to calculate the cost of food sold for the month of December.

Inventory, December 1, 19X1	$12,376
Inventory, December 31, 19X1	15,845
Purchases	76,840
Employee Meals:	
A. General Manager	85
B. Food Department	648
Transfers from the Bar to Kitchen	46
Promotional Meals	256

<u>Required:</u>

1. Calculate the cost of food sold for December 19X1.

2. To which departments would each expense be charged?

Expense	Department
1. Cost of food sold	_____
2. Employee meals—general manager	_____
3. Employee meals—food department	_____
4. Promotional meals	_____

Problem 3.2 Pg 81

Ron Curcio, the owner of Ron's Resort, has hired you to prepare the Resort's income statement for the year ending December 31, 19X1. He has provided you with the balances of each of the general ledger accounts, and has requested you follow the format established in the uniform system of accounts for small hotels, motels and motor hotels.

Vending Machine Revenue	$ 819
Employee Meals, Food Department	443
Cost of Calls, Telephone	22,820
Ending Inventory, Food	15,386
Liability Insurance	3,000
Concessions—Revenue	1,473
Outdoor Advertising	12,121
Ground and Landscaping	12,000
Purchases—Food and Beverage	134,999
Depreciation	76,366
Other Selling Expenses ~Marketing?	17,868
Other Operating Expenses—Food	60,002
Other Operating Expenses—Rooms	151,123
Electric Expense	33,583
Rent Expense	75,000
Water Expense	26,859
Other Operating Expenses—Telephone	1,647
Interest Expense	42,833
Revenues:	
Room	1,075,475
Food and Beverage	418,076
Telephone	53,898
Salaries and Related Expenses:	
Rooms	178,461
Food and Beverage	105,519
Marketing	24,000
Property Operation and Maintenance	20,170
Energy Costs	18,700
Telephone	20,000
Data Processing	25,000
Transportation	10,000
Administrative and General	55,000
Other Departmental Expenses:	
Administrative and General	30,000
Transportation	15,000
Data Processing	15,000
Tax Rate	38%

Required:

Prepare the summary income statement in accordance with the USASH.

Note: The beginning inventory of food was $18,795. The schedules in the appendix at the end of this text may be helpful in determining how some of the above expenses should be categorized for income statement purposes.

ex. Pg 92 **Problem 3.3**

Tim's Tasty Tidbits' August and September 19X1 condensed income statements are as follows:

	August	September
Food Sales	$45,000	$48,000
Beverage Sales	40,000	42,000
Total Sales	85,000	90,000
Cost of Food Sales	15,300	15,840
Cost of Beverage Sales	8,000	9,240
Labor	25,500	28,800
Laundry	4,000	4,200
China, glass, silver	1,000	1,100
Other	16,000	15,500
Total Expenses	69,800	74,680
Net Income	$15,200	$15,320

Customers were served as follows:

Food	10,000	12,000
Beverage	25,000	24,000

Required:

1. Convert the two income statements to common-size income statements.

2. Based on the information provided (including customer information) comment regarding the operating performance of Tim's Tasty Tidbits for the two months.

Problem 3.4

Pat Mulhurn, the founder of Pat's Place, wants to analyze 19X2 year's operations by comparing them to the 19X1 results. To aid him, prepare a comparative income statement using the 19X1 and 19X2 information available.

Pat's Place
Income Statement
For the years ending December 31, 19X1 and 19X2

	19X1	19X2
Revenues		
Rooms	$ 976,000	$1,041,000
Food and Beverage	604,000	626,000
Telephone	50,000	52,000
Total	1,630,000	1,719,000
Direct Expenses		
Rooms	250,000	264,000
Food and Beverage	476,000	507,000
Telephone	68,000	68,000
Total Operational Department Income	836,000	880,000
Undistributed Operating Expenses		
Administrative and General	195,000	206,000
Marketing	65,000	68,000
Property Operation and Maintenance	69,000	68,000
Energy Costs	101,000	102,000
Income Before Fixed Charges	406,000	436,000
Rent, Property Taxes, and Insurance	200,000	201,000
Interest	55,000	52,000
Depreciation and Amortization	116,000	116,000
Income Before Income Taxes	35,000	67,000
Income Taxes	7,000	17,000
Net Income	$ 28,000	$ 50,000

Required:

Prepare the comparative income statements for Pat's Place.

Note: Rearrange the income statement to conform to the USASH format as reflected in Exhibit 3.9

Problem 3.5

Listed below is financial information for the Harby Hotel for the year ended December 31, 19X2.

Account	Account Balance
Commissions—Rooms Department	$ 23,500
Marketing Expense	111,800
Ending Food and Beverage Inventory	53,000
Depreciation and Amortization Expense	91,000
Net Room Revenue	1,560,000
Cost of Sales—Rental and Other Income	9,360
Rent Expense	148,200
Reservation Expense	13,500
Fire Insurance Expense	10,400
Income Taxes—40% pre-tax rate	?
Employee Benefits—Rooms Department	51,000
Food and Beverage Revenue	858,000
Proceeds from Sale of Equipment**	10,000
Other Expense—Telephone Department	6,240
Contract Cleaning—Rooms Department	5,800
Administrative and General Expenses (total)	270,400
Property Taxes	70,200
Food and Beverage Purchases	328,400
Payroll—Telephone Department	15,600
Linen Expense—Rooms Department	8,600
Other Expense—Rental and Other Income	9,360
Beginning Food and Beverage Inventory	38,900
Revenue—Rental and Other Income	119,600
Revenue—Telephone Department	62,400
Data Processing Expenses (total)	34,320
Human Resources Expenses (total)	32,614
Salaries and Wages—Rooms Department	209,000
Interest Expenses	98,800
Payroll—Rental and Other Income	20,800
Free Food and Beverage—Employees*	12,300
Laundry and Drycleaning—Rooms Department	24,800
Other Expenses—Food and Beverage Department	93,600
Other Expenses—Rooms Department	130,000
Property Operation and Maintenance (total)	112,200
Cost of Sales—Telephone Department	46,800
Payroll—Food and Beverage Department	93,600
Energy Costs (total)	159,500

*This has already been recorded as expense in the appropriate departments, except in the determination of the cost of food sold.
**Equipment sold cost $15,000 and had been depreciated by $8,000.

Required:

1. Prepare a rooms departmental statement in accordance with the USASH.

2. Determine the cost of food and beverage sold.

3. Prepare a summary income statement following the USASH.

4 Statement of Changes in Financial Position

Traditionally, the principal financial statements used by hospitality operations have been the income statement, the statement of retained earnings, and the balance sheet. The balance sheet, as discussed in Chapter 2, shows the financial position of the organization at the end of an accounting period. The income statement, as discussed in Chapter 3, reflects the results of operations for an accounting period. The statement of retained earnings indicates the amount of earnings retained in the organization and reflects dividends paid to owners during the most recent accounting period. Although these statements provide extensive financial information, they do not provide answers to such questions as:

1. How much working capital was provided by operations of the hospitality property?

2. What amount of fixed assets was purchased during the year?

3. How much long-term debt was borrowed during the year?

4. What funds were raised by the hospitality property through the sale of capital stock?

5. How much long-term debt was retired or reclassified during the year?

6. How much was invested in long-term investments during the year?

The statement of changes in financial position (SCFP) is designed to answer these questions and more. The SCFP has been a mandatory statement only since 1971. Accounting Principle Board Opinion #19, issued in March, 1971, requires a Statement of Changes in Financial Position when the balance sheet and income statement are issued to owners and/or creditors. The Board in its opinion recognized that the SCFP would most likely be omitted when the financial statements were issued strictly for internal use. Today, the SCFP should be included among the financial statements that are issued to external users. Prior to 1971, some hospitality operations voluntarily issued similar statements titled "Sources and Uses of Funds" or simply "Funds Statements." From time to time, the old titles are still used in informal settings even though "Statement of Changes in Financial Position" is the formal title.

Our discussion of this modern addition to the collection of important financial statements will address the definition of funds, the relationship between the SCFP and successive balance sheets, the objectives of the SCFP, and the notion of changes in working capital. We will also consider how the SCFP is prepared as well as the benefits and alternative formats of this important financial document.

Definition of Funds

Funds may be defined as simply cash, working capital (current assets less current liabilities), or all financial resources.

Under the cash concept of funds, changes in cash between successive balance sheet dates are analyzed. Although the purchase of equipment with cash would be shown using the cash concept of funds, the financing of an equipment purchase with a short-term loan from the supplier would not be reflected on a cash statement. However, even though cash was not used in this financed purchase, it nevertheless represents a change in the operation's financial position. The cash concept of funds is limited in that it does not reflect this kind of change. Thus, the purchase of equipment with cash would be shown under this cash definition of funds; however, the financing of an equipment purchase with a short-term loan from the supplier would not be reflected on a cash statement, because cash was not used.

This shortcoming is overcome by the working capital concept of funds. A statement reflecting changes in working capital shows all transactions affecting working capital. However, a payment to a supplier (accounts payable) is not reflected on this statement, because working capital did not change. The cash payment reduced both the cash account and the accounts payable account; thus, working capital (current assets less current liabilities) was not affected. Further, a statement based only on working capital does not report transactions affecting only noncurrent accounts. For example, the purchase of land with the hospitality property's capital stock is not reflected on a SCFP that is based solely on working capital. Since it fails to reflect these kinds of transactions that influence an operation's financial position, the working capital concept of funds is limited in its ability to report changes in financial position.

The "all financial resources" approach to the SCFP includes not only working capital but also all financing and investing activities that do not affect working capital accounts. Thus, the exchange of capital stock for land by a hotel would be reflected on the SCFP. This approach is required by the Financial Accounting Standards Board, the accounting standards-setting body for the private sector. The APB in Opinion #19 allows a SCFP to be shown on a cash basis so long as changes in other elements of working capital are shown in the body of the statement as well as outlays for the purchase of long-term assets, proceeds from sale of long-term assets; conversion of long-term debt or preferred stock to common stock; insurance, redemption, and repayment of long-term debt; insurance, redemption or purchase of capital stock; and dividends in cash or in kind. The all financial resources concept discussed in this chapter is the most common approach to preparing the SCFP.

Relationship of SCFP to Successive Balance Sheets

The statement of changes in financial position is a major link between successive balance sheets as illustrated in Exhibit 4.1. The statement of retained earnings, reflecting results of operations and dividends declared, reconciles the retained earnings accounts of two

Exhibit 4.1   Relationship of SCFP and Successive Balance Sheets

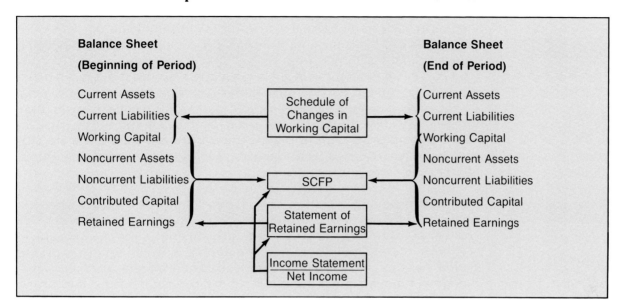

successive balance sheets. Net income from the income statement is "transferred" to the retained earnings account when the temporary income statement accounts are closed at the end of the accounting period, as described in Chapter 1. In addition, net income is shown on the SCFP. The changes in current asset and current liability accounts between two successive balance sheets are shown on a schedule of working capital changes. Finally, the SCFP indirectly reconciles all noncurrent accounts of two successive balance sheets.

Objectives of the SCFP

Like all financial statements, the purpose of the SCFP is to provide management, owners, and other users of the statement with useful information. In this regard, the three major objectives of the SCFP are to:

1. Show funds provided internally from operations.

2. Show funds provided externally from borrowing or the sale of stock.

3. Show long-term investing activities.

The SCFP shows funds provided by operations by adjusting net income or net loss figures from the income statement. One adjustment involves adding back expenses which did not require funds, such as depreciation and amortization. Net income or net loss is also adjusted by activities reported on the income statement which are not part of the property's normal operations. These activities include sales of noncurrent assets such as investments and property and equipment.

A second objective of the SCFP is to show funds provided on a long-term basis from external sources in the form of loans on the sale of capital stock. Financing a new hotel with a long-term loan would be shown on the SCFP. Short-term loans (loans for a period of one year or less) are not shown on the SCFP because these do not result in a change in working capital, as cash and current liabilities are simultaneously increased. For example, a short-term loan of $5,000 results in an increase in cash of $5,000 (thus, current assets by $5,000) and an increase in short-term notes payable by $5,000 (thus, current liabilities by $5,000). The loan results in a zero increase in working capital ($5,000 − $5,000 = 0).

A third objective of the SCFP is to show increases or decreases in long-term investing activities, that is, investments in noncurrent assets such as land, buildings, equipment, and long-term investments. Increases or decreases in short-term investments such as marketable securities (current assets) are not shown on the SCFP, because working capital has not increased or decreased. For example, a $5,000 cash investment in marketable securities results in a simultaneous increase in current assets (marketable securities) and decrease in current assets (cash); therefore, total current assets have not changed, nor has working capital.

Changes in Working Capital

Working capital is the excess of current assets over current liabilities. Current assets include cash, marketable securities, notes receivable, accounts receivable, inventory, and prepaid expenses. They are resources to be used in the coming twelve months for revenue producing activities, for acquiring fixed assets, and for paying obligations. Current liabilities include notes payable, accounts payable, and accrued expenses. They represent obligations at the balance sheet date that must be paid in the coming twelve months. The change in working capital is measured in terms of the amount of working capital at the beginning of the period compared to the end. Exhibit 4.2 illustrates a schedule of changes in working capital. Notice that working capital was $125,883 at the beginning of the year and $19,896 at the end of the year, resulting in a decrease in working capital of $105,987 for the hypothetical Midway Motel. A schedule of changes in working capital in tabulation form similar to Exhibit 4.2 should either accompany the SCFP or be part of the statement itself. Most hospitality operations include it separately from the SCFP rather than integrating the two.

The SCFP does not consider change in the composition of working capital, only change in the amount of working capital. Transactions that occur exclusively within the current asset and/or current liability accounts do not change the amount of working capital, only its composition. For example, purchasing inventory on account results in increasing inventory and increasing accounts payable and, therefore, does not affect working capital.

Exhibit 4.2 Schedule of Working Capital Changes

Schedule of Working Capital Changes Midway Motel			
	December 31 19X2	December 31 19X1	Increase (Decrease)
Current Assets			
Cash	$ 89,278	$ 82,540	$ 6,738
Marketable Securities	—	100,000	(100,000)
Accounts Receivable	3,789	3,811	(22)
Supplies Inventory	11,936	10,833	1,103
Prepaid Insurance	4,667	4,318	349
Total	109,670	201,502	(91,832)
Current Liabilities			
Notes Payable	25,000	—	25,000
Mortgage Payable-Current	50,000	50,000	0
Accounts Payable	6,821	18,776	(11,955)
Accrued Wages	7,953	6,843	1,110
Total	89,774	75,619	14,155
Working Capital	$19,896	$125,883	$(105,987)

Only certain transactions affecting working capital need to be examined in order to prepare a SCFP. These transactions involve both the current accounts (either assets or liabilities) and the noncurrent accounts (noncurrent assets, long-term liabilities, and owners' equity). For example, the purchase of a delivery truck with cash would reduce a current asset account (cash) and increase a noncurrent account (fixed asset—trucks). By identifying the transactions that affect the amount of working capital, the changes in the financial position of the company can be explained.

The change in working capital for the accounting period must be equal to the difference between total sources and uses of funds shown on the SCFP. Thus, if working capital has increased by $10,000, then sources of funds on the SCFP must exceed uses by $10,000. Likewise, if working capital has decreased by $10,000 during the period, then uses of funds on the SCFP must exceed sources by $10,000.

Sources of Funds

The SCFP includes both sources and uses of funds. The major categories of sources of funds and an example of each are listed in Exhibit 4.3.

Decreases in noncurrent assets include sales of fixed assets and/or investments. Often, the key in determining if a transaction counts as a source of funds is to ask: did it increase working capital? For example, a personal computer which originally cost $5,000 (fully depreciated for $5,000) was sold for $1,000. The result is an increase in cash for $1,000, an increase in gain on sale of fixed assets for $1,000, and decrease of $5,000 in the fixed asset and accumulated depreciation accounts. The effect on

Exhibit 4.3 Major Categories of Sources of Funds

Category	Example
1. Decreases in noncurrent assets	Sale of fixed asset for $200,000
2. Increases in noncurrent liabilities	Sale of bonds payable for $500,000
3. Increases in contributed capital	Sale of capital stock for $300,000
4. Income from operations	Net profit of $100,000 plus depreciation of $50,000

working capital is an increase of $1,000. Therefore, the sale of a noncurrent asset (a decrease) resulted in an increase in working capital, thus, a source of funds.

Increases in noncurrent liabilities consist of loans from financial institutions, sale of bonds, and other long-term indebtedness. The result, generally, is an increase in cash and an increase in the long-term debt; thus, current assets have increased without a simultaneous increase in current liabilities, resulting in an increase in working capital. Under the all financial resources concept, the purchase of fixed assets in exchange for a future (long-term) promise to pay, even though no cash is presently paid, results in a source of funds. Working capital has not increased; however, long-term debt has been used to finance the acquisition and should be shown as a source of funds on the SCFP. Incidently, this acquisition of fixed assets is also shown on the SCFP as a use of funds. We will discuss the accounting details of this part of the transaction in the next section of this chapter under "Uses of Funds."

A third source of funds is from contributed capital. The most common contribution of capital is from owners. When a hospitality business sells capital stock, the cash received increases cash and owners' equity accounts. Whether the stock is common or preferred, the contribution is a source of funds. In the infrequent situation where a city may lure a firm to build a hotel by contributing land to the hospitality establishment, the contributed land is treated as a source of funds under the all financial resources of the SCFP.

Finally, working capital provided by operations is a source of funds and is generally the largest source of funds on a continuing basis. Exhibit 4.4 indicates how the working capital provided by operations is typically determined.

Net income is the result of sales which provide cash and/or accounts receivable (current assets) and expenses which use cash and/or increase payables (current liabilities). The result of current assets less current liabilities is working capital; therefore, it is common practice to start the calculation of sources of funds from operations with net income shown on the income statement. However, several elements of the income statement do not use or provide funds; therefore, the net income figure must be adjusted to determine the source of working capital by operations. Both depreciation and amortization expenses reduce net income, but since they do not use working capital, they are added back to net income in determining sources of funds from operations for the SCFP.

The income statement also shows income taxes deducted in deter-

Exhibit 4.4 Determining Working Capital Provided by Operations

Net Income		$XXX
Transactions not affecting working capital:		
Depreciation	$XXX	
Amortization	XXX	
Noncurrent deferred income taxes	XXX	
Loss on sale of noncurrent assets	XXX	
Gains on sale of noncurrent assets	(XXX)	XXX
Working capital provided by operations		$XXX

mining net income. When the income taxes per the income statement exceed the amount of liability to the governmental tax agencies for the year, the firm records the excess as deferred income taxes. This difference generally represents timing differences with respect to payment dates of taxes. Deferred income taxes do not use cash, and if the deferred income taxes is a noncurrent account, it does not affect current liabilities; therefore, working capital is not affected and the increase in the deferred income taxes is added to net income for SCFP purposes.

Two other considerations in calculating the source of funds from operations by using net income are losses and gains on the sale of noncurrent assets. Since hospitality firms are not in business to sell noncurrent assets but to provide products and services to guests, any gains are subtracted from net income and losses are added to net income to determine working capital provided by operations. For example, assume a conveyor oven which cost $15,000 and which had accumulated depreciation of $12,000 is sold for $5,000. The sale is recorded as follows:

Cash	$ 5000	
Accumulated Depreciation—conveyor oven	12000	
Conveyor Oven		$15000
Gain on Sale of Fixed Assets		2000

As a result of this transaction, cash (current assets) has increased by $5,000 without any corresponding increases of current liabilities; therefore, working capital has increased by $5,000. However, the gain of $2,000 is included in net income but is to be subtracted in determining working capital provided by operations. The $5,000 increase in working capital is separately reported as a source of funds as "Proceeds from sale of fixed assets."

Uses of Funds

Exhibit 4.5 lists the three major categories of the uses of funds and provides an example of each. Increases in noncurrent assets include purchases of fixed assets and long-term investments. For example, assume the acquisition of a personal computer results in an increase in

Exhibit 4.5   Major Categories of Uses of Funds

Category	Example
1. Increases in noncurrent assets	Purchase of fixed assets for $500,000
2. Decreases in noncurrent liabilities	Reduction of $100,000 of long-term debt
3. Decreases in owners' equity	Declaration of dividends of $50,000

the equipment account and a decrease in cash. Since cash (current assets) is reduced without a change in current liabilities, working capital is reduced; thus, the acquisition results in a use of funds. An increase in noncurrent assets need not result from cash purchases. Under the all financial resources concept of funds, an increase in noncurrent assets financed with long-term debt and/or capital stock would also be shown as a use of funds on the SCFP.

A second use of funds results from decreases in noncurrent liabilities. When long-term debt is reduced by reclassifying it as a current maturity of long-term debt, working capital is decreased; therefore, the result is a use of funds. Long-term debt may be reduced by refinancing; that is, long-term debt is replaced by other long-term debt. In this situation, even though working capital is not affected, the debt reduction would be reported on the SCFP as a use of funds under the all financial resources concept of funds.

The third use of funds is a decrease in owners' equity. This decrease may result from a cash dividend declaration or transactions involving capital accounts. A cash dividend declaration is based on board of directors' action and results in a legal liability. The accounting entry results in an increase in dividends payable (current liability) and a decrease in retained earnings. Therefore, since current liabilities have increased without a simultaneous change in current assets, working capital has decreased, resulting in a use of funds. The later payment of dividends, resulting in a simultaneous decrease in cash and dividends payable, leaves working capital unchanged. Thus, the cash dividend payment is not a use of funds.

If a hospitality property repurchases its capital stock and retires it or keeps it as treasury stock, the result is a use of funds. The purchase decreases current assets (cash) without affecting current liabilities, resulting in a decrease in working capital.

Preparing the Statement of Changes in Financial Position

The income statement, the statement of retained earnings, and two successive balance sheets from the beginning and end of the accounting period are the principal sources of information needed for preparing the statement of changes in financial position. In addition, details of transactions affecting the change in noncurrent balance sheet accounts must be reviewed. For example, if a comparison of two successive balance sheets shows the fixed assets account, Building, has increased by $500,000, the building account must be analyzed to determine the changes. Simply reflecting the net change of $500,000 on the SCFP is generally not acceptable.

A five-step approach for preparing the SCFP is as follows:

1. Determine change in working capital for the period.

2. Determine how operations for the period have affected working capital.

3. Determine how changes reflected in noncurrent balance sheet accounts have affected funds.

4. Prepare the statement of changes in financial position.

5. Check the accuracy of the statement of changes in financial position.

Exhibits 4.6 and 4.7 contain the Comparative Balance Sheets for December 31, 19X1 and 19X2, and the 19X2 combined Income Statement and Statement of Retained Earnings for the Midway Motel. These exhibits illustrate the five-step approach for preparing the SCFP.

The first step in preparing the statement of changes in financial position is to determine the change in working capital for the accounting period. This is done by developing a schedule from the balance sheets showing each current asset and liability at the beginning and end of the accounting period. From this information, the change in each account and the net change in working capital can be calculated. Exhibit 4.2 gives the schedule for the working capital information for the Midway Motel developed from the year-end balance sheets. This schedule reflects the change in composition of the current accounts but does not reveal why these changes occurred.

The schedule shows that working capital has decreased significantly during the year, from $125,883 at the end of 19X1 to $19,896 at the end of 19X2. In the current asset accounts, the major change is that the marketable securities held at the beginning of the year have been sold. The current liability accounts show two major changes: (1) a new note payable for $25,000, and (2) a decline in the amount of accounts payable of $11,955. The net change of these and all other working capital items has revealed that current assets have decreased and current liabilities have increased. The combined changes in the current assets and current liabilities result in a decrease in working capital of $105,987. To explain the changes in the financial position of a business enterprise, the nature of transactions affecting the amount of working capital must be identified.

The second step in preparing the SCFP is to determine how the income, or loss, for the period (operations) has affected working capital. The income, or loss, reported on the income statement must be adjusted because the accrual method of accounting does not measure the actual change in funds. For example, consider the treatment of depreciation on the income statement. In the accrual method, expenses must be recognized in the accounting period or periods benefited, rather than when the funds expenditure occurred. Therefore, the cost of equipment

Exhibit 4.6   Comparative Balance Sheets

Midway Motel
Comparative Balance Sheets
For December 31, 19X1 and 19X2

	December 31 19X2	December 31 19X1	Increase (Decrease)
Current Assets			
Cash	$ 89,278	$ 82,540	$ 6,738
Marketable Securities	—	100,000	(100,000)
Accounts Receivable	3,789	3,811	(22)
Supplies Inventory	11,936	10,833	1,103
Prepaid Insurance	4,667	4,318	349
Total Current Assets	109,670	201,502	(91,832)
Property and Equipment, at Cost			
Land	262,000	262,000	0
Building	1,927,817	1,572,805	355,012
Equipment and Furniture	241,470	213,843	27,627
	2,431,287	2,048,648	382,639
Less Accumulated Depreciation	411,137	303,227	107,910
	2,020,150	1,745,421	274,729
Total Assets	$2,129,820	$1,946,923	$ 182,897
Current Liabilities			
Notes Payable	$ 25,000	$ —	$ 25,000
Mortgage Payable-Current	50,000	50,000	0
Accounts Payable	6,821	18,776	(11,955)
Accrued Wages	7,953	6,843	1,110
Total Current Liabilities	89,774	75,619	14,155
Long-Term Liabilities			
Mortgage Payable	1,105,399	950,695	154,704
Owners' Equity			
Common Stock, No Par, Authorized 100,000			
Shares, Issued 75,000 Shares	750,000	750,000	0
Retained Earnings	184,647	170,609	14,038
Total Liabilities and Owners' Equity	$2,129,820	$1,946,923	$182,897

purchased in a single accounting period is depreciated over the period of time the operation benefits from its use. With this method, working capital may only be affected in the period that the equipment was purchased. Since depreciation reduces net income on the income statement, depreciation must be added to income, or subtracted from a loss, in order to determine the amount of working capital generated from operations.

Amortization of intangible assets and premium, or discount on long-term debt require similar adjustments. An example of an intangible asset is an initial franchise fee. When the initial fee is paid, it reduces

Exhibit 4.7 Income Statement and Statement of Retained Earnings

Midway Motel
Income Statement and Statement of Retained Earnings
For the year ended December 31, 19X2

Revenues	
Rooms	$1,349,866
Food and Beverage	753,722
Telephone	73,936
Other Operating Income	1,006
Interest Income	785
Total	2,179,315
Costs and Expenses	
Rooms	565,037
Food and Beverage	624,161
Telephone	76,470
Administrative and General	250,677
Property Operation, Maintenance, and Energy Costs	154,478
Property Taxes and Insurance	111,462
Interest Expense	161,087
Depreciation	110,225
Total	2,053,597
Income Before Gain on Sale of Property	125,718
Gain on Sale of Property	3,000
Income Before Income Taxes	128,718
Income Tax	51,180
Net Income	77,538
Retained Earnings at Beginning of Year	170,609
Less: Dividends Declared	63,500
Retained Earnings at End of Year	$184,647

working capital without immediately affecting expense, because it is recorded as a deferred asset. When amortized as an expense over the life of the franchise agreement, it has no effect on working capital, and the amortization expense must be added to earnings for the period when measuring the effect of earnings on working capital.

The net income, or loss, from operations must also be adjusted by the gain or loss on the sale of property, equipment, and long-term investments (noncurrent assets). Gains (losses) from the sale of noncurrent assets are subtracted (added) from net income on the statement of changes in financial position. A question and answer example illustrates this process. A fixed asset with a net book value (cost less accumulated depreciation) of $5,000 is sold for $8,000 cash.

1. What gain, or loss, is recognized on the income statement? Cash received ($8,000) less net book value ($5,000) equals gain ($3,000).

2. What current assets are provided by the transaction? Cash of $8,000.

3. How much does working capital increase because of the sale? By the increase of current assets less the increase of current liabilities. Current assets (cash) increase by $8,000 while current liabilities are not affected. Therefore, working capital (and funds) increases by $8,000.

4. How is net income on the statement of changes in financial position adjusted to reflect the effect of operations on working capital? The sale of the fixed asset is not part of operations as such, so the $3,000 gain must be subtracted from net income. If a loss from the sale of fixed assets had occurred, the loss would be added to net income.

Operations as a source of working capital would require the following adjustments for the Midway Motel.

Net income		$77,538
Add back expenses not requiring working capital:		
Depreciation	$110,225	
Less gain on the sale of equipment	(3,000)	107,225
Working capital provided by operations		$184,763

The third step in preparing the statement of changes in financial position is to determine how changes in the noncurrent assets, noncurrent liabilities, and owners' equity accounts have affected funds. The beginning and ending balance sheets are the initial source of information. Each noncurrent account must be analyzed to determine the nature of its change. The Midway Motel example in Exhibit 4.6 indicates that the following accounts have changed: Building ($355,012), Equipment ($27,627), Accumulated Depreciation ($107,910), Mortgage Payable ($154,704), and Retained Earnings ($14,038).

Each of these noncurrent accounts must be analyzed to determine which transactions affect working capital and thus funds. This is accomplished by reviewing the account in the general ledger and, when necessary, the entry in the appropriate journal.

For the building account in our example, the general ledger shows the following:

Building

1/1/X2	Beginning balance	$1,572,805
5/31/X2	Building addition	355,012
12/31/X2	Ending balance	$1,927,817

The building account increased because of an addition to the building. The $355,012 increase in the account represents a use of funds because it is an increase in a noncurrent asset.

The equipment account and the accumulated depreciation account show the following entries:

Equipment

1/1/X2	Beginning balance	$213,843			
			3/12/X2	Sale	$6,750
7/8/X2	Purchases	34,377			
12/31/X2	Ending balance	$241,470			

Accumulated Depreciation

			1/1/X2	Beginning balance	$303,227
3/12/X2	Sale of equipment	$2,315			
			12/31/X2	Depreciation	110,225
			12/31/X2	Ending balance	$411,137

The equipment account transactions are both a source and a use of funds. The purchases of $34,377 represent a use, while the sale of an equipment item originally costing $6,750 is a source of funds. The equipment general ledger account does not contain enough information to determine the effect of the sale on working capital (funds). The cash receipts journal provides the needed information:

Cash	$7435	
Accumulated depreciation	2315	
Equipment		$6750
Gain on the sale of equipment		3000

The proceeds of $7,435 from the sale represent a source of funds. The gain of $3,000 is treated as a reduction in income when determining the amount of working capital provided from operations. The total depreciation expense of $110,225, shown as a credit entry in the accumulated depreciation account, is added to net income to reflect an increase in working capital from operations.

The mortgage payable (noncurrent) general ledger account shows the following entries:

Mortgage Payable (Noncurrent)

			1/1/X2	Beginning balance	$950,695
			6/12/X2	Increase in mortgage	204,704
12/31/X2	Mortgage re-classification	$50,000			
			12/31/X2	Ending balance	$1,105,399

The increase in the mortgage amount was related to financing of the building addition; this transaction will be disclosed in the SCFP as a source of funds. The $50,000 mortgage reclassification, that is, a reclassification of $50,000 from noncurrent to current, represents a use of funds, as working capital is reduced by $50,000 by the reclassification.

The retained earnings account activity recorded in the general ledger is:

Retained Earnings

			1/1/X2	Beginning balance	$170,609
6/30/X2	Dividends declared	$ 63,500			
			12/31/X2	Earnings for year	77,538
			12/31/X2	Ending balance	$184,647

The retained earnings account shows a use of funds for dividends declared of $63,500. This is a use of funds when dividends were declared since retained earnings were debited and dividends payable (a current liability account) was credited. Earnings for the year are a source of working capital. However, as indicated earlier, they generally require adjustments to arrive at the actual amount of working capital provided by operations.

After all the noncurrent asset accounts have been reviewed, the fourth step is to prepare the statement. The format of this statement can vary, but it generally starts out with sources of funds followed by uses. The bottom line shows the net increase or decrease in working capital. The statement prepared from the Midway Motel example is shown in Exhibit 4.8. Frequently, the working capital schedule, prepared in Step 1, is shown at the bottom of this statement as additional information. Otherwise, it must be disclosed in the footnotes to the financial statements.

The fifth step in preparing the statement is to check its accuracy by comparing the statement's net decrease or increase in working capital with the amount on the schedule (Exhibit 4.2) prepared in Step 1. This provides reasonable assurance that all transactions affecting working capital have been identified and accurately reported.

The Midway Motel illustration did not include changes in the capital stock account. The sale of capital stock is a source of working capital, because cash is increased along with the noncurrent accounts of owners' equity, capital stock, and paid-in capital in excess of par. The repurchase by a firm of its own capital stock is a use of funds, because cash is reduced (and thus, working capital) while the proper capital stock (noncurrent) accounts are also reduced.

When transactions occur only between noncurrent accounts, these changes do not affect working capital. For example, exchanging capital stock for equipment would not affect working capital since it does not involve current accounts. The journal entry for this transaction is:

Equipment	10000	
Capital Stock		10000

Many other transactions involve only noncurrent accounts, such as the following:

Exhibit 4.8   Statement of Changes in Financial Position

Midway Motel
Statement of Changes in Financial Position
For the year ended December 31, 19X2

Sources of Funds	
Funds Provided by Operations:	
Net Income	$ 77,538
Add Expenses Not Requiring Working Capital: Depreciation	110,225
Less: Gain on the Sale of Equipment	3,000
Total from Operations	184,763
Mortgage Payable	204,704
Proceeds from Sale of Equipment	7,435
Total Sources	396,902
Uses of Funds	
Building Addition	355,012
Equipment Purchased	34,377
Dividends Declared	63,500
Mortgage Payable Reclassification	50,000
Total Uses	502,889
Net Decrease in Working Capital	$(105,987)

- Exchange of preferred stock for common stock
- Exchanges—one equipment item for another
- Exchange of long-term debt for capital stock
- Financing fixed asset acquisitions with long-term debt
- Refinancing of long-term debt
- Donation of noncurrent assets to the hospitality firm

Although these types of transactions do not change working capital under the all financial resources concept of funds, they are shown on the statement of changes in financial position. The item exchanged would be listed under sources of working capital, and the item received under uses. For example, a building is financed by a combination of long-term debt and capital stock. For SCFP purposes, "acquisition of building" is a use, while "issuance of capital stock" and "long-term debt borrowing" are sources. In this case, the total sources equal total uses on the SCFP from this transaction.

Major Benefits of the SCFP

The SCFP provides financial information about the hospitality enterprise not directly available from either the balance sheet or income statement. In the Midway Motel illustration, it shows a building addition costing $355,012. Further, Midway's SCFP shows that all internal and external sources of funds were less than fund uses for the building addition, equipment purchased, etc., resulting in a net decrease in working capital of $105,987.

The SCFP aids in evaluating the financing of a hospitality operation by listing its sources of funds. This allows the financial statement user to determine the portions of internal versus external financing. Additionally, the SCFP assists management in detecting any unnecessary use of funds. For example, assume the purchase of operating items for a hotel (particularly china, linen, and repair and maintenance supplies) results in inventory levels exceeding normal operational needs. When inventory levels are excessive, cash is tied up in the storerooms, and the opportunity to use that cash for more beneficial purposes has been lost. The first portion of the SCFP reports the amount of funds that have flowed into the enterprise from operations. The net income or loss reported on the income statement must be adjusted to determine the amount of working capital provided by operations. The external sources of funds are reported after the sources of funds from operations.

Alternative SCFP Formats

Most hospitality enterprises, and United States business firms in general, provide a SCFP which lists sources followed by uses. Alternative SCFP formats may be used to provide the sources and uses of funds. Two alternative approaches are the self-balancing form (Exhibit 4.9) and the change in working capital form (Exhibit 4.10). The self-balancing approach has the decrease in working capital of the Midway Motel of $105,987 added to sources to equal the uses of funds of $502,889. The change in working capital approach simply shows working capital at the beginning and end of the period for the Midway Motel. The working capital at the beginning of the year of $125,883 less the decrease of $105,987 shows the working capital at the end of the year of $19,896.

An interesting and informative approach was used by Marriott Corporation in its annual report for 1985 (Exhibit 4.11). Rather than list sources and uses of funds separately, Marriott reports changes in financial position by type of activity. First, Marriott reports funds from operations and subtracts refurbishments to existing properties resulting in discretionary cash flow. Second, Marriott lists financing activities including new financing and debt payments. Third, investing activities are detailed including investment in property and equipment acquisitions less the proceeds from sale of assets. Next, they list transactions affecting their capital accounts. The change in funds is equaled by the change in working capital accounts as shown at the bottom of their SCFP.

Statement of Cash Flows

Many users of financial reports are more interested in a hospitality operation's actual cash flow than in the flow of funds defined as working

Exhibit 4.9 Self-Balancing Form of SCFP

Midway Motel
Statement of Changes in Financial Position
For the year ended December 31, 19X2

Source of Funds	
Funds Provided by Operations:	
Net Income	$ 77,538
Add Expenses Not Requiring Working Capital: Depreciation	110,225
Less: Gain on Sale of Equipment	3,000
Total from Operations	184,763
Mortgage Payable	204,704
Proceeds from Sale of Equipment	7,435
Decrease in Working Capital	105,987
Total Sources	$502,889
Uses of Funds	
Building Addition	$355,012
Equipment Purchased	34,377
Dividends Declared	63,500
Mortgage Payable Reclassification	50,000
Total Uses	$502,889

capital, or the all financial resources approach just presented. A major reason for this is that obligations are paid with cash, not with working capital. Another reason users are becoming more interested in cash statements is that accrual accounting has become too far removed from the underlying cash flows of a hospitality operation because it uses too many arbitrary allocation devices, such as deferred taxes and depreciation. Many users argue that the net income figure resulting from accrual accounting methods is not an acceptable indicator of earning power. Finally, financial statements do not address inflation, and many users of these documents are looking to a more concrete measure, like cash flow, to evaluate operating performance.

The Revision Committee of the *Uniform System of Accounts for Hotels* (8th edition), has proposed a funds statement that recognizes the sources and uses of cash on an operational/non-operational basis. The proposed statement, the statement of cash flow, identifies the major elements in operating and maintaining a hotel that contribute to the net change in cash from one period to the next.

The statement of cash flow (Exhibit 4.12) discloses the sources of cash receipts by specific category, arising from both operational and non-operational activities. Likewise, cash uses are identified along similar activity lines. Therefore, this statement is distinguished from the SCFP in that it recognizes transactions affecting both balance sheet and income statement accounts.

The Revision Committee is of the opinion that a statement identifying the cash flow, resulting from a hotel's operational as well as

Exhibit 4.10   Change in Working Capital Form of SCFP

Midway Motel
Statement of Changes in Financial Position
For the year ended December 31, 19X2

Working Capital – January 1, 19X2		$125,883
Sources of Funds		
Funds Provided by Operations:		
Net Income	$ 77,538	
Add Expenses Not Requiring Working Capital:		
Depreciation	110,225	
Less: Gain on the Sale of Equipment	3,000	
Total from Operations	184,763	
Mortgage Payable	204,704	
Proceeds from Sale of Equipment	7,435	
Total Sources	396,902	
Uses of Funds		
Building Addition	355,012	
Equipment Purchased	34,377	
Dividends Declared	63,500	
Mortgage Payable Reclassification	50,000	
Total Uses	502,889	
Decrease in Working Capital		105,987
Working Capital – December 31, 19X2		$19,896

non-operational activities, presents data that is useful and is easily understood by both owners and managers of hotels.

Summary

The major objectives of the statement of changes in financial position (SCFP) are to show the sources and uses of funds, and by so doing, link together successive balance sheets. In order to plan for future events, it is vital for management to be aware of the operation's cash and/or working capital position.

There are three major types of funds statements. The first type shows the sources and uses of cash. However, a more in-depth technique examines the changes in working capital (current assets minus current liabilities) accounts. This includes purchases with cash, accounts payable, and short-term notes payable. The final type, the SCFP, includes all working capital accounts, and all financing and investing activity not affecting the working capital accounts. It does not highlight the change in any specific account but shows any overall effect on working capital.

To prepare a SCFP, a five-step approach is recommended. First, determine the change in working capital from the start of the year to the end. Next, compute the total sources provided by operations. In order to

Exhibit 4.11   Consolidated Changes in Financial Position

CHANGES IN FINANCIAL POSITION

Marriott Corporation and Subsidiaries
Fiscal years ended January 3, 1986, December 28, 1984 and December 30, 1983

	1985	1984	1983
		(in millions)	
Operations			
Funds provided from continuing operations:			
Income from continuing operations	$167.4	$135.3	$108.4
Add expenses not requiring current outlay of working capital:			
Depreciation and amortization of property and equipment	111.9	99.2	87.1
Deferred income taxes	71.7	79.5	65.7
Other	21.3	8.5	11.5
Funds provided from continuing operations	372.3	322.5	272.7
Funds provided from discontinued operations	1.1	8.0	21.4
Funds provided from operations	373.4	330.5	294.1
Less refurbishment of existing operations	(56.3)	(52.2)	(48.0)
Discretionary Cash Flow	317.1	278.3	246.1
Financing Activities			
New financing	751.2	489.5	349.3
Maturities and prepayments of debt	(696.9)	(445.8)	(167.0)
	54.3	43.7	182.3
Investing Activities			
Investments in property and equipment	880.6	571.5	432.4
Investments in and advances to affiliates	115.9	212.3	25.6
Acquisitions of businesses	140.5	80.5	19.0
Dispositions of property and equipment of			
discontinued operations, net of tax	(72.6)	(67.0)	—
Proceeds from hotel dispositions and syndications, net of tax	(864.4)	(417.9)	—
Disposals of other property and equipment	(134.1)	(11.9)	(30.8)
Other	325.9	(86.2)	27.3
	391.8	281.3	473.5
Capital and Other Transactions			
Issuance of stock, net	(20.9)	(13.5)	(10.2)
Cash dividends	14.7	12.1	10.2
Purchase of stock for treasury	4.2	93.4	1.0
	(2.0)	92.0	1.0
Increase in Negative Working Capital	$ 18.4	$ 51.3	$ 46.1
Summary of Increase (Decrease) in Negative Working Capital:			
Cash and temporary cash investments	$(24.1)	$ 69.6	$ (2.5)
Receivables, including due from affiliates	(148.5)	(72.7)	(2.4)
Inventories	(36.0)	(16.0)	(6.7)
Prepaid expenses	(1.4)	(9.7)	(8.0)
Short-term loans	3.9	(1.4)	(.3)
Accounts payable and accrued liabilities	216.8	79.7	64.1
Current portion of debt	7.7	1.8	1.9
Increase in Negative Working Capital	$ 18.4	$ 51.3	$ 46.1

The accompanying notes are an integral part of these financial statements.

Courtesy of Marriott Corporation

Exhibit 4.12 Statement of Cash Flow

STATEMENT OF CASH FLOW

	Period Ended	
	19___	19___
OPERATING RECEIPTS	$	$
Guest Receipts		
Cash Sales		
Collection of Accounts Receivable—Trade		
Rentals		
Other	_____	_____
OPERATING DISBURSEMENTS		
Payroll and Related		
Food and Beverage		
Other Merchandise		
Operating Supplies		
Management Fees		
Energy Costs		
Other	_____	_____
Cash from Operations Before Fixed Charges	_____	_____
FIXED CHARGES		
Rent		
Taxes		
Insurance		
Interest Expense	_____	_____
OTHER RECEIPTS		
Collections of Other Receivables		
Proceeds from Sale of Investments		
Proceeds from Outside Borrowing		
Contributions/Advances from Owners		
Proceeds from Sale of Assets		
Other	_____	_____
OTHER DISBURSEMENTS		
Debt Service (Principal)		
Additions to Property and Equipment		
Federal and State Income Taxes		
Distributions to Owners		
Other	_____	_____
INCREASE (DECREASE) IN CASH		
CASH BALANCE, BEGINNING OF PERIOD	_____	_____
CASH BALANCE, END OF PERIOD	$_____	$_____

determine the other sources and uses of funds, examine the noncurrent accounts on the balance sheets. At this point, prepare the statement of changes in financial position. Finally, balance the report by comparing the difference in sources and uses of funds according to the SCFP with the change in working capital calculated in step one.

In order to complete the first step of this process, examine the balance sheets from the beginning and end of the period. Calculate the working capital for each by subtracting the current assets from the current liabilities. The difference between these two amounts is the change in working capital.

The second step analyzes the funds provided by operations, the starting point being the net income for the period as reflected in the income statement. Any non-working capital expenses must be added back to net income, i.e., depreciation and amortization, and any income gains or losses from events other than operations must be added or subtracted, respectively.

The next step examines how the changes in noncurrent balance sheet accounts affect funds. The accounts to be analyzed include all noncurrent assets and liabilities, and the owners' equity section. Sources of funds include, but are not limited to, the sale of capital stock, increases in long-term debt, and the sale of equipment. Uses include the purchase of equipment, declaration of dividends, and the reclassification of long-term debt.

At this point, the SCFP can be prepared, following a format beginning with sources of funds provided by operations, followed by other sources to arrive at total sources. The uses are then totaled, and the difference between sources and uses of funds is calculated. This difference is compared with the change in working capital (step one); the two should be identical. However, the numbers may balance without having recorded all of the sources and uses. The all financial resources approach requires that transactions affecting only noncurrent accounts be reported. For example, although the purchase of a building through increased long-term debt does not directly affect any working capital account, the increase in debt must be shown as a source and the acquisition as a use.

The other type of financial report which is of importance to hotel owners and operators is the statement of cash flow. The statement of cash flow analyzes the change in the cash accounts by examining the balance sheet and the income statement.

Discussion Questions

1. Explain the differences among the three definitions of "funds."

2. What are the major benefits of preparing a statement of changes in financial position?

3. Explain why cash received from an increase in short-term debt, such as a bank loan, does not affect the funds defined as working capital.

4. What are the major sources of funds?

5. Why are gains from sale of equipment subtracted from net income to arrive at "Funds Provided by Operations"?

6. What are the major uses of funds?

7. How do declarations of cash dividends affect the SCFP?

8. What are the steps for preparing an SCFP?

9. If the balance for mortgage payable (long-term debt) was $100,000 and $150,000 at the beginning and end of the year, respectively, what was the effect on the SCFP if only one transaction occurred?

10. State some examples of "transactions" involving only nonworking capital. How are these presented on the SCFP?

Problem 4.1

The owner of the Backdoor Inn desires to prepare a statement of changes in financial position for the year of 19X2 to discuss with his banker in regards to a proposed loan. His accountant has prepared only unclassified balance sheets as follows:

Balance Sheets
Backdoor Inn
December 31, 19X1 and 19X2

	19X1	19X2
Cash	$38,000	$42,000
Marketable Securities	10,000	5,000
Accounts Receivable	49,000	51,000
Inventories	36,000	34,000
Furniture	345,000	443,000
Building	2,000,000	2,000,000
Accumulated Depreciation	(550,000)	(650,000)
Land	380,000	380,000
Total Assets	$2,308,000	$2,305,000
Accounts Payable	$80,000	$76,000
Mortgage Payable (current portion)	80,000	80,000
Mortgage Payable (noncurrent portion)	1,200,000	1,120,000
Common Stock	575,000	575,000
Paid-in Capital in Excess of Par	133,000	133,000
Retained Earnings	240,000	321,000
Total Liabilities and Owners' Equity	$2,308,000	$2,305,000

Required:

1. Calculate working capital at December 31, 19X1.

2. Calculate working capital at December 31, 19X2.

3. Calculate the change in working capital for 19X2.

Problem 4.2

You have been hired by a successful entrepreneur to prepare a statement of changes in financial position for his two-year old hotel, the Illini Inn. The following are copies of the condensed balance sheets and the income statement of the Illini Inn.

Condensed Balance Sheets
Illini Inn
December 31, 19X1 and 19X2

	19X1	19X2
Current Assets	$250,000	$300,000
Property and Equipment (net)	1,400,000	1,500,000
Other Assets	200,000	100,000
Total Assets	$1,850,000	$1,900,000
Current Liabilities	$200,000	$250,000
Long-Term Debt	1,000,000	950,000
Total Liabilities	1,200,000	1,200,000
Owner's Equity	650,000	700,000
Total Liabilities and Owners' Equity	$1,850,000	$1,900,000

Condensed Income Statement
Illini Inn
For the year ended December 31, 19X2

Sales	$1,600,000
Cost of Goods Sold	200,000
Contribution Margin	1,400,000
Undistributed Operating Expenses	950,000
Income Before Fixed Charges	450,000
Depreciation Expense	200,000
Amortization of Preopening Expenses	100,000
Income Before Tax	150,000
Income Tax	50,000
Net Income	$100,000

Additional Information:

1. Equipment was purchased for $300,000.

2. Dividends of $50,000 were declared and paid during 19X2.

3. Long-term debt of $50,000 was reclassified as current at the end of 19X2.

Required:

Prepare a SCFP.

Problem 4.3

Gail Whiting has been operating a hotel for a number of investors who know little about the hospitality industry. Their major concern is not occupancy percentage or net income, but rather flow of funds and liquidity. In order to inform them about these, Ms. Whiting needs a statement of changes in financial position for 19X2. She already knows that $10,000 of funds were provided by operations for 19X2. The following limited information is provided:

1. Current assets increased from $39,500 to $46,000 during 19X2, while current liabilities decreased from $37,500 to $35,500 for the same period.

2. Dividends of $2,000 were declared during the year, while $5,000 of dividends were paid.

3. The long-term debt and the current portion of long-term debt shown on the balance sheet includes the following:

	19X1	19X2
Mortgage Payable (current)	$5,000	$5,000
Notes Payable (long-term)	-0-	5,500
Mortgage Payable (long-term)	100,000	95,000

Note:

Assume there were no other changes in noncurrent balance sheet accounts that require your analysis. Further, assume that all current liabilities are paid during the twelve months following the balance sheet date. Assume the mortgage payable (long-term) is first reclassified as current before the debt is paid.

Required:

1. Determine the change in working capital for 19X2.
2. Prepare the SCFP for Ms. Whiting.

Problem 4.4

The operations of The Freida, a small lodging operation, are becoming more complex. Ms. Martin, the owner, has asked for your help in preparing her statement of changes in financial position. She is able to present you with condensed balance sheets and some additional information.

Condensed Balance Sheets
The Freida
December 31, 19X1 and 19X2

	19X1	19X2
Current Assets	$36,500	$31,500
Investments	10,000	5,000
Equipment	200,000	325,000
Accumulated Depreciation	(20,000)	(40,000)
Total Assets	$226,500	$321,500
Current Liabilities:		
Accounts Payable	$18,000	$21,000
Long-Term Debt (current)	5,000	5,000
Dividends Payable	5,000	5,000
Noncurrent Liabilities:		
Long-Term Debt	75,000	70,000
Notes Payable	-0-	40,000
Common Stock	50,000	100,000
Retained Earnings	73,500	80,500
Total Liabilities and Owners' Equity	$226,500	$321,500

Additional Information:

1. Equipment costing $20,000 depreciated to one half its cost, was sold for $8,000.

2. Common stock, purchased as a long-term investment for $5,000, was sold for $8,000.

3. Dividends declared during 19X2 totaled $7,000.

4. Equipment costing $145,000 was purchased during 19X2.

5. Depreciation expense for 19X2 totaled $30,000.

6. Long-term debt of $5,000 was reclassified as current at the end of 19X2.

7. Common stock of $50,000 was sold and long-term debt of $40,000 was borrowed during 19X2. The Freida generated net income of $14,000 during 19X2.

Required:

1. What is the change in working capital from December 31, 19X1 to December 31, 19X2?

2. Prepare the SCFP as requested by Ms. Martin.

Problem 4.5

Below are the Holly Hotel balance sheets for the years ended December 31, 19X1 and 19X2 and the abbreviated income statements for 19X1 and 19X2.

Balance Sheets
Holly Hotel
December 31, 19X1 and 19X2

	19X1	19X2
Current Assets:		
Cash	$10,000	$15,000
Accounts Receivable (net)	25,000	25,000
Marketable Securities	15,000	15,000
Inventory	8,000	10,000
Total Current Assets	58,000	65,000
Investments	60,000	50,000
Property and Equipment:		
Land	50,000	80,000
Buildings	1,000,000	1,000,000
Equipment	100,000	120,000
Less Accumulated Depreciation	(470,000)	(525,000)
Net Property and Equipment	620,000	675,000
Total Assets	$798,000	$790,000
Current Liabilities:		
Accounts Payable	$12,000	$8,000
Current Maturities of Long-Term Debt	14,000	12,000
Dividends Payable	10,000	-0-
Total Current Liabilities	36,000	20,000
Long-Term Debt	200,000	200,000
Owners' Equity:		
Capital Stock	100,000	80,000
Retained Earnings	462,000	490,000
Total Liabilities and Owners' Equity	$798,000	$790,000

Condensed Income Statements
Holly Hotel
For the years ended December 31, 19X1 and 19X2

	19X1	19X2
Departmental Income	$1,800,000	$2,000,000
Unallocable Expenses Except Depreciation	1,695,000	1,900,000
Depreciation	50,000	55,000
Net Operating Income*	$55,000	$45,000

*Prior to any gains or losses from sale of investments and income taxes.

<u>Additional Information:</u>

1. No equipment was sold during 19X2.

2. Investments costing $10,000 were sold for $15,000 during 19X2.

3. Dividends declared during 19X2 were paid in 19X2. Dividends declared during 19X1 of $10,000 were paid during 19X2.

4. Capital stock of $20,000 was retired for $20,000 during 19X2.

5. Assume all liabilities are paid on a timely basis.

6. Assume that Holly Hotel is subject to income taxes at 25% of pretax income.

7. Assume the only items affecting retained earnings were net income and dividends declared.

<u>Required:</u>

Prepare a SCFP for 19X2.

5 Ratio Analysis

Financial statements issued by hospitality establishments contain considerable financial information. A thorough analysis of this information requires more than simply reading the reported facts. Users of financial statements need to be able to interpret the reported facts and make them yield answers to questions that reveal aspects of the hospitality property's financial situation that could otherwise go unnoticed. This is accomplished through ratio analysis that makes significant comparisons between related facts reported on financial statements. A ratio gives mathematical expression to a significant relationship between two related facts, and is computed by simply dividing one figure by the related figure. By bringing the two facts into relation with each other, ratios generate new information. In this way, ratio analysis goes beyond the figures reported in a financial statement and makes them more meaningful, more informative, and more useful. In particular, ratio analysis generates indicators for evaluating different aspects of the financial situation of a hospitality operation.

Ratio analysis can provide users of financial statements with answers to such questions as:

1. Is there sufficient cash to meet the establishment's obligations for a given time period?

2. Are the profits of the hospitality operation reasonable?

3. Is the level of debt acceptable in comparison to the stockholders' investment?

4. Is the inventory usage adequate?

5. How do the operation's earnings compare to the market price of the hospitality property's stock?

6. Are accounts receivable reasonable in light of credit sales?

7. Is the hospitality establishment able to service its debt?

In this chapter, we will first explain the different kinds of standards against which ratios are compared in order to generate evaluations concerning the financial condition of a hospitality operation. We will also discuss the variety of functions or purposes that ratio analysis serves in interpreting financial statements and the ways in which different ratios are expressed in order to make sense of the information they provide. The bulk of this chapter is devoted to a detailed discussion of the ratios most commonly used to analyze the financial condition of operations in the hospitality industry.

Ratio Standards

Ratio analysis is used to evaluate the favorableness or unfavorableness of various financial conditions. However, the computed ratios alone do not say anything about what is good or bad, acceptable or unacceptable, reasonable or unreasonable. By themselves, ratios are neutral and simply express numerical relationships between related figures. In order to use ratios as indicators or measurements of the success or well-being of a hospitality operation, the computed ratios must be compared against some standard. Only then will the ratios become meaningful and provide users of financial statements with a basis for evaluating the financial conditions.

There are basically three different standards that are used to evaluate the ratios computed for a given operation for a given period. First, many ratios can be compared to corresponding ratios calculated for the prior period in order to discover any significant increases or decreases in the ratios. For example, occupancy percentage (discussed briefly in Chapter 1 and elaborated more fully later in this chapter) for the current year may be compared to occupancy percentage of the prior year in order to determine whether the lodging operation is succeeding in selling more of its available rooms this year than it had previously. This comparison may be useful in evaluating the effectiveness of the property's current marketing plans.

Industry averages provide another useful standard against which to compare ratios. After calculating the return on investment (discussed later in this chapter) for a given property, investors may want to compare this with the average return for similar properties in their particular industry segment. This may give investors an indication of the ability of the property's management to effectively use resources to generate profits for the owners in comparison to other operations in the industry. In addition, managers may want to compare the occupancy percentage or food cost percentage for their own operation to industry averages in order to evaluate their abilities to compete with other operations in their industry segment. As mentioned in previous chapters, published sources of average industry ratios are readily available.

While ratios can be compared against results of a prior period and also against industry averages, ratios are best compared against planned ratio goals. For example, in order to more effectively control the cost of labor, management may project a goal for the current year's labor cost percentage (also discussed in this chapter) that is slightly lower than the previous year's levels. The expectation of a lower labor cost percentage may reflect management's efforts to improve scheduling procedures and other factors related to the cost of labor. By comparing the actual labor cost percentage with the planned goal, management is able to assess the success of its efforts to control labor cost.

Different evaluations may result from comparing ratios against these different standards. For example, a food cost of 33% for the current period may compare favorably with the prior year's ratio of 34% and with an industry average of 36%, but may be judged unfavorably when compared to the operation's planned goal of 32%. Therefore, care must be taken in evaluating the results of operations using ratio analysis. It is necessary to keep in mind not only which standards are being used to evaluate the ratios, but the purposes of the ratio analysis as well.

Purposes of Ratio Analysis

Managers, creditors, and investors may often have different purposes in using ratio analysis to evaluate the information reported in financial statements.

Ratios help managers monitor the operating performances of their operations and evaluate their success in meeting a variety of goals. By tracking a limited number of ratios, hospitality managers are able to maintain a fairly accurate perception of the effectiveness and efficiency of their operations. In a food service operation, most managers compute food cost percentage and labor cost percentage in order to continually monitor the two largest expenses of their operations. In lodging operations, occupancy percentage is one of the key ratios that managers use on a daily basis. Ratios are often used by hospitality establishments to express the goals set for their operations. For example, management may establish ratio goals as follows:

- Maintain a 1.25 to 1 current ratio.

- Debt/equity ratio is not to exceed 1 to 1.

- Maintain return on owner's equity of 15%.

- Maintain fixed asset turnover of 1.2.

These ratios, and many more, will be fully explained later in this chapter. The point here is to notice that ratios are particularly useful to managers as indicators of how well goals are being achieved. When actual results fall short of goals, ratios help indicate where a problem may be. In the food cost percentage example presented earlier in which an actual ratio of 33% compared unfavorably against the planned 32%, additional research is required to determine the cause(s) of the 1% variation. This 1% difference may be due to cost differences, sales mix differences, or a combination of the two. Only additional analysis will determine the actual cause and, as we will see later in the chapter, ratio analysis can contribute significant information to such an investigation.

Creditors use ratio analysis to evaluate the solvency of hospitality operations and to assess the riskiness of future loans. For example, the relationship of current assets to current liabilities, referred to as the current ratio (and discussed in detail later in this chapter), may indicate an establishment's ability to pay its upcoming bills. In addition, creditors sometimes use ratios to express requirements for hospitality operations as part of the conditions set forth for certain financial arrangements they might make. For example, as a condition of a loan, a creditor may require an operation to maintain a current ratio of 2 to 1.

Investors and potential investors use ratios to evaluate the performance of a hospitality operation as they consider their investment decisions. For example, the dividend payout ratio (dividends paid divided by earnings) indicates the percentage of earnings paid out by the hospitality establishment. Potential investors, primarily interested in stock growth, may shy away from investing in properties that pay out "healthy" dividends.

Ratios are used to communicate financial performance. Different ratios communicate different results. Individually, ratios reveal only part of the overall financial condition of an operation. However, collectively, ratios are able to communicate a great deal of information that may not be immediately apparent by simply reading the figures reported in financial statements.

What Ratios Express

In order to understand the information communicated by the different kinds of ratios used in ratio analysis, it is necessary to understand the various ways in which ratios express financial information. Different ratios are read in different ways. For example, many ratios are expressed as a *percentage*. An illustration is the food cost percentage which expresses the cost of food sold in terms of a percent of total food sales. If total food sales for a given year is $430,000, while the cost of food sold is $135,000, then the result of dividing the cost of food sold by the total food sales is .314. Because the food cost percentage is a ratio expressed in terms of a percentage and not a decimal, this figure is multiplied by 100 to yield a 31.4% food cost. Another example is occupancy percentage, resulting from rooms sold divided by rooms available for sale. If a lodging property has 100 rooms available for sale and sells only 50 of them, then 50 divided by 100 yields .5, which is then multiplied by 100 to be expressed as a percentage (50%).

Some other ratios are expressed on a *per unit basis*. For example, the average breakfast check is a ratio expressed as a certain sum per breakfast served. It is calculated by dividing the total breakfast sales by the number of guests served during the breakfast period. Thus, on a given day, if 100 guests were served breakfast and the total revenue during the breakfast period amounted to $490, then the average breakfast check would be $4.90 per meal ($490 divided by 100 equals $4.90).

The proper way to express still other ratios is as a *turnover* of so many times. Seat turnover is one such ratio, determined by dividing the number of guests served during a given period by the number of restaurant seats. If the restaurant in the previous example had a seating capacity of 40 seats, then seat turnover for the breakfast period in which it served 100 guests would be 2.5 times (100 divided by 40 equals 2.5). This means that, during that breakfast period, the restaurant used its entire seating capacity 2.5 times.

Finally, some ratios are expressed as a *coverage* of so many times. The denominator of such a ratio is always set at 1. An example will illustrate this type of ratio expression. The current ratio, determined by dividing current assets by current liabilities, is one of the ratios expressed as a coverage of so many times. For example, if a hospitality operation reported current assets of $100,000 and current liabilities of $81,000 for a given period, then the operation's current ratio at the balance sheet date would be 1.2 to 1 (100,000 divided by 81,000 equals

1.23, rounded to 1.2). This means that the hospitality operation possessed sufficient current assets to cover its current liabilities 1.2 times. Put another way, for every $1 of current liabilities, the operation had $1.20 of current assets.

The proper way to express the various ratios used in ratio analysis depends entirely on the particular ratio and the nature of the significant relationship it expresses between the two facts it relates. The different ways in which different ratios are expressed are a function of how we can make sense out of the new information that results from using ratios. As we discuss the ratios commonly used in the hospitality industry to analyze financial information, pay close attention to how each is expressed. This will help you to make intuitive sense of the nature and uses of each ratio and the different type of information each provides.

Classes of Ratios

Ratios are generally classified by the type of information which they provide. Five common ratio groupings are as follows:

1. Liquidity

2. Solvency

3. Activity

4. Profitability

5. Operating

Liquidity ratios reveal the ability of a hospitality establishment to meet its short-term obligations. Solvency ratios, on the other hand, measure the extent that the enterprise has been financed by debt and is able to meet its long-term obligations. Activity ratios reflect management's ability to use the property's assets, while several profitability ratios show management's overall effectiveness, as measured by returns on sales and investments. Finally, operating ratios assist in analyzing the operations of the hospitality establishment.

The classification of certain ratios may vary. For example, some texts classify the inventory turnover ratio as a liquidity ratio, but this text, and some others, consider it as an activity ratio. Also, profit margin could be classified as an operating ratio, but it is generally included with the profitability group of ratios.

Knowing the meaning of a ratio and how it is used is always more important than knowing its classification. We will now turn to an in-depth discussion of individual ratios. For each ratio discussed, we will consider its purpose, the formula by which it is calculated, the sources of data needed for the ratio's calculation, and the interpretation of ratio results from the varying viewpoints of owners, creditors, and management.

Exhibits 5.1 through 5.3, financial statements of the hypothetical Grand Hotel, will be used throughout our discussion of individual ratios.

Exhibit 5.1   Balance Sheets

Balance Sheets
Grand Hotel
December 31, 19X0, 19X1, 19X2

ASSETS	19X0	19X1	19X2
Current Assets:			
Cash	$ 20,000	$ 21,000	$ 24,000
Marketable Securities	60,000	81,000	145,000
Accounts Receivable (net)	100,000	90,000	140,000
Inventories	14,000	17,000	15,000
Prepaid Expenses	13,000	12,000	14,000
Total Current Assets	207,000	221,000	338,000
Investments	43,000	35,000	40,000
Property and Equipment:			
Land	68,500	68,500	68,500
Buildings	810,000	850,000	880,000
Furniture and Equipment	170,000	170,000	172,000
	1,048,500	1,088,500	1,120,500
Less: Accumulated Depreciation	260,000	300,000	345,000
China, glassware, silver, linen, and uniforms	11,500	20,500	22,800
Total Property and Equipment	800.000	809,000	798,300
Total Assets	$1,050,000	$1,065,000	$1,176,300
LIABILITIES AND OWNERS' EQUITY			
Current Liabilities:			
Accounts Payable	$ 60,000	$ 53,500	$ 71,000
Accrued Income Taxes	30,000	32,000	34,000
Accrued Expenses	70,000	85,200	85,000
Current Portion of Long-Term Debt	25,000	21,500	24,000
Total Current Liabilities	185,000	192,200	214,000
Long-Term Debt:			
Mortgage Payable	425,000	375,000	400,000
Deferred Income Taxes	40,000	42,800	45,000
Total Long-Term Debt	465,000	417,800	445,000
Total Liabilities	650,000	610,000	659,000
Owners' Equity:			
Common Stock	55,000	55,000	55,000
Paid-in Capital in Excess of Par	110,000	110,000	110,000
Retained Earnings	235,000	290,000	352,300
Total Owners' Equity	400,000	455,000	517,300
Total Liabilities and Owners' Equity	$1,050,000	$1,065,000	$1,176,300

Exhibit 5.2   Income Statements

Income Statements Grand Hotel For the years ended December 31, 19X1 and 19X2		
	19X1	**19X2**
Total Revenue	$1,300,000	$1,352,000
Rooms:		
Revenue	$ 780,000	$ 810,000
Payroll and related costs	135,000	145,000
Other Direct Expenses	62,500	60,000
Departmental Income	582,500	605,000
Food and Beverages:		
Revenue	430,000	445,000
Cost of sales	142,000	148,000
Payroll and related costs	175,000	180,000
Other Direct Expenses	43,400	45,000
Departmental Income	69,600	72,000
Telephone:		
Revenue	40,000	42,000
Cost of sales	30,000	31,000
Payroll and related costs	10,000	10,500
Other Direct Expenses	5,000	4,500
Departmental Income	(5,000)	(4,000)
Rentals and Other Income Revenue	50,000	55,000
Total Operated Departments Income	697,100	728,000
Undistributed Operating Expenses:		
Administrative & General	105,000	108,500
Marketing	51,500	55,000
Property Operation & Maintenance	65,250	67,500
Energy Costs	80,250	81,500
	302,000	312,500
Income Before Fixed Charges	395,100	415,500
Rent	20,000	20,000
Property Taxes	20,000	24,000
Insurance	5,500	6,000
Interest	54,000	60,000
Depreciation	60,000	61,000
	159,500	171,000
Income Before Income Taxes	235,600	244,500
Income Taxes	94,300	97,800
Net Income	$ 141,300	$ 146,700

Note: Data processing, human resources, guest entertainment, and transportation expenses are insignificant and are not shown as separate cost centers.

Exhibit 5.3   Statement of Retained Earning and Other Information

Statement of Retained Earnings
and Other Information
Grand Hotel
December 31, 19X1 and 19X2

	19X1	19X2
Retained earnings – beginning of the year	$ 228,700	$ 290,000
Net income	141,300	146,700
Dividends declared	80,000	84,400
Retained earnings – end of the year	$290,000	$352,300

Other Information

	19X1	19X2
Rooms Sold	20,500	21,000
Paid Guests	23,500	24,000
Rooms Occupied by Two or More People	2,400	2,500
Shares of Common Stock Outstanding	55,000	55,000
Food Covers	55,500	56,000

Liquidity Ratios

The ability of a hospitality establishment to meet its current obligations is important in evaluating its financial position. For example, can the Grand Hotel meet its current debt of $214,000 as it becomes due? Several ratios can be computed that suggest answers to this question.

Current Ratio   The most common liquidity ratio is the current ratio, which is the ratio of total current assets to total current liabilities and is expressed as a coverage of so many times. Using figures from Exhibit 5.1, the 19X2 current ratio for the Grand Hotel can be calculated as follows:

$$\text{Current Ratio} = \frac{\text{Current Assets}}{\text{Current Liabilities}}$$

$$= \frac{\$338,000}{\$214,000}$$

$$= \underline{1.58} \text{ times or 1.58 to 1}$$

This result shows that for every $1 of current liabilities, the Grand Hotel has $1.58 of current assets. Thus, there is a cushion of $.58 for every dollar of current debt. A considerable shrinkage of inventory and receivables could occur before the Grand Hotel would be unable to pay its current obligations. By comparison, the 19X1 current ratio for the Grand Hotel was 1.15 times. An increase in the current ratio from 1.15 times to 1.58 times within one year is considerable and would no doubt please creditors. However, would a current ratio of 1.58 times please all interested parties?

Owners/stockholders normally prefer a low current ratio to a high one, because stockholders view investments in most current assets as less productive than investments in noncurrent assets. Since stockholders are primarily concerned with profits, they prefer a relatively low current ratio.

Creditors normally prefer a relatively high current ratio, as this provides assurance that they will receive timely payments from their customers (hospitality enterprises). A subset of creditors, lenders of funds, believe adequate liquidity is so important that they often incorporate a minimum working capital requirement or a minimum current ratio in loan agreements. Violation of this loan provision could result in the lender demanding full payment of the loan.

Management is caught in the middle, trying to satisfy both owners and lenders while, at the same time, maintaining adequate working capital and sufficient liquidity to ensure the smooth operations of the hospitality establishment. Management is able to take action affecting the current ratio. In the case of the Grand Hotel, a current ratio of 2 times could be achieved by selling $90,000 worth of marketable securities on the last day of 19X2 and paying current creditors.[1] Other possible actions to increase a current ratio include:

1.   Obtain long-term loans.

2.   Obtain new owner equity contributions.

3.   Convert noncurrent assets to cash.

4.   Defer declaring dividends and leave the cash in the business.

An extremely high current ratio may mean that accounts receivable are too high because of liberal credit policies and/or slow collections, or it may indicate that inventory is excessive. Since ratios are indicators, management must follow through by analyzing possible contributing factors.

Acid-test Ratio   A more stringent test of liquidity is the acid-test ratio. The acid-test ratio measures liquidity by considering only "quick assets"—cash and near-cash assets. Excluded from current assets are inventories and prepaid expenses in determining the total quick assets. In many industries, inventories are significant and their conversion to cash may take several months. The extremes appear evident in the hospitality industry. In some hospitality operations, especially quick service restaurants, food inventory may be entirely replenished twice a week. On the other hand, the stock of certain alcoholic beverages at some food service operations may be replaced only once in three months.

The difference between the current ratio and the acid-test ratio is a function of the amount of inventory relative to current assets. In some operations, the difference between the current ratio and the acid-test ratio will be minor, while in others, it will be significant. Using relevant figures from Exhibit 5.1, the 19X2 acid-test ratio for the Grand Hotel is computed as follows:

$$\text{Acid-test Ratio} = \frac{\text{Cash, Marketable Securities, Notes \& Accounts Receivable}}{\text{Current Liabilities}}$$

$$= \frac{\$309,000}{\$214,000}$$

$$= \underline{\underline{1.44}} \text{ times}$$

The 19X2 acid-test ratio reveals quick assets of $1.44 for every $1.00 of current liabilities. This is an increase over the 19X1 acid-test ratio of .44 times. Although the acid-test ratio was 1.0 for l9Xl, the Grand Hotel was not in extremely difficult financial straits. Many hospitality establishments are able to operate efficiently and effectively with an acid-test ratio of one, or less than one, for they have minimal amounts of both inventory and accounts receivable.

The viewpoints of owners, creditors, and managers toward the acid-test ratio parallel those held toward the current ratio. That is, owners of hospitality operations prefer a low ratio (generally less than one), creditors prefer a high ratio, and management is again caught in the middle.

Accounts Receivable Turnover

In hospitality operations that extend credit to guests, accounts receivable is generally the largest current asset. Therefore, in an examination of a property's liquidity, the "quality" of its accounts receivable must be considered.

In the normal operating cycle (discussed in Chapter 2), accounts receivable are converted to cash. The accounts receivable turnover measures the rapidity of the conversion. This ratio is determined by dividing revenue by average accounts receivable. A refinement of this ratio uses only charge sales in the numerator; however, quite often charge sales figures are unavailable to outsiders (stockholders, potential stockholders and creditors). Regardless of whether revenue or charge sales are used as the numerator, the calculation should be consistent from period to period. Average accounts receivable is the result of dividing the sum of the beginning of the period and end of the period accounts receivable by two. When a hospitality operation has seasonal sales fluctuations, a preferred approach (when computing the *annual* accounts receivable turnover) is to sum the accounts receivable at the end of each month and divide by 12 to determine the average accounts receivable. Exhibit 5.4 uses relevant figures from Exhibits 5.1 and 5.2 to calculate the accounts receivable turnover for 19X2 of the Grand Hotel.

The accounts receivable turnover of 11.76 times indicates that the total revenue for 19X2 is 11.76 times the average receivables. This is lower than the 19X1 accounts receivable turnover of the Grand Hotel of 13.68 times. Management would generally investigate this difference. The investigation may reveal problems, or that changes in the credit policy and/or collection procedures significantly contributed to the difference.

The faster the accounts receivable are turned over, the more cre-

Exhibit 5.4 Accounts Receivable Turnover

$$\text{Accounts Receivable Turnover} = \frac{\text{Total Revenue}}{\text{Average Accounts Receivable}^*}$$

$$= \frac{1,352,000}{115,000}$$

$$= 11.76 \text{ times}$$

$$^*\text{Average Accounts Receivable} = \frac{\text{Accounts Receivable at Beginning and End of Year}}{2}$$

$$= \frac{90,000 + 140,000}{2}$$

$$= 115,000$$

dence the current and acid-test ratios have in financial analysis. Although the accounts receivable turnover measures the overall rapidity of collections, it fails to address individual accounts. This matter is resolved by preparing an aging of accounts receivable which reflects the status of each account. In an aging schedule, each account is broken down to the period when the charges originated. Like credit sales, this information is generally available only to management. Exhibit 5.5 illustrates an aging of accounts receivable.

Since few hospitality establishments charge interest on their accounts receivable, the opportunity cost of credit sales is the investment dollars that could be generated by investing cash. However, credit terms are extended with the purpose of increasing sales. Therefore, theoretically, the credit policy should be relaxed up to the point where bad debt and additional collection costs equal the additional profit earned by extending credit.

Owners prefer a high accounts receivable turnover to a low turnover as this reflects a lower investment in nonproductive accounts receivable. However, they understand how a tight credit policy and an over-aggressive collections effort may result in lower sales. Further, everything else being the same, a high accounts receivable turnover indicates that accounts receivable are being managed well. Suppliers, like owners, prefer a high accounts receivable turnover, because this means that hospitality establishments will have more cash readily available to pay them. Long-term creditors also see a high accounts receivable turnover as a positive reflection of management. Management desires to maximize the sales of the hospitality operation. However, management realizes that this may result in more accounts receivable and in selling to some less credit-worthy customers. The result is a relatively lower accounts receivable turnover. On the other hand, management must maintain the

Exhibit 5.5 Aging of Accounts Receivable

Aging of Accounts Receivable
Grand Hotel
December 31, 19X2

Firm Name	Total	Days Outstanding				
		0-30	31-60	61-90	91-120	Over 120 days
Ace Co.	$600	$400	$200	$–0–	$–0–	$–0–
Acem Corp.	400	100	–0–	300	–0–	–0–
Ahern, Jim	100	100	–0–	–0–	–0–	–0–
America, Inc.	1,000	950	–0–	–0–	–0–	50
Armadillo Co.	50	–0–	–0–	–0–	50	–0–
⋮						
Zebra Zoo Equip.	80	80	–0–	–0–	–0–	–0–
Total	$145,000	$115,000	$18,000	$7,000	$4,000	$1,000

operation's cash flow and, so, will attempt to manage accounts receivable to achieve an adequate cash flow.

Average Collection Period

A variation of the accounts receivable turnover is the average collection period which is calculated by dividing the accounts receivable turnover into 365 (the number of days in a year). This conversion simply translates the turnover into a more understandable result. For the Grand Hotel, the average collection period for 19X2 is as follows:

$$\text{Average Collection Period} = \frac{365}{\text{Accounts Receivable Turnover}}$$

$$= \frac{365}{11.76}$$

$$= \underline{\underline{31}} \text{ days}$$

The average collection period of 31 days means that on an average of every 31 days throughout 19X2, the Grand Hotel was collecting all its accounts receivable. The 31 days is a four-day increase over the average collection period of 19X1 of 27 days.

What should be the average collection period? Generally, the time allowed for average payments should not exceed the terms of sale by more than 7 to 10 days. Therefore, if the terms of sale are n/30 (entire amount is due in 30 days), the maximum allowable average collection period is 37 to 40 days.

The above discussion assumes all sales are credit sales. However, many hospitality operations have both cash and credit sales. Therefore, the mix of cash and credit sales must be considered when the accounts receivable turnover ratio uses revenue, rather than credit sales, in the numerator. This is accomplished by allowing for cash sales. For example, if sales are 50% cash and 50% credit, then the maximum allowable average collection period should be adjusted. An adjusted maximum allowable average collection period is calculated by multiplying the maximum allowable average collection period by credit sales as a percentage of total sales.

In the previous example of a maximum allowable collection period of 37 to 40 days and 50% credit sales, the adjusted maximum allowable average collection period is 18.5 to 20 days (37 to 40 days x .5). This adjustment can generally only be made by management, because the mix of sales is unknown by other interested parties.

The average collection period preferred by owners, creditors, and management is similar to their preferences for the accounts receivable turnover, because the average collection period is only a variation of the accounts receivable turnover. Therefore, owners and creditors prefer a lower number of days, while management prefers a higher number of days.

Working Capital Turnover Ratio

The final liquidity ratio presented is the working capital turnover ratio which compares working capital (current assets less current liabilities) to revenue. For most businesses, the higher the revenue, the greater the amount of working capital required. Thus, as the revenue rises, working capital is expected to rise also. Exhibit 5.6 uses relevant figures from Exhibits 5.1 and 5.2 to calculate the working capital turnover ratio in 19X2 for the Grand Hotel.

For the Grand Hotel, a working capital turnover of 17.70 times means that working capital of $76,400 was "used" 17.70 times during the year. Everything else being the same, the lower the current ratio, the greater the working capital turnover ratio. Therefore, those establishments in segments of the hospitality industry with virtually no credit sales and a low level of inventory will generally have an extremely high working capital ratio.

Owners would prefer this ratio to be high, as they prefer a low current ratio, thus low working capital. Creditors prefer a lower working capital turnover ratio than owners, because they prefer a relatively high current ratio. Management's preferences fall between owners and creditors. Management desires to maintain an adequate amount of working capital to cover unexpected problems, yet management also desires to maximize profits by using available funds to make long-term investments.

Solvency Ratios

Solvency ratios measure the degree of debt financing by a hospitality enterprise and are partial indicators of the establishment's ability to meet its long-term debt obligations. These ratios reveal the equity cushion that is available to absorb any operating losses. Primary users of these ratios are outsiders, especially lenders who generally prefer less risk rather than more risk. Strong solvency ratios show an operation's financial ability to weather financial storms.

Owners like to use debt to increase their leverage. Leverage is using debt in place of equity dollars to increase the return on the equity dollars already invested. This occurs when the return on the investment exceeds

Exhibit 5.6   Working Capital Turnover

$$\text{Working Capital Turnover} = \frac{\text{Revenue}}{\text{Average Working Capital}}$$

$$= \frac{1,352,000}{76,400^*}$$

$$= \underline{17.70 \text{ times}}$$

Working Capital (WC)	=	Current Assets – Current Liabilities
WC (19X2)	=	$338,000 – $214,000 = $124,00
WC (19X1)	=	221,000 – 192,200 = 28,800

*Average Working Capital = $124,000 + $28,800 divided by 2 = $76,400

Exhibit 5.7   Return on Equity

	High Debt/ Low Equity	High Equity/ Low Debt
Debt	$80	$20
Equity	$20	$80
EBIT	$50	$50
Interest – 15%	12*	3**
Income before taxes	38	47
Income taxes	– 15.20	– 18.80
Net income	$22.80	$28.20

Return per $1 of equity:

$$\frac{\text{Net income}}{\text{equity}} = \frac{22.80}{20} = \$1.14 \qquad \frac{28.20}{80} = \$.35$$

*Debt times interest rate = interest expense   **$20 × .15 = $3
$80 × .15 = $12

the cost of the debt used to finance an investment. When using debt to increase their leverage, owners are, in essence, transferring part of their risk to creditors.

As a further explanation of the concept of leverage, let us consider the following example. Assume that total assets of a lodging facility are $100 and earnings before interest and taxes (EBIT) are $50, and interest is 15% of debt. Further, assume that two possible combinations of debt and equity are $80 of debt and $20 of equity, and the reverse which would be $80 of equity and $20 of debt. Further, assume a tax rate of 40%. The return on equity for each of the two combinations is calculated in Exhibit 5.7.

The calculations in Exhibit 5.7 reveal that each $1 invested by stockholders in the high debt/low equity combination earns $1.14, while every $1 invested by stockholders in the low debt/high equity combination earns only $.35. Therefore, from an owner's perspective, these ratios are leverage ratios.

This class of ratios includes two groups—those based on balance sheet information and those based on income statement information. The first three ratios to be examined (the solvency ratio, the debt-equity ratio, and long-term debt to total capitalization) are based on the balance sheet information. Two other ratios, the number of times interest earned ratio and the fixed charge coverage ratio, are based on information from the income statement and will also be addressed.

Solvency Ratio

A hospitality enterprise is solvent when its assets exceed its liabilities; therefore, the solvency ratio is simply total assets divided by total liabilities. The solvency ratio in 19X2 for the Grand Hotel is determined as follows:

$$\text{Solvency Ratio} = \frac{\text{Total Assets}}{\text{Total Liabilities}}$$

$$= \frac{\$1,176,300}{\$\ 659,000}$$

$$= \underline{\underline{1.78}}\text{ times}$$

Thus, at the end of 19X2, the Grand Hotel has $1.78 of assets for each $1.00 of liabilities or a cushion of $.78. The Grand Hotel's assets could be discounted substantially ($.78 divided by $1.78 = 43.8%) and creditors could be fully paid. The Grand Hotel's solvency ratio at the end of 19X1 was 1.75 times. The difference is relatively minor but the 19X2 ratio would be considered as slightly more favorable from the perspective of creditors.

The greater the leverage (use of debt to finance the assets) used by the hospitality establishment, the lower its solvency ratio. Owners prefer to use leverage in order to maximize their return on their investments. This occurs so long as the earnings from the creditor-financed investment exceeds the cost of the establishment's borrowing. Creditors, on the other hand, prefer a high solvency ratio, as it provides a greater cushion should the establishment experience losses in operations. Managers must satisfy both owners and creditors, thus they desire to finance assets so as to maximize the return on owners' investments while not unduly jeopardizing the establishment's ability to pay creditors.

Debt-equity Ratio

This ratio, one of the most common solvency ratios, compares the hospitality establishment's debt to its net worth (owners' equity). The debt-equity ratio indicates the establishment's ability to withstand adversity and meet its long-term debt obligations. Figures from Exhibit 5.1 can be used to calculate the Grand Hotel's debt equity ratio for 19X2:

$$\text{Debt-equity Ratio} = \frac{\text{Total Liabilities}}{\text{Total Owners' Equity}}$$

$$= \frac{\$659,000}{\$517,300}$$

$$= \underline{\underline{1.27}} \text{ to } 1$$

The Grand Hotel's debt-equity ratio of 1.27 to 1 at the end of 19X2 indicates for each $1 of owners' net worth, the Grand Hotel owed creditors $1.27. The debt-equity ratio for 19X1 for the Grand Hotel was 1.34 to 1. Thus, relative to its net worth, the Grand Hotel reduced its 19X1 debt.

Owners view this ratio similar to the way they view the solvency ratio; that is, they desire to maximize their investment by using leverage. Creditors would favor this trend because their risk is reduced as net worth increases relative to debt. Management, as with the solvency ratio, prefers a middle position between creditors and owners.

Long-term Debt to Total Capitalization Ratio

Still another solvency ratio is the calculation of long-term debt as a percentage of the sum of long-term debt and owners' equity commonly called total capitalization. This ratio is similar to the debt-equity ratio except that current liabilities are excluded in the numerator, and long-term debt is added to the denominator of the debt-equity ratio. Current liabilities are excluded because current assets are normally adequate to cover them, therefore, they are not a long-term concern. Figures from Exhibit 5.1 can be used to calculate the 19X2 long-term debt to total capitalization ratio for the Grand Hotel:

$$\begin{array}{c}\text{Long-term Debt to} \\ \text{Total Capitalization} \\ \text{Ratio}\end{array} = \frac{\text{Long-term Debt}}{\text{Long-term Debt and Owners' Equity}}$$

$$= \frac{\$445,000}{\$962,300}$$

$$= \underline{\underline{46.24\%}}$$

Long-term debt of the Grand Hotel at the end of 19X2 is 46.24% of its total capitalization. This can be compared to 47.87% at the end of 19X1. Creditors would, of course, prefer the lower percentage because it would indicate a reduced risk on their part. Owners, on the other hand, would prefer the higher percentage because of their desire for high returns through the use of leverage.

Number of Times Interest Earned Ratio

This ratio is based on financial figures from the income statement and expresses the number of times interest expense can be covered. The greater the number of times interest is earned, the greater the safety afforded the creditors. Since interest is subtracted to determine taxable income, income taxes are added to net income and interest expense (earnings before interest and taxes, abbreviated as EBIT) to form the numerator of the ratio, while interest expense is the denominator.

Figures from Exhibit 5.1 can be used to calculate the 19X2 number of times interest earned ratio for the Grand Hotel:

$$\begin{matrix} \text{Number of Times} \\ \text{Interest Earned} \\ \text{Ratio} \end{matrix} = \frac{\text{EBIT}}{\text{Interest Expense}}$$

$$= \frac{\$304,500}{\$60,000}$$

$$= \underline{\underline{5.08}} \text{ times}$$

The result of 5.08 times shows that the Grand Hotel could cover its interest expense by over five times. The number of times interest earned ratio in 19X1 for the Grand Hotel was 5.36 times. This two-year trend suggests a slightly more risky position from a creditor's viewpoint. However, in general, a number of times interest earned ratio of greater than 4 reflects a sufficient amount of earnings for a hospitality enterprise to cover the interest expense of its existing debt.

All parties (owners, creditors, and management) prefer a relatively high ratio. Owners are generally less concerned about this ratio than creditors, as long as interest obligations are paid on a timely basis, and leverage is working to their advantage. Creditors and especially lenders prefer a healthy (high) ratio, because this indicates the establishment's ability to meet its interest payments. To the lender, the higher this ratio, the better. Management also prefers a high ratio, but realizes that an extremely high ratio suggests leverage is probably not being optimized for the owners. Therefore, management may prefer a lower ratio than do lenders.

The number of times interest earned ratio fails to consider fixed obligations other than interest expense. Many hospitality firms have long-term leases which require periodic payments similar to interest. This limitation of the number of times interest earned ratio is overcome by the fixed charge coverage ratio.

Fixed Charge Coverage Ratio

This ratio is a variation of the number of times interest earned ratio and considers leases as well as interest expense. Those hospitality establishments that have obtained the use of property and equipment through leases may find this fixed charge coverage ratio to be more useful than the number of times interest earned ratio. This ratio is calculated the same as the number of times interest earned ratio except that lease expense (rent expense) is added to both the numerator and denominator of the equation.

Exhibit 5.8 uses figures from Exhibit 5.1 to calculate the 19X2 fixed charge coverage ratio for the Grand Hotel. The result indicates that earnings prior to lease expense, interest expense, and income taxes cover lease and interest expense 4.06 times. The Grand Hotel's fixed charge coverage ratio for 19X1 was 4.18 times. The change of 0.12 times reflects a minor decrease in the Grand Hotel's ability to cover its fixed costs of interest and lease expense. The viewpoints of owners, creditors, and management are similar to the views they hold regarding changes in the number of times interest earned ratio, discussed in the previous section.

Exhibit 5.8 Fixed Charge Coverage

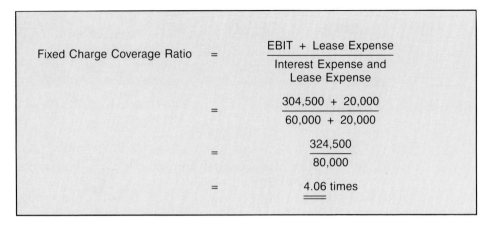

Activity Ratios

Activity ratios measure management's effectiveness in using its resources. Management is entrusted with inventory and fixed assets (and other resources) to generate earnings for owners while providing products and services to guests. Since fixed assets of most lodging facilities constitute a large percentage of the operation's total assets, it is essential to effectively utilize these resources. Inventory, although generally not a significant portion of total assets, must be adequately controlled by management in order to minimize cost of sales expenses.

Inventory Turnover

The inventory turnover shows how quickly the inventory is moving. All things being the same, generally, the quicker the inventory turnover the better, because inventory can be expensive to maintain. Maintenance costs include storage space, freezers, insurance, personnel expense, recordkeeping, and, of course, the opportunity cost of the funds invested in inventory. Inventories held by hospitality operations are highly susceptible to theft and must be carefully controlled. Food and beverage control (Chapter 7) is devoted to this topic.

An inventory turnover should generally be calculated separately for food supplies and beverages. Some food service operations will calculate several beverage turnovers based on the types of beverages available.

Exhibit 5.9 is a condensed food and beverage department statement of the Grand Hotel with food and beverage operations for 19X2 shown separately. Figures from this statement will be used to illustrate the food and beverage turnover ratios.

Exhibit 5.10 calculates the 19X2 food inventory turnover ratio for the Grand Hotel. The food inventory turned over 12.2 times during 19X2, or approximately once per month. The rapidity of food inventory turnover generally depends on the type of food service operation. A quick service restaurant generally experiences a much faster food turnover than does a fine dining establishment. In fact, it may have a food inventory turnover in excess of 200 times for a year. A norm used in the hotel industry for hotels that may have several different types of restaurants and banquets calls for food inventory to turn over four times per month.

Exhibit 5.9 Condensed Food and Beverage Statement

Condensed Food and Beverage Department Statement Grand Hotel For the year of 19X2	Food	Beverage
Sales	$300,000	$145,000
Cost of sales:		
Beginning inventory	11,000	6,000
Purchases	120,000	28,000
Less: Ending inventory	9,000	6,000
Cost of goods used	122,000	28,000
Less: Employee meals	2,000	0
Cost of goods sold	120,000	28,000
Gross Profit	180,000	117,000
Expenses:		
Payroll and related expenses	135,000	45,000
Other expenses	30,000	15,000
Total expenses	165,000	60,000
Departmental income	$15,000	$57,000

Exhibit 5.10 Food Inventory Turnover

$$\text{Food Inventory Turnover} = \frac{\text{Cost of Food Used}}{\text{Average Food Inventory}^*}$$

$$= \frac{122,000}{10,000}$$

$$= 12.2 \text{ times}$$

$$^*\text{Average Food Inventory} = \frac{\text{Beginning and Ending Inventories}}{2}$$

$$= \frac{11,000 + 9,000}{2}$$

$$= 10,000$$

Although a high food inventory turnover is desired, because it means that the food service establishment is able to operate with a relatively small investment in inventory, too high of a turnover may indicate possible stockout problems. Failure to provide desired food items to guests may not only immediately result in disappointed guests, but may also result in negative goodwill if this problem persists. Too low an inventory turnover suggests that food is overstocked, and, in addition to the costs to maintain inventory previously discussed, the potential cost of spoilage may become a problem.

Exhibit 5.11   Beverage Turnover

$$\text{Beverage Turnover Ratio} \quad = \quad \frac{\text{Cost of Beverages Used}}{\text{Average Beverage Inventory}^*}$$

$$= \quad \frac{28,000}{6,000}$$

$$= \quad \underline{\underline{4.67 \text{ times}}}$$

$$^*\text{Average Beverage Turnover} \quad = \quad \frac{\text{Beginning and Ending Inventories}}{2}$$

$$= \quad \frac{6,000 \ + \ 6,000}{2}$$

$$= \quad \underline{\underline{6,000}}$$

Exhibit 5.11 uses figures from Exhibit 5.9 to calculate the 19X2 beverage turnover ratio for the Grand Hotel. The beverage turnover of 4.67 times means that the beverage inventory of $6,000 required restocking approximately every 78 days. This is calculated by dividing 365 days in the year by the beverage turnover of 4.67. Not all beverage items are sold evenly, thus, some items would have to be restocked on a more frequent basis. A norm used in the hotel industry for hotels having several different types of lounges and banquets calls for beverage inventory to turn over 1.25 times per month or 15 times per year.

All parties (owners, creditors, and management) prefer high inventory turnover ratios to low ones, as long as stockouts are avoided. Ideally, as the last inventory item is sold, the shelves are being restocked!

Fixed Asset Turnover

The fixed asset turnover is determined by dividing average total fixed assets into total revenue for the period. A more precise measurement would be to use only revenues related to fixed asset usage in the numerator; however, revenue by source is not available to many financial analysts; so, total revenue is generally used. This ratio measures management's effectiveness in using fixed assets. A high turnover suggests the hospitality enterprise is using its fixed assets effectively to generate revenue, while a low turnover ratio suggests the establishment is not making effective use of its fixed assets and should consider disposing of part of them. A limitation of this ratio is that it places a premium on using older (depreciated) fixed assets since their book value is low. Further, this ratio is affected by the depreciation method employed by the hospitality operation. For example, an operation using an accelerated method of depreciation will show a higher turnover than an operation using the straight-line depreciation method, all other factors being the same.

Exhibit 5.12 uses figures from Exhibits 5.1 and 5.2 to calculate the

Exhibit 5.12   Fixed Asset Turnover

$$\text{Fixed Asset Turnover} = \frac{\text{Total Revenue}}{\text{Average Fixed Assets}^*}$$

$$= \frac{1,352,000}{803,650}$$

$$= 1.68 \text{ times}$$

$$^*\text{Average Fixed Assets} = \frac{\text{Total Fixed Assets at Beginning and End of Year}}{2}$$

$$= \frac{809,000 + 798,300}{2}$$

$$= 803,650$$

19X2 fixed asset turnover ratio for the Grand Hotel. The fixed asset turnover of 1.68 times reveals that revenue was 1.68 times the average total fixed assets. For 19X1, the Grand Hotel's fixed asset turnover was 1.62 times. The change of .06 times, although minor, is viewed as a positive trend.

All parties (owners, creditors, and management) prefer a high fixed asset turnover. Management, however, should resist retaining old and possibly inefficient fixed assets, even though they result in a high fixed asset turnover. The return on assets ratio, discussed in a later section on profitablity ratios, is a partial check against this practice.

Asset Turnover Ratio

Another ratio to measure the efficiency of management's use of assets is the asset turnover ratio. The two previous ratios presented, inventory turnover ratio and fixed assets turnover ratio, concerned a large percentage of the total assets, and now the asset turnover ratio examines the use of total assets in relation to total revenues. Limitations of the fixed asset ratio are also inherent in this ratio to the extent that fixed assets make up total assets. For most hospitality establishments, especially lodging businesses, fixed assets constitute the majority of the operation's total assets.

Exhibit 5.13 uses figures from Exhibits 5.1 and 5.2 to calculate the 19X2 asset turnover ratio for the Grand Hotel. The asset turnover ratio of 1.21 times indicates that each $1 of assets generated $1.21 of revenue in 19X2. The asset turnover ratio for 19X1 was 1.23 times. Thus, the difference between 19X1 and 19X2 is only .02 times, or, virtually no change for the two years.

As with the fixed asset turnover ratio, all concerned parties (owners, creditors, and management) prefer this ratio to be high, because a high

Exhibit 5.13   Asset Turnover

Asset Turnover Ratio	=	$\dfrac{\text{Total Revenues}}{\text{Average Total Assets}^*}$
	=	$\dfrac{1{,}352{,}000}{1{,}120{,}650}$
	=	1.21 times
*Average Total Assets	=	$\dfrac{\text{Total Assets at Beginning and End of Year}}{2}$
	=	$\dfrac{1{,}065{,}000 + 1{,}176{,}300}{2}$
	=	1,120,650

ratio means effective use of assets by management, subject to the limitations discussed previously.

Both the fixed asset turnover and the asset turnover ratios are relatively low for most hospitality segments, especially for hotels and motels. The relatively low ratio is due to the hospitality industry's high dependence on fixed assets and its inability to quickly increase output to meet maximum demand. It is common for many hotels and motels to turn away customers four nights a week due to excessive demand, and operate at an extremely low level of output (less than 50%) the three remaining nights.

Three additional measures of management's ability to efficiently use available assets are occupancy percentage, average occupancy per room, and double occupancy percentage. Although these three ratios are not based on financial information, they are viewed as excellent measures of management's effectiveness in selling space, whether it be rooms in a lodging facility or seats in a food service establishment.

Occupancy Percentage

Occupancy percentage is a major indicator of management's success in selling its "product." It refers to the percentage of rooms sold in relation to rooms available for sale in hotels and motels. In food service operations, it is commonly referred to as seat turnover, and is calculated by dividing the number of people served by the number of seats available. Seat turnover is commonly calculated by meal period. In most food service facilities, different seat turnovers are experienced for different dining periods. However, the occupancy percentage for lodging facilities and the seat turnovers for food service facilities are key measures of facility utilization.

Using the "Other Information" listed in Exhibit 5.3, the annual occupancy percentage of the Grand Hotel can be determined by dividing

Exhibit 5.14   Annual Occupancy Percentage

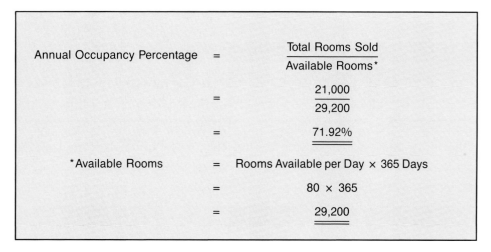

total rooms sold by available rooms for sale. If the Grand Hotel had 80 rooms available for sale each day, its occupancy percentage for 19X2 is calculated as indicated in Exhibit 5.14.

The Grand Hotel's 19X2 annual occupancy percentage of 71.92% was an improvement over the 19X1 annual occupancy percentage of 70.21% when 20,500 rooms were sold. This percentage does not mean that every day 70.21% of the available rooms were sold, only that on the average 70.21% were sold. In fact, it is possible that a hotel could experience 100% occupancy Monday through Thursday and a 33% occupancy Friday through Sunday, with a combined result of 71.29%.

There are many factors affecting occupancy rates in the lodging industry, such as location within an area, geographic location, seasonal factors (both weekly and yearly), rate structure, and type of lodging facility, to mention a few.

Average Occupancy per Room

Another ratio to measure management's ability to use the lodging facilities is the average occupancy per room. This ratio is the result of dividing the number of paid room guests by the number of rooms sold. Generally, as the number of paid guests per room increases, the room rate also increases.

Using figures from the "Other Information" section of Exhibit 5.3, the 19X2 average occupancy per room for the Grand Hotel can be calculated as follows:

$$\text{Average Occupancy per Room} = \frac{\text{Number of Paid Room Guests}}{\text{Number of Rooms Sold}}$$

$$= \frac{24,000}{21,000}$$

$$= \underline{1.14} \text{ Guests}$$

The Grand Hotel's 19X2 average occupancy per room was 1.14

guests. The 19X1 average occupancy per room was slightly higher at 1.15 guests.

The average occupancy per room is generally the highest for resort properties, where it can reach levels as high as 2.0 guests per room, and is lowest for transient lodging facilities.

Double Occupancy Percentage

Another ratio used to measure multiple occupancy of rooms is the double occupancy percentage. This ratio is similar to the average occupancy per room. It is determined by dividing the number of rooms occupied by two or more people by the number of rooms sold.

Using figures from the "Other Information" section of Exhibit 5.3, the double occupancy percentage of the Grand Hotel for 19X2 can be calculated as follows:

$$\frac{\text{Double Occupancy}}{\text{Percentage}} = \frac{\text{Rooms Occupied by Two or More People}}{\text{Rooms Sold}}$$

$$= \frac{2,500}{21,000}$$

$$= \underline{\underline{11.90\%}}$$

The double occupancy percentage for the Grand Hotel during 19X2 indicates 11.90% of the rooms sold were occupied by two or more people. The 19X1 double occupancy percentage for the Grand Hotel was 11.71%; therefore, a minor increase in double occupancy has occurred.

Owners, creditors, and management all prefer high occupancy ratios—occupancy percentage, average occupancy per room, and double occupancy percentage. The higher the occupancy ratios, the greater the use of the facilities. These ratios are considered to be prime indicators of a lodging facility's level of operations. Occupancy ratios are generally computed on a daily basis and are recorded on the daily report of operations.

Profitability Ratios

Profitability ratios reflect the results of all areas of management's responsibilities. All the information conveyed by liquidity, coverage, and leverage ratios impact on the profitability of the hospitality enterprise. The primary purpose of most hospitality operations is the generation of profit. Owners invest for the purpose of increasing their wealth through dividends and through increases in the price of the hospitality establishment's capital stock. Both dividends and stock price are highly dependent upon the profits generated by the operation. Creditors, especially lenders, provide resources to hospitality enterprises to use in the provision of services. Generally, future profits are required to provide cash to repay these lenders. Managers are also extremely interested in profits because their performance is, to a large degree, measured by the operation's bottom line. Excellent services breed goodwill, repeat customers, and other benefits which ultimately result in the desired increase in the operation's profitability.

The profitability ratios we are about to consider measure management's overall effectiveness as shown by returns on sales (profit margin and operating efficiency ratio), returns on assets (return on assets and net return on assets), return on owners' equity (return on owners' equity and return on common stockholders' equity), and lastly, the relationship between net income and the market price of the hospitality establishment's stock (price/earnings ratio).

Profit Margin

Hospitality enterprises are often evaluated in terms of their ability to generate profits on sales. This key ratio, profit margin, is determined by dividing net income by total revenue. It is an overall measurement of management's ability to generate sales and control expenses, thus, yielding the bottom line. In this ratio, net income, as the name implies, is remaining income after all expenses have been deducted, both those controllable by management and expenses directly related to decisions made by the board of directors.

Using figures from Exhibit 5.2, the 19X2 profit margin of the Grand Hotel can be determined as follows:

$$\text{Profit Margin} = \frac{\text{Net Income}}{\text{Total Revenue}}$$

$$= \frac{\$146,700}{\$1,352,000}$$

$$= \underline{\underline{10.85\%}}$$

The Grand Hotel's 19X2 profit margin of 10.85% has remained nearly constant from the 19X1 figure of 10.87%. The 10.85% is quite high compared to a Laventhol & Horwath industry average of approximately 2.5%.[2]

If the profit margin is lower than expected, then expenses and other areas should be reviewed. Poor pricing and sales volume could be contributing to the low ratio. To identify the problem area, the profit margin should be analyzed in addition to operated departmental margins. If the operated departmental margins are satisfactory, the problem would appear to be with overhead expense.

Operating Efficiency Ratio

The operating efficiency ratio (also known as gross operating profit ratio) is a better measure of management's performance than the profit margin. This ratio is the result of dividing income before fixed charges by total revenue. Income before fixed charges is the result of subtracting expenses generally controllable by management from revenue. The remaining fixed charges are expenses relating to the capacity of the hospitality firm, including rent, property taxes, insurance, depreciation, and interest expense. Although these expenses are the result of board of directors' decisions and thus beyond the direct control of active management, management can and should review tax assessments, insurance policies and quotations, and make recommendations to the board of directors that can affect the facility's total profitability. In calculating the operating efficiency ratio, income taxes are excluded also, since fixed charges directly affect income taxes.

Using figures from Exhibit 5.2, the 19X2 operating efficiency ratio of the Grand Hotel can be calculated as follows:

$$\text{Operating Efficiency Ratio} = \frac{\text{Income Before Fixed Charges}}{\text{Total Revenue}}$$

$$= \frac{\$415,500}{\$1,352,000}$$

$$= \underline{\underline{30.73\%}}$$

The operating efficiency ratio shows that nearly $.31 of each $1 of revenue is available for fixed charges, income taxes, and profits. The Grand's operating efficiency ratio was 30.39% for 19X1.

The next group of profitability ratios compare profits to either assets or owners' equity. The result in each case is a percentage and is commonly called a return.

Return on Assets (ROA)

This profitability ratio is a general indicator of the profitability of the hospitality enterprise's assets. Unlike the two preceding profitability ratios drawn only from income statement data, this ratio compares bottom line profits to the total investment, that is, to the total assets. This ratio, or a variation of it, is used by several large conglomerates to measure the performances of their subsidiary corporations operating in the hospitality industry.

Using figures from Exhibits 5.1 and 5.2, the Grand Hotel's 19X2 return on assets is calculated in Exhibit 5.15.

The Grand Hotel's 19X2 ROA is 13.09% which means 13.09 cents of profit for every dollar of average total assets. The 19X1 ROA was 13.36%. Therefore, there was a slight decline in ROA from 19X1 to 19X2.

A very low ROA may result from inadequate profits or excessive assets. A very high ROA may suggest older assets require replacement in the near future, or that additional assets need to be added to support growth in revenues. The determination of low and high is usually based on industry averages and with the hospitality establishment's own ROA profile that is developed over time.

ROA may also be evaluated by reviewing profit margin and asset turnovers, because when these ratios are multiplied by each other they yield ROA:

Profit Margin	x	Asset Turnover	=	ROA
$\dfrac{\text{Net Income}}{\text{Total Revenue}}$	x	$\dfrac{\text{Total Revenue}}{\text{Average Total Assets}}$	=	$\dfrac{\text{Net Income}}{\text{Average Total Assets}}$

Gross Return on Assets (GROA)

Calculating the gross return on assets is a variation of the ROA. This ratio measures the rate of return on assets regardless of financing methods. The calculation of ROA uses net income as its numerator and, therefore, includes the cost of debt-financing of the assets. The computation of the GROA, on the other hand, ignores any debt-financing by using income before interest and income taxes as its numerator. Interest is excluded because it is a financing cost, and income taxes are not

Exhibit 5.15 Return on Assets

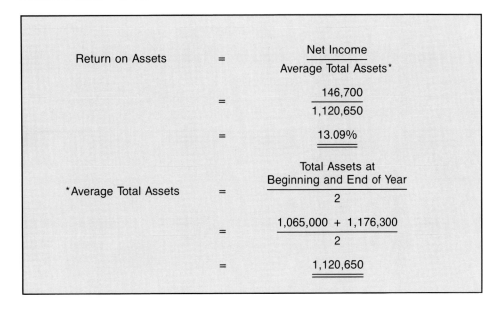

considered because interest expense is deductible in calculating the operation's tax liability.

Using figures from Exhibits 5.2 and 5.3, the Grand Hotel's GROA for 19X2 can be calculated as follows:

$$\text{Gross Return on Assets} = \frac{\text{Earnings Before Interest and Taxes (EBIT)}}{\text{Average Total Assets}}$$

$$= \frac{\$304,500}{\$1,120,650}$$

$$= \underline{27.17\%}$$

The Grand Hotel's GROA of 27.17% indicates a gross return of 27.17 cents for each dollar of average total assets for 19X2. This is a slight decline from 19X1 when GROA was 27.39%.

Return on Owners' Equity

A key profitability ratio is the return on owners' equity (ROE). The ROE ratio compares the profits of the hospitality enterprise to the owners' investment. Included in the denominator is all capital stock plus retained earnings.

Exhibit 5.16 uses relevant figures from Exhibits 5.1 and 5.2 to calculate the 19X2 ROE for the Grand Hotel. In 19X2, for every one dollar of owners' equity, 30.18 cents was earned. The 19X1 ROE for the Grand was even higher at 33.05%. To the owner, this ratio represents the end result of all management's efforts. The ROE reflects management's ability to produce for the owners.

Return on Common Stockholders' Equity

A few hospitality enterprises have issued preferred stock in addition to common stock. A variation of the ROE, when preferred stock has been issued, is the return on common stockholders' equity. It is necessary to compute this ratio only when more than one class of stock has been

Exhibit 5.16   Return on Owner's Equity

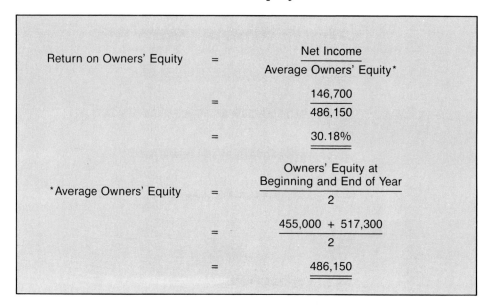

issued. Common stockholders are concerned with what is available to them—net income less preferred dividends paid to preferred stockholders. The ROE ratio is adjusted as follows:

$$\frac{\text{Return on Common}}{\text{Stockholder's Equity}} = \frac{\text{Net Income} - \text{Preferred Dividend}}{\text{Average Common Stockholders' Equity}}$$

Since the Grand Hotel has not issued preferred stock, the calculation of this ratio is not further illustrated, because it would be the same as the previously calculated ROE.

The return to common stockholders is enhanced with the issuance of preferred stock when the return on investment from the use of the preferred stockholders' funds by the hospitality enterprise exceeds the dividends paid to preferred stockholders. From a common stockholder's viewpoint, any time debt or preferred stock can be issued at a "cost" less than the return from investing these "outside funds," the return to common stockholders is increased.

Earnings Per Share

A common profitability ratio shown on hospitality establishments' income statements issued to external users is earnings per share (EPS). The EPS calculation is a function of the capital structure of the hospitality enterprise. If only common stock has been issued, that is, there are no preferred stock or convertible debt or similar dilutive securities, then EPS is determined by dividing net income by the average common shares outstanding. When preferred stock has been issued, preferred dividends are subtracted from net income and the result is divided by the average number of common shares outstanding. If any dilutive securities have been issued, the EPS calculation is considerably more difficult and is beyond the scope of this text.[3]

Using figures from Exhibits 5.1 and 5.2, the 19X2 EPS for the Grand Hotel can be calculated as follows:

$$\text{Earnings Per Share} = \frac{\text{Net Income}}{\substack{\text{Average Common} \\ \text{Shares Outstanding}}}$$

$$= \frac{\$146,700}{55,000}$$

$$= \underline{\$2.67}$$

Simply stated, the 19X2 EPS for the Grand Hotel is $2.67 per common share. In 19X1, the Grand's EPS was $2.57; thus, the Grand's EPS has increased by $.10 from 19X1 to 19X2.

An increase in EPS must be viewed cautiously. The reduction of common stock outstanding by the issuing establishment's purchase of its own stock (treasury stock) will also result in an increased EPS, all other things being equal. Further, EPS is expected to increase as a hospitality enterprise reinvests earnings in its operations because a larger profit can then be generated without a corresponding increase in shares outstanding.

Price Earnings Ratio

The price earnings ratio is often used by financial analysts in presenting investment possibilities in hospitality enterprises. Further, it is shown daily in the Wall Street Journal for all stocks listed on the New York and American Stock Exchanges. The price earnings (PE) ratio is computed by dividing the market price per share by the EPS.

Assume that the market price per share of the Grand Hotel is $25.00 at the end of 19X2. The PE ratio for the Grand Hotel at the end of 19X2 is calculated as follows:

$$\text{Price Earnings Ratio} = \frac{\text{Market Price per Share}}{\text{Earnings per Share}}$$

$$= \frac{\$25}{\$2.67}$$

$$= \underline{9.36}$$

The Grand Hotel's PE ratio of 9.36 indicates that if the 19X2 EPS ratio is maintained, it would take 9.36 years for earnings to equal the market price per share at the end of 19X2.

The PE ratio for different hospitality enterprises may vary significantly. Factors affecting these differences include relative risk, stability of earnings, perceived earnings trend, and perceived growth potential of the stock.

Viewpoints Regarding Profitability Ratios

Owners, creditors, and management obviously prefer high profitability ratios. Owners prefer high profitability ratios because they indicate the return they are receiving from their investments. They will be most concerned about ROE (return on common stockholders' equity if preferred stock has been issued), because ROE measures the precise return on their investments. Although other profitability measures are important to the owner, the ROE is the "bottom line." Other profitability ratios may be relatively low and the ROE may still be excellent. For example, the profit margin could be only 2%, but the ROE could be 20%, based on the following:

Sales	$100
Net Income	$ 2
Owners' Equity	$ 10
Profit Margin	= 2%
ROE	= 20%

If the profitability ratios are not as high as other available investments (with similar risks), stockholders may become dissatisfied and eventually move their funds to other investments. This move, if not checked, will result in lower stock prices, and may pose difficulties for the hospitality enterprise when it desires to raise funds externally.

Creditors also prefer high, stable, or even growing profitability ratios. Although they desire stockholders to receive an excellent return (as measured by ROE), they will look more to the ROA ratio because this ratio considers all assets, not simply claims to a portion of the assets as does ROE. A high and growing ROA represents financial safety and, further, indicates competent management. A high ROA also generally means high profits and cash flow, which suggests safety to the creditor and low risk to the lender.

Managers must keep both creditors and owners happy. Therefore, all profitability ratios are especially important to them. Everything else being the same, the higher the profitability ratios, the better. High ratios also indicate that management is performing effectively and efficiently.

Operating Ratios

Operating ratios assist management in analyzing the operations of a hospitality establishment. Detailed information necessary for computing these ratios is normally not available to owners (owners not actively involved in management) or creditors. These ratios reflect the actual mix of sales (revenue) and make possible comparisons to sales mix objectives. Further, operating ratios relate expenses to revenues and are useful for control purposes. For example, food cost percentage is calculated and compared to the budgeted food cost percentage to evaluate the overall control of food costs. Any significant deviation is investigated to determine the cause (or causes) for the variation between actual results and planned goals.

There are literally hundreds of operating ratios that could be calculated. Consider the following:

- Departmental revenues as a percentage of total revenue (sales mix)

- Expenses as a percentage of total revenue

- Departmental expenses as a percentage of departmental revenues

- Revenues per room occupied, meal sold, etc.

- Annual expenses per room, etc.

Exhibit 5.17, "Certain Operating Ratios Useful in Analysis," suggests over 200 operating ratios.

This section will consider only some of the most critical ratios, several relating to revenues and several relating to expenses. The revenue ratios include the mix of sales, average room rate, and average food service check. The expense ratios include food cost percentage, beverage cost percentage, and labor cost percentage.

Mix of Sales Hospitality establishments, like enterprises in other industries, attempt to generate sales as a means of producing profits. In the lodging segment of the hospitality industry, sales by the rooms department provide a greater contribution toward overhead costs and profits than the same amount of sales in other departments. In a food service operation, the sales mix of entrees yields a given contribution, yet a different sales mix (same sales total) will yield a different (possibly lower) contribution toward overhead and profits. Therefore, it is essential for management to obtain the desired sales mix. To determine the sales mix, departmental revenues are totaled and percentages of the total revenue are calculated for each operated department.

Using figures from Exhibit 5.2, Exhibit 5.18 calculates the 19X2 sales mix for the Grand Hotel. The sales mix of a hospitality operation is best compared to the establishment's objectives as revealed in its budget. A second standard of comparison is the previous period's results. A third involves a comparison to industry averages.

An evaluation of revenue by department is accomplished by determining each department's average sale. For the rooms department, the ratio is the average room rate, and for the food service department, it is the average food service check.

Average Room Rate A key rooms department ratio is the average room rate. Most hotel and motel managers calculate the average room rate even though rates within a property may vary significantly from single rooms to suites, from individual guests to groups and conventions, from weekdays to weekends, and from busy seasons to slack seasons.

Using figures from Exhibits 5.2 and 5.3, the 19X2 average room rate for the Grand Hotel can be calculated as follows:

$$\text{Average Room Rate} = \frac{\text{Rooms Revenue}}{\text{Number of Rooms Sold}}$$

$$= \frac{\$810,000}{21,000}$$

$$= \underline{\underline{\$38.57}}$$

The average room rate for 19X2 is a \$.52 improvement over the Grand Hotel's average room rate for 19X1 of \$38.05 (\$780,000 divided by 20,500 rooms sold). The best standard of comparison to use in evaluating an actual average room rate is the rate budgeted as the goal for the rooms

Exhibit 5.17 Certain Operating Ratios Useful in Analysis

CERTAIN OPERATING RATIOS USEFUL IN ANALYSIS	% of Total Revenues	% of Depart. Revenues	% of Depart. Total Cost	% Change from Prior Period	% Change from Budget	Per Available Room	Per Occupied Room	Per Available Seats	Per Cover/Guest	Per Square Foot	Per Full-time Equiv. Employee	% of Total Salaries & Wages	Per Unit Produced or Used
Total Revenues				•	•	•	•			•	•		
Rooms													
Revenue	•			•	•	•	•				•		
Salary, Wages & Burden		•	•	•	•	•	•					•	
Other Expenses		•	•	•	•	•	•						
Departmental Profit		•		•	•	•	•						
Food													
Revenue	•			•	•	•	•	•	•	•			
Cost of Sales		•	•	•	•				•				
Salary, Wages & Burden		•	•	•	•			•	•			•	
Other Expenses		•	•	•	•				•				
Departmental Profit		•		•	•			•	•	•	•		
Beverage													
Revenue	•			•	•	•	•	•	•	•			
Cost of Sales		•	•	•	•								
Salary, Wages & Burden		•	•	•	•			•				•	
Other Expenses		•	•	•	•								
Departmental Profit		•		•	•			•		•	•		
Minor Departments													
Revenue	•			•	•								
Cost of Sales		•		•	•								
Salary, Wages & Burden		•		•	•						•		
Other Expenses		•		•	•								
Departmental Profit		•		•	•								
Administrative & General													
Salary, Wages & Burden	•			•	•	•	•					•	
Other Expenses	•			•	•	•	•						
Departmental Total Cost	•			•	•	•	•						
Marketing													
Salary, Wages & Burden	•			•	•	•	•					•	
Other Expenses	•			•	•	•	•						
Departmental Total Cost	•			•	•	•	•						

Exhibit 5.17 (continued)

CERTAIN OPERATING RATIOS USEFUL IN ANALYSIS	% of Total Revenues	% of Depart. Revenues	% of Depart. Total Cost	% Change from Prior Period	% Change from Budget	Per Available Room	Per Occupied Room	Per Available Seats	Per Cover/Guest	Per Square Foot	Per Full-time Equiv. Employee	% of Total Salaries & Wages	Per Unit Produced or Used
Property Operation & Maintenance													
Salary, Wages & Burden	•		•	•	•	•					•		
Other Expenses	•		•	•	•	•							
Subtotal Maintenance	•		•	•	•								
Energy Cost	•		•	•	•	•							•
Departmental Total Cost	•		•	•	•	•							
House Laundry													
Salary, Wages & Burden	•		•	•	•	•					•		•
Other Expenses	•		•	•	•	•							•
Departmental Total Cost	•		•	•	•	•							•
Food & Beverage (or Outlets)													
Revenue	•	•	•	•	•	•							
Salary, Wages & Burden		•	•	•							•		
Other Expenses		•	•	•									
Departmental Total Cost		•	•	•									
Total Other Expenses	•		•	•	•	•							
Payroll Burden Items	•		•	•							•	•	
Total Salary & Wages	•		•	•	•	•					•		
Capital Expenses													
Property Taxes	•		•	•	•	•		•					•
Insurance	•		•	•	•	•							•
Rent/Lease	•		•	•	•	•							
Interest	•		•	•	•	•							•
Management Fee	•		•	•	•	•							
Debt Service	•		•	•	•	•							•
FF&E Reserve/Replacement	•		•	•	•	•							

Exhibit 5.18   Sales Mix

Departments	Sales	Percentage of Total
Rooms	$ 810,000	59.9%
Food	300,000	22.2
Beverage	145,000	10.7
Telephone	42,000	3.1
Rentals and Other Income	55,000	4.1
Total	$1,352,000	100.0%

department's operation during the period. This average rate should also be calculated individually for each market segment: business groups, tourists, airline crews, and other categories of guests served.

Average Food Service Check

A key food service ratio is the average food service check. The ratio is determined by dividing total food and beverage revenues by the number of food covers sold during the period.

Using figures from Exhibits 5.2 and 5.3, the average food service check for 19X2 for the Grand Hotel can be calculated as follows:

$$\frac{\text{Average Food}}{\text{Service Check}} = \frac{\text{Total Food and Beverage Revenue}}{\text{Number of Food Covers}}$$

$$= \frac{\$445,000}{56,000}$$

$$= \$7.95$$

The $7.95 average food service check in 19X2 is a $.20 increase over the Grand Hotel's average food service check of $7.75 for 19X1 ($430,000 divided by 55,500 food covers). The average food service check is best compared to the budgeted amount for 19X2. An additional comparison relates this ratio to industry averages.

Additional average checks should be calculated separately for food and beverages. Management may even desire to calculate average check by different dining areas and/or by various meal periods.

Food Cost Percentage

The food cost percentage is a key food service ratio, as it compares the cost of food sold to food sales. Most food service managers rely heavily on this ratio for determining if food costs are reasonable.

Using figures from Exhibits 5.9, the 19X2 food cost percentage for the Grand Hotel is determined as follows:

$$\frac{\text{Food Cost}}{\text{Percentage}} = \frac{\text{Cost of Food Sold}}{\text{Food Sales}}$$

$$= \frac{\$120,000}{\$300,000}$$

$$= \underline{\underline{40\%}}$$

The Grand Hotel's 19X2 food cost percentage of 40 indicates that of every \$1 of food sales, \$.40 goes toward the cost of food sold. This is best compared to the budgeted percentage for the period. A significant difference in either direction should be investigated by management. Management should be just as concerned about a food cost percentage that is significantly lower than budgeted goal as it is about a food cost percentage that exceeds budgeted standards. A lower food cost percentage may indicate that the quality of food served is lower than desired, or that smaller portions are being served than are specified by the standard recipes. A food cost percentage in excess of the objective may be due to poor portion control, excessive food costs, theft, waste, spoilage, and so on.

Beverage Cost Percentage

A key ratio for beverage operations is the beverage cost percentage. This ratio results from dividing the cost of beverages sold by beverage sales.

Using figures from Exhibit 5.9, the 19X2 beverage cost percentage for the Grand Hotel can be calculated as follows:

$$\frac{\text{Beverage Cost}}{\text{Percentage}} = \frac{\text{Cost of Beverages Sold}}{\text{Beverage Sales}}$$

$$= \frac{\$\ 28,000}{\$145,000}$$

$$= \underline{\underline{19.31\%}}$$

The 19X2 beverage cost percentage of 19.31% for the Grand Hotel means that for each \$1 of beverage sales, \$.19 is spent on the cost of beverages served. As with the food cost percentage ratio, this ratio is best compared by management to the goal set for that period. Likewise, any significant variances must be investigated to determine the cause(s). A refinement of this ratio would be beverage cost percentage by type of beverage sold and by beverage outlet.

Labor Cost Percentage

The largest expense in hotels, motels, clubs, and many restaurants is labor. Labor expense includes salaries, wages, bonuses, payroll taxes, and fringe benefits. A general labor cost percentage is determined by dividing total labor costs by total revenue. This general labor cost percentage is simply a benchmark for making broad comparisons. For control purposes, labor costs must be analyzed on a departmental basis. The rooms department labor cost percentage is determined by dividing room department labor cost by room revenue. The food and beverage department labor cost percentage is determined by dividing food and

Exhibit 5.19   Operated Department Labor Cost Percentages

$$\text{Labor Cost Percentage} = \frac{\text{Labor Cost by Departments}}{\text{Department Revenues}}$$

Department	Total Labor Cost	÷	Total Revenue	=	Labor Cost Percentage
Rooms	$145,000		$810,000		17.90%
Food & Beverage	180,000		445,000		40.45%
Telephone	10,500		42,000		25.00%

beverage department labor cost by food and beverage revenue. Other operated department labor cost percentages are similarly determined.

Exhibit 5.19 uses figures from Exhibit 5.2 and 5.9 to calculate the 19X2 operated department labor cost percentages for the Grand Hotel.

The 19X2 labor cost percentages for the Grand Hotel show the food and beverage department with the highest labor cost percentage at 40.45%. In most lodging firms, this is usually the case. The standard for comparing these ratios is the budgeted percentages. Since labor costs are generally the largest expense, they must be tightly controlled. Any significant differences between actual and budgeted labor cost percentages must be carefully investigated by management.

Ratios for other expenses are usually computed as a percentage of revenue. If the expenses are operated department expenses, then the ratio is computed with the operated department revenues in the denominator and the expense in the numerator. An overhead expense ratio will consist of the overhead expense being divided by total revenue. For example, marketing expense percentage is determined by dividing the marketing expense by total revenue. Using figures for the Grand Hotel in 19X2 found in Exhibit 5.2, the marketing expense percentage can be calculated as 4.07%(marketing expenses of $55,000 divided by total revenues of $1,352,000).

Limitations of Ratio Analysis

Ratios are extremely useful to owners, creditors, and management in evaluating the financial condition and operations of hospitality establishments. However, ratios are only indicators. Ratios do not resolve problems or even reveal exactly what the problem is. At best, when they vary significantly from past periods, budgeted standards, or industry averages, ratios can only indicate that there *may be* a problem. Considerably more analysis and investigation is required by users.

Ratios are meaningful when they result from comparing two related numbers. Food cost percentage is meaningful because of the direct relationship between food costs and food sales. A goodwill/cash ratio is somewhat meaningless due to the lack of any meaningful relationship between goodwill and cash.

Ratios are most useful when compared to a standard. A food cost percentage of 32% has little usefulness until it is compared to a standard such as past performance, industry averages, or the budgeted percentages.

Ratios are often used to compare different hospitality establishments. Many ratios, especially operating ratios, will not result in meaningful comparisons if the two firms are in completely different segments of the industry. For example, comparing ratios for a luxury hotel to ratios for a quick service restaurant would serve no meaningful purpose.

In addition, if the accounting procedures used by two separate hospitality establishments differ in several areas, then a comparison of their ratios will likely show differences related to accounting procedures rather than to financial positions or operations.

Even though these limitations are present, a careful use of ratios that acknowledges their shortcomings will result in an enhanced understanding of the financial position and operations of various hospitality establishments.

Computerization

Liquidity, solvency, activity, profitability and operating ratios are by-products of the financial statements discussed in earlier chapters. In this respect, computers can automatically calculate and report these important statistics. The speed of the computers will allow these statistics to be created almost at will, assuming the financial data is stored in the computer. However, many of these ratios need not be calculated on a daily basis; in fact, if they cover too short a period they may not provide important information at all. Although it is difficult for many managers to do, it is important that they determine the key ratios to be calculated and the frequency with which they should be provided. If all the ratios were calculated daily, there would be the risk of "information overload," so much information (and so many reams of paper) provided that the manager would not have the time—or the desire—to look through it to find the valuable items.

Operating ratios, on the other hand, may be very useful when they are prepared more frequently. For example, knowing food cost on a daily or weekly basis might be of great assistance to management. If food cost changes significantly for any day, management will want to know it in order to determine the cause(s) so that corrective action could be taken. Computers can play a major role in information gathering and the preparation of operating ratios. For example, when a hotel's night audit is computerized, many of the lodging statistics are a by-product of the process: average daily rate, occupancy percentage, double occupancy percentage, etc. These statistics can then be compared with the budget to give management a timely (and convenient) measure of the operation's success.

In addition, many other operating ratios can be generated quickly and with almost no manual intervention. The following example shows how this might work. The Grand Hotel has a computerized time clock system. The clocks gather the time in and time out for employees as they enter and leave the building. Once a day, a computer in the accounting department receives yesterday's employee data from the clocks and calculates the total time for each employee. Departmental labor costs can then be determined based upon each employee's hourly rate which is in the payroll system. The computer can even determine overtime, vacation, holiday, or sick pay. It can then report the payroll cost by department and job classification to management. It would also be possible to track labor cost as a percentage of sales, if the daily sales were also entered into the computer. Similar applications apply for food cost, preventive maintenance, and energy costs.

Summary

Ratio analysis permits investors, creditors, and operators to receive more valuable information from the financial statements than they could receive from reviewing the absolute numbers reported in the documents. Vital relationships can be monitored to determine solvency and risk, performance in comparison with other periods, and dividend payout ratios. A combination of ratios can be used to efficiently and effectively communicate more information than that provided by the statements from which they are calculated.

There are five major classifications of ratios: liquidity, solvency, activity, profitability, and operating. Although there is some overlap among these categories, each has a special area of concern. Exhibit 5.20 lists the 30 ratios presented in the chapter and the formulas by which they are calculated. It is important to be familiar with the types of ratios in each category, to know what each ratio measures, and to be aware of the targets or standards against which they are compared.

For example, a number of liquidity ratios focus on the hospitality establishments' ability to cover its short-term debts. However, each person examining the establishment's financial position will have a desired performance in mind. Creditors desire high liquidity ratios indicating that loans will most likely be repaid. Investors, on the other hand, would like lower liquidity ratios since current assets are not as profitable as long-term assets. Management reacts to these pressures by trying to please both groups.

The five ratio classifications vary in importance among the three major users of ratios. Creditors focus on solvency and liquidity; investors consider these ratios, but highlight the profitability ratios. Management uses all types of ratios, but is especially concerned with operation and activity ratios which can be used in evaluating the results of operations.

It is important to realize that a percentage by itself is not meaningful. It is only useful when it is compared to a standard: an industry average, a ratio from a past period, or a budgeted ratio. It is the comparison to budget ratios that is the most useful for management. Any significant

Exhibit 5.20 List of Ratios

Ratio	Formula
1. Current ratio	Current assets/current liabilities
2. Acid-test ratio	Cash, marketable securities, notes and accounts receivable/current liabilities
3. Accounts receivable turnover	Revenue/average accounts receivable
4. Average collection period	365/accounts receivable turnover
5. Working capital turnover	Revenue/average working capital
6. Solvency ratio	Total assets/total liabilities
7. Debt-equity ratio	Total liabilities/total owner's equity
8. Long-term debt to total capitalization ratio	Long-term debt/long-term debt and owner's equity
9. Number of times interest earned ratio	EBIT/interest expense
10. Fixed charge coverage ratio	EBIT + lease expense/interest expense and lease expense
11. Inventory turnover: Food inventory turnover	Cost of food used/average food inventory
Beverage turnover ratio	Cost of beverages used/average beverage inventory
12. Fixed asset turnover	Total revenue/average fixed assets
13. Asset turnover ratio	Total revenues/average total assets
14. Annual occupancy percentage	Total rooms sold/available rooms
15. Average occupancy per room	Number of paid room guests/number of rooms sold
16. Double occupancy percentage	Rooms occupied by more than one person/rooms sold
17. Profit margin	Net income/total revenue
18. Operating efficiency ratio	Income before fixed charges/total revenue
19. Return on assets	Net income/average total assets
20. Gross return on assets	Earnings before interest and taxes (EBIT)/average total assets
21. Return on owners' equity	Net income/average owners' equity
22. Return on common stockholders' equity	Net income – preferred dividend/average common stockholders' equity
23. Earnings per share	Net income/average common shares outstanding
24. Price earnings ratio	Market price per share/earnings per share
25. Mix of sales	Departmental revenues are totaled; percentages of total revenue are calculated for each
26. Average room rate	Room revenue/number of rooms sold
27. Average food service check	Total food and beverage revenue/number of food covers
28. Food cost percentage	Cost of food sold/food sales
29. Beverage cost percentage	Cost of beverages sold/beverage sales
30. Labor cost percentage	Labor cost by department/department revenues

difference should be analyzed to determine its probable causes. Once management has fully investigated areas of concern, as reflected by the ratios, then corrective action can be taken to rectify the problems.

Notes

1. This may be determined mathematically using the following formula:

$$\frac{CA - X}{CL - X} =$$ desired current ratio. Where X indicates the amount of current assets which would be used to retire current liabilities. The calculation for the Grand Hotel is as follows:

$$\frac{338,000 - X}{214,000 - X} = 2; \qquad X = 90,000; \qquad \frac{124,000}{248,000} = 2 \text{ times}$$

2. The Laventhol & Horwath "profit margin" is based on net income before income taxes rather than net income, and is 2.5% for 1984. See Laventhol & Horwath, *U.S. Lodging Industry* (Philadelphia: Laventhol & Horwath, 1985).
3. The interested student is referred to intermediate accounting texts, most of which contain a full discussion of EPS calculations in various situations.

Discussion Questions

1. How does ratio analysis benefit creditors?
2. If you were investing in a hotel, which ratios would be most useful? Why?
3. What are the limitations of ratio analysis?
4. How do the three user groups of ratio analysis react to the solvency ratios?
5. What is leverage, and why may owners want to increase it?
6. What do activity ratios highlight?
7. How is the profit margin calculated? How is it used?
8. Which standard is the most effective for comparison with ratios?
9. Define the ratio expression "turnover."
10. Of what value is the food sales/total sales ratio to the manager of a hotel? To a creditor?

Problem 5.1

The Duke Snyder Motel has operated several years before you became the new manager. In order to better understand the financial situation, you are to examine the financial statements for the year just ended 19X4 and perform ratio analysis. The motel's balance sheet and condensed income statement are below:

Duke Snyder Motel
Balance Sheet
December 31, 19X4

Assets

Current Assets:	
Cash	$95,000
Accounts Receivable	100,000
Inventories	5,000
Total Current Assets	200,000
Property and Equipment:	
Land	60,000
Building (net)	300,000
Furniture & Equipment (net)	80,000
Total Property and Equipment	440,000
Total Assets	$640,000

Liabilities and Owners' Equity

Current Liabilities	$210,000
Long-Term Liabilities	
Note from Owner	40,000
Mortgage Payable	80,000
Total Liabilities	330,000
Owners' Equity	
Common Stock	100,000
Retained Earnings	210,000
Total Owners' Equity	310,000
Total Liabilities and Owners' Equity	$640,000

Duke Snyder Motel
Condensed Income Statement
For the year ended December 31, 19X4

Sales	$1,500,000
Cost of Goods Sold	200,000
Operating Expenses	800,000
Contribution Margin	500,000
Undistributed Operating Expenses	125,000
Income Before Fixed Charges	375,000
Interest	120,000
Other Fixed Charges	162,000
Income Before Taxes	93,000
Income Tax	46,500
Net Income	$46,500

Required:

Calculate the following ratios:

1. Current Ratio

2. Acid-test Ratio

3. Debt-equity Ratio

4. Number of Times Interest Earned Ratio

5. Operating Efficiency Ratio

6. Profit Margin

7. Return on Owner's Equity (assume the only change in owners' equity during 19X4 is the net income of $46,500)

8. Return on Total Assets (assume total assets were $640,000 on January 1, 19X4)

Problem 5.2

The Kirk Gibson Hotel is a 250-room facility with several profit centers. The hotel is open throughout the year, and generally about 2% of the rooms are being repaired or renovated at all times; therefore, assume that they are unavailable for sale. During 19X1, the hotel sold 77,800 rooms and experienced an average occupancy per room of 1.32 people. The accounting department has supplied the following information concerning the food department:

Food Sales	?
Beginning Inventory	?
Ending Inventory	$35,000
Consumption by Employees (free of charge)	5,000
Cost of Sales	312,000
Food Cost %	40%
Food Inventory Turnover	10 times

Required:

Determine the following:

1. Occupancy rate for 19X1

2. Number of paid guests of 19X1

3. Beginning inventory of food

4. Food sales

5. Double occupancy percentage (assume that no more than two persons occupied a double room)

Problem 5.3

The Kaline Hotel's current assets and current liabilities from the past three year's balance sheets are as follows:

	19X1	19X2	19X3
Current Assets:			
Cash	$15,000	$10,000	$8,000
Marketable Securities	30,000	25,000	20,000
Accounts Receivables (net)	70,000	85,000	95,000
Inventory-Food	20,000	22,000	25,000
Prepaid Expenses	10,000	12,000	15,000
Total	$145,000	$154,000	$163,000
Current Liabilities:			
Accounts Payable	$60,000	$62,000	$65,000
Notes Payable	30,000	30,000	30,000
Wages Payable	20,000	22,000	25,000
Taxes Payable	10,000	11,000	12,000
Total	$120,000	$125,000	$132,000
Selected Operations Data:			
Sales (total)	$1,000,000	$1,100,000	$1,200,000
Cost of Food Consumed	150,000	160,000	168,000

Note: Assume 50% of the sales were on account.

Required:

1.   Compute the trend of the following:

    A.   Current Ratio
    B.   Acid-test Ratio
    C.   Accounts Receivable Turnover (19X2 and 19X3 only)
    D.   Inventory Turnover (19X2 and 19X3 only)

2.   Based on the above calculated ratios, comment on the liquidity trend of the Kaline Hotel.

Problem 5.4

The Mickey Mantle Inn commenced operations on January 1, 19X1, and has been operating for two years. Assume you are the new Assistant Manager and desire to gain some insight into financial relationships of your new employer. Balance sheets and condensed income statements for the first two years are provided below.

Balance Sheets
Mickey Mantle Inn
December 31, 19X1 and 19X2

Assets	19X1	19X2
Current Assets		
Cash	$10,000	$15,000
Marketable Securities	-0-	50,000
Accounts Receivable	55,000	60,000
Inventories	10,000	12,000
Total Current Assets	75,000	137,000
Property and Equipment		
Land	100,000	100,000
Building (net)	1,950,000	1,900,000
Furniture & Equipment (net)	240,000	200,000
Total Property & Equipment	2,290,000	2,200,000
Total Assets	$2,365,000	$2,337,000
Liabilities and Owners' Equity		
Current Liabilities	$55,000	$60,000
Long-Term Debt	1,300,000	1,250,000
Total Liabilities	1,355,000	1,310,000
Owners' Equity		
Common Stock	1,000,000	1,000,000
Retained Earnings	10,000	27,000
Total Owners' Equity	1,010,000	1,027,000
Total Liabilities and Owners' Equity	$2,365,000	$2,337,000

Condensed Income Statements
Mickey Mantle Inn
For the years ended December 31, 19X1 and 19X2

	19X1	19X2
Sales	$1,200,000	$1,400,000
Operated Department Expense	620,000	700,000
Operated Department Income	580,000	700,000
Undistributed Operating Expenses	380,000	400,000
Total Income Before Fixed Charges	200,000	300,000
Fixed Charges	185,000	200,000
Income Taxes	5,000	45,000
Net Income	$10,000	$55,000

Required:

1. Calculate the following ratios for both years:

   A. Current Ratio
   B. Solvency Ratio
   C. Profit Margin
   D. Operating Efficiency

2. Also calculate for 19X2 the following ratios:

   A. Fixed Asset Turnover Ratio
   B. Total Assets Turnover Ratio
   C. Accounts Receivable Turnover Ratio
   D. Number of Days Accounts Receivable Outstanding
   E. Return on Total Assets
   F. Return of Owners' Equity

Problem 5.5

The owner of the Billy Martin Motel and Restaurant has asked you to prepare an income statement and balance sheet based on the following:

1. Accounts Receivable = $10,000
2. Accounts Payable = $15,000
3. Current assets consist of cash, accounts receivable, and inventory
4. Current liabilities consist of only accounts payable
5. Current ratio = 1.2 to 1
6. Acid-test Ratio = .8 to 1
7. Accounts receivable turnover = 30 times (all sales are credit sales)
8. Food inventory turnover = 9.625 times
9. Beverage inventory = 6.3525 times
10. Fixed asset turnover = 1 3/47 times
11. Depreciation expense = 10% of book value at year-end
12. Long-term debt = 9 times accounts payable
13. Interest rate = 10%
14. Tax rate = 20%
15. Average room rate = $20.00
16. Average food and beverage check = $5.00
17. Size of motel = 25 rooms
18. Occupancy % = 80%
19. Number of food and beverage checks = 30,800
20. "Undistributed Operating Expenses" = 33 1/3% of total revenues
21. Food cost % = 40%
22. Beverage cost % = 22%
23. Food and beverage labor and other cost % = 30%
24. Rooms labor and other cost % = 40%
25. Food sales = 62 1/2% of total food and beverage sales
26. Debt-equity ratio = 1 to 1
27. Return on owners' equity = 1.330667%

Assume the balance sheet at the beginning of the year is the same as at the end of the year.

6 Internal Control

All business operations require strong internal controls in order to monitor and maintain the quality of goods and services and thereby maximize profits, especially in the long run. For enterprises within the hospitality industry, strong internal controls are critical since (1) many sales transactions involve cash, (2) there are literally hundreds, and for some operations, thousands of transactions in a day, and (3) many employees handle cash at the front desk of the hotel, in the restaurants, and in the beverage operations. However, as we will see in this chapter, internal control includes much more than controls over cash and cash sales. Most successful operations in the hospitality industry involve strong systems of internal control. Some of the questions regarding internal control that will be addressed in this chapter include:

1. How is internal control defined?

2. What are the major objectives of internal control?

3. What are the differences between accounting and administrative controls?

4. What are the characteristics or principles of internal control?

5. How are internal controls documented?

6. How is flowcharting useful in documenting and monitoring internal control?

7. How does the segregation of duties enhance internal control?

8. What methods of internal control are necessary to safeguard cash?

In this chapter, we first provide a formal definition and some examples of internal control. Next, several internal control characteristics of hospitality operations are discussed, followed by the basic requirements of internal accounting control for various accounting functions including cash receipts, cash disbursements, accounts receivable, accounts payable, payroll, inventories, fixed assets, and marketable securities. Next, implementation and review of internal controls is presented, followed by a discussion of internal controls applicable to smaller operations.

Definition and Objectives of Internal Control

There are numerous definitions of internal control, but one of the best known was provided by the American Institute of Certified Public

Accountants (AICPA) as follows: "Internal control comprises the plan of organization and all of the coordinate methods and measures adopted within a business to safeguard its assets, check the accuracy and reliability of its accounting data, promote operational efficiency, and encourage adherence to prescribed managerial policies."[1]

According to this definition, internal control consists of the plan of organization and the methods and measures within the operation to accomplish four major objectives. Several methods and measures used by hospitality operations will be presented in detail later in this chapter. At this point, it is important to realize that each hospitality operation must have a satisfactory plan of organization which should be reduced to writing and be understood by both management and their subordinates. Further, the organizational plan should provide for independence among operating, custodial, and accounting functions in order to both prevent fraudulent conversion and to assist in providing accurate and reliable accounting data. These functions may be illustrated by using a restaurant example. Ideally, food should be stored by custodians and requisitioned for use by operating personnel (preparation personnel). The accounting for the food should be accomplished by accounting personnel. Thus, the storekeepers, preparation personnel, and accountants are separate and independent of each other.

The four AICPA objectives of internal control can be defined as follows:

Safeguard assets. As previously defined in this text, assets are resources such as cash, inventory, equipment, buildings, and land. A major objective of internal control is to safeguard or to protect these assets. This objective includes, but is not necessarily limited to, (1) the protection of existing assets from loss, such as theft, (2) the maintenance of resources, especially equipment, to ensure efficient utilization, and (3) the safeguarding of resources, especially inventories for resale, to prevent waste and spoilage. This objective is achieved by various control procedures and safeguards which include, but are not limited to, the proper use of coolers and freezers for storing food, the use of locks to secure assets, the use of safes and/or vaults for safekeeping cash, limiting access of personnel to various assets, and segregating the operating, custodial, and accounting functions.

Check accuracy and reliability of accounting data. This objective consists of all the checks and balances within the accounting system to ensure accuracy and reliability of accounting information. Accurate and reliable accounting information must not only be available for external reports to owners, governmental agencies, and other outsiders, but is also needed for management's own use in internal operations. For hospitality establishments, this may be best accomplished by adopting a uniform system of accounts. Further, accounting information is most useful when received on a timely basis; therefore, reports for management's use must be prepared and received on a regular basis in order to permit timely management actions.

Promote operational efficiency. Operational efficiency results from providing products and services at a minimum cost. In a hospitality establishment, operational efficiency is promoted and enhanced by training programs and proper supervision. In a lodging operation, for example, rooms will be cleaned at a lower cost when room attendants are properly trained and supervised. In addition, operational efficiency is often improved by the use of mechanical and electronic equipment. Point-of-sale (POS) devices in restaurant operations electronically communicate orders from server stations to both cold and hot preparation areas and often results in greater efficiency. Further, the POS device used in lodging operations will automatically post a restaurant sale to a guest's folio. This automatic function accomplishes the posting with a minimum of labor and eliminates the possibility that the guest will check out without all charges being properly posted to his/her account. Thus, the POS device also results in "safeguarding of assets."

Encourage adherence to prescribed managerial policies. A major objective of internal control is that employees follow managerial policies. For example, most operations have a policy that each hourly employee must clock himself/herself in and out rather than receive assistance from other employees. Employees may be encouraged to follow this policy when the time clock is placed in a location where managerial personnel can observe employees clocking in and out.

At times, there may appear to be a conflict among these objectives. For example, procedures to safeguard assets at a hotel may be so detailed that operational efficiency is reduced. Four signatures required to obtain a case of steaks from the storeroom for serving to guests may forestall theft, yet it may be so time-consuming that increased labor costs far exceed any losses by theft which could result without these elaborate controls. Perfect controls, even if possible, generally would not be cost justified. Management must weigh the cost of instituting a control against the benefit to be received. When the proper trade-off of costs/ benefits is achieved, management is performing both efficiently and effectively.

The four objectives of internal control may be divided between accounting and administrative control. The first two objectives, safeguarding of assets and accuracy and reliability of accounting data, are considered accounting controls, while the last two objectives, promoting operational efficiency and encouraging adherence to managerial policies, are administrative controls. Historically, accountants (especially independent external auditors) focused their attention on internal accounting controls. However, more recently, hospitality establishments are closely reviewing administrative controls which are considered to be more of an operational nature than accounting controls. This trend is highly desirable in order for hospitality operations to achieve their overall objectives of maximizing service to guests and thereby optimizing their profits.

Internal accounting controls are not only highly desirable, they are also the law. The Foreign Corrupt Practices Act of 1977, designed to stop illegal payments by publicly held corporations, contained a provision stating that businesses must devise and maintain a system of adequate internal accounting controls.

Characteristics of Internal Control

The four major objectives of internal control can only be achieved by instituting the numerous methods and measures of control. For example, to help safeguard assets, an operation might maintain a safe for securing cash overnight. Another procedure to safeguard cash may require that cash receipts be deposited with the bank when they total $2,000. Before other methods and measures of an internal control system are discussed, several general characteristics of an internal control system will be presented. These characteristics are sometimes referred to as elements, or principles, of internal control. However, the important point is that they are essential to all effective internal control systems and apply to any business enterprise.

Several characteristics of internal control essential to any effective system are as follows:

- Management leadership
- Organizational structure
- Sound practices
- Competent and trustworthy personnel
- Segregation of duties
- Authorization procedures
- Adequate documents and records
- Procedure manuals
- Physical controls
- Budgets and internal reports
- Independent checks on performances

Management leadership. Key to any hospitality operation's system of internal control is the leadership exerted by management. The operation's highest level policies are established by the board of directors and are communicated and enforced by management. These policies should be clearly stated and communicated to all management levels. In addition, the various management levels are responsible for ensuring that the system of internal control is adequate. The tone they set in communicating and enforcing policies may determine the degree to which employees will accept them and carry them out. Although there may be exceptions to board and top-level management policies, these exceptions should be minimized so as not to render the policies useless.

Organizational structure. Only in the smallest hospitality operations is one person able to exercise personal supervision over all employees. In most establishments, the organizational structure is divided into the functional areas of marketing/sales, production, accounting/finance, and personnel. The organizational structure of an operation is reflected in its organizational chart. Exhibit 6.1 is an organizational chart of a large

Exhibit 6.1 Organization Chart for a Large Lodging Establishment

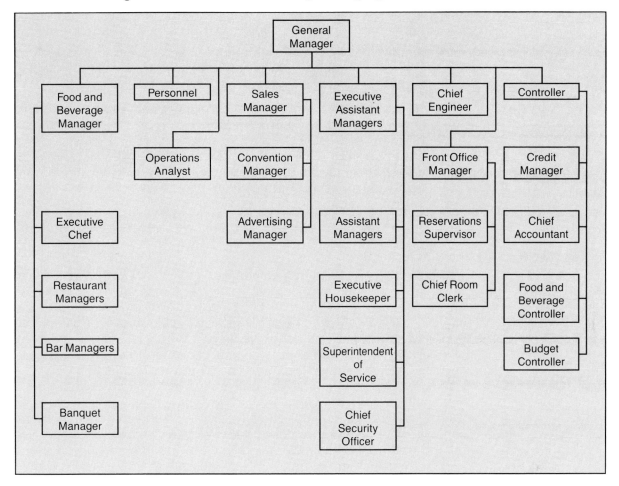

lodging establishment. Personnel must know the organizational chart and follow the chain of command. Management usually has policies to prevent employees from circumventing the chain of command by requiring them to discuss any complaints or suggestions with their immediate supervisors rather than with management officials who are two or three management layers removed from the employee. This approach not only reduces confusion but normally results in greater efficiency for the hospitality operation. The exception to this general rule is when management fraud has occurred. In this extreme case, employees must be able to communicate this to the highest levels of management or to the internal auditors.

In addition to the organizational chart, a job description is generally written for each position. A job description consists of a detailed list of duties for each position. Job descriptions present the "what," not the "how." How a job or duty is performed would be shown in a procedure manual.

Sound practices. Sound practices are policy measures generally set by the board of directors to create an environment for excellent internal control. Several hospitality operations have adopted the following practices:

- Bonding of employees—Employees in a position of trust are covered by fidelity insurance. Some operations carry a blanket bond for minimum coverage on all employees.

- Mandatory vacation policy—Employees are required to take annual vacations. This is rigidly enforced for employees in positions of trust. During their absences, other employees perform the absent employees' duties. If they have engaged in dishonest practices, the replacements may discover them, and management action can be taken.

- Code of conduct—Recently, some operations have required management personnel to follow a code of management conduct prohibiting illegal acts.

Competent and trustworthy personnel. A key characteristic of internal control, perhaps the most important, is personnel. In the hospitality industry, the major difference between competitors is generally the quality of service which is often a function of the quality of personnel. "Service with a smile" may often be more important than the quality of the food served. Personnel must exhibit a caring attitude toward their guests in order for the operation to ensure its success.

An operation's system of internal control may be rendered useless if personnel are not competent and trustworthy. Generally, systems of internal control are not designed to prevent collusion (two or more people working together to defraud the property). Therefore, the selection and training of personnel is vital.

This characteristic of internal control is achieved by proper hiring, training, and supervision. People with potential must be employed at the outset. They must be properly trained in the work to be accomplished. This includes not only communicating what their jobs are and how to do them, but following up to make sure they are properly carried out. In addition, employees must understand the importance of their jobs in relation to the objective of service.

Finally, employees must be properly rewarded for work performed. This includes not only compensation but also praise for "a job well done" and promotions when the person is ready and a position is available.

Segregation of duties. The segregation of duties element of internal control involves the assignment of different personnel for the functions of accounting, custody of assets, and production. Additional segregation of duties is designed within the accounting function. The major objective of segregating duties is the prevention and detection of errors and/or theft.

To illustrate the segregation of duties, consider the following description of a food service operation. A guest's order is taken by a server and recorded on a guest check. A cook prepares the guest's food order from a copy of the guest check provided by the server. The food prepared by the cook was obtained from the storekeeper by means of a requisition submitted earlier in the day based on estimated sales for that day. The guest is given a copy of the guest check and pays the cashier the amount due. The cashier, receiving the cash, records the sale after checking the server's recording. In this example, the functions of order taker (sales), cook (production), storekeeper (custody of assets), and cashier (accounting) are separate. In addition to meeting the internal control objective of safeguarding assets by segregating duties, the objective of operational efficiency is also achieved. Moreover, greater operational efficiency is often achieved by additional segregation of duties. For example, in the production area, a large restaurant will have numerous personnel such as chefs, a garde-manger (one who is in charge of the cold meat production area), a pastry chef, butcher, and a sous chef, among others.

Within the accounting department, the various tasks are divided among accounting personnel to ensure proper checks and balances. For example, different personnel maintain the general ledger than maintain the city ledger and guest ledger. Another example of desired segregation of tasks is that the cash reconciliation is prepared by personnel other than those accounting for cash receipts and/or cash disbursements.

Authorization procedures. Every business transaction needs to be properly authorized by management. Management's authorization may be either general or specific. General authorization is provided by management for employees to follow in the normal course of performing their jobs. For example, in a food service operation, servers are instructed to sell food and beverage items on the menu at the menu prices. No specific approval is required to approve a sale in this case. In addition, a credit card may be accepted for payment of the food purchased by the guest. If the guest's credit card is satisfactory (current, signed, etc.), then the cashier may accept it and process the payment.

Often, management may require specific authorization of a transaction. In these situations, management considers the decision to require its attention when the event occurs. For example, the purchase of fixed assets in excess of $X requires the company president's approval. In this case, the transaction can not be completed without the president's written approval.

Adequate documents and records. Documents for recording transactions are essential to effective internal control. They include such forms as registration cards, folios, server checks, payroll checks, receiving reports, purchase orders, time cards, and room out-of-order reports. Documents should be designed so that they are understood by the preparer and ultimate user. Documents designed for multiple uses will minimize the number of different forms. For example, a server check for a food service operation could be a three-part form with the original copy serving as the "invoice" for the customer, the second copy is used to communicate the order to the production personnel, while the third copy remains as the server's copy. The documents are generally prenumbered to facilitate control. Finally, the documents are prepared when the transaction occurs in order to minimize errors. For example, a voucher is immediately prepared and transferred to the front office when a hotel guest charges a meal to his/her room. This reduces the chance that the guest will check out without paying the food service charge.

Procedure manuals. Each job within the hospitality operation can be reduced to writing. The details of what, how, and when should be included in the procedure manual. The procedure manual serves to encourage consistent job performance, especially for relatively new employees who may be unsure about the details of their jobs. In addition, the procedure manual enables personnel to temporarily fill a position during a regular employee's absence.

Physical controls. Physical controls are a critical element of internal control in achieving the objective of safeguarding assets. Physical controls include security devices and measures for safekeeping assets, such as safes to protect cash and locked storerooms to safeguard inventory. In addition, forms and accounting records need to be secured, a process accomplished by proper storage of assets and limiting access to them. Finally, mechanical and electronic equipment help to safeguard assets by being used in the execution and recording of transactions. For example, cash registers with limited access to tapes help to ensure the prompt and accurate recording of sales transactions in food service and beverage operations.

Budget and internal reports. Budget reports and other internal reports are essential elements of a system of internal control. These reports are an important part of the communications system in the operation. When budgets are used for control purposes, they help to ensure that management's goals will be attained, and when the actual performance falls short of the goals, management is informed and able to take corrective action.

Other reports also alert management to operating performance and enable management to take corrective action as necessary. Exhibit 3.3 in Chapter 3 lists 12 reports including the frequency, content, comparisons, recipient, and purpose of each report. These reports range from those prepared daily (daily report of operations), to weekly (weekly forecasts), to monthly (future bookings reports), and up to annual reports (long-range planning).

Independent checks on performance. This characteristic of internal control is designed to determine that the other elements of the internal control system are functioning properly. In order for the check on performance to be successful, it must be independent, that is, the personnel performing the internal verification must be independent of the personnel responsible for the data that is being checked. In a number of hospitality operations, the independent check on performance is conducted by the internal auditors. In order for the internal audit function to be most successful, the auditors need to be independent of both operations and accounting and report directly to top management.

Another independent check on performance, especially in relation to the accounting function, is the work performed by the independent external auditors. The auditors not only verify financial statements, but also study the internal accounting control system and test it as a basis for how extensive the remaining audit will be.

Finally, independent checks on performance are the result of separation of duties (as discussed earlier in the segregation of duties characteristics). For example, the preparation of the bank reconciliation by personnel independent of those accounting for cash receipts and disbursements constitutes an independent check.

Basics of Internal Accounting Control

Now that the objectives and characteristics of a system of internal control have been discussed, attention is turned to the basic requirements of internal accounting control. Although several methods of control will be discussed for the various accounting functions, the presentation is not intended to be exhaustive. Each hospitality operation must review these areas and determine the methods used to achieve the major objectives of internal control.

Cash Control

Cash is the most vulnerable of all assets; therefore, it is imperative to have an effective system of internal control over cash. Commonly used control procedures include:

1. All bank accounts and authorized check signers must be authorized by the chief financial officer.

2. All bank accounts should be reconciled monthly, and the bank reconciliation should be reviewed by the controller.

3. Bank statements, including cancelled checks, should be received directly from the bank by the person preparing the bank reconciliation. Employees who sign checks or have other accounting duties in connection with cash transactions should not reconcile the bank accounts. The reconciliation procedure should include examination of signatures and endorsements, and tests of the clerical accuracy of cash receipt and disbursement records. Exhibit 6.2 is the Hoosier Hotel's bank reconciliation at December 31, 19X2.

4. The custody of cash should be the responsibility of the general cashier. The accounting for cash received and the review of cash transactions should be assigned to another employee. This segregation of duties provides a check on the cashier's performance.

5. The general cashier must take annual vacations and his or her duties be assumed by another employee.

6. House banks and petty cash funds should be counted at unannounced intervals by employees independent of the cash control function. Special attention should be given to the propriety of noncash items such as IOUs and accommodation checks cashed.

7. Disbursements from petty cash funds should be supported by cash register tapes, invoices, etc. Such supporting data should be

Exhibit 6.2 Bank Reconciliation, Hoosier Hotel

Bank Reconciliation
Hoosier Hotel
December 31, 19X2

Balance per bank statement – 12/31/19X2			$14,622.18
Add: Deposit in Transit			3,641.18
Less: Outstanding checks			
Ck. 4315	$ 18.36		
Ck. 4422	156.14		
Ck. 4429	3,689.18		
Ck. 4440	172.47		
Ck. 4441	396.15		
Ck. 4442	100.00		
Ck. 4443	7.43		
Ck. 4444	799.18		−5,338.91
Other:			
Insufficient funds check received Dec. 31*			+ 324.32
Service charge – December, 19X2**			+ 15.24
Cash balance per books – 12/31/19X2			$13,264.01

Prepared by_____

Approved by_____

*Redeposited January 1, 19X3
**Amount recorded on books in January 19X3, since it was minor in amount.

checked when the fund is replenished and then cancelled to prevent duplicate payment.

Cash Receipts. Commonly used procedures for the internal control of cash receipts include:

1. Accounting and physical control over cash receipts should be established when the cash is first received, whether the cash is received at the front desk, at a profit center such as a coffee shop, or through the mail. For example, incoming mail receipts should be initially listed by an employee independent of both the general cashier and the accounts receivable department. This procedure establishes an independent record that later can be checked against daily bank deposits and the general ledger posting to accounts receivable. Initial control of cash received in the hotel or restaurant is accomplished by using cash registers and front office accounting machines.

2. Restrictive endorsements, such as "For deposit only to Hoosier Hotel's account," should be placed on checks when the checks are first received to guard against obstruction of such cash receipts.

3. Checks or currency should not be handled by employees in the accounts receivable department. Postings to accounts receivable ledger cards should be based on remittance advice or listings of cash receipts.

4. Cash received should be given to the general cashier as soon as is practical. Cash receipts should be deposited daily and intact. They should not be mixed with other cash funds used to pay invoices, incidental expenses, or cash accommodation checks.

5. The general cashier and his/her subordinates should not have any responsibilities regarding the following:

    a. Preparation or mailing of city ledger statements.
    b. Posting accounts receivable records or balancing detail ledgers with general ledger control accounts.
    c. Posting the general ledger.
    d. Authorizing rebates, allowances, discounts, or writing-off uncollectible accounts.
    e. Preparing cash disbursements or reconciling bank accounts.

    All of the above are prohibited to reduce the opportunity for the general cashier and his/her subordinates to practice fraudulent conversion of cash from the operation to their personal use.

6. General instructions for cashiers often include the following:

    a. Cash drawer must be closed after each sale.
    b. Cashiers must circle and initial any overrings on the tape at the time of occurrence.
    c. Cash registers must be locked and keys removed when unattended.
    d. There must be no sales made on an honor system. Cash sales must be rung up when they are made.
    e. Cashiers must not have briefcases, handbags, purses, cosmetic bags, etc., at cashier stations.
    f. Cashiers should immediately inform the manager if they are experiencing problems with the cash register.
    g. Cashiers should verify the amount of cash banks when they receive and sign for them and should not be allowed to count the banks after that time.
    h. Where feasible (or permitted by equipment), items should be rung up separately to permit the cash register to total the sale.

Cash Disbursements. Several procedures adopted by some operations to establish a strong system of internal control over cash disbursements include:

1. Generally, all disbursements should be made by check. An exception is petty cash disbursements.

2. Checks should be prenumbered and used in numerical sequence. In addition, it is desirable to use a check protector to enter the amounts on the checks because this deters anyone from altering the amount.

3. Checks drawn in excess of a minimum amount, such as $50.00, should contain two signatures, while checks less than the minimum may require only one signature. Each check signer should carefully review supporting documents, checking that the documentation has been properly audited and approved. Check signers should not have responsibility for preparing checks and should not have custody of blank checks.

4. When a mechanical check signing device is used, the key should be in the custody of only the employee authorized to use it. An independent record should be maintained of the number of checks processed through the mechanical check signing device, and that number should be reconciled with the numerical sequence of the checks used.

5. Vouchers, invoices, and other documents supporting cash disbursements should be cancelled by stamping them "PAID" when the check is signed. This procedure is designed to avoid duplicate payments should the document become detached from the check copy at a later time.

6. Signed checks and disbursement vouchers should not be returned to the preparer of the check, but should be given to an employee independent of the above functions for immediate mailing.

7. Only authorized check preparers should have access to blank checks. Any voided checks should be mutilated, by removing the signature line, to prevent re-use.

Accounts Receivable

Accounts receivables represent promises to pay the hospitality operation. A critical control in this area is segregation of duties to prevent accounts receivable employees from pocketing cash received in payment of accounts. Several control procedures adopted by some properties for accounts receivable are as follows:

1. Accounts receivable employees should not handle cash received in payment of accounts receivable. Postings to accounts receivable for cash received should be made by accounts receivable department employees from remittance advice or check listings. Control totals for postings should be made independently of accounts receivable department employees for posting by the general ledger clerk to the accounts receivable control account.

2. The total of guest accounts should be reconciled at the end of the month with the independently determined balance in the general ledger control account. These procedures provide protection against manipulation by the accounts receivable department em-

ployees. A common fraudulent practice where cash handling and accounts receivable are not segregated is called lapping. Lapping occurs when an accounts receivable clerk takes cash received on account. The next day, cash received from a second account is posted to the account which was not credited the previous day, and so on. For example, assume Guest A paid $100.00 on account. The accounts receivable clerk practicing lapping takes the $100.00 for personal use. The following day, Guest B pays $150.00. The accounts receivable clerk takes $50.00 for personal use and credits Guest A's account for $100.00. At this point, the accounts receivable clerk has stolen $150.00. This fraudulent activity may continue for quite some time when there is no segregation of duties or other compensating controls.

3. Noncash entries to receivable accounts, such as writing-off an account as uncollectible, should originate with employees or managers who do not handle cash and are not responsible for maintaining accounts receivable.

4. Disputed items should be resolved by the credit manager in conjunction with a member of the hospitality establishment's operating management. Adjustment of accounts receivable should not be delegated to clerical employees on a routine basis.

5. A key feature of control over receivables is an adequate system of internal reporting. Periodically, the accounts receivables should be aged with special collection efforts applied to delinquent accounts. Exhibit 5.5 in Chapter 5 illustrates an aging of accounts receivable. The trend of accounts receivable balances in relation to credit terms should be tracked over time.

6. All collection efforts should be carefully documented, and only uncollectible accounts should be written-off after approval by the controller.[2]

Accounts Payable   Several internal control procedures adopted by some properties in relation to accounts payable are as follows:

1. Vendors' invoices should be routed directly to the accounts payable department. They generally should not be handled or approved by personnel in the purchasing department.

2. Control should be established over vendors' invoices when received. This may be accomplished by the use of a voucher system (see sample in Exhibit 6.3). The voucher system uses prenumbered vouchers which are prepared from vendors' invoices and recorded in a voucher journal. Invoices should be reviewed for possible cash discounts, and the due dates noted to take advantage of any available discounts.

3. Vendors' invoices should be audited as to terms of sale, prices, and goods received by reference to purchase orders and receiving reports. All amount extensions and totals should be checked. The person auditing the vendors' invoices should initial the invoices to indicate the work performed.

Exhibit 6.3   Voucher from Voucher System

	Accounts Payable Voucher		Voucher Number	7321						

Pay To:
Address:

Date Paid

Date Check No.

DATE	DESCRIPTION	AMOUNT	DISCOUNT % AMOUNT	OTHER DEDUCTIONS		NET AMOUNT			ACCOUNT	AMOUNT
				FOR	AMOUNT					

TOTALS

ENTERED ON VOUCHER
RECORDED BY _____

TOTAL CHARGES _____
LESS DISCOUNT _____

PREPARED
BY _____

APPROVED FOR
PAYMENT BY _____

POSTED
BY _____

OTHER DEDUCTIONS _____
AMT. OF CHECK _____

AUDITED
BY _____

4. As discussed previously, all vouchers, invoices, and supporting documents should be cancelled when paid.

5. The accounts payable subsidiary ledger should be maintained by accounting personnel not responsible for the general ledger. The accounts payable subsidiary ledger should be reconciled monthly with the general ledger control account for accounts payable.

6. A monthly trial balance of accounts payable should be prepared for review by the controller. Proper care must be exercised in paying suppliers on a timely basis in order to maintain healthy supplier relationships.

Purchasing and Receiving   As with other areas, the comments in this section concerning internal control of purchasing and receiving are not exhaustive, but cover only a few of the major controls. Chapter 7 contains a more detailed discussion of this area.[3] Several widely adopted control procedures are as follows:

1. To the extent practical, all purchases should be made by the purchasing agent who acts upon approved purchase requisitions from department heads.

2. A written purchase order (PO) system should be used. Copies of the PO should be sent to receiving and accounting. In this way, receiving will be aware of materials ordered, while the accounts

payable department will use the PO in its audit of the vendor's invoice.

3. A receiving department, separate from the purchasing agent, should receive all incoming goods. All materials received should be carefully checked.

4. The receiving department should prepare a receiving report for each vendor's delivery. A copy of the receiving report should be forwarded to the accounts payable department for checking against the vendor's invoice.

Payroll   The largest expense for most hospitality operations is payroll; therefore, controls in this area are critical if the operation is to meet its internal control objectives. Several common control procedures are as follows:

1. Payroll functions should be segregated as follows:

    a. Authorization of employment and wage rates
    b. Reporting hours worked
    c. Preparation of payroll
    d. Signing payroll checks
    e. Distribution of paychecks to employees
    f. Reconciliation of payroll bank accounts

2. The personnel department or executives with hiring/terminating authority should be the only personnel authorizing additions to, or deletions from, the work force. Generally, the personnel department carefully recruits new employees and provides the payroll department with all relevant information regarding newly hired employees.

3. Procedures for reporting time worked should be clearly defined. Time clocks should be used for hourly paid personnel. All time worked by hourly employees should be approved by departmental supervisors.

4. Payrolls generally should be paid by checks rather than with cash. Separate payroll accounts should be maintained. An employee independent of the payroll department should reconcile the payroll bank account.

5. Payroll preparation procedures should include checking the clock used for the department supervisor's approval and rechecking the hours worked.

6. Payroll sheets and paychecks for the employees' net pay should be independently checked.

7. Paychecks should be distributed to employees by personnel independent of the payroll department. In addition, someone other than department heads should distribute the checks to employees.

8. Undelivered paychecks should be given to the controller or a person designated by the controller. This person should not be from the payroll department. The undelivered paychecks should be held for the absent employees until delivered or voided after a specified number of days.

Inventories

Control procedures in regard to purchasing and receiving relate to inventories also. Additional control procedures adopted by some properties include the following:

1. Accounting department employees should maintain inventory records. These employees should not have access to inventory, nor should storekeepers having custody of inventory have access to inventory records.

2. Periodically, a physical inventory is taken by personnel independent of the storekeepers. The physical inventory should be extended by accounting personnel and compared to the book inventory when a perpetual inventory record system is maintained.

3. Taking physical inventory is best accomplished when:
   a. All like items are grouped together in the storeroom.
   b. Pre-printed inventory forms are used when listing all inventory items.
   c. The inventory form is arranged in the same sequence as the inventory items are maintained in the storeroom.
   d. Two individuals should take the physical inventory; one can count the items while the other records the count. (As noted earlier, the personnel should be independent of the storekeepers.)

4. The inventory records must be adjusted for any differences between the books and the physical inventory. The inventory adjustment must be approved by an executive, such as the controller.

5. Any significant overages or shortages of inventory should be investigated, the causes determined, and procedures designed to prevent recurrence of errors disclosed.

6. Other operating controls relating to inventory include the following:
   a. Control must be maintained over physical inventories. This is accomplished by storing inventory in the appropriate facilities; that is, food must be stored at proper temperatures.
   b. Daily inventories and usage are maintained on high priced items.
   c. Access to inventory should be restricted to storekeepers.

            Limiting access is accomplished, in part, by securing inventory in locked facilities.

d.   Personnel handling inventory (storekeepers and production personnel) should leave the facilities by an exit where they can easily be observed by management.

e.   Records of spoilage, over-cooked food, etc., should be maintained for use in reconciling the physical inventory to the book inventory, and for accounting for other discrepancies in food inventory.

Fixed Assets   Fixed assets generally constitute the largest percent of most hospitality operations' assets. These assets are not liquid; however, controls must still be established to maintain these resources for their intended use, that of providing services to guests. Several commonly used control procedures include:

1.   Generally, the board of directors issue formal policies establishing which executives and committees have the authority to purchase these assets.

2.   A work order system should be established for the orderly accumulation of property costs when facilities are acquired. Each approved project is assigned a work order number, and all expenditures are charged to this number as the work progresses.

3.   Accounting records maintained under a typical work order system include the following:

    a.   An expenditure authorization that defines the project scope, purpose, cost justification, and budgeted amount.

    b.   Cost sheets that summarize actual expenditures for comparison to budgeted amounts.

    c.   Supporting evidence of costs charged to the project account. This evidence includes vendors' invoices, material requisitions, and labor time tickets.

4.   General ledger control should be established for each principal classification of property cost and each related depreciation accumulation.

5.   Physical inventories of fixed assets should be taken periodically by personnel independent of the person with custody of the assets or the person maintaining the accounting records. The physical inventory should be compared to the equipment according to the accounting records. Any discrepancies must be resolved and action taken to prevent recurrence of similar errors.

6.   Finally, sales, retirements, or scrapping of fixed assets require formal executive approval. Approval must be from executives not having custody of the fixed asset. Accounting department

personnel must determine that the "retired" assets are removed from the books and proceeds received are properly accounted for.

Marketable Securities

Marketable securities include investments in stocks and bonds of other corporations. Controls over marketable securities often include the following:

1. Accounting department records should identify each marketable security owned, by name and certificate number.

2. All marketable security transactions should be approved by the board of directors or the committee it has designated.

3. Marketable securities should be kept in a safe deposit box to which only the custodian has access.

4. Periodically, independent physical counts of marketable securities should be taken and the count compared to the accounting records.

5. Finally, income from the marketable securities recorded in the accounting records should be compared periodically to what the investment should be generating. For example, a $100,000 bond at 8% interest should provide $8,000 of interest annually.

Implementation and Review of Internal Controls

Top level management is responsible for implementing and maintaining the system of internal controls. This system is critical to the well-being of the hospitality operation; therefore, management must review the system periodically to determine that it is adequate. Once the system is designed and implemented, it may not function properly due to a breakdown in the system. Perhaps various procedures are not being followed because new personnel do not understand them. For example, disputed statements may be returned to the accounts receivable clerk for resolution, because a new employee, who was assigned the responsibility, believes the accounts receivable clerk can resolve any differences most expeditiously.

An adequately implemented internal control system may need restructuring due to changing business conditions and other circumstances. For example, ten years ago, a hospitality operation may have established a cash receipts deposit policy stating that when cash receipts reached $2,000, they were to be deposited with the bank. Due to inflation, the amount might now be revised upwards to $4,000.

Internal controls of an operation may be documented and reviewed by flowcharting and by using internal control questionnaires. A flowchart diagrams the flow of documents through an organization and reveals the origin, processing, and final deposition of each document. In addition, the flowchart shows the separation of duties. Exhibit 6.4 is a simplified flowchart of a payroll system for a club operation.

Flowcharting is useful because it provides a concise overview of the internal control system. It aids in the review of the internal control

Exhibit 6.4 Flowchart of a Payroll System

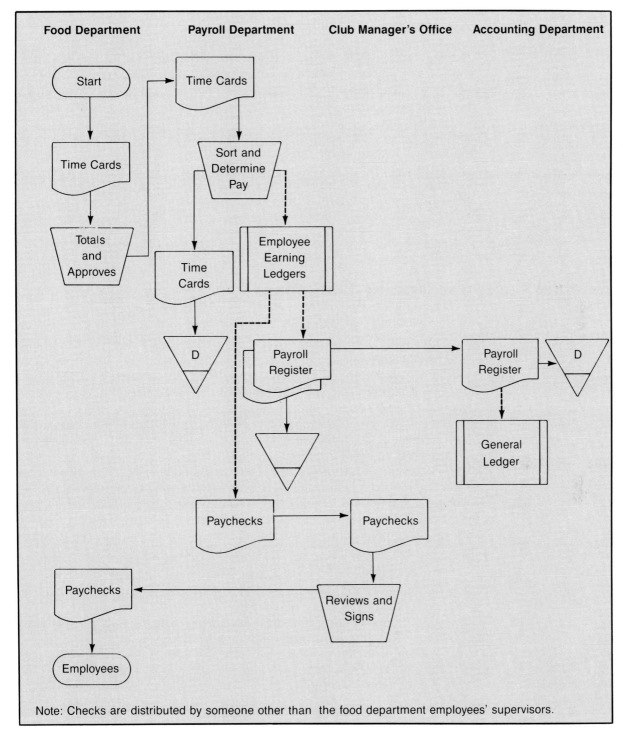

Note: Checks are distributed by someone other than the food department employees' supervisors.

system, enabling management to identify weaknesses for corrective action. The appendix to this chapter contains a discussion of how analytical flowcharts are prepared.

A second device for studying a hospitality operation's system of internal control is the internal control questionnaire (ICQ). The ICQ uses a series of questions about controls in each accounting area as a way of identifying weaknesses. ICQs generally provide complete coverage for each accounting area. However, they do not lend themselves to revealing document flows as do flowcharts. From a practical viewpoint, both flowcharts and ICQs should be used in documenting and reviewing an operation's system of internal control.

Once the review is completed, management must act to strengthen the system of internal control. If a system is documented and reviewed without proper follow-up, then the real value of the review process is lost.

Internal Control in Smaller Operations

Although the hospitality industry has a number of giant firms with system-wide sales exceeding $1,000,000,000, such as Hilton Corporation, Holiday Corporation, Marriott Corporation, McDonalds, Inc., and The Sheraton Corporation, the vast majority of establishments are small. Hospitality operations which have only a few employees do not lend themselves to the elaborate control procedures presented thus far, because there are simply too few people to have the proper segregation of duties required for excellent control.

The key person in internal control in a small operation is the owner or manager. Several duties, if performed by the owner or manager, help to offset what would otherwise be weaknesses in the internal control system. The areas involved and the duties of many small property owners or managers are as follows:

1. Cash Receipts

    a. Open all mail and list cash receipts, retaining one copy of the list.
    b. Deposit all cash daily and compare deposit to the cash receipts debit recorded by the bookkeeper.
    c. Reconcile cash receipts with the cash register tapes.

2. Cash Disbursements

    a. Sign all checks, carefully review documentation, and cancel all supporting documentation.
    b. Use only prenumbered checks and account for them as checks are signed.
    c. Add check disbursements periodically and compare the total to the bookkeeper's cash credit.
    d. Prepare the bank reconciliation.

3. Sales

    a. Keep all cash registers locked and remove cash register tapes.

    b. Compare cash register tape totals to cash debit for the day and the cash receipts deposited.

4. Payroll

    a. Examine the payroll worksheet (or payroll journal), noting employees' names, authorized gross pay, hours worked, deductions, and net pay. Add the payroll and compare the net pay to the cash credit.

    b. Distribute payroll checks.

5. Accounts Receivable

    a. Review aging of accounts receivable.

    b. Compare statements to individual ledger accounts and mail statements.

    c. Resolve all account balances disputed by guests.

6. Inventories

    a. Periodically, supervise or take the physical inventory.

    b. Compare the physical inventory to the perpetual inventory per the books.

    c. Compare cost of goods sold to total sales each month, and investigate any major discrepancies in cost of goods sold percentages.

7. Purchases

    a. On a random basis, review price quotes for inventory items purchased.

    b. Use a purchase order system and account for all purchase orders.

    c. On a random basis, compare purchase orders to receiving reports, and vendors' invoices to vendors' statements.

8. General

    a. Review all general journal entries.

    b. Employ a competent, trustworthy bookkeeper.

    c. Engage an independent auditor to conduct an annual audit and to periodically conduct limited surprise audits of cash, inventory, and accounts receivable.

Computerization

Internal controls are an integral part of any accounting system. Computers can help in several ways to assure adherence to the controls established by management.

First, the accounting software programs can edit the data according to the controls. For example, accounts payable programs can verify whether an invoice has already been paid to help prevent duplicate payments. Other examples in accounts payable include automatically taking discounts offered by vendors, and verifying that a master vendor record has been set up before a vendor can be paid. Similar internal controls can be set into programs for the general ledger, payroll, accounts receivable, fixed assets, and any other functions of accounting. If someone attempts to violate the controls, the computer can record the "error" and "report" it to management. For example, if the payroll program allows payroll checks to be written for no more than $5,000, an attempt to issue a check for $6,000 will be noted by the computer and revealed to management when the "exceptions report" is taken. A good control system will not allow these "violations" except by management override.

A second area where computers can assist management in internal controls is documentation. Word processing, a common use of computers, is an excellent way to create, revise, and distribute policies, procedures, and other documentation relating to internal controls. This is especially helpful in new operations, where controls are being tested, and often revised. In addition, when providing control documentation to new employees or auditors, having the documents on a word processor means they can easily be reproduced on a few moments notice. Since the storage capability of computers is large, records can be kept of not only current controls, but also previous controls as well.

A third application for computers in assisting with internal controls is flowcharting and critical path. For example, there are several flowcharting programs available which can automatically design the exact flowchart for any given set of tasks. In addition, they can lay out a critical path, showing distribution of responsibilities, how long each task should take, and how the individual tasks relate in order to complete the process. One side benefit of this is a simple review of separation of duties. A flowchart and critical path provide overviews of who is responsible for specific functions in an accounting office.

System security is another way to assist with internal controls. Most good data processing systems have a high level of security. They allow system users to access specific functions only. For example, with a good security program, someone handling accounts payable would not be allowed to access payroll. In addition, employees may be allowed to look at an accounts payable vendor master record, but not post invoices. The same can apply to general ledger, payroll, and accounts receivable. Another example of how a system security can assist is in separation of duties. Someone entering invoices into the accounts payable system usually should not be permitted to print the checks. A good security scheme will enforce this control point.

Summary

Internal control is the overall system of protecting the establishment's assets, insuring the accuracy and reliability of its accounting records, promoting the efficient operation of the business, and encouraging adherence to management's policies. It is necessary for an operation to have an adequate internal control system if it is to operate profitably in the long run.

There are four main objectives of every internal control system. The first two, checking the accuracy of accounting data and the safeguarding of assets, are known as accounting controls. These controls ensure that the assets are recorded correctly and that they are safe from loss, whether through negligence or theft. The other two controls are administrative controls. Promoting operational efficiency means that the products and/or services are produced efficiently by the hospitality operation. The last part of internal control stresses adherence to managerial policies; once rules are established, they are only effective if they are followed.

Although there are four major objectives, a strong internal control system has several characteristics. Some of these characteristics relate to the accounting aspects of internal control such as physical control of assets and the development of budgets. Others are more administrative, such as management leadership and organizational structure. Competent and trustworthy personnel are necessary if the operation hopes to be efficient, and also if there is to be adequate physical control of the assets.

Management needs to examine all of the functions of the hospitality operation and establish controls for each. For example, the cash account must have adequate controls because it is highly vulnerable to theft. Management should consider physical controls, segregation of duties, management policies, proper authorization procedures, and adequate checks on performance. If these characteristics of internal control are included in the operation, there will be increased assurance that cash is safeguarded.

Management must consider the costs of internal control policies along with their resultant benefits. A "perfect" system that guarantees no theft of assets would probably be cost prohibitive. This is especially true for smaller operations that do not have adequate personnel to segregate duties. In these instances, management and especially the owners (if they are managing the business) need to be very aware of the precautions available and take an active role in the operation to ensure its success.

Notes

1. Committee on Auditing Procedure, *Internal Control—Elements of a Coordinated System and Its Importance to Management and the Independent Public Accountant* (New York: AICPA, 1949), p. 6.
2. The reader interested in studying detailed procedures regarding the credit function at hotels should consider an article by Ellis Knotts in *Lodging*, June 1979, entitled "Handling the Credit Function at Small Hotels." This article covers credit extension, credit monitoring, and collection of hotel accounts receivable.
3. The reader interested in a detailed explanation of controls for purchasing and receiving should read Chapter 7, "Purchasing and Receiving Controls for Food and Beverages" of Jack D. Ninemeier's *Planning and Control For Food and Beverage Operations* (East Lansing, Mich.: Educational Institute of the American Hotel & Motel Association, 1986).

Discussion Questions

1. What is internal control?

2. What are the four AICPA objectives of internal control?

3. Explain four characteristics of internal control.

4. Which characteristic of internal control is most important? Why have you chosen this one?

5. Why is the control of cash important to a hospitality operation?

6. What is segregation of duties? (Give two examples for a hotel or restaurant.)

7. How can internal control systems be documented and reviewed?

8. How does flowcharting differ from an internal control questionnaire?

9. How can computers be used to strengthen an enterprise's internal control system?

10. Explain three procedures to safeguard inventory.

Problem 6.1

At the Divinity Hotel (DH), a hotel of 150 rooms, the procedure for handling checks returned by the bank marked "insufficient funds," was to carry them as part of the bank balance. That is, when the bank returned a check because payment was refused and charged it to DH's account, no entry was made in the books. The returned check was immediately redeposited and generally these redeposited checks were collected by the bank. At the end of the month, those checks which had not been collected were treated as reconciling items (NSF checks) by the bookkeeper in preparing the bank reconciliation. Later, if the check was collected, the bookkeeper made no formal entry; however, in preparing the next month's bank reconciliation, the bookkeeper reduced the amount of NSF checks. If the check was found to be uncollectible after three months, a journal entry was recorded charging "Bad Debt Expense" and crediting "Cash in Bank."

Required:

1. Explain any deficiencies in the Divinity Hotel's cash control system.

2. Provide the manager with suggestions as to how to improve the system.

Problem 6.2

The Buckeye Motel's books indicated the general checking account at the end of December 19X1 contained $6,523.34, while the bank statement at December 31, 19X1, showed a closing balance of $7,432. The two amounts must be reconciled. Information is provided as follows:

1. Last month's bank reconciliation showed five outstanding checks as follows:

    Ck. 8923— $100.10
    Ck. 8936— 248.15
    Ck. 8944— 194.21
    Ck. 8945— 648.49
    Ck. 8946— 137.75

2. A comparison of the cancelled checks from the bank with the check register revealed five checks written in December 19X1 that had not been paid by the bank as follows:

    Ck. 9164— $384.21
    Ck. 9173— 439.42
    Ck. 9190— 526.14
    Ck. 9191— 422.15
    Ck. 9192—   67.42

3. In addition, three checks were cancelled in December that had been issued in the prior month as follows:

    Ck. 8944— $194.21
    Ck. 8945— 648.49
    Ck. 8946— 137.75

4. Cash receipts of $1,221.75 recorded on the books on December 31, 19X1, were deposited with the bank on January 2, 19X2.

5. Finally, a check for $57.18 received from a guest was returned by the bank on December 31, 19X1, marked "insufficient funds." The check was redeposited on January 2, 19X2. No entry was recorded to reflect the returned check on December 31, 19X1.

<u>Required:</u>

Prepare the December 19X1 bank reconciliation for the Buckeye Motel.

Problem 6.3

At the Morehart Motel, a 200-room property, the books had been entrusted to an old employee, who also did the banking. For nine years, no audit was made, but at that time a friend of the owners "put a bug into the ears" of the partners that it would not hurt to have an audit made for the current year. The audit revealed a cash shortage of over $6,000 for the one year; since the bookkeeper was not bonded, the owners did not wish to go further back in the records. There was ample evidence in the one year's record to send the bookkeeper to prison.

This employee chose one of the crudest methods of covering the manipulations. He deposited in the bank only twice or three times a week during the busy season, and each time he took a few hundred dollars. In the cash receipts journal, he entered the full amount of the cash turned over to him for deposit, but at the same time made an off-setting entry for the shortage in the cash disbursements journal. The latter entries purported to represent checks drawn in payment of food and supply bills and were properly posted to the creditors' accounts in the accounts payable ledger. The auditor promptly discovered the simple manipulation.

Required:

1. Highlight the weaknesses in the internal control system of the Morehart Motel.

2. Offer suggestions to tighten the control.

Problem 6.4

Many Excedrin headaches of the front office manager are caused by the skipper: the guest who departs without paying his bill. The loss from actual skippers is a serious enough matter without having a dishonest employee pocket payments received from departing guests, and marking the deficiencies as "skippers."

But, it will be asked, how can there be a "Fictitious Skipper?" The answer is as follows: Chuck Coors checks in and is assigned to an eighty dollar room. The guest gives no mailing address, for none is requested. The following day Coors, in a hurry to catch his train, runs to the cashier window, and knowing that he had no other charges, throws down four "twenties" saying, "Check me out of 423," and away he goes.

The cashier looks at the bill in the file; he knows that Coors was a stranger, notices that he registered from Chicago; he is quick to realize that it is hard for the credit department to locate anyone with only a city address, so he pockets the four "twenties" and leaves the bill in the file. The next day, room 423 is reported unoccupied. The bill by this time increased to $160 and is charged to "skippers."

In some hotels no effort would be made to locate Coors who left an unpaid bill of $160. Even where the attempt is made, it is usually without success. If Coors is located, the problem is still unsolved. Coors has no receipt; it is a question of his word against the cashier's.

Required:

1. What steps could be taken to adequately control cash in this situation?

Problem 6.5

The practice of paying salaries and wages to employees by individual checks is an improvement over archaic systems which still pay employees with cash not only because it eliminates the necessity of conveying large sums of cash, but it affords a better internal control over these disbursements. However, opportunities for speculation exist even under this system, as is evident from the following case.

At the Wolverine Inn salaries and wages were paid semi-monthly by check to the order of each employee. These checks, drawn on a special payroll bank account, were signed jointly by the accountant and the payroll supervisor.

Transfers for the total amount of the payroll for the period were made semi-monthly to this special account by the check drawn on the regular bank account. In addition to the amounts periodically transferred, there remained a considerable balance from the period, representing the total of the checks which had not been cashed by the employees.

It was necessary for the Wolverine Inn's accountant to be absent several days each month and it was her custom to leave a few signed blank checks to be used in paying employees who might quit during her absence.

With an assured minimum balance in this payroll account and the signed blank checks, the payroll supervisor saw an opportunity and seized it. He drew a check to his own order for an amount within the usual minimum balance. Since he always reconciled the monthly bank statements of this account, he was fairly safe from detection.

Required:

1. Which characteristics of internal control were violated in this situation?

2. How could this theft have been prevented?

Supplemental Reading
Computers in Clubs*

By Michael L. Kasavana, Raymond S. Schmidgall and Michael Speer

Club managers are expected to operate their clubs by providing varied services to members. As their jobs have become increasingly demanding, so too have club managers become more involved in analyzing and controlling the business transactions.

In order to properly control the club's operation, an adequate information system is a prerequisite. A useful tool for understanding and analyzing the club's information system is *flowcharting*. Further, the analysis of the club's information system may indicate using a computer will result in more efficient operations.

Flowcharting Defined

Flowcharting is a graphic means of describing an information system. The flowchart consists of symbols which show what happens to documents and communications as they move through a firm's information system. A flowchart consists of four primary elements: (1) Symbols to show predefined items, steps and actions, (2) flow-lines to highlight document and information flows, (3) identification of areas of responsibility of operating departments and (4) written comments and clarifications that complete the flowchart. The primary elements of a flowchart are illustrated in Exhibit 1.

Purposes of Flowcharting

Flowcharting is a technique aimed at illustrating the information and documentation flows of the firm. An alternative method to accomplish this description involves a less efficient tool called a written narrative. A written narrative is a laborious task and does not lend itself easily to system analysis. A detailed flowchart which may cover only a single page might require as many as six to eight pages in an equivalent written narrative.

Michael L. Kasavana, Ph.D., is an associate professor and **Raymond S. Schmidgall, Ph.D., CPA**, is an assistant professor at the School of Hotel, Restaurant and Institutional Management at Michigan State University, East Lansing, Michigan. **Michael Speer, CPA**, is a consultant with the accounting firm of Laventhol & Horwath, Chicago.

The description of an information system serves three major purposes. First, the flowchart provides an excellent means of documenting the system. An outsider such as an auditor or a new employee can quickly obtain an overview of a given process or subsystem by reviewing its flowchart. If changes in an information system are desirable, these changes can most likely be accomplished through a review of the existing system.

The flowchart is also a means of communication. It is a succinct description which tends to minimize misunderstandings associated with the transmission of information within a system. The importance of this communication capability is reinforced in the training and analytical review of present or planned systems.

Additionally, flowcharting provides a basis by which to analyze the information system of an enterprise. The flowchart indicates information flows by area of responsibility and allows for evaluation and delineation by redundant and overlapping functions. This analysis may lead to revisions, thus, strengthening the overall information system.

Types of Flowcharts

There are three types of flowcharts: (1) Analytical, (2) system, and (3) program. The four primary elements of a flowchart discussed above pertain to an *analytical flowchart* which shows the overall information processing function of a club, such as cash disbursements or purchasing.

This flowchart consists of several vertical columns, one for each department, and contains the flow of documents and information among the various departments. Exhibit 1 is an illustration of an analytical flowchart for purchasing supplies. In Exhibit 1, two copies of a purchase requisition are prepared in the food and beverage department. One copy is filed and the original copy is sent to the assistant manager who functions as the purchasing agent for this club. The assistant manager decides on the vendor based on the lowest price quotation per purchase specifications.

A three-part purchase order is prepared with the original being sent to the vendor, the second copy is sent to the receiving department and the third copy is attached with the original copy of the purchase requisition. Then the third copy of the purchase order and the original copy of the purchase requisition are sent to the accounting department, where they are filed alphabetically. A *system flowchart* is primarily concerned with the data processing needs for one specific task application. The three phases of the data processing cycle (input-process-output) are delineated and the various departments involved may be indirectly referenced. Exhibit 2 contains an illustration of a system flowchart for the recording of a food sale and the updating of a member's account.

The third type of flowchart is the *program flowchart* which is even more specific and detailed than the system flowchart. Although the pro-

gram chart details one specific application into a series of substeps, it presents an even more thorough translation or conversion of input data to output information. The program flowchart is based on an analysis of processing steps with no distinction made between departments.

Exhibit 3 depicts the program flowchart for the determination of an employee's net pay. Note that the program flowchart tends to be more detailed and easier to comprehend than does the analytical flowchart. The program flowchart is important to clubs that desire to streamline their operations by avoiding unnecessary or redundant data handling procedures. Since individual applications are isolated, the program flowchart can be used to identify specific weaknesses within club operations.

Exhibit 1

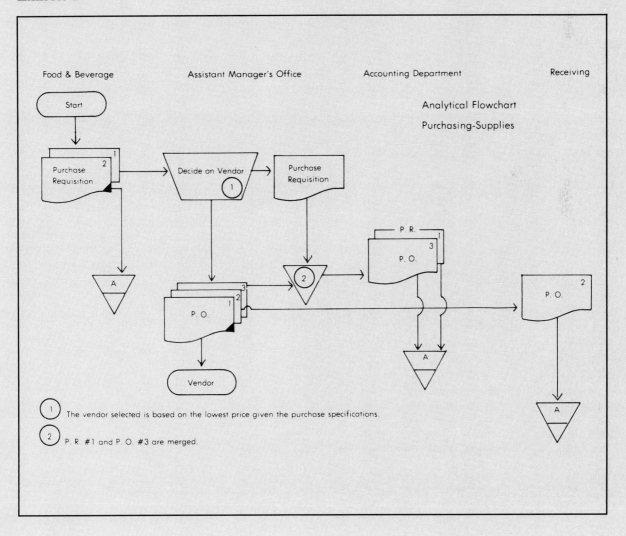

① The vendor selected is based on the lowest price given the purchase specifications.

② P. R. #1 and P. O. #3 are merged.

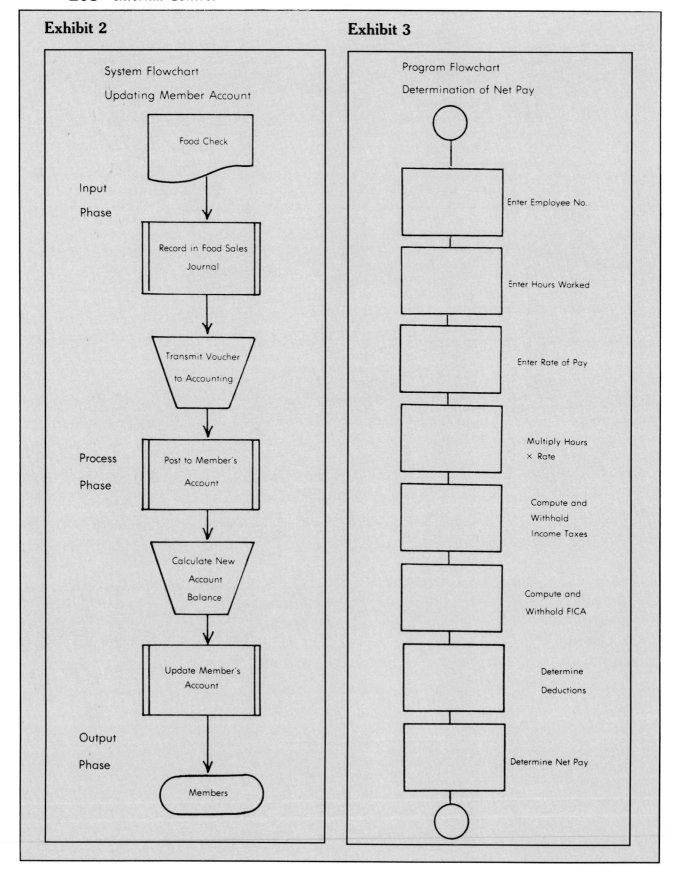

Exhibit 2

System Flowchart

Updating Member Account

Food Check

Input
Phase

Record in Food Sales
Journal

Transmit Voucher
to Accounting

Process
Phase

Post to Member's
Account

Calculate New
Account
Balance

Update Member's
Account

Output
Phase

Members

Exhibit 3

Program Flowchart

Determination of Net Pay

Enter Employee No.

Enter Hours Worked

Enter Rate of Pay

Multiply Hours
× Rate

Compute and
Withhold
Income Taxes

Compute and
Withhold FICA

Determine
Deductions

Determine Net Pay

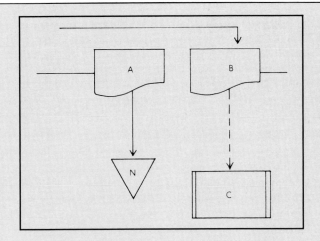

Flowchart Symbols

Standardization in flowcharting symbols results in improved communication of details in an information system. Most of the symbols were established by the United States of America Standards Institute.

The symbols shown are used when preparing analytical flowcharts for nonautomated (non-EDP) information systems. Additional symbols are required when preparing flowcharts for EDP-based information systems.

Flowcharting Techniques

Standardization in flowcharting is not only achieved by using common symbols, but also by drawing flowcharts following established procedures. Several standard techniques are discussed and illustrated below.

* The flowchart should be drawn so that information is shown to move from top to bottom and from left to right. Flowlines should not be slanted.

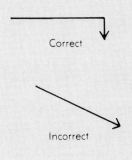

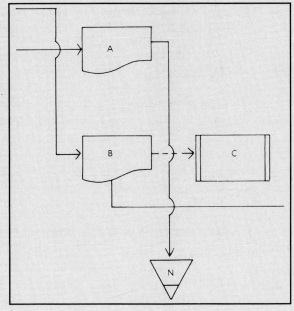

* When drawing flowlines, one should attempt to minimize the crossing of flowlines to reduce confusion. In many situations, various portions of a flowchart can be redrawn to eliminate crossed lines. When crossed lines cannot be avoided, it is desirable to bridge one line over the other.

Two flowcharts shown contain identical document and information flows. However, Flowchart Example 2 is easier to read than Flowchart Example 1.

* The department in which an internal document was created is indicated by darkening of a corner of the document symbol.

* The method for depicting multiple copies of the same document is illustrated below.

Notice the title is written on the first document and the documents are numbered in the upper right corner.

* The flowchart should be divided into columns for each department or function.
* When a document moves from one department to another, the document should be drawn in each department column.
* The type of file should be indicated by placing a letter in the file symbol. The letters indicating various files may be as follows:

Alphabetical	A
Date	D
Numerical	N

Thus a file containing guest records and filed in alphabetical order would be depicted as follows:

* Explanations should be written inside the symbols if there is sufficient space. If additional space is required, an explanation note may be written at the bottom of the column or in a side column. Alternatively, the symbol for annotation of additional information may be used.
* The best flowcharts are generally re-drawn, not drawn. Seldom is a reasonably complex flowchart complete, in final form, on the designer's first attempt. Successive attempts will serve to enhance the flowchart's communication ability and clarity.

Flowcharting Illustrated

To illustrate an analytical flowchart, the payroll system for hourly employees of a club will be used. The food manager, who collects employee time cards on Friday of each week, totals the hours, approves the hours totaled and sends the time cards to the payroll clerk. The payroll clerk determines the employee's pay and all the corresponding deductions and withholdings. The employee earnings ledger is updated and the paychecks are prepared by the payroll clerk.

A payroll register is then prepared by the payroll clerk. The payroll clerk sends the original copy of this register to the general ledger clerk. The general ledger clerk uses the payroll register to record wages and taxes payable in the general ledger and then files the register by date. The payroll clerk files both the time cards by date and the duplicate copy of the payroll register by date.

Finally, the paychecks are sent to the club manager for review and signature. After the checks are signed, they are sent to the food manager for distribution to employees.

Exhibit 4 is a flowchart of this payroll system for hourly employees. Note the distinction between the flow of documents and the flow of information. Further, notice that a distinction is shown between the jobs of the payroll clerk and the general ledger clerk in the accounting department.

After the payroll system has been flowcharted, the flowchart should be studied to determine any weaknesses in the system. Any noted weaknesses should result in a subsequent change in the payroll system.

Summary

Flowcharting is a useful tool for analyzing a club's information system. This analysis will generally result in system changes that may involve the acquisition of a computer.

The flowchart is simply a graphic representation of an information system. It shows interrelationships between paper flow and processing by the use of labeled blocks and keyed symbols connected by lines. The flowchart symbols used in the article should be used to enhance communication via flowcharting.

Several flowcharting techniques are presented, which with practice, will allow even beginning flowcharters to prepare clear and concise flowcharts. Finally, flowcharting is ilustrated using a club's payroll system.

Exhibit 4

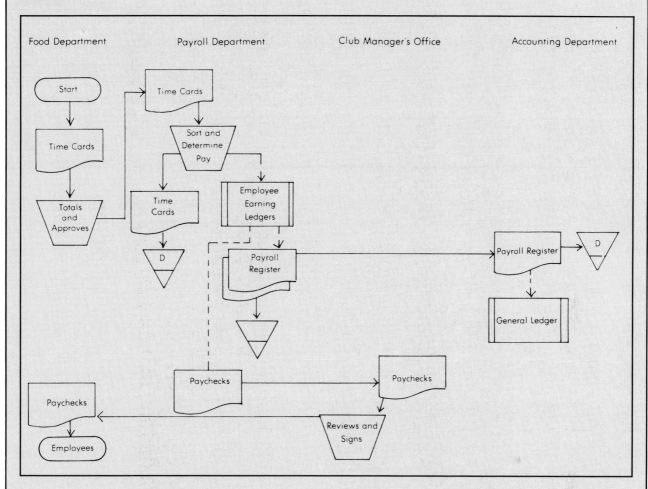

Glossary

Flowchart:

A graphic display of an information system consisting of symbols, flow lines, columns for departments or functions and written comments.

Analytical Flowchart:

A flowchart which shows the overall information processing function of a club, e.g., payroll or purchasing.

System Flowchart:

A flowchart which shows the data processing needs for one specific task application. The input-process-output cycle is shown in this flowchart.

Program Flowchart:

A flowchart detailing one specific application into a series of substeps. It is more detailed than a system flowchart.

Notes

*These articles illustrating flowcharting are reprinted with permission from *Club Management*, January 1982, pp. 20-24, and March 1982, pp. 22-25.

Supplemental Reading
Internal Control Questionnaire
for Financial Reporting: Selected Forms

Reprinted with permission from The Westin Hotels

INTERNAL AUDIT QUESTIONNAIRE

BANK ACCOUNTS

WESTIN HOTELS

Date

QUESTIONS	YES	NO	COMMENTS
1. Are all bank accounts properly authorized and are persons signing checks authorized to sign, and are their signature cards on file?			
2. Are all bank accounts recorded in control accounts in the general ledger?			
3. Are transfers from one bank account to another under accounting control?			
4. Are all bank accounts reconciled regularly? By whom _____.			
5. Does the person reconciling the bank accounts perform any of the following:			
a. sign checks			
b. make deposits			
c. maintain cash receipts or disbursement records			
6. Are bank statements received direct from the bank in unopened envelopes by the employee preparing the reconciliation.			
7. Does the hotel's reconciliation procedure provide for comparison of checks with cash disbursement record?			
8. Are the bank reconciliations reviewed monthly by the controller?			
9. Are any unreconciled variances carried forward on the bank reconciliations?			

WESTIN HOTELS

INTERNAL AUDIT QUESTIONNAIRE

ACCOUNTS RECEIVABLE

Date

QUESTIONS	YES	NO	COMMENTS
1. Are accounts receivable control accounts balanced with detail daily?			
2. Is a trial balance and aging analysis prepared monthly?			
3. Are past due accounts aged accurately on aging analysis?			
4. Are accounts receivable subsidiary ledgers in agreement with general ledger account 0120-1100 - - Accounts Receivable - Guest and Trade?			
5. Are any accounts not being billed?			
6. Are accounts receivable records given proper fireproof protection and restricted access by authorized persons only?			
7. Is accounts receivable insurance in force? Amounts of Coverage?			
8. Are write-offs strictly controlled and approved by the manager and controller?			
9. Is a dollar control maintained on written off accounts?			
10. Are all accounts and checks aged 120 days (120 days from date of charge) except those where the manager accepts responsibility for collection being submitted to the Seattle Credit Office for collection?			
11. Are city ledger payments opened and a deposit prepared by someone without access to accounts receivable records?			
12. Is the computation of Provision for Doubtful accounts in accordance with Westin policy?			
13. Does the hotel adhere to the Fair Credit Billing Act? (AB 54)			
14. All credit balances, as a result of overpayment, are refunded after five businees days.			
15. Any unclaimed or unidentified credit balances are written off to other income account 7401-0000 Other Income.			

INTERNAL AUDIT QUESTIONNAIRE

ACCOUNTS RECEIVABLE

WESTIN HOTELS

Date

QUESTIONS	YES	NO	COMMENTS
16. All room account charges are billed the second business day following check out.			
17. All credit card charges are billed to the credit card companies the second business day following date of charge.			
18. All tour, convention, banquets, and group business is billed as soon as possible, but not later than five days following such business.			
19. Is interest or a service charge being charged on past due accounts?			

INTERNAL AUDIT QUESTIONNAIRE

CREDIT AND COLLECTION AUDIT PROGRAM

WESTIN HOTELS

Date

QUESTIONS	YES	NO	COMMENTS
1. Does hotel forward all "Notification of Bankruptcy" on a customer's account along with a copy of account to Westin Credit office in Seattle? (U.S. hotels only).			
2. Is a properly completed form CO-7 (Rev. 8/84) prepared for all checks and accounts sent to Westin Credit for collection?			
3. Briefly describe hotel's procedure for handling returned checks.			
4. Is a "credit alert list" prepared by the night audit and is there evidence of review and follow-up?			
5. Does the hotel maintain a monthly log for:			
a. Accounts written off?			
b. Accounts recovered.			
c. Bad Debt Morgue?			
6. All political write-offs have been referred to the Treasurer's office for approval prior to write-off.			

WESTIN HOTELS	INTERNAL AUDIT QUESTIONNAIRE		
	HOUSE BANKS		
		Date	

QUESTIONS	YES	NO	COMMENTS
1. Does each cashier have his/her own fund for which they are responsible and over which they have sole custody?			
2. Are properly signed receipts on file for all house funds issued?			
3. Do receipts for house funds contain provision for recording the deposit box assigned to the cashier for storage of the fund when not in use?			
4. Are funds checked at intervals as set forth in the company policy by surprise counts made by responsible officials? Show date of last count in comments.			
5. Do cash count records disclose the inclusion of any questionable items (I.O.U.'s, post-dated checks, returned checks, etc.)?			
6. Does the total of house funds agree with the balance of General Ledger Account 0100-1100 House Funds?			
7. Is an over and short record maintained for each cashier and does the record show evidence of regular review by a hotel executive?			
8. Is the General Cashier's fund maintained on an imprest system?			
9. Does general cashier balance her bank daily?			
10. Does the general cashier fund fluctuate?			
11. Are duplicate keys to cashier banks secure?			
12. Is general cashier's office secure?			
13. Are house banks issued by check?			
14. When house banks are returned, are they deposited to the general bank account through the general cashier's report?			
15. Is there an alarm control when the general cashier closes for the day?			
16. Is there TV surveilance of the general cashier's office?			

INTERNAL AUDIT QUESTIONNAIRE

CASH RECEIPTS

WESTIN HOTELS _____ **Date**

	QUESTIONS	YES	NO	COMMENTS
1	Are cash receipts deposited intact daily?			
2	Is the receipt for the bank deposit compared daily with the cash receipts record? By whom and how is it noted?			
3	Is a witness sheet maintained to record the deposit of the cash turn-in envelopes in the drop safe?			
4	Are two persons present when the drop safe is opened and are the contents compared to the entries on the witness sheet?			
5	Are differences between entries on the witness sheet and contents of the drop safe reconciled and verification noted?			
6	Is the general cashier accompanied to and from the drop safe area by a second party?			
7	Is the transporting of the deposit to the bank subject to adequate security measures and is the deposit made by someone other than the person preparing same. (state method)			
8	Is there a clear separation of duties between the persons preparing the deposit, maintaining the cash receipts journal, the disbursements journal, with signatory powers, and preparing the bank reconciliation?			

Deposit prepared by _____

Date of last vacation_____

Position _____

Bank reconciliations completed by _____

_____

Date of last vacation _____

Position _____

INTERNAL AUDIT QUESTIONNAIRE

CASH RECEIPTS

WESTIN HOTELS

Date

	QUESTIONS	YES	NO	COMMENTS
9	Is a receipt obtained for change requests and due backs? Attach a brief description of the change request and due back system.			
10	Are all checks endorsed with a restrictive endorsement as soon as they are received? (Front Office, Accounts Receivable, Food and Beverage Outlets).			
11	Does the mail opener prepare a list or adding machine tape of city ledger checks prior to sending them to the general cashier.			
12	Are any checks held in Accounts Receivable or by mail opener?			

13	Is a control established over the daily cash receipts prior to their being handled by:
	
	    a. Accounts Receivable
	
	    b. Credit Manager
	
	    c. General Cashier			

14	Are cash receipts for pay station commissions, fat sales, salvage sales, and other miscellaneous revenue properly controlled?			
15	Who replaces the general cashier during vacation or illness?			
16	Are all checks microfilmed prior to deposit to the bank?			
17	If week-end general cashier is normal, is there provision for a night depository?			

7 Food and Beverage Control

After the rooms department, the food and beverage departments are generally the second and third largest revenue producing departments in a lodging facility. In recent years, the average food and beverage sales have totaled nearly one-third of the total sales of hotels and motels. However, the profitability of food and beverage departments is quite low relative to the rooms department. Prior to the allocation of overhead expenses, the food and beverage contribution margin is approximately 20% compared to the rooms department contribution margin of nearly 80%. Therefore, effective control is critical if profitability is to be maximized.

Food and beverage control is among the more difficult responsibilities of managers in the hospitality industry. Food and beverage programs are labor intensive and there are many opportunities for costs to become excessive when there is a lack of attention to the wide range of management details. Additionally, since a large amount of the sales generated is by cash payments, theft of cash is also an ever-present concern. Several questions addressed in this chapter on food and beverage control include:

1. How are food and beverage department staffs organized?

2. What is the relationship between the accounting department and the food and beverage department staffs?

3. What are the five activities in the food control process?

4. What are the objectives of product purchasing?

5. How does the cost of employee meals affect the cost of food sold?

6. How is the "Daily Market Quotation Sheet" used in the purchasing process?

7. What are the objectives of product receiving?

8. When is the "request for credit" form used by food and/or beverage personnel?

This chapter contains answers to these questions and many more that could be asked regarding food and beverage operations. The chapter includes sections on food and beverage department organization, the relationship of food and beverage departments to accounting, and an overview of food and beverage controls. The chapter also discusses problems related to resources to be controlled, product purchasing, product receiving, product storing, product issuing, food preparation and production, beverage production controls, service controls, revenue control systems, and calculating actual food costs.

Organization of Food and Beverage Departments

Exhibit 7.1 presents a sample organization chart that illustrates the rather complex organization required to effectively deliver food and beverage service in a large hotel. Note that there are five primary departments.

- Culinary operations—This department has responsibility for the actual food production for all restaurant outlets, room service, off-site catering (if any), banquet functions, etc., for the hotel.

- Stewarding—This department may be responsible for purchasing (or may work closely with the purchasing department if the latter is separate) and for warewashing, facility clean-up, and related duties.

- Beverage—All alcoholic beverage production and service in all outlets of the property comes under the control of this department.

- Restaurant operations—This department is responsible for the food service function in all outlets of the property and for food and beverage service in the room service department.

- Catering—Working closely with the hotel's marketing and sales division, this department may be responsible for selling banquets and other special functions for groups not needing guestroom or meeting room accommodations. Personnel in this department must work closely with the banquet food preparation staff and are responsible for both the physical arrangements (set-up and tear-down) of banquet rooms and the service of the banquet meals.

All of these duties must be performed by someone in a small hotel as well. The sample organization chart for a food and beverage division in a small property is shown in Exhibit 7.2. You will note that the organization is "flatter" than that in the larger property. There are fewer organizational levels and fewer personnel occupying each position. However, regardless of the size of a property, meals must be produced and served, banquets must be sold, and clean-up duties must be undertaken. As the size of the organization increases, the need for closer coordination and communication among the staff becomes more important.

Exhibits 7.3 and 7.4 provide sample organizational structures of large and small restaurants. In the larger organization, the restaurant manager immediately supervises two positions: the controller (who is responsible for cashiers and a clerk) and the assistant manager (who is responsible for four department heads). The department head positions

Exhibit 7.1 Sample Organizational Chart of the Food and Beverage Division in a Large Hotel

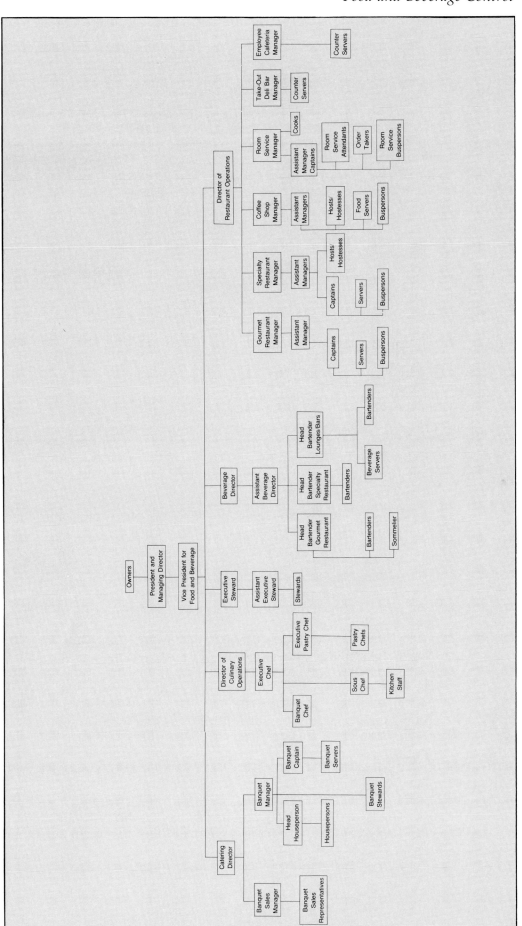

Source: Anthony M. Rey and Ferdinand Wieland, *Managing Service in Food and Beverage Operations* (East Lansing, Mich.: Educational Institute of the American Hotel & Motel Association, 1985), pp. 38–39.

Exhibit 7.2   Sample Organizational Chart of the Food and Beverage Division in a Small Hotel

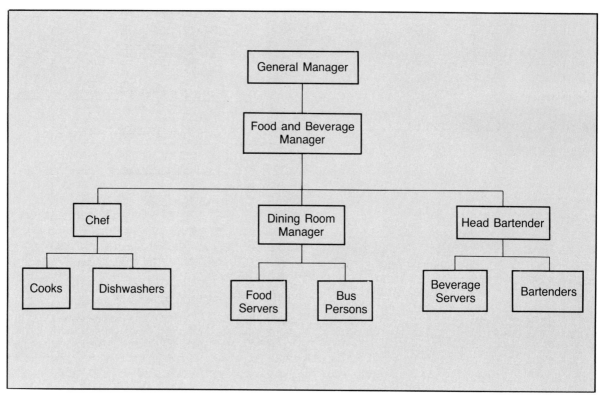

Source: Gerald W. Lattin, *The Lodging and Food Service Industry* (East Lansing, Mich.: Educational Institute of the American Hotel & Motel Association, 1985), p. 147.

involve food production (chef/head cook), purchasing and sanitation (chief steward), beverage production (head bartender), and the front of the house (dining room manager). Each of these department heads also supervises employees. In some cases, fourth-level personnel (sous chef/assistant cook) supervise food service workers. Again, while each of the functions must also be done in the smaller property, the number of required organizational levels and personnel in each position can be reduced.

These organization charts illustrate at least two important facts: (1) While the terminology may differ (cook versus chef and head bartender versus bar manager), the work to be done and the basic positions required do not vary significantly among properties of different sizes or among operations in restaurants and hotels; and (2) A great deal of interaction and cooperation is needed to make things work in food service.

Relationship of Food and Beverage Personnel to Accounting Personnel

The food and beverage manager, along with assistants and supervisors, are part of the "chain of command" in many hospitality organi-

Food and Beverage Control   **223**

Exhibit 7.3   Sample Organizational Chart for a Large Restaurant

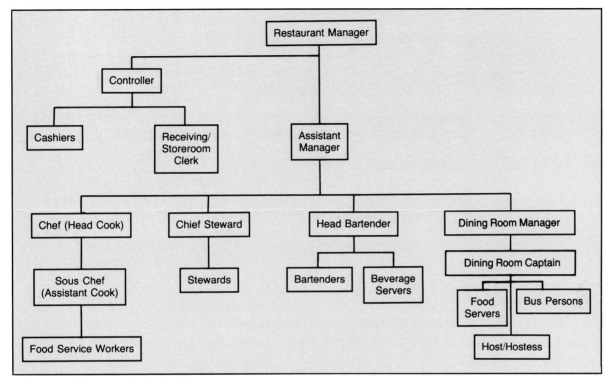

Source: Jack D. Ninemeier, *Principles of Food and Beverage Operations* (East Lansing, Mich.: Educational Institute of the American Hotel & Motel Association, 1984), p. 53.

Exhibit 7.4   Sample Organization Chart for a Small Restaurant

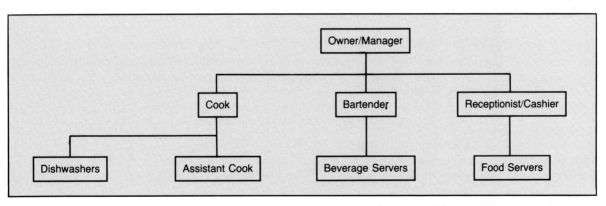

Source: Jack D. Ninemeier, *Principles of Food and Beverage Operations* (East Lansing, Mich.: Educational Institute of the American Hotel & Motel Association, 1984), p. 53.

zations and are directly responsible for revenue generation. It is their responsibility to make decisions about how to maximize the use of limited resources in order to attain budgetary and other goals of their departments.

By contrast, the controller and accounting personnel are in staff positions within the property. As technical experts in a specialized discipline (accounting), they provide advice to managers, such as the food and beverage manager. Working in this capacity, the controller may design and implement information collection systems, "translate" financial information generated through financial reports (such as income and cash flow statements), and present findings along with recommendations to the food and beverage manager.

Working in a staff advisory role, the accounting personnel generate financial information for the food and beverage department's use. Accounting personnel do not make operating decisions or require food and beverage managers to take specific actions based on the information provided. The accounting department personnel assist food and beverage managers in making decisions. Managers use the financial information, along with information from other sources, including their experience, to chart improvement and plan courses of action.

In practice, the above distinction is not always made. For example, in some properties, the food and beverage manager's role includes only "meeting and greeting" guests, supervising or assisting with "hands on" food production, etc. In these properties, the controller is seen as the financial management expert whose job it is to direct economic aspects of the program. At the other extreme, food and beverage managers are considered specialists in all areas affecting operations, including financial management. Unfortunately, some of these managers do not make the most effective use of helpful financial information generated by the accounting department.

A much more effective relationship between the food and beverage manager and the controller occurs when both view each other as "partners" on the property's management team. The food and beverage manager is viewed as an in-house expert in matters pertaining to management and operation of the food and beverage program, while the controller is viewed as an expert in the generation and interpretation of financial information necessary for effective management decision making. Working as a team, both staff members make significant contributions to the attainment of goals established for the food and beverage operation.

As discussed in Chapter 1, there are several areas of accounting emphasis. Managerial accounting is one of the areas that must be understood by the food and beverage manager in order to effectively control the operation. Another area is tax accounting, a highly specialized and frequently changing discipline; responsibility for this area rests with the controller. Methods of inventory valuation and procedures to assess employee meal costs are examples of decisions which affect the operation's profit levels—and the amount of income taxes to be paid! A specialist, such as the controller, is typically responsible for these and related matters.

The food and beverage manager and controller, working as a team, can mutually define procedures to allocate costs to the food and beverage program. Development of budgets, design of source documents and forms for income collection, and development or review of revenue collection methods to reduce the opportunities for theft are among the activities which involve a cooperative working relationship between these two specialists. When problems arise, such as differences between budgeted and actual costs, discussions between the controller and the food and beverage manager about alternatives for problem resolution will frequently yield workable solutions. The controller can often tell how data for actual costs was developed and can help review assumptions made at the time the operating budget was developed. The synergy which arises during these conversations can be of great benefit, not only to the food and beverage manager, but to the hospitality establishment.

The Cycle of Food and Beverage Controls

The cycle of control for food and beverage operations in a hotel or restaurant involves five basic steps: planning, assessing, comparing, acting, and evaluating.

Step One—Planning for the Activity. It is important to establish standards about what revenue/expense levels should be if the food and beverage departments operate according to plans. In many operations, the operating budget (viewed as a "profit plan") provides this information. It reveals, for example, levels of expected revenue and related expenses allocated to the food and beverage operation. If the operating budget is agreed to by the food and beverage manager and higher-level officials (which it should be!), then the budget becomes a "road map" for planning and a source of standard (expected) costs.

Step Two—Assessing Actual Financial Results. The second step in the control cycle requires that actual revenue and operating expense levels be determined. Basically, this is an accounting function which requires the generation of a food and beverage department income statement. As stated previously, it is imperative that the food and beverage manager and the controller cooperatively determine what and how expenses are to be allocated and the level of allowable expenses. Consider problems which arise, for example, when the manager does not separate revenues from different beverage operations and the controller does. As a second example, consider problems which arise if the food and beverage manager includes the cost of employees' meals with costs of food, and the accounting department excludes these costs. (Costs of goods sold calculations will be discussed later in this chapter.)

Step Three—Comparing Financial Information. The third step in the food and beverage cycle of control requires the comparison of standard (expected) financial information (from Step One) with actual financial information (from Step Two). When there is a variance beyond a pre-established level, a control problem is identified. Note that managers must be concerned when there are significant positive or negative variances. For example, if expenses are much lower than expected, this could suggest that product, labor, or other quality levels are not being attained. Likewise, if income levels are sufficiently different than expected, analysis is in order to assess why, so that marketing and other efforts can continue their effectiveness. Obviously, if expenses are higher than expected, everything else being the same, a problem (lower operating profit levels) has been identified. More details of variance analysis are explained and illustrated in Chapter 11 on operations budgeting.

Step Four—Taking Corrective Action. Many observers view this step as the primary element in the control process. Once a problem has been detected, causes of the problem must be eliminated by management. Failure to accomplish this important follow-up step may render the entire control process worthless. Inventory valuation, the locking of storeroom doors, and the use of portion control tools are all physical steps in the control process. As you have seen, however, the three control steps which precede this activity form the foundation for the control system.[1]

Step Five—Evaluating Effectiveness of Corrective Action. After corrective action has been taken, it is important to assess the extent to which the problem (variances between expected and actual revenue/expense levels) has been resolved. Another aspect of control evaluation requires an assurance that there are no "spin-off" effects on other aspects of the food and beverage program. For example, if food costs are too high, they might be reduced by purchasing a lower quality product and/or by utilizing a smaller portion size. While these steps may resolve the food cost problem, they may create new marketing-related problems. Therefore, a total evaluation of the impact of corrective action procedures is necessary.

The control process is diagrammed in Exhibit 7.5. Note that if the evaluation suggests that corrective action has not been effective, the process must be repeated, and alternative corrective plans must be implemented.

Resources to be Controlled

The control process has been defined; however, what exactly must the food and beverage manager control? The basic control process can be used to effectively manage each of the various types of resources available within the food and beverage department, such as products (food and beverage), labor, energy, and other expenses.

Most of this chapter will concentrate on product (food and beverage) control. However, the need to control each resource and the basic procedures to be used are similar; each must receive the food and beverage manager's attention in order to attain the department's financial goals. Note that before one can effectively manage revenue and expenses, it is necessary to know the planned revenue/expense levels in order to compare anticipated results with actual operating information.

Exhibit 7.5   Steps in the Cycle of Food and Beverage Control

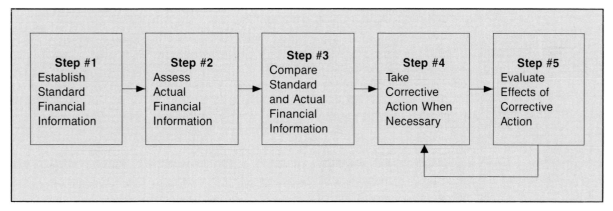

Without this step, it is not possible to define the extent to which a problem is occurring, and it is not possible to assign a priority to the problem resolution task. Given the limited amount of time available, management must first address those operating problems which most hinder efforts to attain the department's goals.

The control process is much more difficult than an analysis of Exhibit 7.5 might suggest. For example, the food and beverage manager may be simultaneously developing an operating budget for the next fiscal year, working with subordinates to identify reasons for variances between planned and actual food, beverage, and energy cost levels, and working with the controller to establish a new revenue control procedure. At the same time, the manager must also supervise ongoing production and service, be involved with organizing, staffing, coordinating, and related management duties, and participate in many activities which involve relationships with other departments. In addition, the food and beverage manager may serve on several hotel committees, such as the executive committee, the planning committee, and the compensation committee. The reader should recognize that even though the focus is on the control process in this chapter, it is only one of a wide range of activities which compete for the time and priorities of the food and beverage manager.

Product control is a systematic process. The elements in a food and beverage operation are shown in Exhibit 7.6. We will examine the basic control procedures for each of these elements.

Purchasing

The major objectives of product purchasing relate to attaining the right quality of products in the right quantities from the right supplier at the right time and at the right price. Thus, the purchasing objective is much more than to simply "get the best price" for required products. There are several purchasing concerns which are integral to product control.

First, purchase specifications should be used to provide an explicit description of the quality characteristics desired in a particular food or beverage item. In multi-unit companies, purchase specifications may be developed at corporate levels with the requirement that they be used in company-operated properties. These may be made available to units owned by franchisees. In single-unit properties, purchase specifications

Exhibit 7.6 Central Control Elements in a Food and Beverage Operation

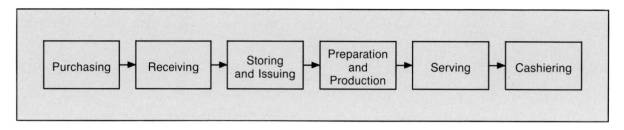

are developed within the unit. Exhibit 7.7 illustrates a sample purchase specification format.

Large hotel and motel properties frequently use a purchasing agent to assist in the procurement of food and beverages. Purchasing agents should have the same staff advisory relationship with department managers as do accounting department personnel. As stated previously, staff specialists provide advice but do not make decisions for the food and beverage manager. Therefore, the purchasing agent can generate product information, interview potentially eligible suppliers, help with "make-buy" studies, and offer recommendations about products to be used and purchase specifications to be developed. However, final responsibility for product selection and quality requirements generally should be left to the food and beverage manager and his or her staff.

It is important to establish guidelines for control of quantities of the food and beverage products to be purchased. For example, if excessive quantities are purchased, there is an increased chance of theft and quality deterioration. Also, funds which could be used for other purposes will be tied up in storage. On the other hand, inadequate quantities will yield stockouts which disrupt production and can cause inconvenience to guests.

Perishable food items should be purchased only in those quantities sufficient to meet immediate anticipated demand. For example, the chef, working with the purchasing manager, may use production forecasts to anticipate demand for certain food items for a seven-day period. After reducing this quantity by the amount currently on hand, it is possible to estimate the additional quantity of products which it will be necessary to order.

Many properties use a daily market quotation sheet when ordering perishable products. With this system, the quantity to be ordered is first assessed. Then several suppliers are contacted (all of whom have received copies of applicable purchase specifications and therefore understand the quality of products desired by the property). Their quoted prices are noted, and the supplier providing the lowest price, on either a by-item or total-order basis, is awarded the order. When orders are awarded on a by-item basis, problems with minimal delivery quantities and additional receiving, recordkeeping, and payment processing duties can arise. However, some properties believe these costs are more than offset by the price savings realized by this purchase method.

Exhibit 7.8 illustrates a sample daily market quotation sheet. To maximize control, the chef and purchasing manager should continuously

Exhibit 7.7 Sample Purchase Specification Format

Purchase Specification Format

_____
(name of food and beverage operation)

1. Product name:_____

2. Product used for:

> Clearly indicate product use (such as olive garnish for beverage, hamburger patty for grill frying for sandwich, etc.)

3. Product general description:

> Provide general quality information about desired product. For example, "iceberg lettuce; heads to be green, firm without spoilage, excessive dirt or damage. No more than 10 outer leaves; packed 24 heads per case."

4. Detailed description:

> Purchaser should state other factors which help to clearly identify desired product. Examples of specific factors, which vary by product being described, include:
>
> - Geographic origin
> - Variety
> - Type
> - Style
>
> - Grade
> - Size
> - Portion size
> - Brand name
>
> - Density
> - Medium of pack
> - Specific gravity
> - Container size
> - Edible yield, trim

5. Product test procedures:

> Test procedures occur at time product is received and as/after product is prepared/used. Thus, for example, products to be at a refrigerated temperature upon delivery can be tested with a thermometer. Portion-cut meat patties can be randomly weighed. Lettuce packed 24 heads per case can be counted.

6. Special instructions and requirements:

> Any additional information needed to clearly indicate quality expectations can be included here. Examples included bidding procedures, if applicable, labeling and/or packaging requirements and delivery and service requirements.

Source: Jack D. Ninemeier, *Purchasing: A Systems Manual for Restaurants, Hotels and Clubs* (Boston, MA: CBI Publishing Company, Inc., 1982).

Exhibit 7.8 Daily Market Quotation Sheet

The Sheraton Corporation — Daily Market Quotation Sheet

Date: _____

ITEM	Stock On Hand	Quantity Ordered	QUOTATIONS
BEEF			
Bottom Rounds			
Corned Brisket			
Chucks, Sq. cut			
Ribs			
Rounds, Steamship			
Strips, Bone-in			
Strips, Boneless			
Tenderloins			
Top Rounds			
Top Sirloin Butts			
VEAL			
Calves Liver			
Veal Legs			
Veal Shoulder			
Veal Sweetbreads			
LAMB			
Lamb Chuck			
Lamb Legs			
Lamb Racks			
POULTRY			
Broilers			
Chicken Breasts			
Chicken Roasting			
Cornish Hens			
Ducks			
Turkeys			
PROVISIONS			
Bacon, Canadian			
Bacon, Sliced			
Ham, Canned			
Ham, Fresh			
Pork Loin, Fresh			
Pork Shoulders			
Pork Tenderloins			
Bologna			

ITEM	Stock On Hand	Quantity Ordered	QUOTATIONS
Frankfurts			
Knockwurst			
Salami			
Sausage, Link			
Sausage, Meat			
Tongue, Beef Smoked			
FISH & SHELLFISH			
Clams, Cherrystone			
Clams, Chowder			
Clams, Littleneck			
Crabmeat, Alaskan K.			
Crabmeat, Lump			
Lobsters, Live			
Oysters			
Scallops, Cape, Gal.			
Scallops, Sea, Gal.			
Shrimp, Green			
Shrimp			
Bass, Striped			
Bluefish			
Cod Fillets			
Finnan Haddie			
Flounder			
Frogs Legs			
Haddock Fillets			
Halibut			
Mackerel			
Red Snapper			
Salmon			
Salmon, Smoked			
Sole, Grey, Fillets			
Sole, Lemon			
Swordfish			
Trout, Brook			

ITEM	Stock On Hand	Quantity Ordered	QUOTATIONS
FRUITS & VEGETABLES			
Asparagus, Jumbo			
Beans, String			
Beets, Bunch			
Broccoli			
Brussels Sprouts			
Cabbage, Green			
Cabbage, Red			
Carrots, Bag			
Cauliflower			
Celery			
Chicory			
Chives			
Corn			
Cucumbers			
Endive, Belgium			
Escarole			
Leeks			
Lettuce, Boston			
Lettuce, Iceberg			
Mint			
Mushrooms			
Onions, Spanish			
Parsley			
Peppers, Choice			
Potatoes, Bag			
Potatoes, Baking			
Potatoes, Peeled			
Potatoes, Sweet			
Romaine			
Scallions			
Schallots			
Spinach			
Squash, Zucchini			
Tomatoes			
Turnips			
Apples, Baking			
Apples, Eating			
Avocado Pears			
Bananas			
Blueberries			
Cherries			
Grapefruit			
Grapes			
Lemons			
Melons, Cantaloupe			
Melons, Cranshaw			
Melons, Honeydew			

ITEM	Stock On Hand	Quantity Ordered	QUOTATIONS
Orange, Juice			
Orange, Table			
Peaches			
Pears			
Pineapple			
Plums			
Raspberries			
Watermelon			
Orange Sections			
Grapefruit Sections			
Pineapple Sections			
Mixed Fruit Sections			
FROZEN VEGETABLES			
Asparagus			
Broccoli Spears			
Beans, Green cut			
Beans, French cut			
Beans, Lima			
Brussel Sprouts			
Carrots			
Cauliflower			
Corn			
Mixed Vegetables			
Peas			
Peas & Carrots			
Potatoes, French Fries			
Spinach			
Squash			
FROZEN FRUITS			
Apples, Sliced			
Blueberries			
Cherries			
Orange Juice			
Peaches, Halves			
Peaches, Sliced			
Raspberries			
Strawberries			

Courtesy of The Sheraton Corporation

review product consumption rates, quantity of stock on hand, and forecasted meals to be served (including banquets).

Typically, nonperishable food and beverage items are purchased with a system that establishes a re-order level for each item. A minimum stock level (par) is determined by considering the normal usage rate, the lead time required for deliveries, planned frequency of orders, and "safety" factors. However, flexibility is always in order, and many factors such as upcoming banquets and/or perceived changes in market selling prices may cause a re-order quantity to be changed.

The "best" price is generally obtained by soliciting information from eligible suppliers, for example, by using a daily market quotation sheet. Large properties accomplish the same objective for the purchase of nonperishable products by soliciting selling price information through the use of a price quotation form. A purchase order, similar to that shown in Exhibit 7.9, is then sent to the supplier selected to provide the product desired.

Alternatively, products with a stable price and large volume (some grocery items such as flour and sugar, and canned and frozen produce) may be purchased with use of a short-term contract. For example, after analysis of price quotations supplied by eligible suppliers, an agreement may be drawn up between the lodging property and a supplier for a three-month period.

It is also possible to negotiate contracts with suppliers of products that experience frequent price changes (dairy and produce items are examples). With one plan, a mark-up based on a wholesale market price is negotiated. Then the supplier agrees to provide products at the wholesale price with the associated mark-up. For example, a supplier may agree to provide dairy products at a cost equal to 10% above the wholesale market price for the area and may agree to this arrangement for a six-month time period.

Generally, it is best to select several vendors to supply products to the property. Competitive pricing and back-up sources of supply are among the advantages. One's experiences with suppliers, their ability to consistently provide products at the required quality and quantity levels, their "philosophy" of doing business, credit arrangements, and time of delivery are among factors to consider when making a supplier selection decision.

Receiving   Product receiving is, perhaps, the most overlooked element in the control process. The receiving activity has several major objectives, including the assurance that:

1.   The quality and condition of products are in agreement with the purchase specifications.

2.   The weight/count is consistent with the quantities ordered.

3.   The weight/count agrees with the quantities for which payment will be requested.

Generally, it is best that all products be received during scheduled hours at one central receiving area. Since some time will be required for

Exhibit 7.9 Sample Purchase Order

Purchase Order

Purchase Order Number:_____   Order Date:_____

Payment Terms_____
From/
To:_____   Ship to:_____
        (supplier)   (name of food service)

_____   _____
        (address)   (address)

Delivery Date:_____

Please Ship:

Quantity Ordered	Description	✔	Units Shipped	Unit Cost	Total Cost

Total Cost_____

IMPORTANT: This Purchase Order expressly limits acceptance to the terms and conditions stated above, noted on the reverse side hereof, and any additional terms and conditions affixed hereto or otherwise referenced. Any additional terms and conditions proposed by seller are objected to and rejected.

_____
Authorized Signature

proper receiving, it may not be possible to accept incoming products during busy periods in small operations which do not have a full-time receiving clerk. In most operations, the receiving area should be relatively large, well lit, and properly ventilated; walls and floors should be of a non-porous, easily cleanable material; scales, carts or dollies for product movement are among the equipment items which should be in the area. Copies of all purchase specifications, daily market quotation sheets, and purchase orders should be available to receiving personnel.

There are several steps necessary for effective receiving. First, the receiver must confirm that the quality characteristics are consistent with those outlined in the purchase specifications. If there is doubt about the acceptability of any product, the receiving clerk should seek advice from the chef or another appropriate manager. It is also necessary to check incoming products against the amount ordered (copies of the daily market quotation sheet for perishable products and the purchase order for nonperishable products can be source documents for this purpose). It is then necessary to confirm that incoming products, including quantities, are properly recorded on the delivery invoice or delivery slip. At this point, it is absolutely imperative that all products be weighed, counted, or measured. Extreme care must be taken to ensure that the property "gets what it pays for." Since the supplier's invoice should be based on the delivery slip information, verifying this information is very important.

All products received should be recorded on a receiving clerk's daily report similar to that shown in Exhibit 7.10. Incoming products can be broken down into type (food and beverages), and purchase values can be quantified for control purposes. For example, in Exhibit 7.10, products which go directly to production, and/or do not enter inventory records, are classified as "food directs," such as fruit, dairy products and other perishable items. By contrast, food products moved into storage areas and placed in storage records are classified as "food stores," such as flour, sugar, and canned items. The cumulative total value of goods received, as detailed on this document, should be verified against applicable supplier invoices to ensure that all liabilities are recorded.

One additional document, a request for credit, such as that shown in Exhibit 7.11, may be necessary at the time of product receiving. It is used to note errors on delivery slips/invoices, such as when information is posted on delivery slips/invoices but not delivered, and/or when products are rejected by the property's receiving staff at the time of receiving.

Special controls are frequently used when high value items such as meat, fish, caviar, champagne, and fine wines are received. These products may be tagged upon receipt. A sample receiving tag is shown in Exhibit 7.12. Use of a receiving tag helps eliminate inadequacies when determining weight or costs as products are issued. Likewise, tags help to facilitate rotation of inventories and can allow for follow-up with a supplier if quality deterioration is noted at the time of issuing and preparation.

Finally, the food and beverage manager should schedule surprise spot-checks at the receiving area to determine that established receiving procedures are followed. The spot-checkers should have sufficient product knowledge, awareness of procedures, and independence to facilitate the surprise "audit."

Storing   The objective of effective product storage is to maintain strict control over products from the time of receipt to preparation. In addition, inventory values must be periodically determined to facilitate preparation of financial statements.

Proper sanitation requirements dictate that storage areas be clean, dry, and well ventilated. Items should be kept off the floor and away from the wall to permit proper air circulation. Incoming products should be placed under and/or behind products already in storage.[2]

If products are tagged or marked at the time of receipt, it will be easier to ensure that they are issued on a first in, first out (FIFO) basis. The food and beverage manager should make frequent tours through all storage areas to help ensure that proper storage practices are consistently followed. In large properties where a food and beverage controller is employed, this responsibility would generally be delegated to him or her by the food and beverage manager.

Several basic control procedures focus on security aspects of storage. For example, only authorized personnel should have access to storage areas. Likewise, a perpetual inventory system can be used for high-cost items to help monitor the quantity of products which should be in storage areas. Even relatively small properties can find ways to

Exhibit 7.10   Receiving Clerk's Daily Report

					Purchase jounal distribution			
Quantity	Unit	Description	Unit price	Total amount	Food Direct	Food Stores	Meat	

The Sheraton Corporation

Date_____

RECEIVING CLERK'S DAILY REPORT   **FOOD**

Signature

Courtesy of The Sheraton Corporation

recognize security concerns at the time of storage. For example, perhaps one compartment of a reach-in refrigerator/freezer can be used for expensive products which should be kept under lock. Alternatively, lockable storage units might be placed inside walk-in refrigerator/freezer areas to safeguard expensive products. Also, "precious storage" (a locked area within a storeroom) might be used for storage of alcoholic beverages, expensive grocery products, buffet chafing units, and other high-cost serviceware.

The emphasis on security aspects of control can be summarized through use of an analogy: how would you control money in a bank vault? If you consider a storage area to be a bank vault and the products within the storage areas to be money, then as a food and beverage manager, you will recognize the priority which must be given to ensure the safekeeping of products while in storage.

Exhibit 7.11   Sample Request for Credit Form

Request for Credit

(prepare in duplicate)   Number: _____

From: _____   To: _____
                                                        (supplier)

_____   _____

_____   _____

_____   _____

Credit should be given on the following:

Invoice Number: _____   Invoice Date: _____

Product	Unit	Number	Price/Unit	Total Price

Reason: Total: _____

_____   _____
(delivery person)   (authorizing signature)

Exhibit 7.12   Sample Receiving Tag

No. *2387*	No. *2387*
Date Received_____	Date Received_____
Item_____Grade_____	Item_____Grade_____
Weight_____lbs_____	Weight_____lbs_____
Extension_____	Extension_____
Dealer_____	Dealer_____

Issuing   To the extent it is practical, no food or beverage product should be issued without a written issue requisition signed by an authorized official. Food requisitions (see Exhibit 7.13) should generally be priced by the storekeeper prior to receipt by the user department. This task will be easier if the product costs have been marked on items at the time of receiving.

Exhibit 7.13   Food Requisition Tag

<table>
<tr><td colspan="6">⟨S⟩ **The Sheraton Corporation**   1451
Food Requisition</td></tr>
<tr><td colspan="4">Department</td><td colspan="2">Date</td></tr>
<tr><td>Quantity</td><td>Item</td><td>Issued</td><td>Unit Price</td><td>Total</td><td></td></tr>
<tr><td></td><td></td><td></td><td></td><td></td><td></td></tr>
<tr><td colspan="6">Total</td></tr>
<tr><td colspan="2">Ordered by</td><td colspan="2">Issued by</td><td colspan="2">Received by</td></tr>
</table>

Courtesy of The Sheraton Corporation

Beverage requisitions (see Exhibit 7.14) typically are accompanied by the empty bottles listed on the requisition form. Issues are made to re-establish a pre-determined bar par. That is, at any time there should be a specified number of bottles of each type of liquor stored behind the bar. These bottles may be full (unopened), opened, or empty, and once each shift (either at the beginning or end), empty bottles are noted on the

Exhibit 7.14   Beverage Requisition Form

The Sheraton Corporation   **BEVERAGE REQUISITION**   No.

BAR: _____   DATE _____

CODE NO.	ITEM	QTY	COST	POTENTIAL	CODE NO.	ITEM	QTY	COST	POTENTIAL	CODE NO.	ITEM	QTY	COST	POTENTIAL	CODE NO.	ITEM	QTY	COST	POTENTIAL
	SCOTCH					**VERMOUTH/APERITIFS**										**BEERS-DOMESTIC**			
100	CHIVAS REGAL				314	DRY SACK				400	BUDWEISER			
101	CUTTY SARK				315	HARV. AMONTILLADO				401	MICHELOB			
102	DEWARS					**VODKAS**				316	BRISTOL CREAM				402	MILLER			
103	J & B				220	FINLANDIA									403	MILLER LITE			
104	J.WALKER RED				221	SMIRNOFF									404	SCHLITZ			
105	J.WALKER BLACK				222	STOLICHNAYA				320	GOLD CAP PORT								
106	PASSPORT																		
107	VAT '69					**RUMS**										**BEERS-IMPORTED**			
					240	BACARDI SILVER									410	BECKS			
					241	BACARDI 151									411	HEINEKEN			
					242	MYERS													
	RYES & BOURBONS										**LIQUEURS**								
140	EARLY TIMES				330	AMARETTO DI SAR.								
141	JACK DANIELS					**TEQUILAS**				331	ANISETTE					**DRAFT BEER-KEGS**			
142	JIM BEAM				260	ARANDAS				332	B & B				421	MICHELOB			
143	OLD GRANDAD				261	CUERVO GOLD				333	BENEDICTINE				421	MILLER LITE			
144	WILD TURKEY									334	CHARTREUSE GREEN								
										335	COINTREAU					**SOFT DRINKS**			
										336	CR. DE CACAO DARK				450	COCA COLA			
					BRANDIES & COGNACS				337	CR. DE CACAO LIGHT				451	CLUB SODA			
	CANADIAN				280	CHRISTIAN BROS.				338	CR.DE MENTHE GREEN				452	GINGER ALE			
170	CANADIAN CLUB				281	COURVOISIER V.S.				339	CR. DE MENTHE WHITE				453	PERRIER			
171	CROWN ROYAL				282	HENNESSY V.S				340	DRAMBUIE				454	TAB			
172	SEAGRAMS V.O.				283	MARTELL***				341	GALLIANO				455	TONIC			
					284	REMY MARTIN V.S.O.P.				342	GRAND MARNIER								
										343	KAHLUA								
	IRISH									344	OUZO					**HOUSE WINES**			
190	BUSHMILLS				345	PERNOD				470	GALLON–RED			
191	JAMESON									346	SAMBUCA				471	GALLON–ROSE			
					VERMOUTH/APERITIFS				347	SOUTHERN COMFORT				472	GALLON–WHITE			
					300	MARTINI SWEET				348	STREGA								
	GINS				301	MARTINI DRY				349	TIA MARIA								
200	BEEFEATER				350	TRIPLE SEC					COST _____			
201	GORDONS															POTENTIAL			
202	TANQUERAY				310	CARPANO									TOTAL REQUISITION COST _____			
					311	DUBONNET									TOTAL REQUISITION POTENTIAL _____			

COST _____	COST _____	COST _____	REQUESTED BY: _____
POTENTIAL _____	POTENTIAL _____	POTENTIAL _____	ISSUED BY: _____
			RECEIVED BY: _____

Courtesy of The Sheraton Corporation

beverage requisition which is reviewed and authorized by the beverage manager before subsequent issuing.

Preparation and Production

Effective preparation procedures rely heavily on accurate sales forecasts. Control of waste is best ensured when food is prepared only in quantities judged necessary to meet forecasted demands. To forecast effectively, a comprehensive analysis of guests' preferences and the number of meals served in the recent past is in order. In properties large enough to justify the position, this activity is frequently the responsibility of the food and beverage controller. In smaller properties, the food and beverage manager and/or chef, aided by sales printouts from the computer, perform this task.

The total volume of meals to be sold can be determined by forecasting volumes by each market segment, such as in-house guests and walk-ins, at each meal period and for each restaurant, room service, banquet service, and other food outlets. In hotels, the basis for in-house meals served to guests is frequently generated from house count (occupancy) estimates generated by the rooms department. This forecast must be adjusted to include the anticipated number of meals to be served to walk-in guests visiting the restaurants. Many properties can develop these estimates for their high-check-average outlets where reservations are mandatory by considering the number of reservations for a specific meal period and then making adjustments based upon this information.

Standard recipes are at the heart of food production control. They dictate the type and amount of each ingredient which is required to prepare each menu item. A sample standard recipe card is shown in Exhibit 7.15. Standard recipes also dictate standard portion sizes which influence the selling price of the menu item. Most properties determine the food cost per portion and adjust this by a mark-up factor to arrive at a base selling price. Pricing is the topic of Chapter 10 and various cost mark-up approaches are presented. Food management personnel must consistently supervise to ensure that standard recipes are used and that planned portion sizes are being served. It is necessary to provide ladles, portion scoops, scales, etc., required to ensure the portion sizes which are desired.

Beverage Production Controls

The bar operation provides the greatest single possibility for product and cash theft in a food and beverage operation. One employee working alone (the bartender) typically takes the guest's order, prepares the order, rings up the sale, collects cash, and operates the cash register. In small operations, this individual may also be responsible for purchasing beverages, issuing to the bar, and even reconciling beverage revenue with the cash register's sales journal tape. The possibilities for theft appear endless, and it should be the objective of every food and beverage director and controller to minimize the opportunity for one person, working alone, to "beat the system."

Details about systems to assess standard and actual beverage costs on a by-bar, by-shift, and by-bartender basis, and systems to provide drinks to service staff are beyond the scope of this chapter. However, basic systems, such as issuing to replenish bar stocks and the control of beverages during times of storage, are essentials of any effective control system. In general, beverage items are purchased with considerably less frequency than food products. In most operations, the variety of beverage products purchased is less and prices are likely to fluctuate less than their food product counterparts. For these reasons, the emphasis on beverage control rests with helping to ensure that the operation receives all revenue that should be generated. Typically, a method employing beverage potential sales information is at the heart of this concern.

A daily beverage potential and actual sales report, such as shown in Exhibit 7.16, captures the information required for this control. If the potential income from the sales of each bottle of alcoholic beverage is known, it becomes easy to compare, on a by-beverage outlet basis, the actual sales with the potential sales. The results of each bar should be monitored on a timely basis. Any outlet showing either significant overage or shortage should be investigated. Potential beverage sales controls also help to indicate whether beverage preparation standards are being followed and whether sales are being properly recorded.

Food and beverage directors and controllers must constantly ask the question, "If I were a dishonest employee, how would I steal from the property?" Answers to this question suggest areas which must be addressed when specific control systems are developed and implemented. Bartenders may collude with beverage servers, free drinks may be given to guests to encourage larger tips, and additional "rounds" of

Exhibit 7.15 Standard Recipe Card

The Sheraton Corporation

STANDARD RECIPE CARD

RECIPE FOR Entrecote Bernaise

Recipe File No. E-4
Restaurant Sample
Sales Price $13.50

Quantity Produced _____
Portion Size 12 ozs.
No. Of Portions Produced 1

Ingredients	Quantity/ Weight	Unit of Purchase	Date:3/3/80 Unit Cost	Total	Date: Unit Cost	Total	Date: Unit Cost	Total	Date: Unit Cost	Total
#180 Striploin (Cost Factor 1.028)	12 ozs.	lb	3.45	3.55						
Small Grilled Tomato	1 each	108/cs	14.00	0.13						
Mushroom Cap	1 each	bag	11.50	0.04						
Watercress	1/2 oz.	Bunch	0.38	0.02						
Broccoli	3 ozs.	lb	0.89	0.17						
Butter	1 oz.	lb	1.54	0.10						
Almonds	1/2 oz.	lb	2.75	0.09						
Baking Potato	1 each	case	8.50	0.12						
Sour Cream	3 oz.	lb	0.58	0.11						
Chopped Chives	1/8 oz	oz.	1.70	0.21						
Bacon Bits	1/2 oz.	lb	2.55	0.08						
Bernaise Sauce (Recipe B-14)	3 ozs.	lb	2.00	0.38						
Subtotal Cost				5.00						
Side Dish: Waldorf Salad (Recipe C-8)				0.22						
Extras: Bread, Butter, etc.				0.16						
Total Cost				$5.38						
Cost Per Portion				$5.83						
Cost % per Portion				39.9%						

Preparation and Garnish (brace spanning Watercress through Bernaise Sauce)

RECIPE COST

Preparation Procedure

1. Broil Steak as Requested
2. Mark Tomato on Top, and Grill
3. Saute Mushroom Cap
4. Garnish Plate with Watercress
5. Boil Broccoli
6. Add Almonds to Melted Butter and Fry Until Golden Brown; Pour Over Broccoli in Serving Dish
7. Cut Surface of Baked Potato; Serve Sour Cream, Chives and Bacon Bits on Side
8. Serve with Bernaise Sauce

Courtesy of The Sheraton Corporation

Exhibit 7.16   Daily Beverage Potential and Actual Sales Report

(S) The Sheraton Corporation	DAILY BEVERAGE POTENTIAL AND ACTUAL SALES REPORT								DATE:_____		___DAYS OF___	
	COMBINED OPERATION		OUTLET____		OUTLET____		OUTLET____		OUTLET____		BANQUET____	
	TODAY	TO DATE										
REQUISITIONS TOTAL												
LESS FULL BOTTLE												
DRINK POTENTIAL												
ADJUSTMENTS: TRANSFERS												
COCKTAIL ADJ.												
OFFICERS CHECKS												
ENTERTAINMENT CHECKS												
WELCOME DRINKS												
HAPPY HOUR												
SODAS/SOFT DRINKS												
BANQUET												
POTENTIAL DRINK SALES												
MONTH TO DATE												
TOTAL ACTUAL SALES												
LESS FULL BOTTLE												
ACTUAL DRINK SALES												
BAR OVER/(SHORT)												
REMARKS:												

Courtesy of The Sheraton Corporation

drinks may be served without recording on pre-check registers, guest checks, or other control tools, and so on. Managers cannot assume that they can identify dishonest employees. They must recognize the potential for product and cash theft and deal with these issues as control systems are monitored. Use of shoppers to pose as guests to note violations of sales/product control systems can also help identify potential problems.

Serving

The task of food and beverage control does not end when products are produced; they must also be served. One important aspect of service relates to revenue control; this topic will be discussed later in the chapter. However, a wide range of other activities must also be addressed. Systems must be in place to safeguard the quality of products being held until service. One aspect of quality, sanitation, demands particular attention at this point. Layout and design concerns, along with equipment availability, must address problems that may arise when a large quantity of food products is ordered.

Communication problems can arise between service and production staff. The mistakes which result may create higher product costs than necessary, as well as guest complaints of ineffective and/or inefficient service. Large operations doing a high volume business frequently make use of an expeditor, typically a member of the management staff, who serves as liaison between production and service staff and turns in orders, arranges plates on service trays, checks for proper portion sizes, assists with necessary garnishes, and so on.

Server stations must be carefully designed to ease the bottlenecks which often result when service gets too busy. It is also important to ensure that supply stations are well-stocked, tables are properly set, and the dining room and its fixtures and furniture are really clean. Service staff must have a thorough knowledge of the food and beverage products which are sold, must be experts in the wide range of guest relations and concerns which can arise, and must be able to work quickly and efficiently.[3]

Revenue Control Systems

Along with product control concerns, the food and beverage manager and controller must also be concerned about the collection of cash. There are many ways that dishonest employees can steal and, of course, the guests themselves may take advantage of flaws in cash collection systems.

The first step of the control process noted the need to define the standard (expected) financial results of operation. In the case of revenue control, the food and beverage manager must know the anticipated revenue level. While there are many ways that this can be accomplished, the most important points are that some system be implemented and that required procedures are consistently followed.

Many properties utilize a prenumbered guest check at the heart of their revenue control system. For example, if guest checks are assigned by number to service staff and all guest checks are accounted for at the end of the shift, then the amount of expected revenue can be determined; expected revenue equals the amount of sales generated from sale of all products on all guest checks. This procedure assumes, of course, that no products are given to service staff without initial entry onto guest checks.

The use of pre-check registers (a pre-check register is basically a cash register without an operating cash drawer) can help in revenue control. After writing the guest's order on the guest check, a server places the guest check in the pre-check register. Entry of information such as server number, product selling cost (a pre-set key often makes both of these entries simultaneously), and other required information enables the machine to print authorizing information on the guest check and, at the same time, enter information onto sales journal tape and/or into memory. This provides the food and beverage manager and controller with a triple check on the amount of revenue which should be generated. The sum of products sold for all guest checks after they are accounted for should equal the amount of sales rung on the pre-check register which should equal the amount of sales recorded on the cash register and cash and charge vouchers deposited in the register's cash drawer.

While this system, with modification as necessary, may work well in many food outlets, different problems arise in the bar. For example, imagine the service concerns that may occur when there are a large number of guests to be served, and the bartender must use guest checks, go through pre-check registers, etc. In practice, an increasing number of beverage outlets use automated beverage dispensing equipment which is tied to the cash register; as drinks are produced, a record is input to the cash register which helps in later reconciliation of the amount of income collected with the number of drinks produced.

Another approach used by an increasing number of food and beverage operators is to hire a bar cashier so that the duties of production and cashiering can be split. While there are still many opportunities for theft (especially if the cashier and bartender collude), additional control elements are introduced into this system as duties are segregated.

Calculating Actual Food Costs

While every aspect of the food and beverage operation requires specialized and consistent controls, special attention is typically given to the food department. It generates a higher level of sales than the beverage department and creates the highest single category of expenses in many operations. The standard (expected) food cost is typically based on the operating budget. However, it is also possible to determine the potential food cost based upon the actual sales mix of items sold. The Potential Food Cost Worksheet shown in Exhibit 7.17 outlines information required and procedures to be used to determine what the food costs should be based upon actual sales. Note that in Exhibit 7.17, the actual number of each menu item sold is multiplied by its total food cost (as calculated from standard recipes). Total sales are also calculated so that a food cost percentage (total cost divided by total sales) can be generated. While Exhibit 7.17 illustrates a form that can be used for manual calculations, computers in some properties allow these calculations to be done electronically. In fact, the information can be accumulated for the entire period to assess the potential food cost for the same period covered by the property's income (departmental operating) statement.

What is food cost? This simple question really has a complicated answer. Exhibit 7.18 identifies many of the elements which must be assessed as financial information regarding food costs is generated for the income statement. Exhibit 7.18 shows that all sales (restaurant and banquet) are first totaled. This information is necessary in order to determine the actual food cost percentage.

The food cost is determined by summing the total value of storeroom and production inventory at the beginning of the fiscal period. Storeroom and direct purchases are added to opening inventory along with transfers of products from the beverage department to the food department. For example, wine used in cooking may generate food income; liquor used in desserts may likewise benefit the food operation. Costs for these products should be borne by the food, not the beverage, department. The sum of inventory, purchases, and beverage to food transfers yields the total food charges ($70,863.95 in Exhibit 7.18).

In order to calculate the actual food cost, some deductions must be made. The value of closing storeroom and production inventories ($12,062) must be deducted. Also, food transfers to the bar, free food to the bar (as might be done for cocktail hours or for marketing promo-

Exhibit 7.17 Potential Food Cost Worksheet

The Sheraton Corporation

POTENTIAL FOOD COST WORKSHEET
Abstract taken from: March 1, 1980 to March 7, 1980

| ITEM | Purchase Price | Cost Factor | Portion Size | COST PER PORTION | | | | Total Cost | Net Menu Price | Number Sold | Total Cost | Total Sales | Cost % |
				Main Item	Preparation & Garnish	Side Dish	Extras						
Appetizers:													
Shrimp Cocktail	6.75	0.215	5 ea.	1.45	0.19	—	—	1.64	4.95	318	521.52	1,574.10	33.1
Lobster Bisque	—	—	8 fl.oz.	0.93	0.10	—	—	1.03	3.75	91	93.73	341.25	27.5
Main Courses:													
Entre Cote Bernaise	3.45	1.028	12 oz.	3.55	1.45	0.22	0.16	5.38	13.50	140	753.20	1,890.00	39.9
Prime Rib of Beef	2.60	—	15/rib	3.99	1.13	0.22	0.16	5.50	14.25	164	902.00	2,337.00	38.6
Breast of Chicken	1.99	0.44	7 oz.	0.88	1.27	0.22	0.16	2.53	9.50	332	839.96	3,154.00	26.6
Desserts:													
Assorted Ice Cream	—	—	2½ oz.	0.34	0.04	—	—	0.38	1.75	85	32.30	148.75	21.7
Fresh Strawberries	—	—	½ pt.	0.51	0.12	—	—	0.63	2.75	187	117.81	514.25	22.9
Beverages:													
Tea	—	—	6 fl.oz.	0.09	—	—	—	0.09	0.75	55	4.95	41.25	12.0
Coffee	—	—	6 fl.oz.	0.15	—	—	—	0.15	0.75	425	63.75	318.75	20.0
Total											$3,329.22	$10,319.35	32.3%

Courtesy of The Sheraton Corporation

Exhibit 7.18 Calculation of Actual Food Cost and Food Cost Percentage

(S) **The Sheraton Corporation**

Hotel _____Sample_____ Location _____ Month ___February 19XX___

Sales:

Restaurant Sales		$103,236.00	
Banquet Sales		55,595.00	
Total Food Sales		$158,831.00	100%

Costs:

Opening Storeroom Inventory	$ 9,678.25		
Opening Production Inventory	2,146.50		
Total Opening Inventory		11,824.75	
Storeroom Purchases	53,623.90		
Direct Purchases	4,770.45		
Total Purchases		58,394.35	
Beverage Transfers to Food		644.85	
Total Charges		70,863.95	

Less:

Closing Storeroom Inventory	9,915.50		
Closing Production Inventory	2,146.50		
Total Closing Inventory		12,062.00	

Credits:

Food Transfers to Bars	249.95		
Gratis to Bars	308.20		
Marketing – Promotion	108.50		
Fruit Baskets	163.65		
Steward Sales	21.75		
Total Credits		852.05	
Total All Credits		12,914.05	

Gross Cost of Food Sold		57,949.90	36.5%
Less: Cost of Employees' Meals		7,204.10	4.6%
Net Cost of Food Sold		$ 50,745.80	31.9%

tions), fruit baskets, and steward sales (food sales to employees) are among the credits which must be deducted from total food charges.

What do all of these deductions from total costs have in common? Simply stated, they initially increased food costs, because they were charged to that department; however, they did not generate food revenue. The food and beverage manager will want to know the food cost which was incurred to generate food revenue. It is for this reason that these credits (deductions from total costs) are made. Note that cost of employee meals (really a labor expense) is also deducted from gross cost of food sold in order to arrive at the net cost of food sold ($50,745.80).

Many properties conclude their actual food cost calculations at this point. An actual food cost percentage can be calculated:

$$\text{Food Cost \%} = \frac{\text{Food Cost}}{\text{Food Sales}}$$

This amount can be compared with the standard cost from the operating budget or other source to determine whether there is a variance and, if so, whether it is excessive and will therefore require corrective action and subsequent evaluation to bring costs more in line with standard costs.

The cost of beverages sold is determined in a similar fashion. As with food, the actual beverage costs are compared with the budgeted cost in order to assess whether, and the extent to which, a problem demanding corrective action has arisen.

Computerization

The computer can be a valuable asset to the food and beverage manager. Many of the control tasks necessary to track performance are very time-consuming when manually performed; when a computer is involved, however, many of the records are updated at the time of production and sale. Timely reports are easily available to help with decision making and corrective actions can be more quickly evaluated.

There are two major types of software programs which can provide assistance in food and beverage control. Pre-cost systems help to control food costs from preparation to service. Pre-check systems tighten control of food and cash during service.[4] The pre-cost system requires only a computer and printer in order to be effective while the pre-check system requires a pre-check register (an electronic cash register without a cash drawer), remote printer in the kitchen, cash register, and CPU. If this hardware is networked, and the programs are compatible, the system will perform both tasks with a minimal amount of intervention from the management.

The pre-cost system takes various data files, combines their information with forecasts of sales, and results in expected food cost. This standard cost can then be compared with actual cost, and any variances can be investigated. The system performs these operations in the following manner:

1. An ingredient file is maintained which contains a description, code number, and cost for each inventory item. This file is used to determine the cost per unit of measure (pound, for example) which will be used throughout the program.

2. A recipe file is established with standard recipes for all items served

in the restaurant. When this information is combined with information from the ingredient file, standard costs are calculated.

3.   Management inputs forecasts of demand for each menu item and the computer calculates the amount of inventory which should be on hand and the standard cost of the forecasted business.

With a system such as this, the inventory costs can be updated, and the standard recipe and food costs will automatically be adjusted. Changes in recipe amounts are easily made. If the system is compatible with the operation, it should keep management's standards up to date, providing them with accurate standards against which to compare actual results while also simplifying the ordering process considerably.

Automated pre-check systems take over when the service begins. The server records guest orders on a note pad and then inputs them into a pre-check register. This equipment should have pre-programmed keys so that the server merely presses a key which is labeled with the proper menu item. This information is then transferred to the kitchen through a remote printer. Without the server even leaving the floor, the kitchen staff can begin preparing the order. When the pre-checking process is initiated, the computer also stores the guest check number along with the items ordered, their prices, and the server number. With adequate control, no food will leave the kitchen without a printed slip; all food removed, therefore, will be recorded in the computer.

When the guests complete their meal, their guest check number can be input into the cash register, the bill totaled, and payment received. This helps to ensure that addition is correct, that all items are included on the final guest check, and that all checks are reconciled. At the end of the shift, a report is produced of all "open" guest check numbers (ones which have been used in the pre-check register which have not been terminated at the cash register) along with the server responsible. Any server with a history of excessive unpaid checks should be closely supervised.

Finally, if both of these systems are integrated, it is possible to generate a standard food cost for the actual sales mix. This is possible because the food items are entered at the pre-check register and the standard costs are available from the recipe file. This information can then be used to compare with actual costs and as a guide in future pricing decisions. For example, computerized menu engineering packages may interface with these programs generating the standard results and graphs automatically. Menu engineering is a pricing approach presented in Chapter 10.

Summary

Food and beverage control is achieved only as managers are diligent in their management efforts. Accounting personnel provide information and may assist food and beverage personnel; however, decision-making concerning food and beverage is the responsibility of the food and beverage staff. The overall control cycle consists of five steps: planning, determining actual results, comparing actual and expected results, taking corrective action, and evaluating the effectiveness of the corrective action.

The control process consists of several elements: (1) purchasing, (2) receiving, (3) storing, (4) issuing, (5) preparation and production, (6) serving and (7) revenue control systems.

Purchasing effectiveness is achieved by the use of purchase specifications, purchasing agents, standardized forms and procedures, and reputable suppliers. Receiving includes making sure that the products received are consistent with what was ordered, both in quality and quantity. Further, the charges should agree with the prices at which the products were ordered. Storage is effective when strict control is exercised over products from the time of receipt until use. Important elements of this function include inspections by management, proper storage facilities, and the use of proper forms. Products should be issued upon written request. More detailed procedures, such as maintaining and monitoring par stocks and returning empty bottles, should be part of the beverage issuing process.

Preparation and production procedures are designed to minimize waste while producing the proper amounts of food needed. Forecasting food sales is a critical element of this process. Service control demands that proper equipment be used, communication problems be minimized, and service staff be properly trained. Revenue control systems are designed to ensure that sales are recorded, and cash or its "equivalent" is collected. The guest check is often at the heart of this control system. Also helpful in this process are pre-check registers.

This chapter closed by discussing the calculation of cost of food sold. The general cost of sales formula of beginning inventory plus purchases less ending inventory must be modified by subtracting credits (such as food transfers) and the cost of employees' meals.

Notes

1. The author is indebted to Dr. Jack D. Ninemeier (Michigan State University) for major input into this chapter. There are a wide range of physical activities helpful in controlling the food and beverage operation during times of purchasing, receiving, storing, issuing, preparation, production, and service. Readers desiring more detailed information about food and beverage control are referred to: Jack D. Ninemeier, *Planning and Control for Food and Beverage Operations*, Second Edition (East Lansing, Mich.: Educational Institute of the American Hotel & Motel Association, 1986).

2. Detailed information about sanitation implications of product control are found in: Ron Cichy, *Sanitation Management* (East Lansing, Mich.: Educational Institute of the American Hotel & Motel Association, 1984).

3. Many details necessary for effective dining service are found in: Anthony M. Rey and Ferdinand Wieland, *Managing Service in Food and Beverage Operations* (East Lansing, Mich.: Educational Institute of the American Hotel & Motel Association, 1985).

4. Interested readers desiring to do further research on computers for food and beverage operations are encouraged to read *Computer Systems for Foodservice Operations*, by Michael L. Kasavana, (N.Y.: Van Nostrand and Reinhold Company Ltd., 1984).

Discussion Questions

1. How do accounting personnel assist food and beverage managers?
2. What are the five activities in the cycle of control in food and beverage operations?
3. How are purchase specifications used in the food control process?
4. How are the roles of a purchasing agent and controller similar as they relate to the food and beverage manager?
5. How do the uses of a daily market quotation sheet and a purchase order differ?
6. What is the major objective of the purchasing function?
7. What are the purposes of tagging high-value items?
8. How do procedures differ for food and beverage issues?
9. How does the pre-check register enhance the revenue control system?
10. How is the net cost of food sales determined?

Problem 7.1

The Lansing Cafe's food cost percentage was calculated at 40% for June, 19X1 by the new assistant food and beverage manager. The calculated food cost percentage differs by 4% from the goal of 36%. The assistant food and beverage manager's calculation included the following information:

Food sales	$100,000
Food inventory, June 1, 19X1	10,000
Food purchase	42,000
Food inventory, June 30, 19X1	13,000

Required:

A. Based on the limited information above, verify the assistant food and beverage manager's calculations.

B. Additional information reviewed reveals the following:

Food provided for marketing purposes	$500
Cost of employee meals	2000
Excessive spoilage due to refrigerator breakdown in June	500

Recalculate the food cost percentage based on the combination of the data used by the assistant food and beverage manager and the above information. Note: the Lansing Cafe desires to exclude excessive spoilage from cost of food sold.

Problem 7.2

The Jackson Inn, in northern Indiana, operates a 100-seat restaurant. Michael, the inn's manager, is concerned about the financial statements he has received from the restaurant management. Although there is an amount recorded for cost of food sold, Michael's investigation has revealed information which was not used in the calculation. He has asked you for some assistance. He provides you with the following information.

Inventory records:	
January 1, 19X1	
Storeroom	$6,321
Production	2,333
December 31, 19X1	
Storeroom	5,878
Production	1,998
Purchases	
Storeroom	188,332
Direct	14,672
Employee meals, food department	20,697
Employee meals, management	1,321
Estimate of fruits used to garnish	
beverages in the bar	1,866
Wines used in cooking food	3,221
Food for free hors d'oeuvres	355
Mints for turn down service (rooms)	$432

Required:

Calculate the cost of food sold for 19X1. Note: follow the form illustrated in Exhibit 7.18.

Problem 7.3

You have been hired by James Joel, the manager, to evaluate the internal control for the Billy Club Restaurant in the Stranger's Inn. While touring the facilities, you see the following actions taking place.

> The restaurant is receiving its regular lunch rush when a supplier's truck arrives. The prep cook signs the receiving voucher, and the dishwasher is pulled from her station to receive today's shipment. In order to keep up with the rush, she stacks the items by the back door for an hour until the dishes are cleaned. At that time, the dishwasher takes the produce to the walk-in refrigerator and stores the dry items in the stock room.

Required:

Outline the weaknesses of the present receiving practices for Mr. Joel.

Problem 7.4

You have just been transferred to the McCartney Hotel as the food and beverage manager. Although last year's sales increased, the property did not experience increased profits. After observing the operation, you have spotted the following:

- The bartender is allowed to go to the back room during very rushed periods to get liquor to replace empty bottles.

- Bottles on the line do not have any identification on them.

- The bartender counts his drawer to make sure that he has enough cash in it to match with the register tape.

- The bartender has been with the restaurant for over five years and the previous manager spoke very highly of him.

Required:

Outline the actions that you plan to take as the food and beverage manager.

Problem 7.5

The owner, Mr. Ringsteen, of the Ross Bar and Grill has hired you to be the operations manager because he is going to have to spend some time on the road. When you were interviewing for the position, he explained that his system was somewhat naive, and that if you had any suggestions, to make them. On your first day of work, you observe the servers taking orders on notepads that they bring from home. They then ask the cooks to prepare the order and wait for the finished food. The food is taken to the guests, and the "guest check" is left at the table. The servers also collect the money and turn it in at the end of their shifts.

Required:

Outline the steps that you will take to tighten the internal control in this situation.

8 Basic Cost Concepts

The word "cost" is used in many different contexts and may convey very different meanings. For example, each of the following expressions uses the term "cost," but each uses it to refer to something different: the cost of a dishwasher was $5,000; the labor cost for the period was $10,000; the cost of damages from the hurricane to the hotel approximated $10,000. In the first expression, "cost" refers to the purchase price for an asset. One asset, cash, was given in exchange for another asset, the dishwasher. The second expression uses "cost" to refer to an expense for the period. Cash, an asset, was paid to employees for services they provided. In this case, assets were not directly exchanged; rather, cash was paid for labor services rendered by employees to generate revenues and accounts receivables. The accounts receivables, when collected, result in cash. In the third expression, the "cost" due to the hurricane refers to a loss—a dissipation of assets without the receipt of other assets either directly or indirectly. Obviously, the term "cost" may have a variety of meanings. For the purposes of this chapter, we will generally use the term cost to mean expenses.

Many cost concepts are frequently considered by managers, as revealed by their interest in the following questions:

1. What are the hotel's fixed costs?

2. Which costs are relevant to purchasing a new micro-computer?

3. What are the variable costs in serving a steak dinner?

4. What is the opportunity cost of adding 25 rooms to the motel?

5. What is the standard cost for catering a banquet for 500 people?

6. What are the controllable costs of the hotel?

7. How are fixed cost portions of mixed costs determined?

8. How are costs allocated to operating departments?

9. Which costs are sunk costs in considering a future purchase?

10. Which costs are relevant in pricing a lobster dinner?

These questions and many others can be answered after studying this chapter's discussion of basic cost concepts. In this chapter we will discuss a variety of cost concepts and consider costs in relation to volume of sales and in relation to operated departments. We will also discuss the separation of mixed costs into fixed and variable elements, provide a simplified approach to the problem of cost allocation, and consider the concept of relevant costs in decision–making. The appendix to this chapter contains a detailed discussion of more advanced approaches to cost allocation, including illustrations of the direct and step methods of cost allocation.

General Nature of Cost

"Cost," considered as an expense, is the reduction of an asset generally for the ultimate purpose of increasing revenues. Costs include cost of food sold, labor expense, supplies expense, utilities, marketing expense, rent expense, depreciation expense, insurance expense, and many other expenses incurred by hospitality establishments as reflected on the income statement. The profit margin for most hospitality operations is less than 10%; therefore, more than 90% of their revenues (ultimately cash) is used to pay these expenses (costs). From management's viewpoint, there are several different types of costs, and it is essential that both the types of costs and their applications are understood.

Costs in Relation to Volume of Sales

One way of viewing costs is to understand how they change in relation to changes in the activity (sales) of the hospitality operation. In this context, costs can be seen as fixed, variable, or mixed (partly fixed and partly variable).

Fixed Costs

Fixed costs are costs which remain constant in the short run, even though sales volume varies. For example, room sales may increase by 5% or food sales may decline by 10% while, in both cases, the fixed costs remain constant. The graph in Exhibit 8.1 plots costs along the vertical axis and sales volume along the horizontal axis. The graph shows that total fixed costs remain constant even though sales volume increases.

Common examples of fixed costs include salaries, rent expense (for example, a machine might be leased for $200 per month), insurance expense (for example, a fire insurance premium may amount to $5,000 for the year), property taxes, depreciation expense, and interest expense. Certain fixed costs may be avoided if a lodging facility closes for part of the year. In these situations, insurance may be reduced, personnel reduced, and so on. Fixed costs avoided in a shut-down situation are called avoidable costs.

Fixed costs can also be related to sales volume in terms of the average fixed cost per unit. For example, if fixed costs total $10,000 for a period and 2,000 rooms are sold during the period, the average fixed cost per room sold is $5.00 ($10,000 divided by 2,000 rooms). However, if 3,000 rooms were sold during the period, then the average fixed cost per room sold would be $3.33 ($10,000 divided by 3,000 rooms). In this example, as the sales volume increases, the fixed cost per unit decreases. The graph in Exhibit 8.2 shows the average fixed cost per unit to be decreasing as sales volume increases.

Exhibit 8.1   Total Fixed Costs

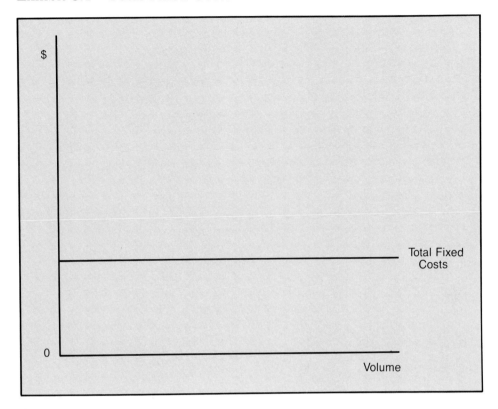

Exhibit 8.2   Fixed Costs per Sales Unit

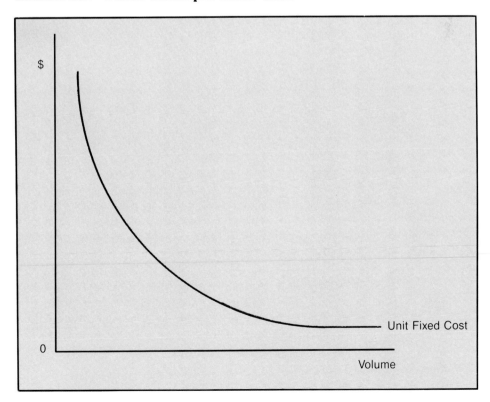

Exhibit 8.3   Total Variable Costs

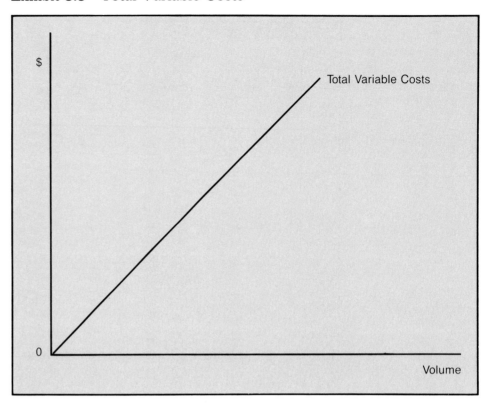

Fixed costs change over longer periods in comparison to other types of expenses. For example, a lease on a machine may change from $200 a month (as mentioned above) to $220 per month. Therefore, over a longer period, many fixed costs change and may be viewed from a long-run perspective as variable costs.

Variable Costs   Variable costs are costs which change proportionately with the volume of business. For example, if food sales increase by 10%, the cost of food sold also may be expected to increase by 10%. Exhibits 8.3 and 8.4 depict total variable cost and variable cost per unit as each relates to sales volume.

The graph in Exhibit 8.3 shows that variable costs are linear; that is, they increase proportionately to total sales. For example, if variable costs are 60% of sales, then variable costs equal $60,000 when total sales equal $100,000, and variable costs equal $600,000 when total sales equal $1,000,000.

If variable costs are strictly defined as costs that vary in exact proportion to total sales, then few, if any, costs are truly variable. However, several costs come close to meeting this definition and may legitimately be considered variable costs. Examples of such variable costs include the cost of food sold, cost of beverages sold, some labor costs, and supplies used in production and service operations.

Exhibit 8.4   Variable Costs per Sales Unit

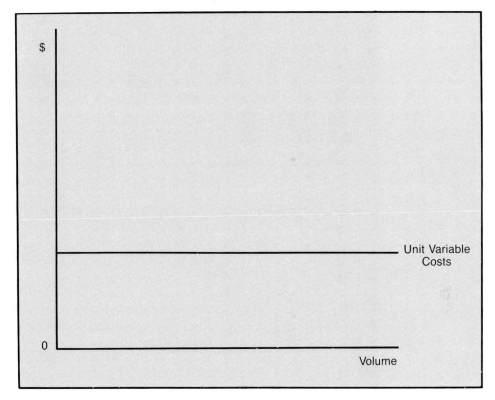

Total variable costs increase with total sales, whereas unit variable costs remain constant as total sales increase. For example, if the cost of food sold is 35%, the cost of sales per $1 of sales is $.35 whether total sales are $1 or $1,000,000. The graph in Exhibit 8.4 shows that unit variable costs are really fixed, that is, their cost per sales dollar remains constant.

Mixed Costs   Many costs are partly fixed and partly variable, that is, they are a mix of both fixed and variable cost elements. These costs are sometimes referred to as semi-variable and/or semi-fixed costs. In this text, we will refer to costs that are partly fixed and partly variable as mixed costs.

The mixed cost's fixed element is determined independently of the activity of the hospitality establishment, while the variable element is assumed to vary proportionately with its volume of sales. Although, in practice, the variable element may not be linearly related to sales activity, the assumption of a linear relationship between variable cost elements and sales volume is generally accepted because any difference is usually considered to be insignificant.

The graph in Exhibit 8.5 depicts the two elements (fixed and variable) of mixed costs. The AO line represents fixed costs, while the slope of the total mixed costs line reflects the variable element of total mixed costs.

Exhibit 8.5 Total Mixed Costs

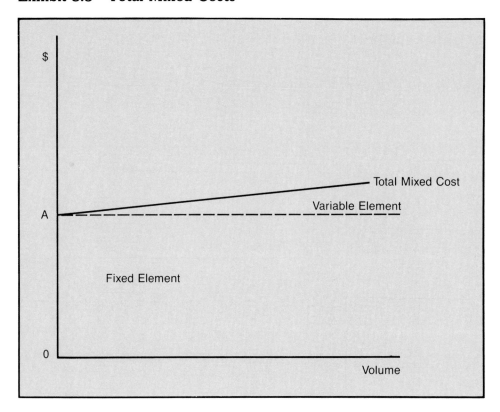

The graph in Exhibit 8.6 shows a decrease in unit mixed costs as sales volume increases. This decrease is not as dramatic as the decrease reflected in fixed costs per sales unit (Exhibit 8.2), because the variable element in mixed costs results in an increase in total mixed costs with each unit sold.

Several examples of mixed costs, including a brief discussion of their fixed and variable elements, are listed in Exhibit 8.7. This list is by no means complete.

Determination of Mixed Cost Elements

When making pricing, marketing, and expansion decisions, it is necessary to estimate the fixed and variable elements of each mixed cost. We will now consider three methods of accomplishing this estimation of mixed cost elements. The methods, which range from a simple to a complex process of estimation, are (1) the high/low two-point method, (2) the scatter diagram, and (3) regression analysis. The maintenance and repair expense of the Mayflower Hotel for 19X1 will be used to illustrate all three methods. Exhibit 8.8 contains the monthly repair and maintenance expense together with rooms sold by month for the hypothetical Mayflower Hotel.

Exhibit 8.6   Mixed Costs per Sales Unit

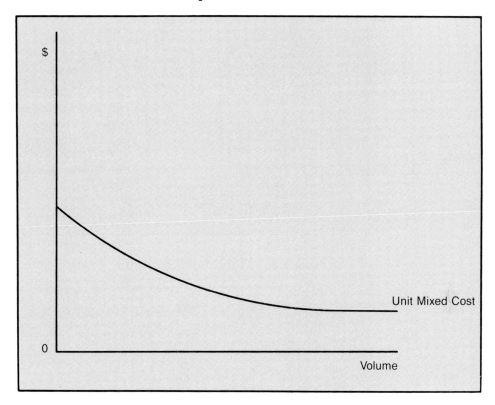

$			

Unit Mixed Cost

0

Volume

High/Low Two-Point Method   The simplest method of estimating the fixed and variable elements of a mixed cost is the high/low two-point approach. The simplicity of this approach stems from the fact that it bases the estimation on data from only two periods. Thus, this method considers only two points over the entire time span of an establishment's operations. The steps involved in this method are as follows:

1.   Select the two extreme periods (possibly months) of activity (e.g., rooms sold) in the time span under consideration (possibly one year).

2.   Calculate the differences in the total mixed cost and activity (e.g., rooms sold) for the two periods.

3.   Divide the mixed cost difference by the activity difference to determine the variable cost per activity unit (e.g., room sold).

4.   Multiply the variable cost per activity unit by the total activity for the period of lowest sales to arrive at the total variable cost for the period of lowest activity.

5.   Subtract the result in Step 4 from the total mixed cost for the period of lowest activity to determine the fixed cost.

6.   Check the answer in Step 5 by repeating Steps 4 and 5 for the period with the greatest activity.

Exhibit 8.7   Fixed and Variable Elements of Mixed Costs

	Elements	
Mixed Cost	**Fixed**	**Variable**
1. Telephone expense	Cost of system/rental of system	Cost of calls
2. Building lease	Fixed cost per square foot of space rented	Percentage of revenue in addition to fixed amount
3. Automobile lease	Fixed cost/day	Additional charge per mile automobile is driven
4. Executive remuneration	Base pay	Bonuses based on sales
5. Repair and maintenance	Minimum amount required to maintain lodging firm at low occupancy	Additional maintenance required with higher occupancy levels

Exhibit 8.8   Monthly Repair and Maintenance Expenses

**19X1 Monthly Repair and Maintenance Expense
Mayflower Hotel**

Month	Repair and Maintenance Expense	Rooms Sold
January	$6,200	1,860
February	6,100	1,820
March	7,000	2,170
April	7,500	2,250
May	8,000	2,480
June	8,500	2,700
July	7,900	2,790
August	8,600	2,800
September	7,000	2,100
October	6,000	1,900
November	6,500	1,800
December	5,900	1,330
Total	$85,200	26,000

7.   Multiply the fixed cost per period by the number of periods in the time span to calculate the fixed costs for the entire time period.

8.   Subtract the total fixed costs from the total mixed costs to determine the total variable costs.

The high/low two-point method is illustrated using data from the Mayflower Hotel's monthly repair and maintenance expense for 19X1 (Exhibit 8.8) as follows:

1. High month—August
   Low month—December

2.

	Repair and Maintenance Expense	Rooms Solds
August	$8,600	2,800
December	5,900	1,330
Difference	$2,700	1,470

3. Variable Cost per Room Sold $= \dfrac{\text{Mixed Cost Difference}}{\text{Rooms Sold Difference}}$

   $$= \frac{2,700}{1,470}$$

   $$= \$1.8367$$

   This result means that for every additional room sold, $1.8367 variable cost of repairs and maintenance will be incurred.

4. Total Variable Cost of Repair and Maintenance Expense for December $=$ (December Rooms Sold) x (Variable Cost)

   $$= 1,330 \times 1.8367$$

   $$= \$2,442.81$$

5. Total Fixed Cost of Repair and Maintenance Expense for December $=$ (Total Repair and Maintenance Cost for December) – (Variable Repair and Maintenance Cost for December)

   $$= \$5,900.00 - \$2,442.81$$

   $$= \$3,457.19$$

6. Check results by using the high month, August.

   Variable Cost
   2,800 x 1.8367 = $5,142.76

   Fixed Costs
   8,600.00 − 5,142.76 = $3,457.24

   Compare the result in Step 5 with Step 6 as follows:

Fixed Costs — Step 6	$3,457.24
Fixed Costs — Step 5	−3,457.19
	.05 (minor difference due to rounding)

7. Calculate total fixed costs for the year.

$$\text{Total Fixed Costs} \quad = \quad \text{Fixed Costs per Month x 12 Months}$$
$$= \quad \$3,457.19 \text{ x } 12$$
$$= \quad \underline{\underline{\$41,486.28}}$$

8. Determine total variable costs of repair and maintenance expense for the year.

$$\text{Total Variable Costs} \quad = \quad \text{Total Mixed Costs} - \text{Total Fixed Costs}$$
$$= \quad \$85,200 - \$41,486.28$$
$$= \quad \underline{\underline{\$43,713.72}}$$

The high/low two-point method considers only two extreme periods and is a fairly simple way of estimating the variable and fixed elements of mixed costs. This approach assumes that the extreme periods are a fair reflection of the high and low points for the entire year; therefore, to the degree they fail to fairly represent the high and low points of activity, the result will be in error. A more accurate approach, though tedious, is the scatter diagram.

Scatter Diagram   The scatter diagram is a detailed approach to determining the fixed and variable elements of a mixed cost. The steps involved in this method are as follows:

1. Prepare a graph with the independent variable (volume) on the horizontal axis and the dependent variable (cost) on the vertical axis.

2. Plot data by period on the graph.

3. Draw a straight line through the points, keeping an equal number of points above and below the line.

4. Extend the line to the vertical axis.

5. The intersection of the vertical axis indicates the fixed costs for the period.

6. Multiply the fixed costs for the period by the number of periods to determine the fixed costs for the time span.

7. Total variable costs are determined by subtracting total fixed costs (Step 6) from total mixed costs.

8. Variable costs per sales unit are determined by dividing total variable costs by total units sold.

Exhibit 8.9 is a scatter diagram of the maintenance and repair expense of the Mayflower Hotel. The scatter diagram was graphed with rooms sold as the independent variable (horizontal axis) and repair and maintenance expense as the dependent variable (vertical axis). Each monthly repair and maintenance expense was plotted and a straight line was drawn through the points. The line would vary depending on who was drawing it; however, it should approximate a "best fit." In this case,

Exhibit 8.9   Scatter Diagram

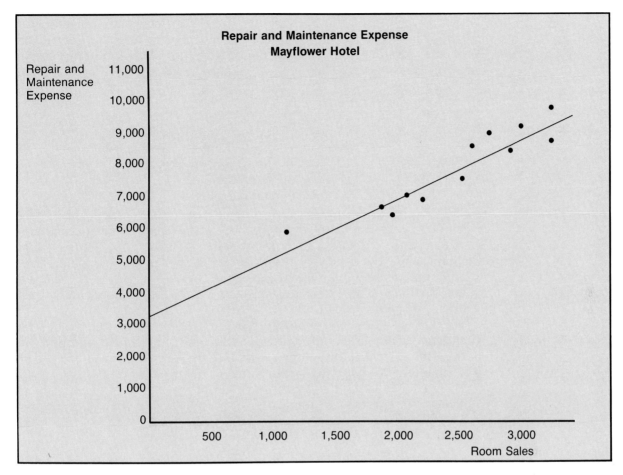

there are five points above the line, five points below the line, and the line intersects two points. The line was extended to the vertical axis which it intercepted at $3,300. The $3,300 is the fixed cost approximation per month. For the year, the estimated fixed costs are $39,600, determined by multiplying $3,300 by 12 months. Therefore, total variable repair and maintenance costs are $45,600, determined by subtracting total fixed costs of $39,600 from total costs of $85,200. Variable repair and maintenance costs per room sold is determined by dividing the total variable costs of $45,600 by the rooms sold for the year of 26,000 to equal $1.75.

The scatter diagram is an improvement over the high/low two-point approach because it includes data from all periods in the time span under consideration. In our example, the calculations used data from 12 months of a year. However, the placement of the straight line between the data points was an approximation rather than a precise measurement. It also took more time to make the "computation." A more precise and accurate approach is accomplished by regression analysis which may (if performed manually) involve even more time in the process of calculating variable and fixed elements of mixed costs.

Regression Analysis   Regression analysis is a mathematical approach to fitting a straight line to data points such that the line is a perfect fit, that is, the difference in the distances of the data points from the line is minimized. Our purpose here is not to draw a straight line, but to calculate total fixed costs and variable costs for a given cost. The formulas used in regression analysis allow us to make the calculation without plotting points or drawing lines.

The formula for a straight line is:

$$y = a + bx$$

$$
\begin{aligned}
\text{where } y &= \text{ the dependent variable} \\
x &= \text{ the independent variable} \\
a &= \text{ fixed amount} \\
b &= \text{ variable amount}
\end{aligned}
$$

For our Mayflower Hotel example, "y" stands for repair and maintenance expense, "x" stands for rooms sold, "a" stands for the fixed cost element, and "b" stands for the variable cost per room sold. Therefore, the total repair and maintenance expense (y) for any period is the fixed cost element (a) plus the variable cost per room sold (b) multiplied by the number of rooms sold (x).

Once we know the monthly fixed cost element of the repair and maintenance expense of the Mayflower Hotel, we multiply that figure by 12 months to calculate the annual total fixed cost element of the repair and maintenance expense for the year.

The formula for determining the monthly fixed cost element is as follows:

$$\text{Fixed Costs} = \frac{(\Sigma y)(\Sigma x^2) - (\Sigma x)(\Sigma xy)}{n(\Sigma x^2) - (\Sigma x)^2}$$

The values within the formula are explained as follows:

Σ means the "sum of." So, Σx and Σy mean the sum of all x values and the sum of all y values, respectively. Σxy means the sum of all x and y values that are multiplied together.
y   stands for the dependent variable.
x   stands for the independent variable.
x^2 means to square each x value.
xy   means to multiply each corresponding x and y value.
n   stands for the number of periods in the time span.

To determine the fixed cost element of the repair and maintenance expense of the Mayflower Hotel for 19X1, all of the above values have been calculated in Exhibit 8.10.

The monthly fixed cost element of repair and maintenance expense of the Mayflower Hotel is determined as follows:

$$
\begin{aligned}
\text{Fixed Cost Element} &= \frac{(85,200)(58,636,800) - (26,000)(189,257,000)}{12(58,636,800) - (26,000)(26,000)} \\[2mm]
&= \frac{4,995,855,360,000 - 4,920,682,000,000}{703,641,600 - 676,000,000}
\end{aligned}
$$

Exhibit 8.10 Calculating Values for Fixed Cost Elements

Determination of Repair and Calculation of Values
for Maintenance Fixed Cost Element
Mayflower Hotel

Month	(x) Rooms Sold	(y) Repair and Maintenance Expense	x^2	xy
January	1,860	$ 6,200	3,459,600	11,532,000
February	1,820	6,100	3,312,400	11,102,000
March	2,170	7,000	4,708,900	15,190,000
April	2,250	7,500	5,062,500	16,875,000
May	2,480	8,000	6,150,400	19,840,000
June	2,700	8,500	7,290,000	22,950,000
July	2,790	7,900	7,784,100	22,041,000
August	2,800	8,600	7,840,000	24,080,000
September	2,100	7,000	4,410,000	14,700,000
October	1,900	6,000	3,610,000	11,400,000
November	1,800	6,500	3,240,000	11,700,000
December	1,330	5,900	1,768,900	7,847,000
Totals	26,000	$85,200	58,636,800	189,257,000

$$= \frac{75,173,360,000}{27,641,600}$$

$$= \underline{\$2,719.57} \text{ per month}$$

Fixed cost per month multiplied by 12 equals the total fixed costs of repair and maintenance expense for 19X1 as follows:

$$\text{Annual Fixed Cost Element} = \$2,719.57 \times 12$$

$$= \underline{\$32,634.84}$$

The total variable costs are determined by subtracting total fixed costs from total costs. Using the total cost figure for the Mayflower Hotel's repair and maintenance expense found in Exhibit 8.8, we can calculate the total variable cost element as follows:

Repair and Maintenance Expense	$ 85,200.00
Total Fixed Cost Element	–32,634.84
Total Variable Cost Element	$ 52,565.16

The variable cost per room sold is determined by solving for the value of b using the formula for a straight line as follows:

$$y = a + bx$$

$$85,200 = 32,634.84 + b(26,000.00)$$

$$b = 2.02174, \text{ or rounded to } \$2.02 \text{ per room sold}$$

Evaluation of the Results   The three methods demonstrated to estimate the fixed and variable elements of the Mayflower Hotel's repair and maintenance expense resulted in the following:

	Fixed	Variable	Total
High/low two-point method	$41,486.28	$43,713.72	$85,200
Scatter diagram	39,600.00	45,600.00	85,200
Regression analysis	32,634.84	52,565.16	85,200

Therefore, there is a difference in the determination of fixed costs between the most simplistic calculation (the high/low two-point method) and the most complex (regression analysis) of $8,851.44. This difference is more than 25% of the low estimate using regression analysis. The major determination of which method to use is based on cost/benefit considerations. The regression analysis method is more precise, but is generally considered to be more laborious (if performed manually). If the additional time (and, therefore, cost) is worth the precision achieved, then the regression analysis approach should be used. With sophisticated calculators and computers, mixed costs are easily analyzed using regression analysis.

Fixed Versus Variable Costs

There are a number of situations in which the management of a hospitality establishment may decide to purchase a good or service whose price may either be fixed or based on a variable cost arrangement. For example, a lease may be either a fixed lease (offered at a fixed price), or a variable lease (offered at a variable price set at a certain percent of revenue). Management's decision whether to select a fixed or variable cost arrangement is based on the cost/benefit considerations involved in the decision. Under a truly fixed arrangement, the cost expended remains fixed regardless of activity and, therefore, management is able to lock in a maximum amount. However, under a variable arrangement, the amount paid depends on the level of activity. The level of activity where the period cost is the same whether the arrangement is fixed or variable is called the indifference point. At this point, everything else being the same, management is indifferent whether the cost is fixed or variable. An example follows to illustrate this concept.

A food service operation has the option of signing an annual fixed lease of $48,000 or obtaining a variable lease set at 5% of revenue. The indifference point is $960,000, determined as follows:

$$\text{Variable Cost \% x Revenue} = \text{Fixed Lease Cost}$$

$$.05(\text{Revenue}) = 48,000$$

$$\text{Revenue} = \frac{48,000}{.05}$$

$$\text{Revenue} = \underline{\underline{\$960,000}}$$

Exhibit 8.11   Indifference Point

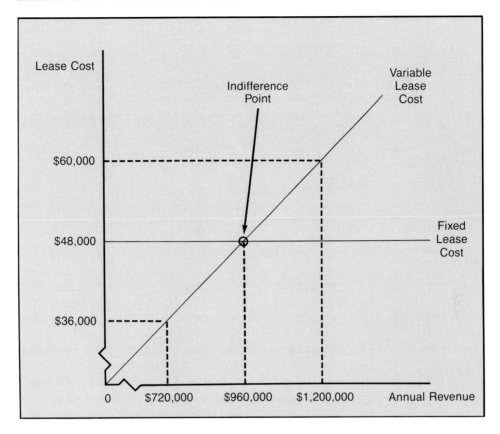

When annual revenue for a period is $960,000, the lease expense will be $48,000, regardless of whether the leasing arrangement was based on fixed or variable rates. Therefore, if annual revenue is expected to exceed $960,000, then management should select a fixed lease in order to minimize its lease expense. Alternatively, if annual revenue is expected to be less than $960,000, a variable lease will result in minimizing lease expense. Exhibit 8.11 is the graphic depiction of this situation. A review of Exhibit 8.11 suggests the following:

1. A decision in favor of a variable lease results in an excess lease expense measured by the vertical distance between the variable lease line and the fixed lease line at any revenue point to the *right* of the indifference point. For example, using the previous illustration, if revenue is $1,200,000, the lease expense from a variable lease is $60,000, or $12,000 greater than for a fixed lease of $48,000 annually.

2. A decision in favor of a fixed lease results in an excess lease expense measured by the vertical distance between the variable lease line and fixed lease line at any revenue point to the *left* of the indifference point. For example, using the previous illustration, if revenue is $720,000, the lease expense is $36,000 or $12,000 less than for a fixed lease.

Direct and Indirect Costs

In Chapter 3, certain expenses were called direct while other expenses were implied to be indirect. In the context of that discussion, we were talking about direct and indirect expenses as they pertained to the operating departments (profit centers) within a lodging establishment. In other words, the objects of direct/indirect expense were considered to be the operating departments that generate income and incur expenses such as the rooms department and the food and beverage department. We indicated that direct costs of the rooms department included payroll and related expenses, commissions, contract cleaning, guest transportation, laundry and dry cleaning, linen, operating supplies, reservations, uniforms, and other expenses as well. In this earlier context, we considered the undistributed operating expenses, management fees, fixed charges, and income taxes to be indirect (overhead) expenses.

However, depending on the object of the incurred expenses, many costs may be both direct and indirect costs. In general, a direct cost is one readily identified to an object, whereas an indirect cost is not readily identified to an object. Therefore, whether a cost is direct or indirect depends upon the context of the discussion and, in particular, on whether the object incurring the cost can be identified in the discussion's context. For instance, when speaking of the service center formed by the general manager's department, the general manager's salary can be ascribed as a direct cost of the service center and can be classified as a subset of administrative and general expense. However, in the context of discussing all operating departments (profit centers) and other service centers (e.g., the marketing department), the general manager's salary would be ascribed as an indirect cost of these other departments, because the object of this cost in those departments cannot be readily identified. This distinction is important because department heads are responsible for the direct costs of their departments since they exercise control over them; however, they are normally not responsible for indirect costs.

Overhead Costs

Overhead costs include all costs other than the direct cost of profit centers (operating departments). Thus, overhead costs are indirect costs when the cost objectives are the profit centers. Overhead costs include the undistributed operating expenses (administrative and general, data processing, human resources, transportation, marketing, guest entertainment, property operation and maintenance, and energy costs), management fees, fixed charges (insurance, rent, depreciation, interest, property taxes, etc.), and income taxes.

In the context of the discussion of the income statement in Chapter 3, overhead costs were not distributed to the profit centers. This is because these expenses were regarded as indirect costs, not readily ascribed to objects in the operating departments. However, management and the board of directors of a hospitality establishment may want overhead costs to be distributed to the profit centers. This process is commonly called cost allocation.

Allocation of Overhead Costs

The appendix to this chapter discusses and illustrates advanced cost allocation approaches. For our purposes here, however, we will consider a more simplified cost allocation approach that allocates overhead costs using a single allocation base, such as square footage, and is referred to as the single allocation base approach (SABA). We will illustrate this approach by using the hypothetical Walters Motor Inn whose unallocated income statement for a typical month is shown in Exhibit 8.12.

Notice the monthly net income for the entire operation is $4,500 while the rooms and food and beverage departments have generated incomes of $34,000 and $14,500, respectively. The only overhead cost that will not be allocated among departments is income tax. All other costs will be allocated based on square footage.

The square footage of the rooms and food and beverage departments are 40,000 and 15,000 square feet, respectively. Therefore, overhead costs will be allocated as follows:

	Square Footage	%
Rooms	40,000	72.73%
Food and Beverage	15,000	27.27%
Total	55,000	100.00%

Exhibit 8.13 shows how the overhead costs are allocated, and Exhibit 8.14 shows the allocated income statement of the Walters Motor Inn. The rooms department's bottom line after cost allocation is $3,453, while the food and beverage department's bottom line is $3,047. If an allocation base, other than square footage, was used, there would have been different cost allocation amounts and, therefore, different departmental income reported after allocation. For example, the Walters Motor Inn employs 14 and 20 people in the rooms and food and beverage departments, respectively. If the SABA had used the number of employees in each department as the allocation base, the rooms department would absorb 41.18% of the overhead costs, and the food and beverage department would absorb 58.82%. The Walters Motor Inn allocated income statement would now appear in very abbreviated form as follows:

	Rooms	Food & Beverage	Total
Departmental Income	$34,000	$14,500	$48,500
Overhead Costs Allocated	17,296	24,704	42,000
Post Allocation Departmental Income	$16,704	$(10,204)	$ 6,500

The above figures show that a different allocation base results in different allocated amounts and, therefore, in different departmental incomes following allocation. Ideally, costs should be allocated based on

Exhibit 8.12   Sample Unallocated Income Statement

Unallocated Income Statement Walters Motor Inn			
	Rooms	Food & Beverage	Total
Revenue	$50,000	$50,000	$100,000
Cost of Sales	0	18,000	18,000
Payroll and Related Expenses	12,000	13,000	25,000
Other Direct Expenses	4,000	4,500	8,500
Total Expenses	16,000	35,500	51,500
Departmental Income	$34,000	$14,500	48,500
Undistributed Operating Expenses:			
Administrative & General			12,000
Marketing			3,000
Property Operation and Maintenance			2,000
Energy Costs			4,000
Total Income Before Fixed Charges			27,500
Insurance			3,000
Depreciation			18,000
			21,000
Income Before Income Taxes			6,500
Income Taxes			2,000
Net Income			$4,500

Note: Data processing, human resources, guest entertainment, and transportation expenses are insignificant and are not shown as separate cost centers.

their usage by the profit centers and the nature of the expense involved. For example, if the hotel is leased on a square footage basis, then square footage appears to be the suitable allocation base for the hotel's rent expense. However, since the general manager's role as "supervisor" is often his or her primary role in managing the hotel, the general manager's salary may be allocated based on the number of employees "supervised," or even payroll expense by department.

The above discussion suggests that a different allocation base be used to allocate different overhead costs among the various departments. This is referred to as the multiple allocation based approach (MABA). MABA is generally preferred to the single allocation based approach (SABA), because MABA allocates overhead costs on the basis of an observed relationship between the cost and the profit center. The appendix to this chapter contains a fairly thorough discussion of two multiple allocation base approaches.

Controllable Costs

In managing subordinates, managers should generally hold the subordinates responsible only for costs they can control. To expect

Exhibit 8.13   Overhead Costs

Overhead Cost Area (2)	Overhead Cost	Percentage		Amount (1)	
		Rooms	Food & Bev.	Rooms	Food & Bev.
A & G	$12,000	72.73%	27.27%	$ 8,728	$ 3,272
Marketing	3,000	72.73	27.27	2,182	818
POM	2,000	72.73	27.27	1,455	545
Energy Costs	4,000	72.73	27.27	2,909	1,091
Insurance	3,000	72.73	27.27	2,182	818
Depreciation	18,000	72.73	27.27	13,091	4,909
Total	$42,000			$30,547	$11,453

Overhead Costs
Walters Motor Inn

(1) All amounts are rounded to the nearest $1.
(2) A & G = administrative & general; POM = property operation and maintenance.

supervisors and department heads to control costs over which they are unable to exert influence seems counterproductive.

Control means to regulate, or to exercise judgment and authority. Control does not mean to eliminate, but to keep within predefined boundaries or limits. Therefore, controllable costs are costs over which a person is able to exercise judgment. For example, the food department manager may exert influence over food usage, personnel preparing and serving food, and supplies used in the production and service of food. Therefore, all of the related costs, that is, cost of food sold, payroll expense, and food and service supplies expense are controllable costs for the food department manager. On the other hand, the food department manager generally has no control over rent paid for the space occupied by the restaurant; so, to the food department manager, rent expense is uncontrollable. However, the board of directors is able to take action regarding the rent expense; therefore, from the board's perspective, rent is a controllable expense.

Several costs cannot be easily influenced or changed in the short run; therefore, these costs are often considered to be uncontrollable. However, these costs can be regulated over the long run, and from this perspective, they can be viewed as controllable. In general, all costs are controllable given (1) sufficient period of time, and (2) high enough level of "management."

The income statement is organized on a responsibility accounting basis. The direct expenses of each profit center are those controllable by the heads of the respective departments. For example, the food and beverage department manager has authority over (and can, therefore, control) the food and beverage cost of sales, payroll and related expenses

Exhibit 8.14   Sample Allocated Income Statement

Allocated Income Statement
Walters Motor Inn

	Rooms	Food & Beverage	Total
Revenue	$50,000	$50,000	$100,000
Cost of Sales	0	18,000	18,000
Payroll and Related Expenses	12,000	13,000	25,000
Other Direct Expenses	4,000	4,500	8,500
Total Expenses	16,000	35,000	51,500
Departmental Income	34,000	14,500	48,500
Allocated Overhead Costs:			
Administrative & General	8,728	3,272	12,000
Marketing	2,182	818	3,000
Property Operation and Maintenance	1,455	545	2,000
Energy Costs	2,909	1,091	4,000
Insurance	2,182	818	3,000
Depreciation	13,091	4,909	18,000
Total	30,547	11,453	42,000
Income Before Income Taxes	$3,453	$3,047	6,500
Income Taxes			2,000
Net Income			$4,500

of the food and beverage department, and other direct expenses of the food and beverage department.

Differential Costs

In decision-making, costs which differ between two alternatives are called differential costs. By focusing on differential costs, decision-makers can narrow the set of cost considerations to those that make a difference between two alternatives. For example, suppose management is considering the installation of a front office computer to replace two obsolete posting machines. In this situation, differential costs include the cost of the computer and any other costs associated with the new computer that differ from the costs involved in using the existing posting machines. Such costs might include labor, utilities, supplies, and insurance. Costs which remain the same between the two decisions are nondifferential and need not be considered in the decision process.

Relevant Costs

Relevant costs are costs which must be considered in a decision-making situation. Three major characteristics of relevant costs are that they must be differential, future, and quantifiable.

The differential characteristic (as discussed previously) demands that the cost between two or more alternatives be different. The future characteristic demands that the costs must not have already occurred, but must be incurred only after the decision is made. Finally, relevant costs must be quantifiable. The unquantifiable preference for Machine A over Machine B is generally not directly considered in the decision-making process. In order for any preference to be relevant to a decision, it should be quantified. The case of Happy Harry's situation of whether to purchase a new range for his food service operation provides a useful illustration of the concept of relevant costs.

Happy Harry, owner of Harry's Place, has been approached by a salesperson who is selling ranges. The salesperson wants to sell Happy Harry a new range and provides the following information:

Cost of new range	= $5,000
Estimated useful life of new range	= 6 years
Operating costs:	
Electricity	= $800 (annually)
Repairs	= $200 (annually)
Labor	= $10,000 (annually)
Est. salvage value at the end of 6 years	= $500

Happy Harry believes his present range, with a major repair job, should last for 6 years. In order to make a rational and informed decision, Happy Harry develops the following data:

Original cost of present range	= $2,000
Est. cost of required major repair of present range	= $1,200
Est. salvage value of present range now	= $300
Est. salvage value of present range at the end of 6 years	= $100
Operating costs of present range:	
Electricity	= $700 (annually)
Repairs	= $500 (annually)
Labor	= $10,000 (annually)

The relevant costs affecting Happy Harry's decision are listed in Exhibit 8.15. Each of these costs are relevant because they are differential, future, and quantifiable. The irrelevant costs fail to include one or more of these characteristics. The cost of the present range is irrelevant because it is not future, and the cost of labor is irrelevant because it is not differential. The process of selecting an alternative is discussed later in this chapter. Exhibit 8.15 simply portrays relevant costs.

Sunk Costs

A sunk cost is a past cost relating to a past decision. A sunk cost may be differential yet irrelevant, because it is not future. In the case of Happy

Harry's decision, the original cost of the old range, $2,000, is a sunk cost and, therefore, irrelevant to Harry's decision-making process.

In many decision-making situations management will review financial records to determine the net book value (cost less accumulated depreciation) of a fixed asset which is to be replaced. This suggests that many managers consider the net book value of a fixed asset, rather than its original cost, to be the sunk cost. However, from the author's perspective, both the original cost and the net book value are sunk costs.

The relevant cost regarding a fixed asset to be replaced is the asset's current value. The current $300 value of Happy Harry's old range and its projected value of $100 at the end of six years are both relevant costs since they meet the three requirements of a relevant cost.

Opportunity Costs

The cost of the best foregone opportunity in a decision-making situation is the opportunity cost. Opportunity costs are among the relevant cost considerations in decision-making situations. If the decision-making is rational, then the opportunity cost is less than the value associated with the outcome of the decision. For example, let's assume that $100,000 may be invested in one of three ways:

	Annual Return
XYZ Corporation Bonds	10%
ABC Company Preferred Stock	12
Uninsured Time Certificate of Deposit	9

For the purposes of this example, let's assume that all three alternatives involve the same amount of risk, that is, the degree of certainty of receiving the specified return is the same for all three investment choices. Further, assume that the ability of each investment to be converted into cash is generally the same for all three alternatives. Everything else being the same, the rational choice is to invest in ABC Company Preferred Stock. The best foregone opportunity is the investment in XYZ Corporation Bonds at 10%. Therefore, the opportunity costs associated with making the rational choice amount to $20,000 over two years ($100,000 x 10% x 2). The choice is a rational one because the return on the alternative selected (ABC Company Preferred Stock) of $24,000 exceeds the opportunity costs of $20,000. The potential return of 9% on the Uninsured Time Certificate of Deposit is not an opportunity cost since it is not the best foregone opportunity; however, it is a relevant cost since it is future, differential, and quantifiable.

Discretionary Costs

Discretionary costs are those costs which managers may choose to avoid during the short run; however, continued avoidance will generally cause problems for the hospitality operation. For example, during a

Exhibit 8.15   Relevant Costs — Happy Harry's

	Alternatives	
"Cost"	Buy New	Keep Old
Cost of new range	$5,000	—
Electricity (annually)	800	$ 700
Repairs (annually)	200	500
Salvage value of present range now	300	—
Salvage value of range (future – end of 6th year)	500	100
Major repair job	—	1,200

recession, educational seminars for executives and public relations advertising might be curtailed. There is generally no immediate impact on operations from these actions; however, if these programs continue to be curtailed into the future, then sales and various expenses may be seriously affected. Discretionary costs are often indirect costs in relation to the operating departments, and decisions to postpone them are typically made by the general manager of a hospitality operation.

Standard Costs

Standard costs are a forecast of what actual costs should be under projected conditions. These standards may serve as comparisons for control purposes and as evaluations of productivity. Normal standard costs are established on a unit basis. For example, standard recipe costs consider the planned cost of a food serving such as a dinner, or an a la carte item. Assume the standard cost for a dinner is $4.50. If 100 dinners are served, then the budgeted cost is $450 ($4.50 x 100). The actual food cost of $475 reveals a $25 variance. If the variance is significant, it is investigated to determine the probable cause(s) and corrective action is taken. (The comparison of budgeted and actual costs will be presented in more detail in Chapter 11 on operations budgeting.)

Decision-Making Situations

Many situations require management to make decisions in which they use the cost concepts presented in this chapter. Several of those decision-making situations are as follows:

1. Which piece of equipment should be purchased?

2. What prices should be set for the hospitality operation's goods and services?

3. Can the hospitality operation ever afford to sell goods and services below cost?

4. During what time periods of a day should the hospitality establishment remain open?

5. When should a seasonal resort close?

6. Which business segment of the hospitality operation should receive the largest amount of funds?

7. Where should the hospitality enterprise expand?

In determining answers to these and other cost-related questions, remember there is no one definitive model for evaluating costs. However, when applied correctly, the cost concepts presented in this chapter are useful in clarifying, and thereby helping to resolve, these problems.

Illustration of Relevant Costs in Management Decisions

The selection process used to purchase a micro-computer will illustrate the application of relevant costs to a decision-making situation. Suppose a hotel desires to purchase a new micro-computer to be used by the controller for planning purposes. Even though the controller should be more productive by utilizing the computer, his/her salary will not change because of the purchase. The costs associated with the purchase of either micro-computer #1 or micro-computer #2 are listed in Exhibit 8.16. Other information to consider includes:

1. Each computer is expected to have a useful life of five years, after which it would be considered completely worthless.

2. The different timing of costs that may be associated with each computer is ignored in this example, as well as any income tax implications. Because these matters affect capital purchases, they will be further discussed in Chapter 14 on capital budgeting.

3. The controller likes the appearance of computer #2 over #1; however, he/she is unable to place any value on this preference.

4. The value to the hotel of the controller's increased productivity is the same regardless of which micro-computer is purchased.

The irrelevant costs are the nondifferential ones which include electricity, supplies, and repairs. All other costs listed for the two computers are relevant, as they are future, differential, and quantifiable. The preference for micro-computer #2 over #1 by the controller is not directly considered since it has not been quantified. However, the controller's preference would become relevant if the difference in cost between the two machines is immaterial; in this situation, machine #2 would be selected due to this unquantified difference. The value of the controller's increased productivity has not been quantified since it is nondifferential between the two computers. In either case, the value to the hotel of this increase in productivity is expected to far exceed the cost

Exhibit 8.16   Illustration of Relevant Costs in Management Decisions

	Micro-computers	
	#1	#2
Costs – Hardware	$3,450	$4,250
Annual operating costs:		
Electricity	100	100
Supplies	200	200
Maintenance contract	200	100
Repairs (not covered by maintenance contract)	50	50
Software	2,000	1,800

of either computer. Exhibit 8.17 reveals a cost analysis useful in deciding which computer to purchase.

Based on the lowest cost alternative, micro-computer #1 would be selected. If the $100 difference between micro-computers #1 and #2 is considered immaterial, then micro-computer #2 most likely would be purchased due to the controller's unquantified preference of micro-computer #2 over #1.

Computerization

Cost analysis is perhaps one of the best uses for the personal computer. With the help of a spreadsheet program, not only can the cost analysis be performed, but "what if" situations can be examined. With cost analysis, any one of the methods described in this chapter can be used. Once the correct formulas are entered into the spreadsheet, it can be used over and over again. With the proper construction of a cost model, variances from month to month can be instantly determined. Variances can be identified by specific cost (e.g., food, room, or maintenance) for further analysis. It might take several hours a month to manually gather the cost information and perform the necessary calculations. With a spreadsheet program, this time can be reduced considerably. Even complex calculations like regression analysis can be done in a matter of seconds.

The "what if" calculations allow the manager to analyze costs and revenues under different circumstances. Exhibit 8.18 shows how a manager might use a "what if" model to determine the best rate to charge guests at a hotel in order to maximize profits. In the example, management made the following assumptions:

$$\text{Room Revenue} = \text{Available Rooms for Sale} \times \text{Average Rate} \times \text{Projected Occupancy}$$

$$\text{Room Variable Expenses} = \text{Available Rooms for Sale} \times \text{Projected Occupancy} \times \$8.40 \text{ per Room.}$$

$$\text{Room Profits} = \text{Room Revenue} - \text{Room Variable Expenses}$$

Exhibit 8.17 Cost Analysis Solution

	Cost Analysis		
		Micro-computers	
Relevant Cost		#1	#2
Hardware		$3,450	$4,250
Operating costs – maintenance contract for 5 years			
$200 x 5		1,000	—
$100 x 5		—	500
Software		2,000	1,800
Total cost		$6,450	$6,550

Management then copied these formulas so that they could see the results in a number of different situations. In this case, management projected that as the room rate increased, the occupancy decreased. However, the lower occupancy is offset by the increased total revenue. In the example, the rate of $52.50 represents the optimum combination of revenues and expenses.

"What if" models can be designed to have a high level of sophistication. For example, in the illustration above, the model could have reflected the effect that the different levels of occupancy would have on the food and beverage operations, telephone revenues, gift shop sales, and other profit centers.

Summary

Although the term "cost" is frequently used, this chapter highlighted the variety of definitions this term can have in the accounting world. In general, a cost as an expense is the reduction of an asset incurred with the intention of increasing revenues. Such costs include labor costs, cost of food sold, depreciation, and others.

There are many specific types of costs. A fixed cost is one which remains constant over a relevant range of operations for the short term. A variable cost is one which changes directly with the level of activity. Depreciation is usually considered a fixed expense, while cost of food sold is assumed to be a variable cost. Many costs are said to be mixed, which is a combination of fixed and variable elements. For example, telephone expense can be divided into a fixed portion (the cost of the system), and a variable portion (the cost of making calls).

Three methods of determining the relative amounts of fixed and variable elements of mixed costs were presented in this chapter. The simplest is the high/low two-point method which examines the change in cost between the periods of lowest and highest activity. A scatter diagram can be used to "eyeball" the relationship between all periods' activities and costs. Regression analysis, the most sophisticated method

Exhibit 8.18   Computer-Generated Rooms Department Rate Analysis

```
                        ROOM DEPARTMENT RATE ANALYSIS

AVAILABLE ROOMS FOR
    SALE              36,500    36,500    36,500    36,500    36,500    36,500

AVERAGE RATE          $40.00    $45.00    $47.50    $50.00    $52.50    $55.00

PROJECTED OCCUPANCY    77.5%     75.0%     72.5%     70.0%     65.0%     60.0%


Room Revenue       $1,131,500 $1,231,875 $1,256,969 $1,277,500 $1,245,563 $1,204,500
Room Variable Expenses 237,615   229,950   222,285   214,620   199,290   183,960
                   --------------------------------------------------------------
Room Profits          893,885 1,001,925 1,034,684 1,062,880 1,046,273 1,020,540
                   ==============================================================
```

addressed, uses equations to determine the appropriate fixed-variable relationship.

Several types of costs are important in decision-making situations. Differential costs are useful when comparing two or more options; they are the costs which are not identical among the various options. Relevant costs also must differ among options. In addition, relevant costs must be quantifiable, and take place in the future. Sunk costs are not considered in decision-making situations because they have already been incurred in the past.

Other costs include controllable and discretionary costs. Controllable costs are costs which can be regulated. The rooms department expenses are controllable by the rooms manager. All costs before management fees and fixed charges are generally considered to be controllable by the general manager. Discretionary costs are controllable and can be avoided in times of financial difficulty. However, it is important to realize that avoiding these expenses can prove detrimental in the long run.

Understanding the relationships among the different types of costs can be very beneficial to a hospitality manager. Different purchase or lease options can be more easily analyzed, operations can be monitored against standards, and costs can be broken into their fixed and variable portions in order to forecast future costs.

Discussion Questions

1. What are some of the different meanings of "cost"?

2. What is the difference between overhead costs and indirect costs?

3. What is an opportunity cost?

4. What technique offers the most accurate method of determining the fixed and variable elements of a mixed cost? Explain.

5. What are the two definitions concerning sunk costs?

6. Which hotel costs are fixed in the short run? the long run?

7. Why would you consider allocating costs to the profit centers?

8. How are relevant costs defined? What is an indirect cost? Give an example.

9. Why are differential costs considered in a decision-making situation?

Problem 8.1

The following monthly income statement had been prepared by Dwayne Kris, CPA, for Troy Caballo, the owner of the Caballo Inn. As Mr. Caballo's private consultant, you are to explain several different cost relationships listed under "Required" below.

Income Statement
Caballo Inn
For the month ended January 31, 19X1

	Net Revenues	Cost of Sales	Payroll and Related Exp.	Other Expenses	Income (Loss)
Rooms	$105,430	$ -0-	$20,000	$ 1,450	$ 83,980
Food	52,400	18,864	15,000	1,000	17,536
Beverage	26,720	6,680	10,000	12,400	(2,360)
Other	4,000	-0-	-0-	-0-	4,000
	$188,550	$25,544	$45,000	$14,850	103,156

Undistributed Operating Expenses:	
Administrative and General	16,720
Data Processing	4,170
Marketing	3,400
Property Operation and Maintenance	5,080
Energy Costs	15,400
Income Before Fixed Charges	58,386
Rent	5,400
Property Taxes	1,220
Insurance	2,000
Interest	3,330
Depreciation	5,500
Income Before Income Taxes	40,936
Income Taxes	15,136
Net Income	$25,800

Required:

1. What are the direct expenses of the rooms department?

2. What is the total of the overhead expenses for the period?

3. Which costs are considered controllable by the general manager or people under his/her supervision?

4. Which costs are considered to be fixed costs?

5. What is the nature of cost of sales?

Problem 8.2

Paul Jones is considering replacing Jones & Smith's dishwasher with an energy-efficient one. Although the old one has a present book value of $2,000, it could only be sold now for $1,500 or, if held for five more years, it could be sold for $500. If Paul decides not to buy the new machine, approximately $300 of repairs must be incurred now on the present dishwasher. The following is a schedule of expected annual expenses for the next five years for each option:

	Options	
	Keep Present Dishwasher	Buy New Dishwasher
Maintenance	$300	$ 100
Labor	9,000	9,000
Energy	700	500
Water	300	300

The new machine would cost $3,450 and is expected to have a salvage value of $1,000 at the end of the five years.

Required:

1. Which costs are sunk?

2. Which costs are irrelevant?

3. What decision should Paul make? (Support your decision with numbers based on the above.)

Problem 8.3

Veronica Jackson desires to analyze labor costs in her restaurant operations. She has the operating statistics for the previous year and has asked for your assistance.

	Customers	Labor Costs
January	4,000	$15,500
February	2,400	10,450
March	3,700	18,500
April	4,450	19,000
May	4,400	19,000
June	4,800	20,250
July	5,000	20,500
August	3,900	18,500
September	3,800	18,000
October	3,100	15,500
November	2,900	15,250
December	3,000	16,650

Required:

1. Using the high-low two-point method, determine the monthly amount of fixed labor costs for Ms. Jackson.

2. What is the variable labor per customer served at Ms. Jackson's restaurant based on the high/low two-point method?

Problem 8.4

Tanya Daniels has been successfully operating her restaurant, The Lions Den, for the past five years. She has to renegotiate her lease and has two options available to her. She can either sign for a $3,000 per month fixed charge or a 5% of revenue variable expense. She has completed next year's budget to "Income Before Lease Expense" and expects annual sales of $1,000,000.

Required:

1. What is the indifference point (annual sales) for these lease options?

2. Which option should Ms. Daniels choose? Why?

Problem 8.5

Tammy's Motor Inn has been open for five months, and Tammy Weaver, the general manager, is conducting some cost analysis. She has not yet determined the amount of fixed and variable expenses the inn is incurring.

The following is a summary of the number of rooms sold and the expenses incurred each month.

	Number of Rooms	Costs
June	3,488	$122,319
July	3,842	128,940
August	3,584	124,320
September	3,333	119,431
October	3,261	117,642

Required:

1. Using regression analysis, determine the fixed cost per month for Tammy's Motor Inn.

2. What is the variable cost per room?

3. If Tammy's Motor Inn expects to sell 3,666 rooms in January of the next year, what are the fixed costs, total variable costs, and total expenses?

Supplemental Reading
Should overhead costs be allocated?*

One of a Series Sponsored by AH&MA's Financial Management Committee
By A. Neal Geller and Raymond S. Schmidgall

Overhead costs are not allocated to profit centers under the *Uniform System of Accounts for Hotels* (USAH). The most recent USAH briefly discusses methods and bases for allocation but neither prescribes nor illustrates the process. The allocation process is fairly complex, and is not well understood by the lodging industry. This article, therefore, has two purposes:

1)   to discuss the advantages and drawbacks of allocation and
2)   to illustrate cost allocation.

Cost allocation is the assignment of overhead costs to operated departments according to benefits received, responsibilities, or other logical measures of use. Such overhead costs as the general manager's salary are spread across profit centers such as rooms and food and beverages.

Please refer at this point to the glossary of terms in Exhibit 1.

Advantages of allocation

The major advantage of cost allocation is that it results in better decision-making by the general and departmental managers. These decisions are improved when based on fully allocated income statements:

PRICING. Pricing is best accomplished when the full costs of an operated department are known.

MARKETING. Management can best determine which services to emphasize after the full costs of each operated department are realized.

***

Dr. A. Neal Geller, *associate professor, School of Hotel Administration, Cornell University, teaches accounting and financial management. His bachelor's and master's degrees are from Cornell, his doctorate, from Syracuse University. Dr. Geller has extensive experience in hotel management, including corporate finance. His consulting work involves financial analysis and planning.*

Dr. Raymond S. Schmidgall *teaches accounting and finance at Michigan State University's department of Hotel, Restaurant and Institutional Management. He is a Certified Public Accountant, a Ph.D. in accounting, a member of AH&MA's Financial Management Committee (as is Neal Geller) and a consultant in accounting and finance.*

CHANGES IN CAPACITY. Expansion or reduction in the capacity of the hotel/motel operation should be based on the profit potential (net of indirect costs) of the operating departments.

STAFFING. More judicious staffing decisions are possible with the full cost of each operated department known to management. In addition, cost allocation provides department heads with more realistic assessments of overhead costs their departments must cover. Without the benefit of fully-allocated income statements, a rooms department manager, for example, may not understand why a 70% contribution from the rooms department is imperative for the firm to realize a profit.

EXHIBIT 1

Glossary of Terms

Cost Center: An area of responsibility for which costs are accumulated; based on costs only and not revenues e.g. the marketing department.

Fixed Charges: Expenses that relate to the capacity of the operation. These include rent, interest, property taxes, insurance, depreciation and amortization. (See page 16, *USAH*)

Indirect Costs: All undistributed operating expenses *and* fixed charges. (See page 16, *USAH*)

Operated Departments: Departments that generate revenue and incur expenses. These include rooms, food & beverage, casino, telephone, etc.

Overhead Costs: Another term commonly used for indirect costs.

Profit Center: Another term commonly used for operated department.

Service Center: A department in a hotel that provides services to other departments. Examples are accounting, payroll, credit, and personnel.

Undistributed Operating Expenses: Operating expenses incurred for the benefit of the operated departments. These traditionally have not been allocated to the operated departments. They include the general categories of administrative and general, marketing, guest entertainment, and property operation, maintenance and energy costs. (See page 16, *USAH*)

Finally, fully-allocated income statements are useful in dealing with government regulations. They provide better information for wage-and-price guidelines, government per-diem rates and general lobbying efforts.

Drawbacks of allocation

The major drawbacks of cost allocation relate primarily to the managers of operated departments and to misunderstandings as to its use. For example:

- Department heads may not understand the process and may resist it.
- Department heads may defer discretionary costs such as repairs, or otherwise strive to achieve short-run profitability at the expense of the long-run profitability of the company.
- Fully-allocated department statements are not appropriate for performance evaluation.

The effects of these drawbacks will be minimized if top-level management will do the following:

1. Explain completely the process of cost allocation and emphasize the benefits to the hotel/motel (or company).
2. Emphasize the importance of management for the long-term rather than focusing all the attention on the current period.
3. Separate department costs in fully-allocated statements between direct and indirect. Further, separate the indirect costs between "controllable by department head"—if any—and "beyond the control of the department head."
4. Stress a team approach to managing the various profit and cost centers of the hotel/motel operation.

Bases of allocation

The USAH contains several suggested bases for cost allocation as you will see in Exhibit 2. A cost allocation base is a factor that determines how much is allocated to a cost objective (department). For example, the rent expense of a hotel may be allocated on the basis of square footage of each department. If the rent expense is $10,000 for the period and the square footage of the rooms and food departments are 18,000 and 6,000 square feet respectively, then 75% ($7,500) would be allocated to the rooms department and 25% ($2,500) to the food department.

It is important to note that the allocation bases should be chosen separately from the allocation method used. While the rent may be allocated to operated departments as shown in the above example, or indirectly through the service centers, the allocation base can be the same. (Again, note Exhibit 2.)

Methods of allocation

The allocation method determines the degree of directness in allocating indirect costs from their cost centers to the profit centers. The three methods listed in USAH are diagrammed and discussed briefly here.

The direct method (see Exhibit 3) results in all indirect costs flowing directly from the cost centers to the profit centers. With this approach, no portion of fixed cost is allocated to service centers. The direct method is simple and easily understood.

The step method (see Exhibit 4) requires a two step allocation process. First, fixed costs are allocated to the profit and service centers. Second, the costs of service centers, including the allocated fixed costs, are allocated to the profit centers. In the second step, the costs of the service centers providing the most services to the other service centers are allocated first.

Once a service center's costs are allocated, no additional costs are allocated to this service center. The step method does not consider the reciprocal provision of services among other service centers. The formula method incorporates this additional refinement. The step method is more realistic than the direct method because it recognizes services provided by some service centers to others.

The formula method also requires two steps in the allocation process (See Exhibit 5). The first step—the allocation of fixed costs—is the same as under the step method. The second step gives full consideration for services rendered by service centers to each other. The second step is generally complex and requires mathematical computations best performed by a computer.

Illustration of allocation

The direct and step methods of cost allocation are illustrated here by using Walters Motor

EXHIBIT 2

Suggested Allocation Bases

ALLOCATED COSTS	ALLOCATION BASES
Rent	1. Percentage applicable to revenue sources 2. Square feet of area occupied (fixed rent)
Real estate taxes	Square feet of area occupied
Insurance—building and contents	1. Square feet of area occupied 2. Square feet plus investment in furniture and fixtures
Interest	Same as insurance
Depreciation—building	Square feet of area occupied
Depreciation—furniture and fixtures	1. Department asset records 2. Square feet of area occupied
Telephone	Number of extensions
Payroll taxes and employee benefits	1. Number of employees 2. Detailed payroll
Administrative and general:	
Executive office	Number of employees
Accounting and control	1. Accumulated costs 2. Number of employees
Security	Square feet of area occupied
Marketing	Ratio to sales
Energy costs	Cubic feet of area occupied
Property operation and maintenance	1. Job orders 2. Square feet of area occupied

Source: *Uniform System of Accounts for Hotels (Seventh Edition)* p. 127.

Inn. The formula method is not illustrated because it is beyond the scope of this article.

The Walters Motor Inn is a 70-room property with food and beverage operations. It uses the *Uniform System of Accounts for Hotels*. To simplify the illustrations, we have included only three undistributed operating expense categories and two fixed charge categories. The Inn's income statement for March, developed in accordance with the USAH, is shown in Exhibit 6. Note that

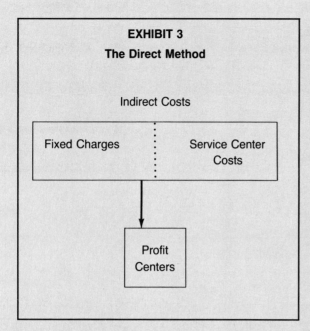

EXHIBIT 3

The Direct Method

Indirect Costs

Fixed Charges · Service Center Costs

Profit Centers

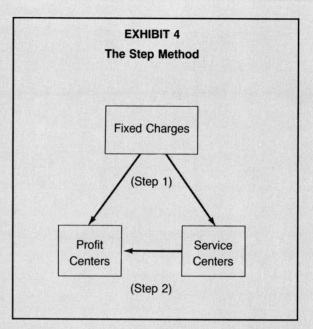

EXHIBIT 4

The Step Method

Fixed Charges

(Step 1)

Profit Centers ← Service Centers

(Step 2)

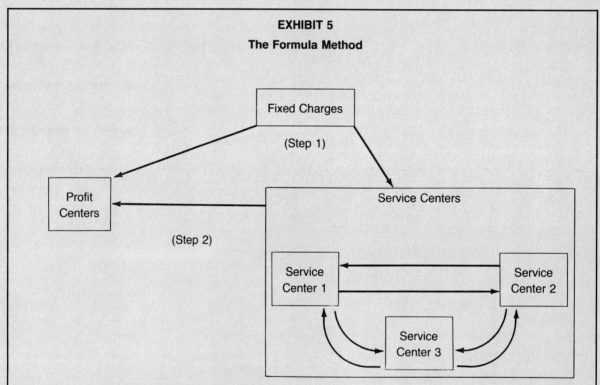

EXHIBIT 5

The Formula Method

Fixed Charges

(Step 1)

Profit Centers

(Step 2)

Service Centers

Service Center 1

Service Center 2

Service Center 3

the indirect expenses have not been allocated to the profit centers so that the rooms and food and beverage departmental incomes, prior to cost allocation, are $34,000 and $14,500 respectively.

Regardless of the allocation method used, a cost allocation base must be selected for each indirect cost. The indirect expenses and the allocation bases selected for cost allocation of the Walters Motor Inn's indirect expenses are shown in Exhibit 6-A.

The bases selected were chosen on recommendations from the USAH. The notable excep-

EXHIBIT 6

Unallocated Income Statement, Walters Motor Inn for the Month of March

	Rooms	Food & Beverage	Total
Revenue	$50,000	$50,000	$100,000
Cost of Sales	-0-	18,000	18,000
Payroll and Related Expenses	12,000	13,000	25,000
Other Direct Expenses	4,000	4,500	8,500
Total Expenses	16,000	35,500	51,500
Departmental Income (Loss)	$34,000	$14,500	48,500

	Payable Related	Other	
Undistributed Operating Expenses:			
Administrative & General (A & G)	$10,000	$2,000	12,000
Marketing	2,000	1,000	3,000
Property Operation, Maintenance and Energy Costs (POM & EC)	2,000	4,000	6,000
Total Income Before Fixed Charges			27,500
Insurance			3,000
Depreciation			18,000
			21,000
Income Before Income Taxes			6,500
Income Taxes			2,000
Net Income			$ 4,500

EXHIBIT 6-A

Indirect Expenses	Bases
Insurance	Book value of fixed assets (BV-FA)
Depreciation	Square footage (SF)
POM & EC	Square footage (SF)
Marketing	Ratio to sales (RS)
A & G	Number of employees (NE)

EXHIBIT 6-B

Department	Book Value of Fixed Assets	Square Footage	Number of Employees
Rooms	$900,000	40,000	14
Food & Beverage	300,000	15,000	20
A & G	50,000	2,500	4
Marketing	30,000	500	1
POM & EC	220,000	2,000	1

tion is Property Operation & Maintenance and Energy Costs. To simplify the illustrations, these two costs (POM and EC) were combined and allocated using one of the recommended bases for property operation and maintenance. The information required to establish the allocation bases for the Walters Motor Inn is shown in Exhibit 6-B.

Illustration of direct method

The direct method of cost allocation is accomplished by allocating all indirect expenses to the profit centers and then preparing the fully-allocated income statement. For the Walters Motor Inn, four bases of allocation are used.

The base for allocating the Inn's insurance is the book value of fixed assets of the rooms and food and beverage departments. The total book value-fixed assets for the two profit centers is $1.2 million of which $900,000 pertains to the rooms and $300,000 pertains to the food and beverage department. Since the book value-fixed assets of

---

EXHIBIT 7

Allocation of Costs—Direct Method

Expense to be Allocated	Amount to be Allocated	Allocation Base	Proportion to		Amounts Allocated to	
			Rooms	Food & Beverage	Rooms	Food & Beverage
Insurance	$ 3,000	BV-FA	.7500	.2500	$ 2,250	$ 750
Depreciation	18,000	SF	.7273	.2727	13,091	4,909
POM & EC	6,000	SF	.7273	.2727	4,364	1,636
Marketing	3,000	RS	.5000	.5000	1,500	1,500
A & G	12,000	NE	.4118	.5882	4,942	7,058
TOTAL	$42,000				$26,147	$15,853

EXHIBIT 8

Fully Allocated Income Statement—Walters Motor Inn Direct Method—For the Month of March

	Rooms	Food & Beverage	Total
Revenue	$50,000	$ 50,000	$100,000
Cost of Sales	-0-	18,000	18,000
Payroll and Related Expenses	12,000	13,000	25,000
Other Direct Expenses	4,000	4,500	8,500
	16,000	35,000	51,500
Departmental Income	34,000	14,500	48,500
Allocated Expenses (from Exhibit 7)	26,147	15,853	42,000
Departmental Income (loss) after Allocation	$ 7,853	$ (1,353)	6,500
Income Taxes			2,000
Net Income			$ 4,500

---

the rooms department is 75% of the combined book value-fixed assets for the two departments ($900,000 divided by $1,200,000), the rooms department is allocated $2,250 of the insurance expenses (.75 x $3,000).

The proportions of other indirect expenses and amounts allocated to the rooms and food and beverage departments were determined in similar fashion using the selected base of allocation as noted previously. Exhibit 7 contains the indirect costs, the amount to be allocated, the allocation base, the proportions to be allocated to rooms and food and beverage, and the amounts allocated to these two departments.

Exhibit 8 contains the fully-allocated income statement. Under this method, the rooms depart-

ment income after allocation is $7,853 while the food and beverage department loss after allocation is ($1,353). Note that income taxes are not allocated to profit centers.

Illustration of step method

The step method of allocation requires two steps:

1. Allocate fixed charges to service centers and profit centers, and,
2. Allocate service center expenses to profit centers.

EXHIBIT 9

Service and Profit Centers	BV-FA	Insurance Proportionate Share of BV-FA	Square Feet	Depreciation Proportionate Share of Sq. Ft.
Rooms	$ 900,000	.6000	40,000	.6667
Food & Beverage	300,000	.2000	15,000	.2500
A & G	50,000	.0333	2,500	.0417
Marketing	30,000	.0200	500	.0083
POM & EC	220,000	.1467	2,000	.0333
TOTAL	$1,500,000	1.0000	60,000	1.0000

EXHIBIT 10

Step 1: Allocation of Fixed Charges to Profit Centers and Service Charges

Fixed Charge	Total Amount	Allocated to Rooms	F&B	A&G	Marketing	POM&EC
Insurance	$ 3,000	$ 1,800	$ 600	$100	$ 60	$ 440
Depreciation	18,000	12,000	4,500	750	150	600
TOTAL	$21,000	$13,800	$5,100	$850	$210	$1,040

Following these steps, the fully-allocated income statement is prepared.

The bases for allocating indirect expenses of the Walters Motor Inn were the same as used to illustrate allocation by the direct method. The difference under the step method is that part of the indirect expenses was first allocated to service centers. Thus, in determining the proportionate share of a base for each cost objective, one must consider both the amounts pertaining to profit centers and to service centers.

The two fixed charges to be allocated are insurance and depreciation. The ratios used to allocate these expenses were calculated as shown in Exhibit 9. Using the ratios thus calculated, the fixed charges were allocated as shown in Exhibit 10.

In step 2, the service center expenses plus the fixed charges allocated to the service centers were allocated to the profit centers. A portion of these new totals was allocated directly to the profit centers with the remaining portion allocated in an established sequence to the service centers until all indirect expenses were allocated to the two profit centers.

Step 2 of the cost allocation of the Walters Motor Inn was accomplished by allocating Administrative and General expenses, Property Operation/Maintenance expenses, Energy Costs, and Marketing expenses. The order is specified on the basis of service centers serving the largest number of service centers.

The Administrative and General expenses to be allocated in Step 2 total $12,850—$12,000 from the unallocated income statement plus $850 of fixed charges allocated in Step 1. Using the number of employees as the allocation base, the $12,850 was allocated to the two remaining service centers and two profit centers as shown in Exhibit 11.

Property Operation/Maintenance and Energy Costs are allocated next under Step 2. The total to be allocated is $7,397. This is the sum of $6,000 from the unallocated income statement, $1,040 from Step 1, and $357 from Administrative and General. The total was allocated to the marketing department and the two profit centers on

EXHIBIT 11

Department	Number of Employees	Proportioned Share of Total Employees	Amount Allocated
Rooms	14	.3889	$ 4,998
Food & Beverage	20	.5555	7,138
POM & EC	1	.0278	357
Marketing	1	.0278	357
TOTAL	36	1.0000	$12,850

EXHIBIT 12

Department	Square Feet	Proportioned Share of Square Footage	Amount Allocated
Rooms	40,000	.7207	$5,331
Food & Beverage	15,000	.2703	1,999
Marketing	500	.0090	67
TOTAL	55,000	1.0000	$7,397

EXHIBIT 13

Step 2: Allocation of Expenses from Service Centers to Profit Centers

	Service Centers			Profit Centers	
	A&G	POM&EC	Marketing	Rooms	Food & Beverage
Unallocated service center costs	$ 12,000	$ 6,000	$ 3,000	$ -0-	$ -0-
Allocated per Step 1	850	1,040	210	13,800	5,100
Costs to be allocated	12,850	7,040	3,210		
A & G	(12,850)	357	357	4,998	7,138
	$ -0-	7,397			
POM & EC		(7,397)	67	5,331	1,999
		$ -0-	3,634		
Marketing			(3,634)	1,817	1,817
TOTAL			$ -0-	$25,946	$16,054

the basis of square footage. The proportionate share and amounts of Property Operation/Maintenance and Energy Costs were calculated as shown in Exhibit 12.

Lastly, the Marketing expense was allocated to the two profit centers on the basis of ratio to sales. Therefore, the total Marketing expense of $3,634 ($3,000 from the unallocated income statement, $210 from Step 1, $357 from Administrative and General, and $67 from Property Operation/Maintenance and Energy Costs) was allocated $1,817 and $1,817 to the food and beverage department. Exhibit 13 shows the step down process (Step 2) of the step method.

The fully-allocated income statement under the step method of cost allocation is shown in

EXHIBIT 14

Fully Allocated Income Statement, Walters Motor Inn
Step Method—For the Month of March

	Rooms	Food & Beverage	Total
Revenue	$50,000	$ 50,000	$100,000
	-----------	-----------	-----------
Cost of Sales	-0-	$ 18,000	$ 18,000
Payroll and Related Expenses	$12,000	13,000	25,000
Other Direct Expenses	4,000	4,500	8,500
	$16,000	$ 35,500	$ 51,500
Departmental Income	$34,000	$ 14,500	$ 48,500
Allocated Expenses (from Exhibit 10)	25,946	16,054	42,000
Departmental Income (loss) after Allocation	$ 8,054	$(1,554)	6,500
Income Taxes			2,000
Net Income			$ 4,500

Exhibit 14. After cost allocation, the rooms department income is $8,054 while the food and beverage department shows a loss of ($1,554).

Conclusion

The precision offered by the allocation procedures discussed and illustrated here increases from the direct to the step methods. So does the cost of preparation.

The decision to use a more sophisticated cost-allocation method must be made following a cost-benefit analysis. Hotel management must determine the value of the more precise information.

Cost allocation is an attention-getting tool. It should not lead to hasty decisions. The results raise a number of questions for management; among them:

— What action should be taken if the departmental income after allocation is negative?
— Should a department's services be cur-
tailed if a loss is shown after a full allocation?
— Should advertising for a department's services be increased if a loss is shown after full allocation?

Management decisions should be made only after careful cost-benefit analysis. Allocation of indirect costs allows management to make such decisions in a more informed and accurate manner.

REFERENCES

Cost Allocation under the Uniform System of Accounts. Cornell Hotel and Restaurant Quarterly. November, 1980 issue. Cornell University, School of Hotel Administration.

Notes

*This article is reprinted with permission from *Lodging*, July 1981, pp. 36-41.

9 Cost-Volume-Profit Analysis

Cost-Volume-Profit (CVP) analysis is a set of analytical tools used to determine the revenue required at any desired profit level. Many businesspeople refer to CVP analysis as a breakeven analysis. However, the breakeven point of a firm is only one point among an infinite number of possible points that can be determined. When properly used, CVP analysis provides useful information about the structure of operations and answers many types of questions such as:

1. What is the breakeven point?

2. What is the profit at 79% occupancy, or any other occupancy level above the breakeven point?

3. How will a $50,000 increase in property taxes next year affect the sales breakeven point?

4. How much must rooms sales increase next year to cover the increase in property taxes and/or other expenses and still achieve the desired profit?

5. How many rooms must be sold to achieve a $100,000 profit?

6. What is the effect on profit if prices increase X%, if variable costs increase X%, or if fixed costs increase X%?

This chapter begins with a definition of CVP analysis followed by a clarification of both the assumptions of the CVP model and the limitations of CVP as an analytical tool. Next, we will describe the relationships depicted in the CVP model, namely the relationships among revenues, variable costs, and fixed costs. We will then illustrate CVP analysis by discussing both the simple situation of a single product offering and the more complex multiple product situation. We will also discuss the effects of income taxes within the CVP model and modify the basic model to more adequately reflect cash flow considerations. Finally, we will consider the topic of the relative mix of fixed and variable costs through a discussion of operating leverage.

CVP Analysis Defined

CVP analysis is a management tool used in decision-making. This tool expresses the relationships among various costs, sales volume, and profits in either graphic or equation form. The graphs or equations assist management in making decisions. A simple example may be used to illustrate this process.

Assume the manager of the Red Cedar Inn, a 10-room motel, would like to know what price must be charged in order to make a profit of $2,000 in a 30-day period. The available information is as follows:

- Variable costs per room sold equal $5.

- If the average price is between $20 and $25, 250 rooms can be sold.

- Fixed costs for a 30-day period are $2,500.

Given these three pieces of information, CVP analysis is able to calculate that the selling price must average $23 in order to attain the goal of a $2,000 profit in a 30-day period. This selling price is determined on the basis of the CVP model by working through the calculations of the following formula:

$$\frac{\text{Selling}}{\text{Price}} = \frac{\text{Variable Costs}}{\text{per Room}} + \frac{\text{Desired Profit} + \text{Fixed Costs}}{\text{Number of Rooms to be Sold}}$$

$$\frac{\text{Selling}}{\text{Price}} = 5 + \frac{2,000 + 2,500}{250}$$

$$\frac{\text{Selling}}{\text{Price}} = 5 + 18$$

$$\frac{\text{Selling}}{\text{Price}} = \$23$$

Since the selling price of $23 suggested by the CVP analysis is within the range of $20 to $25 required to sell the specified number of rooms, the manager will be able to reach the desired goal of a $2,000 profit in 30 days by establishing the price at $23. The Red Cedar Inn's summarized operations budget for the 30-day period is as follows:

Room sales (250 x $23)		$5750
Variable costs (250 x 5)	$1250	
Fixed costs	2500	3750
Profit		$2000

CVP Assumptions and Limitations

CVP analysis, like all mathematical models, is based on several assumptions. When these assumptions do not hold in the actual situations to which the model is applied, then the results of CVP analysis will be suspect. The most common assumptions are as follows:

1. Fixed costs remain fixed during the period being considered. Over time, fixed costs do change; however, it is reasonable to assume fixed costs remain constant over a short time span.

2. Variable costs fluctuate in a linear fashion with revenue during the period under consideration. That is, if revenue increases X%, variable costs also increase X%.

3. Revenues are directly proportional to volume. As unit sales increase by X%, then revenues increase by X%.

4. Mixed costs can be properly divided into their fixed and variable elements. (Several methods to accomplish this task were presented in Chapter 8.)

5. All costs can be assigned to individual operated departments. This assumption limits the ability of CVP analysis to consider joint costs. These are costs which simultaneously benefit two or more operated departments. Joint costs, or a portion thereof, are not eliminated by discontinuing the offering of services such as food, beverage, telephone, etc. Therefore, for the purposes of CVP analysis, joint costs cannot be assigned to individual operated departments. Because of the existence of joint costs, the breakeven point cannot be determined by operated department; but, of course, it can still be determined for the entire operation.

6. The CVP model considers only quantitative factors. Qualitative factors such as employee morale, guest goodwill, etc., are not considered in the CVP analysis; thus, management must carefully consider these qualitative factors prior to making any final decisions.

CVP Relationships

The cost-volume-profit relationships, depicted in CVP equations and graphs, consist of fixed costs, variable costs, and revenues. CVP analysis considers fixed costs to remain constant for the period under consideration. This relationship between fixed costs and levels of sales activity was depicted in Exhibit 8.1 of Chapter 8. Variable costs are assumed to change proportionately with sales; therefore, if sales increase X%, variable costs also increase X%. This relationship was depicted in Exhibit 8.3 of Chapter 8. Finally, CVP analysis considers revenues to increase proportionately with sales; thus, as unit sales increase by X%, revenue increases by X%. This relationship is shown in Exhibit 9.1.

The three elements (fixed costs, variable costs, and revenues) are brought together and their relationships to volume and profits graphically illustrated in Exhibit 9.2. The CVP graph shows dollars on the vertical axis and volume (rooms sales) on the horizontal axis. The fixed cost line is parallel to the horizontal axis from point A. Thus, the amount of the fixed costs would equal the theoretical loss the hospitality operation would suffer if no sales took place. The variable cost line is the broken straight line from point O. This suggests that there are no variable costs when there are no sales and the straight line suggests that variable costs change proportionately with sales. The sum of variable costs and fixed costs equals total costs. The total cost line is drawn from Point A parallel to the variable cost line. This suggests that total costs increase only as variable costs increase, and that variable costs increase only from increased sales.

The revenue line commences from Point O and reflects a linear relationship between revenue and units sold. Point B is the intersection of the total cost line and the revenue line. At Point B, revenues equal total costs which is the breakeven point. The vertical distance between the revenue line and the total cost line to the right of Point B represents

Exhibit 9.1 Graphic Depiction of Revenue

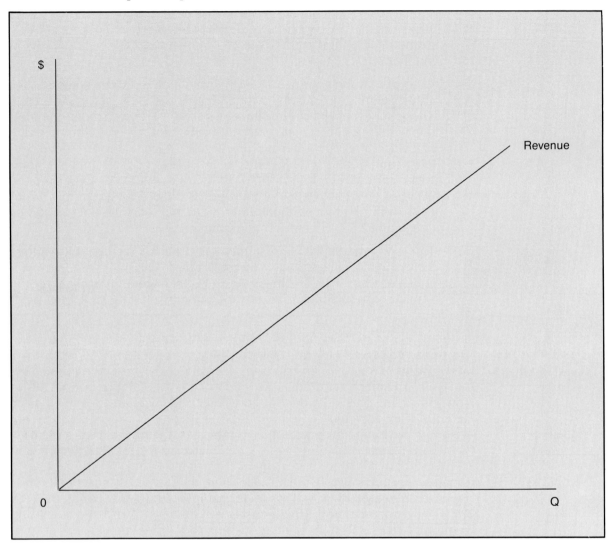

profit, while the vertical distance between these two lines to the left of Point B represents operating loss.

In this way, the CVP model shows the relationship of profit to sales volume and relates both to costs. As the volume of sales increases and reaches the point where the amount of revenue generated by those sales equals the total costs of generating them, then the hospitality operation arrives at its breakeven point. As the volume of sales further increases past the breakeven point, the amount of revenue generated by those sales increases at a faster rate than the costs associated with those sales. Thus, the growing difference between revenue and cost measures the increase of profit in relation to sales volume.

It is important to stress again that the CVP model of the relations of costs, sales volume, and profit is based entirely upon its assumptions about the relationship of costs and revenues to sales volume. Although both costs and revenues are assumed to increase in direct linear

Exhibit 9.2   Cost-Volume-Profit Graph

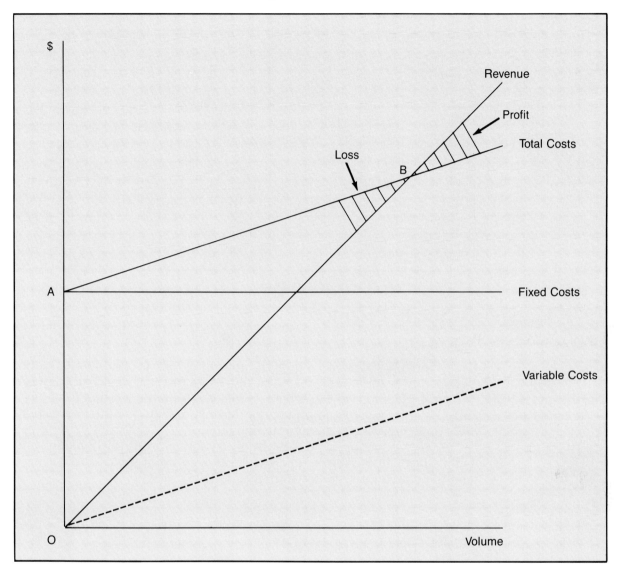

proportion to the increase of sales volume, revenues increase at a faster rate than costs. This is because the starting point for the growth of revenue, prior to any sales, is zero. Costs, on the other hand, begin their proportional growth in relation to sales volume (variable costs) from an already established minimum level required by any amount of sales (fixed costs). Hence, the growth rate of costs in relation to sales is slower than that of revenues. Both revenues and costs increase in proportion to sales, but they do so at different rates due to their different starting levels prior to any sales. It is because of this difference in growth rates of revenues and costs in relation to sales that they are bound to intersect and reach a balance (breakeven point) as sales increase.

Exhibit 9.3 Cost-Volume-Profit Analysis Equation —Single Product

A CVP analysis equation expresses the cost-volume-profit relationships as follows:

$$I_n = SX - VX - F$$

where: I_n = Net income
S = Selling price
X = Units sold
V = Variable cost per unit
F = Total fixed cost per unit

therefore: SX = Total revenue
VX = Total variable costs

CVP Equation—Single Product

("We do not use this")

Pg 301

The CVP graph, although appealing in its simplicity, is not sufficiently precise, and it is often time-consuming to construct a graph for each question to be solved using CVP analysis. Therefore, CVP analysis uses a series of equations that express the mathematical relationships depicted in the graphic model.

A CVP equation expresses the cost-volume-profit relationships and is illustrated in Exhibit 9.3. At the breakeven point, net income is zero and the equation is simply shown as follows:

$$0 = SX - VX - F$$

The equation may be rearranged to solve for any one of the four variables as follows:

		Equation	Determines
X	$=$	$\dfrac{F}{S - V}$	Units Sold at Breakeven
F	$=$	$SX - VX$	Fixed Costs at Breakeven
S	$=$	$\dfrac{F}{X} + V$	Selling Price at Breakeven
V	$=$	$S - \dfrac{F}{X}$	Variable Cost per Unit at Breakeven

This CVP equation assumes the sale of a single product type such as rooms or meals. Most hospitality firms sell a vast array of goods and services. However, before turning to this more complex situation, let's look at an illustration of this simple CVP analysis equation through the following question and answer example.

**CVP
Illustration—
Single Product**

The Michael Motel, a 30-room budget motel, has the following cost and price structure:

- Annual fixed costs equal $90,000.

- Average selling price per room is $20.

- Variable cost per room sold equals $8.

What is the number of rooms sales required for the Michael Motel to breakeven?

$$X = \frac{F}{S - V} \quad \text{(equation for units sold at breakeven)}$$

$$X = \frac{90,000}{20 - 8}$$

$$X = \underline{7,500} \text{ rooms}$$

Exhibit 9.4 depicts the breakeven point of the Michael Motel at 7,500 rooms. The total revenue at the breakeven point is shown as $150,000. Mathematically, it is the result of multiplying the selling price per room by the number of rooms sold which is 7,500 x $20 = $150,000.

What is the occupancy percentage at breakeven for the Michael Motel?

$$\text{Occupancy Percentage} = \frac{\text{Rooms Sold}}{\text{Rooms Available}}$$

$$\text{Occupancy Percentage} = \frac{7,500}{365 \times 30}$$

$$\text{Occupancy Percentage} = \frac{7,500}{10,950}$$

$$\text{Occupancy Percentage} = \underline{68.49\%}$$

If the proprietor desires the Michael Motel to earn $12,000 for the year, how many rooms must be sold?

$$X = \frac{F + I_n}{S - V} \quad \text{(equation for units sold at $12,000 profit level)}$$

$$X = \frac{90,000 + 12,000}{20 - 8}$$

$$X = \frac{102,000}{12}$$

$$X = \underline{8,500} \text{ rooms}$$

Therefore, for $12,000 to be earned in a year, the Michael Motel must sell 1,000 rooms beyond its breakeven point (8,500 − 7,500 = 1,000). The profit earned on these additional sales is the result of the selling price less

Exhibit 9.4   Breakeven Point — Michael Motel

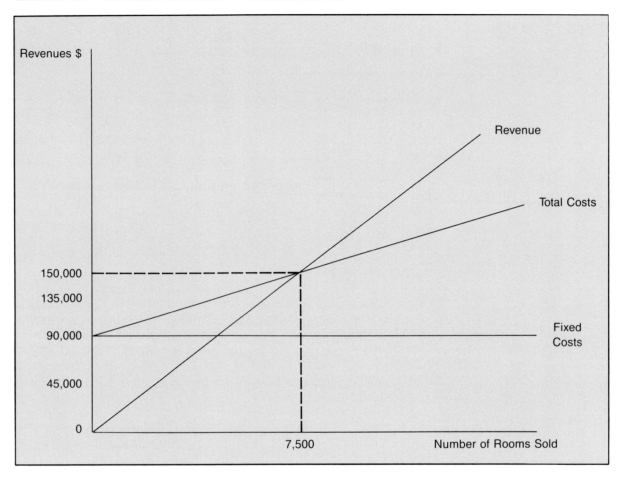

variable cost per room multiplied by the excess rooms (20 − 8 = 12; 12 x 1,000 = $12,000).

The difference between selling price and variable cost per unit is often called contribution margin (CM). In this example, the CM is $12—for each room sold, $12 is available to cover fixed costs or contribute towards profits. Beyond the breakeven point, 1,000 rooms sales resulted in a $12,000 profit (rooms sales beyond breakeven x CM = profit, thus: 1,000 x $12 = $12,000).

Exhibit 9.5 is a graphic depiction of the $12,000 of net income. When total revenue is $170,000 (8,500 x $20), expenses equal $158,000 (calculated by multiplying $8 by 8,500 and then adding $90,000), resulting in a $12,000 net income. The distance between the total revenue line and the total cost line at the 8,500 rooms point represents the net income of $12,000.

Likewise, if rooms sales are less than the 7,500 breakeven point, $12 (CM) is lost per room not sold. For example, we can calculate the loss for the year if the Michael Motel sells only 6,500 rooms. Based on the above information, the answer should be $12,000 (CM x rooms less than breakeven). Using the general formula, the proof is as follows:

Exhibit 9.5 $12,000 Net Income — Michael Motel

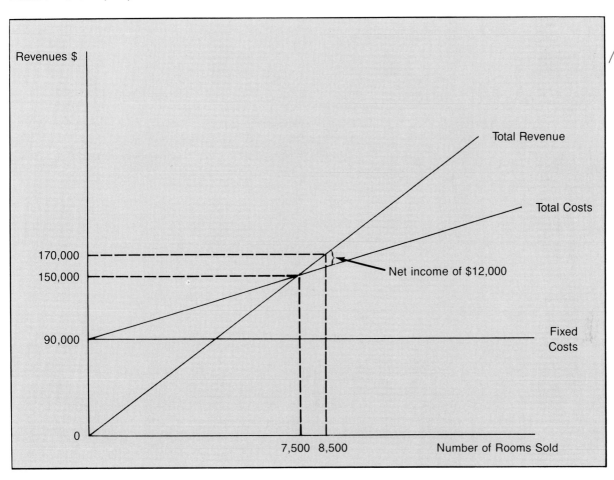

$$I_n = SX - VX - F \quad \text{(general formula)}$$
$$I_n = 20(6,500) - 8(6,500) - 90,000$$
$$I_n = 130,000 - 52,000 - 90,000$$
$$I_n = -\underline{\$12,000}$$

Thus, a loss of $12,000 would be incurred when rooms sales are only 6,500 for the year.

CVP Equation— Multiple Products

Many hospitality operations, especially hotels, sell more than just a single product. In order to determine the operation's breakeven point (or any profit level) using CVP analysis, a different CVP equation is required and is illustrated in Exhibit 9.6.

The contribution margin ratio (CMR) results from dividing CM by the selling price. Using the Michael Motel illustration, CMR is determined as follows:

$$CMR = \frac{CM}{S}$$

Exhibit 9.6 Cost-Volume-Profit Analysis Equation — Multiple Products

$$R = \frac{F + I_n}{CMR_w}$$

where F = Total fixed costs
I_n = Net income
R = Revenue at desired profit level
CMR_w = Weighted average contribution margin ratio

$$CMR = \frac{20 - 8}{20}$$

$$CMR = \frac{12}{20}$$

$$CMR = \underline{\underline{.6}}$$

The CMR means that for every $1 of sales for the Michael Motel, 60% is contributed toward fixed costs and/or profits. However, recall that in a multiple product situation, more than just rooms are being sold. Therefore, the CMR must be a weighted average CMR, that is, an average CMR for all operating departments but weighted to reflect the relative contribution of each department to the establishment's ability to pay fixed costs and/or generate profits. A CMR is determined for each operated department and the weighted average of the various CMRs is determined as illustrated in Exhibit 9.7.

To illustrate the calculation of CMR_w assume the Michael Motel adds a coffee shop. Exhibit 9.8 shows a partial income statement for the Michael Motel after the first year the coffee shop has been in operation. The CMR_w of .5 for the Michael Motel is determined as follows:

$$CMR_w = \frac{R_1}{TR} \times \frac{(R_1 - TV_1)}{R_1} + \frac{R_2}{TR} \times \frac{(R_2 - TV_2)}{R_2}$$

$$CMR_w = \frac{150{,}000}{200{,}000} \times \frac{(150{,}000 - 60{,}000)}{150{,}000} + \frac{50{,}000}{200{,}000} \times \frac{(50{,}000 - 40{,}000)}{50{,}000}$$

$$CMR_w = .75(.6) + .25(.2)$$

$$CMR_w = .45 + .05$$

$$CMR_w = \underline{\underline{.5}}$$

Alternatively, the CMR_w in this case could have been determined by using total revenues and total variable costs as follows:

Exhibit 9.7   Weighted Average Contribution Margin Ratio

$$CMR_w = \frac{R_1}{TR} \frac{(R_1 - TV_1)}{R_1} + \frac{R_2}{TR} \frac{(R_2 - TV_2)}{R_2} + \frac{R_3}{TR} \frac{(R_3 - TV_3)}{R_3}$$

$$\ldots\ldots + \frac{R_n}{TR} \frac{(R_n - TV_n)}{R_n}$$

where

R_1 = Revenue for operated department 1
R_2 = Revenue for operated department 2
R_3 = Revenue for operated department 3
R_n = Revenue for operated department n
TR = Total revenue
TV_1 = Total variable cost for operated department 1
TV_2 = Total variable cost for operated department 2
TV_3 = Total variable cost for operated department 3
TV_n = Total variable cost for operated department n

$$CMR_w = \frac{TR - TV}{TR}$$

$$CMR_w = \frac{200,000 - 100,000}{200,000}$$

$$CMR_w = \underline{\underline{.5}}$$

CVP Illustration— Multiple Products   The following series of questions and answers uses the Michael Motel to illustrate how the CVP calculations are used to analyze profit levels, sales mix, and breakeven points in the more complex, and also more typical, situations where multiple goods and services are sold by hospitality operations. Consider the following information for the Michael Motel:

- Annual fixed costs are $150,000.

- Sales mix is 75% rooms, 25% coffee shop.

- CMR for operated departments are 60% for the Rooms Department and 20% for the Coffee Shop.

What is revenue when the Michael Motel breaks even?

$$R = \frac{F}{CMR_w} \quad \text{(equation for revenue at the breakeven point)}$$

$$R = \frac{150,000}{.5}$$

$$R = \underline{\underline{\$300,000}}$$

Exhibit 9.8   Partial Income Statement — Michael Motel

Operated Department	Revenue	Variable Costs	Contribution Margin
Rooms	$150,000	$ 60,000	$ 90,000
Coffee Shop	50,000	40,000	10,000
	$200,000	$100,000	$100,000

Therefore, the Michael Motel's breakeven point is when revenue is $300,000. Since in this application of CVP analysis, multiple units are being sold, the breakeven point is expressed in dollars, not units sold, which is used when analyzing single product/service operations.

What are Michael Motel's total revenues when a profit of $12,000 is earned?

$$R = \frac{F + I_n}{CMR_w}$$

$$R = \frac{150,000 + 12,000}{.5}$$

$$R = \underline{\underline{\$324,000}}$$

In order for the Michael Motel to earn $12,000, its revenue must increase by $24,000 beyond its breakeven sales of $300,000 ($324,000— $300,000 = $24,000). Alternatively, the additional revenue beyond breakeven could have been determined as follows:

$$\text{Revenue Beyond Breakeven} = \frac{I_n}{CMR_w}$$

$$\text{Revenue Beyond Breakeven} = \frac{12,000}{.5}$$

$$\text{Revenue Beyond Breakeven} = \underline{\underline{\$24,000}}$$

Failure to reach breakeven sales will result in a loss of $.50 for every $1 of sales that falls short of breakeven. For the Michael Motel, total sales of $280,000 will result in a $10,000 loss determined as follows:

$$I_n = R(CMR_w) - F$$

$$I_n = 280,000\,(.5) - 150,000$$

$$I_n = 140,000 - 150,000$$

$$I_n = \underline{\underline{-\$10,000}}$$

Additional Questions and Solutions

If net income is to be $20,000, how much must rooms revenue be, given a ratio of 75% of rooms revenue to total revenue? Solution:

$$R = \frac{F + I_n}{CMR_w}$$

$$R = \frac{150,000 + 20,000}{.5}$$

$$R = 340,000$$

$$\text{Rooms Revenue} = .75R$$

$$\text{Rooms Revenue} = .75(340,000)$$

$$\text{Rooms Revenue} = \$255,000$$

In this situation, rooms revenue must be $255,000. A total revenue of $340,000 is required to yield a net income of $20,000, and 75% of this total revenue represents the contribution of the rooms department ($340,000 x .75 = $255,000).

If room prices increase by 20% and all other elements remain constant, what is the revised breakeven point? (Sales mix = 75% rooms, 25% food)

In this situation, we can expect that the price change will affect the rooms department's relative contribution to the operation's ability to meet fixed costs or profit goals. Therefore, the weighted average CMR must first be recalculated. This is accomplished by recalculating the CMR for the rooms department and then determining the revised CMR_w. The 20% room price increase not only increases the CMR for the rooms department, it also changes the sales mix for the Michael Motel. Solution:

$$\text{Revised CMR for Rooms} = \frac{150,000(1.20) - 60,000}{150,000(1.20)}$$

$$\text{Revised CMR for Rooms} = \frac{180,000 - 60,000}{180,000}$$

$$\text{Revised CMR for Rooms} = 2/3 \text{ or } .66667$$

$$\text{Revised CMR}^w = \frac{180,000}{230,000}(.6667) + \frac{50,000}{230,000}(.2)$$

$$\text{Revised CMR}^w = .5656$$

$$\text{Revenue} = \frac{F}{CMR_w}$$

$$\text{Revenue} = \frac{150,000}{.5656}$$

$$\text{Revenue} = \$265,205.09$$

Thus, the effect on breakeven of a 20% rooms price increase is to reduce the amount of revenue needed to break even from $300,000 to $265,205.09.

If the sales mix changes to 60% rooms and 40% food from the prior mix of 75%rooms and 25% food, what happens to the breakeven point?

Again, the CMR_w must first be revised. The revised CMR_w is divided into total fixed costs to yield the new breakeven point. Solution:

$$\text{Revised } CMR_w = .6(.6) + .4(.2)$$
$$\text{Revised } CMR_w = .36 + .08$$
$$\text{Revised } CMR_w = \underline{\underline{.44}}$$
$$\text{Revenue} = \frac{F}{CMR_w}$$
$$\text{Revenue} = \frac{150,000}{.44}$$
$$\text{Revenue} = \underline{\underline{\$340,909.09}}$$

Thus, the changes in sales mix result in a reduction in the weighted average contribution margin from .50 to .44. This, in turn, results in an increase of $40,909.09 in the amount of revenue needed for the operation to break even ($340,909.09 − $300,000.00 = $40,909.09).

If fixed costs increase by $20,000 and all other factors remain constant, what is the revised breakeven point? (Assume a CMR_w of .5)

In this situation, F is simply increased from $150,000 to $170,000. The new total for fixed costs is then divided by the CMR_w of .5 in order to calculate the new breakeven point. Solution:

$$\text{Revenue} = \frac{170,000}{.5}$$
$$\text{Revenue} = \underline{\underline{\$340,000}}$$

The breakeven point when revenues equal $340,000 could have been determined by dividing the increased fixed costs of $20,000 by .5 (the CMR_w) and adding the result ($40,000) to the original breakeven revenues of $300,000.

If fixed costs increase by $20,000, variable costs decrease by 5 percentage points, and all other factors remain constant, what is the revised breakeven point?

If variable costs decrease by 5 percentage points, then CMR_w increases by the same 5 percentage points; thus, the revised CMR_w is .55. Solution:

$$\text{Revised } CMR_w = \text{Prior } CMR_w + \text{Variable Cost Decrease}$$
$$\text{Revised } CMR_w = .5 + .05$$
$$\text{Revised } CMR_w = \underline{\underline{.55}}$$
$$\text{Revenue} = \frac{170,000}{.55}$$
$$\text{Revenue} = \underline{\underline{\$309,090.90}}$$

Income Taxes and CVP Analysis

Up to this point, the CVP model has treated all costs as either fixed or variable in relation to revenue. However, income taxes vary, not with revenue, but with pretax income. Rather than simply treat income tax as a variable expense (which it is not), the CVP equations can be adjusted to reflect this relationship between income taxes and pretax income. The CVP equations reflect this refinement by substituting I_b, the notation for pretax income, in place of I_n. When I_n and the tax rate (t) are known, I_b can be determined with the following formula:

$$I_b = \frac{I_n}{1 - t}$$

For example, assume the Michael Motel desires to earn $12,000 of net income ($I_n$) and its tax rate is 40%. Pretax income (I_b) is determined as follows:

$$I_b = \frac{I_n}{1 - t}$$

$$I_b = \frac{12,000}{1 - .4}$$

$$I_b = \frac{12,000}{.6}$$

$$I_b = \$20,000^*$$

*Proof:

Pretax income	$20,000
Taxes (40%)	− 8,000
Net income	$12,000

The CVP equation is now altered for income taxes as follows:

$$R = \frac{I_b + F}{CMR_w}$$

This revised CVP analysis equation can be illustrated using the Michael Motel. Assume the following situation:

- Desired net income equals $30,000.
- Annual fixed costs equal $150,000.
- Tax rate equals 40%.
- $CMR_w = .5$

From this information we can calculate the pretax income as follows:

$$I_b = \frac{I_n}{1 - t}$$

$$I_b = \frac{30,000}{1 - .4}$$

$$I_b = \underline{\$50,000}$$

Once we calculate the pretax income as $50,000, we can then use the revised CVP equation to arrive at the breakeven point:

$$R = \frac{I_b + F}{CMR_w}$$

$$R = \frac{50,000 + 150,000}{.5}$$

$$R = \frac{200,000}{.5}$$

$$R = \underline{\$400,000}$$

*Proof:

Revenue	$400,000
Variable costs (50%)	−200,000
Fixed costs	−150,000
Pretax income	50,000
Income taxes	−20,000
Net income	$30,000

When an enterprise breaks even, its net income and pretax income both equal zero. Therefore, the breakeven point for a given operation is the same regardless of the tax rates.

Cash Flow CVP Analysis

In addition to applying CVP analysis to evaluate profit levels, sales mixes, and pretax incomes, managers and owners are also interested in evaluating various levels of cash flow. They are interested in knowing the amount of revenue required to produce a sufficient flow of cash to reach such benchmarks as the breakeven point and other cash flow levels. The CVP analysis equations previously demonstrated may be modified to provide answers to these questions.

The cash flow CVP equation is illustrated in Exhibit 9.9.

The application of CVP analysis to problems involving cash flow can be illustrated using the Michael Motel in light of the following information:

- Fixed costs equal $150,000.

- Tax rate equals 40%.

- CMR_w equals 50%.

Exhibit 9.9   Cash Flow Cost-Volume-Profit Analysis Equation

$$R = \frac{CF_b + F - NCE + NECD}{CMR_w}$$

where

CF_b = Desired cash flow before taxes

F = Fixed costs

NCE = Non-cash expenses – expenses which do not entail cash payments such as depreciation and amortization.

NECD = Non-expense cash disbursements – cash payments which do not relate directly to expenses such as dividend payments.

Other non-expense cash disbursements are for loan payments excluding interest expense, payments for fixed assets, etc. Payment for accounts payable, payroll payable, etc., are considered to relate "directly" to expense, thus, they would not be included in this figure.

Desired positive cash flow is $30,000.

Non-cash expenses equal $10,000. (This is depreciation expense for the period.)

Non-expense cash disbursements equal $20,000.

In this situation, we can calculate the total revenue required to yield the desired positive cash flow of $30,000. But, first, we need to calculate the desired cash flow before taxes:

$$CF_b = \frac{CF}{1-t}$$

$$CF_b = \frac{30,000}{1 - .4}$$

$$CF_b = \underline{\$50,000}$$

We can now calculate the total revenue required to yield the desired cash flow before taxes by using the following formula:

$$R = \frac{CF_b + F - NCE + NECD}{CMR_w}$$

$$R = \frac{50,000 + 150,000 - 10,000 + 20,000}{.5}$$

$$R = \frac{210,000}{.5}$$

$$R = \underline{\$420,000}$$

Exhibit 9.10   Cash Flow — Michael Motel

Cash receipts (revenue)	$420,000
Cash disbursements:	
Variable costs	210,000
Fixed costs	140,000
Non-expenses	20,000
Pretax income	50,000
Cash disbursement (income taxes)	20,000
Positive cash flow	$ 30,000

Therefore, the Michael Motel must have total revenues of $420,000 in order to generate sufficient cash internally to make its payments and to attain the desired positive cash flow level. The proof of our calculations appears in Exhibit 9.10.

Alternatively, the total revenue at which the Michael Motel has the "breakeven" cash flow it desires is determined as follows:

$$CF_b = 0$$

$$R = \frac{CF_b + F - NCE + NECD}{CMR_w}$$

$$R = \frac{0 + 150,000 - 10,000 + 20,000}{.5}$$

$$R = \frac{160,000}{.5}$$

$$R = \$320,000$$

Therefore, the Michael Motel requires a revenue of $320,000 to yield sufficient cash so that it does not have to borrow working capital funds. The cash flow breakeven revenue of $320,000 is $20,000 greater than the breakeven revenue of $300,000 computed previously. The difference is due to the excess of the NECD over NCE divided by the CMR_w ($10,000 divided by .5 equals $20,000).

Comprehensive Problem

The Smith Hotel will be used to more fully illustrate CVP analysis. Exhibit 9.11 contains the summary income statement according to the USASH format for the Smith Hotel for the year ended December 31, 19X1.

For CVP analysis, expenses need to be identified as either variable or fixed. For illustration purposes, the direct expenses of the operated departments for the Smith Hotel are assumed to be variable, while overhead costs (the undistributed operating expenses and fixed charges)

Exhibit 9.11   Summary Income Statement — Smith Motel

Summary Income Statement
Smith Hotel
For the year ended December 31, 19X1

	Revenue	Cost of Sales	Payroll and Related Expenses	Other Expenses	Income (Loss)
Operating Departments:					
Rooms	$4,000,000	$ 0	$ 500,000	$ 300,000	$3,200,000
Food and Beverage	1,800,000	500,000	700,000	200,000	400,000
Telephone	200,000	160,000	30,000	10,000	0
Total	$6,000,000	$660,000	1,230,000	510,000	3,600,000
Undistributed Operating Expenses:					
Administrative and General			100,000	50,000	150,000
Data Processing			50,000	50,000	100,000
Human Resources			30,000	260,000	290,000
Transportation			20,000	40,000	60,000
Marketing			100,000	300,000	400,000
Property Operation and Maintenance			100,000	100,000	200,000
Energy Costs			0	400,000	400,000
Income Before Fixed Charges			$1,630,000	$1,710,000	2,000,000
Rent, Property Taxes and Insurance				$ 200,000	
Interest				1,000,000	
Depreciation				500,000	1,700,000
Income Before Income Taxes					300,000
Income Taxes					120,000
Net Income					$ 180,000

are assumed to be fixed costs. Income tax is a function of income before income taxes. These assumptions are shown in Exhibit 9.12.

Given this information, we will now use CVP analysis to calculate each of the following situations for the Smith Hotel:

1.   Weighted average contribution margin ratio
2.   Breakeven point
3.   Total revenue to yield a net income of $500,000
4.   Rooms revenue when profit equals $500,000
5.   Breakeven point if fixed costs increase by $300,000

Situation #1   Determine the weighted average CMR (CMR$_w$).
From Exhibit 9.12 the CMR$_w$ may be determined as follows:

Exhibit 9.12 Relationship of Revenues, Variable Costs, and Contribution Margin — Smith Motel

Relationship of Revenues, Variable Costs, and Contribution Margin
Smith Hotel
For the year ended December 31, 19X1

	Revenue	Variable Costs	Contribution Margin
Rooms	$4,000,000	$ 800,000	$3,200,000
Food and Beverage	1,800,000	1,400,000	400,000
Telephone	200,000	200,000	0
Total	$6,000,000	$2,400,000	3,600,000
Fixed Costs			3,300,000
Income Before Income Taxes			300,000
Income Taxes			120,000
Net Income			$ 180,000

$$CMR_w = \frac{\text{Contribution Margin*}}{\text{Total Revenue}}$$

$$CMR_w = \frac{3,600,000}{6,000,000}$$

$$CMR_w = \underline{\underline{.6}}$$

*Total operating departments income

Situation #2 Determine the breakeven point.

$$R = \frac{F}{CMR_w}$$

$$R = \frac{3,300,000}{.6}$$

$$R = \underline{\underline{\$5,500,000}}$$

Situation #3 Determine the total revenue required to yield $500,000 of net income. (Assume the sales mix remains constant.)

First, the effect of income taxes on net income must be accounted for, given the Smith Hotel's income tax rate of 40%. The amount of income before income taxes that the hotel must generate in order to achieve the desired net income of $500,000 can be determined as follows:

$$I_b = \frac{I_n}{1 - t}$$

$$I_b = \frac{500,000}{1 - .4}$$

$$I_b = \underline{\underline{\$833,333.33}}$$

Second, the total revenue needed to yield this amount of income before income taxes is calculated as follows:

$$R = \frac{I_b + F}{CMR_w}$$

$$R = \frac{833,333.33 + 3,300,000}{.6}$$

$$R = \frac{4,133,333.33}{.6}$$

$$R = \underline{\underline{\$6,888,888.88}}$$

Situation #4 Determine the amount of room revenue when the Smith Hotel makes $500,000 of net income.

First, from the information provided on the Smith Hotel's summary income statement (Exhibit 9.11), we can determine the relative contribution of rooms revenue to total revenue.

$$\frac{\text{Rooms Revenue}}{\text{Total Revenue}} = \frac{4,000,000}{6,000,000}$$

$$= \underline{\underline{.6667}}$$

Second, we can then multiply .6667 by the total revenue and arrive at the required rooms revenue as part of the total revenue for the Smith Hotel to achieve $500,000 of net income.

$$\text{Room Revenue} = 6,888,888.83 \times .6667$$

$$\text{Room Revenue} = \underline{\$4,592,822.18}$$

Situation #5 Determine the breakeven point for the Smith Hotel if fixed costs increase by $300,000 and all other things remain constant.

The breakeven point is determined as follows:

$$R = \frac{F}{CMR_w}$$

$$R = \frac{3,600,000}{.6}$$

$$R = \underline{\underline{\$6,000,000}}$$

Note the Smith Hotel's breakeven point has increased from $5,500,000 to $6,000,000 when its fixed costs increased by $300,000. Alternatively, the new breakeven point could have been determined by dividing the increased fixed costs ($300,000) by the CMR_w and adding the result to the previously calculated breakeven point of $5,500,000 as follows:

$$R = \$5,500,000 + \frac{300,000}{.6}$$

$$R = \underline{\$6,000,000}$$

Operating Leverage

Operating leverage is the extent to which an operation's expenses are fixed rather than variable. When an operation substitutes fixed costs for variable costs, it is highly levered. Being highly levered means a relatively small increase in sales beyond the breakeven point results in a large increase in net income. However, failure to reach the breakeven point results in a relatively large net loss.

If an operation has a high level of variable costs relative to fixed costs, it is said to have low operating leverage. A relatively small increase in sales beyond the breakeven point results in a small increase in net income. On the other hand, failure to reach the breakeven point results in a relatively small net loss.

For example, consider the cost structures of two competing hospitality operations illustrated in Exhibit 9.13.

Note that both hospitality properties will break even when their revenue equals $500,000. However, Property A has a CMR of 40% (100% − 60% = 40%), while Property B has a CMR of 60% (100% − 40% = 60%). This reveals that for each revenue dollar over the shared breakeven point, Property A will earn only $.40 while Property B will earn $.60. On the other hand, for each revenue dollar under the breakeven point, Property A loses $.40 while Property B loses $.60. Therefore, Property B has a high operating leverage compared to Property A. Both Properties A and B identify the same breakeven point as the difference between revenues and expenses, and, for both properties, the costs of failure equal the rewards of success. They both risk as much as they gain, but for Property B, the stakes are higher. Property B is more highly levered.

Exhibit 9.14 is a graphical representation of the cost structures of Properties A and B and reflects identical breakeven points for Properties A and B. However, it is the vertical distance between the total revenue and total cost lines that measures the degree of profitability for each property. Since Property B is more highly levered, the distance between the total cost and total revenue lines is greater at all operating levels, compared to Property A, except at the breakeven point.

The degree of operating leverage desired by a hospitality property reflects the degree of risk that the operation desires to take. All other things being the same, the more highly levered the operation, the greater the risk. However, the greater the risk, the greater the expected returns as reflected in Exhibit 9.14. Property B is taking more risk, but potentially may earn considerably more profit than Property A. On the other hand, Property B risks losing considerably more than Property A. For example, if sales are $800,000 for both operations, Property A earns $120,000 of profit ($300,000 x .4 = $120,000) while Property B generates $180,000 of profit ($300,000 x .6 = $180,000). However, if sales were only $200,000, Property A would lose $120,000 ($500,000 − $200,000 = $300,000;

Exhibit 9.13 Cost Structures of Properties A and B

| | Firm A | | Firm B | |
	$	%	$	%
Revenues	$500,000	100%	$500,000	100%
Variable costs	300,000	60	200,000	40
Fixed costs	200,000	40	300,000	60
Net income	$ 0	0%	$ 0	0%

$300,000 x .4 = $120,000), while Property B would lose $180,000 ($500,000 − $200,000 = $300,000; $300,000 x .6 = $180,000).

Computerization

As mentioned in Chapter 8, spreadsheet programs can perform very extensive and sophisticated calculations, including the formulas discussed in this chapter. For example, the breakeven calculation could easily be entered into a spreadsheet and multiple levels of calculations could be performed quickly and accurately. As in the "what if" models in Chapter 8, these formulas can be repeated many times in the same model to determine the optimum solution to a question. In the case of CVP analysis, the breakeven point could be easily determined, and then the analysis could be conducted to find the revenues which would generate the desired net income.

Multiple product CVP analysis is also ideally suited to spreadsheet programs. Contribution margins for each profit center can be quickly determined and combined to create a total picture for the business. Exhibit 9.15 shows how this might be done with the Salem Hotel Company. Expanding upon the model shown in Chapter 8, the effects of the lower occupancy also caused a reduction in food and beverage revenues. Food and beverage revenues equals the product of available rooms for sale x projected occupancy x $15 average check. This is based on past performance that suggests an average of $15 dollars of food and beverage sales per room sold. The food and beverage variable expenses equals food and beverage revenue x .75.

With any reduction in business, variable costs would also be reduced. The effect is that profitability peaks at 70% occupancy and the combined contribution margin is 69.8%.

With this information, the breakeven point of the hotel is shown for each of the occupancy, revenue, and expense levels in the analysis. The breakeven point at the maximum profitability level is $1,089,305. Some managers might, however, prefer to operate under the scenario of $55 room rate and 50% occupancy because it has the lowest breakeven point and, all other things being equal, is, therefore, the least risky option. By changing the revenue and expense line in the analysis, the contribution margin is calculated automatically, as well as the breakeven point.

Exhibit 9.14 Operating Leverage of Properties A and B

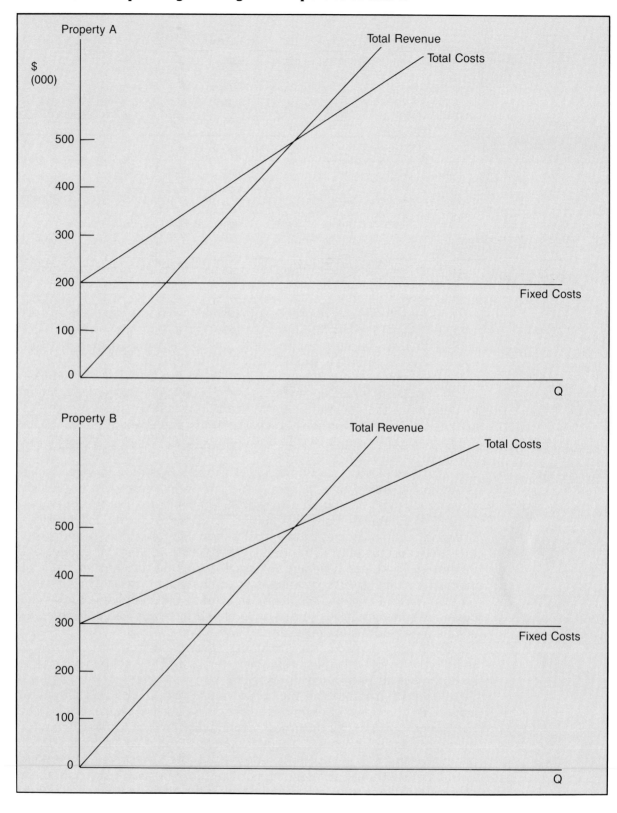

Exhibit 9.15 Computer-Generated Rooms Department Rate Analysis — Salem Hotel Company

Room Department Rate Analysis
Salem Hotel Company

Available Rooms for Sale	36,500	36,500	36,500	36,500	36,500	36,500
Average Rate	$40.00	$45.00	$47.50	$50.00	$52.50	$55.00
Projected Occupancy	77.5%	75.0%	72.5%	70.0%	65.0%	60.0%
Room Revenue	$1,131,500	$1,231,875	$1,256,969	$1,277,500	$1,245,563	$1,204,500
Room Variable Expense	237,615	229,950	222,285	214,620	199,290	183,960
Room Profits	893,885	1,001,925	1,034,684	1,062,880	1,046,273	1,020,540
F&B Revenues	424,313	410,625	396,938	383,250	355,875	328,500
F&B Variable Expenses	318,234	307,969	297,703	287,438	266,906	246,375
F&B Profits	106,079	102,656	99,235	95,812	88,969	82,125
Total Departmental Profits	999,964	1,104,581	1,133,919	1,158,692	1,135,242	1,102,665
Contribution Margin Ratio	64.3%	67.2%	68.6%	69.8%	70.9%	71.9%
Fixed Expenses	$ 760,000	$ 760,000	$ 760,000	$ 760,000	$ 760,000	$ 760,000
Breakeven Point*	$1,182,461	$1,130,112	$1,108,518	$1,089,305	$1,072,100	$1,056,604

*Breakeven point was calculated by the computer using the formula which divided Fixed Expenses by the quantity (1 – Contribution Margin Ratio).

Summary

Cost-volume-profit (CVP) analysis is an analytical tool used by managers to examine the relationships among costs, revenues, and sales volume. By expressing these relationships in graphic form or by using mathematical equations, management can determine an operation's breakeven point, sales requirements for a specified net income level, and/or the mix of sales within the operation.

In order to use CVP to determine the breakeven point, various relationships must be understood. First, fixed costs are constant; they will not fluctuate within the range of operating activity being studied. Both variable costs and revenue fluctuate linearly with sales volume; that is, a percentage increase in sales volume (e.g., rooms sold) will result in the same percentage increase in revenue and variable expenses. In a "shut-down" situation (when the sales are zero), there are no variable costs or revenues, but the fixed costs will be at their constant level; therefore, the theoretical bottom line for such a shut-down period will be a net loss equal to the fixed costs of the period.

The breakeven point is defined as the level of sales which generates revenue equal to total costs. The balance between revenues and costs at the breakeven point is expressed in the following equation: *Revenues = Fixed Costs + Variable Costs*. CVP analysis allows management selling a single product/service (for example, only rooms) to arrive at this breakeven level of revenues with the aid of the equation:

$$X = \frac{F}{(S - V)}$$

The $S - V$ element of the equation is the contribution margin, which is the amount of money generated by the sale that may be applied to cover fixed cost, or, beyond the breakeven point, to contribute to profit. Therefore, the equation reflects the fixed cost divided by the dollars provided to cover fixed costs per sales unit.

In the more complex situation where more than one good or service is sold, the CVP formula is as follows:

$$R = \frac{F + I_n}{CMR_w}$$

The CMR_w element of the equation reflects the weighted-average of the CMRs for the profit centers. The CVP formulas for the multiple products operation may be used to determine breakeven points by substituting 0 for I_n. This formula may further be modified by substituting I_b for I_n to consider income taxes.

Once the CVP relationship is understood, it can become a vital tool offering aid in a number of situations. It can provide management with benchmark sales levels—the breakeven level, the amount to provide a required net income, or the required level to provide for cash needs—prices, or sales mix. It can be used to examine the differences between levels of sales or costs. It can also be used to examine different cost structures, as the effect of differences in the CMR can be seen over different sales levels.

Discussion Questions

1. What are the assumptions underlying the CVP analysis?

2. What does the term S-V represent in the CVP equation? How does its use differ from that of the CMR?

3. Draw a CVP graph of the following operation: F = \$10; S = \$1; V = \$.50. What is the meaning of the regions (between the total revenue and total cost lines) to the left and right of 20 units sold?

4. What is income before taxes for a hospitality operation which generates no sales during a period?

5. What is the advantage of using the CVP equations to express the relationships over graphing the relationships?

6. How does CMR for a single department, or for an enterprise selling only one product/service, differ from a weighted-average CMR (CMR_w)? How is CMR_w determined?

7. What part of the CVP equation used to determine the breakeven point must be changed in order to produce the answer in terms of sales dollars versus sales units? Why is this so?

8. Define the term "sales mix." How does this affect CMR_w?

9. Explain why non-cash expenses should be subtracted in the CVP formula used to determine the revenue level at the cash flow breakeven point.

10. If, by changing an operation's sales mix, the CMR_w decreases, how is the breakeven level of sales affected?

Problem 9.1

Keith Jones is considering investing $1,500,000 in a 60-room motel, The Olympia Inn. Based on his market research, he has determined that a reasonable room rate for the region is $39.95. He projects variable costs to be $12.00 per room, and his annual fixed costs are estimated at $400,000.

Required:

1. Determine the number of rooms sales required for The Olympia Inn to break even.

2. Assuming all 60 rooms will be available 365 days during the year, what is The Olympia Inn's projected breakeven occupancy percentage?

3. How many rooms must be sold if Mr. Jones is to make a 15% return on his investment? (Assume there is no tax effect.)

Problem 9.2

Sid Gull, the owner/operator of the Iowa Inn, is interested in determining the level of sales necessary to realize a net income of $500,000 next year. He has compiled records on each department's sales and costs, and assumes the sales mix will be the same next year. The major department, the rooms department, had sales of $2,500,000, and its contribution margin was $1,750,000. The coffee shop, Josh's Mug, had sales of $750,000 and variable costs of $300,000. The restaurant, Chateau Stacie, had sales of $1,200,000 and variable costs of $750,000. Mr. Gull assumes the fixed costs will be $1,000,000.

Required:

1. What is the weighted average contribution margin?

2. What is the required level of total sales to generate $500,000 net income? (Assume there are no income taxes.)

3. What is the required level of total sales to generate $500,000 net income if the income tax rate is 50%?

Problem 9.3

Dustin Gordon, the executive vice president of COB, is considering expanding the company's operations into the hospitality industry. The company's goals include diversification, but also require an 18% return on their investment after taxes. Mr. Gordon has studied a hotel property which yields the following results:

A. The rooms department generates 80% of the sales, and operates with a contribution margin ratio (CMR) of 76%.

B. The food and beverage department generates the other 20% of sales, and has a CMR of 55%.

C. Fixed costs per year are estimated to be $240,000.

D. In order to purchase the hotel, COB would have to invest $1,500,000.

E. COB's tax rate is 40%.

Required:

What level of sales is required before Mr. Gordon would recommend investing in the hotel to COB's board of directors?

Problem 9.4

Stephanie Miller, an experienced businessperson and consultant, realizes the importance of cash flow. Therefore, whenever she is requested to provide a client with a breakeven level of sales, she also provides them with a cash flow "breakeven analysis." The present owner has provided Ms. Miller with the following information for BMS, Inc.

Monthly Condensed Income Statement
BMS Inc.

Rooms Revenue		$100,000
F&B Revenue		40,000
Total Revenue		140,000
Departmental Expenses		
Rooms	$20,000	
F&B	20,000	
Total Departmental Expense		40,000
Contribution Margin		100,000
Fixed Costs		
Interest Expense	10,000	
Depreciation	20,000	
Other Fixed Costs	50,000	
Total Fixed Costs		80,000
Income Before Tax		20,000
Tax		5,000
Net Income		$15,000

Other Information:

1. Assume the tax rate to be constant over any level of pretax income.

2. The monthly mortgage payment is $15,000 of which $10,000 is interest expense.

3. All inventories are purchased on a cash basis and are expensed when purchased since they are insignificant.

4. There is no major change in current assets, other than cash, or current liabilities from month to month.

Required:

You are to assist Ms. Miller in:

1. Determining the level of sales required to provide BMS, Inc. with $40,000 net income.

2. Determining the level of sales required to provide BMS, Inc. with $10,000 positive cash flow for a month.

Problem 9.5

Edwin and Carla's Dude Ranch (ECDR) is a 40-room hotel near Denver with a 30-seat restaurant and stables (a profit center). Edwin and Carla Cass, the owners, are interested in having you use the CVP analysis to aid them in determining various sales levels for their resort. The following is a summary of the most recent annual income statement.

Condensed Income Statement
Edwin and Carla's Dude Ranch
For the year ended December 31, 19X5

	Rooms	Food	Stables	Total
Revenue	$500,000	$200,000	$5,000	$705,000
Variable Expenses	150,000	150,000	4,000	304,000
Contribution Margin	$350,000	$50,000	$1,000	401,000
Fixed Expense				151,000
Income Tax				125,000
Net Income				$125,000

Required:

1.   What is the food department's contribution margin ratio (CMR)?

2.   What is the weighted average CMR for ECDR?

3.   What is the breakeven point?

4.   The Casses wish to increase net income by $30,000 and feel this can be done by increasing room sales *only*. Determine the necessary increase in room sales to meet this requirement.

5.   Assume (independent of #4) that revenue from the stables can be increased, but only with a $500 increase in advertising (a fixed cost) for brochures to go in each room. What level of sales from the stables must be generated to cover this cost?

6.   Assume that the brochures mentioned in #5 are used as a direct mailing. The cost would now be $1,500 to cover printing and mailing, but sales for each department would increase. Assuming room sales, food sales, and stable revenue remain at 5:2:.05, how much must revenue increase for net income to remain constant?

10 Cost Approaches to Pricing

Pricing is one of the most difficult decisions made by hospitality managers. If prices are set too high, lower demand may result in reduced sales. When prices are set too low, demand may be high, but lowered sales revenue is likely to result in costs not being covered. Either way, the hospitality operation's profitability may be placed in jeopardy. How can a hospitality manager ensure that prices are neither too high nor too low?

Needless to say, anyone can set prices, but to establish prices which result in revenues being maximized is extremely difficult. Some managers would suggest that the process of setting effective prices for products and services in any segment of the hospitality industry involves a bit of luck. There may be no completely scientific method guaranteed to determine the best prices to successfully maximize profits for a hospitality operation. However, good managers will seek to establish a rational basis for their pricing decisions. General approaches to the pricing problem provide ways of using relevant information and the manager's knowledge of the relationships among sales, costs, and profits to establish a reasonable basis for effective pricing.

Our discussion of cost approaches to pricing in this chapter will answer many of the important questions that come to mind regarding the pricing process, such as the following:

1. Which costs are relevant in the pricing decision?

2. What is the common weakness of informal pricing methods?

3. What are the common cost methods of pricing rooms?

4. What are common methods of pricing food and beverages?

5. How may popularity and profitability be considered in setting food prices?

6. Will departmental revenue maximization result in revenue maximization for the hospitality firm?

7. What is price elasticity of demand?

8. What is integrated pricing?

We will begin this chapter with a discussion of the importance of pricing and the need for profits by both profit-oriented and nonprofit-oriented operations. Next, we will explain and illustrate the concept of the price elasticity of demand. We will then consider a variety of approaches to pricing both rooms and meals, discuss the effect of sales mix on profits, and address the topic of integrated pricing.

Importance of Pricing

A major determinant of a hospitality establishment's profitability is its prices. Whether prices are set too low or too high, the result is the same—a failure to maximize profits. When prices are below what the market is willing to pay, the establishment will realize less revenues than it could generate through its operations. Alternatively, prices set too high will reduce sales and, thereby, fail to achieve the operation's potential for profit. Another factor to consider when setting prices is the "positioning" of the establishment's offerings within the marketplace. Prices set too low may tend to degrade the quality of products, whereas inflated prices may tend to reduce the perceived value of products from the guest's perspective. Therefore, management's goal is to set prices which result in profit maximization.

Profits should not simply result because revenues happen to exceed expenses. Profits should occur because revenues generated, based on prices and units sold, exceed expenses incurred. The emphasis should not be defensive, that is, keep costs down to make a profit. Aggressive management should generate sufficient revenues to cover costs. Cost containment is a respectable secondary objective after marketing efforts are undertaken to achieve a reasonably high level of sales.

As the title of this chapter suggests, prices will be approached from a cost perspective. The author does not suggest, nor even imply, that noncost factors such as market demand and competition are irrelevant; in some situations they may be critical to the pricing decision.

Profit-oriented operations desire to make profits for such reasons as expanding operations, providing owners with a return on capital invested, and increasing the share prices of stock. Many nonprofit-oriented operations must make a profit (often it may be called "revenue in excess of expenses") for expanding operations, replacing fixed assets, and upgrading services. Since both types of operations need to generate profits, their approaches to pricing will not necessarily be different. The differences generally relate to costs and type of demand. For example, some nonprofit food service operations, including some in the institutional setting, do not have to cover many capital costs such as interest expenses, property taxes, or depreciation. Further, the demand for the products and/or services may be different. The demand for food service in a hospital is quite different than the demand for food service in most hotels or restaurants. Many nonprofit operations have less direct competition, so they may have greater leeway in pricing their products and/or services.

The emphasis in this chapter will be on commercial (profit-oriented) operations. However, since we will be discussing approaches to pricing that are cost–oriented, our discussion will apply to nonprofit-oriented operations as well.

Price Elasticity of Demand

The concept of the price elasticity of demand provides a means for measuring how sensitive demand is to changes in price. In general, as the selling price of a product or service decreases, everything else being the same, more is expected to be sold. When the price of a product is increased, only rarely is more of the product sold, everything else being the same, and even then there may be other factors which account for the increased demand.

The demand for a product or service may be characterized as elastic or inelastic. Every operation desires to have an inelastic demand for its products and/or services. That is, when prices are increased, the percentage reduction in quantity demanded is less than the percentage of the price increase so that revenue is increased and generally profits are increased as well. If the reverse occurs, that is, the percentage of price change is less than the percentage change in demand, then the demand is characterized as elastic.

Exhibit 10.1 illustrates the price elasticity of demand formula for mathematically determining whether the type of demand is elastic or inelastic. The base quantity demanded (Q_o) is the number of units sold during a given period prior to changing prices. The change in quantity demanded ($\triangle Q$) is the change in the number of units sold during the period the prices were changed in comparison to the prior period. The base price (P_o) is the price of the product and/or service for the period prior to the price change. The change in price ($\triangle P$) is the change in price from the base price.

If the elasticity of demand exceeds 1, the demand is characterized as elastic, that is, it is sensitive to price changes. With an elastic demand, the percentage change in quantity demanded exceeds the percentage change in price.

If the result is less than 1, demand is known to be inelastic, that is, a percentage price change results in a less percentage change in quantity demanded. If a hospitality operation has an inelastic demand for its products and/or services, then it is able to increase its prices without having a comparable effect on the quantity demanded. An inelastic demand results in increases of revenue when prices are increased even though there may be some decrease in quantity demanded.

Let's look at an example illustrating the calculation of price elasticity of demand. A budget motel sold 1,000 rooms during a recent 30-day period at $20 per room. For the next 30-day period, the price was increased to $22, and 950 rooms were sold. The demand for the budget motel over this time period is considered to be inelastic since the calculated price elasticity of demand is less than one. The calculation of price elasticity of demand is as follows:

$$\text{Price Elasticity of Demand} = \frac{50}{1,000} \text{ divided by } \frac{2}{20}$$

$$\text{Price Elasticity of Demand} = .05 \text{ divided by } .1$$

$$\text{Price Elasticity of Demand} = \underline{\underline{.5}}$$

Notice that the negative change in quantity is ignored since it is almost always the case that price decreases result in increases in quantity demanded and vice versa.

In general, the demand for products and services in the lodging and

Exhibit 10.1 Price Elasticity of Demand Formula

$$\text{Price Elasticity of Demand} = \frac{\dfrac{\text{Change in Quantity Demanded}}{\text{Base Quantity}}}{\dfrac{\text{Change in Base Price}}{\text{Base Price}}}$$

$$\text{Price Elasticity of Demand} = \frac{\dfrac{\triangle Q}{Q_o}}{\dfrac{\triangle P}{P_o}}$$

where:

$\triangle Q$	=	Change in quantity demanded
Q_o	=	Base quantity demanded
$\triangle P$	=	Change in price
P_o	=	Base price

the commercial food service segments of the hospitality industry are considered to be elastic. Generally, demand will be elastic where competition is high due to the presence of many operations, and where the products and/or services offered are fairly standardized. On the other hand, where competition is low (or even nonexistent), or an operation has greatly differentiated its products and/or services, then demand may be inelastic. At the extreme, some resorts, clubs, high-check-average restaurants, and luxury hotels are known to have an inelastic demand for their products and services. Generally, quick service restaurants and medium priced hotels/motels are considered to have elastic demand for their products and services. However, these are generalizations, and there are exceptions.

Although this analysis of demand/price relationships assumes other things are the same, seldom do hospitality operations increase prices without effectively advertising their products so as to counter potential decreased demand. Therefore, the concept of the price elasticity of demand tends to be more theoretical than practical in nature.

Informal Pricing Approaches

There are several informal approaches to setting prices for selling food, beverages, and rooms. Since each of these approaches, by itself, ignores the cost of providing the "product," they are only briefly presented here as a point of departure for our discussion of more scientific approaches to setting prices.

Several managers have priced their products based on what the competition charges. If the competition charges $80 for a room night, or an average of $20 for a dinner, then those are the prices set by managers using competitive pricing. When the competition changes their prices, then managers using this pricing approach follow suit. A variation of this approach is changing prices when the leading hospitality operation changes its prices.

Although these approaches may seem reasonable when there is considerable competition in a market, they ignore the many differences that exist among hospitality operations such as location, product quality, atmosphere, customer goodwill, etc. In addition, they ignore the cost of producing the products and services sold. Different hospitality operations must consider their own cost structures when making pricing decisions. A dominant operation with a low cost structure may "cause" competitors to go bankrupt if they ignore their own costs and price their products following the competitive approach.

Another informal pricing approach used by some managers is "intuition." Intuitive pricing is based on what the manager feels the guest is willing to pay. Generally, managers using this approach rely on their past experience regarding guests' reactions to prices. However, as with competitive pricing, intuition ignores costs and may result in failure to both recover costs and generate a reasonable profit.

A third approach is psychological pricing. Here, prices are established based on "what the guest expects to pay." This approach may be used by relatively exclusive locations and by operators who think that the guest believes "the more that is paid the better the product." Although psychological pricing does possess a certain merit, it fails to consider underlying costs and, therefore, may not result in profit maximization.

Finally, the trial and error pricing approach first sets a product price, monitors guests' reactions, and then adjusts the price based on the guests' reactions. This approach appears to fully consider the operation's guests; however, problems with this method include:

- Guests' reactions may take relatively longer periods of time than the manager would like to allow.

- Frequent changes in prices, based on guests' reactions may result in price confusion to guests.

- There are many outside, uncontrollable factors that affect guests' purchase decisions. An example illustrates this last problem: a 10% price increase in rooms may appear to be too high if occupancy is down by more than 10% over the next 30 days. However, other factors that may be part of the consumer decision include competition, new lodging establishments, weather conditions (especially if the lodging facility is a resort), and so on.

- The trial and error approach fails to consider costs.

Although all of the informal price approaches have some merit, they are most useful only when coupled with cost approaches we are now going to consider.

Mark-up Approaches to Pricing

A major method of pricing food and beverages is marking up the cost of the goods sold. The mark-up is designed to cover all nonproduct costs, such as labor, utilities, supplies, interest expense, taxes, and also to provide the desired profit.

Under the mark-up approaches to pricing are ingredient mark-up and prime ingredient mark-up. The ingredient mark-up approach attempts to consider all product costs while only the cost of the major ingredient is considered in the prime ingredient mark-up approach.

The four steps to the ingredient cost approach are as follows:

1. Determine the ingredient costs.

2. Determine the multiple to use in marking up the ingredient costs.

3. Multiply the ingredient costs by the multiple resulting in the desired price.

4. Consider if the price appears reasonable based on the market.

The multiple determined in step two is generally based on the desired product cost percentage and is calculated as follows:

$$\text{Multiple} = \frac{1}{\text{Desired Product Cost Percentage}}$$

For example, if a product cost percentage of 40% is desired, the multiple would be 2.5, determined as follows:

$$\text{Multiple} = \frac{1}{\text{Desired Product Cost Percentage}}$$
$$\text{Multiple} = \frac{1}{.40}$$
$$\text{Multiple} = \underline{\underline{2.5}}$$

The ingredient cost approach can be illustrated using ingredient cost figures for a chicken dinner listed in Exhibit 10.2. Assuming a desired multiple of 3.5, the price of the chicken dinner is determined as follows:

$$\text{Price} = \text{Ingredients' Cost x Multiple}$$
$$\text{Price} = 1.32 \times 3.5$$
$$\text{Price} = \underline{\underline{\$4.62}}$$

If the result appears reasonable based on the market for chicken dinners, then the chicken dinner is sold for about $4.62.

The prime ingredient approach differs only in that the cost of the prime ingredient is marked up rather than the total cost of all ingredients. In addition, the multiple used, all other things being equal, would be greater than the multiple used when considering the total cost

Exhibit 10.2   Chicken Dinner Ingredients/Costs

Ingredient	Cost
Chicken – 2 pieces	$ .59
Baked potato with sour cream	.19
Roll and butter	.09
Vegetable	.15
Salad with dressing	.18
Coffee – refills free	.12
Total cost	$1.32

of all ingredients. The multiple used would generally be based on past experience, i.e., what multiple has provided adequate cost coverage and desired profit. Using the same chicken dinner example, the prime ingredient cost is chicken with a cost of $.59. Using an arbitrary multiple of 7.8, the chicken dinner is priced at $4.60 calculated as follows:

$$\text{Price} = \text{Prime Ingredient Cost x Multiple}$$

$$\text{Price} = \$.59 \times 7.8$$

$$\text{Price} = \underline{\$4.60}$$

If the cost of chicken in the above example increases to $.69 for the dinner portion, then the new price would be $5.38 ($.69 x 7.8). The prime ingredient approach assumes that the costs of all other ingredients change in proportion to the prime ingredient, that is, when the prime ingredient's cost increases 10%, then other ingredients' costs have also increased 10%. When changes in the other ingredients' cost percentage differ from the prime ingredient's, then the product cost percentage will differ from the established goal.

When pricing is based on a cost approach, four modifying factors to consider are historical prices, perceived price/value relationships, competition, and price rounding. First, prices that have been charged in the past must be considered when pricing the hospitality operation's products. A dramatic change dictated by a cost approach may seem unrealistic to the consumer. For example, if a breakfast meal was mistakenly priced at $1.49 for five years, and the realistic price should be $3.49, the food service operation may be "forced" to slowly move from $1.49 to $3.49 by implementing several price increases over a period of time.

Second, the guest must perceive that the value of the product and/or service is reasonably priced. Many guests in the 1980s appear to be more value-conscious than ever. Most are willing to pay prices much higher than a few years ago, but they also demand value for the price paid.

Third, the competition cannot be ignored. If an operation's product is viewed as substantially the same as a competitor's, then everything else being equal, the prices would have to be similar. For example, an operation's price calculations for a gourmet burger may suggest a $4.50 selling price; however, if a strong nearby competitor is charging $3.50 for a very similar product, everything else being the same, then competition would appear to force a price reduction. However, remember it is extremely difficult for everything else to be the same: the location is at least slightly different, one burger may be fresher, and so on.

Finally, the price may be modified for price rounding, that is, the item's price will be rounded to the nearest $.25 or possibly up to $X.95. For example, using the prime ingredient approach, the chicken dinner would be priced at $4.60; however, the price most likely would be rounded to $4.75, or even to $4.95.

Pricing Rooms

Two well-known cost approaches to pricing rooms are the $1 per $1,000 approach and the Hubbart Formula approach.

$1 per $1,000 Approach

The $1 per $1,000 approach sets the price of a room at $1 for each $1,000 project cost per room. For example, assume the average project cost of a hotel for each room was $80,000. Using the $1 per $1,000 approach results in a price of $80 per room. Doubles, suites, singles, and so on would be priced differently but the average would be $80.

This approach fails to consider the value of facilities when it emphasizes the project cost. A well-maintained hotel worth $100,000 per room today may have been constructed at $20,000 per room forty years ago. The $1 per $1,000 approach would suggest a price of $20 per room; however, a much higher rate would appear to be appropriate. This approach also fails to consider all the services which guests pay for in a hotel complex such as food, beverages, telephone, laundry, etc. If a hotel is able to earn a positive contribution from these services (and the successful ones do), then the need for higher prices for rooms is reduced.

Hubbart Formula

A more recently developed cost approach is the Hubbart Formula which is a bottom-up approach to pricing rooms. In determining the average price per room, this approach considers costs, desired profits, and expected rooms sold. In other words, this approach starts with desired profit, adds income taxes, and then adds fixed charges followed by operating overhead expenses and direct operating expenses. It is called bottom-up because the first item, profit, is at the bottom of the income statement. The second item, income taxes, is the next item from the bottom of the income statement, and so on. The approach involves the following eight steps:

1. Calculate the desired profit by multiplying the desired rate of return by the owners' investment (ROI).

2. Calculate pretax profits by dividing desired profit (Step 1) by (1 minus tax rate).

3. Calculate fixed charges and management fees. This calculation includes estimating depreciation, interest expense, property taxes, insurance, amortization, rent, and management fees.

4. Calculate undistributed operating expenses. This calculation includes estimating administrative and general, data processing, human resources, transportation, marketing, guest entertainment, property operation and maintenance, and energy costs.

5. Estimate non-room operating department income or losses.

6. Calculate the required rooms departmental income. The sum of pretax profits (Step 2), fixed charges and management fees (Step 3), undistributed operating expense (Step 4), and other operating department losses less other operating department income (Step 5) equals the required rooms department income.

7. Determine the rooms department revenue. The required rooms department income (Step 6) plus rooms department direct expenses of payroll and related expenses, plus other direct expenses, equals rooms department revenue.

8. Calculate the average room rate by dividing rooms department revenue (Step 7) by expected rooms to be sold.

Illustration of the Hubbart Formula

The Harkins Hotel, a 200-room hotel, is projected to cost $9,900,000 inclusive of land, building, equipment, and furniture, and an additional $100,000 is needed for working capital purposes. The hotel is financed with a loan of $7,500,000 at 12% interest with the owners providing cash of $2,500,000. The owners desire a 15% annual return on their investment. A 75% occupancy is estimated, thus, 54,750 rooms will be sold during the year (200 x .75 x 365). The income tax rate is 40%. Additional expenses are estimated as follows:

Property taxes	$ 250,000
Insurance	50,000
Depreciation	300,000
Administrative & general	300,000
Data processing	120,000
Human resources	80,000
Transportation	40,000
Marketing expense	200,000
Property operation and maintenance	200,000
Energy costs	300,000

The other operating departments' income or losses are estimated as follows:

Food and beverage	$ 150,000
Telephone	(50,000) loss
Rentals and other income	100,000

Room department direct expenses are $10 per room sold.

Exhibit 10.3 contains the calculations used in the Hubbart Formula and reveals an average room rate of $67.81.

The formula for calculating room rates for singles and doubles,

Exhibit 10.3   Calculation of Average Room Rate Using Hubbart Formula

Item	Calculation	Amount
Desired net income	Owners' Investment × ROI 2,500,000 × .15 = 375,000	$375,000
Pretax income	Pretax income = $\frac{\text{net income}}{1-t}$ Pretax income = $\frac{375,000}{1-.4}$ Pretax income = $625,000	$625,000
Interest expense	Principal × int. rate × time = int. exp. 7,500,000 × .12 × 1 = 900,000	900,000
Income before interest and taxes		1,525,000
Estimated depreciation, property taxes, and insurance		600,000
Income before fixed charges		2,125,000
Undistributed operating expense		1,240,000
Required operated departments income		3,365,000
Departmental results excluding rooms		
Less: Food and beverage income		(150,000)
Rentals and other income		(100,000)
Plus: Telephone department loss		50,000
Rooms department income		3,165,000
Rooms department direct expense	54,750 × $10 = 547,500	547,500
Rooms revenue		3,712,500
		÷ 54,750
Required average room rate		$67.81

Exhibit 10.4   Determining Single and Double Room Rates from an Average Room Rate

Singles Sold (x) + Doubles Sold (x + y) = Average Rate (Rooms Sold)

where:

x	=	Price of single
y	=	Price of differential between singles and doubles
x + y	=	Price of doubles

where the doubles are sold at a differential of "y" from singles, is shown in Exhibit 10.4. For the Harkins Hotel, a double occupancy rate of 40% and a price differential of $10 would result in the calculation of single and double rates as follows:

$$
\begin{aligned}
\text{Doubles sold in one day} &= \text{(double occ.) (rooms sold per day)} \\
\text{Doubles sold in one day} &= .4(200)(.75) \\
\text{Doubles sold in one day} &= \underline{\underline{60}} \\[4pt]
\text{Singles sold in one day} &= 150 - 60 \\
&= \underline{\underline{90}}
\end{aligned}
$$

$$
\begin{aligned}
90x + 60(x + 10) &= (67.81)(150) \\
90x + 60x + 600 &= 10{,}171.5 \\
150x &= 9{,}571.5 \\
x &= \frac{9{,}571.5}{150} \\[6pt]
\underline{\text{Single Rate}} &= \underline{\underline{\$63.81}} \\[6pt]
\underline{\text{Double Rate}} &= \$63.81 + 10.00 \\
\underline{\text{Double Rate}} &= \underline{\underline{\$73.81}}
\end{aligned}
$$

Alternatively, the double rate could be set as a percentage of the single rate. When this is the case, the formula is slightly altered as follows:

Avg. Rate = Singles Sold (x) + Doubles Sold (x) (1 + Markup %)

The percentage mark-up is simply the percentage difference of the double rate over the single rate. To illustrate this approach, let's again use the Harkins Hotel example. Assume a 40% double occupancy and a markup of 15%.

$$
\begin{aligned}
90x + 60(x)(1.15) &= (67.81)(150) \\
90x + 69x &= 10{,}171.5 \\
159x &= 10{,}171.5 \\
x &= \frac{10{,}171.5}{159} \\[6pt]
\underline{\text{Single Rate}} &= \underline{\underline{\$63.97}} \\[6pt]
\underline{\text{Double Rate}} &= 63.97(1.15) \\
\underline{\text{Double Rate}} &= \underline{\underline{\$73.57}}
\end{aligned}
$$

Bottom-Up Approach to Pricing Meals

The bottom-up approach used to price rooms (Hubbart Formula) may also be used to determine the average meal price for restaurants. Seven steps for determining the required food revenue are as follows:

1. Determine desired net income by multiplying investment by desired return on owners' investment (ROI).

2. Determine pretax profit by dividing the desired net income by 1 minus the tax rate.

3. Determine fixed charges.[1]

4. Determine controllable expenses.

5. Determine food revenue by first adding figures from Steps 2-4 and then dividing this sum by 1 minus the desired food cost percentage.

6. Determine meals to be served by multiplying days open by seats and by seat turnover for the day.

7. Determine price of the average meal by dividing the total food revenue by the estimated number of meals to be served.

To illustrate the average restaurant meal price calculation, Morgans, a 100-seat restaurant, will be used. Information regarding Morgans is found in Exhibit 10.5.

Exhibit 10.6 shows that the average meal price for Morgans inclusive of beverage sales, desserts, etc., is $18.22, given the above costs and the seat turnover of 2. In those calculations, total food revenue is determined by dividing total expenses and net income (prior to cost of food sold) by 1 minus the cost of food sold percentage. If management could turn the seats faster, everything else being the same, then the average meal price required to provide the owners with the desired 12% return will be reduced. For example, if the seat turnover could be increased to 3, then the average meal price is determined as follows:

$$\text{Average Meal Price} = \frac{\text{Food Revenue}}{\text{Meals Sold}}$$

$$\text{Average Meal Price} = \frac{1,140,477}{93,900}$$

$$\text{Average Meal Price} = \$12.15$$

On the other hand, a less frequent turnover requires a higher average meal price, all other things being the same. For Morgans, a lower seat turnover of 1.5 requires an average meal price of $24.29.

The entire discussion of the bottom-up approach to pricing meals has centered on average meal prices. Few food service establishments price all meals at one price, or even all meals for a given meal period at one price. However, the average meal price per meal period can be determined as follows:

1. Calculate the revenue by meal period by multiplying the estimated percentage by meal period by total food revenue.

2. Divide the revenue by meal period by the meals sold by meal period.

3. Meals sold per meal period is calculated by multiplying the days the food service business is open by the seat turnover and by the number of seats.

Once again, Morgans is used to illustrate these calculations.

Exhibit 10.5   Essential Factors for Determining the Average Meal Price at Morgans

Item	Amount	Other
Owner's investment	$200,000	Desired ROI = 12%
Funds borrowed	500,000	Interest Rate = 10%
Tax rate	—	30%
Fixed charges (excluding interest)	100,000	Annual amount
Controllable expenses	500,000	Annual amount
Cost of food sold percentage	—	40%
Seat turnover	—	2 times per day
Days open (closed one day per week)	—	313 days

Exhibit 10.6   Calculation of Average Meal Price for Morgans

Item	Calculation	Amount
Desired net income	200,000 × .12	$ 24,000
Pretax profits	$\frac{24,000}{1-.3} = \frac{24,000}{.7}$	$ 34,286
Interest	500,000 × .10 × 1	50,000
Other fixed charges		100,000
Controllable expenses		500,000
Total expenses and net income prior to cost of food sold		$ 684,286
Total food revenue	$\frac{684,286}{.6}$	$1,140,477
Meals sold	313 × 100 × 2	62,600
Average meal price	($1,140,477 ÷ 62,600)	$ 18.22

Assume management estimates the total food revenue to be divided between lunch and dinner revenue as 40% and 60%, respectively. Further, assume the luncheon seat turnover is 1.25 while the dinner seat turnover is .75. Using the total revenue for Morgans as calculated in Exhibit 10.6, the average meal prices by meal period are determined as follows:

Revenue by meal period:

Lunch 40% x $1,140,477	=	456,191
Dinner 60% x $1,140,477	=	684,286
Total	=	$1,140,477

Exhibit 10.7   Sales Mix Alternatives and Number of Meals

| | **Sales Mix Alternatives** | | |
	#1	#2	#3
Chicken	500	300	200
Fish	200	300	300
Steak	300	400	500
Total	1,000	1,000	1,000

Meals sold by meal period:

$$\text{Lunch } 313 \times 100 \times 1.25 \quad = \quad 39,125$$

$$\text{Dinner } 313 \times 100 \times .75 \quad = \quad 23,475$$

Average meal prices by meal period:

$$\text{Average Meal Prices by Meal Period} = \frac{\text{Meal Period Revenue}}{\text{Meals Sold}}$$

$$\text{Lunch} = \frac{456,191}{39,125}$$

$$\text{Lunch} = \$11.66$$

$$\text{Dinner} = \frac{684,286}{23,475}$$

$$\text{Dinner} = \$29.15$$

Food Sales Mix and Gross Profit

Traditionally, restaurateurs have placed heavy emphasis on food cost percentage. The multiple in the mark-up approach used to price meals for many restaurants was set at 2.5 times, so that a 40% cost of food sold could be achieved. This emphasis resulted in many managers evaluating the profitability of their food service operations by reviewing the food cost percentage. However, the food cost percentage is not the best guide to evaluating food sales, as will be shown below.

Consider a restaurant that may sell one of three alternative sales mixes for the week as listed in Exhibit 10.7. Notice in each sales mix, the same number of meals are served. Exhibit 10.8 shows the total revenue, total cost of food sold, the gross profit, and food cost percentage for each alternative.

Exhibit 10.9 compares the three alternatives. The sales mix with the lowest total food cost percentage is mix #1 at 39.56%, while mix #3 has the highest at 41.99%, or nearly 2.5% greater than mix #1. If the most desirable mix is based on food cost percentage, then mix #1 is selected. However, under mix #3, the gross profit is $4,670 compared to a low of $4,140 for mix #1. Gross profit generated by mix #3 is $530 more than the

Exhibit 10.8 Profitability of Three Sales Mix Alternatives

	Selling Price	Cost Per Meal	Meals Sold	Revenue	Total Cost of Food	Gross Profit
Alternative #1						
Chicken	$4.95	$1.65	500	$2,475	$825	$1,650
Fish	6.95	2.75	200	1,390	550	840
Steak	9.95	4.45	300	2,985	1,335	1,650
Total			1,000	$6,850	$2,710	$4,140
		Food cost % =	$\frac{2,710}{6,850}$ = 39.56%			
Alternative #2						
Chicken	$4.95	$1.65	300	$1,485	$495	$990
Fish	6.95	2.75	300	2,085	825	1,260
Steak	9.95	4.45	400	3,980	1,780	2,200
Total			1,000	$7,550	$3,100	$4,450
		Food cost % =	$\frac{3,100}{7,550}$ = 41.06%			
Alternative #3						
Chicken	$4.95	$1.65	200	$990	$330	$660
Fish	6.95	2.75	300	2,085	825	1,260
Steak	9.95	4.45	500	4,975	2,225	2,750
Total			1,000	$8,050	$3,380	$4,670
		Food cost % =	$\frac{3,380}{8,050}$ = 41.99%			

profit generated by mix #1. Therefore, all other things being the same, mix #3 is preferred, because a higher gross profit means a higher net income.

Exhibit 10.10 reveals the average gross profit for the three sales mix alternatives. The gross margin sold reflects the average gross profit per meal sold. The average gross margin under sales mix #3 ($4.67) is $.53 and $.22 higher than under mixes #1 and #2, respectively. Based on these results, fewer meals could be sold in mixes #3 and #2 than under mix #1, yet, the same gross profit under mix #1 still would be earned:

$$\frac{\text{Gross Profit} - \text{mix \#1}}{\text{Gross Margin} - \text{Other Sales Mix Alternative}}$$

Mix #2 to Mix #1

$$\frac{\$4,140}{\$4.45} = 930.34 \text{ meals}$$

Thus, under sales mix #2, 930.34 meals sold at an average gross margin of $4.45 yields $4,140 of gross profit, which is the same as generated under mix #1 when 1,000 meals are sold.

Exhibit 10.9   Comparison of Sales Mix Alternatives

Sales Mix Alternative	Total Revenue	Total Cost of Food	Gross Profit	Food Cost %
1	$6,850	$2,710	$4,140	39.56%
2	7,550	3,100	4,450	41.06
3	8,050	3,380	4,670	41.99

Exhibit 10.10   Average Gross Profit of Three Sales Alternatives

Sales Mix	Gross Profit	Meals Sold	Gross Margin
1	$4,140	1,000	$4.14
2	4,450	1,000	4.45
3	4,670	1,000	4.67

Exhibit 10.11   Gross Profit Graph for Three Sales Mix Alternatives

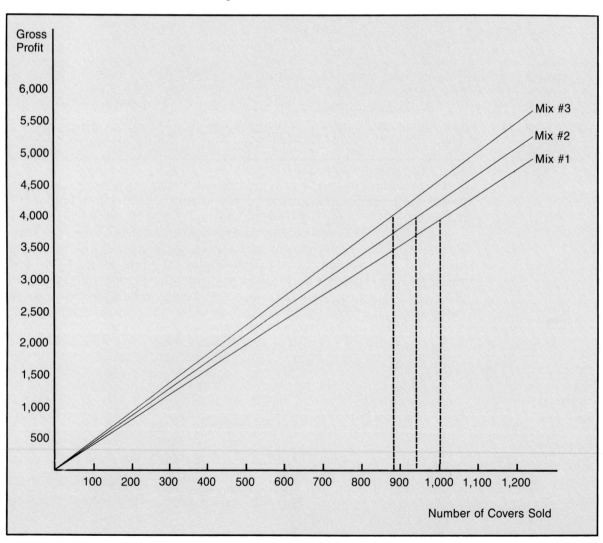

$$\underline{\text{Mix \#3 to Mix \#1}}$$

$$\frac{\$4,140}{\$4.67} = \underline{886.51 \text{ meals}}$$

This shows that under sales mix #3, 886.51 meals sold at an average gross margin of $4.67 yields $4,140, the same gross profit generated with mix #1 when 1,000 meals are sold.

These results are more clearly reflected in the graph found in Exhibit 10.11. The gross profit is related to meals sold in sales mixes #1 through #3. Gross profit increases progressively from sales mix #1 to sales mix #3. The same gross profit for sales mix #1 can be achieved by sales mixes #2 and #3 with considerably fewer meals sold.

Menu Engineering

A relatively new method of menu analysis and food pricing has been coined "menu engineering."[2] This sophisticated and fairly complex approach considers both the profitability and popularity of competing menu items. The emphasis is on gross margin (called contribution margin by Kasavana and Smith), and, for all practical purposes, food cost percentages are ignored. This emphasis on gross margin rather than food cost percentage is justified based on the fact that managers bank dollars, not percentages.

Menu engineering requires the manager to know each menu item's food cost, selling price, and quantity sold over a specific period of time. The menu item's gross margin (selling price minus food cost) is characterized as either high or low, in relation to the average gross margin for all competing menu items sold.

For example, assume a menu item X has a gross margin of $3.00 when the average gross margin for the menu is $3.50, then menu item X is classified as having a low gross margin. If menu item Y has a gross margin of $4.50, then it is classified as high for profitability purposes.

Each menu item is further classified by popularity (high or low) based on the item's menu mix percentage; that is, the menu item count for each menu item as a percentage of the total menu items sold. The dividing point for determining high and low popularity is calculated as follows:

$$70\% \, \frac{(1)}{n}$$

where n equals the number of competing menu items.

Therefore, if there are 10 competing items on a menu, the dividing point is 7% determined as follows:

$$70\% \, \frac{(1)}{10} = \underline{7\%}$$

Given a ten-item menu, any menu items with unit sales of less than 7%

Exhibit 10.12   Profitability/Popularity Classification of Menu Items

Profitability	Popularity	Classification
High	High	Stars
High	Low	Puzzles
Low	High	Plowhorses
Low	Low	Dogs

of the total items sold would be classified as having a low popularity, while any equal to, or greater than, 7% would be classified as having high popularity. The profitability and popularity classifications for each menu item result in four categories of menu items as shown in Exhibit 10.12.

Exhibit 10.13 is a menu engineering worksheet useful for determining the classification of each menu item. A more complete discussion of menu engineering, including a comprehensive example, is contained in the appendix to this chapter.

Integrated Pricing

Many businesses in the hospitality industry, especially the lodging sector, have several revenue producing departments (profit centers). Prices must be set for products and/or services in each profit center so as to optimize the operation's net income. Allowing each profit center to price its products independently may fail to optimize the operation's profits. For example, the swimming pool department manager may decide to institute a direct charge to guests. This new pricing policy may maximize swimming pool revenues, but, at the same time, guests may opt for other hotels where pool privileges are provided at no additional cost. Therefore, the revenue for other profit centers, rooms and food and beverage, is lost from guests who select competing hotels because of the new pool charge policy.

Prices for all departments must be established so as to optimize the operation's net income. This will generally result in some profit centers not maximizing their revenues and thus not maximizing their departmental incomes. This integrated approach is essential and can only be accomplished by the general manager and profit center managers coordinating their pricing.

Computerization

Many of the pricing methods discussed in this chapter do not require sophisticated mathematical models to determine the desired price. However, even simple tasks can waste valuable time when they

Exhibit 10.13   Menu Engineering Worksheet

Menu Engineering Worksheet

Restaurant: _____

Date: _____

Meal Period: _____

(A) Menu Item Name	(B) Number Sold (MM)	(C) Menu Mix %	(D) Item Food Cost	(E) Item Selling Price	(F) Item CM (E-D)	(G) Menu Costs (D*B)	(H) Menu Revenues (E*B)	(L) Menu CM (F*B)	(P) CM Category	(R) MM% Category	(S) Menu Item Classification
Column Totals:	N					I	J	M			

Additional Computations:

K = I/J   O = M/N   Q = (100%/items)(70%)

Exhibit 10.14 Computer-Generated Hubbart Formula Worksheet

INPUTS:	Alternatives				
	1	**2**	**3**	**4**	**5**
Investment	$2,000,000	$2,000,000	$2,000,000	$2,000,000	$2,000,000
ROI	16.0%	16.0%	16.0%	12.0%	16.0%
Tax Rate	46.0%	46.0%	46.0%	46.0%	46.0%
Long-Term Debt	4,000,000	4,000,000	4,000,000	4,000,000	4,000,000
Interest Rate	15.0%	15.0%	15.0%	15.0%	15.0%
Estimated Fixed Charges (excluding interest expense)	60,000	60,000	60,000	60,000	85,000
Undistributed Operating Expenses	600,000	600,000	600,000	600,000	650,000
Departmental Profits Food	135,000	135,000	135,000	135,000	135,000
Telephone	10,000	10,000	10,000	10,000	10,000
Rooms Department Variable Costs per Rooms Sold	$15	$15	$15	$15	$18
Number of Rooms	200	200	200	200	200
Occupancy Rate	75%	80%	65%	75%	60%
Hubbart Calculation					
Desired Net Income	$320,000	$320,000	$320,000	$240,000	$320,000
Pretax Income	592,593	592,593	592,593	444,444	592,593
Interest Expense	600,000	600,000	600,000	600,000	600,000
Income Before Fixed Charges	1,252,593	1,252,593	1,252,593	1,104,444	1,277,593
Required Room Dept. Income	1,707,593	1,707,593	1,707,593	1,559,444	1,782,593
Rooms Revenue	2,528,843	2,583,593	2,419,343	2,380,694	2,570,993
Required Average Rate	$46.19	$44.24	$50.99	$43.48	$58.70

must be repeated many times. Because the standard formulas are frequently used by firms, their computerization could be beneficial for a manager. This is especially true when management wants to view a number of scenarios in order to determine the "best" pricing options.

The Hubbart Formula can be translated into a computerized worksheet with relative ease. By entering each of the "inputs" into the formula separately, as shown in Exhibit 10.14, management can vary assumptions and see the results of their "what if" questions. In the past, the number of scenarios considered was seriously limited by the time that a staff member could devote to "number crunching," now, suggestions can be calculated almost at will.

The personal computer also can be a tool for food and beverage outlets. There are menu engineering packages available which will calculate the contribution margins and menu mix percentages after the user inputs the menu items' sales prices, costs, and demands. Then, they determine the classification of each menu item and print the menu engineering graph for the manager. More sophisticated systems will interface a personal computer with the point of sale register and with the inventory information. Having done this, it is possible to generate not only the outputs of menu engineering, but also to gather all of the inputs. When this type of a system is utilized, management can generate daily sales and cost reports so that pricing decisions can be made at any time. This is especially useful for restaurants which offer a large number of specials, or vary their entrees based on market availability.

Summary

An optimal pricing structure can play a large role in the profitability of a hospitality operation. If rooms are underpriced, profits are lost; if meals are overpriced, demand may decrease causing a decrease in profits. Management needs to be aware of these effects and set prices accordingly.

The relationship between the percentage change in price and the resulting percentage change in demand is called elasticity. In order to determine the price elasticity of demand for a product, the manager utilizes this formula:

$$\frac{\text{Change in Quantity Demanded}}{\text{Base Quantity}} \quad \text{divided by} \quad \frac{\text{Change in Price}}{\text{Base Price}}$$

If the result is greater than 1, the demand for the product is said to be elastic. In other words, a change in price results in a larger percentage change in the quantity demanded. Inelastic demand results when the change in price is greater than the percentage change in demand, and the formula results in an answer less than 1. Every manager would prefer to have products with inelastic demand. When this is the case, a raise in prices results in increased revenues because the percentage decrease in demand is less than the percentage increase in prices.

There are a number of informal pricing methods which are used by management. One is to price items based on what the competition charges. Other managers assume they know the price the public will accept and use "intuition." Still another method is psychological pricing by which managers determine what they think customers expect to pay.

These methods, although frequently used, fail to examine some vital aspects of the operation; they do not examine costs. More technical methods, such as the mark-up and the bottom-up approaches, all start with costs and determine prices to ensure that the result is adequate net income.

The mark-up approach begins with the cost and, based on the desired product cost percentage, multiplies it by the mark-up. There are two variations of this approach. One sets a mark-up factor to mark up the total cost of the meal; the other multiplies the prime ingredient cost by a factor. The result of either of these approaches should be a price that will not only cover the food cost but also the labor and other costs.

The Hubbart Formula is a method used to price rooms. It begins with the required return on the investment and adds to it the costs of the operations including taxes, management fees, fixed charges, undistributed operating expenses, and other departmental income. Using this approach, departmental income (or losses) from other profit centers are added to (or subtracted from) the total indirect expenses of the hotel to determine the required rooms department income. The direct expenses of the rooms department plus the required rooms department income equal the required rooms department revenue. The average price per room is calculated by dividing the required rooms department revenue by the number of rooms expected to be sold during the period.

The cost approaches appear rigorous and objective; however, they generally are based on estimates. Further, when the proposed price is computed on the basis of one of the cost approaches presented, careful consideration must be given to prices being charged by the competition prior to the implementation of any price changes. Differences in price must be supported by a different offering, such as a better location, more amenities, and so on. Finally, in a multi-product situation, such as a hotel, prices of the various products, food, beverages, and rooms, must be set on an integrated basis.

Notes

1. Based on terminology used in the *Uniform System of Accounts for Restaurants* (Washington, D.C.: National Restaurant Association, 1983).
2. Michael L. Kasavana and Donald I. Smith, *Menu Engineering—A Practical Guide to Menu Analysis (Lansing, Mich.: Hospitality Publications, 1982).*

Discussion Questions

1. What are five methods of informal pricing?

2. What disadvantages are inherent with informal pricing?

3. How is the cost mark-up factor often calculated?

4. What is the difference between the mark-up and the prime ingredient mark-up pricing methods?

5. What is price elasticity of demand?

6. What is the philosophy behind bottom-up pricing?

7. What does menu engineering consider in its review of menu items?

8. What is the relation between contribution margins and cost percentages?

9. How is the $1 per $1,000 technique used to price rooms?

10. Which pricing method is the most applicable for restaurants? Why?

Problem 10.1

Kristy's has been charging an average of $45 for its hotel rooms and has operated at an 80% occupancy. A recent average room price increase to $50 has been proposed. The general manager expects the occupancy to decline to 77% as a result of the price increase.

Required:

1.   Compute the price elasticity of demand.

2.   How is demand characterized for Kristy's, based on your calculations in #1.

Problem 10.2

Erica's Eatery enjoys a strong market position in a midwestern city. Erica Eastman, the owner, desires to maintain the high quality of service as well as excellent profits. Therefore, food items are marked up by a factor of 3.5 while beverages are to have a beverage cost percentage of 20%. Assume that a new item, chicken continental, has a $2.25 food cost, and a drink to be tested, the Great Escape, has a beverage cost of $.48.

Required:

Determine the selling price of both the chicken continental and the Great Escape by using the mark-up method.

Problem 10.3

Monica's Motel, a 100-room property constructed in 19X1 for $680,000, has just been purchased by a new firm, Lodging Limited, which is reconsidering the motel's pricing structure.

The motel was purchased with $800,000 of long-term debt and $400,000 equity. Lodging Limited is in the 35% tax bracket and requires a 15% return on its equity investment. The accountant for Lodging Limited has estimated annual fixed charges and undistributed operating expenses to be $600,000 and annual rooms department expenses of $125,000 when occupancy is 68%. There are no other operated departments and any other income is deemed immaterial.

Assume the hotel will operate 365 days during the year and have a 68% room occupancy.

Required:

1.   Determine the average room rate by the $1 per $1,000 method.

2.   Determine the average room rate by the Hubbart Formula.

Problem 10.4

Josie's Place Inn, a proposed 30-room motel with a restaurant, fully equipped, will cost $750,000 to construct. An estimated additional $50,000 will be invested in the business as working capital. Of the total $800,000 investment, $400,000 is to be secured from the Columbo Federal Bank at the rate of 10% interest. The projected occupancy rate is 80% for the year. The owners desire a 15% return on equity after the corporation pays income taxes of 25%. The estimated undistributable expenses, not including income taxes and interest expense total $480,000. The estimated direct expenses of the rooms department are $7 for each room sold. Consider a year to have 365 days.

Required:

1. Determine the average price of a room using the Hubbart Formula assuming the contribution from the restaurant department is $-0-.

2. If the double rooms are sold at a premium of $10 over singles, what is the price of singles and doubles? Assume a double occupancy rate of 40%.

3. If the restaurant generates a department profit of $20,000 per year, how much may average room rates be decreased and still meet the owners' financial goals?

Problem 10.5

Bobbie's Place has not changed its menu in three years. Recently, the owner, Bobbie Schmidt, read about menu engineering and desires your assistance in analyzing the dinner menu. The seven dinner entrees, their selling prices, costs, and the menu counts for a recent month are as follows:

	Selling Price	Food Cost	Number Sold
Sirloin steak	$ 9.95	$3.00	240
King crab	15.95	6.00	50
Lobster	18.45	8.00	60
Prime rib	14.50	4.25	300
Whitefish	8.75	2.50	80
New York strip	12.45	5.75	180
Chicken a la king	8.50	2.60	280

Required:

1. Complete a menu engineering worksheet using the format of Exhibit 10.13.

2. What recommendations would you offer the owner based on your analysis?

Note: Review of the menu engineering discussion in the appendix to this chapter would be helpful in working this problem.

Supplemental Reading
Menu Engineering*
What to do with plowhorses, stars, puzzles and dogs

By Donald Smith, Director,
Michigan State's School of Hotel, Restaurant & Institutional Management

A menu is a portfolio of items. The way you manage this portfolio determines what your consumer demand and profit contribution margin will be. The key to any menu's success is whether or not it produces more customers and more contribution dollars.

Menu engineering is a tool foodservice operators can use to evaluate one menu against another. It requires that the operator know each menu item's total product cost, selling price, and quantity sold over a specific period of time. A menu item's revenue contribution margin and sales activity is categorized as either relatively high or low. Each menu item is classified and evaluated for both its marketing (popularity) and pricing (profit) success.

By categorizing and classifying menu items through logical mathematical procedures, menu engineering enables the operator to make the right decisions.

Food cost percentages

Most foodservice operators have been conditioned to judge profitability by cost of goods percentages. To establish a total product cost in a foodservice operation, management must know three key pricing factors: standard recipe cost, garnish cost, and supplementary food cost.

Standard recipe cost. The cost of all products used to produce one standard portion of a menu item. For example, New York Strip Steak may be served as a 10 oz. portion of 180A strip loin extra short. At $6 per pound, the cost of the standard 10 oz. portion would be $3.75 ($6 lb./10 oz. equals 5/8 lb. x $6 equals $3.75).

Garnish cost. Products used in garnishing the standard recipe for each item to enhance eye appeal and flavor. For example, parsley, fruit, lobster butter, mushroom caps and onion rings. The New York Strip Steak might be garnished with onion rings and mushroom caps.

Supplementary food cost. Foods that are included with menu items regardless of selection or sales price. Many restaurants offer bread, butter, salad (including salad dressing) and po-

tato with all menu items. Supplementary foods can account for a substantial cost factor.

The total product cost for a standard portion of New York Strip Steak might be as follows:

Standard recipe cost	$3.75
Garnish cost	.18
Supplementary food cost	.57
	$4.50

Once management analyzes the total cost of each menu item, the menu's potential cost of goods can be determined. The potential cost of goods is the total cost if all items purchased are sold, and if no foods are incorrectly portioned, stolen, or otherwise wasted. Obviously, potential cost of goods sold and actual costs will vary. Variance—usually from one to three percent—depends on the type of restaurant and the effectiveness of management control. Actual food costs are determined by purchases and inventory at the end of an accounting period.

As a rule of thumb, the variance in potential and actual cost of goods at fast food operations is one half to one percentage point; at table service and specialty restaurants, it is two to two and a half percentage points. Any larger variance should signal management that a problem exists.

To determine each menu item's food cost percentage, the item's total product cost for a standard portion is divided by its selling price. The food cost percentage for the entire menu is determined by dividing the menu's total food cost by total revenues.

Cost percentages, however, should not be the sole means of evaluating food profitability. Illustration 1 ranks the menu items at Johny's Grill, a hypothetical restaurant that we will use as a case study. The menu items are ranked from highest to lowest contribution margin. For our purposes, contribution margin is the amount left over after subtracting the item's total standard portion cost from its selling price.

As you can see, low food cost percentages do not necessarily indicate profitability. The chicken entree has the lowest food cost percentage, 31%, but yields only a $2.74 contribution margin. The lobster tail entree produces the highest contribu-

1. Items Ranked by Contribution Margin

(A) CM Classification	(B) Menu Item	(C) CM	(D) Food Cost %
1. HIGH	Lobster Tail	4.65	41%
2. HIGH	Prime Rib (20 oz.)	4.30	46%
3. HIGH	NY Strip Steak	4.00	41%
4. HIGH	Top Sirloin Steak	3.65	39%
5. LOW	Shrimp	3.05	41%
6. LOW	Red Snapper	3.00	39%
7. LOW	Prime Rib (12 oz.)	3.00	45%
8. LOW	Chicken	2.74	31%
9. LOW	Chopped Sirloin	2.55	41%
10. LOW	Tenderloin Tips	2.45	42%

2. Menu A: When Chicken is Most Popular Item

	Menu Mix	Cost	Income
Chicken	1000	$1500	$ 4,500
Steak	400	1200	2,800
Lobster	300	1350	2,700
	1700	$4050	$10,000

Potential Food Cost: $\frac{4050}{10,000} = 40.5\%$

Contribution Margin: $5,950

Average C.M. per Guest: $3.50

3. Menu B: When Steak is Most Popular Item

	Menu Mix	Cost	Income
Chicken	300	$ 450	$ 1,350
Steak	800	2400	5,600
Lobster	600	2700	5,400
	1700	$5550	$12,350

Potential Food Cost: $\frac{5550}{12350} = 44.9\%$

Contribution Margin: $6,850

Average C.M. per Guest: $4.03

tion margin—$4.65—and has a food cost percentage of 41%.

Illustrations 2 and 3 show the importance of tracking the effects of varied consumer demand—menu mix—on contribution margin and potential food cost. Each menu contains the same three entrees prepared with similar standard recipe and product costs. The total number of covers sold is the same for each menu—1,700—but the consumer purchase pattern, menu mix, is different.

In Illustration 2, Menu A, the chicken entree is the most popular item. It produces, however, only $4,500 in income when 1,000 covers are sold. Menu A's food cost percentage is 40.5%, its average contribution margin per guest is $3.50, and it generates a total contribution margin of $5,950.

In Illustration 3, Menu B, the steak entree is the most popular item. With only 800 covers sold, it produces income of $5,600. Menu B's food cost percentage is 44.9%, but its average contribution margin per guest is $4.03. It generates a total contribution margin—$6,850—higher than Menu A.

The menu with the lowest cost of goods percentage is the least profitable as a result of menu mix. The more a foodservice operator can shift demand to higher contribution margin items, the greater the menu's total contribution margin will be.

Gathering information

Every attempt to improve your menu begins with a statistical evaluation of your current situation. A foodservice operator's objective is to make the next menu more profitable and appealing to the guest. In order to do this, management must consider:

- The wants and needs of the target market
- What menu items to offer
- How to describe menu items
- How to cost and price each item
- How and where to place each item on the menu
- How to graphically design the complete menu

Management needs accurate information to answer these questions. Hence, the first step in menu engineering is to systematically gather information about each current menu item. This should include standard recipe cost and direct labor cost.

All recipes require lesser or greater time and skill depending on the product recipe and stage of raw or readiness of the ingredients. For our purposes in this article, we will treat direct labor, a semi-variable cost, as a fixed cost. The subject of direct labor input to each menu item will not be discussed.

Using menu engineering

Lets see how menu engineering works in actual practice. Johny's Grill is a table specialty restaurant with ten items on its dinner menu. Illustration 4 shows how menu engineering was used to analyze Johny's menu for a 30-day period.

1. First, the operator lists all menu entrees in column A. Only entree items are listed. Do not list appetizers, desserts or other side items. Do not list alcoholic beverage sales on this list. The ratio of food to beverage sales is a key to successful merchandising in most restaurants. The analysis of beverage sales, however, should be done separately. While we separate purchases for the purposes of our menu analysis, the successful operator is always concerned with the guests' total expenditure.

Daily specials must also be analyzed separately. By listing purchases of daily specials separately, their impact on the menu is more easily

identified. If the operator's suggestive selling program is effective, daily specials should become popular with relatively high contribution margins.

2. The total number of purchases for each item is listed in column B, menu mix. All purchases are listed on a per person basis.

3. Each item's sales is divided by the total number of purchases—3,000 in this case—to determine that item's menu mix percentage, column C.

4. In column D, each item's menu mix percentage is categorized as either high or low. Any menu item that is lower than 70% of the menu mix average percentage is considered low. Any item that is 70% or above the average is considered high. On a ten-item menu, for example, each item would theoretically get 10% of the mix. On a 20-item menu the average would be 5%. For Johny's ten-item menu, we multiply 10% times 70% to get the desired menu mix percentage rate of .07, or 7%. Any item 7% or higher is considered high. Any item less than 7% is low.

5. Each item's published menu selling price is listed in column E.

6. Each item's standard food cost is listed in column F. An item's standard portion cost is composed of standard recipe costs, garnish cost, and supplemental food cost. Not all items, however, will have all three cost components.

7. The contribution margin for each item is listed in column G. Contribution margins are determined by subtracting the item's standard food cost (column F) from its selling price (column E).

8. In column H we determine the total menu revenues by multiplying the number of purchases of each item (column B) by its selling price (column E).

9. In column I we determine the total menu food cost by multiplying each item's standard food cost (column F) by the number of items purchased (column B).

10. The total menu contribution margin is listed in column J. This is determined by multiplying each item's contribution margin (column G) times the item's total number of purchases (column B).

11. In column K we list the contribution margin percentage for each item. This is determined by dividing each item's contribution margin by the total menu contribution margin which is the total of column J, $9,644.80.

12. Each item's contribution margin is categorized as either high or low in column L, depending upon whether or not the item exceeds

4. How Menu Engineering Was Used to Analyze a Menu for a 30-Day Period

A Menu Item	B Menu Mix	C MM%	D MM% Category	E Menu Price	F Food Cost	G CM
Shrimp	210	7%	H	$7.95	$4.90	3.05
Chicken	420	14	H	4.95	2.21	2.74
Chopped Sirloin	90	3	L	4.50	1.95	2.55
Prime Rib/12 oz.	600	20	H	7.95	4.95	3.00
Prime Rib/20 oz.	60	2	L	9.95	5.65	4.30
New York Strip	360	12	H	8.50	4.50	4.00
Top Sirloin	510	17	H	7.95	4.30	3.65
Red Snapper	240	8	H	6.95	3.95	3.00
Lobster Tail	150	5	L	9.50	4.95	4.55
Tenderloin Tips	360	12	H	6.45	4.00	2.45
TOTALS	3,000	100%				

Potential Food Cost: 56.17%

the menu's average contribution margin. The menu's average contribution margin is determined by dividing the total contribution margin—$9,664.80—column J, by the total number of items sold, 3,000. The average contribution margin for Johny's Grill is $3.22.

13. We use all the data we have gathered to classify each item into categories in column M. Each menu item is classified as either a Star, Plow Horse, Puzzle, or Dog. These classifications are standard marketing theory terms (see below).

14. In column N we list the decisions made on each item. Should the item be retained, repositioned, replaced, or repriced?

The four key menu categories

When accurate information has been gathered and analyzed for each menu item as we have done in Illustration 4, the items are then categorized for decision making. All menu items can be grouped into four categories: Stars, Plow Horses, Puzzles and Dogs.

Stars. Menu items high in both popularity and contribution margin. Stars are the most popular items on your menu. They may be your signature items.

Plow Horses. Menu items high in popularity but low in contribution margin. Plow horses are demand generators. They may be the lead items on your menu or your signature items. They are often significant to the restaurant's popularity with price conscious buyers.

Puzzles. Menu items low in popularity but high in contribution margin. In other words, Puzzles yield a high profit per item sold, but they are hard to sell.

Dogs. Menu items low in popularity and low in contribution margin. These are your losers. They are unpopular, and they generate little profit.

How to use the categories

Once you have grouped your menu into the four key categories, you are ready to make decisions. Each category must be analyzed and evaluated separately.

Stars. You must maintain rigid specifications for quality, quantity, and presentation of all Star items. Locate them in a highly visible position on the menu. Test them occasionally for price inelasticity. Are guests willing to pay more for these items, and still buy them in significant quantity? The Super Stars of your menu—highest priced Stars—may be less price sensitive than any other items on the menu. If so, these items may be able to carry a larger portion of any increase in cost of goods and labor.

Plow Horses. These items are often an important reason for a restaurant's popularity. Increase their prices carefully. If Plow Horses are

H Total Menu Revenues	I Menu Food Cost	J Menu CM	K CM%	L CM Category	M Class	N Action Taken
$ 1,669.50	$ 1,029.00	$ 640.50	6.6	L	Plowhorse	Carefully increase price
2,079.00	928.20	1,150.80	11.9	L	Plowhorse	Retain as low price leader
405.00	175.50	229.50	2.4	L	Dog	Eliminate
4,770.00	2,970.00	1,800.00	18.6	L	Plowhorse	Retain
597.00	339.00	258.00	2.7	H	Puzzle	Increase Price
3,060.00	1,620.00	1,440.00	14.9	H	Star	Increase Price
4,054.50	2,193.00	1,861.50	19.3	H	Star	Retain
1,668.00	948.00	720.00	7.4	L	Plowhorse	Increase Price
1,425.00	742.50	682.50	7.1	H	Puzzle	Test by lowering price as special to see if demand increases
2,322.00	1,440.00	882.00	9.1	L	Plowhorse	Increase price in stages
$22,050.00	$12,385.20	$9,664.80	100%			

Average Contribution Margin: $3.22

highly price sensitive, attempt to pass only the cost of goods increase on to the menu price. Or, consider placing the increase on to a Super Star item. Test for a negative effect on demand (elasticity). Make any price increase in stages (from $4.55 to $4.75 then $4.95). If it is necessary to increase prices, pass through only the additional cost. Do not add more. Relocate non-signature and low contribution margin Plow Horses to a lower profile position on the menu. Attempt to shift demand to more profitable items by merchandising and menu positioning. If the item is an image maker or signature item, hold its current price as long as possible in periods of high price sensitivity.

Determine the direct labor cost of each Plow Horse to establish its labor and skill intensiveness. If the item requires high skills or is labor intensive, consider a price increase or substitution. Also, consider reducing the item's standard portion without making the difference noticeable. Merchandise the Plow Horse by packaging it with side items to increase its contribution margin. Another option is to use the item to create a "better value alternative." For example, prime ribs can be sold by the inch, and steaks can be sold by the ounce. This offers guests an opportunity to spend more, and get more value.

Puzzles. Take them off the menu. Particularly if a Puzzle is low in popularity, requires costly or additional inventory, has poor shelf life,

requires skilled or labor intensive preparation, and is of inconsistent quality. Another option is to reposition the Puzzle and feature it in a more popular location on the menu. You can try adding value to the item through Table D'Hote packaging. Rename it. A Puzzle's popularity can be affected by what it is called, especially if the name can be made to sound familiar.

Decrease the Puzzle's price. The item may have a contribution margin that is too high and is facing price resistance. Care must be taken, however, not to lower the contribution margin to a point where the Puzzle draws menu share from a Star. Increase the item's price and test for inelasticity. A Puzzle that has relatively high popularity may be inelastic.

Limit the number of Puzzles you allow on your menu. Puzzles can create difficulties in quality consistency, slow production down, and cause inventory and cost problems. You must accurately evaluate the effect Puzzle items have on your image. Do they enhance your image?

Dogs. Eliminate all Dog items if possible. Foodservice operators are often intimidated by influential guests to carry a Dog on the item. The way to solve this problem is to carry the item in inventory (assuming it has a shelf life) but not on the menu. The special guest is offered the opportunity to have the item made to order upon request. Charge extra for this service. Raise the Dog's price to Puzzle status. Some items in the

Dog category may have market potential. These tend to be the more popular Dogs, and may be converted to Puzzles.

Whenever possible, replace Dogs with more popular items. You may have too many items. It is not unusual to discover a number of highly unpopular menu items with little, if any, relation to other more popular and profitable items held in inventory. Do not be afraid to terminate Dogs, especially when demand is not satisfactory.

Developing new menu items

There are three reasons to add new menu items. To increase demand, to increase contribution margins, and to create greater market share for your operation.

Each new menu item should be carefully considered and pre-tested as a special before adding it to the menu. When adding new items, attempt to build off of products already in inventory. Try to develop new items that require low skills, and are not labor intensive. Add items that have the growth potential to become highly popular. Items not easily prepared at home—roasts and fish, for example—have good potential. Make sure food cost for the new item is relatively stable. And finally, aim for items with low food cost and good plate coverage. This will allow you to give the item a lower price and still maintain a high contribution margin.

Increase demand. Add a menu item with already proven popularity to increase frequency or broaden your market. For example, salad bars have high appeal to light eaters, and have proven their effectiveness in both fast food and specialty restaurants. Eggs and omelettes are also items with high popularity. Another way to increase demand is by adding a signature item that cannot be found anywhere else.

Increase contribution margin. Try to add new items with high contribution margins, espe-cially if they do not require additional inventory. For example, 20 oz. prime rib is a particularly good item to add when smaller cuts are already being served.

Signature items. Signature items, like Plow Horses, may be the most important reason for your restaurant's popularity. These are items found only at your operation, the specialty of the house. Properly developed and merchan-dised, they can create greater market share, and bring prestige and visibility to your operation. Add signature items with the utmost care.

Summary and conclusion

Menu engineering provides management with a tool to evaluate the effectiveness of its current menu, and to make decisions on menu pricing, content and design. It is a step-by-step process that helps management develop a menu with both popularity and profits.

Every attempt to improve your menu must begin with a statistical analysis of your current situation. By categorizing and classifying menu items through logical mathematical procedures, menu engineering enables the operator to make the right decisions.

The key to any menu's success is whether or not it produces more customers and more contri-bution dollars. A foodservice operator's objective must always be to make the next menu more profitable and appealing to the guest.

Notes

*This article is reprinted with permission from Hospitality Publications, Okemos, Mich., 1982.

11 Operations Budgeting

Every rational manager plans for the future. Some plans are formal while others are informal. Budgets are simply formal plans reduced to dollars. Budgets provide answers to many questions including the following:

1. What are the forecasted revenues for the month?

2. What is the budgeted labor for the year?

3. How many rooms are expected to be sold during February, and what is the expected average room rate?

4. What is the budgeted telephone department operating income for the month?

5. What is the estimated depreciation for the year?

6. How close were actual food and beverage revenues to the budgeted amounts for March?

7. What is the projected net income for the year?

This chapter is divided into two major sections. The first section investigates reasons for budgeting, the process of preparing the operations budget, and also the idea of budgeting horizons. The second part of the chapter focuses on budgetary control and how hospitality operations make use of budget reports in the budgetary control process. The Sands Motel, a hypothetical small lodging operation, is used to illustrate both budget preparation and control.

Types of Budgets

There are several types of budgets prepared by hospitality operations. The operations budget, the topic of this chapter, is also referred to as the revenue and expense budget, because it includes management's plans for generating revenues and incurring expenses for a given period. The operations budget includes not only operating department budgets (budgets for rooms, food and beverage, telephone, and other profit centers) but also budgets for service centers such as marketing, accounting, and human resources. In addition, the operations budget includes the planned expenses for depreciation, interest expense, and other fixed charges. Thus, the operations budget is a detailed operating plan by profit centers, cost centers within profit centers (such as the housekeeping department within the rooms department), and service centers. It includes all revenues and all expenses which appear on the summary income statement and related subsidiary schedules that we discussed in Chapter 3. Annual operating budgets are normally subdivided into monthly periods, and certain information is reduced to a daily basis for management's use in controlling operations. Thus, the operations budget enables management to accomplish two of its major functions: planning and control.

Capital budgeting pertains to planning for the acquisition of equipment, land, buildings, and other fixed assets. Capital budgeting procedures used by hospitality operations are the topic of Chapter 14.

The cash budget is management's plan for cash receipts and disbursements. It includes the projection of cash to be received, usually by monthly periods. Also, certain information is reduced to a weekly or even daily basis for management's use in controlling operations. We will discuss cash budgeting in Chapter 13 of this text.

Budgeting Horizons

The annual operations budget must be subdivided into monthly plans in order for management to effectively use it as an aid in monitoring operations. The monthly plans allow management to measure the operation's overall performance several times throughout the year. However, certain elements of the monthly plan are reduced to weekly and daily bases. For example, many lodging operations have daily revenue plans which differ by property, by day of the week, and by season. The daily revenue is compared to these daily revenue goals on the daily report of operations. Any significant differences (variances) require analysis, determination of causes, and, if necessary, corrective action. (Variance analysis will be discussed later in this chapter.) In addition, every month all revenue and expense amounts are compared to the budgeted amounts, and all significant variances are analyzed and explained.

Alternatives to the monthly budgets for a year are thirteen 4-week segments and the 4-4-5 quarterly plan. The corporation using thirteen 4-week periods simply divides the 52 weeks of the year into thirteen 4-week periods. The 4-4-5 plan consists of two 4-week plans followed by one 5-week which equal the thirteen weeks in a quarter. Four of these quarterly plans serve as the annual operations budget.

Many hospitality organizations also prepare operations budgets on a long-range basis. A common long-range period is five years. A five-year plan consists of five annual plans. The annual plans for the 2nd through 5th years are much less detailed than the current year's annual plan. When long-range budgets are used, the next year's budget serves as a starting point for preparing the operations budget. The long-range budget procedure is used to review and update the next four years and add the fifth year to the plan.

Long-range planning, also referred to as strategic planning, is recognized as essential to controlled growth of major hospitality organizations. It not only considers revenues and expenses (as do annual operating plans), but also evaluates and selects among major alternatives those which provide long-range direction to the hospitality operation. Major directional considerations may include the following:

- Evaluating whether a proposed acquisition will have a synergistic effect on existing operations or whether it will hinder or detract from existing operations.

- Determining whether the hospitality operation should expand into foreign markets.

- Determining whether a quick-service restaurant chain should add breakfast to its existing lunch and dinner offerings.

- Considering whether a single-property operation should add rooms, or possibly expand to include another property.

Reasons for Budgeting

Many smaller organizations in the hospitality industry have not formalized their operations budgets. Often, the overall goals, sales objectives, expense projections, and the desired bottom line remain "in the head" of the owner/manager. However, there are many reasons why every hospitality operation should use formalized budgeting, several of which are briefly described below:

1. Budgeting requires management to examine alternatives before selecting a particular course of action. For example, there are pricing alternatives for each product and/or service sold. Also, there are many different marketing decisions that must be made, such as where to advertise, how much to advertise, how to promote, when to promote, and so on. There are also several approaches to staffing, each of which will affect the quality of service provided. In nearly every revenue and expense area, several courses of action are available to hospitality operations. Budgeting provides management with an effective means of evaluating these alternatives.

2. Budgeting provides hospitality operations with a standard of comparison. At the end of the accounting period management is able to compare actual operating results to a formal plan. Significant variances may be analyzed to suggest the probable cause, or causes, which require additional investigation and possibly corrective action. Preparation of budgets is independent of budgetary control; however, budgets not used for control purposes result in an inefficient use of the budget process.

3. Budgeting enables management to look forward, especially where strategic planning is concerned. Too often, management is either solving current problems or reviewing the past. Budgeting requires management to anticipate the future. Future considerations may be both external and internal. External considerations include the economy, inflation, and major competition while internal considerations are primarily the hospitality operation's reactions to external

considerations. Hospitality operations should aggressively attempt to shape their environment rather than merely react to it.

4. When participative budgeting is practiced, the budget process involves all levels of management. This involvement should motivate the lower level managers as they have real input in the process rather than blindly adhering to budget numbers that are imposed upon them. Too often, autocratic budgeting approaches result in "unsuccessful" managers who blame the budget preparers (higher level managers) instead of accepting responsibility for poor operating results.

5. The budget process provides a channel of communication whereby the hospitality operation's objectives are communicated to the lowest managerial levels. In addition, lower level managers are able to react to these objectives and suggest operational goals such as rooms sold, rooms revenue, rooms labor expense, and so on. When the budget is used as a standard of comparison, the operating results are also communicated to lower level managers. This allows for feedback to these managers as the operating results are compared to the periodic plan. Further, lower level managers are required to explain significant variances—why they exist, what the cause(s) are, and what action is to be taken.

6. Finally, to the degree that prices are a function of costs, the budget process provides estimates of future expenses enabling managers to set their prices in relation to their expenses. Price changes can be the result of advanced planning, thereby allowing such changes to be properly implemented. Price changes made on the spur of the moment often result in "unprofessional" price execution, such as penciled changes on menus, a poorly informed service staff who often misquote prices, and other similar situations.

Personnel Responsible for Budget Preparation

The complete budget process includes both budget preparation and budgetary control. The former is before the fact while the latter is accomplished at the end of a period of operations. The major purpose of budgeting is to allow management to accomplish its functions: planning, execution, and control.

In most hospitality organizations, the board of directors approves the operating budget which has been delegated to the chief executive officer (CEO). The CEO generally enlists the controller to coordinate the budget preparation process; however, budgeting is not a financial function where bookkeepers, accountants, and the controller have the sole responsibility for preparing the budget. The controller facilitates the budget preparation process by initially providing information to operating managers. The major input for the budget should come from operating department (profit centers) managers working with their lower level managers and from service department managers.

The controller receives the department managers' operating plans and formulates them into a comprehensive operating budget. These are then reviewed by the CEO and a budget committee (if one exists). If the comprehensive operating budget is satisfactory in meeting financial goals, it is presented to the board of directors by the CEO with the assistance of the controller. If it is not satisfactory, then the elements requiring change are returned to the appropriate department heads for review and change. This process may continue several times until a satisfactory budget is prepared.

The final budget should be the result of an overall team effort rather than a decree dictated by the CEO. This participative management approach should result in maximizing departmental managers' motivation.

The Budget Preparation Process

The major elements in the budget preparation process are as follows:

- Financial objectives
- Revenue forecasts
- Expense forecasts
- Determination of forecasted net income

The operations budget process begins with the board of directors of the hospitality organization establishing financial objectives. A major financial objective set by many organizations, both hospitality and business firms in general, is long-term profit maximization. Long-term profit maximization may mean that the operation does not maximize its profits for the next year. For example, in the next year, profits may be increased by reducing public relations efforts and major maintenance projects; however, in the long run, cuts in these programs may disturb the financial well-being of the hospitality establishment. An alternative objective set by institutional food service operations (e.g., hospital food service) is cost containment. The food service revenue generated by many of these operations is limited, therefore cost containment is critical to enable these operators to break even.

Another objective may be to provide high quality service even if it means incurring higher labor costs than allowable to maximize profits. Other objectives set by hospitality organizations have been (1) to be the top establishment in its segment of the hospitality industry, (2) to be the fastest growing establishment, and/or (3) to be recognized as the hospitality operation with the best reputation.

Many more objectives could be listed; however, critical to budget preparation is the establishment of the major objectives by the board of directors. These are then communicated to the CEO and are the basis for formulating the operating budget.

Forecasting revenue is the next step in preparing the operations budget. In order for managers of profit centers to be able to forecast revenue for their departments, they must be provided with information regarding the economic environment and detailed historical financial results of their departments. Information regarding the economic environment includes such items as:

- Expected inflation for the next year
- Ability of the operation to pass on cost increases to guests
- Changes in competitive conditions—for example, the emergence of new competitors, the closing of former competitors, and so on
- Expected levels of guest spending for products/services offered by the hospitality operation
- Business travel trends
- Tourist travel trends

For operations in foreign countries, in addition to the above considerations, other factors such as wage/price controls expected for the next year and the political environment may need to be considered.

In order for this information to be useful, it must be operationalized; that is, it must be reduced to usable numbers. For example, regarding inflation and the ability of the operation to increase its prices, the information received by department heads may be phrased as follows: inflation is expected to be 6% for the next year and prices of all products and services may be increased by an average maximum of 5%, with a 2.5% increase effective January 1 and July 1.

Forecasting Revenue

Historical financial information often serves as the foundation from which managers build their revenue forecasts. This type of budgeting has been referred to as "incremental budgeting." For example, rooms revenue of a hotel for 19X1 through 19X4 is shown in Exhibit 11.1.

From year 19X1 to 19X4, the amount of revenue increased from $1,000,000 to $1,331,000; however, the percentage increase was 10% for each year. Therefore, if future conditions appear to be similar to what they were in prior years, the rooms revenue for 19X5 would be budgeted at $1,464,100 which is a 10% increase over 19X4.

An alternative approach to budgeting revenue based on increasing the current year's revenue by a percentage is to base the revenue projection on unit sales and prices. This approach considers the two variables of unit sales and prices separately. For example, rooms revenue for a lodging property for years 19X1 through 19X4 appears in Exhibit 11.2.

An analysis of past financial information shows that occupancy percentage increased 2% from 19X1 to 19X2, 1% from 19X2 to 19X3, and 2% from 19X3 to 19X4. The average room rates have increased by $2, $3, and $4 over the past three years, respectively. Therefore, assuming the future prospects appear reasonable, the considerations for forecasting rooms revenues for 19X5 may use a 1% increase in occupancy percentage and a $5 increase average room rate as the basis for forecasting 19X5 rooms revenues. The formula for forecasting rooms revenue is as follows:

Rooms Available	x	Occupancy Percentage	x	Average Rate	=	Forecasted Rooms Revenue
36,500	x	.76	x	$54	=	$ 1,497,960

Exhibit 11.1 Rooms Revenue Increases

	Amount	Increase over prior year	
		Amount	%
19X1	$1,000,000	—	—
19X2	1,100,000	100,000	10
19X3	1,210,000	110,000	10
19X4	1,331,000	121,000	10

Exhibit 11.2 Rooms Revenue 19X1 through 19X2

Year	Rooms Sold	Occ. %	Average Room Rates	Rooms Revenues
19X1	25,550	70	$40	$1,022,000
19X2	26,280	72	42	1,103,760
19X3	26,645	73	45	1,199,025
10X4	27,375	75	49	1,341,375

This simplistic approach to forecasting rooms revenue is meant only to illustrate the process. A more detailed (and proper) approach would include further considerations such as: different types of rooms available and their rates, different room rates charged to different guests (e.g., convention groups, business travelers, and tourists), different rates charged on weeknights versus weekends, and different rates charged based on seasonality (especially for hotels subject to seasonal changes). These are just a few of the details considered by lodging operations in forecasting rooms revenues. In addition, managers of other profit centers, such as food and beverage, telephone, and the gift shop, must forecast their revenues for the year.

Estimating Expenses

The next step in the budget formulation process is estimating expenses. Since expenses are categorized both in relation to operated departments (direct/indirect) and how they react to changes in volume (fixed/variable), the forecasting of expenses is similar to the approach used in forecasting revenue. However, before department heads are able to estimate expenses, they must be provided information regarding the following:

1. Expected cost increases for supplies, food, beverages, and other expenses

2. Labor increases including the cost of fringe benefits and payroll taxes

Department heads of profit centers estimate their variable expenses in relation to the projected revenue of their departments. For example, historically, the food and beverage department may have incurred food costs at 35% of food sales. For the next year, the food department manager decides to budget at 35%; therefore, the food sales multiplied by 35% results in the projected cost of food sales. Other variable expenses are estimated similarly. Fixed expenses are projected on the basis of past experience and expected changes. For example, assume supervisors in the food department were paid salaries of $85,000 for the past year. The new salary level of the supervisors is $90,000 plus another half-time equivalent to be added at a cost of $8,000 for the next year. Thus, the fixed cost of supervisor salaries for the next year is set at $98,000. Other fixed expenses are similarly projected.

While the profit center managers are projecting expenses for their departments the service center department heads are estimating expenses for their departments. The service departments in a hotel comprise the general expense categories of administrative and general, marketing, property operation and maintenance, energy costs, human relations, data processing, and transportation. Department heads of service centers will estimate their expenses based on past experience and expected future changes. Generally, the historical amounts are adjusted to reflect higher costs. For example, the accounting department salaries of a hotel for 19X1 were $150,000. Salary increases for 19X2 are limited to an average of 5%; therefore, the 19X2 accounting department salaries budget is set at $150,000 + ($150,000 x .05) = $157,500.

A relatively new budgeting approach, zero-base budgeting (ZBB), is applicable in budgeting for service departments. ZBB, unlike the incremental approach, requires all expenses to be justified. In other words, the assumption is that each department starts with zero dollars (zero base) and must justify all budgeted amounts. Let's look at an example that illustrates the differences between the incremental and the ZBB approaches to budgeting.

The marketing department of a hotel had a total departmental budget of $500,000 in 19X1. In 19X2, cost increases are expected to average 5%, and advertising in the monthly city magazine is expected to cost $500 per month. Under the incremental approach the marketing budget would be set at $531,000, determined as follows:

$$\$500,000 + 500(12) + 500,000(.05) = \$531,000$$

Under ZBB, the marketing department would have to justify every dollar budgeted; that is, documentation would be required showing that all budgeted amounts are cost justified. This means all payroll costs, supplies, advertising, etc., would have to be shown to yield greater benefits than their cost.

The ZBB approach to budgeting in hotels appears to be limited to the service departments. However, the total cost of these departments is approximately 25%of the average hotel's total revenue, thus the total amount can be rather considerable for a hotel.

More detailed discussion of ZBB is beyond the scope of this text; however, the interested student is encouraged to read Peter A. Pyrrh's *Zero-Base Budgeting*[1] and also Lee M. Kruel's article applying ZBB to hotels, entitled "Zero-Base Budgeting of Hotel Indirect Expenses."[2]

Projecting Fixed Charges

The next step in the budget formulation process is the projection of fixed charges. Fixed charges include depreciation, insurance expense,

Exhibit 11.3   Interest Expense Budget 19X2

Debt	Principal	Interest Rate	Time	Amount
Mortgage payment	$500,000	12%	Year	$60,000
Loan from partner A	500,000	18	Year	90,000
Working capital				
loans	200,000	20	6 mo.	10,000
			Total	$160,000

property taxes, rent expense, and similar expenses. These expenses are fixed and are projected based on past experience and expected changes for the next year.

For example, assume interest expense for a hotel was $215,000 for 19X1. Exhibit 11.3 illustrates how the interest expense budget for 19X2 is determined by estimating interest expense based on current and projected borrowings. Based on calculations in Exhibit 11.3, the interest expense budgeted for 19X2 is $160,000.

The final step is for the controller to formulate the entire budget based on submissions from operated departments and service departments. The forecasted net income is a result of this process. If this bottom line is acceptable to the board of directors, then the budget formulation is completed. If the bottom line is not acceptable, then department heads are required to rework their budgets to provide a budget acceptable to the board. Many changes may be proposed in this "rework" process, such as price changes, marketing changes, and cost reductions, just to mention a few.

Budget Formulation Illustrated

A very simplified lodging example will be used to illustrate the preparation of an operations budget. The Sands Motel is a 20-room lodging facility which does not sell food and beverages. Each room is equipped with a telephone. Thus, the Sands Motel has two profit centers, the rooms department and telephone department. The Sands Motel also has two service centers, administration and a combined maintenance and energy cost department.

The board of directors has established the major financial goal of generating a minimum net income of 15% of sales. The income statements for the past three years are contained in Exhibit 11.4, and an analysis of this financial information appears in Exhibit 11.5.

Economic environment information relevant to the Sands Motel in 19X4 is summarized as follows:

- No new firms are expected to compete with the Sands Motel.

- Overall consumer demand for motel rooms is expected to remain relatively constant.

- Inflation is expected to be about 5% in the next year.

The major findings and projections for 19X4 are as follows:

Exhibit 11.4   Income Statements — Sands Motel

Income Statements
Sands Motel
For the years of 19X1-19X3

	19X1	19X2	19X3
Revenues:			
Rooms	$146,438	$158,634	$171,654
Telephone	2,962	3,466	4,246
Total	149,400	162,100	175,900
Departmental Expenses:			
Rooms:			
Payroll	21,966	23,000	27,465
Laundry	1,464	1,600	1,735
Linen	2,929	3,150	4,324
Commissions	1,470	1,578	1,650
All Other Expenses	1,500	2,380	2,575
Total	29,329	31,708	37,749
Telephone	2,850	3,350	4,285
Total	32,179	35,058	42,034
Departmental Income:			
Rooms	117,109	126,926	133,905
Telephone	112	116	(39)
Total	117,221	127,042	133,866
Undistributed Operating Expenses:			
Administration	27,470	30,105	32,795
Maintenance and Energy Costs	16,952	19,292	21,775
Total	44,422	49,397	54,570
Income Before Fixed Costs	72,799	77,645	79,296
Depreciation	15,000	15,000	15,500
Property Taxes	5,000	5,500	6,000
Insurance	5,000	5,000	5,000
Interest Expense	15,000	16,000	15,000
Income Before Income Taxes	32,799	36,145	37,796
Income Taxes	9,840	10,844	11,339
Net Income	$22,959	$25,301	$26,457

Item	Analytical Findings	Projection for 19X4
1. Rooms Revenue		
Occupancy Percentage	There is no new competition for next year and the Sands has been acquiring 1% more of the market each year for the last three years. Assume	71%

Exhibit 11.5   Analysis of Income Statements — Sands Motel

Analysis of Income Statements
Sands Motel
For the years of 19X1-19X3

	19X1	19X2	19X3
Rooms Sold	4,964	5,036	5,124
Occ. %	68	69	70
Average Rate	$29.50	$31,50	$33.50
Rooms Revenue	$146,438	$158,634	$171,654
Telephone revenue as a % of room revenue	2%	2.2%	2.5%
Rooms expenses %			
Payroll	15%	14.5%	16%
Laundry	1	1	1
Linen	2	2	2.5
Commissions	1	1	1
All other expenses	1	1.5	1.5
Total	20%	20%	22%
Administration			
Payroll			
Fixed	$20,000	$22,000	$24,000
Variable	3%	3%	2.5%
Other	2%	2%	2.5%
Maintenance and Energy Costs			
Maintenance			
Fixed	$4,000	$4,500	$5,000
Variable	3%	3%	3%
Energy Costs			
Fixed	$1,000	$1,500	$2,000
Variable	5%	5.2%	5.4%
Fixed Charges			

Depreciation – based on cost of fixed assets, expected lives, and straight-line method of depreciation
Property taxes – historically has increased by $500 for 19X1 through 19X3
Insurance – a three-year policy for 19X1-19X3 was quoted at $5,000 per year
Interest expense – based on amount borrowed and prevailing interest rates
Income taxes – based on 30% of income before income taxes

	19X1	19X2	19X3
Profit Margin %	15.36%	15.61%	15.04%

	an additional 1% increase in 19X4.	
Average Room Rate	This has increased by $2 each year and the Sands Motel has still increased its occupancy percentage. An additional $2 increase appears to be reasonable for 19X4. Note: The $2 increase is 6% of the	$35.50

$33.50 average price for 19X3 and exceeds the expected inflation of 5%.

2. Telephone Revenue	This has increased from 2% to 2.5%. Another .2% increase appears reasonable for 19X4.	2.7%
3. Rooms Expenses Payroll	This has fluctuated significantly due to labor unrest. Major pay increases this past year appear to be satisfying the two room attendants and part-time front office personnel. Keep the payroll percentage for 19X4 at 19X3 levels.	16%
Laundry	This has remained constant at 1% of rooms revenue for three years.	1%
Linen	A .5% increase was experienced in 19X3 due to major purchases. The prior 2% appears adequate for 19X4.	2%
Commissions	The average for the past three years has been 1%. Continue to use 1% as an estimate for 19X4.	1%
All Other Expenses	These have stabilized for the past two years at 1.5%. This appears reasonable.	1.5%
4. Telephone Expense	This has nearly equalled telephone revenue each year. A breakeven situation is reasonable for 19X4.	100% of telephone revenue
5. Administration Payroll	The fixed portion has increased approximately $2,000 per year from 19X1-19X3. A $3,000 increase is scheduled for 19X4 to reward the general manager. Variable labor (as a percentage of total revenue) is expected to be 3% for 19X4.	$27,000 and 3%
Other	Although this increased to 2.5% in 19X3, it is expected to return to the previous level of 2% in 19X4.	2%

6. Maintenance and
   Energy Costs

Maintenance	The fixed portion of part-time workers' pay has increased $500 each year over three years. An increase of $1,000 is scheduled for 19X4. Variable maintenance of 3% appears adequate for 19X4.	$6,000 and 3%
Energy Costs	The fixed portion has increased approximately $500 each year since 19X1. Therefore, the estimated fixed portion should be increased accordingly for 19X4. The variable portion has increased .2% from 19X1-19X3. Energy costs are expected to be moderate in 19X4 and 5.4% appears reasonable.	$2,500 and 5.4%

7. Fixed Charges

Depreciation	The accountant's calculation of depreciation for 19X4 is $15,000 for existing fixed assets and an additional $700 for a new microcomputer to be purchased in 19X4.	$15,700
Property Taxes	This assessed valuation is expected to increase by 10% for 19X4. The tax rate is not expected to change; therefore, increase property taxes for 19X4 to $6,600.	$6,600
Insurance	The current three-year insurance policy expires on December 31. The new three-year policy requires a $6,000 annual premium each year.	$6,000
Interest Expense	The flexible interest rate presently at 15% is expected to average 14.5% for 19X4. The average debt outstanding for 19X4 will be $90,000. $90,000 x .145 = $13,050.	$13,050
Income Taxes	Income taxes for 19X1-19X3 were 30% of the income before income taxes. Due to reduced rates, the tax rate for 19X4 will be 25%.	25% of pretax income

Exhibit 11.6 Sample Operations Budget Worksheet

Operations-Budget (Worksheet)
Sands Motel
For the year of 19X4

	Calculation	Amount
Revenue		
Rooms	365 × 20 × .71 × 35.50	$183,996
Telephone	183,996 × .027	4,968
Total		188,964
Departmental Expenses		
Rooms		
Payroll	183,996 × .16	29,439
Laundry	183,996 × .01	1,840
Linen	183,996 × .02	3,680
Commissions	183,996 × .01	1,840
All other expenses	183,996 × .015	2,760
Total		39,559
Telephone	(same as telephone revenue)	4,968
Departmental Income		
Rooms		144,437
Telephone		—0—
Total		144,437
Undistributed Operating Expenses		
Administration	27,000 + .05 (188,964)	36,448
Maintenance and Energy Costs	8,500 + .084 (188,964)	24,373
Total		60,821
Total Income Before Fixed Costs		83,616
Insurance		6,000
Property Taxes		6,600
Depreciation		15,700
Interest Expense		13,050
Income Before Income Taxes		42,266
Income Taxes	42,266 × .30	12,680
Net Income		$29,586

The operations budget for 19X4 is shown in Exhibit 11.6. The projected 19X4 net income for the Sands Motel of $29,586 is 15.6% of sales which exceeds the minimum requirement of 15%.

Flexible Budgets

The budgets we have discussed so far have been either fixed or static, in that only one level of activity was planned. However, no matter how sophisticated the budget process, it is improbable that the level of activity budgeted will be realized exactly. Therefore, when a fixed budget is used, variances from several budget line items, specifically for revenues and variable expenses, can almost always be expected. An alternative approach is to budget on several different levels of activity. For example, a hotel may budget at several occupancy levels such as 69%, 71%, 73%, even though it is believed that the level of activity is most likely to be at the 71% level. With flexible budgeting, revenue and variable expenses change with each level of activity while fixed expenses remain constant.

Exhibit 11.7 contains three condensed operations budgets for the Sands Motel. The flexible budgeting reflects occupancy at 69%, 71%, and 73%. The static budget for the Sands Motel (Exhibit 11.6) was based on 71% occupancy. The kinds of observations that should be made in relation to flexible budgeting reflected in Exhibit 11.7 include:

- Revenues increased/decreased with occupancy.

- Departmental expenses increased/decreased with occupancy.

- Undistributed operating expenses increased/decreased only slightly since a major portion of these expenses is fixed.

- Fixed expenses remained constant as expected.

- Net income changed with activity but not as much as revenue.

- Net income as a percentage of total revenue for the three levels of activity is as follows:

At 69% occupancy:
$$\frac{\text{Net Income}}{\text{Total Revenue}} = \frac{27,237}{183,641} = \underline{\underline{14.8\%}}$$

At 71% occupancy:
$$\frac{\text{Net Income}}{\text{Total Revenue}} = \frac{29,586}{188,964} = \underline{\underline{15.7\%}}$$

At 73% occupancy:
$$\frac{\text{Net Income}}{\text{Total Revenue}} = \frac{31,935}{194,287} = \underline{\underline{16.4\%}}$$

Therefore, the minimum required profit margin percentage of 15% can only be realized at the two budgeted occupancy levels of 71% and 73%. Without making changes to the 69% occupancy budget, the 15% profit margin will not be achieved.

Budgetary Control

In order for budgets to be used effectively for control purposes, budget reports must be prepared periodically (generally on a monthly basis) for each level of financial responsibility. In a hotel, this would normally require budget reports for profit, cost, and service centers.

Budget reports may take many forms. Exhibit 11.8, supplied by The Sheraton Corporation, is prepared monthly and is the summary of the entire hotel operations. It is used by the hotel top management and is also made available to corporate executives and financial analysts. Note not only that absolute dollars are shown for current month and year-to-

Exhibit 11.7 Flexible Operations Budget — Sands Motel

Flexible Operations Budget
Sands Motel
For the year of 19X4

	Activity Levels – Occupancy %		
	69%	71%	73%
Revenue			
Rooms	$178,813	$183,996	$189,179
Telephone	4,828	4,968	5,108
Total	183,641	188,964	194,287
Departmental Expenses			
Rooms	38,445	39,559	40,673
Telephone	4,828	4,968	5,108
Total	43,273	44,527	45,781
Departmental Income			
Rooms	140,368	144,437	148,506
Telephone	0	0	0
Total	140,368	144,437	148,506
Undistributed Operating Expenses			
Administration	36,182	36,448	36,714
Maintenance and Energy Costs	23,926	24,373	24,820
Total	60,108	60,821	61,534
Total Income Before Fixed Costs	80,260	83,616	86,972
Insurance	6,000	6,000	6,000
Property Taxes	6,600	6,600	6,600
Depreciation	15,700	15,700	15,700
Interest	13,050	13,050	13,050
Income Before Income Taxes	38,910	42,266	45,622
Income Taxes	11,673	12,680	13,687
Net Income	$27,237	$29,586	$31,935

date but relative percentages to total revenue and individual department expenses as a percentage of departmental revenue are also given. Besides variances from budget on both a dollar basis and a percentage basis, variances from last year's actual are also shown in order to put the budget in perspective and to provide management with significant trend information.

Exhibit 11.9 is a departmental budget report for the rooms department. It provides a further breakdown of the elements that make up revenues, wages, benefits, and other costs of sales. It also provides various rooms statistics. Besides being available to corporate management this report goes to the next level of management below the general manager and controller.

In order for the reports to be useful, they must be timely and relevant. Budget reports issued weeks after the end of the accounting

Exhibit 11.8   Monthly Summary Income Statement

Monthly Summary Income Statement

		CURRENT MONTH							YEAR TO DATE				
Actual		Variance From Budget		Variance From Last Year				Actual		Variance From Budget		Variance From Last Year	
$	%	$	%	$	%			$	%	$	%	$	%
	100					Stats – Rooms Available			100				
						Rooms Occupied							
						Average Room Rate							
	100					Total Revenue -- Including TVA							
	100					Excluding TVA			100				
						Rooms – Revenues			100				
						Wages & Benefits							
						Other Expenses							
						Departmental Profit							
	100					Food – Revenues			100				
						Cost of Sales							
						Wages – Benefits							
						Other Expenses							
						Departmental Profit							
	100					Beverage – Revenues			100				
						Cost of Sales							
						Wages & Benefits							
						Other Expenses							
						Departmental Profit							
						Food & Beverage Other Income							
						Convention Services Deptl. Profit							
						Total Food & Bev. Profit							
						Minor Operated Departmental Profit							
						Casino Deptl. Profit							
						Rents and Other Income							
						Total Operated Departmental Profit							
						Overhead Departments							
						Administrative & General							
						Marketing							
						Property Operation							
						Total Overhead Departments							
						Gross Operating Profit (Loss)							
						Capital Expenses							
						Taxes							
						Insurance							
						Rent Non-Affiliate							
						Int. & Debt Exp. Non-Affiliate							
						(Int. Income) – Non-Affiliate							
						Other (Adds) & Deductions							
						Total Capital Exp. & Other							
						Cash Earnings (Loss)							
						Depreciation/Replacement Reserve							
						(Deferral) of First Year Loss							
						Amortization 1st Yr. Loss/Pre-Open Exp.							
						Profit: Before Sheraton Charges							
						Rent – Affiliate							
						Int. Exp. (Inc.) Affil. – Net							
						Marketing Fee							
						License Fee							
						Mgmt. Fee – Basic							
						Management Fee – Incentive							
						Total Fees							
						Pretext Profit (Loss) Operations							
						Income Taxes							
						(Gain)/Loss Translation							
						Net Operations							

Courtesy of The Sheraton Corporation

Exhibit 11.9   Monthly Income Statement — Rooms Department

Monthly Income Statement

··········CURRENT MONTH··········						ROOMS DEPARTMENT	···········YEAR TO DATE···········					
Actual		Variance From Budget		Variance From Last Year			Actual		Variance From Budget		Variance From Last Year	
$	%	$	%	$	%		$	%	$	%	$	%
						Revenues						
						Transient – Regular						
						– Group						
						– Airline Crew						
						Extra Room Revenue						
						Total Revenues						
						Expenses						
						Salaries & Wages						
						Benefits						
						Total Wages & Benefits						
						Other Expenses						
						Linen China Glass Silver						
						Contract & Dry Cleaning						
						Operating Supplies						
						Laundry						
						Uniforms						
						Rooms Commission						
						Reservation						
						Miscellaneous						
						Total Other Expenses						
						Total Expenses						
						Departmental Profit						
						Rooms Statistics						
						Total Rooms in Hotel						
						Available for Guest Use						
						Occupied (Overall)						
						Transient – Regular						
						– Group						
						– Comp						
						– Airline Crew						
						Trans Units Occupied						
						Trans Units Double Occupied						
						Average Rate – Overall						
						Transient – Regular						
						– Group						
						– Airline Crew						

Courtesy of The Sheraton Corporation

period are too late to allow managers to investigate variances, determine causes, and take action in a timely fashion. Relevant financial information includes only the revenues and expenses for which the individual department head is held responsible. For example, to include allocated overhead expenses such as "administrative and general" salaries on a rooms department budget report is rather meaningless from a control viewpoint, because the rooms department manager is unable to exercise judgment to affect these allocated costs. Further, they detract from the expenses which the rooms department manager can take action to control. Relevant reporting also requires sufficient detail to allow reasonable judgments regarding budget variances; however, information overload generally results in management's failure to act properly. There are five steps in the budgetary control process:

1. Determination of variances

2. Determination of significant variances

3. Analysis of significant variances

4. Determination of problems

5. Action to correct problems

Determination of Variances

Variances are the result of comparing actual results to the budget. This is accomplished by the preparation of the budget report discussed previously. The budget report should disclose both monthly variances and year-to-date variances; however, major attention for variance analysis is generally focused on monthly variances, because the year-to-date variances are essentially the summation of monthly variances.

Exhibit 11.10 is the January 19X4 summary budget report for the Sands Motel. This budget report contains only monthly financial information and not separate year-to-date numbers, as January is the first month of the fiscal year for the Sands Motel.

Variances shown on this report include both dollar variances and percentage variances. The dollar variances result from subtracting the actual results from the budget figures. For example, rooms revenue for the Sands Motel was $14,940, while the budgeted rooms revenue was $15,620, resulting in a difference of $680. The difference is bracketed to reflect an unfavorable variance. The dollar variances are considered either favorable or unfavorable based on situations presented in Exhibit 11.11.

Percentage variances are determined by dividing the dollar variance by the budgeted amount. For rooms revenue (Exhibit 11.10), the (4.35%) is the result of dividing $(680) by $15,620. Variances should be determined for all line items on budget reports along with an indication of whether the variance is favorable or unfavorable. The kind of variance can be indicated by marking it "+" for favorable and "-" for unfavorable, "F" for favorable and "U" for unfavorable, or placing parentheses around unfavorable variances and simply showing the differences without parentheses for favorable variances as shown in Exhibit 11.10. In addition, some enterprises simply asterisk unfavorable variances.

Determination of Significant Variances

Virtually all budgeted revenue and expense items on a budget report will differ from the actual amounts, with the possible exception of fixed expenses. This is only to be expected, because any budgeting process, however sophisticated, is not perfect. However, simply because a variance exists does not mean that management should analyze the variance and follow through with appropriate corrective actions. Only significant variances require this kind of management analysis and action.

Criteria used to determine which variances are significant are

Exhibit 11.10   Summary Budget Report — Sands Motel

Summary Budget Report
Sands Motel
For January 19X4

	Budget	Actual	Variances $	Variances %
Revenue				
Rooms	$15,620	$14,940	$ (680)	(4.35)%
Telephone	429	414	(15)	(3.50)
Total	16,049	15,354	(695)	(4.33)
Departmental Expenses				
Rooms				
Payroll	2,500	2,243	257	10.28
Laundry	156	150	6	3.85
Linen	313	300	13	4.15
Commissions	156	150	6	3.85
All other expenses	234	200	34	14.53
Total	3,359	3,043	316	9.41
Telephone	422	380	42	9.95
Total	3,781	3,423	358	9.47
Departmental Income				
Rooms	12,268	11,911	(357)	(2.91)
Telephone	0	20	20	NA
Total	12,268	11,931	(337)	(2.75)
Undistributed Operating Expenses				
Administration	3,052	2,961	91	2.98
Maintenance and energy costs	2,169	2,220	(51)	(2.35)
Total Income Before Fixed Charges	7,047	6,750	(297)	(4.21)
Insurance	500	500	0	—
Property Taxes	550	550	0	—
Depreciation	1,308	1,308	0	—
Interest Expense	1,087	1,087	0	—
Income Before Income Taxes	3,602	3,305	(297)	(8.25)
Income Taxes	1,081	992	89	8.23
Net Income	$2,521	$2,313	$(208)	(8.25)%

referred to as significance criteria and are generally expressed in terms of both dollar and percentage differences. Dollar and percentage differences should be used jointly due to the weakness of each when used separately. Dollar differences fail to recognize the magnitude of the base. For example, a large hotel may have a $1,000 difference in rooms revenue from the budgeted amount. Yet the $1,000 difference based on a budget of $1,000,000 results in a percentage difference of only .1% (one-tenth of 1%). Most managers would agree this is insignificant. However, if the

Exhibit 11.11   Evaluating Dollar Variance Situations

	Situation	**Variance**
Revenues	Actual exceeds budget	Favorable
	Budget exceeds actual	Unfavorable
Expenses	Budget exceeds actual	Favorable
	Actual exceeds budget	Unfavorable

rooms revenue budget for the period was $10,000, a $1,000 difference would result in a percentage difference of 10% which most managers would consider significant. This suggests that variances should be considered significant based on the percentage difference. However, the percentage difference also, at times, fails. For example, assume the budget for an expense is $10. A dollar difference of $2 results in a 20% percentage difference. The percentage difference appears significant, but generally, little (if any) managerial time should be spent analyzing and investigating a $2 difference.

Therefore, the dollar and percentage differences should be used jointly in determining which variances are significant. The size of the significance criteria will differ among hospitality properties in relation to size of the operation and the controllability of certain revenue or expense items. In general, the larger the operation the larger the dollar difference criteria. Also, the greater the control exercised over the item, the smaller the criteria.

For example, a large hospitality operation may set significance criteria as follows:

Revenue	$1,000 and 4%
Variable expense	$500 and 2%
Fixed expense	$50 and 1%

A smaller hospitality operation may set significance criteria as follows:

Revenue	$200 and 4%
Variable expense	$100 and 2%
Fixed expense	$50 and 1%

Notice that the change in criteria, based on size of operation, is generally the dollar difference. Both significance criteria change as the item becomes more "controllable."

To illustrate the determination of significant variances, the significance criteria above for a smaller hospitality operation will be applied to the Sands Motel's January 19X4 budget report (Exhibit 11.10). The following revenue and expense items have significant variances:

1. The unfavorable $680 difference between the budgeted rooms revenue and the actual rooms revenue exceeds the dollar difference

criterion of $200, and the unfavorable 4.35% percentage difference exceeds the percentage difference criterion of 4%.

2. The favorable $257 difference between the budgeted rooms payroll expense and the actual rooms payroll expense exceeds the dollar difference criterion of $100, and the favorable 10.28% difference exceeds the percentage difference criterion of 2%.

3. Several rooms expense variances such as laundry, linen, and commissions exceed the percentage difference criterion, but do not exceed the dollar difference criterion, so they are not considered significant; therefore, they will not be subjected to variance analysis.

Variance Analysis

Variance analysis is the process of analyzing variances to determine the general cause(s) of the variance. For example, the analysis of a revenue variance will reveal differences due to price and/or volume, but it does not reveal just why the price and/or volume variances exist. The analysis of variable labor expense will reveal differences due to rate, efficiency, and volume but, again, the exact cause of rate, efficiency, and volume variances is not disclosed. Additional investigation by management is required to determine the exact cause(s) of the variance. For example, an unfavorable labor rate variance may be due to staffing problems, or excessive overtime pay, or a combination of these two factors.

Variance analysis will be presented for three general areas—revenue, cost of goods sold, and variable labor. The basic models presented in these areas can be applied to other similar areas. For each area, formulas, a graph, and an illustration will be provided. In addition, the two significant variances of the Sands Motel, rooms-revenue and rooms-payroll expense, will be analyzed.

Revenue Variance Analysis

Revenue variances occur because of price and volume differences; thus, the variances relating to revenue are called price variance and volume variance. The formulas for these variances are as follows:

Price Variance = Budgeted Volume x (Actual Price − Budgeted Price)
$$PV = BV(AP - BP)$$

Volume Variance = Budgeted Price x (Actual Volume − Budgeted Volume)
$$VV = BP(AV - BV)$$

A minor variance due to the interrelationship of the price and volume variance is the price-volume variance calculated as follows:

Price-Volume Variance = (Actual Price − Budgeted Price) x (Actual Volume − Budgeted Volume)
$$P\text{-}VV = (AP - BP)(AV - BV)$$

These formulas are illustrated by using the Sample Motel whose

Exhibit 11.12   Rooms Revenue: Budget and Actual — Sample Motel

	Room Nights	Average Price	Total
Budget	400	$20	$8,000
Actual	450	18	8,100
Difference	50	$2	$ 100(F)

budget and actual monthly results for rooms revenue appear in Exhibit 11.12.

The budget variance of $100 ($8,100 − $8,000) is favorable. Variance analysis will be conducted to determine the general cause(s) of this variance; that is, price, volume, or the interrelationship of the two. The price variance for the Sample Motel is determined as follows:

$$PV = BV(AP - BP)$$
$$PV = 400(18 - 20)$$
$$PV = 400(-2)$$
$$PV = \$-\underline{800}(U)$$

The price variance of $800 is unfavorable because the average price charged per room night of $18 was $2 less than the budgeted average price of $20.

The volume variance (VV) is computed as follows:

$$VV = BP(AV - BV)$$
$$VV = 20(450 - 400)$$
$$VV = 20(50)$$
$$VV = \$\underline{1,000}(F)$$

The volume variance of $1,000 is favorable, because 50 more rooms per night were sold than planned.

The price-volume variance is determined as follows:

$$
\begin{aligned}
\text{P-VV} &= (AP - BP)(AV - BV) \\
\text{P-VV} &= (18 - 20)(450 - 400) \\
\text{P-VV} &= -2(50) \\
\text{P-VV} &= \$-\underline{100}(U)
\end{aligned}
$$

The price-volume variance is due to the interrelationship of the volume and price variances. Two dollars per room less than budgeted multiplied by the 50 excess rooms results in an unfavorable $100 price-volume variance.

The sum of the three variances equals the budget variance of $100 for room revenue as follows:

$$
\begin{aligned}
\text{VV} &= \$1,000(F) \\
\text{PV} &= -800(U) \\
\text{P-VV} &= -100(U) \\
\text{Total} &= \underline{100}(F)
\end{aligned}
$$

Exhibit 11.13   Revenue Variance Analysis — Sample Motel

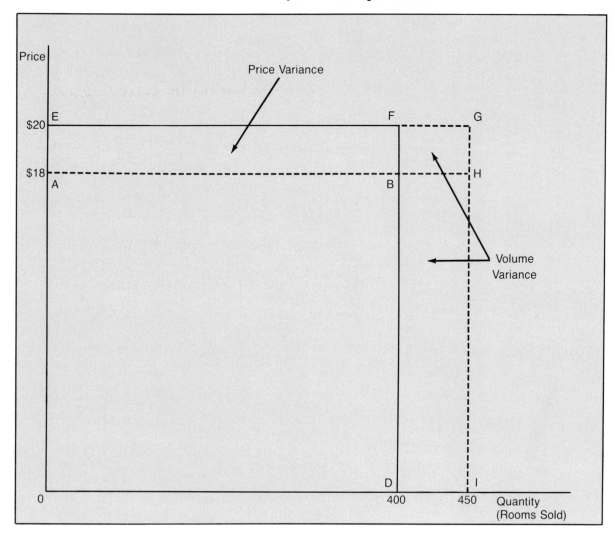

The price-volume variance in the analysis of revenue variances will be unfavorable when the price and volume variances are different; that is, one is favorable and the other is unfavorable. When the price and volume variances are the same, that is, either both are favorable or both are unfavorable, then the price-volume variance will be favorable.

Exhibit 11.13 is a graphic depiction of the revenue variance analysis for the Sample Motel. The area inside the solid line rectangle (OEFD) represents the budgeted amount while the area inside the broken line rectangle (OAHI) represents the actual amount of rooms revenue. The price variance is the area inside the rectangle AEFB while the volume variance is the area inside the rectangle DFGI. The price-volume variance is the area inside the small rectangle BFGH.

Cost of Goods Sold Analysis

The cost of goods sold variance occurs because of differences due to cost and volume. That is, the amount paid for the goods sold (food and/or beverage) differs from the budget, and the total amount sold differs from the budgeted sales. The detailed variances related to the cost of goods are called the cost variance, the volume variance, and the cost-volume variance. The formulas for these variances are as follows:

Cost Variance = Budgeted Volume x (Budgeted Cost − Actual Cost)
$$CV = BV(BC - AC)$$

Volume Variance = Budgeted Cost x (Budgeted Volume − Actual Volume)
$$VV = BC(BV - AV)$$

Cost-Volume Variance = (Budgeted Cost − Actual Cost) x (Budgeted Volume − Actual Volume)
$$C\text{-}VV = (BC - AC)(BV - AV)$$

The cost-volume variance results from the interrelationship of the cost and volume variances.

The analysis of the cost of goods sold variance formulas is illustrated by using a food service example. The Sample Restaurant, open only for dinner, had cost of food sold results and budgeted amounts for January as shown in Exhibit 11.14. The budget variance of $1,120 is analyzed using variance analysis as follows:

The cost variance is determined as follows:

$$CV = BV(BC - AC)$$
$$CV = 3,000(4.00 - 4.10)$$
$$CV = 3,000(- .10)$$
$$CV = \$\underline{\underline{-300}}(U)$$

The cost variance of $300 is unfavorable because the cost per cover of 3,000 covers exceeded budget by $.10.

The volume variance is determined as follows:

$$VV = BC(BV - AV)$$
$$VV = 4(3,000 - 3,200)$$
$$VV = 4(-200)$$
$$VV = \$\underline{\underline{-800}}(U)$$

The volume variance of $800 is also unfavorable because excessive volume results in greater costs than budgeted. Remember this is from an expense perspective. Excessive volume from a revenue perspective is favorable.

The cost-volume variance is determined as follows:

$$C\text{-}VV = (BC - AC)(BV - AV)$$
$$C\text{-}VV = (4.00 - 4.10)(3,000 - 3,200)$$
$$C\text{-}VV = (-.10)(-200)$$
$$C\text{-}VV = \$\underline{\underline{20}}(U)$$

The cost-volume variance of $20 is also unfavorable even though the mathematical sign of the result is positive. The cost-volume variance will be unfavorable when the other two variances (cost and volume) are the same, that is, both are favorable or unfavorable. When the cost and volume variance differ, that is, one is favorable and the other unfavorable, then the cost-volume variance will be favorable.

Exhibit 11.14   Cost of Food Sold: Budget and Actual — Sample Restaurant

	Covers	Average Cost Per Cover	Total Cost
Budget	3,000	$4.00	$12,000
Actual	3,200	4.10	13,120
Difference	200	$ .10	$ 1,120(U)

The sum of the three variances is $1,120:

Cost Variance	=	$300(U)
Volume Variance	=	+800(U)
Cost-Volume Variance	=	+20(U)
Total		$1,120(U)

This sum equals the budget variance shown above of $1,120. These results show that of the total $1,120, only $300 is due to cost "overruns." Further investigation should be undertaken to determine why there were excessive food costs of $300. The volume variance of $800 should be more than offset by the favorable volume variance for the Sample Restaurant food revenue. The cost-volume variance of $20 is due to the interrelationship of cost and volume. It is insignificant and requires no additional management attention.

Exhibit 11.15 is a graphic depiction of the cost of food sold variance analysis. The original budget of $12,000 for cost of food sold is represented by the rectangle of OABC while the actual food cost for the period is the rectangle of ODFH. Therefore, the difference between these two rectangles is the budget variance. The budget variance is divided among the three variances of cost, volume, and cost-volume. The cost variance is represented by the area inside the ADEB rectangle; the volume variance is represented by the area inside the BGHC rectangle; and the cost-volume variance is represented by the area inside the BEFG rectangle.

Variable Labor Variance Analysis

Variable labor expense is labor expense that varies directly with activity as discussed in Chapter 8. Variable labor increases as sales increase, and decreases as sales decrease. In a lodging operation, the use of room attendants to clean rooms is a clear example of variable labor. Everything else being the same, the more rooms to be cleaned, the more room attendants' hours are necessary to clean the rooms; therefore, the greater the room attendants' wages. In a food service situation, servers' wages are generally treated as as variable labor expense. Again, the greater the number of guests to be served food, the greater the number of servers; therefore, the greater the server expense. The remainder of the discussion of labor in this section will pertain to variable labor, however we will simply refer to it as labor expense.

Exhibit 11.15. Cost of Food Sold Variance Analysis — Sample Restaurant

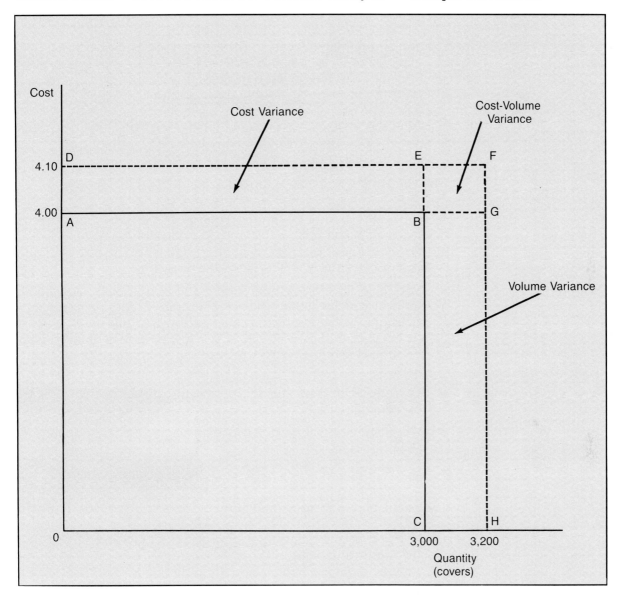

Labor expense variances result from three general causes—volume, rate, and efficiency. All budget variances for labor expense may be divided among these three areas. Volume variances result when there is a different volume of work than forecasted. Rate variances result when the average wage rate is different than planned. Efficiency variances result when the amount of work performed by the labor force on an hourly basis differs from the forecast. Of course, as with revenue variance analysis and with cost of goods sold variance analysis, there is a variance due to the interrelationship of the major elements of the budget variance. The formulas for these variances are as follows:

Volume Variance = Budgeted Rate x (Budgeted Time − Allowable Time for Actual Output)

$$VV = BR(BT - ATAO)$$

Rate Variance = Budgeted Time x (Budgeted Rate − Actual Rate)

$$RV = BT(BR - AR)$$

Efficiency Variance = Budgeted Rate x (Allowable Time for Actual Output − Actual Time)

$$EV = BR(ATAO - AT)$$

Rate − Volume Variance = (Budgeted Time − Actual Time) x (Budgeted Rate − Actual Rate)

$$R - VV = (BT - AT)(BR - AR)$$

The elements within these formulas are defined as follows:

- Budgeted Time (BT)—hours required to perform work per the budget. For example, if the work standard for serving meals is 15 customers/hour per server, then servers would require 40 hours to serve 600 meals (600 divided by 15 = 40).

- Allowable Time for Actual Output (ATAO)—hours allowable to perform work based on the actual output. This is determined in the same way as budgeted time, except that the work is actual versus budget. For example, if 660 meals were actually served, the allowable time given a work standard of 15 meals/hour would be 44 (660 divided by 15 = 44).

- Budgeted Rate (BR)—the average wage rates budgeted per hour for labor services.

- Actual Rate (AR)—the actual average wage rate paid per hour for labor services.

- Actual Time (AT)—the number of hours actually worked.

The calculation of these formulas are illustrated in Exhibit 11.16. The work standard for servers of the Sample Restaurant is serving 15 meals per hour. Therefore, on the average, a meal should be served every four minutes (60 minutes divided by 15 = 4).

The volume variance is determined as follows:

$$VV = BR(BT - ATAO)$$

where
$$BR = \text{Budgeted Rate}$$
$$BT = \text{Budgeted Time}$$
$$ATAO = \text{Allowable Time for Actual Output}$$

$$VV = 2.50(200 - 213\tfrac{1}{3})$$

where 213⅓ for ATAO is determined by dividing the work standard of 15 covers per hour into the 3,200 covers served

$$VV = 2.50(- 13\tfrac{1}{3})$$
$$VV = \$\underline{-33.33}(U)$$

The volume variance of $33.33 is unfavorable, because more covers were served than budgeted. Normally, the volume variance is beyond

Exhibit 11.16   Labor Expense: Budget and Actual — Sample Restaurant

	Covers	Time/ Cover	Total Time	Hourly Wage	Total
Budget	3,000	4 min.	200 hrs.	$2.50	$500
Actual	3,200	5 min.	266 ⅔	2.40	640
Difference	200	1 min.	66 ⅔ min.	$ .10	$140(U)

the control of the supervisor of personnel to which the labor expense pertains. Therefore, this should be isolated and generally not further pursued from an expense perspective. In addition, an unfavorable volume variance should be more than offset by the volume variance for the related food sales.

The rate variance for the Sample Restaurant is determined as follows:

$$RV = BT(BR - AR)$$
$$RV = 200(\$2.50 - \$2.40)$$
$$RV = 200(\$.10)$$
$$RV = \$20(F)$$

The rate variance of $20 is favorable due to the average pay rate per hour of $2.40 being $.10 per hour less than the budgeted $2.50 per hour. The credit for this is normally given to the labor supervisor responsible for scheduling and managing labor.

The efficiency variance for the Sample Restaurant is determined as follows:

$$EV = BR(ATAO - AT)$$
$$EV = \$2.50(213⅓ - 266⅔)$$
$$EV = \$2.50(- 53⅓)$$
$$EV = \$-133.33(U)$$

The efficiency variance of $133.33 is unfavorable, because an average of one minute more was spent serving a meal than was originally planned. The supervisor must determine why this occurred. It could have been due to new employees who were inefficient in their work, the excess volume may have resulted in inefficiency due to work overload, or perhaps there were other factors. Once the specific cause(s) are determined, the manager can take corrective action to ensure a future reoccurrence is avoided.

The rate-volume variance is determined as follows:

$$R\text{-}VV = (BT - AT)(BR - AR)$$
$$R\text{-}VV = (200 - 266⅔)(\$2.50 - \$2.40)$$
$$R\text{-}VV = (- 66⅔)(\$.10)$$
$$R\text{-}VV = \$-6.66(F)$$

The rate-volume variance of $6.66 is favorable even though the mathematic sign "-" seems to indicate otherwise. This compound variance is favorable when the individual variances within it differ. In this case, the rate variance was favorable; however, the "time" variance was unfavorable.

The sum of the four variances equals the budget variance of $140(U) as follows:

Volume Variance	$33.33(U)
Rate Variance	20.00(F)
Efficiency Variance	133.33(U)
Rate-Volume Variance	6.66(F)
Total	$140.00(U)

Exhibit 11.17 is a graphic depiction of the labor variance analysis of the Sample Restaurant. The budget for labor expense is represented by the solid line forming rectangle ODEC, while the actual labor expense is represented by the broken line forming rectangle OAGH. The rate variance is represented by the area inside the ADEB rectangle. The volume variance is represented by the area inside the CEIJ rectangle. The area inside the JIFH rectangle represents the efficiency variance. And, the rate-volume variance is represented by the area inside the EFGB rectangle.

Variance Analysis of Sands Motel's Significant Variances

Exhibit 11.18 contains the analysis of the unfavorable rooms revenue variance of $680. The breakdown is as follows:

Due to unfavorable volume differences	$887.50(U)
Due to favorable pricing differences	220.00(F)
Compound variance	12.50(U)
Total	$680.00(U)

Management needs to investigate the causes of the failure to sell 25 additional rooms. This failure was partially offset by a favorable price variance.

If the volume variance was due to controllable causes such as price resistance or rooms unavailable due to being out-of-order or simply not clean when desired by potential guests, then management action can be taken. If, on the other hand, the causes were beyond management's control, such as weather-related factors, then no specific management action appears to be required.

The other significant variance of the Sands Motel requiring analysis was rooms-payroll which was favorable during January 19X4, at $257. An analysis of rooms labor revealed the following:

	Budget	Actual	Difference
Room attendants	$ 737	$ 581	$ 156(F)
Front office	1,763	1,662	101(F)
Total	$2,500	$2,243	$257(F)

Since the largest portion relates to room attendants' wages, only this portion is analyzed for illustrative purposes in Exhibit 11.19. The analysis

Exhibit 11.17   Labor Variance Analysis — Sample Restaurant

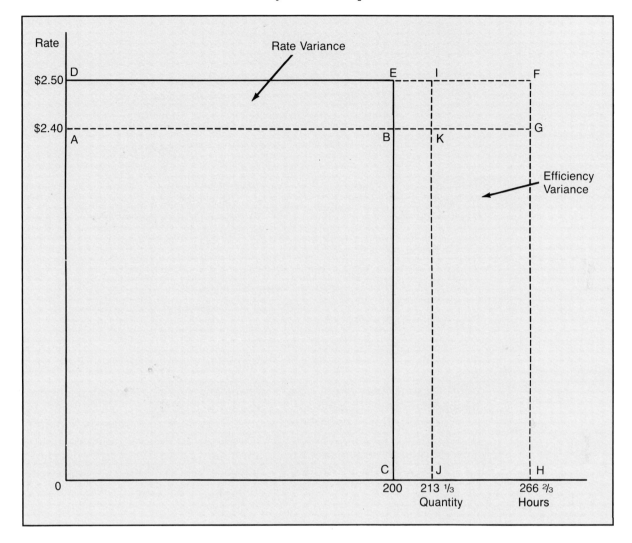

of the $156 variance reveals favorable volume, rate, and efficiency variances.

Determination of Problems and Management Action

The next step in the budgetary control process is for management to investigate variance analysis results in an effort to determine the cause(s) of the variances. For example, the analysis of the room attendants' labor variance may reveal a significant portion of an unfavorable variance is due to rate. Management must further investigate the rate variance to determine why the average rate paid was higher than budgeted. It may have been due to scheduling more higher paid room attendants than originally planned, perhaps room attendants worked overtime, or some

Exhibit 11.18   Rooms Revenue Variance Analysis — Sands Motel

Analysis of Rooms Revenue Variance
Sands Motel
January 19X4

	Room Nights	Price	Total
Budget	440	$35.50	$15,620
Actual	415	36.00	4,940
Difference	25	$ .50	$ 680 (U)

Volume Variance

VV = BP (AV – BV)
VV = 35.50 (415-440)
VV = $887.50 (U)

Price Variance

PV = BV (AP – BP)
PV = 440 (36.00 – 35.50)
PV = $220 (F)

Price – Volume Variance

P-VV = (AV – BV) (AP – BP)
P-VV = (415-440) (36.00 – 35.50)
P-VV = $12.50 (U)

other reasons may exist. Each significant variance requires further management investigation to determine the cause(s).

The final step to complete the budgetary control process is hospitality managers taking action to correct the problem. For example, if a major cause of the rate variance for room attendants is that excessive overtime is paid, this may be controlled by requiring all overtime to be approved a specified number of hours in advance by the next highest management level.

Reforecasting

Regardless of the extensive efforts and the sophisticated methods used in formulating operations budgets, most large hospitality properties reforecast their expected operations as they progress through the budget year. This reforecasting is necessary only when the actual results begin to vary significantly from the budget due to changes that occur after the budget is prepared. Some organizations will start reforecasting at the beginning of the budget year and continue to reforecast every month for the entire year.

Reforecasting at The Sheraton Corporation

Reforecasting at Sheraton is a continuing process that begins immediately with the new year and involves a three-step process as follows:

1.   Three Months Outlook

2.   Advanced Information for Outlook

3.   Weekly Activity Report

Exhibit 11.19   Rooms Payroll Variance Analysis — Sands Motel

Analysis of Room Payroll Variance
Sands Motel
January 19X4

	Room Nights	Time/ Room	Total Time	Hourly Wages	Total
Budget	440	30 min.	220 hrs.	$3.35	$737
Actual	415	28 min.	193 ⅔	3.00	581
Difference	25	2 min.	26 ⅓	$.35	$156

Volume Variance

$VV = BR(BT - ATAO)$

$VV = 3.35(220 - 207.5)$

$VV = 3.35(12.5)$

$VV = \$41.88$ (F)

Rate Variance

$RV = BT(BR - AR)$

$RV = 220(3.35 - 3.00)$

$RV = 220(.35)$

$RV = \$77$ (F)

Efficiency Variance

$EV = BR(ATAO - AT)$

$EV = 3.35(207.5 - 193.67)$

$EV = 3.35(13.83)$

$EV = \$46.33$ (F)

Rate-Volume Variance

$R\text{-}VV = (BT - AT)(BR - AR)$

$R\text{-}VV = (220 - 193.67)(3.35 - 3.00)$

$R\text{-}VV = (26.33)(.35)$

$R\text{-}VV = \$9.22$ (U)

Summation of Variances

Volume Variance	$41.88 (F)
Rate Variance	77.00 (F)
Efficiency Variance	46.33 (F)
Rate-Volume Variance	9.22 (U)
	155.99
Rounding Difference	.01
Total	$156.00

The Three Months Outlook. Exhibit 11.20 is a short-term forecast used to update the annual budget on an ongoing basis. It is prepared monthly and covers the following ninety-day period. The budget continues to be the standard against which goal achievement is measured. The Outlook process enables management to evaluate the hotel's immediate future, and to react accordingly by determining objectives, making plans, and assigning responsibilities. The general manager should be able to judge the performance of his/her team members relative to their outlook commitments.

The Three Months Outlook blends two types of forecast into its report format:

- Sales Forecast (revenues, occupancy, and average rate)
- Profit and Loss Forecast (complete P & L)

Exhibit 11.20 Three Months Outlook

THREE MONTH OUTLOOK

HOTEL_____ LOCATION_____

Months:			19			19			19
Report 000.0	OUTLOOK	BUDGET	LAST YEAR	Outlook	Budget	Last Year	Outlook	Budget	Last Year

Statistics

% Occupancy %									
Average Room Rate $									
No. Rooms Occupied									
No. Rooms Available									
Total Revenue (Excl TVA) $									
Total Revenue (Incl TVA)									

Operated Departments	$	%	$	%	$	%				
Room –Revenues		100		100		100				
–Wages & Benefits										
–Other expenses										
–Departmental Profit										
Food –Revenues (Excl. O/L)		100		100		100				
–Cost of Sales										
–Wages & Benefits										
–Other Expenses										
–Departmental Profit										
Beverage –Revenues (Excl O/L)		100		100		100				
–Cost of Sales										
–Wages & Benefits										
–Other Expenses										
–Departmental Profit										
Food & Beverage Other Income										
–Food & Bev. Dept'l Prof										
Casino Departmental Profit										
Minor Operated Dept. Profit										
Convention Services Dept. Profit										
Rents & Other Income										
Total Operated Departments										
Overhead Departments										
Administrative & General										
Marketing										
Property Operation										
Total Overhead Departments										
Gross Operating Profit										
Taxes										
Insurance										
Rent Non-Affiliate										
Interest & Dept. Exp. Non-Affiliate										
(Interest Income) Non-Affiliate										
Other (Adds) & Deductions										
Cash Earnings (Loss)										
Depreciation/Replacement Reserve										
(Deferral) of First Year Loss										
Amortization of First Year Loss/Pre. Op.										
Profit Before Sheraton Charges										
Rent-Affiliate										
Inf. Exp. (Inc.) Affil.-Net										
Profit Before Sheraton Fees										
Fee License										
Management Basic										
Management Incentive										
Marketing										
Total Sheraton Fees										
Pretax Profit (Loss) Operations)										

Equivalent Full Time Employees	Outlook	Budget	Last Year
Salaries & Wages			
Benefits			
Total Compensation			

Joint Ventures			
Joint Venture Pretax Profit	Outlook	Budget	Last Year
Partner(s) Equity			
Sheraton Gross Equity Before Deferral/Amort.			
Def./(Amort.) 1st Year Equity Loss			
(Def.)/Amort Fee Income			
Sheraton Net Equity			

International Hotels Only Rate of Exchange
Outlook U.S.
$1.00_____
Budget U.S.
$1.00_____
Last Year U.S.
$1.00_____

Controller _____   Date _____   General Manager _____   Date _____

Courtesy of The Sheraton Corporation

While the general manager is the final approval authority, the hotel controller is responsible for overall coordination of the report preparation.

The Advanced Information for Outlook. Exhibit 11.21 is prepared each month in conjunction with the Three Months Outlook; its purpose is to provide the home office with a breakout of certain key outlook and budget figures on a month-to-date by week basis for the following month. The report is the basis for preparation by the home office of a consolidated report each week comparing month-to-date actual results with outlook and budget.

The Weekly Activity Report. Exhibit 11.22 is a calculated estimate of each hotel's key financial results. With the exception of fiscal year beginning and ending dates, the reporting periods cover 7-day time frames from Thursday through Wednesday. The reported information is on a cumulative (month-to-date) basis.

Each hotel utilizes its Weekly Activity Report as a primary source of financial performance, engaging in a review of its profit & loss statement before the approved information is transmitted to headquarters.

At headquarters, the "on-line" information enters directly into a computer which generates a report showing actual results with variances to Budget and Outlook.

In addition to the Three Month Outlook, reforecasting is also done on a total year basis at least twice a year for Strategic and Operating Plans.

Budgeting at Multi-Unit Hospitality Enterprises

This chapter has been oriented toward operations budgeting at a single hotel property. However, both lodging and food service chains continue to increase their dominance in their respective hospitality segments. The chains in the foodservice industry account for more than 50% of the hotel food service sales, and in the lodging industry giants such as Holiday Corporation and Marriott experience over $1 billion lodging sales annually.

Recent research[3] on budgeting at multi-unit food service chains revealed the following significant results:

1. A majority of companies develop their overall corporate budgets using the bottom-up approach, i.e., restaurant managers develop individual budgets that are "cumulated" through successive company layers until an overall corporate budget is proposed. The most common reasons cited for using the bottom-up approach were (1) the need to increase the feeling of unit level "ownership" in the budget, and (2) the ability of restaurant level personnel to recognize specific problems affecting lower organizational levels.

2. A significant minority develop their budgets at the corporate level and then "dictate" the budgets to the lower levels in the corporate structure. The major reason cited for the top-down approach was

Exhibit 11.21 Advanced Information for Outlook/Fiscal Budget

ADVANCED INFORMATION FOR OUTLOOK/FISCAL BUDGET
(Reported in U.S. Dollars and round to nearest thousand)

INFORMATION FROM HOTEL:

LOCATION:

PERIOD FROM: TO:

Signed: _____
                                                    Hotel Controller

Date: _____

Refer to Financial Reports Calendar for Due Date.

MONTHLY OUTLOOK

Hotel Res. No.	Month	Title Rev. P/L	Excl. TVA	Rate	Avg. Occ.	% Fees	Equity	Hash Total
7 Days	MO/							
14 Days	MO/							
21 Days	MO/							
28 Days	MO/							
35 Days	MO/							

/W1
/W2
/W3
/W4
/W5

MONTHLY BUDGET

7 Days	MB/							
14 Days	MB/							
21 Days	MB/							
28 Days	MB/							
35 Days	MB/							

/W1
/W2
/W3
/W4
/W5

International Hotels Only – Rate of Exchange:
Outlook U.S. $1.00 =
Budget U.S. $1.00 =

Total Revenue Excl. TVA | Occupancy

Month		
Month 2		
Month 3		

Total Month Outlook
MPWR | COMP

Month: First three letters of the month being reported.

Total Rev: Total revenue excluding TVA's where applicable.

P/L: Owned & Leased report pre-tax income before Inter Co. Items. ie: before fees.
Managed & non-consolidated report gross operating profit.

Avg. Rate & %OCC: enter without decimals, ie: 28.70 Enter as 2870 76.2 enter as 762

Fees: Consolidated-Joint Ventures/Partnerships will report fees weekly.
Non-Consolidated will report fees weekly.

Equity: Consolidated & Non-consolidated Joint Ventures/Partnerships will report this field weekly.

MPWR: Average equivalent 40 hour employees, round to nearest whole number.

Comp: Total salaries/wages/benefits.

Courtesy of The Sheraton Corporation

Exhibit 11.22 Weekly Activity Report

WEEKLY ACTIVITY REPORT
IN THOUSANDS OF DOLLARS

The Sheraton Corporation

FOR THE MONTH OF
WEEK ENDING DATE

WEEK

PAGE
OF

HOTELS

REVENUE

	THIS WEEK			MONTH TO DATE		
		VARIANCE			VARIANCE	
ACTUAL	BUDGET	OUTLOOK	ACTUAL	BUDGET	OUTLOOK	

*PROFIT (LOSS)

	THIS WEEK			MONTH TO DATE		
		VARIANCE			VARIANCE	
ACTUAL	BUDGET	OUTLOOK	ACTUAL	BUDGET	OUTLOOK	

AVG. ROOM RATE

MONTH TO DATE		
	VARIANCE	
ACTUAL	BUDGET	OUTLOOK

%OCCUPANCY

MONTH TO DATE		
	VARIANCE	
ACTUAL	BUDGET	OUTLOOK

that the sum of the individual restaurant budgets would not meet corporate expectations.

3. Whether the budgeting approach is bottom-up or top-down, most companies at the corporate level set financial goals before the budget process begins.

4. The major differences in budgeting by chains versus the single unit organization included:

    ● Greater need for coordination

    ● Greater volume of information to be processed

    ● Use of more sophisticated and frequently computerized procedures

    ● Greater amount of time required

    ● Unique procedures to allocate costs between organization levels

    ● Greater extent of management attention to budget process

Budgeting at The Sheraton Corporation

Budgeting at The Sheraton Corporation involves a three–stage process as follows:

1. Long Range Strategic Plans

2. Shorter Term Operating Plans

3. Detailed Monthly Budgets for the following year.

The Strategic Plan is done each spring and is a projection of the financial objectives of the corporation over the next five years. It is generally a top-down approach with corporate strategies defined in the areas of marketing, development, and financial performance. The hotels participate individually by providing seven-year summary financial statements to their divisions' offices showing Prior Year Actual, Current Year Budget, Forecast, Variance, and Projected Earnings for the next five years (Exhibit 11.23).

The One Year Operating Plan is done in the fall and is a refinement of Plan Year I of the Strategic Plan. Standardized workpapers are provided to each hotel for use in developing detailed backup for their Plan Year I revenue and expense projections. These workpapers are then subject to review by division operations and support staffs prior to final acceptance of the Operating Plan as local management's formal commitment to achieve these goals during the next year.

Upon final acceptance of the hotel's Operating Plan, the Annual Income Statement for Plan Year I automatically becomes the fixed budget against which actual performance will be measured for the next fiscal year. The budget is input into the computer at the corporate headquarters after breaking down the Annual Income Statement by month and by

Exhibit 11.23 Strategic Plan: Comparative Income Statement

Sheraton Weighted Avg. Exchange Rate–US $1	LINE NO.	PRIOR YEAR ACTUAL 19___	% of Rev	CURRENT YEAR 19___ BUDGET	% of Rev	FORECAST	% of Rev	VARIANCE	PLAN YEAR I 19___	% of Rev	PLAN YEAR II 19___	% of Rev	PLAN YEAR III 19___	% of Rev	PLAN YEAR IV 19___	% of Rev	PLAN YEAR V 19___	% of Rev
	1																	
Total Revenue – Including TVA	2																	
Excluding TVA	3		100		100		100			100		100		100		100		100
Rooms – Revenues	4		100		100		100			100		100		100		100		100
Wages & Benefits	5																	
Other Expenses	6																	
Departmental Profit	7																	
Food Revenues	8		100		100		100			100		100		100		100		100
Cost of Sales	9																	
Wages–Benefits	10																	
Other Expenses	11																	
Departmental Profit	12																	
Beverage Revenues	13		100		100		100			100		100		100		100		100
Costs of Sales	14																	
Wages & Benefits	15		100		100		100			100		100		100		100		100
Other Expenses	16																	
Departmental Profit	17																	
Food & Beverage Other Income	18																	
Convention Services Deptl. Profit	19																	
Total Food & Bev. Profit	20																	
Minor Operated Deptl. Profit	21																	
Casino Departmental Profit	22																	
Rents and Other Income	23																	
Total Operated Deptl. Profit	24																	
Overhead Departments	25																	
Administrative & General	26																	
Marketing	27																	
Property Operation	28																	
Total Overhead Departments	29																	
Gross Operating Profit (Loss)	30																	
Capital Expenses	31																	
Taxes	32																	
Insurance	33																	
Rent Non-Affiliate	34																	
Int. & Debt Exp. Non-Affiliate	35																	
(Int. Income) – Non-Affiliate	36																	
Other (Adds) & Deductions	37																	
Total Capital Exp. & Other	38																	
Cash Earnings (Loss)	39																	
Depreciation/Replacement Reserve	40																	
(Deferral) of First Year Loss	41																	
Amortization 1st Yr. Loss/Pre-Open Exp.	42																	
Profit Before Sheraton Charges	43																	
Rent – Affiliate	44																	
Int. Exp. (Inc.) Affil. – Net	45																	
Marketing Fee	46																	
License Fee	47																	
Mgmt. Fee – Basic	48																	
Management Fee – Incentive	49																	
Total Fees	50																	
Pretax Profit (Loss) Operations	51																	
Income Taxes	52																	
(Gain)/Loss Translation	53																	
Net Operations	54																	
Memo Sheraton Gross Equity	55																	
Def./(Amort) 1st Yr. Equity Loss	56																	
(Def)/Amort. Fee Income	57																	
Sheraton Net Equity	58																	
Total Salaries, Wages, Benefits	59																	
Avg. Equiv. Full-Time Employees	60																	
Headcount at 12/31	61																	
Overall Occupancy %	62																	
Average Rate	63																	
No. of Rooms Available	64																	
No. of Rooms Occupied	65																	
No. of Rooms at Year End	66																	
	67																	

19___ STRATEGIC PLAN

COMPARATIVE INCOME STATEMENT (Round to Nearest Thousand)

(HOTEL NAME)

FRS NO. ______

(DATE) (REV NO)

Courtesy of The Sheraton Corporation

departmental components on forms provided to the hotels for that purpose.

Summary

The budgetary process can be valuable to the operation of a hospitality establishment. In order to formulate a budget, the establishment's goals must be stated and each department must look ahead and estimate future performance. As the actual period progresses, management can compare operating results to the budget, and significant differences can be studied. This process forces management to set future goals and to strive to see that they become realized.

In order to formulate a budget, each department estimates its revenues and expenses. This is done by observing past trends and projecting them for another year. The manager must also take into account forces in the economy, new developments in the market, and other significant events which will affect the operation. These projections are then combined to form a budget for the next period's operations. At this point, the budgeted results are compared with the establishment's goals, and the budget is adjusted until these goals are met.

Once completed, the budget becomes a control tool. As the periods progress, management compares the budget with actual performance. The differences between each line item are calculated, and the significant differences are analyzed. Significance depends on both absolute dollar differences and percentage differences. The analysis includes dividing each into its components including price and volume for revenues and rate, volume, and efficiency in the case of labor. Any deficiencies can then be addressed by management, and corrective action can be taken to keep the operations heading toward the predefined goals.

Notes

1. Peter A. Pyrrh, *Zero-Base Budgeting* (New York: John Wiley & Sons, 1973).
2. Lee M. Kruel, "Zero-Base Budgeting of Hotel Indirect Expense," *The Cornell Hotel & Restaurant Administration Quarterly* (November 1978): pp. 11-14.
3. Schmidgall, Raymond S. and Jack D. Ninemeier, "Foodservice Budgeting: How the Chains Do It," *The Cornell Hotel & Restaurant Administration Quarterly* (February 1986): pp. 51-55.

Discussion Questions

1. Explain four future items which should be considered when formulating a budget.

2. How does a budget help an establishment to realize its operating goals?

3. How is the budget formulated?

4. Why should budgets be prepared at various levels of sales?

5. What constitutes a "significant" variance?

6. What does the volume variance highlight for management?

7. Why is an increase in volume favorable in revenue analysis and unfavorable in cost analysis?

8. Explain the formula: $EV = BR(ATAO - AT)$.

9. What items should be considered when preparing the rooms revenue section of the budget?

10. State three possible goals an establishment could set for its operations.

Problem 11.1

Jackie Jackson is the rooms department manager of Waverly Motor Hotel and is preparing a condensed 19X6 annual budget. She has the following information upon which to base her estimates.

- Estimated occupancy percentage: 75%

- Rooms: 100

- Average rate: $37.00

- Labor: Variable: $5.00/room
  Fixed: $200,000 (annual)

- Other operating expenses: $2.50/room

Required:

1. Prepare a condensed budget for the rooms department. (Assume the hotel is open 365 days a year.)

2. The Waverly's management requires that the department have a departmental profit of at least $400,000 and a departmental profit of 40% of revenue. Will Ms. Jackson's condensed budget projections be acceptable to the hotel's management?

Problem 11.2

Barbara Collins is the manager of Shives, a fine dining restaurant, and is preparing next year's budget. She wants to examine three different levels of sales as follows: $700,000, $1,000,000, and $1,300,000. The following information upon which to make the calculations is provided.

- Food cost percentage: 45%
- Labor: Variable: 23%
  Fixed: $80,000
- Other operating expenses: 8%
- Fixed charges: $100,000
- Income taxes: 30% of pretax income

Required:

1. Assist her by preparing the condensed operating budget for Shives at the three levels of sales indicated above.

2. Comment briefly regarding the impact of different levels of sales on the restaurant's profits.

Problem 11.3

The Mica Motel (MM), open 365 days a year, consists of an 80-room motel with a 60-seat coffee shop. J. D. Mica provides you with the following information:

1.   Of the 80 rooms, 60 are doubles and 20 are singles.

2.   The doubles are sold for $22 each while the singles are sold for $18 each.

3.   Forecasted occupancy is 84% for doubles and 78% for singles.

4.   The average occupancy per room is 1.8. (Only one person stays in a single but two or more may stay in a double for $22/night.)

5.   Forty percent of those staying in the singles eat breakfast in the coffee shop while twenty percent of those staying in the doubles eat breakfast at the MM. (There is no walk-in business for breakfast.) The average check is $2.80.

6.   The lunch and dinner business have seat turnovers and average checks as follows:

	Lunch		Dinner	
	Turnover	Aver. Ck.	Turnover	Aver. Ck.
Mon.-Fri.	1¼	$4.20	1	$10.75
Sat.	½	4.50	1	12.50
Sun.	1½	5.50	½	11.25

7.   The first day of the year for which you are to prepare the budget is Monday.

8.   The food cost percentage is estimated to be 35%.

9.   The labor cost percentages are as follows:
Rooms: 20%
Food: 38%

10.   Other direct expenses of the operated departments are as follows:
Rooms: 10%
Food: 12%

11.   Undistributed operating expenses include:
$100,000 of fixed expenses and the remainder is 10% of total revenue

12.   Other fixed costs include the following:
Property taxes $30,000
Depreciation   60,000
Interest   50,000

13.   The MM's average income tax rate is 30% of income before income taxes.

Required:

Prepare, in reasonable form, the operating budget for the year.

Problem 11.4

For the week of June 6, Melvin Mince, the manager of Melvin's Hotel in northwestern Illinois, budgeted 600 hours for room attendants to clean rooms. This budget was based on a work standard of cleaning one room every 36 minutes. The rooms attendants actually worked 660 hours cleaning 1,050 rooms. The budgeted wage rate for room attendants is $3.40 per hour. The wages paid to room attendants totaled $2,178.00.

Required:

1. What is the amount of the budget variance?

2. What is the amount of the volume variance?

3. What is the amount of the efficiency variance?

4. What is the amount of the rate variance?

Problem 11.5

Stacy Konrad, the manager of the Double K Motel, has done the preliminary budget analysis, but is not sure how to evaluate the results. The following diagram is a depiction of the labor expense for the Double K.

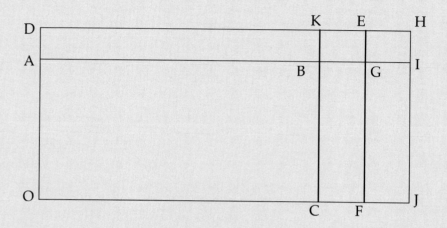

OABC = Budget for room attendants' wages
OF = Actual hours
OJ = Allowable time for actual output
OD = Actual rate

Required:

1. Which rectangle represents the rate variance?
2. How is the compound variance represented?
3. Which rectangle represents the volume variance?
4. Which rectangle represents the efficiency variance?

12 Forecasting Sales

Every hospitality manager's job includes forecasting, which is the calculation and prediction of future events such as sales for the following day, week, or month. Forecasting is necessary in order to plan the most effective and efficient ways to meet expected sales volume. For example, if the food and beverage manager of a hotel forecasts 500 dinner guests, then food, beverages, and other supplies must be obtained, and the appropriate personnel must be scheduled to prepare and serve the food and beverages to the guests. Generally, the accuracy of sales forecasts is a major determinant of the cost effectiveness of the hospitality operation. For example, if 400 meals are forecast and 500 guests show up, the food and beverage provisions may not be adequate, nor may be the number of employees scheduled to work. This may result in poor service and overtime wages. On the other hand, if 600 meals had been forecast, service would probably have been outstanding; however, due to possibly excessive labor costs, efficiency would have been reduced. The general topic of forecasting raises several questions such as:

1. How important is forecasting?

2. Is forecasting limited to financial forecasts?

3. How is forecasting conducted by unit managers in the hospitality industry?

4. How does forecasting enable management to be successful?

5. What are the limitations to forecasting?

6. How does forecasting differ from planning?

7. What is the difference between seasonal and cyclical patterns?

8. How do quantitative and qualitative forecasting methods differ?

9. How is a moving average calculated?

10. When are causal forecasting approaches most useful in the hospitality industry?

This chapter begins by explaining the distinction between implicit and explicit forecasts. A general discussion of forecasting in the hospitality industry is followed by identifying the personnel who are responsible for preparing forecasts. Next, we turn to the nature of forecasting itself, focusing on the underlying patterns of data used in forecasts and providing an overview of various forecasting methods. The problem of selecting a forecasting method appropriate to individual hospitality operations is given special consideration. Finally, we will illustrate the chapter's discussion of forecasting by providing case studies of how forecasts are prepared by three different hospitality operations.

Implicit Versus Explicit Forecasts

Some hospitality managers may insist that they do not believe in forecasting. However, their actions almost always prove otherwise. For example, when the manager makes a "snap decision" to replace an inoperative piece of equipment, such as a range, he or she is implicitly forecasting that profits will be higher if a new range is purchased.

This intuitive approach to managing may be useful since unforeseen events often occur and must be resolved quickly; however, to manage in this fashion on a daily basis would be less than optimal. It is generally more useful to forecast consciously. Implicit forecasts are unsystematic, imprecise, and difficult to evaluate rationally, while explicit forecasts are systematic, may be reasonably reliable and accurate, and are easier to evaluate rationally.

Forecasting in the Hospitality Industry

A major function of management is planning, and a subset of the planning function is forecasting. Forecasting is generally used to predict what will happen in a given set of circumstances. The forecast gives an idea of expected results if management makes no changes in the way things are done. In planning, forecasts are used to help make decisions about which circumstances will be most desirable for the hospitality operation. Thus, if a forecast shows rooms demand will decrease next month, management should prepare an action plan to prevent rooms sales from declining. After the action plan is completed, a new forecast must be made to reflect the impact of the action plan.

Planning, and thus forecasting, is pervasive in hospitality operations. In a hotel operation, rooms sales and the food and beverage sales account for approximately 80% of the total sales activity of a hotel. Sales are forecast for several years in long-range budgets by many operations, especially chains in both the food service and lodging segments of the hospitality industry. At the other extreme, sales are forecast for months, days, parts of a day, and sometimes even on an hourly basis, since management must plan to service the forecasted sales.

Hospitality establishments also provide estimates of future activity in management reports to stockholders which include both qualitative and quantitative forecasts. For example, Marriott Corporation included the following in a recent Annual Report[1]:

> "We seek to build and maintain Marriott's reputation as a premier company in lodging, food service, and related business areas."
> "We are confident we can continue 20% earnings per share growth and maintain return on equity over 20%."
> "Marriott will add 25,000 luxury priced rooms by 1988."

Personnel Responsible for Forecasting

Forecasting of sales and related expenses is not the sole responsibility of the accounting department but involves management personnel in other departments as well. For example, at Hilton Hotels, the year-ahead forecast includes input from (1) the sales director's forecast of group rooms business, (2) the front office manager's forecast of rooms occupancy from all other sources, (3) a joint forecast of rooms business by the sales director and front office manager, and (4) a general manager and management team review. Additionally, Hilton Hotels personnel prepare month-ahead forecasts, 10-day forecasts, and long-range projections for five years. The financial controller participates in all these forecasts.[2]

Heads of other revenue producing departments, such as food service, are involved in forecasting sales of their respective departments. In fact, management personnel at virtually all levels (corporate, division, area, etc.) are involved in making forecasts.

The Nature of Forecasting

In order to appreciate forecasting, its nature and limitations must be understood. First, forecasting deals with the future. A forecast made now is for activity during a future period, be it tonight's dinner sales, tomorrow's rooms sales, etc. Both the future aspect and the time period are involved. A forecast today for tomorrow's sales is generally much easier than an estimate today of next year's sales. The more removed the forecast period is from the date the forecast is made, the greater the difficulty in making the forecast.

Second, forecasting involves uncertainty. If management were certain about what circumstances would exist during the forecasted period, the forecast preparation would be a trivial matter. Virtually all situations faced by managers involve uncertainty; therefore, judgments are made and information gathered on which to base the forecast. For example, assume rooms sales for a major hotel must be forecast for one year in advance. The manager (forecaster) may be uncertain as to competition, guest demand, room rates, etc. Nevertheless, using the best information available and his or her best judgment, X rooms at an average room rate of $Y are forecasted to be sold.

Third, forecasting generally relies on information contained in historical data. Historical activity, for example past sales, may not be a strong indicator of future activity; still, it is considered a reasonable starting point. When historical data appears to be irrelevant to the future time period, the forecasts should be modified appropriately. For example, a successful world's fair might have had a major impact on hotel occupancies for several months; however, in projecting future hotel occupancies, this factor affecting historical information must be carefully considered.

Fourth, by their nature, forecasts are generally less accurate than desired. However, due to factors already discussed, this should be expected. Rather than discarding forecasts due to their inaccuracy, management should consider using more sophisticated forecasting models when their cost is justified, updating forecasts as necessary, and/or planning more carefully based on the forecasted projections.

Naive forecasting models, such as the most recent value plus 5%, may have been adequate in the past when a hospitality operation was small; however, more sophisticated models may be appropriate as the operation expands both in physical size and revenues. Forecasts must be revised as soon as there is a change in the circumstances on which the forecasts were based. For example, an enhanced food and beverage reputation due to favorable publicity may call for reforecasting next month's food and beverage sales.

Finally, management must plan to cover a deviation of an additional X% from the forecasted levels. Past experience may be the best indication of the required planning. For example, if actual sales historically have differed by an additional 10% from projected sales, management should order sufficient provisions to cover such a deviation for the projected activity.

Underlying Pattern of the Data

Most forecasting methods assume some pattern exists in past data that can be identified and used in making the forecast. The methods to be presented in this chapter make explicit assumptions about the type of underlying pattern; thus, the manager in forecasting must attempt to match the pattern with the most appropriate forecasting method. Three types of pattern are trend, seasonal, and cyclical.

The trend pattern is simply a projection of the long-run estimate of the activity being evaluated. The trend pattern of the data is often shown for several years. Exhibit 12.1 shows a trend for rooms sales of a hypothetical hotel. The trend of rooms sales of this hotel is an increasing one and could be determined by using methods presented later in this chapter.

A seasonal pattern exists when a series of data fluctuates according to some seasonal pattern. The season may be monthly, the four seasons of the year, or, as discussed previously in Chapter 1, the days of the week. Seasonal patterns exist in the hospitality industry primarily due to forces external to the industry. For example, many summer resort hotels on Mackinac Island (Michigan) experience high occupancy during the summer months but are closed during the months of October through April. The manager of a hospitality operation affected by seasonal business swings must fully appreciate this impact in order to manage efficiently. The seasonal pattern for a hypothetical hotel is shown in Exhibit 12.1.

The final underlying pattern of data is called cyclical. Cyclical patterns are movements about a trend line that generally occur over a period of more than one year. Exhibit 12.1 shows that the cyclical pattern is similar to a seasonal pattern except for the length of the pattern.

The cyclical pattern is the most difficult to predict because, unlike a seasonal pattern, it does not repeat itself at constant intervals. A cyclical

Exhibit 12.1 Underlying Patterns of Data for a Hypothetical Hotel

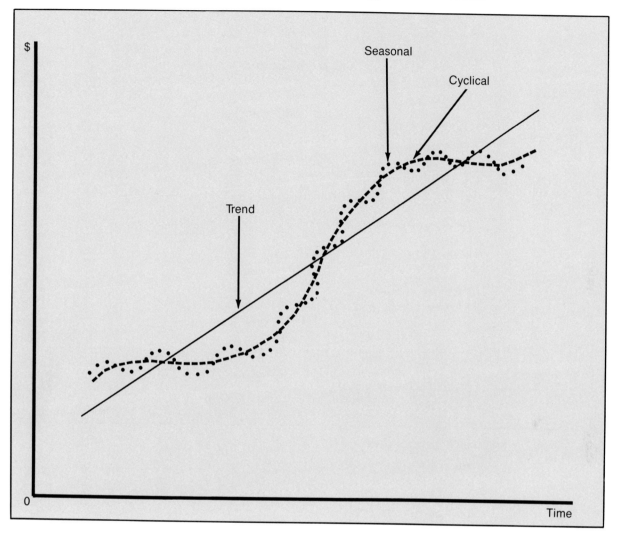

pattern can be observed in the annual lodging revenues (constant dollars) for 1967-84 as shown in Exhibit 12.2. The graph shows growth of annual revenues from just under $10 billion to nearly $16 billion over 18 years. However, several fairly dramatic declines and increases are reflected.

Finally, random variations are also present in all historical data. By definition, there is no pattern in random variations, and they occur for reasons that the hospitality manager cannot anticipate regardless of the sophistication of forecasting methods. Therefore, the actual observed result is a combination of trend and randomness. So long as randomness exists, uncertainty will be present. However, when the forecaster is able to identify the exact pattern of the underlying data, the random deviations are minimized.

Exhibit 12.2   Annual Lodging Revenues 1967–84 — Constant Dollars

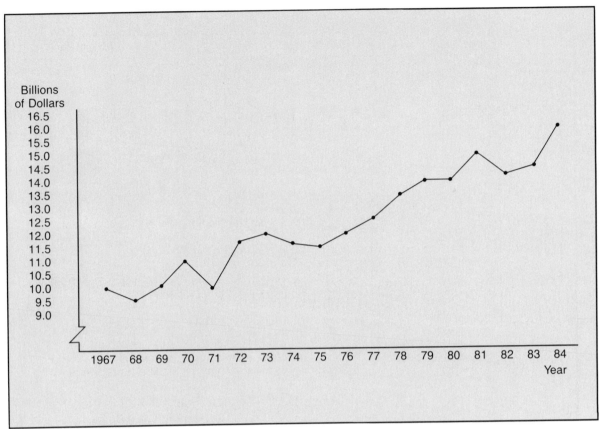

Source: Adapted from the *National Income and Products Accounts of the United States*, U.S. Dept. of Commerce.

Overview of Forecasting Methods

There are numerous ways to forecast, ranging from the simple, unsophisticated method of intuition to complex approaches such as econometric models, where sets of two or more multiple regression equations are used. Explicit forecasting methods may be classified as shown in Exhibit 12.3.

The first breakdown is between informal and formal forecasting methods. Informal methods are based on intuition and lack systematic procedures transferable to other forecasters. Formal forecasting methods outline steps to be followed so they can be applied repeatedly. Formal forecasting methods are divided between qualitative methods and quantitative methods, as shown in Exhibit 12.3. The quantitative methods, which will be the thrust of the remainder of this chapter, are further divided between causal and time series approaches.

Exhibit 12.3   Forecasting Methods

Approaches				Brief Description
Informal forecasting				Ad hoc, judgmental or intuitive methods
Formal Forecasting	Quantitative Methods	Causal Methods	Regression Analysis	Independent variables are related to the dependent variable using least squares: $y = A + Bx_1 + Cx_2$. Approaches include simple linear regression, multiple linear regression, and nonlinear regression.
			Econometrics	A system of interdependent regression equations describing one or more economic sectors.
		Time Series	Naive	Simple rules such as forecast equals last period's actual activity.
			Smoothing	Based on average past values of a time series (moving average) or weighting more recent past values of a time series (exponential smoothing).
			Decomposition	A time series that is broken down into trend, cyclical, seasonality, and randomness.
	Qualitative Methods		Market Research	Gathering information from potential customers regarding a "new" product or service.
			Juries of Executive Opinion	Top executives jointly prepare forecasts.
			Salesforce Estimates	A bottom-up approach to aggregating unit managers' forecasts.
			Delphi Method	A formal process conducted with a group of experts to achieve consensus on future events as they affect the company's markets.

The time series approaches always assume that a pattern recurs over time which, when identified, may be used to forecast values for any subsequent time period. For example, if a seasonal pattern of December hotel occupancies of 30% below the monthly average has been identified, then the estimated hotel occupancy for December of the following year would most likely be 30% below the monthly average for that year.

Time series approaches assume the underlying pattern can be identified solely on the basis of historical data from that series and do not consider the potential effects of certain decisions, such as pricing and advertising, that the manager makes for the future periods. Time series approaches, presented in this chapter, include naive methods and smoothing methods.

The causal approaches assume that the value of a certain variable is a function of other variables. For example, the sales of food and beverages in a hotel are a function, among other things, of hotel occupancy. Thus, food and beverage sales forecast, in part, is based on forecasted rooms sales. Causal methods include single and multiple regression methods and econometric models. Only the single regression approach will be presented in this text.[3]

Naive Methods

The simplest time series approach to forecasting is to use the most recently observed value as a forecast. For example, a food service manager's sales projections for the current month of $50,000 may be based upon the $50,000 sales of the prior month. This naive approach to forecasting assumes there is no seasonality affecting sales. To take seasonality into account, a forecaster might use sales from the same month of the previous year as a base and either add or subtract a certain percentage.

For example, assume a hotel's January 19X1 rooms sales totaled $150,000. The projection for January 19X2, using an anticipated 10% increase due to expected increased rooms sales and prices, would be $165,000, computed as follows:

$$\text{Base } (1 + 10\%) = \text{Forecast for January 19X2}$$
$$150,000 \ (1.1) \quad = \underline{\underline{\$165,000}}$$

Although these naive methods are based on very simple rules, they may provide reasonably accurate forecasts, especially for estimates of up to one year. In some cases, more sophisticated methods do not sufficiently improve the accuracy of forecasts, compared with these naive approaches, to justify their use—especially in light of their higher costs.

Moving Averages

In some cases, the major cause of variations among data used in making forecasts is randomness. Since managers do not make business decisions based on randomness that may never again happen, they attempt to remove the random effect by averaging the data from specified time periods. One such approach to forecasting is the moving average, which is expressed mathematically as follows:

$$\text{Moving Average} = \frac{\text{Activity in Previous n Periods}}{n}$$

where n is the number of periods in the moving average

Exhibit 12.4   Weekly Meals Served — Bank of Hospitality

Week	Actual Meals Served
1	1,000
2	900
3	950
4	1,050
5	1,025
6	1,000
7	975
8	1,000
9	950
10	1,025
11	1,000
12	1,050

This moving average method is illustrated using the contract food service operation at the Bank of Hospitality. Service Company, the contract feeding company, serves lunch five days a week at the Bank of Hospitality, and the manager needs to estimate sales for the 13th week. Exhibit 12.4 reveals weekly sales for weeks 1-12. Using a three-week moving average, the estimate for the number of meals to be served during the 13th week is 1,025, determined as follows:

$$\text{3-Week Moving Average} \quad = \quad \frac{1,025 + 1,000 + 1,050}{3}$$

$$\text{3-Week Moving Average} \quad = \quad \underline{\underline{1,025}} \text{ meals}$$

As new weekly results become available, they are used in calculating the average by adding the most recent week and dropping the earliest week. In this way, the calculated average is a "moving" one because it is continually updated to include only the most recent observations for the specified number of time periods. For example, if 950 meals were served during week 13 at the Bank of Hospitality, then the forecast of 1,000 for week 14, using the three-week moving average, would be calculated as follows:

$$\text{Forecast for Week 14} \quad = \quad \frac{\text{Sum Sales for Weeks 11-13}}{3}$$

$$\text{Forecast for Week 14} \quad = \quad \frac{1,000 + 1,050 + 950}{3}$$

$$\text{Forecast for Week 14} \quad = \quad \underline{\underline{1,000}} \text{ meals}$$

Alternatively, more weeks could be used to determine the weekly forecast. For example, a 12-week moving average to estimate meals to be sold during the 13th week results in a forecast of 994, determined as follows:

$$\text{12-Week Moving Average} = \frac{\text{Actual Weekly Sales for Weeks 1-12}}{12}$$

$$\text{12-Week Moving Average} = \frac{11,925}{12}$$

$$\text{12-Week Moving Average} = 993.75, \text{ rounded to } \underline{\underline{994}}$$

It should be noted that the more periods averaged, the less effect the random variations will have on the forecast. This can be seen in the above illustration. The three-week moving average forecast for week 13 was 1,025 meals, compared to the 12-week moving average forecast of 994. In this case, since the actual sales during the 13th week turned out to be 950 meals, the 12-week moving average forecast of 994 was more accurate than the forecast based on only three weeks. The increased accuracy is due to minimizing the effect of random variations by using data covering a greater number of time periods.

Although the moving average approach to forecasting is often considered to be more accurate and reliable than the naive methods, there are some disadvantages associated with this approach. One limitation is the need to store and continually update the historical data covering the most recent number of time periods used in calculating the moving average. This requirement would be quite costly for a large retail business, such as Sears or K-Mart, which would have to keep track of sales data for a large number of different items. However, in the hospitality industry the cost of storing and maintaining historical data for moving average forecasts is not unreasonable, since a comparatively small number of different items are sold by hotels and restaurants.

A more serious limitation is that the moving average method gives equal weight to each of the observations gathered over the specified number of time periods. Many managers would agree that the data from the most recent time periods contain more information about what will happen in the future and, therefore, should be given relatively more weight than the older observations that are calculated into the moving average. The exponential smoothing approach to forecasting not only satisfies this concern to count recent data more heavily than older data, but also eliminates the need for storing all of the historical data covering the specified time period.

Exponential Smoothing

Exponential smoothing is a forecasting method that uses a smoothing constant and recent actual and forecasted activity to estimate future activity. This approach has widespread appeal among business forecasters because it incorporates the intuitively appealing logic of "if the forecast for a particular period was too high, reduce it for the next period; if it was too low, raise it!"

When the exponential smoothing method is used, the hospitality manager requires only three types of data as follows:

1. The forecast from the prior period

2. The actual activity that resulted from this forecasted period

3. A smoothing constant

Both the forecast from the prior period and the actual activity from this period are readily available; however, the smoothing constant requires the manager to identify what is a good response rate. The smoothing constant, which will be between 0 and 1, should be small if sales have been relatively stable in the past, and large if the product/ service is experiencing rapid growth.

The general formula for exponential smoothing is as follows:

New Forecast = Past Forecast + Smoothing Constant (Actual Demand
− Past Forecast)

Using the previous illustration with the Bank of Hospitality, the weekly sales will be projected for week 13 using the exponential smoothing method of forecasting. Assume the forecasted sales for week 12 were 1,020 and that .1 is the smoothing constant. The forecasted sales for week 13 of 1,023 meals is determined as follows:

Week 13 Forecast = Week 12 Forecast + .1 (Week 12 Actual Sales
− Week 12 Forecast)

Week 13 Forecast = 1,020 + .1 (1,050 − 1,020)

Week 13 Forecast = <u>1,023</u> meals

The exponential smoothing method presented in this text is only one of several such approaches.[4] Exponential smoothing techniques are most useful when only short-term forecasts are required, and when reasonably accurate rather than precise forecasts are acceptable.

Causal Forecasting Approaches

Causal forecasting approaches include both single and multiple regression as well as econometric models; however, in this text, we will discuss only single regression analysis.

Regression analysis involves estimating an activity within the hospitality operation on the basis of other activities or factors that are assumed to be causes, or highly reliable indicators, of the levels of activity. The activity to be forecasted (such as food sales) is the dependent, unknown variable, while the basis on which the forecast is made (such as room sales and/or advertising expenses) is the independent, known variable. Regression analysis is used to predict the dependent variable given the value of the independent variable.

The level of demand to be estimated is thought to depend upon, or be closely related to, the independent variable. In order to forecast the operation's demand, the closeness of the variables needs to be determined. For example, how closely related is a lodging property's rooms sales to food sales in its restaurant operation?

Two measures of closeness are the coefficient of correlation and the coefficient of determination. The coefficient of correlation is the measure of the relation between the dependent and independent variables, such as food sales and rooms sales. The formula for determining the coefficient of correlation is as follows:

$$r = \frac{n\Sigma xy - \Sigma x \Sigma y}{\sqrt{[n\Sigma x^2 - (\Sigma x)^2][n\Sigma y^2 - (\Sigma y)^2]}}$$

	Room Guests	Meals Served
January	4,060	5,200
February	4,100	5,360
March	4,200	5,720
April	4,250	5,430
May	4,200	5,680
June	4,150	5,520
July	4,300	5,800
August	4,350	5,910
September	4,400	6,020
October	4,200	5,840
November	4,080	5,510
December	3,600	5,020

In this equation, "r" stands for a positive relationship value between 0 and +1. The closer the r value is to +1, the stronger the relationship between the dependent and independent variables being measured.

The square of the coefficient of correlation, r, is the coefficient of determination. This measure reflects the extent to which the change in the independent variable explains the change in the dependent variable.

Regression analysis is illustrated using the hypothetical Forest Hotel. Exhibit 12.5 contains the number of room guests and meals served in the dining room for 19X1. Using the regression equation of

$$y = a + bx$$

where

y = Meals served
a = Meals served to nonhotel registrants
b = Average number of meals served to each hotel guest
x = Number of hotel room guests

Using formulas[5] to determine a and b, given the data in Exhibit 12.5, the regression equation becomes

$$y = 398 + 1.247(x)$$

This equation indicates that 398 people not registered as guests at the Forest Hotel dine there weekly and, further, that each registered room guest eats 1.247 meals at the hotel each day.

Assuming the sales forecast for the first week of January, 19X2 is 3,000 rooms at an average occupancy per room of 1.5 people, the projected meals to be sold is determined as follows:

Forecasted Meals Sold	=	398 + 1.247(3000)(1.5)
Forecasted Meals Sold	=	398 + 5,612
Forecasted Meals Sold	=	6,010

The forecasted 6,010 meals to be sold during the first week of January, 19X2 includes 398 meals for diners not registered as guests and 5,612 meals for hotel guests.

Regression analysis forecasting used when two or more independent variables are related to the dependent variable is called multiple regression analysis. For example, the manager of the food and beverage department at a lodging operation may desire to forecast food sales, which are highly dependent upon the number of room guests and advertising expenditures. Although multiple regression analysis is both interesting and challenging, it is beyond the scope of this text.[6]

Regression analysis techniques are useful for making forecasts for up to two years. In addition, the usefulness of these approaches is a function of satisfactory dependent and independent variables; that is, the higher the correlation of the dependent and independent variables, the greater the probability regression analysis will yield meaningful forecasts.

Limitations of Quantitative Forecasting Methods

Although time series forecasting and causal forecasting can be quite useful, they have limitations. First, they are virtually useless when data are scarce, such as the opening of a new hotel or restaurant, or the opening of a new dining room in a hotel. In these instances, there is no sales history for the newly opened facility from which to collect the data needed to forecast demand. Secondly, they assume historical trends will continue into the future and are unable to consider unforeseeable, unexpected occurrences, such as the energy crisis in the early 1970's and its impact on highway lodging properties.

Qualitative Forecasting Techniques

When the limitations of quantitative approaches significantly affect a hospitality operation, qualitative forecasting methods are useful. These methods emphasize human judgment. Information is gathered in as logical, unbiased, and systematic a way as possible, and then judgment is brought to bear on the activity being forecasted. Qualitative forecasting methods include marketing research, jury of executive opinion, salesforce estimates, and the Delphi method.

Marketing research systematically gathers, records, and analyzes data related to a hospitality operation's marketing of products and services. Large hotel chains generally conduct extensive market research prior to opening a new property to determine whether there is adequate demand. This market research provides data which can then be used in preparing formal sales forecasts.

The jury of executive opinion technique uses key financial, marketing, and operations executives to estimate sales for the forecast period. Generally, the executives are given expected economic conditions and changes in the establishment's services prior to independently making their sales forecasts. The president's role can be to reconcile differences among the executives' opinions.

Salesforce estimates is a technique similar to the jury of executive opinion in that opinions of corporate personnel are obtained. However, in this case, the input is from lower echelon personnel who estimate their next year's sales. This approach could be used by multi-unit food service operations. Unit managers would be polled, and their immediate superiors would review and discuss these estimates with each unit manager.

Then, the separate sales estimates would be combined to create a sales forecast for the food service operation.

The Delphi technique is used for making technical forecasts which are generally futuristic in nature. This technique involves obtaining opinions from a group of experts to achieve consensus on future events that might affect an operation's markets. Rather than meeting together at one place, the group interacts anonymously. Questionnaires are often used. The responses are then analyzed and resubmitted to the experts for a second round of opinions. This process may continue for several rounds.

Selection of a Forecasting Method

The specific forecasting method that a hospitality operation adopts will depend on several factors; however, the two most important are the method's effectiveness in providing usable projections from available data, and the cost of using the method. Different methods will, of course, be used for different purposes as suggested throughout this chapter. Smaller establishments, lacking personnel with forecasting skills, will likely adopt the less sophisticated, but still highly useful, naive methods. On the other hand, larger establishments may find the more sophisticated methods to be the most effective; although these approaches may appear more costly, they may actually be less costly in the long run when used by the many diverse operations managed by larger establishments.

In addition to the effectiveness and cost of different forecasting methods, other factors relevant to selecting an appropriate approach to forecasting include:

- Frequency with which forecasts will be updated

- Turnaround required for an updated forecast

- Size and complexity of the hospitality operation

- Forecasting skills of personnel involved in making forecasts

- Purposes for which the forecasts are made

Forecasting Cases

To illustrate forecasting in hospitality industry firms, three companies from different segments have contributed overviews of one facet of forecasting at their companies. The case illustration from Canteen Corporation, which serves the business and industry segment of the hospitality industry, was provided by Mr. Donald R. Finger, Assistant Corporate Controller of Canteen Corporation. It focuses on forecasting at the unit level for a four-week period. A brief description of the calculation of the sales dollars is included as well as the two major expenses, cost of food sold and labor expense. Included with the case is their food forecast form and a copy of a 1986 operations budget for one of their restaurants.

The second case is from Pizza Hut, and it was prepared by Don

Meyer and Mark Willoughby, members of the accounting staff of Pizza Hut Inc. Its focus is their weekly sales forecast. This forecast is prepared by starting with the average of the past three weeks (effectively a three-week moving average); however, it is adjusted based on several factors, such as local advertising. A major purpose of this forecast is scheduling labor. Included with the case are several forms, including a Labor Scheduling Grid. This form is used to determine the number and types of personnel required on an hourly basis given the sales forecast.

The Stouffer Hotels illustration was provided by Raymond O. Holmes, Vice President/Controller of Stouffer Hotels. Its focus is the sales forecast for the annual budget. This case details the various managers' roles in forecasting sales for the annual budget. Forms included are the "Hotel Room Forecast" and the "Rooms Forecast Reconciliation and Casualty Report." The guidelines for completing these reports are also included to illustrate this facet of budgeting.

The three cases cover three segments of the hospitality industry and three time periods—weekly, monthly (four weeks), and annual. They are just a sampling of budgeting practices in hospitality corporations in the 1980s.

Canteen Corporation— Forecasting By Unit Managers

Canteen Corporation is a major competitor in the growing B&I (business and industry) segment of the hospitality industry. With over 1,600 operating units, sales in excess of $1.4 billion, and 20,000 employees, Canteen operates in all of the 50 states and Canada. Owned by Transworld Corporation, Canteen provides foodservice at the Kennedy Space Center, Yellowstone National Park and other numerous national and state parks, several Stadiums such as Yankee and Kansas City, small and large colleges, elementary schools, correctional facilities, banks, hospitals, and industrial plants.

Forecasting at Canteen is conducted at each management level including unit, district, region, and corporate. Forecasting at the unit level (the focus of this section) includes a profit and loss forecast for the next four periods. Canteen operating quarters are 4-4-5, that is, four weeks, four weeks, and five weeks, followed by another 4-4-5, etc. Although forecasting varies by region, division, and operation, it is the responsibility of the manager of the unit.

A major use of the four-period profit and loss forecast is for control purposes, with the major emphasis on the bottom line. However, in addition, copies are provided to higher level management for their use in monitoring the operating unit's performance. The sales forecast is prepared by considering:

1. Operating days in the period

2. Projected customer count (The past two years of prior experience is considered with emphasis placed on the most recent year in addition to the present population, e.g., student enrollment at the school.)

3. Check average (The check average of the prior period is generally used as adjusted for known price increases.)

The sales dollars forecast is estimated as follows:

Operating Days x Projected Customer Count x
Check Average = Forecasted Sales

The two major expenses are cost of food sold and labor expense. Cost of food sold is estimated by multiplying the target food cost percentage by the net sales (gross sales less sales tax). Labor expense is forecasted by multiplying the expected labor hours by the appropriate hourly wages.

Finally, the major measures of performance are (1) the bottom line, (2) cost of food ratio determined by dividing cost of food by gross sales, and (3) sales per labor hour determined by dividing gross sales by the total labor hours. A food forecast form used by unit managers is shown in Exhibit 12.6. Exhibit 12.7 is the 1986 Budget for a Canteen Corporation operation.

Pizza Hut—A Case in Forecasting

Pizza Hut is the largest retail distributor of pizza in the world, with a distribution of over 4,000 units, including 2,000 corporate-owned units and 2,000 franchised units. Though this makes the Wichita, Kansas headquartered Pizza Hut one of the largest multi-unit food chains, it is owned by an even larger firm, Pepsico. Incidentally, Pepsico also owns the largest Mexican food chain, Taco Bell, which systemwide has in excess of 2,100 units.

The typical Pizza Hut operation consists of approximately 100 seats, 2,300 square footage, and has 25 employees. Pizza Hut's major items, familiar to most pizza lovers, include deep pan pizza, personal pan pizza, and its recently introduced priazzo.

Forecasting pervades the entire organization; however, the emphasis in this case is on the store manager. The major forecasting by a unit manager is the preparation of the weekly sales forecast which is reviewed and approved by his/her area supervisor. Area supervisors use unit sales forecasts in preparing their area sales forecasts which then are used by district managers in preparing district forecasts, etc. The major uses of the weekly sales forecast by the unit manager are labor scheduling and preparing product ingredients for each day.

The weekly sales forecast is detailed by hour for each day. The manager starts with historical data—the average of the daily-hourly sales for the past three weeks. This historical hourly sales average is adjusted for several factors as follows:

- Advertising in local papers

- Local marketing, such as a Cub Scout troop of 20 boys is expected between 6-7 p.m. on Tuesday

- Seasonality—including weather changes, time of year, and holidays

- Media advertising

- Trend for the past few weeks

Pizza Hut does not prescribe a formalized approach for adjusting the historical data for the above factors but allows unit managers to use their judgment.[7]

Exhibit 12.6   Food Forecast

Operation Number:____ / ____ / ____ / ____ /   Submitted By: _____ / ____

Operation Name: _____   Approved By: _____ / ____

P / L: _____

Mgmt. Fee: _____

Period: _____

Weekly: _____

		Prior Period				Period # ____		Period # ____		Period # ____		Period # ____	
		Forecast		Actual									
		Amt.	%	Amt.	%	Amt.	%	Amt.	%	Amt.	%	Amt.	%
*Gross Sales:	0												
Net Sales:	+		100		100		100		100		100		100
Product Cost:	−												
Variable Labor:	+												
Central Bkpng:	+												
Fringe:	+												
Sub Total:	+												
Semi-Var. Labor:	+												
DMF:	+												
Fringe:	+												
Sub Total:	+												
Total Labor Cost:	−												
Commission Pd/Rent:	−												
Repair/Replacemt:	−												
Depreciation:	−												
Investment Charge:	−												
Other Direct:	−												
O/H & Mgmt. Fee:	−												
Misc. & Vend Income:	+												
Profit/Contract:	±												
Amount Due–(To)Fm:	±												
O/H & Mgmt. Fee:	±												
Investment Charge:	−												
DMT Expense:	−												
Pretax P/(L):	±												

Total Operating Days: _____ _____   _____ _____   _____ _____   _____ _____

Partial Shutdown Da: _____ _____   _____ _____   _____ _____   _____ _____

Hol./Full Shutdown: _____ _____   _____ _____   _____ _____   _____ _____

Population: _____ _____   _____ _____   _____ _____   _____ _____

Customer Count/Day: _____ _____   _____ _____   _____ _____   _____ _____

Participation Rate: _____ _____   _____ _____   _____ _____   _____ _____

Check Average: _____ _____   _____ _____   _____ _____   _____ _____

Hourly Hours/Day: _____ _____   _____ _____   _____ _____   _____ _____

Average Hourly Rate: _____ _____   _____ _____   _____ _____   _____ _____

*Total Hours/Day: _____ _____   _____ _____   _____ _____   _____ _____

*SPH: _____ _____   _____ _____   _____ _____   _____ _____

Event	Date	***Critical Milestones***	Event	Date
_____	____/____		_____	____/____
_____	____/____		_____	____/____

Exhibit 12.7 1986 Budget P & L — Final

06/24/85 at 19.95.28

.0000 Description	Line	January Amt	%	February Amt	%	March Amt	%	April Amt	%	May Amt	%
—SALES—											
Food and Bar Items	010	6.1	105.2	9.0	105.9	10.1	106.3	8.1	106.6	8.5	106.3
Sales Tax	030	0.3-	5.2	0.5-	5.9	0.6-	6.3	0.5-	6.6	0.5-	6.3
Net Sales		5.8	100.0	8.5	100.0	9.5	100.0	7.6	100.0	8.0	100.0
Product Cost	040	3.2	55.2	4.6	54.1	5.3	55.8	4.1	53.9	4.4	55.0
Gross Profit		2.6	44.8	3.9	45.9	4.2	44.2	3.5	46.1	3.6	45.0
—VAR. COSTS - DIR.—											
Labor	050	2.3	39.7	3.5	41.2	3.8	40.0	2.9	38.2	2.9	36.3
Fringe	060	1.3	22.4	1.3	15.3	1.5	15.8	1.2	15.8	1.2	15.0
Total Pers. Cost/Dir		3.6	62.1	4.8	56.5	5.3	55.8	4.1	53.9	4.1	51.3
—SEMI-VAR. COSTS—											
Labor	070	0.0		0.0		0.2	2.1	0.2	2.6	0.2	2.5
Fringe	080	0.0		0.0		0.1	1.1	0.1	1.3	0.1	1.3
Tot. Pers. Cost/Su		0.0		0.0		0.3	3.2	0.3	3.90	0.3	3.8
Total Pers. Costs		3.6	62.1	4.8	56.5	5.6	58.9	4.4	57.9	4.4	55.0
Mds. Equip. Replace	100	0.0		0.0		0.0		0.0		0.0	
Rental Expense	110	0.1	1.7	0.1	1.2	0.1	1.1	0.1	1.3	0.1	1.3
Advertising	130	0.0		0.0		0.0		0.0		0.1	1.3
Outside Services	170	0.2	3.4	0.2	2.4	0.2	2.1	0.1	1.3	0.1	1.3
Other Taxes & Insurance	200	0.0		0.0		0.0		0.0		0.0	
Laundry & Cleaning	210	0.2	3.4	0.3	3.5	0.2	2.1	0.1	1.3	0.3	3.8
Other Direct	230	0.1	1.7	0.1	1.2	0.1	1.1	0.1	1.3	0.0	
Total Semi-Var		0.6	10.3	0.7	8.2	0.9	9.5	0.7	9.2	0.9	11.3
P&L Before Oh/Fee		1.6-	27.6	1.6-	18.8	2.0-	21.1	1.3-	17.1	1.4-	17.5
Overhead & Fee Exp.	240	0.4	6.9	0.5	5.9	0.6	6.3	0.5	6.6	0.5	6.3
Profit/Contract		2.0-	34.5	2.1-	24.7	2.6-	27.4	1.8-	23.7	1.9-	23.8
Prof/Cont Aft Sub5		2.0-	34.5	2.1-	24.7	2.6-	27.4	1.8-	23.7	1.9-	23.8
Amount Due from Acct	280	2.0	34.5	2.1	24.7	2.6	27.4	1.8	23.7	1.9	23.8
Contractual P/L		0.0		0.0		0.0		0.0		0.0	
—INCOME RETAINED—											
Overhead & Fee Inc.	310	0.4	6.9	0.5	5.9	0.6	6.3	0.5	6.6	0.5	6.3
Total Inc. Retained		0.4	6.9	0.5	5.9	0.6	6.3	0.5	6.6	0.5	6.3
—OTHER COSTS—											
Personnel Costs	340	0.3	5.2	0.5	5.9	0.3	3.2	0.2	2.6	0.2	2.5
Inv. & Oh. Chg./Cr.	380	0.1	1.7	0.1	1.2	0.1	1.1	0.1	1.3	0.1	1.3
Computer Exp. Alloc.	400	0.0		0.0		0.0		0.0		0.0	
Total Other Costs		0.4	6.9	0.6	7.1	0.4	4.2	0.3	3.9	0.3	3.8
Pre-Tax Profit		0.0		0.1-	1.2	0.2	2.1	0.2	2.6	0.2	2.5

Courtesy of Canteen Corporation

—FORECAST—

	June		July		August		September		October		November		December		Total Year	
	Amt	%	Amt	%	Amt	%	Amt	%	Amt	%	Amt	%	Amt	%	Amt	%
	10.3	106.2	7.7	105.5	4.2	105.0	10.4	106.1	8.6	106.2	8.7	106.1	10.0	106.4	101.7	106.0
	0.6-	6.2	0.4-	5.5	0.2-	5.0	0.6-	6.1	0.5-	6.2	0.5-	6.1	0.6-	6.4	5.8-	6.0
	9.7	100.0	7.3	100.0	4.0	100.0	9.8	100.0	8.1	100.0	8.2	100.0	9.4	100.0	95.9	100.0
	5.3	54.6	4.0	54.8	2.2	55.0	5.4	55.1	4.4	54.3	4.5	54.9	5.1	54.3	52.5	54.7
	4.4	45.4	3.3	45.2	1.8	45.0	4.4	44.9	3.7	45.7	3.7	45.1	4.3	45.7	43.4	45.3
	2.9	29.9	2.3	31.5	1.3	32.5	2.9	29.6	2.4	29.6	2.5	30.5	2.8	29.8	32.5	33.9
	1.4	14.4	1.1	15.1	1.1	27.5	1.4	14.3	1.1	13.6	1.1	13.4	1.4	14.9	15.1	15.7
	4.3	44.3	3.4	46.6	2.4	60.0	4.3	43.9	3.5	43.2	3.6	43.9	4.2	44.7	47.6	49.6
	0.2	2.1	0.2	2.7	0.2	5.0	0.2	2.0	0.2	2.5	0.2	2.4	0.2	2.1	2.0	2.1
	0.0		0.1	1.4	0.0		0.1	1.0	0.0		0.1	1.2	0.0		0.6	.6
	0.2	2.1	0.3	4.1	0.2	5.0	0.3	3.1	0.2	2.5	0.3	3.7	0.2.	2.1	2.6	2.7
	4.5	46.4	3.7	50.7	2.6	65.0	4.6	46.9	3.7	45.7	3.9	47.6	4.4	46.8	50.2	52.3
	0.1	1.0	0.0		0.0		0.1	1.0	0.0		0.1	1.2	0.1	1.1	0.4	.4
	0.1	1.0	0.1	1.4	0.1	2.5	0.1	1.0	0.1	1.2	0.1	1.2	0.1	1.1	1.2	1.3
	0.0		0.0		0.0		0.0		0.0		0.0		0.0		0.1	0.1
	0.3	3.1	0.0		0.1	2.5	0.2	2.0	0.0		0.1	1.2	0.2	2.1	1.7	1.8
	0.0		0.0		0.0		0.1	1.0	0.0		0.0		0.1	1.1	0.2	0.2
	0.0		0.3	4.1	0.2	5.0	0.0		0.3	3.7	0.3	3.7	0.0		2.2	2.3
	0.2	2.1	0.2	2.7	0.2	5.0	0.2	2.0	0.2	2.5	0.0		0.2	2.1	1.6	1.7
	0.9	9.3	0.9	12.3	0.8	20.0	1.0	10.2	0.8	9.9	0.9	11.0	0.9	9.6	10.0	10.4
	0.8-	8.2	1.0-	13.7	1.4-	35.0	0.9-	9.2	0.6-	7.4	0.8-	9.8	0.8-	8.5	14.2-	14.8
	0.6	6.2	0.5	6.8	0.2	5.0	0.6	6.1	0.5	6.2	0.5	6.1	0.6	6.4	6.0	6.3
	1.4-	14.4	1.5-	20.5	1.6-	40.0	1.5-	15.3	1.1-	13.6	1.3-	15.9	1.4-	14.9	20.2-	21.1
	1.4-	14.4	1.5-	20.5	1.6-	40.0	1.5-	15.3	1.1-	13.6	1.3-	15.9	1.4-	14.9	20.2-	21.1
	1.4	14.4	1.5	20.5	1.6	40.0	1.5	15.3	1.1	13.6	1.3	15.9	1.4	14.9	20.2	21.1
	0.0		0.0		0.0		0.0		0.0		0.0		0.0		0.0	
	0.6	6.2	0.5	6.8	0.2	5.0	0.6	6.2	0.5	6.2	0.5	6.1	0.6	6.4	6.0	6.3
	0.6	6.2	0.5	6.8	0.2	5.0	0.6	6.1	0.5	6.2	0.5	6.1	0.6	6.4	6.0	6.3
	0.3	3.1	0.2	2.7	0.2	5.0	0.3	3.1	0.2	2.5	0.2	2.4	0.3	3.2	3.2	3.3
	0.1	1.0	0.1	1.4	0.1	2.5	0.1	1.0	0.0		0.0		0.0		0.9	0.9
	0.0		0.0		0.0		0.0		0.0		0.1	1.2	0.1	1.1	0.2	0.2
	0.4	4.1	0.3	4.1	0.3	7.5	0.4	4.1	0.2	2.5	0.3	3.7	0.4	4.3	4.3	4.5
	0.2	2.1	0.2	2.7	0.1-	2.5	0.2	2.0	0.3	3.7	0.2	2.4	0.2	2.1	1.7	1.8

Exhibit 12.8   Hourly Reading Sheet

	**HOURLY READING SHEET**																	

HOURLY READING SHEET

DAY		MARKETING WINDOW: LOCAL PROMOTION:																
Date	Open-12	12-1 PM	1-2 PM	2-3 PM	3-4 PM	4-5 PM	5-6 PM	6-7 PM	7-8 PM	8-9 PM	9-10 PM	10-11 PM	11-12 PM	12-1 AM	PROMO $	TOTAL SALES	COMMENTS

Courtesy of Pizza Hut, Inc.

The forecasting form used by unit managers is titled the "Hourly Reading Sheet," Exhibit 12.8. After this is completed based on the discussion above, the "Daily Labor Worksheet," Exhibit 12.9, is completed in part by using a Labor Scheduling Grid similar to the illustration in Exhibit 12.10.

For example, assume a Pizza Hut restaurant forecast $250 of hourly sales between 6 and 7 p.m. The required staffing includes 10 people based on the labor scheduling grid column 9 as follows: 2—production, 3—service, 1—register/telephone, 1—bus/dishwasher, 1—production leader, 1—host/hostess, and 1—floor manager.

Forecasting at Stouffer Hotels

Stouffer Hotels, a member of the Stouffer Group owned by Nestle Inc., a Switzerland based conglomerate, operates 24 hotels. Ten hotels are owned or partially owned and operated, while 14 other hotels are under a management agreement. Collectively, 9,000 rooms are operated by Stouffer Hotels with total revenues in excess of $250,000,000. Some Stouffer Hotels are: The Mayflower (Washington, D.C.), Wailea Beach in Maui, and Denver Concourse in Denver, Colorado.

As most hotel corporations, Stouffer Hotels have major objectives to provide excellent service and achieve reasonable profits. This is

Exhibit 12.9   Daily Labor Worksheet

DAILY LABOR WORKSHEET   Day:_____   Period_____

RESTAURANT NO.	PAN DOUGH	SPECIAL EVENTS/MARKETING	MARKETING WINDOW _____
	• # PPP's ____ x .0225 = ____	WK _____	
	• Morning Pan Batches (A.M.) ____	WK _____	
	• Afternoon Pan Batches (P.M.) ____	WK _____	
		WK _____	

HOUR		6	7	8	9	10	11	12	1	2	3	4	5	6	7	8	9	10	11	12	1	2		Promo $/Hrs.	Total Sales/Hrs.
PROJECTED SALES		PPP Hours	Basic Open	A.M. Pan	P.M. Pan														Close All.	Disc Hrs.				
GRID HOURS (DIRECT)			2.5																						
SCHEDULED DIRECT HOURS																									

JOB #	IN	OUT	6	7	8	9	10	11	12	1	2	3	4	5	6	7	8	9	10	11	12	1	2	3	IN	OUT	JOB #

Courtesy of Pizza Hut, Inc.

Exhibit 12.10 Personal Pan Pizza Labor Scheduling Grid

PERSONAL PAN PIZZA
LABOR SCHEDULING GRID
6/28/84

COLUMN NUMBER	1	2.	3	4	5	6	7	8	9	10	11	12	13	14	15	16
PROJECTED	0	41	60	85	116	152	175	197	238	289	332	376	437	503	595	634
HOURLY	TO	TO	TO	TO	TO	TO	TO	TO	TO	TO	TO	TO	TO	TO	TO	TO
NET SALES	40	59	84	115	151	174	196	237	288	331	375	436	502	594	633	673
PRODUCTION PERSON	0	1	1	1	1	1	1	1	2	2	2	2	2	2	3	3
SERVICE PERSON	1	1	2	2	2	2	3	3	3	4	4	4	4	4	4	5
REGISTER/TELEPHONE	0	0	0	0	1	1	1	1	1	1	2	2	2	3	3	3
BUS/DISHWASHER	0	0	0	0	0	0	0	1	1	1	1	1	2	2	2	2
BEVERAGE PERSON	0	0	0	0	0	0	0	0	0	0	0	1	1	1	1	1
PRODUCTION LEADER	1	1	1	1	1	1	1	1	1	1	1	1	1	1	1	1
HOST/HOSTESS	0	0	0	1	1	1	1	1	1	1	1	1	1	1	1	1
FLOOR MANAGER	0	0	0	0	0	1	1	1	1	1	1	1	1	1	1	1
TOTAL	2	3	4	5	6	7	8	9	10	11	12	13	14	15	16	17

OPENING ALLOWANCE

\# OF 6" PIZZAS PREPPED × .0225 HRS. = LUNCH PREP HOURS

Courtesy of Pizza Hut, Inc.

achieved, in part, by forecasting and even reforecasting throughout the management organization. At the hotel level, forecasting is utilized in the preparation of the annual budget, the monthly reforecast, and the 10-day forecast. The annual budget is self-explanatory; however, the reforecast is management's forecast every month for the following twelve months. Included in the reforecast are occupancy percentages and revenue/expense figures down through gross operating profit. The 10-day forecast is oriented to forecasting room, and food and beverage sales for the next 10 days to assist department heads in scheduling labor and comparing back the actual figures to forecasts.

This case will focus on the sales forecasts as part of the annual budget. The sales forecasts result from a cooperative effort of the Director of Sales or Marketing, General Manager and or Assistant General Manager, Senior Assistant Manager, Reservations Manager, Food and Beverage Manager and Controller which comprise the budget committee.

First, the room sales forecast includes forecast of group business for the next year. The Director of Sales considers (1) sales booked and (2) tentative group sales. A major factor used regarding tentative group sales is prior years' experience.

The definite business is reviewed and reduced by wash factors that have been developed from prior experience with the specific group or other similar groups.

The next is the tentative business. A double wash factor has to be applied as these are groups where contracts have gone out to clients but have not been returned. The sales department first weighs the probability of the group to sign. If it is felt they will sign, a factor is decided on along with the wash down factor and this combined factor is used to determine the number of room nights to project.

The third piece of the group business is the pick-up factor. Normally, three years is used unless past or present economic conditions distort one or more of these years. The booking "pace" (i.e., tentative and definite rooms and books in any month for each of future months being forecasted) is compared to actual results. From this, a historical tentative pick-up percentage is developed and applied to the month being forecasted.

The Reservations Manager estimates the expected non-group business. Consistent in this forecast is historical data and confirmed reservations. For Reservations Managers to have valid information, they compile anywhere from three to five years of experience showing, by month, how many reservations were booked for future months, and then compared to how many rooms actually materialized for those future months. This building process will establish a lead time rate, which then can be used in developing the pattern of historical information versus actual. This same timing process is followed with the groups so that as the budgeted year approaches, you can compare group room nights booked for the future year versus prior years' results which provides a trend as to whether the hotel is on target or not. In addition to the overall patterns by month, the Reservation Manager would have all this information by day to be able to pinpoint when the hotel will be full (e.g., Monday, Tuesday, and Wednesday, or Tuesday, Wednesday, and Thursday, etc.) so that the hotel can begin developing special promotions to fill in the valley periods.

Also considered by the Reservations Manager in forecasting non-group room sales are week-end packages, such as "Summer Family" and any special community events scheduled on particular week-ends.

The occupancy percentage and average rates are developed between the Director of Sales and the Reservations Manager. This is done by scheduling all groups that are definite and tentatives, laying in the pick-up groups required and then using historical information for the average number of individual travelers for each day. This base gives the hotel the estimated daily occupancy and average transient rate.

This forecast is compared to the occupancy percentages and average rates which have been established by the General Manager and approved by the Vice President-Operations. Occupancy and average rates are developed from prior years, current economic conditions, and competition. If the numbers prepared by the Director of Sales and the Reservation Manager differ, then a review is made of the forecast and appropriate adjustments are made.

After the initial rooms forecast is developed, it is reviewed by the budget committee. Once the room sales forecast is deemed acceptable, the food and beverage sales are forecast.

The food and beverage forecast is prepared by the Food and Beverage Manager, and cost analyst based on the room sales forecast and historical information, including covers by occupancy percentage and reviewing group functions which reduce outlet use. Also, they put in the special holiday meals (e.g., Thanksgiving buffet).

The food and beverage forecast consists of banquet sales, and food and beverage outlet sales. The banquet sales estimates are based on confirmed bookings and business that might be picked-up.

The definite Banquet business is taken from the catering book. This includes both definite group business and booked local business. Pick-up in Food and Beverage Banquet Sales is related to forecasted group room pick-up formulated by the Rooms Department. Average number of guests per room pick-up is multiplied by the average Food and Beverage Banquet check projected. Banquet Sales not associated with Room Sales should also be considered. These sales are projected based on special community events, holidays (i.e., Easter, Mother's Day, Thanksgiving), plus known pick-up from historical records for weddings, birthday parties, and community events.

The Food and Beverage Outlet Managers would look at historical information as to covers by day, covers by occupied rooms, taking into consideration banquet activities to reduce the guest base where banquet functions are scheduled. A good system of guest tracking would be able to determine a base of local clientele which would be used as the first step in building the number of covers that could be expected in a food and beverage outlet. This would be done by meal period as shown in the following example.

Outlet covers are derived by meal period: breakfast, lunch, and dinner. These covers are determined based upon the number of guests in the hotel. For example, if the hotel is 80% occupied (400 rooms), on a particular day and there are 1.2 persons per occupied room, there are 480 guests in the hotel. Of these 480 guests, we've forecasted 100 will be attending a banquet breakfast, leaving 380 guests available. From past historical data, we know 30% will have breakfast in Restaurant A. (NOTE: the 30% is weighted for outside business—non-hotel guests.) Our projected number of food covers for Restaurant A, breakfast meal period is 114 (380 x 30%). The average check is determined from prior year trends, i.e., last year was $9.50 and this year prices are increased 8% to $10.26. Note that the previous night occupancies are used for calculating breakfast covers.

After the room sales, and food and beverage sales are forecast, other hotel revenues such as telephone, gift shop, are estimated as well as the expenses of hotel operations. The other operating department revenues can be developed from the number of rooms occupied.

The "Hotel Room Forecast" (Exhibit 12.11) and "Rooms Forecast Reconciliation and Casualty Report" (Exhibit 12.12) are used as worksheets in the forecasting process. Via completing data required on each of these documents, each hotel compiles a 12 month day-by-day forecast as a guideline in order to maximize room revenue and occupancy.

Exhibit 12.11 Hotel Room Forecast

HOTEL ROOM FORECAST   Form #H1065 03

HOTEL NAME _____   MONTH OF _____   19____

DAY	S	S	M	T	W	T	F	S	S	M	T	W	T	F	S	S	M	T	W	T	F	S	S	M	T	W	T	F	S	S	M	T	W	T	F	TOTAL ROOM NIGHTS
LAST YEAR																																				
Group																																				
Contract																																				
Transient																																				
TOTAL																																				
THIS YEAR																																				
Group Allocation																																				
Actual Definite																																				
Actual Tentative																																				
Group Actual																																				
± Allocation																																				
TOTAL GROUP FORECAST																																				
Forcasted Transient																																				
Forcasted Contract																																				
TOTAL FORECAST																																				
FORECASTED OCC. %																																				
Actual Group																																				
Actual Contract																																				
Actual Transient																																				
ACTUAL TOTAL																																				
ACTUAL OCC. %																																				

Courtesy of Stouffer Hotels

Computerization

Many of the forecasting methods discussed in this chapter would take a great deal of time to manually calculate. However, with the help of a computer and forecasting programs, they can be generated almost immediately. Even general software packages such as electronic spreadsheets can calculate averages and perform trend extrapolation.

Exhibit 12.13 shows how management at the Jefferson Motel forecasts future room sales using moving averages. In order to do this, management first collects historical information—the number of rooms sold and the average rate for the last three weeks' business—and this information is entered into the computer. At this point, the computer generates a forecast for the fourth week's sales by calculating the average of the same day of the week over the previous three weeks. In this case, it was estimated that 93 rooms would be sold on Monday which is the average of 90, 95, and 93 (rounded to the nearest whole number). This information could be used for labor scheduling, or to calculate the forecast of revenues. Average rate is calculated in the same fashion, and the forecast of sales is the product of forecast room rate and rooms sold.

This worksheet can then be used to compare actual to forecast. For example, although 93 rooms were forecast to be sold on Monday, 95 rooms were actually sold, and management entered the actual results into the computer. When this number was input, the computer generated the variance figure between forecast and actual, and the forecast for

Exhibit 12.12   Rooms Forecast Reconciliation and Casualty Report

"Rooms Forecast Reconciliation and Casualty Report"

Hotel: *Solon Hotel (400)*   Forecast: _____
Month: *February 1985*   Actual: *XX*

CRO Status
C = Closed Out
P = Partial Available
A = All available
S = Sell Thru

Day	Date	Opening # Rooms	6 PM Arr.	GTD Arr.	Total Arr.	Due Outs	(6 PM Group Arr.)	(GTD Group Arr.)	R1 # Rooms Tonight	# CXL	% CXL	# 6 PM No-Shows	% 6 PM No-Shows	# GTD No-Shows	% GTD No-Shows	Stay Overs	Unexpected Departures	# Rooms Proj. Tonight	R2 # Rooms to Sell	E.S.P. R1 + R2	CRO Status	# Walk-ins
Sa	2/2	144	15	18	34	96	—	6	81	4	11.8	3	20.0	5	27.8	6	5	70	330	411	A	3
Su	3	73	297	106	133	70	—	51	136	4	3.0	6	22.2	3	2.8	1	4	120	280	416	A	34
Mo	4	154	14	136	150	35	—	39	269	16	10.7	—	—	4	2.9	2	2	249	151	420	A	24
Tu	5	273	19	161	180	81	—	36	372	21	11.7	2	10.5	5	3.1	6	6	344	56	428	A	38
We	6	382	12	175	187	162	—	70	407	24	13.3	5	83.3	3	1.7	7	10	372	28	435	P	6
Th	7	378	17	48	65	126	—	13	317	9	13.9	7	41.2	4	8.3	2	10	289	111	428	A	12
Fr	8	301	32	58	90	203	—	19	188	8	8.9	5	15.6	5	8.6	3	32	141	259	447	A	7
Sa	9	148	42	48	90	108	—	13	130	10	11.1	4	9.5	7	14.6	8	5	112	288	418	A	0
Su	10	112	15	99	114	104	—	53	122	4	3.5	4	26.7	2	2.0	1	2	111	289	411	A	34
Mo	11	145	26	164	190	40	—	65	295	2	1.1	2	7.7	—	—	—	6	285	115	410	A	0
Tu	12	285	12	158	170	106	—	54	349	20	11.8	2	16.7	3	1.9	2	13	313	87	436	A	28
We	13	341	11	167	178	141	—	67	378	20	11.2	4	36.4	3	1.8	4	10	345	55	433	A	14
Th	14	359	10	69	79	177	—	6	261	9	11.4	3	30.0	6	8.7	2	22	223	177	438	A	30
Fr	15	253	47	66	113	246	—	25	120	12	10.6	9	19.1	14	21.2	1	6	80	320	440	A	10
Sa	16	90	57	56	113	46	—	39	157	7	6.2	15	26.3	3	5.4	7	4	135	265	422	A	12
Su	17	147	19	64	83	101	—	50	129	5	6.0	15	23.4	2	3.1	3	11	99	301	430	A	33
Mo	18/H	132	7	135	142	92	—	76	182	6	4.2	6	85.7	2	2.2	1	4	165	235	417	A	40
Tu	19	205	9	107	116	45	—	8	276	14	12.1	4	44.4	12	11.2	2	5	243	157	433	A	30
We	20	273	12	311	323	201	—	228	385	15	4.7	2	16.7	6	1.9	3	15	362	38	423	P	20
Th	21	382	9	36	95	86	—	40	391	9	9.5	2	22.2	4	4.7	7	15	368	32	423	P	11
Fr	22	379	11	22	33	339	—	9	73	7	21.2	6	54.6	4	18.2	—	2	54	346	419	A	16
Sa	23	121	12	41	53	90	—	35	84	—	—	7	58.3	2	4.9	5	3	77	323	407	A	12
Su	24	89	17	85	102	35	—	38	156	1	1.0	6	35.3	2	2.4	—	2	145	255	411	A	3
Mo	25	148	26	122	148	24	—	14	272	21	14.2	4	15.4	5	4.1	1	3	240	160	432	A	28
Tu	26	268	19	171	190	75	—	12	383	22	11.6	2	10.5	9	5.3	4	13	341	59	442	A	41
We	27	382	19	189	208	189	—	69	401	20	9.6	4	21.1	6	3.2	15	36	350	50	451	A	36
Th	28	386	18	103	121	211	—	15	296	19	15.7	5	27.8	7	6.8	5	20	250	150	446	A	31
Fr	3/1	281	15	71	86	236	—	53	131	6	7.0	3	20.0	1	1.4	1	4	118	282	413	A	19

Courtesy of Stouffer Hotels

the fifth week's rooms sold (the average of the second, third and fourth week's rooms sold). In this manner, management can enter each week's actual figures to calculate the next week's forecast. As a side effect, this also provides management with a record of performance which can be used in future periods as needed.

As an extension of this worksheet, management also has the computer generate a graph of the variance between actual and forecast room sales. (See Exhibit 12.14) This very quickly highlights the week's results; although the weekday sales were close to forecast, the weekend sales were substantially below forecast. This graph is used because it

Exhibit 12.13   Moving Average Forecast Worksheet — Jefferson Motel

Moving Average Forecast Worksheet
Jefferson Motel

ROOMS SOLD DAY	Historical Week 1	Week 2	Week 3	X	Forecast Week 4	Actual Week 4	Variance	X	Forecast Week 5	Actual Week 5	Variance
Monday	90	95	93	X	93	95	2	X	94		
Tuesday	92	90	92	X	91	92	1	X	91		
Wednesday	99	94	95	X	96	94	−1	X	95		
Thursday	89	85	99	X	91	94	3	X	92		
Friday	51	40	44	X	45	40	−5	X	43		
Saturday	33	30	32	X	32	30	−2	X	31		
Sunday	45	50	51	X	49	52	3	X	50		

AVERAGE RATE DAY	Historical Week 1	Week 2	Week 3	X	Forecast Week 4	Actual Week 4	Variance	X	Forecast Week 5		
Monday	$62.50	$61.50	$63.00	X	$62.33	$61.52	($0.81)	X	$62.28		
Tuesday	62.50	65.00	64.90	X	64.13	62.89	−1.24	X	64.68		
Wednesday	65.00	65.00	65.50	X	65.17	65.70	0.53	X	65.22		
Thursday	62.50	61.00	62.50	X	62.00	62.50	0.50	X	61.83		
Friday	50.00	47.00	43.00	X	46.67	44.44	−2.23	X	45.56		
Saturday	47.80	49.00	40.00	X	45.60	41.25	−4.35	X	44.87		
Sunday	$60.00	$59.80	$62.50	X	$60.77	$65.23	$4.46	X	$61.02		

SALES INFORMATION

DAY	Forecast Week 4	Actual Week 4	Variance	X	Forecast Week 5	Actual Week 5	Variance
Monday	$5.776.22	$5,844.40	$68.18	X	$5,826.43		
Tuesday	5.857.51	5.785.88	−71.63	X	5,892.86		
Wednesday	6,256.00	6.175.80	−80.20	X	6,196.11		
Thursday	5,642.00	5,875.00	233.00	X	5,668.06		
Friday	2,100.00	1.777.60	−322.40	X	1,958.89		
Saturday	1,444.00	1,237.50	−206.50	X	1,400.84		
Sunday	$2,957.31	$3,391.96	$434.65	X	$3,044.33		

quickly alerts management to potential problems, and they can take timely actions to prevent any major events from happening unexpectedly.

Management could also use the computer to generate more sophisticated forecasts. There are programs available which perform linear regression, exponential smoothing, multiple regression, and many other methods mentioned in this chapter.[8]

Exhibit 12.14   Forecast vs. Actual — Jefferson Motel

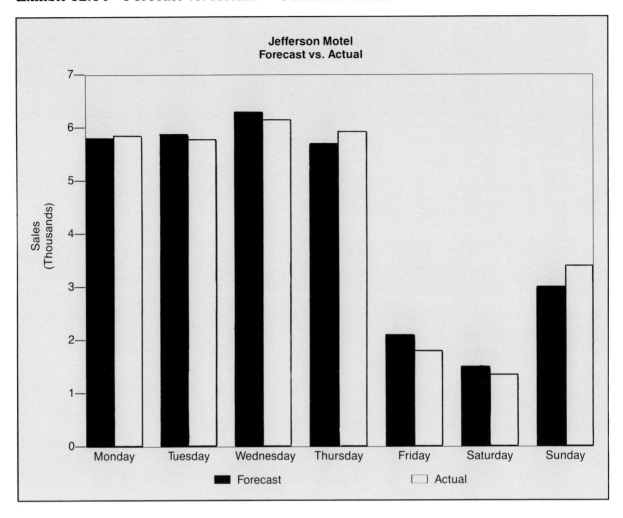

Summary

Forecasting is simply the process of estimating the levels of some future activity such as sales. After an initial sales forecast has been made, the hospitality operation must plan to ensure the desired outcome is achieved.

Forecasts may be implicit or explicit. Implicit forecasts are implied by the expectations reflected by managers' actions when no explicit forecast has been made. In this chapter, we were concerned with deliberate attempts to estimate levels of future activities (explicit forecasts) to provide managers with rational foundations for planning.

Since forecasting deals with the future, it inevitably involves uncertainty. In addition, since forecasts are made on the basis of historical data, they are predicated on the risky assumption that the past will be indicative of the future.

Patterns in existing data include trend, seasonal, and cyclical. A trend is simply the long-run projection of an activity being evaluated.

Seasonal patterns exist when a series of data fluctuates according to a seasonal pattern, such as seasons of the year, while cyclical patterns represent movements along a trend line.

Forecasting methods covered in the chapter included both quantitative and qualitative approaches, with the emphasis on the former. Quantitative methods discussed included naive methods, moving averages, exponential smoothing, and regression analysis. Limitations of quantitative methods, such as scarce data and the inability to consider unforeseeable or unexpected occurrences, sometimes render quantitative methods less useful. When these limitations are significant, qualitative methods may be used. The qualitative methods covered briefly in this chapter included marketing research, jury of executive opinion, salesforce estimates, and the Delphi technique.

Finally, forecasting techniques used by unit-level management at three hospitality operations were presented. The three operations—Canteen Corp., Pizza Hut, Inc., and Stouffers Hotels—were intentionally selected from three different segments of the hospitality industry: business and industry food service, commercial food service, and hotels, respectively. Although they were chosen to illustrate different applications of forecasting methods, they are not necessarily representative of their respective segments.

Notes

1. *Marriott Corporation Annual Report 1984*, p. 2.
2. "How to Forecast Sales," *Lodging*, January 1981, p. 41-46.
3. The reader interested in pursuing forecasting approaches shown in Exhibit 16.3, not discussed in this chapter, should consider *Forecasting Methods and Applications* by Steven C. Wheelwright and Spyros Makridakis, published by John Wiley & Sons, 1978.
4. Steven C. Wheelwright and Spyros Makridakis, *Forecasting Methods for Management*, 3rd Ed. (New York: John Wiley & Sons, 1980).
5. $$a = \frac{n\Sigma xy - \Sigma x \Sigma y}{n\Sigma x^2 - (\Sigma x)^2}$$

   $$b = \frac{(\Sigma y)(\Sigma x)^2 - (\Sigma x)(\Sigma xy)}{n(\Sigma x)^2 - (\Sigma x)^2}$$
6. The interested reader should consider *Forecasting Methods for Management*, 3rd Ed., by Wheelwright and Makridakis.
7. At the writing of this book, Pizza Hut is exploring the use of computer-assisted forecasting models.
8. For more information on the use of spreadsheet programs for forecasting, see *Financial Management with Lotus 1-2-3*, by Hugh S. McLaughlin and J. Russell Boulding published by Prentice-Hall, 1986.

Discussion Questions

1. What is the difference between implicit and explicit forecasts?

2. How do forecasting and planning differ?

3. What are the purposes and limitations of forecasting?

4. How do cyclical and seasonal patterns of data differ?

5. What are the differences between quantitative and qualitative forecasting methods?

6. How do causal forecasting methods differ from time series methods?

7. How is a moving average calculated?

8. When are exponential smoothing techniques most useful?

9. How can regression analysis be used to forecast food revenue based on occupancy percentage?

Problem 12.1

Mr. Jim Wheat, manager of the Plains Motel, has decided to forecast monthly room sales for the next three years. The monthly sales for 19X1 were as follows:

January	$194,321	July	$185,197
February	187,296	August	180,200
March	198,431	September	206,711
April	197,911	October	215,840
May	215,640	November	201,612
June	210,411	December	165,411

Jim believes that sales will increase 5% in 19X2, another 5% in 19X3, and still another 6% in 19X4.

Required:

Based on the above information, prepare the three-year sales forecast by month for the Plains Motel.

Problem 12.2

Servco operates the hot lunch program at Acres Elementary School. The weekly sales forecast necessary for ordering food provisions and scheduling labor is based on a three weeks moving average, i.e., Monday's forecast is based on the average sales of the prior three Mondays. The forecast is modified based on a number of factors, including weather. The weather modification is that sales are expected to increase moderately as the school year progresses into cooler (even cold) weather and decrease moderately with warmer weather in the spring. In addition, rainy days result in significant increases in sales.

The sales for weeks 4 through 6 were as follows:

	Week 4	Week 5	Week 6
Monday	$450	$460	$475
Tuesday	420	435	440
Wednesday	440	438	520
Thursday	430	445	450
Friday	410	420	435

Required:

Based on the above results, answer the following questions:

1. What type of weather trend do the above figures suggest? Why?
2. Which day did it appear to rain?

Problem 12.3

This problem is a continuation of Problem 12.2. Karin Smith, manager of Servco, desires assistance in preparing the sales forecast for Week 7. To prepare the weekly sales forecast, the days' sales of the prior three weeks are averaged and modified by ±$20 for expected weather changes. In addition, if a rainy day is expected, an additional $70 of sales is expected.

Required:

Prepare the weekly sales forecast by day for Week 7. Assume the winter season is approaching, that is, it is expected that Week 7 will be cooler than Week 6. Further, use $450 for sales for Wednesday of Week 6 in place of actual sales of $520. Finally, assume Monday of Week 7 is expected to be a rainy day.

Problem 12.4

The Wilderness Inn uses the exponential smoothing method presented in this chapter to forecast total weekly sales. Darlene Jones, the manager, has supplied you with past forecasts and actual sales as follows:

	Forecast	Actual Sales
Week 1	$10,400	$12,400
Week 2	10,800	11,000
Week 3	10,840	10,940
Week 4	10,860	11,360
Week 5	10,960	10,560
Week 6	10,880	11,580

Required:

1. Based on the above information, what is the smoothing constant?

2. Using the smoothing constant (determined in 1), forecast sales for Week 7.

3. Assuming the smoothing constant is .5, what would be the forecasted sales for Week 7?

Problem 12.5

The Evergreen Hotel, a 200-room lodging facility, uses regression analysis to forecast dining room meals. Larry Spruce, the manager, has indicated the regression equations used are as follows:

$$y = 50 + .42x \text{ (breakfast)}$$
$$y = 200 + .21x \text{ (lunch)}$$
$$y = 450 + .35x \text{ (dinner)}$$

where y equals forecasted meals and
x equals the number of hotel guests

Further, the average check in the hotel's dining room is expected to be as follows:

breakfast	-	$3.25
lunch	-	$6.50
dinner	-	$12.95

Required:

Forecast sales by meal period when the occupancy percentage is expected to be 85% (all rooms are available for sale) and the average occupancy per room is expected to be 1.58.

Appendix

The ability to forecast, with a reasonable degree of accuracy, the number of rooms that may be occupied and the number of guests to be served in the dining rooms of a hotel for a future period is an important aspect of management. Those two revenue sources make up at least 75 percent to 80 percent of the total, and directly influence a very significant portion of the variable cost of operations. In this article, I will illustrate two methods used in making forecasts: analysis of a time series and regression analysis. Each provides a systematic and disciplined approach to forecasting.

These methods are based upon the generally accepted concept that what has occurred previously under similar circumstances is the best basis for a forecast, provided it is modified by current events and good judgment. The techniques will be used to analyze information through December, 1980 and to forecast results for January-June, 1981. Since the actual results for that period are known, the accuracy of the forecast can be tested.

FORECASTING
Rooms Occupancy and Food Covers by Analyzing Trends

by John D. Lesure, CPA, Laventhol & Horwath

Editor's Note: *This article is sponsored by AH&MA's Financial Management Committee. It is based on an actual experience in forecasting occupancy and covers at a 352-room property operated by a committee member's company. Part I, on forecasting rooms occupancy, appears in this issue; part II, on forecasting covers, in the January 1982 issue.*

Part One

A time series is a set of numbers representing the measurement of activity during time intervals, normally equal in duration. The number of rooms occupied monthly since 1976 in the Suburban Motor Inn shown in Illustration 1 is a time series. This table contains valuable information for the analyst. Since the property contains 352 rooms, it is possible to compute monthly percentages of occupancy from the data and compare those common-sized figures. This can be done by means of a chart (Illustration 2), which shows that there are very wide month-to-month variations. Observation of the numbers and a few calculations also reveals other information:

1. The arithmetic mean (average) of the number of rooms occupied monthly from January, 1976 to May, 1981 was 8,058 or 75.2 percent of rooms available.
2. During the 5-year period, March and June were consistently the best months, with April also showing above average occupancy.

3. The weakest month has been December and in November there has consistently been a sharp drop from the previous month.
4. There are irregular variations. For example, in 1978, rooms occupied in February exceeded the total for January; also, on October 1978, the number fell below the mean for that year although it was well above in 1979 and 1980.
5. The monthly mean of rooms occupied rose in 1977 and 1978 and then dropped in 1979 and 1980.

Thus, the time series shows the following variations for analysis:

1. A trend or tendency to go either up or down over a long range period.
2. Month-to-month differences, some quite sharp, caused by fluctuations in travel patterns and demand, generally called seasonal variations.
3. Irregular surges that may be caused by a variety of outside influences including but not limited to, the economy, gasoline shortages, strikes and bad weather.

By analyzing these factors, we create a basis for forecasting.

Time Series Rooms Occupied Monthly
1976–1981

	1976	1977	1978	1979	1980	TOTAL 1976–1980	1981
January	8,075	8,402	8,555	8,249	7,889	41,170	7,344
February	8,003	8,240	8,870	8,732	8,368	42,213	8,220
March	8,555	9,068	9,166	9,428	9,024	45,241	9,101
April	8,226	8,469	9,039	8,987	8,490	43,211	8,300
May	8,097	8,424	8,697	8,468	8,086	41,772	8,479
June	8,543	8,965	9,082	8,670	8,406	43,666	8,681
July	8,249	8,664	8,642	7,933	7,824	41,312	
August	8,097	8,500	8,664	8,359	8,031	41,651	
September	7,392	7,688	7,931	7,793	7,476	37,780	
October	7,889	8,282	8,271	8,424	8,108	40,974	
November	6,336	6,970	7,054	6,801	6,716	33,877	
December	5,849	6,023	6,034	5,663	5,412	28,981	
TOTAL	93,311	97,695	100,005	97,507	93,830	482,348	50,125
MEAN	7,776	8,141	8,334	8,126	7,819	8,039	8,354

Analysis of the Time Series: Trend

If you hold a ruler on the high or low points of the monthly occupancy ("actual" line) in the chart (Illustration 2) you can see the downward trend. However, the very wide monthly fluctuations tend to obscure the overall tendency, so we prepare a moving average in order to clarify the direction. The "moving average" line on the chart is the moving average percentage of occupancy for the period January, 1979 to May, 1981, and it shows clearly the downward trend in occupancy. Because each point is the arithmetic mean of the occupancies for the previous 12 months, it is called a 12-month moving average. The period can be any suitable length; a 12-month period was selected as being the one that most closely fits the cycles of business in the lodging industry. The 12 month moving average of a series of numbers XI, X2, X3 is obtained by the formula:

$$\frac{X_1 + X_2 \ldots X_{12,}}{12}$$

$$\frac{X_2 + X_3 \ldots X_{13,}}{12}$$

$$\frac{X_3 + X_4 \ldots X_{14,} \ldots}{12}$$

This simply means that the figures for the first 12 months are added and divided by 12 to obtain the starting point. Then as each new monthly figure is added, the occupancy for the same month of the previous year is dropped, and the total divided by 12 to obtain the next mean. The process is continued through the entire series. Illustration 3 shows the 12-month moving average (mean) number of rooms occupied for the period January, 1977 through May, 1981. Since the first 12 months are used to obtain the starting point the data are lost.

It is clear from the numbers that the trend has been generally downward since January, 1979.

Analysis of the Time Series: Seasonal Index

The seasonal fluctuations can best be illustrated by comparisons with the monthly number of rooms occupied for each year. For example, in 1976 the mean was 7,776 and the number of rooms occupied monthly ranged from only 5,849 in December (25 percent less) to 8,555 in March (10 percent more). Only in October was the number really close to the mean, 1.5 percent more.

A seasonal index expresses the relationship between the number of rooms occupied in one

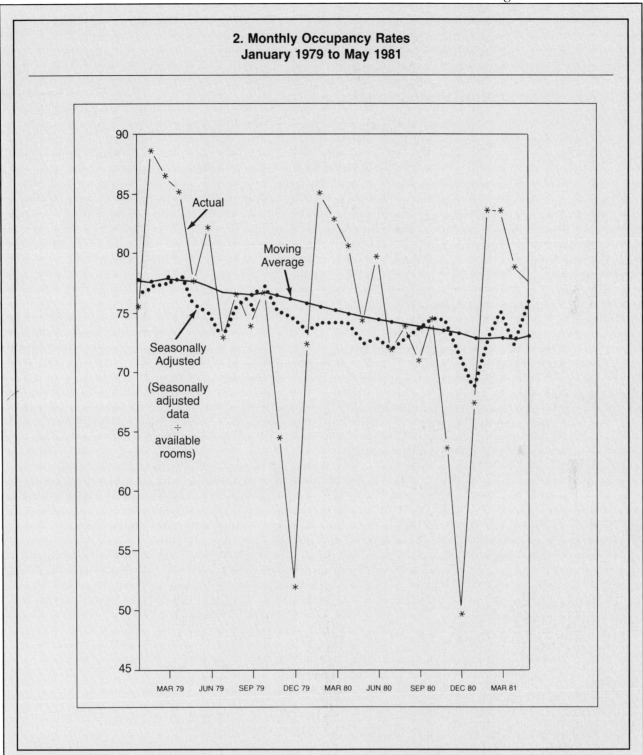

**2. Monthly Occupancy Rates
January 1979 to May 1981**

month and the monthly mean for the year. It may be computed in several ways, and Illustration 4 shows one way which consists of the following steps:

1. The number of occupied rooms each month is divided by the arithmetic mean for the year and the ratio is entered in the table. (For example, 8,075 rooms

		3. Twelve-Month Moving Average				
		Rooms Occupied				
	1976	1977	1978	1979	1980	1981
January		7,803	8,154	8,308	8,096	7,774
February		7,823	8,207	8,297	8,065	7,761
March		7,866	8,215	8,319	8,032	7,768
April		7,886	8,262	8,314	7,990	7,752
May		7,913	8,285	8,295	7,958	7,785
June		7,948	8,295	8,261	7,936	7,808
July		7,983	8,293	8,202	7,927	
August		8,017	8,307	8,176	7,900	
September		8,041	8,327	8,165	7,874	
October		8,074	8,326	8,178	7,847	
November		8,127	8,333	8,157	7,840	
December	7,776	8,141	8,334	8,126	7,819	

occupied in January, 1976 divided by the mean of 7,776 equals 1.038.)

2. The arithmetic mean for each month is obtained by adding the ratios for that month for each year and dividing by 5. (i.e. the 5 years considered 1976-1980)

3. Minor adjustments are made to the means for each month so that they total 12.000.

The result of these calculations is a list of monthly ratios that enable us to estimate the number of occupied rooms for a month, if we can forecast the monthly mean for the year. These ratios also enable us to perform another calculation that reveals the cyclical or irregular increases and decreases in monthly occupancy brought about by outside influences. Using the ratios we can "deseasonalize" the original time series leaving numbers that are "seasonally adjusted." In other words, the monthly number of rooms that we would expect to be occupied if there was no seasonal influence. Illustration 5 shows the adjusted data. The number of occupied rooms for each month from January, 1976 to May, 1981 has been divided by the appropriate monthly mean.

(Example: January 1976 = $\frac{8,075}{1.024}$ = 7,886)

Analysis of Time Series: Irregular Index

It is apparent from the table (Illustration 5)

that there is another factor that influences the activity besides the trend and the seasonal changes in demand. This can also be seen in the chart (Illustration 2) by the way the "seasonally adjusted" line moves above and below the trend line, although it follows the generally downward tendency of that line. By removing the seasonal fluctuations from the occupancy ("actual" line), we have smoothed out the sharp fluctuations; if we also remove the trend ("moving average" line) we will have only the irregular increases and decreases left. That is the next step in our analysis and it provides the numbers in the table, Illustration 6.

In order to determine whether or not there are discernable cycles in the irregular increases and decreases, the variances above and below zero are plotted. The result is shown in Illustration 7. By studying the chart and ignoring the minor month-to-month fluctuations, we can discern a cycle that reached a peak in July, 1977, dropped to a low in July, 1979 and has begun to return to reach a point above zero, possibly by July, 1981. It is also apparent that predicting the month-to-month fluctuations would be virtually impossible. However, how important is this index in making a forecast?

In Illustration 6 the arithmetic mean of the monthly irregularities has been computed and in only one case does the ratio show a variation of as much as 1 percent—for December the mean is .989 or −1.1 percent. Further analysis of the chart (Illustration 7) shows that in 3 instances the variance exceeded 5 percent (which could be

4. Seasonal Index

| | Ratio of Monthly Occupied Rooms To Annual Means | | | | | Monthly |
	1976	1977	1978	1979	1980	Mean
January	1.038	1.032	1.027	1.015	1.009	1.024
February	1.029	1.012	1.064	1.075	1.070	1.050
March	1.100	1.114	1.100	1.160	1.154	1.126
April	1.058	1.040	1.085	1.106	1.086	1.075
May	1.041	1.035	1.044	1.042	1.034	1.039
June	1.099	1.101	1.090	1.067	1.075	1.086
July	1.061	1.064	1.037	976	1.001	1.028
August	1.041	1.044	1.040	1.029	1.027	1.036
September	.951	.944	.952	.959	.956	.952
October	1.015	1.017	.992	1.037	1.037	1.020
November	.815	.856	.846	.837	.859	.843
December	.752	.740	.724	.697	.692	.721

5. Seasonally Adjusted Data
Monthly Occupied Rooms ÷ Seasonal Index (Monthly Mean)

	1976	1977	1978	1979	1980	1981
January	7,886	8,205	8,354	8,056	7,704	7,172
February	7,622	7,848	8,448	8,316	7,970	7,829
March	7,598	8,053	8,140	8,373	8,014	8,083
April	7,652	7,878	8,408	8,360	7,898	7,721
May	7,793	8,108	8,371	8,150	7,782	8,161
June	7,866	8,255	8,363	7,983	7,740	7,994
July	8,024	8,428	8,407	7,717	7,611	
August	7,816	8,205	8,363	8,069	7,752	
September	7,765	8,076	8,331	8,186	7,853	
October	7,734	8,120	8,109	8,259	7,949	
November	7,516	8,268	8,368	8,068	7,976	
December	8,112	8,354	8,369	7,854	7,506	

significant), but that a majority of the points are within 2.5 percent (33 out of 48). In short, the following conclusions can be drawn:

1. In addition to a long-range trend and regular seasonal fluctuations, there is an irregular or cyclical variation.
2. Except that the current tendency of the index shown in Illustration 7 is upward, there is no readily apparent basis for estimating it, other than analysis of a much more extended time series.

4. Although allowance for the irregular variation can be made by using the mean of the monthly ratios for the past 4 years, we can expect fluctuations of as much as 5 percent. However, the chances are better than 2 out of 3 that the variation will not exceed + or 2.5 percent.

We are now in a position to make forecasts of the number of rooms occupied for January through June, 1981 based on the following formula:

6. Computation of Irregular or Cyclical Index

Ratio of Seasonally Adjusted Data to Trend

	1976	1977	1978	1979	1980	Mean
January		1.052	1.025	.970	.952	.999
February		1.003	1.029	1.002	.988	1.006
March		1.024	.991	1.006	.998	1.005
April		.999	1.018	1.006	.988	1.003
May		1.025	1.010	.983	.978	.999
June		1.039	1.008	.966	.975	.997
July		1.056	1.014	.941	.960	.993
August		1.023	1.007	.987	.981	1.000
September		1.004	1.000	1.003	.997	1.001
October		1.006	.974	1.010	1.013	1.001
November		1.017	1.004	.989	1.016	1.007
December	1.043	1.026	1.004	.967	.960	.989

7. Cyclical Variations after "Deseasonalized" Numbers are Divided by Trend

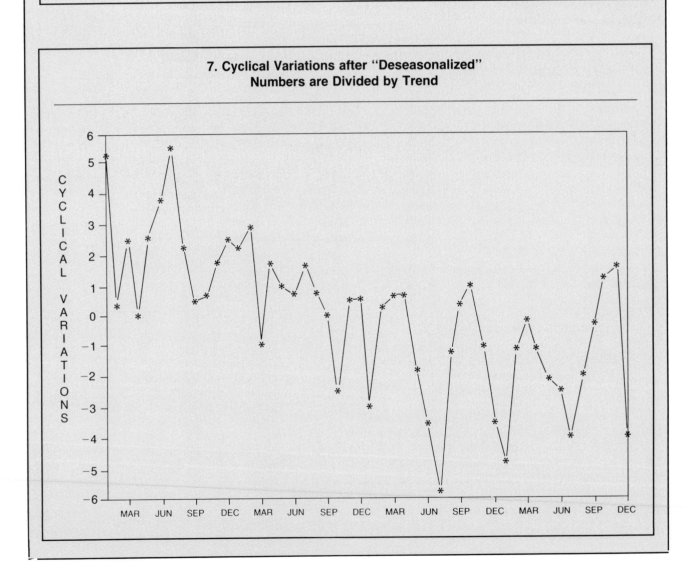

8. Forecast of Rooms Occupied

Month	Trend	×	Index	×	Seasonal Cyclical Index	=	Forecast	Actual	Percentage Variance
January 1981	7,819		1.024		.999		7,999	7,344	8.9 %
February	7,774		1.050		1.006		8,212	8,220	(.1)
March	7,761		1.126		1.005		8,783	9,101	(3.5)
April	7,768		1.075		1.003		8,376	8,300	.9
May	7,752		1.039		.999		8,046	8,479	(5.1)
June	7,785		1.086		.997		8,429	8,681	(2.9)
Total—6 Months							49,845	50,125	(.6)%

Estimate = T (Trend) x S (Seasonal index)
x C (Cyclical or Irregular index)

The trend figure is the most recent point in the 12-month moving average; for January, 1981 that would be December, 1980: 7,819 (Illustration 3). The seasonal index for January is 1.024 (Illustration 4), and the cyclical index is the arithmetic mean for January, .999 (Illustration 6). The appropriate numbers are attained from the tables for the other months and the forecast and comparison with the actual results are shown in Illustration 8. The month-to-month variances are compared with the actual cyclical variations in the following table, together with some explanations for the fluctuations:

Month	Variance in Forecast	Cyclical Variation	Possible Explanation
January, 1981	+8.9	−7.7	Severe storm
February	−.1	+.9	Trips delayed from January
March	−3.5	+4.1	Economic recovery?
April	+.9	−.4	Easter?
May	−5.1	+4.8	Group Business
June	×2.9	+2.4	Lower gasoline prices; supply plentiful

In each case, the variance in the forecast can be nearly completely explained by the cyclical variation and the importance of that index is apparent. Although the estimates are within acceptable limits of the actual results, a much more extensive analysis as a basis for establishing a reliable cyclical index might be justified.

Part Two

In the November issue, I illustrated the forecasting of rooms occupancy by the analysis of a time series (the previous five years) at a 352-room hotel. On the following pages, I illustrate food cover forecasting at the same hotel.

The method used in the food cover forecast is a less time-consuming technique. It is known as linear regression analysis, and relies not only on past experience but assumes a continuing relationship between two variables:

1. number of persons served in the dining rooms (excluding banquets) and
2. number of guests.

Illustration 1 shows the number of persons served in the dining rooms (excluding banquets) and the number of room guests at the 352-room hotel in our case study. Statistics used are for 1979 and 1980.

The Scatter Diagram

In order to determine if there is a relationship between the variables, we prepare a visual presentation called a scatter diagram (Illustration 2). The number of room guests is shown on the X or horizontal axis of the chart and the number of persons served is shown on the Y or vertical axis.

For each monthly relationship we have made a point on the chart. For example, in January 1979 we find the point on the X axis where the number of guests is 11,425 and the point on the Y axis where the number of persons served is 10,125. We then place a point on the chart where a line drawn horizontally from point Y (10,125) will intersect a line drawn vertically from point X (11,425). The same procedure is followed for each pair of variables until all 24 data points have been entered.

It is now apparent that as the number of room guests increases (i.e. moves to the right) the number of persons served also increases (moves upward). Since the points appear to run in a line, the relationship is called linear, and since the number of persons served increases as the number of guests increases, the relationship or correlation is positive. If one variable declined as the other increased, it would be a negative correlation.

The Least Square Line

In order for the chart to be useful, a line must be drawn that comes closest to each of the points in the diagram. That could be done visually by moving a straight edge around on the diagram until there are approximately as many points to the left and above the line as there are to the right and below. However, there is a formula that will enable us to determine where the line should be

1. Number of Room Guests and Number of Persons Served in Dining Rooms (Excluding Banquets)

	1979 Room Guests	1979 Persons Served In Dining Rooms	1980 Room Guests	1980 Persons Served In Dining Rooms
JANUARY	11,425	10,125	10,518	10,317
FEBRUARY	12,191	10,707	11,402	10,206
MARCH	13,294	11,545	12,368	10,721
APRIL	12,595	11,014	12,126	12,134
MAY	11,733	10,389	11,206	9,905
JUNE	12,093	10,632	12,396	10,668
JULY	10,925	9,745	11,182	9,459
AUGUST	11,600	10,258	11,461	9,113
SEPTEMBER	10,703	9,576	9,846	8,304
OCTOBER	11,703	10,336	10,361	8,825
NOVEMBER	9,130	8,380	9,156	8,811
DECEMBER	7,326	7,009	6,907	6,822

2. Number of Persons Served in Dining Rooms Versus Number of Room Guests

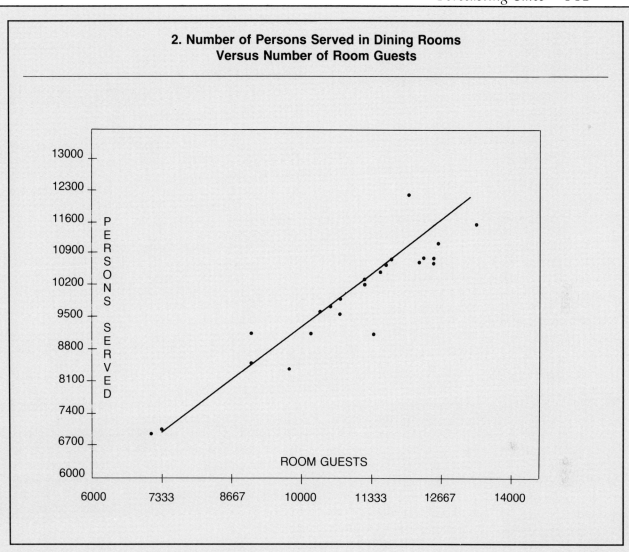

drawn. The formula is based on the concept that the line of "best fit" (i.e. the one coming closest to each point) is the one for which the sum of the squares of all of the distances from the points to the line (called deviations) is the lowest. The distances are squared because the square of a negative deviation (one below and to the right) is a positive number. That line is referred to as the least square line and is determined by the formula:

$$Y = A + BX$$

In our example,

Y = number of persons served in the dining room

A = number of persons served who are not registered in the hotel

B = change in number of persons served for each increase in number of room guests

X = number of room guests

Since we are using one variable (X) to determine another (Y), this is called regression analysis and most programmable calculators have a standard program for a linear regression. We therefore enter the 24 pairs of variables in a calculator which solves the problem as follows:

Y (persons served) = 1,438 + .76 times X (room guests)

This means that in 1979 and 1980, the number of persons served monthly in the dining rooms consisted of 1,438 non-registered guests plus .76 persons served for each room guest, or stated another way, 76 percent of the room guests had one meal. If we assume that the same relationship will continue in 1981, we can use that formula to estimate the number of persons served each month based upon a forecast of room guests.

The calculator and the linear regression program gives us the following information on the reliability of the relationship between the variables:

- The **coefficient of correlation**, which is the measure of the relationship between the variables is + .93. If all of the points on the scatter diagram fell on the line, the correlation coefficient would be +1 since the relationship is positive. Our "fit" of .93 is very close.
- The **coefficient of determination** is + .86. This is the square of .93 and it represents the extent to which changes in one variable (in this case number of room guests) explain changes in the other (number of persons served). In other words, 86 percent of the variations in the number of persons served in 1979 and 1980 can be explained by changes in the number of room guests during the period.

Since both coefficients are quite high on a scale of 0 to +1, we are confident that the relationship between the variables is a good one, and that the formula can be used in forecasting. We can prove this by testing the accuracy of the formula. We can substitute actual figures from our case study hotel for X (number of room guests in the formula), solve for Y (number of persons served), and see how close the number obtained comes to the actual figures.

The number of room guests at our case study hotel in February 1980 was 11,402. Assume we do not know the actual number of persons served in the dining rooms. What is Y?

$$Y = 1,438 + .76 \times 11,402$$
$$Y = 10,034$$

The actual number of persons served during this month was 10,206. Using the formula, we are able to obtain a forecast for the number of persons served—10,034—that is 99% of the number actual served, for a variation of −.1, proof that the least square line can be used as a basis for estimating.

Using the Formula

Using the least square line is somewhat tedious and only approximate. However, the formula can be used to estimate the number of persons served if we first estimate the number of room guests. We have previously estimated the number of rooms occupied, and we can convert that to the number of guests. In order to do so we need an index which is the ratio of the number of guests for each month divided by the number of rooms occupied for that month. This is also based on past performance and the result of the compilation is shown in Illustration 3. For each month, the total number of guests for the five years 1976-1980 has been divided by the total number of rooms occupied during the same period that was shown in Illustration I in Part I. (November issue)

We can now prepare a forecast for the months of January-June, 1981, based upon our estimates of the number of rooms occupied. The forecast of the number of rooms occupied is first multiplied by the appropriate ratio of guests to rooms and the number of guests is then substituted for X in the formula: Y = 1,438 + .76 times X in order to compute the number of persons served. The results are shown in Illustration 4 together with the actual number of persons served and the variances. Once again our estimate for the 6 months is quite accurate, although the monthly variances, while tolerable, range up to 8.5 percent.

Conclusions

The detailed analysis of the fluctuations in the demand for rooms and in the number of persons served in the dining rooms provides a basis for estimates of activity in future periods. The basic formulas are reasonably reliable but experience may dictate the use of additional factors. For example, more emphasis might be placed on current trends and market conditions. The results are only as reliable as the data on which they are based and the care with which the information is used. Reliable estimates help department heads plan the use of resources to meet customer demands. However, no formula can substitute for experienced judgment and forecasts should always be subject to the adjustments dictated by changing trends and other circumstances.

3. Number of Room Guests and Ratio of Guests to Rooms Occupied

	1976	1977	1978	1979	1980	Total	Ratio To Rooms Occupied
January	11,150	11,668	11,910	11,425	10,518	56,671	1.3765
February	11,035	11,411	12,410	12,191	11,402	58,449	1.3846
March	11,910	12,724	12,879	13,294	12,368	63,175	1.3964
April	11,389	11,774	12,678	12,595	12,126	60,562	1.4015
May	11,184	11,703	12,135	11,773	11,206	58,001	1.3885
June	11,891	12,560	12,746	12,093	12,396	61,686	1.4127
July	11,425	12,083	12,048	10,925	11,182	57,663	1.3958
August	11,184	11,823	12,083	11,600	11,461	58,151	1.3961
September	10,067	10,536	10,921	10,703	9,846	52,073	1.3603
October	10,855	11,478	11,460	11,703	10,361	55,857	1.3632
November	8,393	9,398	9,531	9,130	9,156	45,608	1.3463
December	7,621	7,897	7,915	7,326	6,907	37,666	1.2997

4. Forecast of Number of Persons Served Compared with Actual

	Rooms Occupied*	Ratio Of Guests	Number Of Guests	Number Of Persons Served** Forecast	Actual	Variance
January, 1981	7,999	1.3765	11,011	9,806	9,035	+8.5%
February	8,212	1.3846	11,371	10,080	10,090	− .1
March	8,783	1.3964	12,265	10,759	11,151	−3.5
April	8,376	1.4015	11,739	10,360	10,186	+1.7
May	8,046	1.3885	11,172	9,929	10,402	−4.6
June	8,429	1.4127	11,908	10,488	10,525	− .4
Total 6 Months				61,422	61,389	− .1%

*From Illustration 8, November issue.

**In main dining room and coffee shop. Does not include banquets.

13 Cash Management

Cash management refers to the management of a hospitality operation's cash balances (currency and demand deposits), cash flow (cash receipts and disbursements), and short-term investments in securities. Cash management is critical to both large and small hospitality operations. Failure to have sufficient cash can result in bankruptcy as the enterprise simply is unable to pay its bills when they become due. This chapter will address many questions regarding cash management such as:

1. What is the distinction between income and cash flows?
2. What is contained in a cash budget?
3. How are cash receipts forecasted?
4. How do short-term and long-term cash budgeting approaches differ?
5. What are the relevant factors to consider when investing working capital funds?
6. What are compensating balances?
7. How does a lockbox system speed cash flows?
8. Why is depreciation expense not relevant in cash flow considerations?
9. Why are investors interested in cash flow?
10. How are other (non-cash) current assets related to cash flow?

Our discussion of cash management will identify the uses and importance of cash in a hospitality operation. We will consider the distinction between income and cash flows and explain what is meant by negative cash flows. This chapter will focus on basic approaches to using cash budgets for planning purposes. We will also address the major areas of hospitality operations affecting the process of cash budgeting, such as management of working capital including accounts receivable, inventory, and current liabilities. Finally, we will address the special considerations of integrated cash management for multi-unit operations.

Cash and Its Importance

In hospitality establishments, cash consists of petty cash funds, cash on hand for operational purposes, and cash in the bank. Cash on hand includes both house banks and undeposited cash receipts from guests. Cash in the bank includes demand deposits. Some operations also include time deposits and certificates of deposit as cash. In our discussion, all of these elements will be considered as cash.

Petty cash funds are established for making minor cash purchases. These funds are normally maintained on an imprest basis, that is, they are replenished by the amount of disbursements since the previous replenishment.

House banks are maintained in order to facilitate cash transactions with guests. Each cash drawer must consist of a minimum amount. For food service operations using server banking, each server's bank must consist of a sufficient amount of cash to transact business with guests. Added together, the house banks in a hotel may total several thousand dollars. Since house banks do not generate earnings directly but only facilitate cash transactions, these cash balances should be minimized.

Ideally, the hospitality operation's cash balance in a demand deposit account with a bank should be zero. That is, amounts should be deposited daily to equal the amounts paid by the bank for the depositing establishment. However, cash received and cash disbursed is generally not uniform because the cash receipts for a day seldom equal the cash disbursements for the same day. Therefore, most operations maintain balances in their checking accounts to meet checks drawn on their accounts. The reason for keeping these cash balances is commonly referred to as a transaction motive.

The size of cash balances in checking accounts is also influenced by bankers. Some bankers demand that depositors maintain substantial amounts in their accounts to cover bank services and also to serve as compensating balances for bank loans. For example, an operation may receive a loan for $100,000 and be required to maintain a 10% compensating balance. This means $10,000 ($100,000 x 10%) must be maintained in the checking account. Since no interest is earned on the compensating balance, the effective cost of the loan is higher than its stated interest rate. The effective cost is determined as follows:

$$\text{Effective Interest Rate} = \frac{\text{Annual Interest on Loan}}{\text{Loan} - \text{Compensating Balance Requirement}}$$

For example, assume a hotel received a one-year loan of $100,000 at 10% with a compensating balance requirement of $10,000. The effective interest rate is 11.1%. Annual interest of $10,000 and the effective interest rate are determined as follows:

$$\text{Interest} = \text{Principal x Rate x Time}$$

$$\text{Interest} = 100,000 \text{ x } 10\% \text{ x } 1 \text{ year}$$

$$\text{Interest} = \$10,000$$

$$\text{Effective Interest Rate} = \frac{\$10,000}{100,000 - 10,000}$$

$$\text{Effective Interest Rate} = \frac{10,000}{90,000}$$

$$\text{Effective Interest Rate} = \underline{\underline{11.1\%}}$$

Exhibit 13.1   Sample Condensed Income Statement and Cash Flow Statements —
Rambles Restaurant

Condensed Income Statement and Cash Flow Statements
Rambles Restaurant
For the year ended December 31, 19X3

Income Statement		Cash Flow Statement	
Sales	$600,000	Cash Receipts:	
Cost of Food Sold	200,000	Cash Sales	$300,000
Payroll Cost	200,000	Collection of Accounts	
Other Operating Expense	100,000	Receivable	300,000
Depreciation	50,000	Total	600,000
Interest	25,000	Cash Disbursements:	
Income Taxes	10,000	Purchases of Food	200,000
		Payment of Payroll	200,000
Net Income	$15,000	Payment of Operating Costs	100,000
		Payment of Income Taxes	10,000
		Payment for Equipment	50,000
		Mortgage Payment	50,000
		Dividends Paid	10,000
		Total	620,000
		Excess Cash Disbursements	$20,000

Aggressive financial managers attempt to keep cash balances at a minimum, given the in-house cash needs and banking requirements. The cost of excessive cash in-house or in checking accounts is the opportunity cost. The opportunity cost equals the earnings available if the cash were invested. For example, if a hospitality operation had an average balance through the year in its checking account of $40,000 when the banker requires only $25,000, the opportunity cost is the interest that could be earned on $15,000. If 10% could be earned, then the opportunity cost is $1,500 annually ($15,000 x 10%).

While cash is important to operators in order to pay bills as they come due and as compensating balances to satisfy bankers, investors also have a keen interest in the operation's cash position. Many invest in the stock of corporations in order to increase their wealth in at least two ways. First, dividends received provide them with cash, and second, their wealth is increased as the corporations' stock prices increase. However, our focus here is on dividends. Corporations are able to pay cash dividends only as cash is available. Therefore, investors interested in investing in corporations for dividends will review final statements to determine that the operation appears to have sufficient cash to pay dividends, and that the operation will be operated in a manner that will allow dividend payments in the future.

Distinction Between Income and Cash Flows

Income flows result from operations generating revenues and incurring expenses. These flows are shown on the income statement and reflect the results of operations. Cash flows result from the receipt and disbursement of cash. It is possible for an operation to generate profits (income flow), yet have a negative cash flow (cash disbursements exceed cash receipts). This is illustrated in the situation of Rambles Restaurant as shown in Exhibit 13.1.

Rambles Restaurant generated net income flows of $15,000 as shown on the income statement; however, cash disbursements exceeded cash receipts by $20,000. In this simplified illustration, the differences in income and cash flows are as follows:

Income Flows	Cash Flows
1. Depreciation $50,000	1. Depreciation has no effect on cash flows.
2. Interest expense $25,000	2. Interest expense is part of the mortgage payment of $50,000. The $25,000 difference between the mortgage payment and the interest expense is the principal reduction portion of the mortgage payment.
3. The purchase of equipment has no direct effect on income flows. The write-off (depreciation) will affect income flows over several future years.	3. Payment for equipment purchase of $50,000 (purchased in the last month of the year)
4. Dividends do not affect income flows.	4. Dividends paid of $10,000

Therefore, the *cash* outflows listed above of $110,000 (mortgage payment $50,000, payment for equipment $50,000, and dividends paid $10,000) exceed the sum of the two *income* outflows of depreciation and interest expense of $75,000. The difference of $35,000 ($110,000 − $75,000) is the same as the difference between the income flows (net income of $15,000) and cash flows (net cash outflow of $20,000). Note that all other cash flows and income flows are the same in this simplified example. In more complex situations, there generally will be additional differences between income and cash flows.

A hospitality operation may have negative cash flows for short periods of time as long as cash reserves are adequate to cover the deficits. However, over long periods, negative cash flows will most likely result in failure, even if the income flows were positive.

Most businesses, including hospitality establishments, have peaks and valleys in their operations. Generally, during the peak periods, more cash is required as cash is tied up in inventories and especially accounts receivable. Therefore, cash planning is important to ensure sufficient cash at all times. Cash planning is achieved by preparing cash budgets for several months in the future.

Cash Budgeting

Cash budgets are prepared to reflect the estimated cash receipts and cash disbursements for the period. If the estimated cash receipts and beginning cash (estimated available cash) are not sufficient to cover projected cash disbursements, management must take action. Even if estimated available cash is greater than the projected cash disbursements, the projected cash balance must be reviewed to determine if it is a sufficient buffer for any cash receipt shortfalls and/or cash disbursements in excess of what has been planned. If the estimated cash balance is insufficient, then the operation must plan to increase cash receipts, decrease cash disbursements, or a combination of both. If the estimated cash balance at the end of the period appears to be excessive, then the excess cash should be temporarily invested until needed at a later time.

The five factors management should consider when investing excess cash are risk, return, liquidity, cost, and size. Risk refers to the probability of losing the investment. Management should generally take a minimum risk when investing, especially when investing short-run funds. For example, investments in government securities such as Treasury Bills are considered to be risk-free. Return refers to the rate of return that can be received on the funds. Generally, the greater the risk and the longer the period of the investment, the greater the return. Liquidity refers to the ability to convert the investment to cash. When temporary cash is invested, it should generally be invested in fairly liquid investments so it can be quickly liquidated as required. Cost refers to the brokerage cost of investing, while size refers to the amount of funds available for investing. Generally, as the amount of funds available for investing increases, the return available increases.

In certain situations, cash may be in short supply and a cash deficit may be projected. The cash budget prepared for several months in the future should reflect this condition, thus allowing management to act on a timely basis. Various management actions to cover temporary deficits include obtaining short-term bank loans, obtaining loans from stockholders, deferring equipment purchases, and deferring payment of dividends.

There are two basic approaches to cash budgeting: the cash receipts and disbursements method and the adjusted net income approach. The method selected is primarily a function of the length of time for which the cash budget is prepared.

Cash Receipts and Disbursements Approach

The cash receipts and disbursements method is useful when forecasting cash receipts for any length of time up to six months in the future. It shows the direct sources of cash receipts, that is, cash receipts from cash sales, collection of accounts receivable, bank loans, sale of capital stock, etc. It also reveals the direct uses of cash, for example, payment of food purchases, payment of payroll, mortgage payments, and dividend payments. Because the cash receipts and disbursement method reflects the direct sources and uses of cash, it is readily understood by management. However, it should generally not be used

Exhibit 13.2   Cash Budget — Cash Receipts and Disbursements Approach

Cash Budget
Cash Receipts and Disbursements Approach
For the months of Jan.-June, 19X1

	January	February	March	April	May	June
Estimated Cash – Beginning	$	$	$	$	$	$
Est. Cash Receipts:						
Cash Sales						
Collection of Accounts Rec.						
Proceeds from Bank Loans						
Proceeds from Sale of Fixed Assets						
Other						
Total						
Est. Cash Available						
Est. Cash Disbursements for:						
Inventory						
Payroll						
Operating Expenses						
Taxes						
Insurance						
Mortgage Payments						
Dividends						
Other						
Total						
Estimated Cash Ending						
Minimum Cash Required						
Cash Excess or Shortage	$	$	$	$	$	$

for periods exceeding six months in the future because the reliability of "more distant" figures rapidly decreases, especially when actual operations differ significantly from the operations budget.

The basic format of a cash budget based on the cash receipts and disbursements approach is shown in Exhibit 13.2. This format consists of two major sections, estimated cash receipts and estimated cash disbursements. Estimated cash receipts are added to the "estimated cash—beginning" resulting in the "estimated cash available" for the period. Estimated cash disbursements are subtracted from estimated cash available resulting in "estimated cash—ending." This figure is compared to the minimum cash required to identify any shortage or excess. The process of estimating cash receipts and cash disbursements will be presented later in this chapter.

Adjusted Net Income Approach

The adjusted net income approach is generally preferred for cash budgeting over longer periods of time than the cash receipts and disbursements method. It also reflects the estimated cash balance for management's evaluation. In addition to its usefulness for longer periods of time, it emphasizes external, as opposed to internal, sources of funds. The format of a prepared cash budget using the adjusted net income approach is shown in Exhibit 13.3.

The adjusted net income method is an indirect approach to cash budgeting because the sources and uses related to operations are indirect rather than direct (as is the case with the cash receipts and disbursements approach). This approach has two major sections, sources and uses. The sources section consists of internal sources, primarily cash from operations which is chiefly reflected by net income plus income tax expense, depreciation, and similar types of expenses. Several other sources of funds include proceeds from bank loans, sale of capital stock, and similar types of sources. The sum of the beginning cash and the sources of cash equals estimated cash available.

The second major section is uses of cash. The uses of cash, as shown in Exhibit 13.3, are subtracted from "cash—beginning of year" plus sources of cash, equaling "estimated cash—end of year." The "estimated cash—end of year" is compared to the minimum cash requirement to determine any cash excess or shortage.

The adjusted net income approach focuses directly on changes in accounts receivable, inventories, and current liabilities. This requires management to consider the amount of cash tied up in accounts receivable and inventory and cash "provided" by current liabilities. Therefore, this approach encourages closer management review of these working capital accounts.

From a practical viewpoint, both cash budgeting approaches are useful. The cash receipts and disbursements approach should be used for short-term budgets prepared on a month-by-month or even a week-by-week basis. The adjusted net income approach is useful for long-term budgets. Many hospitality establishments will prepare cash budgets for long-range periods corresponding to the long-range operations budgets.

Information for Cash Budgeting

The operations budget is the major source of information required in preparing a cash budget. For example, cash sales for a period are estimated based on total sales for the period and the estimated percentage of the sales that will be cash sales.

In addition to the operations budget, further information required is as follows:

- Estimated percentages of sales that are cash and credit sales.

- Estimated collection experience for credit sales, that is, when the credit sales will be collected. For example, the collection experience may be 30% in the month of sale, 60% in the following month, and the remaining 10% in the second month following the month of the sale.

- Estimated other cash receipts including bank loans, sale of capital stock, and proceeds from sale of fixed assets and investments.

Exhibit 13.3   Cash Budget — Adjusted Net Income Approach

**Cash Budget
Adjusted Net Income Approach
For the year ended December 31, 19X1**

Cash – beginning of year		$
Sources of Cash:		
Net Income	$	
Add: Income Tax Expense		
Depreciation		
Amortization		
Other	_____	
Other Sources:		
Proceeds from bank loans		
Sale of fixed assets		
Sale of capital stock		
Other		_____
Total		_____
Uses of Cash:		
Increase in accounts receivable		
Increase in inventories		
Decrease in current liabilities		
Purchase of fixed assets		
Income taxes paid		
Reduction in long-term debt		
Other		_____
Total		_____
Estimated Cash – end of year		_____
Minimum Cash Requirement		_____
Cash Excess or Shortage		$ _____

- Estimated payments for inventory items. For example, 10% of the purchases may be paid in the month purchased, while 90% are paid in the following month.

- Estimated payroll payments. A monthly payroll where all employees are paid on the last day of the month for that month means simply using the payroll expense estimates from the operations budget. However, payroll paid any other way requires considerably more calculations.

- The payment schedules for other operating periods must be considered. Some operating expenses, such as utilities, are generally paid in the month following the month it is expensed. Operating supplies are often paid for prior to the recognition of the expense when hospitality operations carry them as "supplies—inventory." Each type of expense requires review to determine when the related cash expenditure is made.

- Capital expenses such as property taxes and insurance are often paid only once or twice a year. In these cases, the payment date, not the expense from the operations budget, is the important information required.

- A schedule of debt payments (not part of the operations budget) is required to determine total debt payments.

- Additional information required includes, but may not be limited to, forecasted dividend payments and forecasted fixed asset and investment purchases.

Illustration—
Cash Receipts
and
Disbursements
Approach

The Greenery, a hypothetical 100-seat restaurant, will be used to illustrate the cash receipts and disbursements approach to cash budgeting. In this illustration, cash budgets will be prepared for the three-month period of April-June, 19X1. Exhibit 13.4 contains the Greenery's operations budget for March-July, 19X1.

At the Greenery, cash receipts and sales relationships are as follows:

1. Cash sales represent 50% of each month's sales. Therefore, the Greenery's estimated cash receipts from cash sales in April are $30,000 ($60,000 x .50).

2. Charge sales represent the remaining 50%. Twenty percent of the charge sales are collected in the month of the sale, while the remaining 80% are collected in the following month. The Greenery's estimated cash receipts from the charge sales in April total $6,000 ($60,000 x .50 x .20). In addition, March charge sales yield $25,200 of cash receipts in April ($63,000 x .50 x .80).

3. The Greenery receives cash each month for the projected interest income. Therefore, the Greenery's cash receipts from interest income total $2,000 for April.

The Greenery's cash disbursements and expenses have the following relationships:

1. Food purchases (cost of sales) are paid during the current month as follows:

> 70% of cost of sales of current month
> 30% of cost of sales of prior month

The Greenery's cash disbursements for food during April total $20,300 as follows:

March cost of sales x .3 = ($21,000 x .3) = $ 6,300
April cost of sales x .7 = ($20,000 x .7) = $14,000
                                              $20,300

2. Salaries, wages, and fringe benefits are paid in the month they are expensed. The April cash disbursements for salaries, wages, and fringe benefits total $18,500.

Exhibit 13.4 Operations Budget — The Greenery

Operations Budget
The Greenery
For the months of March-July, 19X1

	March	April	May	June	July
Sales	$63,000	$60,000	$65,000	$70,000	$75,000
Cost of Sales	21,000	20,000	21,700	23,400	25,000
Gross Profit	42,000	40,000	43,300	46,600	50,000
Interest Income	2,000	2,000	2,000	2,000	2,100
Total Income	44,000	42,000	45,300	48,600	52,100
Controllable Expenses					
Salaries and wages	17,000	16,000	18,000	19,000	20,000
Employee benefits	3,000	2,500	3,000	3,000	3,500
Direct operating expenses	3,000	2,500	2,500	2,500	3,000
Marketing	4,000	4,200	4,000	4,500	5,000
Energy Costs	3,000	2,500	2,000	2,000	2,200
Administrative & general	2,000	1,800	1,700	1,800	2,000
Repairs and maintenance	1,000	1,000	1,000	1,000	1,000
Income before Occupation Costs, Interest, and Depreciation	11,000	11,500	13,100	14,800	15,400
Occupation Costs	4,000	4,000	4,000	4,000	4,000
Interest	1,000	1,000	1,000	1,000	1,000
Depreciation	1,700	1,700	1,700	1,700	1,700
Income Before Income Taxes	4,300	4,800	6,400	8,100	8,700
Income Taxes	1,400	1,600	2,100	2,700	2,900
Net Income	$ 2,900	$ 3,200	$ 4,300	$ 5,400	$ 5,800

3. With the exception of marketing, 50% of all remaining controllable expenses are paid in the month expensed. The other 50% are paid in the following month. The Greenery's cash disbursements in April of $8,400 for these expenses are shown in Exhibit 13.5.

4. Marketing expense is paid for as follows:

    In January, $24,000 was paid to an advertising agency for $2,000 of advertising each month of 19X1. The remaining marketing expense (per the operations budget) is paid for during the month it is expensed. Therefore, $2,200 ($4,200 − $2,000) is paid for marketing expense by the Greenery in April 19X1.

5. Occupation costs of $4,000 per month are paid during the month incurred.

6. Interest expense of $1,000 for April is part of a mortgage payment of $2,000 per month.

7. Depreciation is a write-off of fixed assets and requires no cash flow.

8. Income taxes are paid quarterly. The tax expense for April-June is paid in June.

Exhibit 13.5   Estimated Cash Disbursements — The Greenery

Estimated Cash Disbursements in April for Various Controllable Expenses The Greenery			
	From March	For April	Total
Direct Operating Expenses	$1,500	$1,250	$2,750
Energy Costs	1,500	1,250	2,750
Administrative & General	1,000	900	1,900
Repairs & Maintenance	500	500	1,000
Total	$4,500	$3,900	$8,400

Other information includes the following:

1.   Assume cash at the beginning of April is $5,000.

2.   Equipment costing $5,000 is scheduled for purchase in May and is to be paid for in June.

The Greenery's three-month cash budget for April-June, 19X1, is shown in Exhibit 13.6 and explanations for each cash budget line item are shown in Exhibit 13.7.

The Greenery has a relatively healthy cash flow, as cash at the beginning of the quarter (April 1) of $5,000 is projected to increase to $18,430 by the end of the quarter (June 30). If the Greenery's management considers cash at the end of any month to be in excess of its cash needs, then it should be invested. Many hospitality establishments establish a minimum cash balance requirement, and any cash in excess of the minimum is available to invest on a temporary basis if needed for future operations, or, alternatively, it may be paid to the owners. The minimum cash balance ideally could be $-0- so long as daily cash inflow equalled daily cash outflow. However, this ideal situation is seldom achieved, so a cushion is maintained. Assume the Greenery maintains a cash cushion of $5,000 at the end of each month. The projected cash available to invest at the end of April-June, 19X1, is determined in Exhibit 13.8.

Thus, the Greenery is projected to have excess cash for investing of $7,800 and $7,310 in April and May, respectively. However, in June, temporary investments of $2,960 must be liquidated to provide the $5,000 minimum cash balance at June 30, 19X1.

Illustration— Adjusted Net Income Approach

The Greenery is also used to illustrate the adjusted net income approach to cash budgeting. Since this approach is used for preparing long-term cash budgets, the cash budgets for years 19X1-19X3 will be shown. Exhibit 13.9 contains the Greenery's operations budgets for 19X1-19X3.

In addition to the operations budgets for three years, information

Exhibit 13.6   Cash Budget — The Greenery

Cash Budget
The Greenery
For the months of April-June, 19X1

	April	May	June
Cash – beginning of the month	$ 5,000	$12,800	$ 20,110
Estimated cash receipts:			
Cash sales	30,000	32,500	35,000
Collection of accounts receivable	31,200	30,500	33,000
Interest received	2,000	2,000	2,000
Total	63,200	65,000	70,000
Estimated available cash	68,200	77,800	90,110
Estimated cash disbursements:			
Food purchases	20,300	21,190	22,890
Salaries, wages, and fringe benefits	18,500	21,000	22,000
Direct operating expenses	2,750	2,500	2,500
Marketing	2,200	2,000	2,500
Energy costs	2,750	2,250	2,000
Administrative & general	1,900	1,750	1,750
Repairs and maintenance	1,000	1,000	1,000
Occupation costs	4,000	4,000	4,000
Mortgage payment	2,000	2,000	2,000
Income taxes	0	0	6,400
Payment of equipment purchase	0	0	5,000
Total	55,400	57,690	72,040
Estimated cash – end of month	$ 12,800	$ 20,110	$ 18,070

required to prepare cash budgets using the adjusted net income approach is as follows:

1. Equipment acquisitions, which will be purchased with cash, are projected at $10,000 per year for 19X1-19X3.

2. Distributions to owners are projected at 50% of net income.

3. Mortgage payments are estimated to be $30,000 per year for 19X1-19X3.

4. The annual change in various current assets and current liabilities is estimated as follows:

	19X1	19X2	19X3
Accounts receivable	+2,000	+3,000	+4,000
Inventory	+1,000	+1,500	+1,500
Current liabilities	+2,000	+3,000	+3,500

The Greenery's long-range cash budget for 19X1-19X3 is shown in Exhibit 13.10. Overall, the cash budget shows a substantial increase in cash from $5,000 at the beginning of 19X1 to $86,650 at the end of 19X3. This fully considers the distribution of 50% of net income to owners, the cash purchase of $10,000 of equipment each year, and the reduction in

Exhibit 13.7 Explanation of Cash Budget Line Items — The Greenery

Explanation of Cash Budget Line Items
April – June, 19X1
The Greenery

Monthly Budgets

Line Item	April	May	June
Cash – beginning of the month (BOM)	$5,000 – based on assumption provided	$12,800 – cash-EOM, April 19X1	$20,110 – cash-EOM, May 19X1
Cash sales	$30,000 – April sales x .5 = 60,000 x .5 = $30,000	$32,500 – May sales x .5 = 65,000 x .5 = $32,500	$35,000 – June sales x .5 = 70,000 x .5 = $35,000
Collection of accounts receivable	$31,200 – April sales x .5 x .2 = 60,000 x .5 x .2 = $6,000 March sales x .5 x .8 = 63,000 x .5 x .8 = $25,200	$30,500 – May sales x .5 x .2 = 65,000 x .5 x .2 = $6,500 April sales x .5 x .8 = 60,000 x .5 x .8 = $24,000	$33,000 – June sales x .5 x .2 = 70,000 x .5 x .2 = $7,000 May sales x .5 x .2 = 65,000 x .5 x .8 = $26,000
Interest received	$2,000	$2,000	$2,000
Estimated cash available	$68,200 – cash-BOM + total estimated cash receipts = 5,000 + 63,200 = $68,200	$77,800 – cash-BOM + total estimated cash receipts = 12,800 + 65,000 = $77,800	$90,110 – cash-BOM + total estimated cash receipts = 20,110 + 70,000 = $90,110
Food purchases	$20,300 – March exp. x .3 = 21,000 x .3 = $6,300 April exp. x .7 = 20,000 x .7 = $14,000	$21,190 – April exp. x .3 = 20,000 x .3 = $6,000 May exp. x .7 = 21,700 x .7 = $15,190	$22,890 – May exp. x .3 = 21,700 x .3 = $6,510 June exp. x .7 = 23,400 x .7 = $16,380
Salaries, wages, and fringe benefits	$18,500 – 16,000 + 2,500 = $18,500	$21,000 – 18,000 + 3,000 = $21,000	$22,000 – 19,000 + 3,000 = $22,000
Direct operating expenses	$2,750 – March exp. x .5 = 3,000 x .5 = $1,500 April exp. x .5 = 2,500 x .5 = $1,250	$2,500 – April exp. x .5 = 2,500 x .5 = $1,250 May exp. x .5 = 2,500 x .5 = $1,250	$2,500 – May exp. x .5 = 2,500 x .5 = $1,250 June exp. x .5 = 2,500 x .5 = $1,250
Marketing expenses	$2,200 – Exp. for April – 2,000 = 4,200 – 2,000 = $2,200	$2,000 – May exp. – 2,000 = 4,000 – 2,000 = $2,000	$2,500 – June exp. – 2,000 = 4,500 – 2,000 = $2,500
Energy costs	$2,750 – March exp. x .5 + April exp. x .5 = (3,000 x .5) + (2,500 x .5) = 1,500 + 1,250 = $2,750	$2,250 – April exp. x .5 + May exp. x .5 = (2,500 x .5) + (2,000 x .5) = 1,250 + 1,000 = $2,250	$2,000 – May exp. x .5 + June exp. x .5 = (2,000 x .5) + (2,000 x .5) = 1,000 + 1,000 = $2,000
Administrative & general	$1,900 – March exp. x .5 + April exp. x .5 = (2,000 x .5) + (1,800 x .5) = 1,000 + 900 = $1,900	$1,750 – April exp. x .5 + May exp. x .5 = (1,800 x .5) + (1,700 x .5) = 900 + 850 = $1,750	$1,750 – May exp. x .5 + June exp. x .5 = (1,700 x .5) + (1,800 x .5) = 850 + 900 = $1,750

Exhibit 13.7 (continued)

Repairs and Maintenance	$1,000 – March exp. x .5 + April exp. x .5 = (1,000 x .5) + (1,000 x .5) = 500 + 500 = $1,000	$1,000 – April exp. x .5 + May exp. x .5 = (1,000 x .5) + (1,000 x .5) = 500 + 500 = $1,000	$1,000 – May exp. x .5 + June exp. x .5 = (1,000 x .5) + (1,000 x .5) = 500 + 500 = $1,000
Occupation costs	$4,000	$4,000	$4,000
Mortgage payment	$2,000	$2,000	$2,000
Income taxes	$ 0	$ 0	$6,400 – April-June exp. = 1,600 + 2,100 + 2,700 = $6,400
Purchase of equipment	$ 0	$ 0	$5,000
Estimated cash – EOM	$12,800 – Est. available cash – est. cash disb. = 68,200 – 55,400 = $12,800	$20,110 – Est. available cash – est. cash disb. = 77,800 – 57,690 = $20,110	$18,070 – Est. available cash – est. cash disb. = 90,110 – 72,040 = $18,070
		Monthly Budgets	
Line Item	April	May	June

long-term debt of $15,000 each year. The Greenery's management must consider the best uses of the excess funds reflected by the cash budget. The factors relevant to investing for a short period are appropriate in a long-term situation, although less importance is placed on liquidity than was considered when investing short-term funds.

Management of Working Capital

Closely related to the management of cash is the management of working capital. Working capital (current assets less current liabilities) is directly related to cash. Exhibit 13.11 depicts the effect of working capital on cash. These relationships assume that other activities (such as sales and expenses) remain constant. For example, if marketable securities decrease, everything else being the same, then cash would increase. Therefore, it is imperative that managers of hospitality operations understand the management of these elements of working capital.

Accounts Receivable

Accounts receivable arise from sales on accounts. Hospitality operations would prefer to transact only cash sales; however, in order to increase sales, credit is often extended to guests. Credit commences when the guest checks into a room without paying for the room. Credit continues until the guest pays the bill which may occur at the time of

Exhibit 13.8   Cash Availabile to Invest — The Greenery

Project Cash Available to Invest
The Greenery
For the months of April-June, 19X1

	April	May	June
Cash – BOM	$ 5,000	$ 5,000	$ 5,000
Plus: Total Estimated Cash Receipts	68,200	65,000	70,000
Less: Total Estimated Disbursements	55,400	57,690	71,680
Preliminary Cash EOM	17,800	12,310	(3,320)
Less: Cash Cushion	5,000	5,000	5,000
Excess Cash for Investing	$12,800	$7,310	($1,680)*

*If the excess cash is invested in April and May, The Greenery should prepare to liquidate $1,680 of these investments to maintain the desired cash cushion of $5,000 at the end of June.

check-out or after the guest leaves the hotel. Credit should be monitored while the guest stays at the hotel. Details of this process are beyond the scope of this text; however, Ellis Knotts provides guidance in this area.[1]

Statements should be mailed for accounts receivable periodically, normally monthly. A series of collection letters should be used to speed collection of accounts receivable. Delinquent accounts should be turned over to collection agencies only when all reasonable collection efforts have been expended by the hospitality operation, because collection fees may range from 30% to 50% of the delinquent amount.

To speed the flow of cash from accounts receivable to the bank, a lockbox system should be used in many instances. This system consists of a post office box from which bank personnel collect all incoming mail and deposit any checks directly in the property's account with the bank. This process may speed up the cash flow from collection of accounts receivable up to three days. In addition, control over mail cash receipts is enhanced, because no company personnel have access to this cash. However, the bank does charge for this service, generally on the basis of checks handled. Therefore, the cost of handling small checks may exceed the benefits of having the cash deposited in the property's checking account sooner than if the property's personnel handled these cash receipts.

A formula for considering the financial costs and benefits of a lockbox system provides a breakeven amount; that is, the amount of a receivables account, which when invested for the number of days cash flow is speeded-up, yields income equal to the added cost of the lockbox system. The formula is as follows:

$$B = \frac{C}{I \times T}$$

where B = Breakeven Amount

C = Bank Charge per Item

I = Daily Interest Rate

T = Change in Time

Exhibit 13.9 Long-Range Operations Budget — The Greenery

Long-Range Operations Budget
The Greenery
For the years of 19X1-19X3

	19X1	19X2	19X3
Sales	$730,000	$850,000	$1,000,000
Cost of sales	240,000	270,000	320,000
Gross profit	490,000	580,000	680,000
Interest income	25,000	30,000	35,000
Total income	515,000	610,000	715,000
Controllable expenses:			
Salaries and wages	200,000	240,000	300,000
Employee benefits	25,000	30,000	35,000
Direct operating expenses	28,000	30,000	32,000
Marketing	40,000	50,000	60,000
Energy costs	30,000	35,000	40,000
Administrative & general	20,000	25,000	30,000
Repairs and maintenance	12,000	14,000	16,000
Total	355,000	424,000	513,000
Income before Occupation Costs, Interest, and Depreciation	160,000	186,000	202,000
Occupation Costs	50,000	50,000	50,000
Interest	15,000	15,000	15,000
Depreciation	20,000	22,000	24,000
Income before income taxes	75,000	99,000	113,000
Income taxes*	25,000	33,000	37,700
Net income	$50,000	$66,000	$75,300

*The income taxes paid each year is the same as the income tax expense in the long-range operations budget.

An example may best illustrate the breakeven amount. Assume a hotel desires to know the breakeven amount from a lockbox system where a bank charges $.20 for each mail receipt processed, funds can be invested at 12% per annum, and a lockbox system speeds mail cash receipts to its bank account two days faster than by having company personnel process the mail receipts. The breakeven amount is $304.14, determined as follows:

$$B = \frac{.20}{\frac{.12 \times 2}{365}}$$

$$B = \frac{.20}{.0003288 \times 2}$$

Exhibit 13.10 Long-Range Cash Budget — The Greenery

Long-Range Cash Budget The Greenery For the years of 19X1-19X3		19X1	19X2	19X3
Cash – beginning of the year		$ 5,000	$ 24,000	$ 52,000
Sources of cash:				
Net income		50,000	66,000	75,300
Add: Depreciation		20,000	22,000	24,000
Increase in current liabilities		2,000	3,000	3,500
	Total	72,000	91,000	102,800
Uses of cash:				
Increase in accounts receivable		2,000	3,000	4,000
Increase in inventory		1,000	1,500	1,500
Distributions to owners		25,000	33,000	37,650
Purchase of fixed assets		10,000	10,000	10,000
Reduction in long-term debt		15,000	15,000	15,000
	Total	53,000	62,500	68,150
Estimated cash – end of year		$ 24,000	$ 51,500	$ 86,650

$$B = \frac{.20}{.0006576}$$

$$B = \underline{\$304.14}$$

The result shows that this hotel will benefit financially by using a lockbox system for processing mail receipts which are greater than $304.14. Therefore, this hotel should instruct its debtors with balances greater than $304.14 to mail their checks to its lockbox (P.O. Box XX), while debtors owing less than $304.14 should send their payments to the hospitality operation for company personnel to process. This assumes company personnel and related expenses are fixed and will not change by processing more or fewer mail cash receipts.

Accounts receivable, especially city ledger accounts, are monitored by the use of ratio analysis and the preparation of an aging schedule of accounts receivable. Three useful ratios, discussed in Chapter 5 on financial ratios, are accounts receivable to sales, accounts receivable turnover, and number of days accounts receivable outstanding (which is a variation of the accounts receivable turnover). The ratios are useful in detecting changes in the overall accounts as they relate to sales.

An aging of accounts receivable (see Exhibit 5.5 in Chapter 5 for an example of an aging schedule) is useful for monitoring delinquent accounts. Maximum efforts should be exerted to collect the oldest, thus the most delinquent, accounts. The aging schedule is also useful for estimating the uncollectible accounts, at the end of the accounting period.

Exhibit 13.11   The Effect of Working Capital on Cash

Increases in cash result as:
- marketable securities decrease
- accounts receivable decrease
- inventory decreases
- current liability increase

Decreases in cash result as:
- marketable securities increase
- accounts receivable increase
- inventory increases
- current liabilities decrease

Inventory

Inventory is viewed by some as a necessary evil. Hospitality operations must maintain an inventory of food and beverages even though there is a relatively high cost to store this inventory. The benefit of having food and beverages for sale is reasonably obvious, that is, food and beverages are generally sold at several times their cost.

However, the non-product costs of inventory need to be considered so that management will exercise tight control in this area. Several costs directly related to inventory include storage, insurance, and personnel. Storage space is required for keeping inventory, and many inventory items must be stored in temperature controlled environments. Certain inventory items have a limited shelf life; thus, personnel need to closely monitor these items. Inventory must be counted periodically which also requires personnel, thus, payroll dollars. Overall cost increases when, in spite of management's best efforts, some inventory spoils and must be discarded. Insurance to cover inventory, although not expensive, is still another cost. In addition to these costs, there is the opportunity cost of inventory. If funds were not tied up in inventory, they could be invested to provide a return to the hospitality operation. Therefore, management must closely monitor inventory to keep it at a minimum yet still have products available when customers desire to make purchases.

Common means of monitoring inventory include the inventory ratios discussed in Chapter 5. The most common ratio is inventory turnover, calculated by dividing average inventory into cost of sales, yielding the turnover. This ratio should be computed not only for food but also for each category of beverages. The results are most meaningful when compared to the planned ratios and to ratios for past periods. The ratios can assist management in detecting unfavorable trends. For example, a food inventory turnover of 2, 1.8, and 1.6 for three successive months suggests a major change in food inventory for the operations. Management should determine if the inventory is excessive and take the appropriate actions to correct the situation.

Current Liabilities

A considerable portion of current assets is financed by current liabilities in hospitality operations. The current ratio, computed by dividing current assets by current liabilities, of approximately 1 to 1 for hospitality operations, especially in the lodging sector, reflects this situation. Trade credit is free, that is, suppliers do not charge interest to hospitality operations for amounts owed in the normal course of business. Everything else being the same, the longer a property has to pay its bills, the greater the reliance on trade credit to finance its operations.

Current liabilities consist primarily of trade payables, taxes payable, accrued wages, and the current portion of long-term debt. The remainder of this section focuses on trade payables, as the other payables generally must be paid on stipulated dates.

Trade payables resulting from purchases on account generally require payment in 30 days. Exceptions to this are when suppliers offer cash discounts. Cash discounts are offered to hospitality operations to encourage them to pay their accounts early. For example, a supplier may provide a 2% cash discount if the invoice is paid within ten days of the invoice date. Thus, the terms of sale per the invoice are simply shown as 2/10, n/30. The n/30 means that if the invoice is not paid within ten days of the invoice date, then the entire amount is due within 30 days from the invoice date. The effective interest rate of the cash discount is determined as follows:

$$\text{Effective Interest Rate} = \frac{\text{Cash Discount}}{\text{Invoice Amount} - \text{Cash Discount}} \times \frac{\text{Days in Year}}{\substack{\text{Difference between end} \\ \text{of discount period and} \\ \text{``final'' due day}}}$$

The following example illustrates the calculation of the effective interest rate. A hotel purchases a posting machine for $8,000 and is offered terms of 3/10, n/30. The effective interest rate of 56.45% is the result of:

$$
\begin{aligned}
\text{Effective Interest Rate} &= \frac{240^*}{8,000 - 240} \times \frac{365}{20} \\[2mm]
&= \frac{240}{7,760} \times \frac{365}{20} \\[2mm]
&= .03093 \times 18.25 \\[2mm]
&= \underline{\underline{56.45\%}}
\end{aligned}
$$

*Cash Discount = $8,000 x .03 = $240

Thus, the hotel would be wise to borrow funds to pay the invoice within the cash discount period as long as the interest rate was less than 56.45%.

In general, management should pay bills only when they are due, except when cash discounts are available for early payments. The payment of invoices earlier than required results in a higher cost of doing business since the cash expended could have been invested. However, the intangible factor of supplier relations must also be considered by management. Keeping on favorable terms with suppliers is especially advantageous when the hotel or restaurant desires special favors such as receiving inventory two days sooner than normally available, and so on.

Integrated Cash Management for Multi-Unit Operations

So far, our discussion of cash management could most easily be applied to a single-unit operation. However, for multi-unit operations, an integrated cash management system should generally be installed.

An integrated cash management system consists of centralizing cash receipts and especially cash disbursements in the corporate office. Cash receipts, although initially received by the individual unit, are moved quickly to the corporate office. Cash disbursements, for the most part, are made from the corporate office banking accounts (e.g., payroll checks are prepared at the corporate office).

An integrated cash system's primary goal is to minimize the amount of cash held by the hospitality operation. Cash balances at individual units may be reduced by having a centralized cash disbursement system through which, where practical, supplier invoices and payroll are disbursed using the corporate office checking accounts. The checking accounts at the individual operations become, in essence, cash clearing accounts. That is, cash deposited in these accounts is quickly transferred to the corporate office bank accounts, and the cash balances of the individual unit checking accounts are maintained at minimum levels to facilitate required local disbursements. As cash balances are reduced at the individual operating units, more cash is accumulated at the corporate level. Financial expertise is available at the corporate office which results in increased financial returns from superior investments. This, in part, results from large pools of cash being available which increase the multi-unit's bargaining power with financial institutions.

An integrated cash management system results in better allocation of funds throughout the operation. When some properties require cash, excess cash is funneled to the needy properties by the corporate office rather than the property negotiating with the local banker for a short-term loan.

Caraux and Geller suggest that an integrated cash system improves control over collection and disbursement procedures of multi-unit operations.[2] For example, individual properties may pay invoices prior to their due dates; however, a centralized system allows for proper monitoring of cash disbursements.

An integrated cash management system consists of cash forecasting including the preparation of cash budgets at both the unit and corporate levels. Both short- and long-term budgets should be prepared at both levels. The banking system is centralized, as has been mentioned, with considerable interest in transferring cash to corporate accounts. In addition, some hospitality operations have their own credit card systems, although most choose to work directly with major credit card companies.

Computerization

As this chapter has pointed out, cash management is very important to a business. Management must control cash daily, making sure that there is sufficient cash to meet the needs of the business, yet not an excess amount that is unproductive. Many large companies, including hotel firms, have people assigned to just such a function. Yet, the typical hotel or restaurant is too small to have an employee assigned to manage the company's cash; the labor cost would exceed the benefits derived.

A method to control the cash easily and quickly can often be implemented with the help of a computer. For example, the cash forecast shown in Exhibits 13.6 and 13.7 can be computerized and used for weekly, or even daily, analysis. A general cash budget can be developed using the operating budget of the company as a starting point. Because many of the line items in the operating budget affect the cash budget, if the budget process is already computerized, it is possible to have a tentative cash budget be an automatic outflow of the process for managerial review and modification.

For control, this cash budget can be used for weekly and monthly forecasting of cash needs. The budget can reflect expected cash activity based upon cash incomes and outflows. Cash needed for major expenditures can also be projected in this plan, allowing for the anticipation of unusual items as well as daily transactions. While it would take hours to develop such a plan manually every week, a computer can simplify the process and do it in just a few moments. Assuming some basic ratios do not change, such as percentage of cash sales, average check sales, and cost of sales, a cash budget can be quickly developed whenever necessary. This will allow the manager to oversee what cash is required, and decide how to invest any extra cash on hand. Exhibit 13.12 shows how this might be done for a food service operation.

Summary

Cash is a very important asset for hospitality operations. Although it may earn no interest, cash is used to pay debts, make disbursements, and facilitate guest transactions. Management must try to minimize the operation's cash holdings by investing them in revenue producing assets while, at the same time, not jeopardizing its operations. This chapter highlighted a number of tools to aid in this task including cash budgets, the treatment of other current assets, and an integrated cash system.

Cash budgets are formulated to estimate the operation's future cash position. Two approaches, the cash receipts and disbursements method, and the adjusted net income approach, both estimate the cash balance at the end of the period and give management the information necessary for planning when a surplus or deficit is forecasted.

The cash receipts and disbursements method is a direct approach which examines all cash inflows and outflows. Items found in this budget would include, but not be limited to, the following: the amount of cash sales in the period, collection of accounts receivable, dividends and interest received, the operating expenses which were paid for during

Exhibit 13.12   Computer-Generated Monthly Cash Budget

ABC Restaurant Company
Monthly Cash Budget
Month of July, 19X1

	Week 1	Week 2	Week 3	Week 4
Covers Served Restaurant	1,500	1,590	1,350	1,530
Covers Served Banquet	125	333	250	400
Average Price/Cover Rest.	$12.40	$12.40	$12.40	$12.40
Average Price/Cover Banquet	$14.10	$14.10	$14.10	$14.10
Bev Checks Restaurant	900	954	810	918
Bev Checks Banquet	38	100	75	120
Ave. Bev. Sale Restaurant	$ 6.00	$ 6.00	$ 6.00	$ 6.00
Ave. Bev. Sale Banquet	$ 3.25	$ 3.25	$ 3.25	$ 3.25
Cash – Beginning of Week	$ 1,600	$ 6,784	$12,215	$13,961
Estimated Cash Receipts:				
Cash & Credit Card Sales	24,417	26,695	22,542	25,988
A/R Collections	2,199	3,397	2,966	1,854
Interest on Investments	6	6	6	6
Total Receipts	26,622	30,098	25,514	27,848
Estimated Cash Available	28,222	36,882	37,729	41,809
Estimated Cash Expenditures				
Food Purchases	6,951	8,074	6,740	8,050
Beverage Purchases	1,104	1,210	1,021	1,180
Salaries, Wages, & Benefits	8,507	10,056	8,369	10,089
Direct Operating Expenses	1,346	1,468	1,240	1,429
Marketing & Advertising	300	300	300	300
Administration & General	1,597	1,806	1,531	1,671
Credit Card Commissions	551	601	507	585
Energy Costs	532	602	510	557
Repairs & Maintenance	300	300	300	300
Occupation Costs	250	250	250	250
Mortgage Payment	0	0	0	3,500
Capital Purchases	0	0	3,000	0
Income Tax Allowance	0	0	0	4,625
Total Cash Expenditures	21,438	24,667	23,768	32,536
Estimated Cash – End of Week	$ 6,784	$12,215	$13,961	$ 9,273

the period, and dividends paid. This type of budget is most useful for short-term periods because the estimates upon which it is based are less reliable the further the projections are made into the future.

The adjusted net income approach to cash budgeting is used for periods beyond six months. The projected operations for each future year are adjusted to reflect cash flows. This approach also considers any expected changes in current accounts and any capital expenditures. Management should examine excess funds, estimated by this approach, and determine the appropriate way to invest them.

Management must also monitor the activity in other current accounts in order to optimize the operation's liquidity position. Accounts receivable should be analyzed to ensure their timely collection. Inventory is expensive to store but is valuable to operations, so it should be monitored. Often, this is done by analyzing the turnover ratio. Current liabilities should be studied with special consideration given to trade discounts. All of these procedures will aid management in cash control and overall operational efficiency.

In addition, several additional cash management procedures which can be used in multi-unit operations are presented in this chapter. The main goal of an integrated cash system is to minimize the total cash holdings of the hospitality operation. This is accomplished by maintaining a central account to which all receipts are deposited and from which all disbursements are made. Even when hospitality operations have this central account, it is important for them to make budgets, both for the long- and short-term horizons, and constantly update these as information becomes available.

Notes

1. For the person interested in studying this area, Ellis Knotts has discussed this topic in "Handling the Credit Function at Small Hotels," *Lodging*, June 1979.
2. Caraux and Geller provide a fairly detailed discussion of an integrated cash management system for multi-unit firms in their article titled "Cash Management: A Total System Approach for the Hotel Industry," in the November 1977 issue of *The Cornell Hotel & Restaurant Administration Quarterly*.

Discussion Questions

1. What is meant by an "imprest basis?"

2. How is cash used by hospitality operations?

3. What are three items which exemplify the differences between income and cash flows?

4. What are the two different types of cash budget formats, and why would you use one over the other?

5. What are five informational items needed to prepare a cash budget using the cash receipts and disbursements approach?

6. What should management consider when investing excess cash?

7. Why must you analyze other current asset accounts when using the adjusted net income approach to cash budgeting?

8. How soon should you turn delinquent accounts receivable over to a collection agency? Why?

9. What is the value of a lockbox system to a hospitality operation?

10. What is an integrated cash management system?

Problem 13.1

Warren Peace, owner of the War 'N Peace Motel, is considering using a lockbox system for some of his collections of accounts receivable. He can program his computer to send statements with different return addresses depending on the amount of the balance, and has the following information from the bank regarding a lockbox system:

Collection charge/item by bank:	25¢
Annual interest rate on cash invested with the bank:	9%

He has estimated that using the lockbox would speed up collections by 3 days. Further, assume a year has 365 days.

Required:

What is the breakeven amount, that is, the amount at which W. Peace would be indifferent as to whether a customer sent the check directly to the motel or the post office box (part of the lockbox system)?

Problem 13.2

Amy Jason is the accountant for the Jason Junction Inn and is unfamiliar with trade discounts.

Required:

1. Explain what "2/10, n/30" means.
2. What is the effective rate of interest of terms of sales of "2/10, n/30"?

Problem 13.3

Use the following information to formulate a simplified cash budget for Heidi's Place.

	Dec.	Jan.	Feb.	Mar.
Sales	$40,000	$40,000	$50,000	$75,000
Inventory Purchases	15,000	17,000	18,000	30,000
Other Cash Expenses	15,000	15,000	22,000	37,000
Capital Purchases (With cash)	-0-	-0-	10,000	-0

Sales: 60% of the sales are cash while the remaining 40% are credit sales. One half of the credit sales are collected in the month of sale and one half in the next month.

Purchases: 80% of the purchases are paid in the month of the purchase while 20% are paid in the next month.

Inventory: Assume other cash expenses and capital purchases are paid for during the month indicated above (e.g., other cash expenses of $5,000 for December were paid in December).

Assume the beginning cash balance of January 1 is $5,000.

Required:

Prepare a cash budget using the cash receipts and disbursements approach for the months of January-March.

Problem 13.4

Beth McNight is the manager of the Night Time Inn and has completed the operating budget for the next 3 years as shown below. She is now ready to prepare the cash budget.

	Operating Budgets 19X1-19X3		
	19X1	19X2	19X3
Sales	$1,000,000	$1,200,000	$1,500,000
Direct Expenses	450,000	550,000	650,000
Depreciation	200,000	200,000	200,000
Other Fixed Expenses	250,000	250,000	350,000
Income Before Taxes	100,000	200,000	300,000
Income Tax	40,000	100,000	150,000
Net Income	$60,000	$100,000	$150,000

Additional information includes:

A. Dividends paid in a given year are estimated to be 30% of net income for that year.

B. The following is a summary of the only current accounts which are expected to change:

	19X1	19X2	19X3
Accounts Receivable	+10,000	+5,000	+20,000
Accounts Payable	−5,000	+5,000	+10,000

C. A major piece of equipment which costs $50,000 is scheduled for purchase during 19X3. Beth McNight desires to purchase the machine with company cash rather than borrow the necessary funds.

D. The cash balance at the beginning of 19X1 is $10,000.

E. Assume the income tax for each year is paid in the year it is shown as expense.

Required:

Prepare cash budgets for 19X1-19X3 for the Night Time Inn using the adjusted net income approach.

Problem 13.5

Claude Ziggy, owner of Ziggy's Diner, desires your assistance in preparing a cash budget for his restaurant. He estimates cash on July 1 will be $2,400. He desires to maintain a minimum of cash at the end of each month equal to one week's (7 days) disbursements of the next month, not including disbursements relating to working capital loans. (Assume disbursements are made evenly throughout a month.)

Total monthly sales are as follows:

March	$50,000
April	120,000
May	120,000
June	150,000
July (est.)	159,000
August (est.)	180,000
September (est.)	142,000
October (est.)	90,000

The sales are 40% cash and 60% regular credit. Regular credit sales are collected as follows:

Month of sale	10%
Month after sale	60%
Second month after sale	20%
Third month after sale	8%
Bad debts	2%
TOTAL	100%

Interest income of $1,000 is expected to be received in August. In September, the firm plans to sell some extra equipment. The chef estimates the equipment will bring $2,000. The book value of the equipment is $1,000. During September, 1,000 shares of capital stock with $1 par value are to be sold for $5 per share. Cash is to be received in September for the stock sales.

Payments for food are made one month after the sale and the food cost percentage is 35%. Beverages are purchased and paid for one month in advance and the beverage cost percent is 25%. Beverage sales are 50% of food sales.

Labor is paid during the month wages are earned and represent 40% of total sales. Fixed expenses, except for insurance, depreciation, and property taxes are $8,000 per month and are paid on a monthly basis.

Insurance premiums of $3,000 are paid quarterly in January, April, July and October of each year.

The property taxes of $20,000 for the year are paid in two installments of $10,000 each in July and December. Depreciation expense is $3,000 per month.

The Board of Directors is expected to declare a dividend share of $.25 in July payable in August (20,000 shares are outstanding).

In September, the firm plans to acquire fixed assets using cash totaling $20,000. If the firm is to borrow cash to maintain the desired cash balances, it must do so in increments of $1,000. The rate of interest is 12% and funds borrowed and interest pertaining thereto must be paid back in 30 days. (Assume the funds borrowed, if any, are paid back in the subsequent month.) Assume a year has 365 days when calculating interest on short-term loans.

Required:

Prepare a monthly cash budget for Ziggy's Diner for July-September using the cash receipts and disbursements approach.

14 Capital Budgeting

The hospitality industry, especially the lodging segment, is fixed-asset-intensive. This means that the majority of the assets of hospitality operations are fixed instead of current because of the considerable portion of their funds that are invested in inventories and receivables. This sets hospitality operations apart from many manufacturing firms that have the majority of their assets as current rather than as fixed. Since establishments in the hospitality industry are so fixed-asset-intensive, capital budgeting becomes an important management concern.

Capital budgeting is the process of determining the amount to spend on fixed assets and which fixed assets to purchase. Capital budgeting addresses such questions as:

1.   What piece of equipment among several alternatives should be purchased?

2.   Should old equipment be replaced with new?

3.   What is meant by the time value of money?

4.   How is cash flow computed from an investment?

5.   How is payback computed?

6.   When is the net present value method preferred to the internal rate of return method?

7.   How are alternative investments with different lives considered in the capital budgeting process?

8.   Which fixed assets are purchased under capital rationing?

We'll begin our consideration of the capital budget by comparing it to the operations budget and identifying various types of decisions involving capital budgeting. We will then focus on the concept of the time value of money and the computation of cash flow and payback from fixed asset investments. We'll explain different models of capital budgets and see how they apply to choices among various kinds of projects. Finally, we will discuss capital rationing and identify special problems with capital budgeting.

Relationship of Capital Budget to Operations Budget

Preparing the operations budget (covered in Chapter 11) is a prerequisite to capital budgeting for equipment. If the operations budget suggests that sales will increase beyond what present equipment is reasonably able to produce, then the present equipment has become functionally obsolete and must be replaced. For example, if a restaurant's budget is based on a realistic assumption that breakfast business will sizeably increase, it may be necessary to invest in a large rotary toaster instead of continuing to use a four-piece drop-in toaster.

Capital budgets are prepared not only for the current year, but also are often projected for several years into the future. Construction projects undertaken by some hotel properties may take up to 24 months to complete. Even though capital budgets may be prepared for several years, they must be reviewed annually to consider the impact of changing economic conditions. The capital budget is adjusted as new information becomes available regarding changes in demand for the hospitality operation's goods and services, technological changes, and changes in the cost of providing goods and services. Evaluating past capital budgeting decisions in light of such current information is useful in determining whether those projects should be continued, expanded, reduced in scope, or possibly even terminated. Such current information may also affect the capital budgeting process itself and cause revisions in the capital budgeting process.

Types of Capital Budgeting Decisions

Capital budgeting decisions are made for a variety of reasons. Some are the result of meeting government requirements. For example, the Occupational Safety & Health Administration (OSHA) requires certain safety equipment and guards on meat cutting equipment. The hospitality operation may spend several hundreds or even thousands of dollars in order to upgrade equipment and meet OSHA's requirements. Regardless of the potential profit or cost savings (if any) from this upgrading of equipment, the government regulation "forces" the hospitality operation to make the expenditure.

A second capital budgeting decision is acquiring an asset to reduce the operation's costs. For example, a lodging operation may have leased vehicles to provide airport transportation. However, to reduce this cost, a van could be purchased.

A third capital budgeting decision is acquiring fixed assets to increase sales. For example, a lodging operation may add a wing of 100 rooms or expand a dining facility from 75 to 150 seats. As a result of this expansion, both sales and expenses are increased, and, if the proper decision is made, total profits should increase to justify the capital expenditure.

The fourth capital budgeting decision is replacing an existing fixed asset. This replacement may be required because the present fixed asset is fully used up or functionally obsolete, or perhaps the replacement is simply more economical.

All four kinds of capital budgeting decisions require significant expenditures resulting in fixed assets. The return on the expenditures will accrue over an extended period of time and the expenditures should generally be cost justified in the sense that the expected benefits will exceed the cost. The more sophisticated capital budgeting models require a comparison of current cost expenditure for the fixed asset against a future stream of funds. In order to compare current year expenditures to future years' income, the future years' income must be placed on an equal basis. The process for accomplishing this involves the time value of money.

Time Value of Money

The saying, "$100 today is worth more than $100 a year from now" is true, because $100 today could be invested to provide $100 plus the interest for one year in the future. If the $100 can be invested at 12% annual interest, then the $100 can be worth $112 in one year. This is determined as follows:

Principal	+	(Principal	x	Time	x	Interest Rate)	=	Total
100	+	(100	x	1	x	.12)	=	$\underline{\$112}$

Principal is the sum of dollars at the beginning of the investment period ($100 in this case). Time is expressed in terms of years, as long as an annual interest rate is used. The interest rate is expressed in decimal form, so 12% is shown as .12. The interest of $12 plus the original principal of $100 equals the amount available one year hence of $112.

A shorter formula for calculating a future value is as follows:

$$F = A(1+i)^n$$

where F = Future Value
       A = Present Amount
       i = Interest Rate
       n = Number of Years

One hundred dollars invested at 12% for two years will yield $125.44 determined as follows:

$$F = 100(1+.12)^2$$
$$F = 100(1.2544)$$
$$F = \underline{\$125.44}$$

The present value of a future amount is the present amount which must be invested at X% interest to yield the future amount. For example, what is the present value of $100 one year hence when the interest rate is 12%? The formula to determine the present value of the future amount is as follows:

$$P = F \frac{(1)}{(1+i)^n}$$

where P = Present Amount
       F = Future Amount
       i = Interest Rate
       n = Number of Years

Therefore, the present value of $100 one year hence (assuming an interest rate of 12%) is $89.29 determined as follows:

$$P = F \quad \frac{(1)}{(1+i)^n}$$

$$P = 100 \quad \frac{(1)}{(1+.12)^1}$$

$$P = 100(.8929)$$

$$P = \underline{\$89.29}$$

The present value of $100 two years hence (assuming an interest rate of 12%) is $79.72 determined as follows:

$$P = F \quad \frac{(1)}{(1+i)^n}$$

$$P = 100 \quad \frac{(1)}{(1+.12)^2}$$

$$P = 100(.7972)$$

$$P = \underline{\$79.72}$$

An alternative to using this formula to calculate the present value of a future amount is to use a table of present value factors, such as that found in Exhibit 14.1. The present value factors in Exhibit 14.1 are based on future amounts at the end of the period. For example, the present value of $100 a year from now at 15% interest is $86.96. This is determined by finding the number in the 15% column and the period one row (0.8696) and multiplying it by 100. The present value of $100 today is simply $100.

Most capital investments provide a stream of receipts for several years. When the amounts are equal at equal intervals, such as the end of each year, the stream is referred to as an annuity. Exhibit 14.2 shows the calculation of the present value of an annuity of $10,000 due at the end of each year for five years. The present value factors used in the calculation are from the present value table presented in Exhibit 14.1.

The present value of an annuity will vary significantly based on the interest rate (also called the discount rate) and the timing of the future receipts. Everything else being the same, the higher the discount rate, the lower the present value. Likewise, everything else being the same, the more distant the receipt, the smaller the present value.

An alternative to multiplying each future amount by the present value factor from the present value table in Exhibit 14.1 is to sum the present factors and make one multiplication. This is illustrated in Exhibit 14.3. Thus, the $33,522 calculated in Exhibit 14.3 equals the calculation performed in Exhibit 14.2. Rather than using the present values from Exhibit 14.1, present values of an annuity are provided in Exhibit 14.4. As a check on your understanding of the present value of an annuity table, locate the present value factor for five years and 15%. As you would expect, it is 3.3522. Thus, the present value of an annuity table is nothing more than a summation of present value factors from Exhibit 14.1. However, this table of present values of an annuity will save considerable time, especially when streams of receipts for several years must be calculated.

A problem which "requires" the use of both present value factors (Exhibit 14.1) and present value of an annuity factors (Exhibit 14.4) is included in Exhibit 14.5. This problem is solved by treating the stream of

Exhibit 14.1   Table of Present Value Factors

Period	1%	2%	3%	4%	5%	6%	7%	8%	9%	10%	12%	14%	15%	16%	18%
1	.9901	.9804	.9709	.9615	.9524	.9434	.9346	.9259	.9174	.9091	.8929	.8772	.8696	.8621	.8475
2	.9803	.9612	.9426	.9246	.9070	.8900	.8734	.8573	.8417	.8264	.7972	.7695	.7561	.7432	.7182
3	.9706	.9423	.9151	.8890	.8638	.8396	.8163	.7938	.7722	.7513	.7118	.6750	.6575	.6407	.6086
4	.9610	.9238	.8885	.8548	.8227	.7921	.7629	.7350	.7084	.6830	.6355	.5921	.5718	.5523	.5158
5	.9515	.9057	.8626	.8219	.7835	.7473	.7130	.6806	.6499	.6209	.5674	.5194	.4972	.4761	.4371
6	.9420	.8880	.8375	.7903	.7462	.7050	.6663	.6302	.5963	.5645	.5066	.4556	.4323	.4104	.3704
7	.9327	.8706	.8131	.7599	.7107	.6651	.6227	.5835	.5470	.5132	.4523	.3996	.3759	.3538	.3139
8	.9235	.8535	.7894	.7307	.6768	.6274	.5820	.5403	.5019	.4665	.4039	.3506	.3269	.3050	.2660
9	.9143	.8368	.7664	.7026	.6446	.5919	.5439	.5002	.4604	.4241	.3606	.3075	.2843	.2630	.2255
10	.9053	.8203	.7441	.6756	.6139	.5584	.5083	.4632	.4224	.3855	.3220	.2697	.2472	.2267	.1911
11	.8963	.8043	.7224	.6496	.5847	.5268	.4751	.4289	.3875	.3505	.2875	.2366	.2149	.1954	.1619
12	.8874	.7885	.7014	.6246	.5568	.4970	.4440	.3971	.3555	.3186	.2567	.2076	.1869	.1685	.1372
13	.8787	.7730	.6810	.6006	.5303	.4688	.4150	.3677	.3262	.2897	.2292	.1821	.1625	.1452	.1163
14	.8700	.7579	.6611	.5775	.5051	.4423	.3878	.3405	.2992	.2633	.2046	.1597	.1413	.1252	.0985
15	.8613	.7430	.6419	.5553	.4810	.4173	.3624	.3152	.2745	.2394	.1827	.1401	.1229	.1079	.0835
16	.8528	.7284	.6232	.5339	.4581	.3936	.3387	.2919	.2519	.2176	.1631	.1229	.1069	.0930	.0708
17	.8444	.7142	.6050	.5134	.4363	.3714	.3166	.2703	.2311	.1978	.1456	.1078	.0929	.0802	.0600
18	.8360	.7002	.5874	.4936	.4155	.3503	.2959	.2502	.2120	.1799	.1300	.0946	.0808	.0691	.0508
19	.8277	.6864	.5703	.4746	.3957	.3305	.2765	.2317	.1945	.1635	.1161	.0829	.0703	.0596	.0431
20	.8195	.6730	.5537	.4564	.3769	.3118	.2584	.2145	.1784	.1486	.1037	.0728	.0611	.0514	.0365
25	.7798	.6095	.4776	.3751	.2953	.2330	.1842	.1460	.1160	.0923	.0588	.0378	.0304	.0245	.0160
30	.7419	.5521	.4120	.3083	.2314	.1741	.1314	.0994	.0754	.0573	.0334	.0196	.0151	.0116	.0070
40	.6717	.4529	.3066	.2083	.1420	.0972	.0668	.0460	.0318	.0221	.0107	.0053	.0037	.0026	.0013
50	.6080	.3715	.2281	.1407	.0872	.0543	.0339	.0213	.0134	.0085	.0035	.0014	.0009	.0006	.0003
60	.5504	.3048	.1697	.0951	.0535	.0303	.0173	.0099	.0057	.0033	.0011	.0004	.0002	.0001	•

receipts as a $10,000 annuity and two separate payments of $5,000 and $10,000 due at the end of years two and four, respectively.

Cash Flow in Capital Budgeting

In most capital budgeting decisions, an investment results only when the future cash flow from the investment justifies the expenditure. Therefore, the concern is with the cash flow from the proposed investment. From the hospitality operation's perspective, the incremental cash flow is the focus rather than the operation's cash flow. Incremental cash flow is simply the change in the cash flow of the operation resulting from the investment. Cash flow relating to an investment includes the following:

Exhibit 14.2   Present Value of a $10,000 Five-Year Annuity

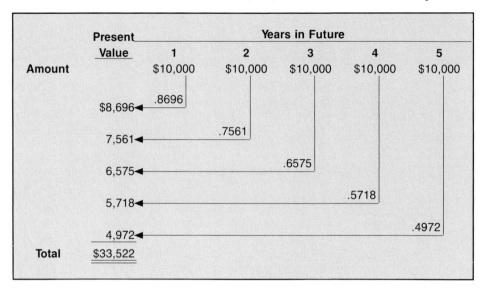

Exhibit 14.3   Shortcut Calculations of the Present Value of a $10,000 Five-Year Annuity

Years Hence	Present Value Factors at 15%
1	.8696
2	.7561
3	.6575
4	.5718
5	+ .4972
	3.3522
3.3522 × 10,000 =	$33.522

- Investment initial cost (cash outflow)

- Investment revenues (cash inflow)

- Investment expenses except depreciation (cash outflow)

Depreciation expense results from writing-off the costs of the investment; however, it is not a cash outflow and, therefore, does not affect the capital budgeting decision. It is used in determining the income taxes relating to the investment since the IRS allows depreciation to be deducted in computing taxable income.

Exhibit 14.6 illustrates the relevant cash flows of a proposed investment of the hypothetical Hampton Hotel. The Hampton Hotel is considering installing a game room. Since space is available with only minor modifications, the focus is on the cost of machines and related future revenues and expenses. Depreciation of $7,500 per year is used only in determining the pretax income from the investment. The cash flow

Exhibit 14.4 Table of Present Values of an Annuity

Number of Payments	1%	2%	3%	4%	5%	6%	7%	8%	9%	10%	12%	14%	15%	16%	18%
1	0.9901	0.9804	0.9709	0.9615	0.9524	0.9434	0.9346	0.9259	0.9174	0.9091	0.8929	0.8772	0.8696	0.8621	0.8475
2	1.9704	1.9416	1.9135	1.8861	1.8594	1.8334	1.8080	1.7833	1.7591	1.7355	1.6901	1.6467	1.6257	1.6052	1.5656
3	2.9410	2.8839	2.8286	2.7751	2.7232	2.6730	2.6243	2.5771	2.5313	2.4869	2.4018	2.3216	2.2832	2.2459	2.1743
4	3.9020	3.8077	3.7171	3.6299	3.5460	3.4651	3.3872	3.3121	3.2397	3.1699	3.0373	2.9137	2.8550	2.7982	2.6901
5	4.8534	4.7135	4.5797	4.4518	4.3295	4.2124	4.1002	3.9927	3.8897	3.7908	3.6048	3.4331	3.3522	3.2743	3.1273
6	5.7955	5.6014	5.4172	5.2421	5.0757	4.9173	4.7665	4.6229	4.4859	4.3553	4.1114	3.8887	3.7845	3.6847	3.4976
7	6.7282	6.4720	6.2303	6.0021	5.7864	5.5824	5.3893	5.2064	5.0330	4.8684	4.5638	4.2883	4.1604	4.0386	3.8115
8	7.6517	7.3255	7.0197	6.7327	6.4632	6.2098	5.9713	5.7466	5.5348	5.3349	4.9676	4.6389	4.4873	4.3436	4.0776
9	8.5660	8.1622	7.7861	7.4353	7.1078	6.8017	6.5152	6.2469	5.9952	5.7590	5.3282	4.9464	4.7716	4.6065	4.3030
10	9.4713	8.9826	8.5302	8.1109	7.7217	7.3601	7.0236	6.7101	6.4177	6.1446	5.6502	5.2161	5.0188	4.8332	4.4941
11	10.3676	9.7868	9.2526	8.7605	8.3064	7.8869	7.4987	7.1390	6.8052	6.4951	5.9377	5.4527	5.2337	5.0286	4.6560
12	11.2551	10.5753	9.9540	9.3851	8.8633	8.3838	7.9427	7.5361	7.1607	6.8137	6.1944	5.6603	5.4206	5.1971	4.7932
13	12.1337	11.3484	10.6350	9.9856	9.3936	8.8527	8.3577	7.9038	7.4869	7.1034	6.4235	5.8424	5.5831	5.3423	4.9095
14	13.0037	12.1062	11.2961	20.5631	9.8986	9.2950	8.7455	8.2442	7.7862	7.3667	6.6282	6.0021	5.7245	5.4675	5.0081
15	13.8651	12.8493	11.9379	11.1184	10.3797	9.7122	9.1079	8.5595	8.0607	7.6061	6.8109	6.1422	5.8474	5.5755	5.0916
16	14.7179	13.5777	12.5611	11.6523	10.8378	10.1059	9.4468	8.8514	8.3126	7.8237	6.9740	6.2651	5.9542	5.6685	5.1624
17	15.5623	14.2919	13.1661	12.1657	11.2741	10.4773	9.7632	9.1216	8.5436	8.0216	7.1196	6.3729	6.0472	5.7487	5.2223
18	16.3983	14.9920	13.7535	12.6593	11.6896	10.8276	10.0591	9.3719	8.7556	8.2014	7.2497	6.4674	6.1280	5.8178	5.2732
19	17.2260	15.6785	14.3238	13.1339	12.0853	11.1581	10.3356	9.6036	8.9501	8.3649	7.3658	6.5504	6.1982	5.8775	5.3162
20	18.0456	16.3514	14.8775	13.5903	12.4622	11.4699	10.5940	9.8181	9.1285	8.5136	7.4694	6.6231	6.2593	5.9288	5.3527
25	22.0232	19.5235	17.4131	15.6221	14.0939	12.7834	11.6536	10.6748	9.8226	9.0770	7.8431	6.8729	6.4641	6.0971	5.4669
30	25.8077	22.3965	19.6004	17.2920	15.3725	13.7648	12.4090	11.2578	10.2737	9.4269	8.0552	7.0027	6.5660	6.1772	5.5168
40	32.8347	27.3555	23.1148	19.7928	17.1591	15.0463	13.3317	11.9246	10.7574	9.7791	8.2438	7.1050	6.6418	6.2335	5.5482
50	39.1961	31.4236	25.7298	21.4822	18.2559	15.7619	13.8007	12.2335	10.9617	9.9148	8.3045	7.1327	6.6605	6.2463	5.5541
60	44.9550	34.7609	27.6756	22.6235	18.9293	16.1614	14.0392	12.3766	11.0480	9.9672	8.3240	7.1401	6.6651	6.2482	5.5553

generated by the investment in game machines is $35,400 for three years, resulting in an incremental net cash flow of $14,400 after the cost of the machines is subtracted. The means of financing the game machines is not considered. In capital budgeting models, the discount rate includes the interest cost, if any.

Capital Budgeting Models

Managers in hospitality operations use several different models in making capital budgeting decisions. The models vary from simple to sophisticated. The simple models are accounting data of return (ARR) and payback, while more sophisticated models, which require the discounting of future cash flows, are net present value (NPV) and

Exhibit 14.5   Present Value of a Stream of Unequal Future Receipts

Problem:

Determine the present value of receipts from an investment using a 15% discount factor which provides the following stream of income.

Years Hence	Amount
0	$10.000
1	10,000
2	15,000
3	10,000
4	20,000
5	10,000

Solution:

Years Hence	Amount	Annuity	Excess of Annuity
0	$10,000	$10,000	0
1	10,000	10,000	0
2	15,000	10,000	5000
3	10,000	10,000	0
4	20,000	10,000	10,000
5	10,000	10,000	0

Calculation:

Present Value of amount due today	=	$10,000	
Present Value of the $10,000 annuity for 5 years			
10,000 × 3.3522	=	33,522	
Present Value of $5,000 due 2 years hence			
5000 × .7561	=	3,781	
Present Value of $10,000 due 4 years hence			
10,000 × .5718	=	5,718	
	TOTAL	$53,021	

internal rate of return (IRR). The advantages and disadvantages of each model will now be addressed and illustrated using the investment-related data in Exhibit 14.7.

Accounting Rate of Return

The ARR model considers the average annual project income (project revenues less project expense generated by the investment) and the average investment. The calculation of ARR is simply:

$$\text{ARR} = \frac{\text{Average Annual Project Income}}{\text{Average Investment}}$$

The average annual project income is the total project income over its life divided by the number of years, while average investment is project cost less salvage value divided by two. The proposed investment

Exhibit 14.6   Cash Flows from Game Room — Hampton Hotel

Cost of machines	$21,000
Life of machines	3 years
Tax rate	40%
Salvage value of machines	—0—
Annual revenues	$ 25,000
Related annual expenses excluding depreciation and income taxes	$10,000
Method of depreciation	Straight-line

Cash Flow Calculation

	Years		
	1	2	3
Revenues	$25,000	$25,000	$25,000
Expenses except for depreciation and income taxes	10,000	10,000	10,000
Income taxes	3,200(1)	3,200(1)	3,200(1)
Cash flow	$11,800	$11,800	$11,800

Net cash flow is determined as follows:

Cash flows from above – 11,800 × 3 =	$35,400
Cost of machines	21,000
Net Cash Flow	$14,400

(1) Income taxes:

Predepreciation income	$15,000
Less: depreciation	7,000(2)
Taxable income	8,000
Tax rate	× .40
Income taxes	$ 3,200

(2) Annual depreciation $= \dfrac{\text{Cost} - \text{Salvage Value}}{\text{Life}} = \dfrac{21,000 - 0}{3} = \$7,000$

is accepted if the ARR exceeds the minimum ARR required. For example, a 52% ARR results in project acceptance when the minimum ARR is 40%.

The ARR model can be illustrated by using the Hampton Hotel's proposed investment in pizza equipment illustrated in Exhibit 14.7. The total project income over the five-year period is $89,000 which results in an average annual project income of $17,800. The average investment is $25,000, determined as follows:

$$\text{Average Investment} = \frac{\text{Project Cost} - \text{Salvage}}{2}$$

Exhibit 14.7   Proposed Investment in Pizza Equipment — Hampton Hotel

Investment		Accept/Reject Criteria		
Cost of Equipment	$48,000	ARR	=	40%
Installation costs	2,000	Payback	=	3 years
		IRR	=	15%
Total	$50,000	NPV	=	0

Depreciation Consideration		Depreciation Percentages	
Salvage Value	$—0—	Year	
Life for tax purposes 5 years		1	15%
		2	22%
		3	21%
		4	21%
		5	21%

Estimated Project Revenue and Expense

	YEARS				
	1	2	3	4	5
Project Revenues	$100,000	$120,000	$140,000	$160,000	$180,000
Project Expenses:					
Labor	25,500	26,200	33,900	37,100	40,300
Cost of product	25,000	30,000	35,000	40,000	45,000
Supplies	5,000	6,000	7,000	8,000	9,000
Utilities	4,000	4,800	5,600	6,400	7,200
Depreciation	7,500	11,000	10,500	10,500	10,500
Other operating expenses	11,000	12,000	14,000	16,000	18,000
Income taxes	11,000	15,000	17,000	21,000	25,000
Project Income	$11,000	$15,000	$17,000	$21,000	$25,000

Total Project Income for Years 1-5 = $89,000

Cash Flow:					
Investment profit	$11,000	$15,000	$17,000	$21,000	$25,000
Add: Depreciation	7,500	11,000	10,500	10,500	10,500
Total	$18,500	$26,000	$27,500	$31,500	$35,500

$$\text{Average Investment} = \frac{50,000 - 0}{2}$$

$$\text{Average Investment} = \underline{\$25,000}$$

The ARR of 71.2% is determined as follows:

$$\text{ARR} = \frac{\text{Average Annual Project Income}}{\text{Average Investment}}$$

$$\text{ARR} = \frac{17,800}{25,000}$$

$$\text{ARR} = \underline{71.2\%}$$

Since the project ARR of 71.2% exceeds the required minimum of 40%, if the Hampton Hotel used this capital budgeting model, management would invest in the pizza equipment.

Some managers consider ARR to be useful because it relies on accounting income and, thus, it is easy to calculate and easy to understand. However, these advantages are more than offset by its disadvantages: ARR fails to consider cash flows, or the time value of money.

Payback

The payback model compares annual cash flows to the project cost to determine a payback period as follows:

$$\text{Payback Period} = \frac{\text{Project Cost}}{\text{Annual Cash Flows}}$$

If the calculated payback period is equal to or less than the payback objective, then the project is accepted. The payback model is reasonably popular in the hospitality industry because it is conceptually simple. Management simply sets the payback period at the determined length of time required for the operation to get its money back from the project. Also, the payback model is often used as a screening device in conjunction with more sophisticated models. Some operations will not consider evaluating proposed projects using the NPV or IRR approaches unless their initial review using the payback model suggests that the proposed project is viable.

The payback period is determined as follows:

1. Set project cost equal to project cash flows for years 1 through n, where n is the last year (or portion thereof) required for project cash flows to equal the project cost.

2. Payback period = number of years of project cash flows required to equal the project cost.

Using figures from Exhibit 14.7, the payback period for the Hampton Hotel's proposed investment in pizza equipment can be calculated as follows:

$$\text{Project Cost} \quad = \quad \text{Project Cash Flows for Years 1, 2, and .2 of}$$
$$\text{year 3}$$
$$\$50,000 \quad = \quad \$18,500 + \$26,000 + \$5,500$$
$$\$50,000 \quad = \quad \$50,000$$

The final $5,500 of project cash flows is .2 of the third year's project cash flows of $27,500. Therefore, the payback period is 2.2 years. Since the payback period of 2.2 years is less than the accept/reject criterion of 3 years as stated in Exhibit 14.7, based on the payback model, the Hampton Hotel would invest in the proposed pizza project.

Disadvantages to the payback model that require careful consideration are that it fails to consider either the time value of money or the project flows after the payback period. The latter disadvantage is readily apparent when comparing two mutually exclusive projects (A & B) as shown in Exhibit 14.8.

Based on the payback method, project A would be accepted rather than project B, because the payback period of 2.33 years for project A is less than 2.6 years for project B. However, the excess cash flows of $5,000 and $15,000 for projects A and B, respectively, suggests an error. The calculation of the present value of all cash flows of $10,986 and $15,833 for projects A and B, respectively, is convincing. If this is not readily clear, it will be as we now turn to consider the net present value model.

Net Present Value Model

Both the NPV and IRR models overcome the weaknesses of the previous models in that they consider the time value of money. The net present value approach discounts cash flows to their present value. The net present value is calculated by subtracting the project cost from the present value of the discounted cash flow stream. The project is accepted if the NPV is equal to, or greater than, zero. If the capital budgeting decision considers mutually exclusive alternatives, the alternative with the highest NPV is accepted and other alternatives are rejected.

The advantage of the NPV model over the two models presented previously is the consideration of cash flows and the time value of money. Some managers have suggested that a disadvantage of the NPV model is its complexity. This argument may have been convincing to hospitality operations in the past, but as the hospitality industry continues to mature, the best methods of capital budgeting must be used (and they will be) if decision-making is to be optimized.

The NPV model is illustrated using the Hampton Hotel's proposed investment in pizza equipment (Exhibit 14.7). Assume a discount rate of 15% is used. Exhibit 14.9 shows the net present value to be $39,491. Therefore, the Hampton Hotel, based on the NPV model, should make the proposed investment, because NPV is positive.

Internal Rate of Return

A capital budgeting approach that considers cash flows and the time value of money and results in the determination of the rate of return earned by a proposed project is the IRR model. In determining IRR, the net present value of cash flows is set at zero and the "discount rate" is determined. The formula is as follows:

$$0 \quad = \quad \frac{CF_1}{1+r} \quad + \quad \frac{CF_2}{(1+r)^2} \quad + \quad \frac{CF_n}{(1+r)^n} \quad - \quad PC$$

Exhibit 14.8 **Comparison of Two Mutually Exclusive Projects — Payback Model**

	Project Cost Cash Flows	
Years Hence	Project A	Project B
0	$10,000	$10,000
1	5,000	3,000
2	4,000	4,000
3	3,000	5,000
4	2,000	6,000
5	1,000	7,000
Payback Period	2.33 years	2.60 years
Excess Cash Flow: Cash flow generated beyond payback period	$5,000	$15,000
Present value of all cash discounted at 15%	$10,986	$15,833

Exhibit 14.9 **Illustration of NVP — Proposed Investment in Pizza Equipment by Hampton Hotel**

Years Hence	Cash Flow	P.V. Factor (15%)	Present Value of Cash Flow
0	$(50,000)	1.0000	$(50,000)
1	18,500	.8696	16,088
2	26,000	.7561	19,659
3	27,500	.6575	18,081
4	31,500	.5718	18,012
5	35,500	.4972	17,651
		Net Present Value	$39,491

where CF = Cash Flow
    r = Internal Rate of Return
  PC = Project Cost

Assume a proposed project costs $6,850 and is expected to yield a cash flow stream of $3,000 for three years. The internal rate of return is 15%, determined as follows:

$$0 = \frac{CF_1}{1+r} + \frac{CF_2}{(1+r)^2} + \frac{CF_3}{(1+r)^3} - PC$$

$$0 = \frac{3,000}{1.15} + \frac{3,000}{(1.15)^2} + \frac{3,000}{(1.15)^3} - 6,850$$

Exhibit 14.10   Illustration of IRR — Proposed Investment in Pizza Equipment by Hampton Hotel

Years Hence	Cash Flow	41%		42%	
		PV Factor (1)	PV Cash Flow	PV Factor (1)	PV Cash Flow
0	$(50,000)	1.000	$(50,000)	1.000	$(50,000)
1	18,500	.7092	13,120	.7042	13,028
2	26,000	.5030	13,078	.4960	12,896
3	27,500	.3568	9,812	.3493	9,606
4	31,500	.2530	7,970	.2459	7,746
5	35,500	.1749	6,369	.1732	6,149
		Total	$ 349		$ (575)

(1) PV factors determined by the formula:

$$\frac{1}{(1 + r)^1} \, , \quad \frac{1}{(1 + r)^2} \, , \quad \frac{1}{(1 + r)^3} \, , \quad \frac{1}{(1 + r)^4} \quad \text{and} \quad \frac{1}{(1 + r)^5}$$

PV factor for 1 year at 41% is determined by dividing 1 by $(1.41)^1$ to equal .7092

$$0 \quad = \quad 2,609 \quad + \quad 2,268 \quad + \quad 1,973 \quad - \quad 6,850$$
$$0 \quad = \quad \underline{\underline{0}}$$

Using the IRR model, a project is accepted if the IRR is equal to, or greater than, the established minimum IRR, which is also commonly called "hurdle rate" by hospitality financial managers.

Like the NPV model, the IRR model is superior to the ARR and payback approaches because it considers the time value of money. The IRR is also superior to the ARR model because it considers cash flows. When there is a capital budgeting decision involving mutually exclusive projects, results from the IRR model may conflict with the NPV approach. This may occur because of the IRR's assumption that all project cash flows are reinvested at the internal rate of return. Since operations normally invest in the most profitable projects first, one should not assume other projects would result in the same return. This conflict will be discussed in greater detail in a later section of this chapter.

The IRR model is illustrated using the proposed investment by the Hampton Hotel in pizza equipment. Although the brief illustration of IRR above may have appeared simple, in practice, calculations are by trial and error. Various discount rates are tried until the approximate net present value is found to be zero. Computers can be very helpful in regard to these trial and error calculations. The manual approach is illustrated in Exhibit 14.10.

The exact IRR lies between 41% and 42%. Interpolation would result in approximate determination of 41.5%. Since the IRR of 41.5% exceeds the target of 15%, using this capital budgeting model, the Hampton Hotel should invest in the proposed pizza equipment.

Comparison of NPV and IRR Models

As discussed previously, the NPV and IRR models are preferred to the simplistic ARR and payback models. However, which is preferred, NPV or IRR? The NPV and IRR models, when applied in most situations, provide the same solution whether the situation considers a single project or mutually exclusive projects. However, in some of the latter situations, the NPV could suggest one project while the IRR model suggests a different project. This results from the assumed reinvestment rates of each model. The NPV model assumes reinvestment at the discount rate used (15% in the Hampton Hotel problem), while the IRR model assumes reinvestment at the computed IRR (41.5% in the Hampton Hotel problem). As stated previously, if the superior projects are first selected, then it is doubtful that reinvestment would be at the calculated IRR. Most likely, reinvestment will be at a lower rate. Therefore, when mutually exclusive projects are considered, the NPV approach is most useful.

The NPV is generally easier to compute than the IRR. However, computers and calculators have reduced the laborious calculations of the IRR model. On the other hand, many industry financial managers prefer the IRR model because the results are easier to interpret.

Mutually Exclusive Projects With Different Lives

To this point in our discussion, mutually exclusive projects were assumed to have the same useful life. However, in reality, many mutually exclusive projects do not have equal lives; therefore, three alternative approaches to decision-making are as follows:

1. Assume the shorter-lived project is replaced with another project whose combined lives equals the life of the mutually exclusive longer-lived project.

2. Assume the longer-lived project is disposed of at the end of the shorter-lived project's life.

3. Ignore the differences in lives of the two mutually exclusive projects.

This third alternative is reasonable only if the lives are both long and the differences are inconsequential. For example, a difference of one year for proposed projects with fourteen- and fifteen-year lives may be immaterial.

The first alternative is illustrated in Exhibit 14.11. In this example, a hotel is considering whether to replace its laundry washer with Machine A, which has a ten-year life, or with Machine B, which has a five-year life and no salvage value. At the end of Machine B's life, Machine C, which will have a five-year life, will be acquired. In addition, Machines A and C are considered worthless at the end of their lives, therefore, they have a zero salvage value. Thus, the life of Machine A (ten years) equals the combined lives of Machines B and C. The capital budgeting model and discount rate used are NPV and 15%, respectively. The results suggest

**Exhibit 14.11 Comparison of Machine Acquisitions with Different Lives —
Alternative One**

	Cash Flows		
	Alternative A	Alternative B	
Years Hence	Machine A (1)	Machine B (2)	Machine C (3)
0	$(15,000)	$(6,000)	
1	3,000	3,000	
2	3,000	3,000	
3	3,000	3,000	
4	3,000	3,000	
5	3,000	3,000	$(11,000)
6	3,000		3,000
7	3,000		3,000
8	3,000		3,000
9	3,000		3,000
10	3,000		3,000

NPV – Alternative A

NPV = 3000 (5.0188) – 15,000

NPV = 15,056 – 15,000

NPV = $56

NPV – Alternative B

NPV = 3000 (5.0188) – 6000 – 11,000 (.4972)

NPV = 15,056 – 6,000 – 5,469

NPV = $3,587

(1) Machine A costs $15,000 and provides a project cash flow of $3,000 per year for its ten-year life.

(2) Machine B costs $6,000 and provides a project cash flow of $3,000 per year for its five-year life of years 1 through 5.

(3) Machine C (purchased to replace Machine B) costs $11,000 at the end of year five and provides project cash flow of $3,000 per year for its five-year life of years 6 through 10.

that Machine B be purchased now followed by Machine C at the end of year five.

The second alternative, that of assuming the longer-lived project is disposed of at the end of the short-lived project's life, is illustrated in Exhibit 14.12. The same situation is assumed as in Exhibit 14.11 except the comparison is only for five years as Machine B is totally used at the end of year five. In addition, at the end of year five, Machine A is assumed to have a salvage value of $7,000. The NPV of Machines A and B are $29 and $4,057, respectively. Therefore, based on the available information, Machine B would be purchased.

Capital Rationing

Up to this point, no limit on projects has been discussed so long as the project returns exceeded the reject criteria. In reality, there are often limited funds available. For example, a parent corporation may limit funds provided to a subsidiary corporation, or a corporation may limit funds provided to a division. This concept of limited funds for capital purposes, regardless of the expected profitability of the projects, is called capital rationing. Under capital rationing, the combination of projects should be selected with the highest net present value.

Exhibit 14.12 Comparison of Machine Acquisitions with Different Lives —
Alternative Two

Machine A costs $15,000 and provides project cash flow of $3,000 per year for five years and then may be sold for $7,000. Machine B costs $6,000 and provides project cash flow of $3,000 per year for five years. At the end of five years, the machine is worthless.

	Cash Flows	
Years Hence	**Machine A**	**Machine B**
0	$(15,000)	$(6,000)
1	3,000	3,000
2	3,000	3,000
3	3,000	3,000
4	3,000	3,000
5	10,000	3,000

NPV – Machine A	**NPV – Machine B**
NPV = 3,000 (3.3522) + 10,000 (.4972) – 15,000	NPV = 3,000 (3.3522) – 6,000
NPV = 10,057 + 4972 – 15,000	NPV = 10,057 – 6,000
NPV = 15,029 – 15,000	NPV = $4,057
NPV = $29	

Exhibit 14.13 considers five proposed projects and calculates several possible combinations and their NPVs. In this illustration, projects B and C are considered to be mutually exclusive and only $150,000 is available for capital projects.

The optimum combination is projects A, B, & E, because this yields the highest combined NPV of $60,000. Other feasible combinations result in a lower NPV. In the several combinations where all funds would not be spent on projects, excess funds would be invested at the going interest rate; however, the present value of the return on the excess funds would be the amount invested, thus there would be no related NPV on these excess funds. (This assumes the going interest rate is equal to the discount rate.)

Computerization

Spreadsheet programs on personal computers have automated many of the calculations discussed in this chapter. The internal rate of return, return on investment, and net present value calculations have been simplified into short computer instructions which execute the calculations automatically. For example, using Lotus 1-2-3, the "functions" typed to calculate the three formulas mentioned above are:

Exhibit 14.13   Capital Rationing — Five Proposed Projects

Project	Project Cost	NPV
A	$ 60,000	$30,000
B	70,000	20,000
C	50,000	15,000
D	100,000	40,000
E	20,000	10,000

Combination	Total Investment	Total NPV
A, B, & E	$150,000	$60,000
A, C, & E	130,000	55,000
A & B	130,000	50,000
A & C	110,000	45,000
C & D	150,000	55,000
D & E	120,000	50,000

Internal Rate of Return = @IRR(i, V1 . . .Vn)
  i = Guess at a rate of return
  V1 . . .Vn = Range of cash flows, starting with the first and ending with the last

Net Present Value = @NPV(i, V1 . . .Vn)
  i = Interest rate to be used
  V1 . . .Vn = Range of cash flows, starting with the first and ending with the last

Return on Investment = @NPV(i, V1 . . .Vn)—I
  I = Amount of a single investment
  i = Return on investment rate
  V1 . . .Vn = Range of cash flows, starting with the first and ending with the last

Exhibit 14.14 is an example of how some of these functions could be used. The first section examines two telephone systems by looking at their estimated cash savings due to decreased expenses over the system presently in use. The lower section demonstrates how a spreadsheet can compare various investments. It shows the two options' internal rates of return and states which option should be chosen.

There are two basic advantages to using a spreadsheet program to perform these calculations. First, once the format of the model is set, it can be used repeatedly. This ensures consistency in the evaluation of all projects. The model represents a standard methodology for determining which investments provide the best returns. Second, it is very quick and accurate. The actual calculation by a computer takes only a few seconds and it is correct every time (assuming the formulas and data have been entered correctly). The computer makes for the more efficient use of

Exhibit 14.14 Computer-Generated Telephone Investment Analysis

	Washington Hotel Company Telephone Investment Analysis				
			Year:		
Proposed Telephone System 1 Investment = $70,000 Cash Savings:	**19X1**	**19X2**	**19X3**	**19X4**	**19X5**
Long Distance Charges	$45,000	$46,350	$47,741	$49,173	$50,648
Yearly Maintenance	10,800	11,340	11,907	12,502	13,127
Depreciation	20,000	20,000	20,000	20,000	20,000
Total Pretax Savings	75,800	77,690	79,648	81,675	83,775
Plus Salvage Value					7,300
Net Pretax Cash Savings	75,800	77,690	79,648	81,675	91,075
Less Taxes @ 46%	(34,868)	(35,737)	(36,638)	(37,571)	(41,895)
Net Aftertax Savings	40,932	41,953	43,010	44,105	49,181
Less Depreciation Savings	20,000	20,000	20,000	20,000	20,000
Net Aftertax Cash Flow	$20,932	$21,953	$23,010	$24,105	$29,181
Net Present Value at 12%:	$14,444				
Proposed Telephone System 2 Investment = $75,000 Cost Savings:					
Long Distance Charges	$48,000	$49,440	$50,923	$52,451	$54,024
Yearly Maintenance	8,400	8,820	9,261	9,724	10,210
Depreciation	15,000	15,000	15,000	15,000	15,000
Total Pretax Savings	71,400	73,260	75,184	77,175	79,234
Plus Salvage Value					5,000
Net Pretax Cash Savings	71,400	73,260	75,184	77,175	79,234
Less Taxes @ 46%	(32,844)	(33,700)	(34,585)	(35,501)	(36,448)
Net Aftertax Savings	38,556	39,560	40,599	41,675	42,786
Less Depreciation Savings	15,000	15,000	15,000	15,000	15,000
Net Aftertax Cash Flow	$23,556	$24,560	$25,599	$26,675	$27,786
Net Present Value at 12%:	$16,552				

Net Present Value Information						
Cash Flows:						
Option 1:	($70,000)	$20,932	$21,932	$23,010	$24,105	$29,181
Option 2:	($75,000)	$23,556	$24,560	$25,599	$26,675	$27,786
Internal Rate of Return:						
Option 1:	19.6%		Choose Option:	2		
Option 2:	20.3%					

management time, which should be spent evaluating projects, not calculating numbers.

Summary

Management must carefully consider many necessary additions or changes in fixed assets in order to operate their businesses effectively.

Projects are evaluated based on their costs and corresponding revenues. Projects which generate the most money for the firm should be accepted and the others should be rejected. This process is called capital budgeting.

Capital budgeting is appropriate in a number of decision-making processes. It can be used when purchasing equipment to meet government standards or to replace existing equipment. It is also valuable when considering the purchase of equipment which could either increase the operation's revenues or decrease its costs. In each of these cases, budgeting is performed to determine if the revenues (or cost savings) generated by the equipment are greater than the corresponding expenditures, or to decide which option is the best for the operation. By using capital budgeting models, management takes an active stance to maximize the operation's profits.

Four capital budgeting approaches were examined in this chapter: accounting rate of return, payback, net present value, and internal rate of return. ARR is defined as the average annual project income divided by the average investment. Although it is a simple method, it does have a number of deficiencies and is, therefore, not used frequently. The payback method is also simple and is used more than the ARR in the hospitality industry. It examines the cash flows generated by the equipment and determines the number of years' cash flows required to recover the investment. The NPV approach looks at the cash flows relating to the project and discounts them to their present value. A project with NPV equal to, or greater than, zero is accepted. The final approach discussed, IRR, examines the cash flows to determine the rate of return the investment generates. In other words, it sets the project NPV equal to zero and calculates the discount rate.

The NPV and IRR methods are more complex than the ARR and payback approaches, but they also provide more valuable results. They both examine cash flows and recognize the time value of money. The major difference between the two is that IRR, somewhat unrealistically, assumes that the project cash flows will be reinvested in projects which generate the same return. Thus, when mutually exclusive projects are analyzed, the NPV method is preferred over the IRR.

Discussion Questions

1. What is capital budgeting?

2. What are four situations which might require capital budgeting?

3. Explain the statement "$1 today is worth more than $1 a year from now."

4. Explain how to use the payback method of capital budgeting.

5. Define project cash flow.

6. What are the disadvantages of using the payback method of capital budgeting?

7. How can two mutually exclusive projects with different lengths of lives be analyzed?

8. Explain the accept/reject criterion for the NPV and IRR methods of capital budgeting.

9. Which method of capital budgeting is the most effective? Explain your choice.

10. What is capital rationing?

Problem 14.1

Martice Smith and Associates is considering investing $5,000,000 in a new motel and has predicted the following income stream over its 10-year life.

YEAR	NET INCOME
1	$(245,000)
2	(115,600)
3	18,400
4	276,320
5	455,000
6	1,066,700
7	1,150,000
8	1,069,300
9	1,055,700
10	1,000,250

The motel is expected to have no salvage value at the end of its 10-year life.

Required:

1. Using the ARR method, what is the rate of return for this project?

2. If Martice Smith and Associates requires a 35% return on its investment, should this motel be purchased?

Problem 14.2

Carol Rollins, owner of Carollins, is considering buying an energy efficient oven for her restaurant. However, she is concerned that the cost savings adequately offset the purchase price; she would prefer the project to have no more than a 2.5 year payback period. She is basing her decision on the following information:

PROJECT COST: $23,500
COST SAVINGS:

	Years				
	1	2	3	4	5
Energy	$2,000	$2,500	$3,000	$3,000	$3,000
Maintenance	3,000	3,000	2,000	1,000	1,000
TOTAL	$5,000	$5,500	$5,000	$4,000	$4,000

Required:

1. Determine if Ms. Rollins should invest in this oven.

2. If there was an estimated cash savings of $4,500 for each year, would this oven be purchased, based on the payback criterion?

Problem 14.3

Susie Reed, the owner of the Wild Life, an amusement park, is contemplating purchasing a new roller coaster/water combination ride for $1,500,000. She has determined that it would increase park revenues by $300,000 a year because of its originality, but it will cost approximately $70,000 a year to operate.
Assume a 15% discount rate and a 10-year life for the equipment.

Required:

1. Use the NPV model to determine if the equipment should be purchased.

Problem 14.4

The Jonathan Club is considering adding pizza to its menu. However, a conveyor oven will have to be purchased which will cost $20,000. It has an estimated 7-year life and Jon Jones, the manager, has determined that the club could sell approximately $50,000 worth of pizzas each year with a food cost of 35%, labor cost of 30% and other negligible operating costs. At the end of 7 years the conveyor oven should be able to bring $2,000 at an auction.

Required:

1. If the club requires a 15% return on investment, use the IRR method to determine if the machine should be purchased.

Problem 14.5

Jason and Jamie Hills, owners of the Hills Hotel, are considering upgrading their front office equipment by purchasing a new front office machine. The _annual_ operating costs for front office machines are as follows:

COST	PRESENT MACHINE	PROPOSED MACHINE
Labor	$15,000	$12,000
Maintenance	500	200
Utilities	500	600
Insurance	60	100

The present machine has a present market value of $3,000 and will be useful for the next five years, but be worth $-0- at the end of five years. The proposed machine will cost $15,000.

To simplify the problem, assume both machines would be depreciated by using the straight-line method of depreciation. Assume a discount rate of 12% and a tax rate of 30%. Further, assume the proposed machine will be worth $5,000 at the end of year five.

Required:

1. Using the NPV model, should the new machine be purchased? (Show all your work!)

15 Lease Accounting

Acquiring the right to use equipment, buildings, or land without ownership is achieved by leasing. Leasing is often a means of acquiring the use of resources when purchase is not possible or desirable. A food service chain may lease space for a restaurant in a shopping mall since that space is not for sale. Equipment may be leased for even a single day by a hotel for a special function. Numerous other examples of leasing could be provided. This chapter will address several questions regarding lease accounting, such as:

1.   What are the advantages and disadvantages of leasing resources?

2.   What are executory costs in relation to leases?

3.   How are leases classified for accounting purposes?

4.   What are criteria for capitalizing leases?

5.   How are leasehold improvements amortized?

6.   What is a triple-net lease?

7.   What is meant by a firm's incremental interest rate?

8.   What is a sale and leaseback?

9.   How are ratios affected by the accounting for leases?

10.   What are several common provisions of lease agreements?

In this chapter, we will first consider the various uses of leases in the hospitality industry and discuss some of their advantages and disadvantages, as well as some provisions commonly found in all leases. We will focus on the differences between operating leases and capital leases and present guidelines for accounting for the different types of leasing arrangements. Finally, we will investigate the effects leases may have on a hospitality operation's financial statements and financial ratios.

Leases and Their Uses

A lease is simply defined as an agreement conveying the right to use resources (equipment, buildings, and/or land) for specified purposes and limited periods of time. From an operational perspective, the equipment is available for use, and operating personnel generally have little concern whether it was purchased or leased. Lease agreements govern the parties to the lease and contain several provisions to be covered later in this chapter. The two parties to most leases are the lessor and the lessee. The lessor owns the property and conveys the right of its use to the lessee in exchange for periodic cash payments called rent.

Leasing is popular with businesses in general in the United States, and with the hospitality industry in particular. Restaurants lease space in shopping malls, lodging companies lease hotels, and gambling casinos lease slot machines, just to mention a few leasing situations.

Historically, several hotel companies have leased many of their hotels. A common lease arrangement by Holiday Corporation during the 1950s and 1960s was the variable lease which resulted in Holiday Corporation (lessee) paying the lessors a percentage of rooms revenue, food revenue, and beverage revenue. For example, a 25-5-5 lease resulted in the lessee paying the lessor 25% of rooms revenue, 5% of food revenue, and 5% of beverage revenue. Since these rental payments were based on revenues, most of the financial risk of the hotel property was shouldered by the lodging operation itself. All other operational expenses are paid by the lessee prior to any profit generation.

Leasing of hotels, quite popular in the 1950s and 1960s, is less popular today. In the 1980s, few hotels have signed new leases; instead, they manage hotels under a "management contract" arrangement. These contracts often result in substantial payments to hotel companies from gross revenues similar to what hotel companies paid lessors for leased properties.[1]

In part, the extent of the leasing by hotel and food service companies is revealed in footnotes to their annual financial statements. Holiday Corporation in its 1984 annual financial statements, reported rental expenses for 1984 for all its leases to be $59,716,000. (Its total revenues for 1984 were $1,759,818,000.) Marriott Corporation revealed 1985 rent expense of $103,700,000 in its 1985 Annual Report. In addition, it also showed payments to owners of leased and managed hotels of $283,100,000. Total Marriott sales in 1985 exceeded $4.2 billion. The lease footnote from Marriott's 1985 Annual Report is shown in Exhibit 15.1

Advantages and Disadvantages of Leases

There are several advantages and disadvantages to leasing. First, several advantages will be presented, followed by some disadvantages.

- Leasing conserves working capital, because little or no cash is generally deposited to lease property, while cash equal to 20-40% of the purchase price is required when purchasing property. Therefore, for the cash-strapped operation, leasing may be the only reasonable way of "obtaining" the desired property.

- Leasing often involves less red tape than acquiring the property through external financing. Although a lease agreement must be prepared, it usually is less involved than the numerous documents required in a purchase, especially when financing is required.

- Leasing permits quicker changes in equipment, especially when equipment becomes functionally obsolete due to technological innovations. However, the lessee can not expect this ability to be cost free. The greater the probability of technological obsoles-

Exhibit 15.1   Leases Footnote — Marriott Corporation

LEASES

Minimum future rentals under non-cancelable leases (primarily real estate and shopping center space), including leases on Howard Johnson Company units which have been identified for disposition, are (in millions):

Fiscal Year	Capital Leases	Operating Leases
1986	$ 17.4	$ 72.1
1987	16.6	68.7
1988	15.8	63.6
1989	14.9	58.5
1990	13.3	53.5
Thereafter	83.4	350.8
Total minimum lease payments	161.4	$667.2
Amount representing interest	(73.0)	
Present value of minimum lease payments	88.4	
Current portion of capital lease obligations	(10.1)	
Long-term capital lease obligations	$ 78.3	

These future rentals have not been reduced by minimum sublease rentals of $114.6 million payable to the company under non-cancelable subleases.

Most leases contain one or more renewal options, generally for five or 10-year periods.

Rent expense consists of:

	1985	1984	1983
	(in millions)		
Minimum rentals in operating leases	$ 61.9	$ 52.2	$ 50.4
Additional rentals based on sales			
—operating leases	40.4	35.9	29.0
—capital leases	1.4	1.7	2.5
	$103.7	$ 89.8	$ 81.9
Payments to owners of leased and managed hotels	$283.1	$233.6	$182.7

Source: Marriott Corporation *Annual Report* 1985.

cence, the greater the lease payment, all other things being the same.

● Leasing allows the lessee to receive tax benefits which otherwise may not be available. For example, an unprofitable operation may not be able to use tax credits available to purchasers of certain qualifying equipment. However, a lessor, who can use the tax credits in a competitive environment, will pass on part of the tax credit in the form of lower rental payments to the lessee.

● Leasing generally places less restrictive contracts on the lessee than financial institutions often place on long-term borrowers to finance property purchases.

- Leasing has less impact on financial ratios, especially when the leases are not capitalized. Property acquired for use through operational leases is not shown on the balance sheet nor are the future rent obligations, although some footnote disclosure may be required. For this reason, leases are often referred to as off-balance-sheet-financing.

- Operating leases may result in obtaining resources without following a capital budget.

Therefore, in several cases, leasing may be a lower overall cost alternative for many hospitality operations. However, there are also disadvantages to leasing, such as:

- Any residual value of the leased property benefits the lessor unless the lessee has the opportunity to acquire the leased property at the end of the lease.

- The cost of leasing in some situations is higher than purchasing. This is especially true when there are only a limited number of lessors, and the economic situation is less than competitive. An operation may be saddled with extended payments for equipment which becomes dysfunctional or obsolete.

- Disposal of a financial lease before the end of the lease period often results in additional costs. These additional costs are not present if the property is owned.

This discussion of advantages and disadvantages of leasing is not exhaustive but only provides several of the major advantages and disadvantages. The student interested in pursuing this topic in greater detail is encouraged to read books devoted entirely to leasing.[2]

Provisions of Lease Contracts

Each lease results from negotiations between the lessor and lessee. As a result, the specific needs of each party are met—resulting in a unique document. However, all lease contracts normally contain several provisions such as the following:

1. Term of lease—The term of a lease may be as short as a few hours for renting a piece of equipment to as long as several decades as is common with real estate.

2. Purpose of lease—The stated purpose generally limits the lessee to using the property for limited purposes. For example, a restaurant lease may state "the lessee shall use the leased premises as a restaurant and for no other purpose without first having obtained the written consent of the lessor to any other purpose."

3. Rental payments—The lease specifies the rent payment, its frequency, when it is due, and any adjustments. For example, adjustments for inflation are often based on the consumer price index for a given city. Any contingent rent is also specified. For example, a lease may stipulate that contingent rent equal to 3% of all annual food and beverage sales in excess of $700,000 is due the 15th day of the first month after the end of the fiscal year per the lease.

4. Renewal options—Many leases contain a clause allowing the lessee the option to renew the lease for additional time periods. For example, a lease may state "an option to renew this lease for an additional five-year period on the expiration of the leasing term upon giving lessor a 90-day notice in writing prior to the expiration of the lease."

5. Obligations for property taxes, insurance, and maintenance (executory costs)—Leases, especially long-term leases, specify who shall pay the property taxes, insurance, and maintenance on the leased property. A lease in which the lessee is obligated to pay property taxes, insurance, and maintenance is commonly called a triple-net lease.

6. Other provisions include:

    - Right of lessor to inspect lessee's books, especially when part of the lease payment is tied to sales or some other operational figure.

    - Lessor's obligations to restore facilities damaged by fire, tornadoes, and similar "acts of nature."

    - Lessee's opportunity to sublease the leased property.

    - Lessee's opportunity to make payments lessor is responsible for, such as principal and interest payments to preclude default on lessor's financing of the leased property.

    - Security deposits, if any, required of the lessee.

    - Indemnity clauses protecting the lessor.

    - Investment tax credit, when appropriate.

The appendix to this chapter contains a sample lease which is included only as an example and is not intended to be representative of hotel leases. However, the reader, upon careful study, will note that the lease contains several of the above mentioned provisions.

Lease Accounting   Historically, leases were accounted for simply as executory contracts, that is, the rental expense was generally recognized with the passage of time. Leases were not capitalized as assets, nor were liabilities recognized for the lessee's obligations under lease contracts. However, as leases became more sophisticated, and since the economic substance of many lease transactions was the same as a sale/purchase transaction, many accountants have argued for a change in lease accounting.

The Accounting Principles Board, the past accounting rule-making body, issued four opinions regarding lease accounting. The Financial Accounting Standards Board (FASB), the present rule-making body, has issued eight statements relating to lease accounting. A major result of these rules is that many long-term leases are capitalized, that is, they are recorded as fixed assets.

Most of the remainder of this chapter contains guidelines for accounting for leases by lessees. Accounting for leases by lessors is beyond the scope of this text. Our discussion is meant to cover major elements of lease accounting and is certainly not exhaustive. The student interested in the study of accounting for leases beyond the coverage in this text should consult an intermediate accounting text and/or FASB statements.[3]

Classification of Leases

In general, leases are classified by lessees for accounting purposes as either operating leases or as capital leases. At the extremes, operating leases differ substantially from capital leases. Operating leases are normally, but not always, of relatively short duration, and the lessor retains the responsibility for executory costs, that is, paying property taxes, insuring, and maintaining the property. They can be cancelled rather painlessly. On the other hand, capital leases are of relatively long duration, and the lessee often assumes responsibility for property taxes, insurance, and maintenance. In addition, they are generally noncancellable, or at least fairly costly to cancel. However, problems arise regarding leases which are not at these extremes. For accounting purposes, whether a lease is an operating lease or a capital lease determines the accounting for the lease. Capital leases are capitalized, that is, the lease is recorded as an asset with recognition of a liability, while operating leases are not capitalized, but the lease payment is generally recorded as rent expense.

The FASB established four capitalization criteria for reviewing noncancellable leases. If any one of the four criteria are met, the lessee must classify and account for the lease as a capital lease. The criteria are as follows:

1. The property is transferred to the lessee by the end of the lease term, hereafter referred to as "title transfer provision."

2. The lease contains a bargain purchase option, hereafter referred to as "bargain purchase provision."

3. The lease term is equal to 75% or more of the estimated economic life of the leased property, hereafter referred to as "economic life provision."

4. The present value of minimum lease payments (excluding executory costs) equals or exceeds 90% of the excess of fair market value of the leased property over any investment tax credit retained by the lessor, hereafter referred to as "value recovery provision."

Leases not meeting any of the four criteria are accounted for by lessees as operating leases which will be explained in the following section of this chapter. Prior to the discussion of accounting for operating leases, several terms used in the four capitalization criteria should be explained.

In the bargain purchase provision, a bargain purchase means the purchase price at the end of the lease is substantially less than the leased property's expected market value at the date the option is to be exercised. The bargain price is generally considered to be substantially less only if the difference, for all practical purposes, ensures that the bargain purchase option will be exercised.

The "economic life" term contained in the economic life provision refers to the useful life of the leased property. Several terms in the value recovery provision requiring explanation are as follows:

- Present value—refers to determining present value as discussed in the prior chapter on Capital Budgeting.

- Minimum lease payments—consist of minimum rental payments during the lease term and any bargain purchase option. If no bargain purchase option exists, the minimum lease payments include any guarantee of residual value by the lessee or any amount payable by the lessee for failure to renew the lease. Minimum lease payments do not include contingent rent such as a percentage of sales since the rental payment is contingent on sales.

- Executory costs—are also excluded in determining minimum rental payments when the lease specifies that the lease payments include these costs. As mentioned before, executory costs include property taxes, insurance, and maintenance costs related to the leased item.

- Fair market value—represents the amount the leased item would cost if it was purchased rather than leased.

- Investment tax credit—is a credit which the federal government allows against the federal income tax liability of the hospitality operation. Generally, up to 10% of the cost of qualifying equipment can be taken as a credit. In general, it applies only to personal property, such as equipment, as compared to real property, such as land and buildings.

- Residual value—refers to the estimated market value of the leased item at the end of the lease term. When the residual value is guaranteed by the lessee, then the lessee is ultimately liable to the lessor for the residual value.

Accounting for Operating Leases

Operating leases are accounted for as simple rental agreements, that is, expense is generally recognized when the rent is paid. For example, if a restaurant company leases space in a shopping mall for $5,000 per month and pays rent on the first day of each month, the monthly rental payment would be recorded as follows:

Rent Expense	$5000	
Cash		$5000

When rent is paid in advance, it should be recorded in a prepaid rent account. For example, if the restaurant company had paid three months' rent in advance, the proper entry would be as follows:

Rent Expense	$5000	
Prepaid Rent	10000	
Cash		$15000

This accounting entry recognizes rent expense for the current month and delays recognition (based on the matching principle as discussed in Chapter 1) of rent for the following two months. In the event rent is paid for a period beyond twelve months from the balance sheet date, the rental payment should be recorded as "Deferred Rent" and shown as a deferred charge on the balance sheet. Any rent paid for future periods is recognized during the period it relates to by an adjusting entry. For example, in the restaurant company illustration above, the adjusting entry to recognize the second month's rent would be as follows:

Rent Expense	$5000	
Prepaid Rent		$5000

Accounting for Capital Leases

Capital leases are similar to a purchase of a fixed asset; therefore, the accounting for capital leases recognizes an asset and applicable liabilities. The amount to be recorded as an asset and a liability is the present value of future minimum lease payments as defined previously. The lease payments are discounted using the lessee's incremental borrowing rate, or, if known, the lessor's implicit rate of interest in the lease, but only if this is lower than the lessee's incremental borrowing rate. Generally, the former is used, because the lessee does not know the lessor's implicit interest rate in the lease. The lessee's incremental borrowing rate is the rate of interest the lessee would have to pay if he or she were financing the purchase of the item to be leased. When leases are capitalized, they are recorded for an amount equal to the present value of the minimum lease payments.

Any executory costs included with the lease payments must be excluded in determining the present value of minimum lease payments, while a bargain purchase option or a lessee's guaranteed residual value must be included. For example, a lease agreement may require a monthly payment of $1,000 of which $200 is for maintenance. This $200 for maintenance is excluded in determining the present value of minimum lease payments. On the other hand, if the lessee guarantees a residual value of $2,000 for the lease, the present value of $2,000 should be included in determining the present value of minimum lease payments.

When subsequent lease payments are made by the lessee, the lease obligation is reduced by the difference between the lease payment, excluding executory costs, and the interest on the lease obligation. The interest is calculated by using the effective interest method which results in a constant rate of interest throughout the lease term. This is accomplished by multiplying the interest rate used in discounting the minimum lease payments by the lease obligation for the lease period. For example, assume a lease payment is $5,000 for the month, including $500 for property taxes, and the lease obligation for the period is $480,000. Further, assume the lessee's incremental borrowing rate is 10%. The entry to record the lease payment is as follows:

Property tax expense	$500	
Interest expense	4000	
Lease obligations	500	
Cash		$5000

The interest expense of $4,000 is determined as follows:

$$I = \text{Lease Obligation} \times \text{Incremental Borrowing Rate} \times \text{Time}$$

$$I = 480,000 \times .10 \times \frac{1}{12}$$

$$I = \underline{\underline{\$4,000}}$$

Therefore, the lease obligation is debited by $500 which is determined as follows:

$$\text{Reduction in Lease Obligation} = \text{Lease Payment} - \text{Executory Costs} - \text{Interest Expense}$$

$$= 5,000 - 500 - 4,000$$

$$= \underline{\underline{\$500}}$$

Illustration of Accounting for Capital Leases

The Chambers Hotel signs a lease agreement with a major computer manufacturer to use a front office computer for a five-year period beginning January 1, 19X1. Provisions of the lease agreement and other relevant facts for classifying the lease are as follows:

1. The term of the lease is 5 years commencing on January 1, 19X1. The lease is noncancellable.

2. Annual payments of $55,000 are due at the beginning of each year for five years.

3. The leased computer has a fair market value at January 1, 19X1, of $200,000.

4. The estimated economic life of the leased equipment is seven years, and there is no expected residual value.

5. Chambers Hotel is to pay directly all executory costs except for annual maintenance of $10,000 which is included in the annual lease payments.

6. The lease contains no renewal options, bargain purchase options, and the equipment reverts to the lessor at the end of the lease.

7. Chambers Hotel's incremental borrowing rate is 12%.

8. Chambers Hotel depreciates its own computer equipment on a straight-line basis.

9. The lessor's implicit rate of return on leasing the computer to Chambers Hotel is unknown.

10. Assume that tax credits do not exist.

The Chambers Hotel must determine whether the lease should be capitalized by comparing the lease provisions to the FASB lease capitalization rules. If any one of the four rules is met, then the lease is to be capitalized. Exhibit 15.2 contains the comparison of the lease provisions to the FASB rules and, on the basis of rule #4, the lease should be capitalized as the present value of lease payments, excluding executory

Exhibit 15.2 FASB Lease Capitalization Criteria

<table>
<tr><td colspan="3" align="center">**FASB Lease Capitalization Criteria
and the lease of computer equipment
by the Chambers Hotel**</td></tr>
<tr><td align="center">**Lease Capitalization
Criteria**</td><td align="center">**Computer Lease
Provisions**</td><td align="center">**Capitalize
Yes/No**</td></tr>
<tr><td>1. Title transfer provision</td><td>Item 6 states the "equipment reverts
to the lessor at the end of the lease."</td><td align="center">No</td></tr>
<tr><td>2. Bargain purchase provision</td><td>Item 6 states the lease contains no
bargain purchase options</td><td align="center">No</td></tr>
<tr><td>3. Economic life provision</td><td>Life of lease
Useful life of equipment =
5/7 = 71.4%; 71.4% < 75%</td><td align="center">No</td></tr>
<tr><td>4. Value recovery provision</td><td>45,000 (4.0373) =
200,000 (.9) =
excess of PV of lease payments over
90% of FMV is</td><td>$181,678
(180,000)

$1,678</td></tr>
</table>

<table>
<tr><td></td><td align="right">Yes</td></tr>
</table>

costs, exceeds 90% of the fair market value of the leased equipment. The present value of the five lease payments is calculated in Exhibit 15.3.

The present value of the five lease payments is greater than 90% of the fair market value of the leased equipment as calculated below:

Fair market value of leased equipment	$200,000
90% factor	x .9
	180,000
Present value of lease payments	181,678
Excess of lease payments	$1,678

The journal entry to record the capitalization of the leased equipment accompanied by the first payment of $55,000 is as follows:

Leased equipment under capital leases	$181678	
Prepaid maintenance	10000	
Cash		$55000
Obligations under capital leases		136678

This single entry consists of the capitalization of the lease at $181,678, the recognition of the related liability at $136,678, and the initial payment for $55,000, of which $10,000 relates to maintenance and the remaining $45,000 to the lease. Alternatively, the single entry could have been recognized in two parts as follows:

**Exhibit 15.3 Present Value of Five Lease Payments —
Chambers Hotel**

Annual lease payments	$ 55,000
Less: Amount for executory costs	10,000
Net lease payment	45,000
Present value of an annuity of 1 for 5 years at 12%	
Plus: Present value factor for initial payment 3.0373 +	
1.0000	x 4.0373
	$181,678

(1) Capitalization of lease

Leased equipment under capital leases	$181678	
Obligations under capital leases		$181678

(2) Lease payment

Obligations under capital leases	$45000	
Prepaid maintenance	10000	
Cash		$55000

The prepaid maintenance would be written off throughout the year to maintenance expense by a monthly entry of:

Maintenance expense	$833	
Prepaid maintenance		$833

Future payments will result in the recognition of interest expense, the reduction of the obligation under capital leases, and prepayment of maintenance for the next year. In practice, at year-end (December 31, 19X1), interest expense would be accrued by debiting interest expense by $16,401 and crediting accrued interest by $16,401 because of the matching principle.

The Chambers Hotel would record its second lease payment on January 1, 19X2 as follows:

Interest expense	$16401	
Obligations under capital leases	28599	
Prepaid maintenance	10000	
Cash		$55000

The interest expense of $16,401 results from multiplying the $136,678, recorded as "Obligations under capital leases" throughout the year, by the Chambers Hotel's incremental borrowing rate of 12% as follows:

$$\$136,678 \times .12 = \underline{\$16,401}$$

The reduction in the liability, "Obligations under capital leases" of $28,599 is the difference between *net* lease payment of $45,000 and the interest expense of $16,401.

The leased equipment should be depreciated over its lease term of five years. The entry for depreciation expense (based on straight-line) on an annual basis would be as follows:

Depreciation expense	$36336
Accumulated depreciation—capital leases	$36336

This entry assumes a zero salvage value as the equipment reverts back to the lessor at the end of the lease term.

At the end of the five-year term, the leased equipment is returned to the lessor and the two accounts "Leased equipment under capital leases" and "Accumulated depreciation—capital leases", each at $181,678, are reduced to zero as follows:

Accumulated depreciation—capital leases	$181678
Leased equipment under capital leases	$181678

Throughout the five-year period, the following expenses related to the leased item, and specifically this lease, were incurred:

Maintenance—$10,000/year	$50,000
Depreciation—the capitalized cost of the lease	181,678
Interest expense—the sum of the five net lease payments less the capitalized cost of the lease: 225,000 − 181,678	43,322
Total Expense	$275,000

Notice the total expense equals the five annual payments of $55,000 ($55,000 x 5 = $275,000).

Leasehold Improvements

Buildings which are leased for several years, such as restaurants in shopping malls, often require extensive "improvements" prior to the commencement of operations. Often the space leased is not capitalized, since none of the four capitalization criteria are met; however, any improvements to the space should be capitalized as "leasehold improvements." For example, the cost of walls, ceilings, carpeting, and lighting installed in leased space is capitalized. The leasehold improvement is recognized as an intangible asset, and the cost should be amortized against revenue over the lesser of the life of the lease or the life of the leasehold improvement. For example, assume the Chambers Hotel leased three acres of adjoining land for parking facilities and the land was improved by adding storm sewers, sidewalks, lighting, pavement, etc., at the cost of $200,000. Assume the life of the improvement is 10 years while the land was leased for 30 years. The *annual* amortization of the leasehold improvement would be 1/10 of the cost—$20,000 per year for 10 years. This expense is generally recognized monthly (1/12 of annual amortization) as follows:

Amortization of leasehold improvement	$1667	
Leasehold improvement		$1667

Sale and Leasebacks

Sale and leasebacks are transactions whereby an owner of real estate agrees with an investor to sell the real estate to the investor and simultaneously lease it back for a future period of time. Therefore, the use of the property continues without interruption.

The major reason for sale and leaseback transactions is to raise capital which previously was tied up in the property. The investors in these transactions generally are simply looking for a financial return, as they have no interest in managing hospitality operations. In the case of insurance companies, many state laws preclude them from operating other businesses; however, the sale and leaseback arrangements allow insurance companies as investors to partially reap the benefits of the hospitality industry by investing in appreciating properties.

In a sale and leaseback transaction, the property is sold to the investor (lessor) at market value, and then it is leased back to the seller (lessee) for an amount equal to the investor's cost plus a reasonable return.

From the lessee's perspective, the lease should be accounted for based on the four criteria for classification of leases as discussed previously. If profit is experienced by the seller (lessee) from the sale of the now leased assets, such profit should generally be deferred and amortized over the lease term, while losses should normally be recognized in their entirety when the sale and leaseback agreement is signed. The student interested in more detailed discussion of this topic is encouraged to consult an intermediate accounting text.

Leases and Their Effect on Financial Ratios

Whether a leased item is accounted for as a capital lease or as an operating lease can have a major impact on the financial statements, especially the balance sheet. Therefore, several financial ratios are also affected. Property leased under an operating lease is not shown on the balance sheet, while property leased under a capital lease is reflected on the balance sheet. The balance sheet disclosure of capital leases includes both assets and liabilities. Therefore, most financial ratios involving noncurrent assets and long-term liabilities are affected by how leases are accounted for. In general, because of the negative impact on ratios of leases accounted for as capital leases, hospitality operations desire to treat leased property as operating leases whenever possible. Four financial ratios affected by capitalizing leases are shown in Exhibit 15.4.

The effect of treating leased property as operating leases is generally to reduce these ratios, that is, the ratios suggest a less desirable situation than if the leases had been accounted for as operating leases. Thus, it

Exhibit 15.4   Financial Ratios Most Affected by Lease Accounting

Ratio	Ratio Formula	How lease accounted for as capital lease affects ratio
1. Asset turnover	revenue ÷ average total assets	Capitalizing leases results in increasing the average total assets, therefore reducing the asset turnover ratio.
2. Return on assets	net income ÷ average total assets	(Same as for asset turnover)
3. Debt-equity ratio	total debt ÷ total equity	Capitalizing leases results in increasing the total debt, therefore increasing the debt-equity ratio when it is greater than 1
4. Number of times interest earned ratio	earnings before interest and taxes ÷ interest expense	Capitalizing leases results in increased interest expenses, therefore this ratio is generally reduced.

should not be surprising that many hospitality operations prefer not to capitalize leases and, in fact, may negotiate lease provisions so that the lease does not qualify as a capital lease under any of the four capitalization criteria established by the FASB.

Summary

Leasing is a special type of financing utilized by many hospitality businesses. By entering into this agreement, the lessee has the right to use specific resources for a limited period of time for a specific purpose. The advantages for the lessee include the conservation of working capital, the benefits of tax deductions which might otherwise not be available, and, in some cases, a favorable effect on the balance sheet ratios. In exchange for these advantages, the lessee must make some sacrifices. In many instances, the residual value of the property remains with the lessee, there may be substantial penalties for termination of the lease contract, and the cost of leasing may be higher than if the leased item is purchased. It is up to the operator contemplating a lease arrangement to weigh the advantages and disadvantages before entering into the contract; in many cases in the hospitality industry, the lease contract proves advantageous.

There are many aspects common to most leases. Provisions contained in most lease contracts include the length and purpose of the contract, the specific rent payments, any obligations of the lessee, and renewal options.

When deciding between leasing or purchasing an asset, many businesses consider how the agreement will affect the financial statements. Depending upon the terms of the lease, it will either be capitalized (be recorded on the balance sheet as an asset and liability) or be treated as an operational lease (be expensed as the payments are made). If capitalized, the assets and liabilities increase, and the net income should also increase in order to maintain a constant return on assets. Some managers avoid capital leases because of this type of effect.

In addition to accounting for the initial lease, any leasehold improvements must be recorded and subsequently amortized over the shorter of the life of the lease or the improvement.

All of the variations to the lease agreement must be studied by management before any contract is signed. Establishments judged solely on their operation ratios will probably be more interested in whether or not a lease is capitalized. Other establishments will value the difference between the total lease payments and the benefits of having a present cash flow. The final decision must be made by management. Historically, leases have been a popular way to finance assets, and the trend indicates that leases will continue as viable means of hospitality financing, especially for equipment.

Notes

1. The reader interested in studying management contracts is referred to James J. Eyster's *The Negotiation and Administration of Hotel Management Contracts*, 2nd Edition, Cornell University, 1981.
2. Two books on the topic of leasing are: Pietrat Elgers and John J. Clark, *The Lease-Buy Decision* (New York: The Free Press, 1980); T. M. Clarke, *Leasing* (London: McGraw-Hill Book Company, 1978).
3. Consider Jay M. Smith, Jr. and K. Fred Skouser's *Intermediate Accounting*, 7th Edition (Cincinnati: South-Wester Publishing Co., 1981) or Donald E. Keiso and Jerry J. Weygandt, *Intermediate Accounting* (New York: John Wiley & Sons, 1983). Also, *Accounting for Leases* (Stamford, Conn.: Financial Accounting Standards Board, 1980)—which contains FASB statements 13, 17, 22, 23, 26, 27, 28, and 29, and related interpretations 19, 21, 23, 24, 26, and 27.

Discussion Questions

1. What are three major advantages of lease financing to the lessee?

2. What are some provisions common to most leases?

3. What are the FASB's four criteria used to determine if a lease is a capital or operating lease?

4. Assume a hotel operation enters into a capital lease agreement. What effect will it have on the debt to equity ratio?

5. What major effects do capital leases, as compared to operating leases, have on an operation's balance sheet?

6. What are leasehold improvements?

7. What is a sale and leaseback agreement?

8. What are lease executory costs and how do they influence the determination of whether a lessee should capitalize a lease?

9. How may investment tax credit influence the capitalization of a lease?

10. At what value is a capitalized lease recorded?

Problem 15.1

Jimmy Ko, proprietor of Jimmy's Place, has recently leased a computer which does not meet any of the accounting requirements specified by the FASB for capitalizing the lease. The three-year lease contract requires Jimmy to make an original payment of $4,000 on July 1, 19X1 for the first and last month's rent expense of $2,000 each.

On August 1, 19X1, Jimmy is required to make the next month's payment of $2,000. Jimmy's Place maintains its books on a strict accrual accounting basis.

Required:

1. Prepare the journal entry to record the original payment for July 1, 19X1.

2. Prepare the adjusting journal entry for July 31, 19X1.

3. What is the proper journal entry to record the August 1, 19X1 payment?

Problem 15.2

Bob and Audrey Read are the owners/operators of Resort Kove, a small hotel in central Ohio. On July 1, 19X1, they entered into a lease arrangement with Larose Leasing for a wide screen TV for the beverage operation. The lease provides for the equipment to become the property of Resort Kove at the end of the five-year lease period. The lease payments are $4,161 annually payable at the beginning of each year. Assume that the Read's average rate of borrowing is 10% while their incremental rate is 12%. The first year's payment is made on July 1, 19X1.

Required:

1. Prepare the journal entry to record the capitalization of the lease and the first lease payment.

2. Prepare the journal entry for July 1, 19X2, to record the second annual payment.

Problem 15.3

Brian's Bungalow on January 1, 19X1, leased a 100-room motel property for 25 years. The estimated life of the property is 35 years. The lease of the motel is not capitalized since it does not meet any of the FASB's requirements. A posting machine was leased on July 1, 19X2, for a five-year period. The machine's life is 7 years, and the property reverts to lessor at the end of 5 years. The cost of the posting machine, if purchased, would be $6,000; annual lease payments are $1,525 payable at the beginning of each year. Brian's has an incremental borrowing rate of 12% and the present value of $1 for 4 periods is 3.0373.

The rooms are to be renovated effective July 1, 19X2, at a cost of $2,000 per room. The life of the renovation is estimated at 30 years.

Required:

1. Should the lease of the posting machine be capitalized? If so, at what amount?

2. Should the renovation be capitalized? If so, at what amount?

3. If the renovation is capitalized, what is the annual amortization?

Problem 15.4

The Irish Inn is contemplating the purchase or the lease of a new dryer. Tip O'Reilly, owner of the Irish Inn, believes that the lease would not be capitalized and thus his financial ratios would not be adversely affected by the lease. He has asked you to examine the proposed arrangement which is as follows:

Term of Lease:	5 years
Est. life of dryer:	8 years
Average cost of debt:	11%
Incremental cost of debt:	12%
Lease payments due:	
—1st payment due at signing of lease (January 1, 19X1)	
—next 4 payments annually beginning at January 1, 19X2	
Annual lease payment amounts:	$1,000
First lease payment amount:	$1,000
Investment tax credit (ITC):	10%
ITC retained by:	lessor
Fair market value:	$4,500
Option to buy at the end of lease:	no option
Will the dryer be given to the lessee at the end of the lease term?	no

Required:

1. Is the owner correct in his belief? (Show all your work in arriving at your decision!)

2. What is the present value of the lease payment stream?

3. Prepare the journal entry to record the lease *assuming it will be capitalized.*

4. What is the amount of interest for 19X1?

5. What is the amount of interest over the life of the lease (19X1-19X5)?

Problem 15.5

The King's Inn's financial situation at the end of 19X3 and 19X4 is summarized as follows:

	19X3	19X4
Total property and equipment (fixed assets)	$5,800,000	$6,000,000
Total assets	$6,500,000	$6,750,000
Interest expense (for the year)	$600,000	$625,000
Income taxes (for the year)	$400,000	$420,000
Net income (for the year)	$500,000	$550,000

On January 1, the King's Inn leased adjoining sporting facilities for its guests' use. The lease was negotiated so that the lease was not capitalized since none of the capitalization criteria were met. However, if they had been met, the above accounts would have been affected at the end of 19X4 as follows:

Total property and equipment—increased by—$850,000
Total assets—increased by—$850,000
Interest expense for 19X4—increased by—$100,000

Note: income taxes and net income would not be affected as rent expense (for operating leases) and would equal the depreciation and interest expense (for the capitalized lease).

Required:

1. Calculate the following ratios given the King's Inn did *not* capitalize the lease of the sporting facilities:

    1. Return on fixed assets
    2. Return on total assets
    3. Number of times interest earned

2. Calculate the same ratios (part 1) for the King's Inn assuming the lease was capitalized.

3. Based on your calculations, was the King's Inn wise in negotiating an operating lease? Why?

Appendix
Sample Lease

Lease Intended for Security

This LEASE INTENDED FOR SECURITY ("Lease") dated as of _____, is between _____ a Delaware corporation, with its principal office at _____ ("Lessor") and _____, a _____, with its principal office at _____ ("Lessee").

Lessor agrees to acquire and to lease and to sell to Lessee and Lessee agrees to hire and purchase from Lessor certain personal property (the "Units" and individually a "Unit") described in the Schedule (the "Schedule") attached hereto and made a part hereof, upon the terms and conditions hereinafter set forth:

Section 1.   Procurement, Delivery and Acceptance.

1.1   Lessee has ordered or shall order the Units pursuant to one or more purchase orders or other contracts of sale ("Purchase Agreements" and individually a "Purchase Agreement") from one or more vendors ("Vendors" and individually a "Vendor"). Prior to the earlier of the time that title to any Unit has been transferred by the applicable Vendor or the "Delivery Date" (as hereinafter defined) Lessee shall assign to Lessor all the right, title and interest of Lessee in and to the applicable Purchase Agreement insofar as it relates to such Unit by execution and delivery to Lessor of a Purchase Agreement Assignment substantially in the form of Exhibit A hereto. The Delivery Date of each Unit shall be the date on which the Unit is first placed in service by Lessee. Lessor agrees to accept the assignment and, subject to the conditions of Section 1.2, assume the obligations of Lessee under the Purchase Agreement to purchase and pay for such Unit, but no other duties or obligations of Lessee thereunder; provided, however, that Lessee shall remain liable to Vendor in respect of its duties and obligations in accordance with the Purchase Agreement. Lessee represents and warrants in connection with the assignment of any Purchase Agreement that (a) Lessee has the right to assign the Purchase Agreement as set forth herein, (b) the right, title and interest of Lessee in the Purchase Agreement so assigned shall be free

from all claims, liens, security interests and encumbrances, (c) Lessee will warrant and defend the assignment against lawful claims and demands of all persons and (d) the Purchase Agreement contains no conditions under which Vendor may reclaim title to any Unit after delivery, acceptance and payment therefor.

1.2 The obligation of Lessor to pay for each Unit is subject to the following conditions:

(a)   Lessee shall have accepted such Unit on the Delivery Date thereof;

(b)   the Delivery Date for such Unit shall be during the Utilization Period set forth in the Schedule; and

(c)   there shall exist, as of the Delivery Date of such Unit no Event of Default nor any event which with notice or lapse of time or both, would become an Event of Default.

If any of the foregoing conditions have not been met with respect to any Unit, Lessor shall assign, transfer and set over unto Lessee all the right, title and interest of Lessor in and to such Unit and the Purchase Agreement insofar as it relates to such Unit.

1.3 Lessee shall execute and deliver to Lessor, within 15 days of the Delivery Date of each Unit accepted by Lessee, an Acceptance Supplement in the form of Exhibit B hereto, confirming the Delivery Date of such Unit and the acceptance of such Unit as of the Delivery Date. Each Acceptance Supplement shall be accompanied by the invoice relating to any Unit covered by such Acceptance Supplement if it has been received. If the invoice has not been received, Lessee shall, within 5 days of its receipt (unless otherwise specified by Lessor), forward it to Lessor.

1.4 As soon as possible, but no later than the first assignment by Lessee of a Purchase Agreement hereunder, Lessee shall deliver to Lessor in form and substance satisfactory to Lessor:

(a)   a certificate evidencing Lessee's authority to enter into and perform its obligations under this Lease;

(b)   a certificate as to the incumbency of the person or persons authorized to execute and deliver this Lease and any other agreements or documents required hereunder, including the signatures of such persons;

(c) certificates of insurance, loss payable endorsements or other evidence acceptable to Lessor that Lessee has complied with the provisions of Section 7 of this Lease;

(d) as to any Unit which will be installed or affixed on any real property, a Consent to Removal in the form of Exhibit C hereto; and

(e) such other documents as may be reasonably requested by Lessor.

Section 2. Term, Rent and Payment.

2.1 The term of this Lease as to each Unit shall commence on the Delivery Date in respect thereof and continue as specified in the Schedule.

2.2 Lessee shall pay to Lessor rental for each Unit in the amounts and at the times set forth in the Schedule.

2.3 Rent and all other sums due Lessor hereunder shall be paid at the principal office of Lessor set forth above.

2.4 This Lease is a net lease and Lessee shall not be entitled to any abatement or reduction of rent or any setoff against rent, whether arising by reason of any past, present or future claims of any nature by Lessee against Lessor or otherwise. Except as otherwise expressly provided herein, this Lease shall not terminate, nor shall the obligations of Lessor or Lessee be otherwise affected by reason of any defect in, damage to, loss of possession or use or destruction of any Unit, however caused, by the attachment of any lien, encumbrance, security interest or other right or claim of any third party to any Unit, by any prohibition or restriction of or interference with Lessee's use of the Unit by any person or entity, or by the insolvency of or the commencement by or against Lessee of any bankrupty, reorganization or similar proceeding, or for any other cause, whether similar or dissimilar to the foregoing, any present or future law to the contrary notwithstanding. It is the intention of the parties that all rent and other amounts payable by Lessee hereunder shall be payable in all events in the manner and at the times herein provided unless Lessee's obligations in respect thereof have been terminated pursuant to the express provisions of this Lease.

Section 3. Warranties.

LESSEE ACKNOWLEDGES AND AGREES THAT (a) EACH UNIT IS OF A SIZE, DESIGN, CAPACITY AND MANUFACTURE SELECTED BY LESSEE, (b) LESSEE IS SATISFIED THAT THE SAME IS SUITABLE FOR ITS PURPOSES, (c) LESSOR IS NOT A MANUFACTURER THEREOF NOR A DEALER IN PROPERTY OF SUCH KIND AND (d) LESSOR HAS NOT MADE, AND DOES NOT HEREBY MAKE, ANY REPRESENTATION OR WARRANTY OR COVENANT WITH RESPECT TO THE TITLE, MERCHANTABILITY, CONDITION, QUALITY, DESCRIPTION, DURABILITY OR SUITABILITY OF ANY SUCH UNIT IN ANY RESPECT OR IN CONNECTION WITH OR FOR THE PURPOSES AND USES OF LESSEE. Lessor hereby assigns to Lessee, to the extent assignable, any warranties, covenants and representations of Vendor with respect to any Unit, provided that any action taken by Lessee by reason thereof shall be at the expense of Lessee and shall be consistent with Lessee's obligations pursuant to Section 2 hereunder.

Section 4. Possession, Use and Maintenance.

4.1 Lessee shall not (a) use, operate, maintain or store any Unit improperly, carelessly or in violation of any applicable law or regulation of any governmental authority, (b) abandon any Unit, (c) sublease any Unit or permit the use thereof by anyone other than Lessee without the prior written consent of Lessor, which consent shall not be unreasonably withheld, (d) permit any Unit to be removed from the location specified in the Schedule without the prior written consent of Lessor, (e) affix or place any Unit to or on any other personal property or to or on any real property without first obtaining and delivering to Lessor such waivers as Lessor may reasonably require to assure Lessor's legal title and security interest and right to remove such Unit free from any lien, encumbrance or right of distraint, or any other claim which may be asserted by any third party, or (f) sell, assign or transfer, or directly or indirectly create, incur or suffer to exist any lien, claim, security interest or encumbrance of any kind on any of its rights hereunder or in any Unit.

4.2 Lessee shall at its expense at all times during the term of this Lease maintain the Units in good operating order, repair, condition and appearance.

4.3 Lessee shall not alter any Unit or affix or place any accessory, equipment or device on any Unit, if such alteration or addition would impair the originally intended function or use or reduce the value of any such Unit. All repairs, parts, supplies, accessories, equipment and devices furnished, affixed or installed to or on any Unit, excluding temporary replacements, shall thereupon become subject to the security interest of Lessor. If no Event of Default has occurred and is continuing, Lessee may remove at its expense any such accessories, equipment and devices at the expiration of the term of this Lease with respect to such Unit, provided such parts, accessories, equipment or devices are readily removable and provided that such removal will not impair the originally intended function or use of such Unit.

4.4 If Lessor supplies Lessee with labels, plates or other markings, stating that the Units are leased from Lessor, Lessee shall affix and keep the same upon a prominent place on the Units during the term of this Lease.

4.5 Upon prior notice to Lessee, Lessor shall have the right at all reasonable times to inspect any Unit and observe its use.

Section 5.   General Tax Indemnity.

5.1 Lessee agrees to pay or reimburse Lessor for, and to indemnify and hold Lessor harmless from, all fees (including, but not limited to, license, documentation, recording or registration fees), and all sales, use, gross receipts, personal property, occupational, value added or other taxes, levies, imposts, duties, assessments, charges or withholdings of any nature whatsoever, together with any penalties, fines or additions to tax, or interest thereon (all of the foregoing being hereafter referred to as "Impositions"), arising at any time prior to or during the term of this Lease, or upon any termination of this Lease or upon the return of the Units to Lessor, and levied or imposed upon Lessor, directly or otherwise, by any federal, state or local government or taxing authority in the United States or by any foreign country or foreign or international taxing authority upon or with respect to (a) any Unit, (b) the exportation, importation, registration, purchase, ownership, delivery, leasing, possession, use, operation, storage, maintenance, repair, return, sale, transfer of title or other disposition thereof, (c) the rentals, receipts, or earnings arising from any Unit, or (d) this Lease or any payment made hereunder, excluding, however, taxes measured by Lessor's net income imposed or levied by the United States or any state thereof

but not excluding any such net income taxes which by the terms of the statute imposing such tax expressly relieve Lessee or Lessor from the payment of any Impositions which Lessee would otherwise have been obligated to pay, reimburse or indemnify.

5.2 Lessee agrees to pay on or before the time or times prescribed by law any Impositions (except any Impositions excluded by Section 5.1) provided, however, that Lessee shall be under no obligation to pay any such Imposition so long as Lessee is contesting such Imposition in good faith and by appropriate legal proceedings and the nonpayment thereof does not, in the opinion of Lessor, adversely affect the title, property, use, disposition or other rights of Lessor with respect to the Units. If any Impositions (except any Impositions excluded by Section 5.1) shall have been charged or levied against Lessor directly and paid by Lessor, Lessee shall reimburse Lessor on presentation of an invoice therefor.

5.3 If Lessor shall not be entitled to a corresponding and equal deduction with respect to any Imposition which Lessee is required to pay or reimburse under Sections 5.1 or 5.2 and which payment or reimbursement constitutes income to Lessor, then Lessee shall also pay to Lessor the amount of any Impositions which Lessor is obligated to pay in respect of (a) such payment or reimbursement by Lessee and (b) any payment by Lessee made pursuant to this Section 5.3.

5.4 Lessee shall prepare and file, in a manner satisfactory to Lessor, any reports or returns which may be required with respect to the Units.

Section 6.   Risk of Loss; Waiver and Indemnity.

6.1 In the event that any Unit shall be or become worn out, lost, stolen, destroyed or irreparably damaged, from any cause whatsoever, or taken or requisitioned by condemnation or otherwise (any such occurrence being hereinafter called a "Casualty Occurrence") prior to or during the term of this Lease as to such Unit, Lessee shall give Lessor prompt notice thereof. On the first rental payment date following such Casualty Occurrence or, if there is no such rental payment date, 30 days after such Casualty Occurrence, Lessee shall pay to Lessor an amount equal to the then "Balance Due" (as hereinafter defined) for such Unit. The Balance due for each Unit is the sum of

    (a)   any and all amounts with respect to such Unit which under the terms of this

Lease may be then due or which may have accrued to such payment date (computing the rental for any number of days less than a full rental period by a fraction of which the numerator is such number of days and the denominator is the total number of days in such full rental period); plus

(b) before the Base Date for such Unit as set forth in the Schedule, the amount Lessor is obligated to pay for such Unit, and thereafter, the sum of (i) the present value, as of such payment date, of the entire unpaid balance of all rental for such Unit which would otherwise have accrued hereunder from such payment date to the end of the term of this Lease as to such Unit, and (ii) the present value, as of such payment date, of the amount of the mandatory or optional payment required or permitted to be paid by Lessee to Lessor at the end of the term of this Lease in accordance with the Schedule. Such present values are to be computed in each case by discounting at the Implicit Interest Rate set forth in the Schedule.

Upon the making of such payment by Lessee in respect of any Unit, the rental for such Unit shall cease to accrue, the term of this Lease as to such Unit shall terminate and Lessee shall be entitled to possession of such Unit. Provided that Lessor has received the Balance Due for such Unit, Lessee shall be entitled to the proceeds of any recovery in respect of such Unit from insurance or otherwise, and Lessor, subject to the rights of any insurer insuring the Units as provided herein, shall execute and deliver, to Lessee, or to its assignee or nominee, a bill of sale (without representations or warranties except that such Unit is free and clear of all claims, liens, security interests and other encumbrances by or in favor of any person claiming by, through or under Lessor) for such Unit, and such other documents as may be required to release such Unit from the terms of this Lease and to transfer title thereto to Lessee or such assignee or nominee, in such form as may reasonably be requested by Lessee, all at Lessee's expense. Except as hereinabove in this Section 6.1 provided, Lessee shall not be released from its obligations hereunder in the event of, and shall bear the risk of, any Casualty Occurrence to any Unit prior to or during the term of this Lease with respect to such Unit.

6.2 Lessee hereby waives and releases any claim now or hereafter existing against Lessor on account of, and agrees to indemnify, reimburse and hold Lessor harmless from, any and all claims (including, but not limited to, claims relating to patent infringement and claims based upon strict liability in tort), losses, liabilities, demands, suits, judgments or causes of action, and all legal proceedings, and any costs or expenses in connection therewith, including allocated charges, costs and expenses of the Legal Department of Bank of America National Trust and Savings Association and any other attorneys' fees and expenses incurred by Lessor, which may result from or arise in any manner out of the delivery, condition, use or operation of any Unit prior to or during the term of this Lease as to such Unit, or which may be attributable to any defect in any Unit, arising from the material or any article used therein or from the design, testing or use thereof, or from any maintenance, service, repair, overhaul or testing of any Unit regardless of when such defect shall be discovered, whether or not such Unit is in the possession of Lessee and no matter where it is located.

Section 7. Insurance.

Lessee, at its own cost and expense, shall keep each Unit insured against all risks, in no event for less than the amount set forth in Section 6.1 (b) with respect to such Unit, and shall maintain public liability insurance against such risks and for such amounts as Lessor may require. All such insurance shall be in such form and with such companies as Lessor shall approve, shall specify Lessor and Lessee as insureds and shall provide that such insurance may not be cancellable as to Lessor or altered in any way which would affect the interest of Lessor, without at least ten days prior written notice to Lessor. All liability insurance shall be primary, without right of contribution from any other insurance carried by Lessor. All insurance covering loss or damage to the Units shall contain a "breach of warranty" provision satisfactory to Lessor and shall provide that all amounts payable by reason of loss or damage to the Units shall be payable solely to Lessor.

Section 8. Default.

8.1 The following shall constitute events of default ("Events of Default") hereunder:

(a) Lessee shall fail to make any payments to Lessor when due hereunder;

(b) Any representation or warranty of Lessee contained herein or in any document furnished to Lessor in connection herewith shall be incorrect or misleading in any material respect when made;

(c) Lessee shall fail to observe or perform any other covenant, agreement or warranty made by Lessee hereunder and such failure shall continue for _____ days after written notice thereof to Lessee;

(d) Any default shall occur under any other agreement between Lessee and Lessor or under any agreement between Lessee and any affiliate of Lessor;

(e) Lessee shall make an assignment for the benefit of creditors or shall file any petition or action under any bankruptcy, reorganization, insolvency or moratorium law, or any other law or laws for the relief of, or relating to, debtors; or

(f) Any involuntary petition shall be filed under any bankruptcy statute against Lessee, or any receiver, trustee, custodian or similar official shall be appointed to take possession of the properties of Lessee, unless such petition or appointment is set aside or withdrawn or ceases to be in effect within sixty days from the date of said filing or appointment.

8.2 If any Event of Default shall occur, Lessor, at its option, may,

(a) proceed by appropriate court action or actions either at law or in equity, to enforce performance by Lessee of the applicable covenants of this Lease or to recover damages for the breach thereof; or

(b) by notice in writing to Lessee terminate this Lease, but Lessee shall remain liable as hereinafter provided; Lessor may, at its option, do any one or more of the following: (i) declare the aggregate Balance Due with respect to the Units immediately due and payable and recover any damages and expense in addition thereto which Lessor shall have sustained by reason of the breach of any covenant, representation or warranty contained in this Lease other

than for the payment of rental; (ii) enforce the security interest given hereunder pursuant to the Uniform Commercial Code or any other law; (iv) require Lessee to return the Units as provided in Section 9 hereof.

8.3 Lessor shall have any and all rights given to a secured party by law, and may, but is not required to, sell the Units in one or more sales. Lessor may purchase at such sale. Lessee acknowledges that sales for cash or on credit to a wholesaler, retailer or user of the Units, or at public or private auction, are all commercially reasonable. The proceeds of such sale shall be applied in the following order: First, to the reasonable expenses of retaking, holding, preparing for sale and selling, including the allocated charges, costs and expenses of the Legal Department of _____ and any other attorneys' fees and expenses incurred by Lessor; Second, to the amounts, except those specified below, which under the terms of this Lease are due or have accrued; Third, to late charges; and Fourth, to the aggregate Balance Due. Any surplus shall be paid to the person or persons entitled thereto. If there is a deficiency, Lessee will promptly pay the same to Lessor.

8.4 Lessee agrees to pay all allocated charges, costs and expenses of the Legal Department of _____ and any other attorneys' fees, expenses or out-of-pocket costs incurred by Lessor in enforcing this Lease.

8.5 The remedies hereunder provided in favor of Lessor shall not be deemed exclusive, but shall be cumulative, and shall be in addition to all other remedies in its favor existing at law or in equity.

8.6 If Lessee fails to perform any of its agreements contained herein, Lessor may perform such agreement, and expenses incurred by Lessor in connection with such performance shall be payable by Lessee upon demand.

Section 9. Return of Units.

If Lessor shall rightfully demand possession of any Unit pursuant to this Lease or otherwise, Lessee, at its expense, shall forthwith deliver possession of such Unit to Lessor, at the option of Lessor (a) by delivering such Unit, appropriately protected and in the condition required by Section 4 of this Lease, to Lessor at such place as may be specified by Lessor within the county in which the Unit was originally delivered or, if the Unit has been moved to another county in accordance with this Lease, within such other county, or (b) by loading such Unit, appropriately protected and in the condition required by Section 4 of this Lease, on board such carrier as Lessor shall specify and shipping the same, freight collect, to the destination designated by Lessor.

Section 10. Assignment.

All or any of the right, title or interest of Lessor in and to this Lease and the rights, benefits and advantages of Lessor hereunder, including the rights to receive payment of rental or any other payment hereunder, and title to the Units, may be assigned or transferred by Lessor at any time. Any such assignment or transfer shall be subject and subordinate to the terms and provisions of this Lease and the rights and interests of Lessee hereunder. No assignment of this Lease or any right or obligation hereunder may be made by Lessee or any assignee of Lessee without the prior written consent of Lessor.

Section 11. Ownership, Security Interest and Further Assurances.

Unless assigned by Lessor, or applicable law otherwise provides, title to and ownership of the Units shall remain in Lessor as security for the obligations of Lessee hereunder until Lessee has fulfilled all of its obligations hereunder. Lessee hereby grants to Lessor a continuing security interest in the Units to secure the payment of all sums due hereunder and agrees, at its expense, to do any further act and execute, acknowledge, deliver, file, register and record any further documents which Lessor may reasonably request in order to protect Lessor's title to and security interest in the Units and Lessor's rights and benefits under this Lease.

Section 12. Late Payments.

Lessee shall pay to Lessor, on demand, interest at the rate set forth in the Schedule on the amount of any payment not made when due hereunder from the date due until payment is made.

Section 13. Effect of Waiver.

No delay or omission to exercise any right,

power or remedy accruing to Lessor upon any breach or default of Lessee hereunder shall impair any such right, power or remedy nor shall it be construed to be a waiver of such breach or default, or an acquiescence therein or of or in any similar breach or default thereafter occurring, nor shall any waiver of any single breach or default be deemed a waiver of any other breach or default theretofore or thereafter occuring. Any waiver, permit, consent or approval of any kind or character on the part of Lessor of any breach or default under this Lease must be in writing specifically set forth.

Section 14. Survival of Covenants.

All covenants of Lessee under Sections 1, 2, 4, 5, 6, 8, 9, and 12 shall survive the expiration or termination of this Lease to the extent required for their full observance and performance.

Section 15. Applicable Law.

This Lease shall be governed by and construed under the laws of California.

Section 16. Effect and Modification of Lease.

This Lease exclusively and completely states the rights of Lessor and Lessee with respect to the leasing of the Units and supersedes all prior agreements, oral or written, with respect thereto. No variation or modification of this Lease shall be valid unless in writing.

Section 17. Financial Information.

Lessee shall keep its books and records in accordance with generally accepted accounting principles and practices consistently applied and shall deliver to Lessor its annual audited financial statements and such other unaudited quarterly financial statements as may be reasonably requested by Lessor. Credit information relating to Lessee may be disseminated among Lessor and any of its affiliates.

Section 18. Notices.

All demands, notices and other communications hereunder shall be in writing and shall be deemed to have been duly given when personally delivered or when deposited in the mail, first class postage prepaid, or delivered to a telegraph office, charges prepaid, addressd to each party at the address set forth below the signature of such party on the signature page, or at such other address as may hereafter be furnished in writing by either party to the other.

Section 19. Counterparts.

Two counterparts of this Lease have been executed by the parties hereto. One counterpart has been prominently marked "Lessor's Copy." One counterpart has been prominently marked "Lessee's Copy." Only the counterpart marked "Lessor's Copy" shall evidence a monetary obligation of Lessee.

IN WITNESS WHEREOF, the parties hereto have executed this Lease as of the day and year first above written.

By_____   By_____

Title_____   Title_____

By_____   By_____

Title_____   Title_____

Address:_____   Address:_____

SCHEDULE TO LEASE INTENDED FOR SECURITY
DATED AS OF _____, 19____
BETWEEN _____ AND ___

A. Description of Units.

Telephone System.

B. Purchase Price.

Purchase Price with respect to each Unit shall mean the amount Lessor is obligated to pay for such Unit. Without the prior written consent of Lessor, the sum of the Purchase Prices of all Units leased hereunder shall not exceed $500,000.

C. Term.

The lease term for each Unit shall consist of an Interim Term followed immediately by a Base Term. The Interim Term for each Unit shall commence on the Delivery Date in respect thereof and shall continue until the Base Date for such Unit. The Base Term for each Unit shall commence on the Base Date for such Unit and shall continue for eighty four (84) months. The Base Date for each Unit shall be the first day of the month following the respective Delivery Date.

D. Rental.

Supplemental Rental: Lessor agrees to advance funds for the purchase of the Units prior to the Delivery Date of such Units, provided with respect to each advance, Lessee executes and delivers to Lessor, no later than ten days prior to the date of such advance, a Request for Advance substantially in the form attached hereto as Exhibit D. With respect to each such advance, Supplemental Rental shall accrue from the date of such advance to, but not including, the Delivery Date of the Units for which such advance was made at a rate per annum equal to one hundred twenty percent (120%) of Bank of _____ "Prime Rate" (the rate of interest publicly announced from time to time by Bank of _____, as its Prime Rate, with any change in the Prime Rate to take effect on the day specified in the public announcement of such change), computed on the funds so advanced and based on a year of 365/366 days and actual days elapsed. Supplemental Rental for such Units shall be payable when billed by Lessor.

If Lessee shall fail to accept, pursuant to Section 1.2 of the Lease, any Unit for which Lessor shall have advanced funds as set forth above, Lessee shall, on demand of Lessor, purchase any such Unit from Lessor for the amount of the funds advanced by Lessor or which Lessor may be obligated to advance and any other costs or obligations incurred by Lessor in connection therewith, plus all accrued and unpaid rentals at the rate set forth above with respect to such Unit to the date of purchase of such Unit by Lessee from Lessor.

Interim Rental: For each day of the Interim Term, Lessee shall pay rental for each Unit equal to 0.0638% of the Purchase Price of such Unit actually paid on or before such day, payable when billed by Lessor.

Base Rental: During the Base Term, Lessee shall pay rental for each Unit, in consecutive monthly installments commencing on the Base Date for such Unit. Each rental payment for each Unit shall be in an amount equal to 1.914% of the Purchase Price of such Unit.

E. Utilization Period.

All Delivery Dates for Units leased hereunder must occur between December 1, 1982 and January 31, 1983, inclusive.

F. Interest on Late Payments.

The interest rate on late payments shall be 19% per annum.

G. Location.

The Units shall be located in _____.

H. Implicit Interest Rate.

The Implicit Interest Rate is 15.27% per annum compounded Monthly.

I. Commitment Fee.

Lessee shall pay to Lessor a non-refundable commitment fee of 1% of $500,000 on the date of execution of this Lease.

J. Purchase Provision.

At the end of the lease term for a Unit, as set forth in this Schedule, provided that this Lease has not been earlier terminated with respect to such Unit, Lessee shall purchase such Unit for a price equal to 1% of the original Purchase Price of such Unit.

Upon Lessee's payment of the Purchase Price, Lessor shall execute and deliver, to Lessee or its assignee or nominee, a bill of sale (without representations or warranties except that such Unit is free and clear of all claims, liens, security interests and other encumbrances by or in favor of any person claiming by, through or under Lessor) for such Unit, and such other documents as may be required to release such Unit from the terms and scope of this Lease and to transfer title thereto to Lessee or such assignee or nominee, in such form as may reasonably be requested by Lessee, all at Lessee's expense.

16 Income Taxes

The most disliked expenditure made by hospitality operations and most investors is for taxes. The dislike for taxes is no recent phenomenon, as the Bible suggests Roman tax collectors were held in low regard during the first century A.D. Most businesses, and many individuals as well, have come to accept taxes as a necessary evil; however, where legally possible, they avoid paying them. It is the duty of the managers of hospitality operations to pay minimal taxes in order to increase the financial returns of the owners of the hospitality enterprises. Questions regarding taxes addressed in this chapter are as follows:

1.   Are taxes a major consideration when purchasing capital assets?

2.   What is the difference between "income exclusion" and "deductions"?

3.   How do deductions differ from tax credits?

4.   Is tax avoidance legal?

5.   How does tax avoidance and tax evasion differ?

6.   What are the advantages of a sole proprietorship form of organization?

7.   What is double taxation?

8.   How can double taxation be avoided by a corporate form of organization?

9.   What is a limited partnership and what are the advantages over a general partnership?

10. What federal tax forms are filed by each type of organization form?

This chapter includes a discussion of the effect of taxes on business decisions and a very brief history and statement of objectives of federal income taxes. Next, tax basics for the individual taxpayer are covered. Tax avoidance and tax evasion are discussed, followed by an overview, including advantages and disadvantages, of the various forms of organization—sole proprietorships, partnerships, and corporations. Also included in this chapter is a discussion of cash versus accrual accounting and accounting income versus taxable income. Even though this chapter is titled "Income Taxes" other taxes discussed briefly are state and municipal taxes and property taxes.

It is not our purpose here to attempt to explain all of the ramifications of the various tax laws, some of which can be very complex, but rather to raise the reader's awareness that taxes must be considered as a significant element in the economic decisions of business entities.

Permeating Force in Economic Business Decisions

Managers of hospitality operations must realize that taxes are an important consideration in most major financial decisions. For example, the purchase of furniture and equipment may be delayed because a new tax incentive enacted by Congress becomes effective the following year. This is not to suggest that a decision to invest in fixed assets be delayed simply because of a tax advantage. Other business goals may indicate that the purchase should be made immediately. However, when current business objectives allow a choice of timing, management should plan acquisitions to gain any added tax advantage which will ultimately lower the net cost of acquiring the property. Similarly, dispositions of marketable securities, investments, fixed assets, or even an entire business demand that the tax effects of the transaction and alternatives be fully considered.

In addition to considering federal income taxes, managers must recognize the potential effects of other taxes which include state and city income taxes, property taxes, and so on. Although these additional taxes are important, this chapter's orientation is toward federal income taxes. Later in the chapter, state and city income taxes and property taxes will be discussed briefly.

History and Objectives of Federal Income Taxes

While the federal government first used an income tax during the Civil War to raise revenue, it was the Sixteenth Amendment in 1913 that put aside all questions of the constitutionality of such a tax and cleared the way for the federal income tax as we know it today. Since 1913, Congress has made amendments to the original law and charged the Treasury Department with its enforcement through its branch, the Internal Revenue Service (IRS).

Up until the late 1960's, major tax law changes were infrequently enacted. Seven to ten year spans without significant change were common. In recent years, however, massive changes have been made to the Internal Revenue Code nearly every year.

The primary objective of income taxes has been, and continues to be, to raise revenue necessary for the operation of the federal government. Over the years, this goal has been expanded at various times to stimulate certain aspects of the economy, to achieve full employment, and to accomplish a variety of social goals.

With this diversity of objectives in our federal tax system, as well as the fact that federal, state, and city taxes may consume in excess of 50% of a business's earnings, management must be ever vigilant to the effect that tax rules may have on business decisions. A major purpose of the various hospitality associations, such as the American Hotel & Motel

Association and the National Restaurant Association, is to lobby for tax legislation most beneficial to hospitality industry operations.

Tax Basics

Taxes are levied on individuals and corporations. Corporations are separate legal entities; however, they are owned ultimately by individual investors. Therefore, tax decisions regarding corporations are often based on the ultimate impact they may have on the individual. For example, the use of an accelerated method of depreciation reduces taxable income which reduces taxes (therefore, cash paid in taxes), allowing for more cash to be invested and/or more cash dividends to be paid to investors. Thus, a brief discussion of individual income taxes is warranted.

The individual income tax return is Form 1040 (see the example in Exhibit 16.3). In 1985, Form 1040 or one of its variations, Form 1040A or Form 1040EZ, was required of individuals with gross incomes above IRS minimums. An individual's tax is determined as follows:

> Income
> Less: Exclusions from Gross Income
> Equals: Gross Income
> Less: Adjustments to Income
> Equals: Adjusted Gross Income (AGI)
> Less: Deductions
> Less: Amount for Exemptions
> Equals: Taxable Income
> Taxable Income x Tax Rates = Federal Income Taxes
> Less: Tax Credits
> Plus: Other Federal Taxes
> Equals: Total Tax

In addition to Form 1040, several schedules, as appropriate, are required to be filed, such as Schedule C which summarizes the sole proprietor's hospitality business for the year. However, taxes and the various schedules are too varied and detailed to discuss in this chapter. The following brief discussion covers the major elements of the Form 1040.

Income, Exclusions, Adjustments

Income on Form 1040 includes, but is not limited to, wages, salaries, and tips, as shown on Form W-2, interest and dividend income, business income (loss) from a sole proprietorship, capital gains (losses), rents, royalties, partnership income (loss), and S Corporation income (loss). Exclusions from income shown on the tax forms include amounts for dividends and a portion of long-term capital gains. Certain income classified as nontaxable income, such as interest from state and local government bonds, is not reported on the individual's tax return. Income less exclusions equals gross income. Gross income less adjustments to gross income equals adjusted gross income (AGI). Adjustments to gross income include, but are not limited to, qualifying moving expenses, unreimbursed employee business expenses, and individual retirement account deductions.

Deductions, Exemptions, and Taxable Income

Deductions are itemized by individual taxpayers if the total exceeds minimal amounts specified by the tax code. For example, in 1985, it was generally beneficial for married taxpayers who filed a joint return to itemize if their deductions exceeded $3,540. Itemized deductions include medical and dental expenses which exceed 5% of AGI, taxes paid during the tax year such as state and local income taxes, real estate taxes, sales tax, interest expense, contributions to charitable organizations, limited amounts for casualty and theft losses, and miscellaneous deductions such as union and professional dues and tax preparation fees.

In 1985, $1,040 was subtracted for each exemption. In general, a taxpayer is allowed one exemption for himself/herself and each dependent. The current law provides for an annual adjustment of the exemption allowance based on the inflation rate.

Taxes and Credits

Taxes are determined based on taxable income in a variety of ways as provided by the tax code. In addition, the code provides for minimum taxes when certain taxpayers otherwise would not have to pay income taxes.

Credits deductible from income taxes include credit for child and dependent care expenses, foreign tax credit, and investment tax credit. The credits are generally deducted directly from the taxes calculated on taxable income. Other taxes to be included are self-employment tax, which is commonly known as social security for the sole proprietor, and also social security taxes on tip income not reported to the employer. Taxes less credits plus other taxes equals the total tax for the individual.

The tax code is quite complex as are the many forms and schedules required in completing an individual's tax return. Many tax experts offer their services to assist taxpayers in completing their returns. Individuals with fairly complex returns should consider obtaining tax preparation assistance in order to minimize their income taxes.

A Taxing Illustration

Warren and Beth Schmidt have two children and own Snicker's Restaurant, an unincorporated business. Exhibit 16.1 is a summarized income statement of their restaurant operation which is managed by Warren. In addition, Beth earns $10,000 as a part-time education specialist at the local community college. Her W-2 showed $1,500 was withheld for federal income taxes. Exhibit 16.2 shows other income, adjustments to income, deductions, and other taxes for the Schmidts. Exhibits 16.3 through 16.5 are for the Schmidt's Form 1040, Schedule A, and Schedule C, respectively. Schedule W—Deduction for a Married Couple When Both Work, Schedule SE—Computation of Social Security Self-Employment Tax, and Form 4562—Depreciation, must be filed with the Schmidt's return but are not included as exhibits here, though the results are included on the exhibits as appropriate. For example, the total depreciation of $20,000 from Form 4562 (form not included) is shown on line 12 of Schedule C (Exhibit 16.5).

Notice that income from the restaurant, shown on Schedule C, is entered on Form 1040, line 12. Further, note a refund of $680 is due the Schmidts since they overpaid their taxes during 1985.

**Exhibit 16.1   Summarized Income Statement —
Snicker's Restaurant**

**Summarized Income Statement
Snicker's Restaurant
For the year ended December 31, 1985**

Sales		$700,000
Cost of Sales		300,000
Gross Profit		400,000
Controllable Expenses:		
Payroll	$180,000	
Employee Benefits	18,000	
Laundry	5,000	
Supplies	10,000	
Utilities	30,000	
Advertising	12,000	
Car Expenses	8,000	
Legal and Professional	8,000	
Office Expense	3,000	
Telephone	3,000	
Travel	5,000	
Dues and Publications	1,000	
Profit Sharing Plans	8,000	
Repairs and Maintenance	10,000	301,000
Income Before Occupation Costs		99,000
Rent		20,000
Property Taxes		6,000
Insurance		6,000
Interest		10,000
Depreciation		20,000
Income Before Taxes		$37,000

Tax Avoidance

The orderly planning of a transaction to mitigate the impact of taxes or avoid the application of taxes completely is entirely legal and should be aggressively pursued. Judge Learned Hand stated it well:

> Over and over again courts have said there is nothing sinister in so arranging one's affairs as to keep taxes as low as possible. Everybody does so, rich or poor; and all do right, for nobody owes any public duty to pay more than the law demands: taxes are enforced extractions, not voluntary contributions. To demand more in the name of morals is mere cant.[1]

Management can and should cast the hospitality operation's business transactions in such a manner as to achieve the lowest possible tax cost within the constraints of other business considerations and the

Exhibit 16.2 Information Regarding the Schmidt's Income

Other Income:

Interest income of $250

Adjustments:

An IRA of $2,000 (for Warren Schmidt)

Deduction for married couple when both work $1,000*

Deductions:

Medical –

Prescribed drugs	$ 250
Doctor bills, etc	1,000

Taxes –

Property taxes – house	$1,500
Sales tax	334
Sales tax – new car	400

Interest –

Mortgage on house	$3,600
Credit cards	100

Contributions	$2,000
Professional dues – Beth	$ 100
Tax return preparation fee for 1984 tax return	$ 100

Other Taxes:

Self-employment tax	$1,615**
Federal taxes paid during year by Warren	$7,000

*Per Schedule W (not included)

**Per Schedule SE (not included)

prevailing tax laws and regulations. This is simply good tax planning which is good business management!

For example, consider the purchase or sale of a hotel, restaurant, or other hospitality establishment. A seller operating in the corporate form of ownership must decide whether to sell the stock of the company or its assets. Assuming a gain on the transaction, the after-tax differences can be dramatic based on the decision to sell either stock or assets. Even in a situation generating an overall loss, tax recognition of gain may be required on certain elements of the transaction based solely on the decision made to sell assets rather than stock.

Conversely, a buyer will be concerned about acquiring stock of a corporation where the tax value of the underlying assets is substantially below the selling price of the stock. In that situation, the buyer's goal generally is to acquire the assets of the corporation at their fair market value in order to preserve this higher base for future depreciation purposes.

Exhibit 16.3 1985 Income Tax Return — Warren and Beth Schmidt

Form 1040 Department of the Treasury—Internal Revenue Service
U.S. Individual Income Tax Return 1985

For the year January 1–December 31, 1985, or other tax year beginning , 1985, ending , 19 | OMB No. 1545-0074

Your first name and initial (if joint return, also give spouse's name and initial) | Last name
Warren B. and Beth J. | Schmidt

Your social security number
333 33 3333

Present home address (number and street, including apartment number, or rural route)
1415 Redbird Ave.

Spouse's social security number
334 34 3334

City, town or post office, state, and ZIP code
Topeka, XXX XXXXX

Your occupation: Restaurateur
Spouse's occupation: Education Specialist

Presidential Election Campaign ▶ Do you want $1 to go to this fund? Yes ☐ No ☒ — Note: Checking "Yes" will not change your tax or reduce your refund.
If joint return, does your spouse want $1 to go to this fund? Yes ☐ No ☒

For Privacy Act and Paperwork Reduction Act Notice, see Instructions.

Filing Status (Check only one box)
1 ☐ Single
2 ☒ Married filing joint return (even if only one had income)
3 ☐ Married filing separate return. Enter spouse's social security no. above and full name here ▶
4 ☐ Head of household (with qualifying person). (See page 5 of Instructions.) If the qualifying person is your unmarried child but not your dependent, write child's name here ▶
5 ☐ Qualifying widow(er) with dependent child (year spouse died ▶ 19) (See page 6 of Instructions.)

Exemptions
6a ☒ Yourself — 65 or over ☐ — Blind ☐ | Enter number of boxes checked on 6a and 6b ▶ 2
b ☒ Spouse — 65 or over ☐ — Blind ☐ | Enter number of children listed on 6c ▶ 2
c First names of your dependent children who lived with you (see page 6): Ami, Heidi | Enter number of children listed on 6d
d First names of your dependent children who did not live with you (see page 6).
(If pre-1985 agreement, check here ▶ ☐) | Add numbers entered in boxes above ▶ 4
e Other dependents:
(1) Name | (2) Relationship | (3) Number of months lived in your home | (4) Did dependent have income of $1,040 or more? | (5) Did you provide more than one half of dependent's support?
f Total number of exemptions claimed (also complete line 36)

Income
7 Wages, salaries, tips, etc. (Attach Form(s) W-2) | 7 | 10,000
8 Interest income (also attach Schedule B if over $400) | 8 | 250
9a Dividends (also attach Schedule B if over $400) | 9a
b Exclusion | 9b | 9c
10 Taxable refunds of state and local income taxes, if any, from the worksheet on page 9 of Instructions | 10
11 Alimony received | 11
12 Business income or (loss) (attach Schedule C) | 12 | 37,000
13 Capital gain or (loss) (attach Schedule D) | 13
14 40% of capital gain distributions not reported on line 13 (see page 9 of Instructions) | 14
15 Other gains or (losses) (attach Form 4797) | 15
16 Fully taxable pensions, IRA distributions, and annuities not reported on line 17 (see page 9) | 16
17a Other pensions and annuities, including rollovers. Total received | 17a
b Taxable amount, if any, from the worksheet on page 10 of Instructions | 17b
18 Rents, royalties, partnerships, estates, trusts, etc. (attach Schedule E) | 18
19 Farm income or (loss) (attach Schedule F) | 19
20a Unemployment compensation (insurance). Total received | 20a
b Taxable amount, if any, from the worksheet on page 10 of Instructions | 20b
21a Social security benefits (see page 10). Total received | 21a
b Taxable amount, if any, from worksheet on page 11 | 21b
22 Other income (list type and amount—see page 11 of Instructions) | 22
23 Add lines 7 through 22. This is your **total income** ▶ | 23 | 47,250

Adjustments to Income
24 Moving expense (attach Form 3903 or 3903F) | 24
25 Employee business expenses (attach Form 2106) | 25
26 IRA deduction, from the worksheet on page 12 | 26 | 2,000
27 Keogh retirement plan deduction | 27
28 Penalty on early withdrawal of savings | 28
29 Alimony paid (recipient's last name and social security no.) | 29
30 Deduction for a married couple when both work (attach Schedule W) | 30 | 1,000
31 Add lines 24 through 30. These are your **total adjustments** ▶ | 31 | 3,000

Adjusted Gross Income
32 Subtract line 31 from line 23. This is your **adjusted gross income**. If this line is less than $11,000 and a child lived with you, see "Earned Income Credit" (line 59) on page 16 of Instructions. If you want IRS to figure your tax, see page 13 of Instructions | 32 | 44,250

Form 1040 (1985) | Page 2

33 Amount from line 32 (adjusted gross income) | 33 | 44,250
34a If you itemize, attach Schedule A (Form 1040) and enter the amount from Schedule A, line 26 | 34a | 4,594
Caution: If you have unearned income and can be claimed as a dependent on your parents return, check here ▶ ☐ and see page 13 of Instructions. Also see page 13 if you are married filing a separate return and your spouse itemizes deductions, or you are a dual-status alien.
b If you do not itemize but you made charitable contributions, enter your cash contributions here. (If you gave $3,000 or more to any one organization, see page 14.) | 34b
c Enter your noncash contributions (you must attach Form 8283 if over $500) | 34c
d Add lines 34b and 34c. Enter the total | 34d
e Divide the amount on line 34d by 2. Enter the result here | 34e
35 Subtract line 34a or line 34e, whichever applies, from line 33 | 35 | 39,656
36 Multiply $1,040 by the total number of exemptions claimed on line 6f (see page 14) | 36 | 4,160
37 **Taxable income.** Subtract line 36 from line 35. Enter the result (but not less than zero) | 37 | 35,496
38 Enter tax here. Check if from ☐ Tax Table, ☐ Tax Rate Schedule X, Y, or Z, or ☐ Schedule G | 38 | 6,205
39 Additional taxes. (See page 14 of Instructions.) Enter here and check if from ☐ Form 4972, or ☐ Form 5544 | 39
40 Add lines 38 and 39. Enter the total | 40 | 6,205

Credits
41 Credit for child and dependent care expenses (attach Form 2441) | 41
42 Credit for the elderly and the permanently and totally disabled (attach Schedule R) | 42
43 Residential energy credit (attach Form 5695) | 43
44 Partial credit for political contributions for which you have receipts | 44
45 Add lines 41 through 44. These are your total personal credits | 45 | –0–
46 Subtract line 45 from line 40. Enter the result (but not less than zero) | 46 | 6,205
47 Foreign tax credit (attach Form 1116) | 47
48 General business credit. Check if from ☐ Form 3800, ☐ Form 3468, ☐ Form 5884, ☐ Form 6478 | 48
49 Add lines 47 and 48. These are your total business and other credits | 49 | –0–
50 Subtract line 49 from line 46. Enter the result (but not less than zero) | 50 | 6,205

Other Taxes (Including Advance EIC Payments)
51 Self-employment tax (attach Schedule SE) | 51 | 1,615
52 Alternative minimum tax (attach Form 6251) | 52
53 Tax from recapture of investment credit (attach Form 4255) | 53
54 Social security tax on tip income not reported to employer (attach Form 4137) | 54
55 Tax on an IRA (attach Form 5329) | 55
56 Add lines 50 through 55. This is your **total tax** ▶ | 56 | 7,820

Payments (Attach Forms W-2, W-2G, and W-2P to front)
57 Federal income tax withheld | 57
58 1985 estimated tax payments and amount applied from 1984 return | 58 | 1,500
59 Earned income credit (see page 16) | 59
60 Amount paid with Form 4868 | 60
61 Excess social security tax and RRTA tax withheld (two or more employers) | 61
62 Credit for Federal tax on gasoline and special fuels (attach Form 4136) | 62
63 Regulated Investment Company credit (attach Form 2439) | 63
64 Add lines 57 through 63. These are your **total payments** ▶ | 64 | 7,000

Refund or Amount You Owe
65 If line 64 is larger than line 56, enter amount **OVERPAID** | 65
66 Amount of line 65 to be **REFUNDED TO YOU** ▶ | 66
67 Amount of line 65 to be applied to your 1986 estimated tax | 67
68 If line 56 is larger than line 64, enter **AMOUNT YOU OWE**. Attach check or money order for full amount payable to "Internal Revenue Service." Write your social security number and "1985 Form 1040" on it. Check ▶ ☐ if Form 2210 (2210F) is attached. See page 17 Penalty: $ | 68 | 680

Please Sign Here
Under penalties of perjury, I declare that I have examined this return and accompanying schedules and statements, and to the best of my knowledge and belief, they are true, correct, and complete. Declaration of preparer (other than taxpayer) is based on all information of which preparer has any knowledge.
Your signature | Date
Spouse's signature (if filing jointly, BOTH must sign)

Paid Preparer's Use Only
Preparer's signature | Date | Check if self-employed ☐ | Preparer's social security no.
Firm's name (or yours, if self-employed) and address | E.I. No. | ZIP code

☆ U.S. GOVERNMENT PRINTING OFFICE: 1985-483-072

**Exhibit 16.4   1985 Schedule A — Itemized Deductions —
Warren and Beth Schmidt**

SCHEDULES A&B (Form 1040) Department of the Treasury Internal Revenue Service (O)	Schedule A—Itemized Deductions (Schedule B is on back) ▶ Attach to Form 1040. ▶ See Instructions for Schedules A and B (Form 1040).		OMB No. 1545-0074 1985 07

Name(s) as shown on Form 1040   Warren B. and Beth J. Schmidt   Your social security number

Medical and Dental Expenses (Do not include expenses reimbursed or paid by others.) (See Instructions on page 19.)	1 Prescription medicines and drugs; and insulin	1	250	
	2 a Doctors, dentists, nurses, hospitals, insurance premiums you paid for medical and dental care, etc.	2a	1,000	
	b Transportation and lodging	2b		
	c Other (list—include hearing aids, dentures, eyeglasses, etc.) ▶	2c		
	3 Add lines 1 through 2c, and write the total here	3	1,250	
	4 Multiply the amount on Form 1040, line 33, by 5% (.05)	4	2,212	
	5 Subtract line 4 from line 3. If zero or less, write -0-. **Total medical and dental** ▶	5		-0-
Taxes You Paid (See Instructions on page 20.)	6 State and local income taxes	6	-0-	
	7 Real estate taxes	7	1,500	
	8 a General sales tax (see sales tax tables in instruction booklet)	8a	334	
	b General sales tax on motor vehicles	8b	400	
	9 Other taxes (list—include personal property taxes) ▶	9		
	10 Add the amounts on lines 6 through 9. Write the total here. **Total taxes** ▶	10		2,234
Interest You Paid (See Instructions on page 20.)	11 a Home mortgage interest you paid to financial institutions	11a	3,600	
	b Home mortgage interest you paid to individuals (show that person's name and address) ▶	11b		
	12 Total credit card and charge account interest you paid	12	100	
	13 Other interest you paid (list) ▶	13		
	14 Add the amounts on lines 11a through 13. Write the total here. **Total interest** ▶	14		3,700
Contributions You Made (See Instructions on page 21.)	15 a Cash contributions. (If you gave $3,000 or more to any one organization, report those contributions on line 15b.)	15a	2,000	
	b Cash contributions totaling $3,000 or more to any one organization. (Show to whom you gave and how much you gave.) ▶	15b		
	16 Other than cash. (You must attach Form 8283 if over $500.)	16		
	17 Carryover from prior year	17		
	18 Add the amounts on lines 15a through 17. Write the total here. **Total contributions** ▶	18		2,000
Casualty and Theft Losses	19 Total casualty or theft loss(es). (You must attach Form 4684 or similar statement.) (See page 21 of Instructions.)	19		
Miscellaneous Deductions (See Instructions on page 21.)	20 Union and professional dues	20	100	
	21 Tax return preparation fee	21	100	
	22 Other (list type and amount) ▶	22		
	23 Add the amounts on lines 20 through 22. Write the total here. **Total miscellaneous** ▶	23		200
Summary of Itemized Deductions (See Instructions on page 22.)	24 Add the amounts on lines 5, 10, 14, 18, 19, and 23. Write your answer here.	24		8,134
	25 If you checked Form 1040 { Filing Status box 2 or 5, write $3,540 / Filing Status box 1 or 4, write $2,390 / Filing Status box 3, write $1,770 }	25		3,540
	26 Subtract line 25 from line 24. Write your answer here and on Form 1040, line 34a. (If line 25 is more than line 24, see the Instructions for line 26 on page 22.) ▶	26		4,594

For Paperwork Reduction Act Notice, see Form 1040 Instructions.   Schedule A (Form 1040) 1985

Even if the stock must be acquired, it will probably be possible to affect a tax reorganization to realize a step-up in tax basis. The point is that management must be aware that, with proper tax planning, tax laws frequently allow for the realization of most of the opposing goals of both buyer and seller. To recognize these opportunities for tax planning and avoid excessive or burdensome taxes is perfectly legal and represents a key responsibility of management.

Exhibit 16.5 **1985 Schedule C—Profit or (Loss) from Business or Profession (Sole Proprietorship) — Warren and Beth Schmidt**

SCHEDULE C (Form 1040) Department of the Treasury Internal Revenue Service (3)	**Profit or (Loss) From Business or Profession** (Sole Proprietorship) Partnerships, Joint Ventures, etc., Must File Form 1065. ▶ Attach to Form 1040 or Form 1041. ▶ See Instructions for Schedule C (Form 1040).	OMB No. 1545-0074 19**85** 09

me of proprietor: Warren B. and Beth J. Schmidt   Social security number: 333 33 3333

A Principal business or profession, including product or service (see Instructions)
Foodservice sales

B Principal business code from page 2: 3079

C Business name and address ▶ Snicker's Restaurant
1979 Main St., Topeka, XXX   XXXXX

D Employer ID number

E Method(s) used to value closing inventory:
(1) ☒ Cost   (2) ☐ Lower of cost or market   (3) ☐ Other (attach explanation)

	Yes	No
F Accounting method: (1) ☒ Cash (2) ☐ Accrual (3) ☐ Other (specify) ▶		
G Was there any change in determining quantities, costs, or valuations between opening and closing inventory? If "Yes," attach explanation.		X
H Did you deduct expenses for an office in your home?		X

Part I   Income

1 **a** Gross receipts or sales	1a	700,000
b Less: Returns and allowances	1b	–0–
c Subtract line 1b from line 1a and enter the balance here	1c	700,000
2 Cost of goods sold and/or operations (from Part III, line 8)	2	300,000
3 Subtract line 2 from line 1c and enter the **gross profit** here	3	400,000
4 **a** Windfall Profit Tax Credit or Refund received in 1985 (see Instructions)	4a	
b Other income	4b	–0–
5 Add lines 3, 4a, and 4b. This is the **gross income** ▶	5	400,000

Part II   Deductions

6 Advertising	12,000	22 Pension and profit-sharing plans		8,000
7 Bad debts from sales or services (Cash method taxpayers, see Instructions)		23 Rent on business property		20,000
		24 Repairs		10,000
8 Bank service charges		25 Supplies (not included in Part III below)		10,000
9 Car and truck expenses	8,000	26 Taxes (Do not include Windfall Profit Tax here. See line 30.)		6,000
10 Commissions		27 Travel and entertainment		5,000
11 Depletion		28 Utilities and telephone		33,000
12 Depreciation and section 179 deduction from Form 4562 (not included in Part III below)	20,000	29 **a** Wages	180,000	
		b Jobs credit	–0–	
13 Dues and publications	1,000	**c** Subtract line 29b from 29a		180,000
14 Employee benefit programs	18,000	30 Windfall Profit Tax withheld in 1985		
15 Freight (not included in Part III below)		31 Other expenses (specify):		
16 Insurance	6,000	**a**		
17 Laundry and cleaning	5,000	**b**		
18 Legal and professional services	8,000	**c**		
19 Mortgage interest paid to financial institutions (see Instructions)	10,000	**d**		
20 Office expense	3,000	**e**		
21 Other interest		**f**		
		g		
32 Add amounts in columns for lines 6 through 31g. These are the **total deductions** ▶			32	363,000

33 **Net profit or (loss).** Subtract line 32 from line 5 and enter the result. If a profit, enter on Form 1040, line 12, and on Schedule SE, Part I, line 2 (or Form 1041, line 5). If a loss, you **MUST** go on to line 34	33	37,000

34 If you have a loss, you **MUST** answer this question. "Do you have amounts for which you are not at risk in this business (see Instructions)?" ☐ Yes ☐ No
If "Yes," you **MUST** attach **Form 6198.** If "No," enter the loss on Form 1040, line 12, and on Schedule SE, Part I, line 2 (or Form 1041, line 5).

Part III   Cost of Goods Sold and/or Operations (See Schedule C Instructions for Part III)

1 Inventory at beginning of year (if different from last year's closing inventory, attach explanation)	1	–0–
2 Purchases less cost of items withdrawn for personal use	2	300,000
3 Cost of labor (do not include salary paid to yourself)	3	–0–
4 Materials and supplies	4	–0–
5 Other costs	5	–0–
6 Add lines 1 through 5	6	300,000
7 Less: Inventory at end of year	7	–0–
8 **Cost of goods sold and/or operations.** Subtract line 7 from line 6. Enter here and in Part I, line 2, above.	8	300,000

For Paperwork Reduction Act Notice, see Form 1040 Instructions.   Schedule C (Form 1040) 1985

Tax evasion, on the other hand, is the fraudulent denial or concealment of a current or future tax liability, such as the underreporting of income or claiming unsubstantiated or excessive deductions. For example, underreporting of income—and an evasion of tax—occurs when revenues, dividends, interest, fees, or profits from business transactions, or the sale of property, is not reported or is underreported. Similarly, evasion of taxes occurs when nondeductible expenses, such as personal expenses or costs related to personal use of business property (e.g., automobiles), are deducted on tax returns as business expenses. Activities of this nature are illegal and are untenable for the management of any business.

Form of Organization

The importance of addressing tax considerations in the early stages of a particular transaction is, perhaps, best illustrated in the need to consider taxes when starting a business. One of the basic decisions a businessperson must make is determining the legal form of operation: sole proprietorship, partnership, corporation, or some of their hybrid forms such as limited partnership and S Corporation.

Each of these entities offers both tax and nontax advantages and disadvantages. Tax considerations, however, are only one factor in the decision process. There are practical business and legal considerations, as well as government regulatory requirements, which bear on the final decision. The following sections briefly discuss the forms of business organization shown in Exhibit 16.6 and the major advantages and limitations for each.

Sole Proprietorship

In terms of sheer numbers, the sole proprietorship form of operation is the most frequently encountered in the hospitality industry. However, in a recent year, revenues from corporate lodging businesses totaled nearly two-thirds of the total lodging revenue across the United States.[2]

As the name implies, in a sole proprietorship the business is owned by a single individual. Its popularity stems from the ease with which it is formed. Establishing a sole proprietorship may only require filing an assumed business name statement with the proper authorities such as the county government, and filing a Schedule C on the owner's federal, state, and local tax returns.

Advantages of the sole proprietorship type of organization include the following:

1. Proprietorship eliminates double taxation, as income is reported only on the owner's individual tax return. Expected losses during start-up and the early years can offset other income of the owner.

2. Losses that exceed the owner's other income may result in net operating losses that can be used to recover some, or all, of the owner's prior years' taxes.

3. Business credits, such as investment tax credit, retain their character and are used directly by the owner.

4. The owner is able to maintain complete control over the business by being the sole owner.

Several disadvantages of this type of organization that may discourage a hospitality business owner from operating as a sole proprietor are as follows:

Exhibit 16.6   Operating Forms for Hospitality Businesses

	Sole Proprietorship	Partnership		Corporation	
		General	**Limited**	**Regular**	**S Corporation**
Instrument of Creation	None (assumed name statement may be required)	Agreement – oral or written	Certificate of limited partnership	Articles of incorporation	Articles of incorporation, file election with IRS
Organizational Documents	None	Partnership Agreement	Certificate of limited partnership agreement	Articles of incorporation, by-laws, minutes	Articles of incorporation, bylaws, minutes
Type of Tax Return	Schedule C for Form 1040	Form 1065	Form 1065	Form 1120	Form 1120S
Tax Rates	Individual	Individual	Individual	Corporate	Individual
Limited Liability	No	No	Yes – Limited Partners; No – General Partners	Yes	Yes
Recognition of Losses	Owner	Partners	Partners	Corporation	Shareholders

1. Hospitality industries may be risky. The sole proprietor does not enjoy the limited liability available with some other organizational forms; that is, he/she is personally liable for obligations of the business. However, adequate insurance can at least partially alleviate this problem.

2. Certain fringe benefits are severely limited or completely disallowed if they are for the benefit of the sole proprietor.

3. The transfer of a portion of the ownership interest in a sole proprietorship requires a change to either partnership or corporate form. In addition, the continuity of the business is not assured at the death of the owner. By contrast, a corporate form of organization is legally separate from its owners.

4. Generally, owners are unable to raise large amounts of capital due to the sole proprietorship type of organization, while a corporation may be able to issue stock and/or sell bonds.

The sole proprietorship may be an ideal form of organization if the anticipated risk is minimal and is covered by insurance, if the owner is either unable or unwilling to maintain the necessary organizational documents and tax returns of more complicated business entities, and if the business does not require extensive borrowing.

Partnerships	The partnership type of organization consists of two or more owners joined together in a noncorporate manner for the purpose of operating a business. A partnership form retains most of the tax as well as nontax advantages and disadvantages of a sole proprietorship. The advantages are as follows:

1.	Greater financial strength is provided by having more than one owner. The added capital can provide greater resources for expansion of the business.

2.	Partnership arrangements allow flexibility in the allocation of profits, losses, and certain tax benefits among owners. Such allocations must be reasonable and justified as having economic substance in order to satisfy the IRS.

3.	Profits, losses, and tax credits pass through the partnership entity to the owners' individual returns, thus avoiding double taxation.

4.	Capital gains pass to owners in the partnership as capital items rather than dividends (as with a corporation) which are taxable at ordinary income tax rates.

Major disadvantages of the partnership form of operation are as follows:

1.	Partners are taxed on their share of the profits whether or not cash is distributed to them.

2.	Partners may become frustrated in sharing the decision-making process which can prove cumbersome. Partners may hold different opinions, and theoretically, each has an equal right to manage the business.

3.	Partners generally have unlimited legal liability for obligations of the business. This can be a significant factor where uninsurable business risks exist. This last disadvantage may be partially overcome within the partnership form by the use of a limited partnership form of organization.

Limited Partnerships	A limited partnership is a partnership of two or more individuals having at least one general partner and at least one limited partner. Unlike a general partnership agreement, which can be oral, the limited partnership must be in writing, and the certificate of limited partnership must be filed with the proper governmental authorities. Most states regulate the public sale of limited partnership interests. Further, public offerings must be filed with the Securities and Exchange Commission; thus, sizable legal fees may be incurred. Smaller private issues generally seek an exemption from registration.

The major unique feature of limited partnerships is the limited liability afforded to limited partners. The limited partners' liabilities are limited to their investments. However, to ensure this feature, limited partners cannot actively participate in controlling or managing the hospitality business.

In recent years, the limited partnership has become an attractive financing vehicle for the expansion of hospitality operations. Limited partnerships have been formed for specific projects, with the hospitality establishment acting as the general partner and investors as the limited partners. Thus, the use of the limited partnership enables the hospitality establishment to obtain needed capital and still maintain control over the hospitality operations.

Basic tax advantages available to general partners are also available to limited partners. Nontax advantages available to limited partners which are not available to general partners include the limited liabilities (discussed previously), and within certain limits, the limited partners' interests may be assigned without prior approval of general partners.

Corporations   A corporation is a legal entity created by a state or another political authority. The corporation receives a charter or articles of incorporation and has basic attributes of (1) an exclusive name, (2) continued existence independent of its stockholders, (3) paid-in capital represented by transferred shares of capital stock, (4) limited liability for its owners, and (4) overall control vested in its directors.

While hospitality businesses organized as sole proprietorships account for the largest number of businesses, hospitality corporations account for the greatest volume in terms of sales, assets, profits, and employees. Several hospitality corporations, such as Holiday Corporation, Marriott Corporation, and McDonald's, Inc., have annual sales in excess of $1 billion. The major advantages of the corporate form over other forms discussed previously are as follows:

1. Shareholders' liability is normally limited to their investment.

2. Owners are taxed only on distributed profits.

3. If the corporation is sold or liquidated, the gain may be taxed to the owners at long-term capital gain rates.

4. Employees can be motivated by equity participation, such as stock bonus plans and stock options, and by certain tax-favored fringe benefits.

5. Equity capital can be raised by selling capital stock to the public.

6. A corporation can use its stock to acquire other companies and thereby offer the sellers a tax-free exchange.

7. For smaller corporations, tax rates are generally lower than individual rates.

8. There is free transferability of capital stock by owners.

9. The corporation's life continues irrespective of the owners.

As with other forms of business organization, there are disadvantages to the corporate form. Several are as follows:

1. Double taxation—corporate profits are taxed as well as dividends paid to stockholders. Exhibit 16.7 shows that, based on 1985 tax rates, the effective tax rate on corporate pretax income *in excess of* $100,000 could be as high as 73%. The calculations assume the

Exhibit 16.7 Illustration of Double Taxation

	Dollars	Percentage
Corporate Pretax Income over $100,000	$100,000	100%
Less: Corporate Tax (46%)	46,000	46
Dividend Distribution	54,000	54
Less: Individual Income Taxes (50%)	27,000	27
After-Tax Benefit to Stockholder	$ 27,000	27%

individual taxpayer's marginal tax rate is 50%, and that all after-tax profits are distributed. Thus, the corporate tax of 46% plus the individual tax of 27% (50% of 54%), equal 73%, the effective tax rate.[3] If the above business had been unincorporated, the maximum effective tax rate would have been only 50%. Therefore, the maximum potential cost of double taxation is $23,000 for every $100,000 of pretax profits, or 23%.

2.   Another potential disadvantage of the corporate form is the inability to pass through to owners favorable tax attributes, such as operating losses and tax credits, that might be more advantageous to owners than to the hospitality corporation.

S Corporation

The tax drawbacks of the corporate form of operation can be overcome by the corporation filing as an S Corporation for tax purposes. In essence, this allows the corporation to be taxed in the same manner as a partnership.

The philosophy behind the S Corporation provisions of the internal revenue code is that a firm should be able to select its form of organization free of tax considerations. The S Corporation is a hybrid form allowing the highly desired limited liability for owners but avoiding the corporate "curse" of double taxation.

To qualify as an S Corporation, the corporation must meet several tests including, but not limited to, (1) having 35 or fewer stockholders, (2) the corporation must be a domestic corporation that is not a member of a controlled group, and (3) the corporation can have only one class of stock.

The S Corporation form of organization can be most useful when corporate losses are anticipated and owners have taxable income that can absorb the losses or when corporations are profitable without having uses for extra capital that may be taxed on accumulated earnings. Since profits are passed through to stockholders, this potential problem is overcome by the subchapter S election.

Accounting Methods

After deciding on the legal form of operation, management must determine which accounting method best reflects their type of business and provides optimum ability to minimize or postpone taxes by effectively timing the recognition of income and deduction of expenses. The manager should be aware that there are different types of accounting methods available, depending on the nature of the business.

Cash Versus Accrual Method

Current tax laws permit use of the cash method of measuring taxable income if inventories are not a significant factor in the operation of the business. Under this method, items of income and expense are generally reported for tax purposes when cash is actually received for an item of income, or paid out for an expense item.

Even under the cash method, there are exceptions. For example, fixed assets must generally be depreciated over the life of the asset rather than being deducted as an expense in the year paid. Exhibit 16.3 shows that Snicker's Restaurant was on a cash basis. For tax purposes, inventories of food were $-0- as shown on Schedule C; however, there was depreciation of $20,000 for 1985.

A cash basis taxpayer has some flexibility in the reporting of income and expenses. The timing of income collection, or the payment of expenses, can be controlled to some extent, particularly near year-end.

The accrual method of accounting reports income when it is earned rather than when the cash is collected. It reflects expenses when they are incurred rather than when they are paid. As is the case with many areas of tax law, there are exceptions to the general rule.

Under the accrual method, some items of income are taxed when collected rather than when earned; for example, advance rentals. Similarly, an expense item must be fixed and determinable before it can be deducted for tax purposes. Estimated expenses, while generally acceptable for financial accounting, may not be deducted for tax reporting until all factors which affect the expense item have become "fixed and determinable."

Installment Sales Method

For financial accounting purposes, when goods or property are sold on the installment method, that is, the sales price is received in periodic payments over time, the entire sales price is recognized at the time of sale, and the entire cost of goods sold deducted as an expense of sale. Tax reporting, however, allows for a choice to be made to recognize the profit on sales made on the installment method ratably as cash is received. This method is frequently chosen upon the sale of a business, such as a hotel or restaurant.

Accounting Income Versus Taxable Income

Thus far, the importance of tax planning for a transaction at an early stage of its development has been emphasized. In addition, several options available for selecting the legal entity within which to conduct a business have been presented. Having selected the entity, the method of accounting (cash versus accrual) most suitable for mitigating the tax costs of operation is chosen. All of these choices are made in concert with the overall business objectives of the operation.

These various choices can cause differences in the amount and timing of income or expenses reported in financial statements from the amount reported in the tax return. There are other tax requirements or choices that can cause further differences in the amount or timing of the reporting of income and expense.

Accelerated Depreciation

Tax legislation in 1981 and 1982 liberalized tax depreciation rules with enactment of an Accelerated Cost Recovery System (ACRS) which provides for faster "recovery" (depreciation) of capital expenditures.

Under financial accounting, a building may be depreciated over thirty years (or more). ACRS currently allows recovery for tax purposes over nineteen years. Similarly, furniture and equipment may be depreciated over seven to ten years (or more) for financial accounting purposes, while the same items are depreciated for tax purposes over five years under ACRS. Thus, the timing of reporting net income for financial purposes can be significantly different than taxable income.

This situation will be reversed in the later years of an asset's life. The deduction for depreciation will be greater for financial accounting than for tax accounting. At the end of the asset's life, the deduction for depreciation will be the same in total for both book and tax accounting. The point to remember is the timing of the deduction.

Exhibit 16.8 uses a purchase of $1,000,000 of equipment to illustrate the difference between ACRS recovery expense and depreciation using the straight-line method. For tax purposes, the ACRS allows the cost of the equipment to be recovered over five years, while for financial reporting purposes, assume the hospitality operation chooses to depreciate the equipment over ten years using the straight-line method. In the first five years, ACRS results in $500,000 more expense than straight-line method, while the reverse results in the later five years.

Pre-Opening Expenses

For many years, hospitality firms were able to deduct, for tax purposes, many of the expenses as they were incurred prior to the formal opening of a new hotel, even if such expenses were deferred for financial reporting purposes. This was especially true if the operation was not the first hotel in the business.

In recent years, however, the courts have generally decided against current deductibility of such expenses, and the law and regulations have been tightened significantly. Because of the complexity of the area, a manager should consult with his/her tax advisor to ensure the proper tax position is taken.

First Year Losses

First year losses of a hospitality operation are usually capitalized as a deferred charge and amortized over several years for financial accounting purposes. However, for tax purposes, such costs are generally deductible as incurred so taxable income is lower than financial accounting income, improving cash flow of the company by the deferral of taxes. This situation reverses as the first year losses are amortized for financial accounting with no offsetting amortization for tax accounting, producing a higher taxable income than book income and a corresponding higher payment of tax.

Loss Carrybacks and Carryforwards

A final example of differences between financial and tax accounting is the treatment of operating losses sustained by a business. Current tax laws allow a net operating loss to be carried back and applied as a deduction against prior taxable income in order to obtain a refund of

Exhibit 16.8 Depreciation of Equipment for Tax and Financial Reporting Purposes

Year	ACRS Recovery[1]	Straight-Line Recovery[2]	Difference
19X1	$ 150,000	$ 100,000	$ 50,000
19X2	220,000	100,000	120,000
19X3	210,000	100,000	110,000
19X4	210,000	100,000	110,000
19X5	210,000	100,000	110,000
19X6	0	100,000	(100,000)
19X7	0	100,000	(100,000)
19X8	0	100,000	(100,000)
19X9	0	100,000	(100,000)
19X0	0	100,000	(100,000)
Total	$1,000,000	$1,000,000	$0

[1]The recovery rates are as follows:

1st year	– 15%
2nd year	– 22
3rd year	– 21
4th year	– 21
5th year	– 21
Total	100%

[2]Assuming a zero salvage value. Annual depreciation is determined by dividing the cost ($1,000,000) by the life (10 years) to equal the annual depreciation ($100,000).

taxes previously paid. A loss may be carried back three years and carried forward fifteen years.

For financial accounting purposes, an operating loss incurred by a business will generally flow through to reported earnings as this pre-tax book loss may be reduced, in certain situations, by the tax benefit up to the amount of previously paid taxes. Financial accounting rules permit the recording of tax benefit on an operating loss if it can be carried back and utilized against prior years' taxable income.

For example, assume an enterprise incurs a $100,000 pre-tax loss which can be carried back against prior years' taxable income. Further assume that $30,000 of prior paid taxes can be recovered. The pre-tax loss is then reduced by the $30,000 recovery.

State and Municipal Taxes

Until recently, managers paid little attention to state and local taxes because rates were low and the aggregate dollars did not warrant serious study. This has changed in recent years as state and local governments have been increasing tax rates and seeking new areas to generate tax revenue in order to fund the increasing demand for services placed on them by their constituents. Today's manager realizes state and local taxes provide ever-increasing opportunities for tax planning to reduce the overall tax burden.

The financial manager of a multi-state operation should be aware that the manner in which business is conducted in a state determines whether and how the business is subject to that state's tax laws. Early tax planning is the key to success here, as it is in all areas of tax planning.

Another planning opportunity in a multi-corporate form of business is present when one unit is profitable and a second is unprofitable due to a start-up situation or to other reasons. The manager should investigate whether state tax laws allow consolidation of operations to offset the income of one corporation with the loss of another to minimize the total tax burden. If state laws do not permit consolidation and the mix of profit and loss operations is expected to continue for some time, the manager will want to consider whether a corporate reorganization is desirable to merge the loss operation into the profitable one to achieve the same tax results as the filing of a consolidated return.

As noted above, other business objectives should be weighed and the decision of whether to reorganize the corporate structure through merger would be tempered by any competing goals of a non-tax nature that may take precedence.

Property Taxes

Taxes levied on real estate and personal property such as furniture, fixtures, and equipment are commonly called property taxes. In recent years, property taxes for hotels have approximated 3.0% of gross revenue, which may seem insignificant. However, a reduction of .5% to 2.5% in property taxes for a hotel with $20,000,000 sales would save the hotel $100,000.

Property taxes are generally levied at the local levels, that is, by county and/or city. The tax is a function of assessed valuation and the tax rate. Property taxes differ by state and locality; the State of Michigan will be used for illustration purposes to show the calculation of property taxes.

The general property tax formula in Michigan is:

$$\text{Property Taxes} = \frac{\text{Assessed Valuation}}{1,000} \times \text{Tax Rate}$$

In this formula, the assessed valuation is the value placed on the property to be taxed by the tax assessor. The tax rate is stated in mills, which is tax dollars per $1,000 of assessed valuation. Assume Rocky's Hotel had an assessed valuation of $10,000,000 and a tax rate of 50 mills. The annual property tax would be calculated as follows:

$$\text{Property Taxes} = \frac{10,000,000}{1,000} \times 50$$

$$\text{Property Taxes} = 10,000 \times 50$$

$$\text{Property Taxes} = \underline{\$500,000}$$

Although property taxes are normally viewed as a fixed cost, not controllable by management, the assessed valuation should be challenged when it is considered to be excessive. For example, in Michigan, the assessed valuation by law is to be 50% of market value. Using Rocky's Hotel, assume it had recently been purchased for $18,000,000. Based on Michigan law, the assessed valuation for Rocky's Hotel should be reduced to $9,000,000, which is 50% of the market price. The $1,000,000 assessed valuation reduction, given the tax rate of 50 mills, reduces property taxes by $50,000 annually.

Summary

Income taxes are charged by governments to raise revenue to provide their constituents with services and to achieve a variety of social goals. Both individuals and businesses pay taxes. Most financial business decisions have tax implications, and hospitality managers must have knowledge of taxes in order to make optimal decisions.

Federal income taxes are based on a self-reporting system, whereby the taxpayer prepares the appropriate tax forms. For the individual, tax considerations include income, adjustments to income, deductions, exemptions, credits, other taxes, and taxes paid. Form 1040, Form 1040A, or Form 1040EZ must be filed by all qualifying taxpayers.

A major goal is tax avoidance which is a legal approach to reduce taxes, while tax evasion results from illegal means of reducing taxes.

A major tax consideration is the form of organization used by a business. The sole proprietorship, partnership, and corporation are major forms, while hybrid forms include limited partnership and S Corporation. There are advantages and disadvantages of each form of organization. The disadvantage of individual unlimited liability can be overcome by incorporating; however, incorporation results in double taxation. Avoiding double taxation and unlimited liability can be achieved by filing as an S Corporation; however, S Corporations are limited to one type of stock and 35 or fewer stockholders. Thus, the type of business organization used will have some disadvantages, but given the size, goals, and riskiness of the business, a form should be chosen which minimizes the disadvantages while maximizing the advantages.

The discussion of accounting income versus taxable income included depreciation, pre-opening expenses, first year losses, and loss carryback and carryforward. In addition, state and municipal taxes, including property taxes, were discussed. The hospitality manager must be alert to reducing these taxes when possible.

Notes

1. Commissioner v. Newman (CA-2), 47-1 USTC 99175, 159 Fed.(2d)848.
2. Albert J. Gomes, *Hospitality in Transition*, New York: AH&MA, 1985.

Discussion Questions

1. What are five types of income that must be reported on an individual's tax return?

2. How do "deductions" differ from "tax credits"?

3. What are the major advantages of a sole proprietorship?

4. What are the major advantages of a corporation?

5. How may the disadvantage of unlimited liability be overcome in selecting a form of organization?

6. Why are limited partnerships so useful in raising capital funds for hospitality operations?

7. How does accelerated depreciation, as opposed to straight-line depreciation, save profitable hospitality firms tax dollars?

8. What are two limitations to S Corporations?

9. What is double taxation?

10. When is the sole proprietorship form preferred?

Problem 16.1

Leslie Boyer is considering opening a franchised quick service restaurant (QSR). He believes in a typical year he will gross nearly $1,200,000 and net $100,000 prior to payment of income taxes. Angela, his wife, is expected to have taxable income of $100,000 from her apartment rentals. Her business is not incorporated. Leslie desires to avoid double taxation but also wants to limit his liability.

Required:

1. What form of organization do you suggest?

2. How *may* the liability problem be "overcome" without incorporating?

Problem 16.2

Based on the information in the prior problem, ignore exemptions and personal deductions and calculate income taxes for the Boyers and their businesses in the following situations:

A.   Assume the Boyers' average tax rate is 46%, and that both QSR and the real estate businesses are unincorporated.

B.   Assume the Boyers' average tax rate is 46%, the average corporate rate is 40%, and the QSR is incorporated.

C.   Assume the same situation as B above, and that the QSR pays Leslie $50,000 of dividends that are taxed at the Boyers' average tax rate.

D.   Assume the Boyers' average tax rate is 46%, the average corporate rate is 40%, and the QSR is incorporated but is treated as an S Corporation for tax purposes.

Problem 16.3

Nicole Bustle is earning a mint selling real estate. During the past five years, she has had average taxable income annually of $200,000. Her husband, Richie, is anxious to open a 100-unit motor hotel. The feasibility study conducted for the lodging facility suggests losses of $150,000, $100,000, and $50,000 for the first three years, respectively. The following three years, the motor hotel is expected to generate pre-tax profits of $100,000 per year. Assume the Bustles' average tax rate is 45%. Further, assume the average corporate tax rate is 25%, and that corporate tax losses can be carried forward for up to five years.

Required:

Based on the above information, how should Richie Bustle organize his motor hotel business? Note: consider providing "tax savings" to support your answer.

Problem 16.4

J. Deere Restaurants, Inc. is undecided whether to use the cash or accrual method of accounting for tax purposes. The chairperson, John Deere, has provided you with the following information:

	Basis	
	Cash	Accrual
Sales	$1,000,000	$1,100,000
Cost of Sales	350,000	325,000
Labor	300,000	310,000
Other Expenses (excluding taxes)	200,000	190,000

John believes the approach which minimizes taxes for the first year is the preferred method. Assume that the taxes for J. Deere Restaurants, Inc. will be based on the following tax structure:

Taxable Income	Marginal Tax Rate
$ 0—25,000	15%
25,000—50,000	18
50,000—75,000	30
75,000—100,000	40
over 100,000	46

Required:

Determine which method J. Deere Restaurants, Inc. should use.

Problem 16.5

The Celtic Corporation has purchased $2,000,000 worth of equipment for its hotels in the current year. The President, Fred Boston, has heard that using the ACRS recovery versus straight-line offers cash savings. Assume the equipment could be "depreciated" over five years for tax purposes using the recovery rates shown in Exhibit 16.8. Alternatively, assume it could be depreciated over 10 years using the straight-line method and have a salvage value of $-0-. Further, assume the marginal tax rate for the Celtic Corporation is 46%, and that taxes saved due to the difference in ACRS and straight-line depreciation are invested at the end of each year at 10% interest compounded annually.

Required:

1. Determine the amount of the "tax savings fund" from taxes saved based on the above and interest earned over the first five years.

2. Calculate the interest earned over the ten-year period. Assume that for the 6th through 10th years the taxes paid due to excess straight-line depreciation over ACRS comes at the end of each year from the "tax savings fund."

Appendix A
Uniform Systems Schedules

ROOMS—SCHEDULE 1

	Current Period
REVENUE	
Transient—Regular	$
Transient—Group	
Permanent	
Other	
Total Revenue	
ALLOWANCES	
NET REVENUE	
EXPENSES	
Salaries and Wages	
Employee Benefits	
Total Payroll and Related Expenses	
Other Expenses	
Commissions	
Contract Cleaning	
Guest Transportation	
Laundry and Dry Cleaning	
Linen	
Operating Supplies	
Reservations	
Uniforms	
Other	
Total Other Expenses	
DEPARTMENTAL INCOME (LOSS)	$

FOOD AND BEVERAGE—SCHEDULE 2

	Current Period		
	Food	Beverage	Total
REVENUE	$	$	$
ALLOWANCES			
NET REVENUE			
COST OF FOOD AND BEVERAGE SALES			
Cost of Food and Beverage Consumed			
Less: Cost of Employee Meals			
Net Cost of Food and Beverage Sales			
OTHER INCOME			
Meeting Room Rentals			
Cover Charges			
Miscellaneous Banquet Income			
Miscellaneous Other Income			
Other Cost of Sales			
Net Other Income			
GROSS PROFIT (LOSS)	$	$	$
EXPENSES			
Salaries and Wages	$	$	$
Employee Benefits			
Total Payroll and Related Expenses	$	$	$
Other Expenses			
China, Glassware, Silver, and Linen			
Contract Cleaning			
Kitchen Fuel			
Laundry and Dry Cleaning			
Licenses			
Music and Entertainment			
Operating Supplies			
Uniforms			
Other			
Total Other Expenses			
DEPARTMENTAL INCOME (LOSS)			$

TELEPHONE—SCHEDULE 3

	Current Period
REVENUE	
Local	$
Long-Distance	
Service Charges	
Pay Station	————
Total Revenue	
ALLOWANCES	————
NET REVENUE	————
COST OF CALLS	
Local	
Long-Distance	————
Total Cost of Calls	————
GROSS PROFIT (LOSS)	————
EXPENSES	
Salaries and Wages	
Employee Benefits	————
Total Payroll and Related Expenses	————
Other Expenses	
Printing and Stationery	
Uniforms	
Other	————
Total Other Expenses	————
DEPARTMENTAL INCOME (LOSS)	$ ————

GIFT SHOP—SCHEDULE 4

	Current Period
REVENUE	$_____
ALLOWANCES	_____
NET REVENUE	_____
COST OF MERCHANDISE SOLD	_____
GROSS PROFIT (LOSS)	_____
EXPENSES	
Salaries and Wages	
Employee Benefits	_____
Total Payroll and Related Expenses	_____
Other Expenses	
Operating Supplies	
Uniforms	
Other	_____
Total Other Expenses	_____
DEPARTMENTAL INCOME (LOSS)	$_____

GARAGE AND PARKING—SCHEDULE 5

	Current Period
REVENUE	
Parking and Storage	$
Merchandise	
Other	————
Total Revenue	
ALLOWANCES	————
NET REVENUE	————
COST OF MERCHANDISE SOLD	————
GROSS PROFIT (LOSS)	————
EXPENSES	
Salaries and Wages	
Employee Benefits	————
Total Payroll and Related Expenses	————
Other Expenses	
Licenses	
Management Fee	
Operating Supplies	
Uniforms	
Other	————
Total Other Expenses	————
DEPARTMENTAL INCOME (LOSS)	$ ————

OTHER OPERATED DEPARTMENTS—SCHEDULE ___

	Current Period
REVENUE	
Services	$ _____
Sales of Merchandise	
Total Revenue	
ALLOWANCES	_____
NET REVENUE	_____
COST OF MERCHANDISE SOLD	_____
GROSS PROFIT (LOSS)	_____
EXPENSES	
Salaries and Wages	
Employee Benefits	
Total Payroll and Related Expenses	_____
Other Expenses	
China and Glassware	
Contract Services	
Laundry	
Linen	
Operating Supplies	
Uniforms	
Other	_____
Total Other Expenses	_____
DEPARTMENTAL INCOME (LOSS)	$ _____

RENTALS AND OTHER INCOME—SCHEDULE 6

	Current Period
SPACE RENTALS	
Clubs	$
Offices	
Stores	
Other	
Total Rentals	
CONCESSIONS	
Total Concessions	
COMMISSIONS	
Laundry	
Valet	
Games and Vending Machines	
In-house Movies	
Other	
Total Commissions	
CASH DISCOUNTS EARNED	
ELECTRONIC GAMES AND PINBALL MACHINES	
FORFEITED ADVANCE DEPOSITS	
INTEREST INCOME	
SALVAGE	
VENDING MACHINES	
OTHER	
TOTAL RENTALS AND OTHER INCOME	$

ADMINISTRATIVE AND GENERAL—SCHEDULE 7

	Current Period
SALARIES AND WAGES	$
EMPLOYEE BENEFITS	
Total Payroll and Related Expenses	
OTHER EXPENSES	
Credit Card Commissions	
Data Processing	
Dues and Subscriptions	
Human Resources	
Insurance—General	
Operating Supplies	
Postage and Telegrams	
Professional Fees	
Provision for Doubtful Accounts	
Travel and Entertainment	
Other	
Total Other Expenses	
TOTAL ADMINISTRATIVE AND GENERAL EXPENSES	$

DATA PROCESSING—SCHEDULE 8

	Current Period
SALARIES AND WAGES	$
EMPLOYEE BENEFITS	
Total Payroll and Related Expenses	
OTHER EXPENSES	
Dues and Subscriptions	
Training	
Maintenance	
Hardware	
Software	
Operating Supplies	
Service Bureau Fees	
Other	
Total Other Expenses	
TOTAL DATA PROCESSING EXPENSES	$

HUMAN RESOURCES—SCHEDULE 9

	Current Period
SALARIES AND WAGES	$
EMPLOYEE BENEFITS	
Total Payroll and Related Expenses	
OTHER EXPENSES	
Dues and Subscriptions	
Employee Housing	
Employee Relations	
Medical Expenses	
Operating Supplies	
Recruitment	
Relocation	
Training	
Transportation	
Other	
Total Other Expenses	
TOTAL HUMAN RESOURCES EXPENSES	$

TRANSPORTATION—SCHEDULE 10

	Current Period
SALARIES AND WAGES	$
EMPLOYEE BENEFITS	
Total Payroll and Related Expenses	
OTHER EXPENSES	
Fuel and Oil	
Insurance	
Operating Supplies	
Repairs and Maintenance	
Uniforms	
Other	
Total Other Expenses	
TOTAL TRANSPORTATION EXPENSES	$

MARKETING—SCHEDULE 11

	Current Period
SALES	
Salaries and Wages	$
Employee Benefits	
Total Payroll and Related Expenses	
Other Expenses	
Total Sales	
RESERVATIONS	
Salaries and Wages	
Employee Benefits	
Total Payroll and Related Expenses	
Other Expenses	
Total Reservations	
ADVERTISING AND MERCHANDISING	
Direct Mail	
In-house Graphics	
Outdoor	
Point-of-Sale Material	
Print	
Radio and Television	
Selling Aids	
Other	
Total Advertising and Merchandising	
FEES AND COMMISSIONS	
Agency Fees	
Franchise Fees	
Other	
Total Fees and Commissions	
MISCELLANEOUS MARKETING EXPENSES	
TOTAL OTHER EXPENSES	
TOTAL MARKETING EXPENSES	$

PROPERTY OPERATION AND MAINTENANCE—SCHEDULE 12

	Current Period
SALARIES AND WAGES	$
EMPLOYEE BENEFITS	
Total Payroll and Related Expenses	
OTHER EXPENSES	
Building Supplies	
Electrical and Mechanical Equipment	
Engineering Supplies	
Furniture, Fixtures, Equipment, and Decor	
Grounds and Landscaping	
Operating Supplies	
Removal of Waste Matter	
Swimming Pool	
Uniforms	
Other	
Total Other Expenses	
TOTAL PROPERTY OPERATION AND MAINTENANCE	$

ENERGY COSTS—SCHEDULE 13

	Current Period
Electric Current	$
Fuel	
Steam	
Water	_____
TOTAL ENERGY COSTS	$

FIXED CHARGES—SCHEDULE 14

RENT, PROPERTY TAXES, AND INSURANCE

	Current Period
RENT	
Land and Buildings	$
Data Processing Equipment	
Telephone Equipment	
Other Equipment	_____
Total	_____
TAXES OTHER THAN INCOME AND PAYROLL	
Real Estate Taxes	
Personal Property Taxes	
Utility Taxes	
Business and Occupation Taxes	
Other	_____
Total	_____
INSURANCE ON BUILDING AND CONTENTS	_____
TOTAL RENT, PROPERTY TAXES, AND INSURANCE	$

INTEREST EXPENSE

	Current Period
Mortgages	$
Notes Payable	
Interest on Capital Leases	
Other Long-Term Debt	
Amortization of Deferred Financing Costs	
Other	_____
Total	$

DEPRECIATION AND AMORTIZATION

	Current Period
Buildings and Improvements	$
Leaseholds and Leasehold Improvements	
Furnishings and Equipment	
Capital Leases	
Preopening Expenses	
Other	_____
Total	$
GAIN OR LOSS ON SALE OF PROPERTY	$

INCOME TAXES—SCHEDULE 15

	Current Period
FEDERAL	
Current	$
Deferred	
Total	
STATE	
Current	
Deferred	
Total	
OTHER	
Current	
Deferred	
Total	
TOTAL FEDERAL AND STATE INCOME TAXES	$

SALARIES AND WAGES—SCHEDULE 16

	Current Period	
	Number of Employees	Amount
ROOMS		
Management		$
Front Office		
Housekeeping		
Service		
Security		
Total (Schedule 1)		$
FOOD AND BEVERAGE		
Management		$
Kitchen		
Service		
Other		
Total (Schedule 2)		$
TELEPHONE (Schedule 3)		$
GIFT SHOP (Schedule 4)		$
GARAGE AND PARKING (Schedule 5)		$
OTHER OPERATED DEPARTMENTS (Schedule _)		$
ADMINISTRATIVE AND GENERAL		
Manager's Office		$
Accounting Office		
Credit Office		
Front Office Bookkeeping		
Night Auditors		
Receiving Clerks		
Timekeepers		
Total (Schedule 7)		$
DATA PROCESSING (Schedule 8)		$
HUMAN RESOURCES (Schedule 9)		$
TRANSPORTATION (Schedule 10)		$
MARKETING (Schedule 11)		$
PROPERTY OPERATION AND MAINTENANCE		
Management		$
Engineers		
Grounds		
Office and Storeroom		
Other		
Total (Schedule 12)		$
HOUSE LAUNDRY		
Managers and Assistants		$
Finishing		
Washing		
Other		
Total (Schedule 18)		$
TOTAL SALARIES AND WAGES		$

	Schedule B-17
PAYROLL TAXES AND EMPLOYEE BENEFITS	

Current
Period

Payroll Taxes $
   Federal Retirement
   Federal Unemployment
   State Unemployment   _____
      Total Payroll Taxes   _____

Employee Benefits
   Nonunion Insurance
   Nonunion Pension
   Profit Sharing
   Union Insurance
   Union Pension
   Worker's Compensation Insurance
   Other   _____
      Total Employee Benefits   _____

Total Payroll Taxes and Employee Benefits $_____

Charged to Departments $

Rooms	Schedule B-1
Food and Beverage	Schedule B-2
Telephone	Schedule B-3
Gift Shop	Schedule B-4
Garage and Parking	Schedule B-5
Other Operated Departments	Schedule B-
Administrative and General	Schedule B-7
Data Processing	Schedule B-8
Human Resources	Schedule B-9
Transportation	Schedule B-10
Marketing	Schedule B-11
Property Operations and Maintenance	Schedule B-12
House Laundry	Schedule B-18

Total Payroll Taxes and Employee Benefits $_____

HOUSE LAUNDRY   **Schedule B-18**

Current
Period

Salaries and Wages $ _____

Employee Benefits   _____
       Total Payroll and Related Expenses   _____

Other Expenses
    Cleaning Supplies
    Laundry Supplies
    Printing and Stationery
    Uniforms
    Other   _____
       Total Other Expenses   _____

Credits
    Cost of Guest Laundry
    Cost of Concessionaires' Laundry   _____
       Total Credits   _____

Cost of House Laundry $_____

Charged to Departments
    Rooms   Schedule B-1 $
    Food and Beverage   Schedule B-2
    Other Departments   Schedule B-   _____
       Total $_____

Appendix B
Essentials of Computer Systems

The introduction of a computer system can significantly change the way hospitality business is charted and conducted. Every business collects and analyzes data about its operations. A computer system enables management to speed up the process by which useful information is made available to decision makers. In addition, a computer system can streamline the process of collecting and recording data and expand the ways in which information is organized and reported.

How much does a manager need to know about a computer to operate one? About as much as a motorist needs to know about auto mechanics to drive a car. The automobile responds to the driver's "commands." As long as the driver understands what the vehicle will do when the lever is pulled, the accelerator pushed, the wheel turned, etc., the car ought to perform correctly. In addition, if the motorist knows some basics of auto mechanics and some emergency maintenance techniques, the car ought to perform better and longer. In the same way, if a manager understands how the computer responds to commands and some basics about its operation, it can be an effective tool in managing information needs. While all businesses use some information system, a computerized system enables management to achieve its goals much more easily.

This appendix outlines the basics of computer operation by examining general information concepts and needs, computer hardware and software, data security, and human factors involved in computerizing functions within a hospitality operation.

Data and Information

Hospitality managers are bombarded with facts—data—throughout the day. These isolated bits of data are meaningless until they are related to each other—processed—in a way that converts them into useful information. When the collection of facts bombarding hospitality managers daily is analyzed and organized into information, they can provide significant insights and guide decisions affecting the operation. The objective of all information systems, including computerized ones, is to transform this data into information—and to do so on a timely basis so that the results are still useful to the manager.

There are three distinct types of data. One

type is called "alpha" because it consists of only letters of the alphabet. For example, the name of a menu item, a server, or a hotel guest are all types of alpha data. A second kind of data is called "numeric" because it consists of only numbers. Menu prices, room numbers, guest check serial numbers, and occupancy percentages are all numeric data. The third form of data is termed "alphanumeric" since it involves both letters and numbers in the same data entry. A hotel's street address, a menu item description, and personnel records are examples of hospitality alphanumerics.

Why is information so important to the hospitality operation? What does it do? First, information provides knowledge related to operations, service, labor, finance, and other areas of concern. Second, information reduces uncertainty with respect to decision making. Third, information presents feedback which enables corrective action. A survey of customers leaving a restaurant, for example, may offer management information about the business, reduce uncertainty about guest satisfaction, and provide important operational feedback. Information, one of an operation's most valuable resources, is the outcome of data processing.

Data Processing

Regardless of the degree of automation, all businesses use some form of data processing. Data processing is primarily concerned with the transformation of raw, isolated facts (data) into comprehensive, useful information. This occurs constantly—not only in business but everyday life as well. Everyone processes data. For example, when people receive their paychecks, they might consider all of the items they would like to purchase, what the cost of those purchases is, and the difference between the check and total purchases. If the paycheck is larger than the expenditures, a person might decide to place the extra in a savings account. If, on the other hand, expenditures are greater than the paycheck, the person has to reconsider the purchase options—or, perhaps, decide to take out a loan. A collection of data (purchase costs and paycheck amount) has been processed (totaled and compared) and, thus, transformed into information (deficit or surplus) useful in making decisions (what to buy). This conversion is accomplished through procedures referred to as input, process, and output. In the above situation, the paycheck and the purchase options are inputs; the calculation of the different expenditures is the processing; and the deficit or surplus is the output. It is the sequential combination of these factors that compose the basic data processing cycle.

Data Processing Cycle

During input, data are captured and coded to simplify subsequent processing functions. During processing, input data is mathematically manipulated or logically arranged to generate meaningful output. The output, then, can be stored (saved for future reference) and/or reported for immediate use. The basic data processing cycle is presented in Exhibit B-1.

The data processing cycle occurs almost constantly and is not limited to computer applications. Standard recipes, used to convert raw ingredients into menu items, can be seen as data processing techniques. Ingredients and their corresponding quantities are typical (alphanumeric) inputs to recipe production. During processing, by following the recipe's instructions the desired recipe output—a number of standard portions per batch—will result.

Objectives of Data Processing

The objectives of data processing include minimizing turnaround time (elapsed time from input to output), and minimizing the number of times the same piece of data is handled. An efficiently designed data processing system provides managers with rapid access to the information they need to make timely and effective decisions. Inquiry and search procedures should be performed within an acceptable response time. For example, if a front desk clerk needs to find out in which room a guest is registered, the answer should be generated quickly. Also, a busy food and beverage manager, who wants to spot check inventory of the most expensive ingredients immediately following a meal period, would appreciate the speed and accuracy of an effective data processing design. Computer systems are able to minimize turnaround time for almost all data processing tasks.

Reducing the number of times data must be rehandled enhances both the speed and the accuracy of data processing tasks. Consider the

Exhibit B-1   Data Processing Cycle

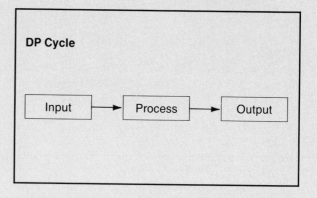

difference between a manual accounting system and a computerized one. In the manual system, an invoice received is first recorded in a journal. Next, the amount is carried over to a ledger. Amounts in the ledger are then used to calculate the financial statements. During any of these steps it is possible for a bookkeeper to write the wrong number, write a number's digits in the wrong order (transpose them), calculate a total incorrectly, etc. In the computerized system, however, the invoice amount is entered only once. The amount can then be accessed by the programs which prepare the journal, ledger, and financial statements. Therefore, if the number is entered correctly, all of the subsequent statements will be correct. If it is entered incorrectly, but the mistake corrected, the correction automatically flows from the journal through to the financial statements. With electronic data processing, there are fewer opportunities for the types of errors to occur that happen when the same data must be rehandled for a variety of different tasks. And, if there is an error, electronic data processing can perform again all the affected tasks almost instantaneously once the error is corrected. The speed, accuracy, and efficiency required for an effective information system are often best achieved through electronic data processing.

Electronic Data Processing

The difference between data processing (DP) and electronic data processing (EDP) lies in the automation of the process and the addition of a memory unit. Electronic data processing employs a computer system for its base of operation. The automation of input, process, and output components results in faster and more efficient opera-

Exhibit B-2 Electronic Data Processing Cycle

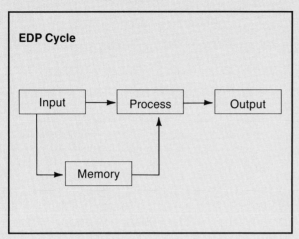

Exhibit B-3 Computer Hardware Components

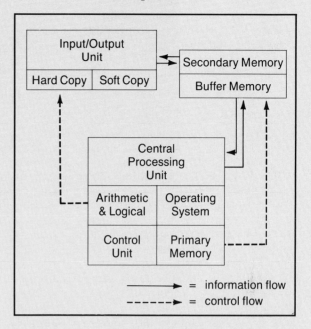

tions. The inclusion of a memory unit enables storage of instructions and data for more reliable and thorough analysis. Exhibit B-2 shows how the addition of memory affects the data processing cycle. This cycle is referred to as the EDP cycle.

What is a Computer? A computer is a managerial tool capable of processing large quantities of data very rapidly and accurately. It can perform arithmetic (addition, subtraction, multiplication, and division) and logical (ranking, sorting, and assembling) operations. The advantages of a computer include: speed, accuracy, retention, and control. Computers process data much more quickly than any other method while maintaining an incredible level of precision. In addition, they are capable of storing and retrieving tremendous amounts of information, and bringing discipline to and controlling procedures otherwise overlooked.

Computer systems are composed of a variety of component parts. It is important that these components be well understood in order to ensure optimal system design and operation. Managers who understand the functions of each component and are comfortable with the computer's operations are more in control of this valuable tool. This knowledge enables them to more effectively verbalize needs or requests when they decide which computer system best suits their operation or when they want to expand the data processing functions their system already performs.

A knowledge of computer jargon (frequently termed "computerese") is extremely helpful in expressing the functions desired from a computer system and in understanding the functioning of the system itself. This section introduces many of these computer terms by explaining the concepts of hardware, software, communication devices, information security, and the human factors involved in computing.

Hardware

The physical equipment found in a computer system is called hardware. Computer hardware is visible, movable, and easy to distinguish. In order to have a computer system, three components are required: the input/output unit, the secondary memory unit, and the central processing unit. Exhibit B-3 shows how these three components are related and indicates their major elements.

The input/output (I/O) unit allows the user to interact with the system. The user can input data and receive output information through a variety of electronic devices. The most common I/O device at work in the hospitality industry is the CRT. (CRT is the acronym for cathode ray tube; that term is very infrequently used now.) The CRT unit is composed of a television-like video screen and a typewriter keyboard. As data is entered through the keyboard, it is displayed on the screen. The CRT operator can edit and verify the on-screen input prior to transmitting it for processing.

Another popular I/O device is the teletype terminal (TTY). The teletype is less expensive than the CRT and does not include a video display component. Instead, input is entered over the keyboard and printed on a roll of paper. As the operator enters data into the system, a printed report can be made at the TTY console. The entered data is then communicated to a remote unit for processing. After processing, the information is relayed back to the TTY and printed on paper. For example, the housekeeping department of a hotel might use TTYs to communicate with the front desk and keep them up-to-date on room status. In this case, the housekeeping department needs some record of the messages sent, but does not require all the capabilities of a CRT. Therefore, the extra cost for a CRT is not justified.

Other types of I/O equipment include keyboard and operator display units such as electronic cash registers (ECR) and line printing terminals. A hotel's food and beverage operation might use ECRs to communicate with the front office. In a computerized hotel system, restaurant charges can be entered into a point-of-sale device in the restaurant and transmitted to the front office where guest folios are automatically updated with the charges.

One important difference between I/O devices is the type of output they produce. CRTs display output on a monitor for the user to examine; this type of output is referred to as "soft copy" because it cannot be handled by the operator or removed from the computer. Printers, however, generate a paper copy of the output which is called a "hard copy." Many systems are designed so that they can produce both types of output. For example, a computer at a hotel's front desk might have a CRT which the clerk can use to view a soft copy of guest folios during check-in and check-out times. However, when the guest checks out, a hard copy of the folio will be generated from a printer so that the guest can keep a copy. Obviously, output displayed on a screen (CRT) is much more temporary and its use more constricted than output printed on paper. Generally hospitality managers obtain essential reports in hard copy form, allowing storage outside the computer and providing a base for information backup.

The central processing unit (CPU) is the most important and expensive hardware component found within a computer system. It is the "brains" of the system and is responsible for controlling all other system components. As shown in Exhibit B-3, the CPU is composed of four subunits. The first subunit is the arithmetic and logical unit (ALU) which performs all the mathematical, sorting, and processing functions.

A second subunit, referred to as the control unit, is responsible for determining which devices in the computer system are accessible to and/or by the CPU. If a device is capable of interacting directly with the CPU, it is said to be "on-line"; "off-line" describes the condition in which there is no established connection between a system device and the CPU. It is interesting to note that although computer devices may be switched on (powered-up) they are not necessarily on-line. For example, when a printer is connected to a computer and turned on, the operator can switch the printer to either on-line or off-line status. The printer will respond to commands from the CPU only when it is on-line.

The third subunit of the CPU is the operating system (OS). The operating system is responsible for orchestrating the hardware and the software within the system. It establishes the system's priorities and directs its resources to effectively accomplish desired tasks. This concept is discussed in greater depth later in this appendix.

The final subunit of the CPU is the primary memory unit which contains permanent programs designed into the system by the manufacturer. The CPU comes equipped with its own set of commands and instructions. These commands are the most basic ones recognized by the computer. To ensure they are not altered by the user, these programs are stored within the computer in a read-only memory (ROM) format. This means that the computer can "read" or understand the information stored in these memory chips, but no one can "write" or save anything in this area of the computer's memory. Since the primary memory is composed of a limited syntax (vocabulary), the computer only recognizes its own pre-programmed commands. If a user tries to enter a different command, the computer will not recognize the input and will respond by reporting that a "syntax error" has occurred. For example, some personal computers will start a program's operation if the user types "GO"; others require the user to type "RUN." If the user types the wrong command, the computer will respond with a message such as "UNDEFINED COMMAND" to alert the user to the problem. Since these commands are specified by the computer manufacturer, different machines utilize different commands. This is why software designed for one brand of computer will not work on other brands; since the primary memories are different, some of the commands are not recognized by the other brands.

Another type of memory, the secondary memory unit, is used to store data and programs needed by the user. Types of secondary memory include diskettes and cassettes. Diskettes are small magnetic plates enclosed in protective coverings. They are frequently referred to as "floppy disks" because they are very flexible. The computer is able to transfer ("write") data from its working memory to the diskette by adjusting its magnetic surface. Once encoded on the diskette, the data can be permanently stored; the user can remove the diskette from the computer and access the data it contains at some other time or with some other (compatible) computer. The computer retrieves ("reads") data from diskettes by scanning the magnetic surface and translating the electronic code into a form the computer can understand. Cassettes are similar to diskettes in that they store data on a magnetic surface. However, they are made of long tape and are read much like an audio cassette tape.

Information in secondary memory can be accessed in either a sequential or random manner. Secondary memory units that are accessed sequentially depend on magnetic tape as their storage media. Their operation is similar to a tape recorder; if someone wants to know what was recorded five minutes ago, the tape must be rewound and played forward while the listener searches for the desired recording. Similarly, computer systems with sequentially accessed secondary memory units record and retrieve transactions in the order in which they are entered. This is not a feasible storage medium for most hospitality applications. Guests do not enter and leave food service operations in exact sequences. Employees do not sign in and out in ascending order by identification number; nor do inventory items become depleted in any specific order. The best secondary memory approach for the hospitality industry involves random access media.

Disks and diskettes are two types of secondary storage media that provide random access memory (RAM) appropriate for hospitality applications. Disks are either installed as a permanent part of the computer (these are called "hard disks" or "fixed disks" when installed in personal computers) or, in large computer systems, can be "loaded"—attached—to disk drives as needed. Data can be stored on the disk in any order, and the disk drive unit remembers where each piece of data is placed. By definition, any

data stored on RAM media should be accessible in the identical amount of time, regardless of whether it was placed there one second, week, month, or year ago. Random access memory works especially well in hospitality operations since their clientele, menu items, inventory items, check ins, and so on, occur in random fashion.

Another important component of secondary memory is referred to as buffer memory. Buffer memory is a temporary storage area that stores data which cannot yet be placed into the permanent portion of the memory unit. For example, a restaurant employing remote kitchen printers uses buffer memory to receive orders entered through precheck terminals and awaiting printing at a work station. Since the terminals process and transmit their data at extremely high speeds and kitchen printers tend to be relatively slow devices, an order entered but not immediately printed might risk being lost. The buffer memory (also called a network controller) receives order entry data and holds that data until the appropriate printer becomes available. Other examples of buffer memory use include the intermediate computations in a complex program, and programs known as "scratch pads" which allow the operator to use the computer as a calendar or calculator without interrupting the operations in session at the time. Buffer memory is an important part of the secondary memory unit and one that should not be overlooked.

Although every computer must have each of the three components mentioned, the size and capacity of various computers varies greatly. When computers were first invented, they filled large rooms with electronic tubes and required specific atmosphere control. There are still computers that large; however, they are capable of doing more than all of the original ones combined. Now it is possible to get the same sophistication that the first computers offered in a hand held calculator. This is possible because the electronic tubes mentioned above have been replaced with magnetic chips, no larger than one's fingernail, which can hold as much information as hundreds of tubes. Because of this great size reduction, many small hospitality operations find that their needs can be met by a minicomputer, or even by a microcomputer which is better known as a "personal computer." This term is used for the smallest computers on the market. Despite their small size, they contain the same types of components as the larger machines and may also have additional options such as hard disks, color monitors, graphics printers, and so on.

The major advantages of microcomputers include their low price (a complete system can be purchased for less than $2,500) and the large amount of software available to operate on them. Their major disadvantage, however, is their limited storage capacity—in both secondary and internal memory areas. As a result of this limited memory capacity, some of the more sophisticated programs a hospitality operation may want to use will not run on a microcomputer. If this is the case, the hospitality operation may want to use a minicomputer. Although the difference between mini and microcomputers is becoming increasingly difficult to spot, minicomputers generally have much larger memory capacities. Hospitality operations needing a computer with even larger internal memory capacity and external storage media are more likely to choose a mainframe computer. Mainframe computers are the largest computer systems currently available and can be programmed to handle the extensive amounts of data that a large hospitality operation is likely to generate.

Software

The instructions within a computer system are called software. Software basically tells the hardware what to do, how to do it, and when to do it. To enable rapid data processing, these directives must be written in a language the computer is programmed to understand. There are two basic types of computer languages—high level and low level languages. High level languages (e.g., BASIC, COBOL, FORTRAN, C, and others) are the most sophisticated because a relatively simple command gets the computer to perform complex procedures that involve a number of different operations. For example, some computer languages recognize the word "SORT" and respond to this command by taking a list of separate items and arranging them in some predetermined fashion. High level languages are easy for a novice programmer to work with because they are similar to the user's own spoken language.

At its most basic level, however, a computer is really only able to distinguish between positive or negative electronic charges. This means that a computer is not able to understand the commands of a high level language directly; it must first interpret or compile them into a form that the computer can understand. All computers have low level languages programmed into them because it is at this most basic level that its opera-

tions are carried out. Low level languages are usually referred to as machine languages because they do not require interpreting or compiling before the machines can understand them. The computer can directly distinguish their instructions. There are a variety of low level machine languages, and which language a given computer utilizes depends on the type of compiler or interpreter it has available. These languages are very complex and require a skilled programmer for their development. In general, programs written in machine languages cost more to develop but operate faster than their high level language equivalents.

There are basically two different types of computer software: system software and application software. System software is developed and installed by the system's manufacturer. Its primary purpose is diagnostics, error detection, and error correction. The display of a syntax error message, for example, is not left to the user to program into the system. It comes preprogrammed by the manufacturer as part of the system's software package. System software aids the system in start-up and in establishing continuous operation.

Application software, on the other hand, is purchased separately from the computer and provides programs that allow the computer to perform specific tasks. Although the computer will run without application software, it will not be able to perform those tasks for which it was purchased. For example, application software is required in order for the computer to accomplish the necessary functions involved in maintaining a data base or generating reports. Therefore, when purchasing a computer system, choosing application software is more important than the choice of computer hardware. The user first needs to determine what functions or tasks the system will be required to perform and what application software will best accomplish those tasks. Only then is the user in a position to decide which computer hardware is needed to run the required software. Not all application software is available for every computer brand, and the compatibility of software and hardware is a critical factor in purchase decisions. By focusing first on which application software will best meet the needs of the hospitality operation, managers can ensure that the computer system they purchase accomplishes all the desired tasks.

The design of application software incorporates a plan to achieve a particular purpose. This plan is referred to as an "algorithm," which means "formula," and involves a logical procedure beginning with input data and concluding with output information. An algorithm must be reliable and accurate. Consider the calculation of a food cost percentage. The basic formula is: food cost divided by food revenues. The application software must be capable of computing food cost based upon clearly defined relationships (beginning inventory plus purchases minus ending inventory) and charting food revenues (number of items sold at various selling prices). The actual division of costs by revenues completes the algorithm function.

There are two levels of application software; some software is very application-specific while others can be used for many tasks. For example, a restaurant manager can purchase a software package designed to perform menu engineering. This type of application software performs all of the necessary calculations involved in menu engineering and prints a graph displaying the results. This software has one specific purpose and requires no additional programming by the manager to perform that task; all that is required is input data for the program to work with. On the other hand, a spreadsheet program can be used for a number of different applications. Although the manager needs to program the spreadsheet to accomplish desired tasks, it can perform many different kinds of mathematical calculations, including menu engineering. It can also produce graphs and generate a variety of different reports. Spreadsheets were discussed in Chapter 5. Other types of application software capable of performing a variety of tasks include word processing packages and data base programs.

Word processing packages allow computers to function as advanced typewriters. Users can type on the keyboard while everything is displayed on the computer's monitor and stored in the CPU's temporary memory. Editing is fairly simple because the computer updates the temporary memory whenever changes are made. For example, lines can be added and inserted into the text, words deleted, spelling errors corrected, and whole blocks of text moved from one place to another. In addition, some word processing packages assist writers by checking for spelling errors, providing a built-in thesaurus, and performing some mathematical functions. At any time, the text entered with a word processor can be stored on a secondary memory device, such as a diskette, and be accessed later for further additions or editing. This makes it simpler to write long works at different times. It also makes it possible to type form letters, or other documents that are used repeatedly, only once and to make

any necessary changes or additions prior to printing. Other available features include certain kinds of data base management useful in accomplishing a variety of tasks that involve inserting variable information into prepared documents. For example, a list of guests and their addresses can be stored in a data base and merged with the prepared document to create "personalized" letters sent to each guest for marketing purposes. The letter is only typed once but, as a copy is printed for each guest, the guest's name and address appears in the salutation.

Data base packages are software programs which allow users to store facts about their businesses for future use. The data base provides a means of organizing related facts and arranging them in ways that facilitate searches, updates, and reports. Each fact in a data base is stored in a separate "field," and the fields are arranged in groups so that related facts are stored together in a "record." The data base as a whole is a collection of different records. For example, an inventory data base might be set up for inventory control. This data base would contain one record for each inventory item, and each record would contain a number of fields such as the item's name, number, reorder quantity, number on hand, price per inventory quantity, and so on. The user can then arrange this data for any number of applications: inventory check sheets could be generated to assist in physical inventory, variance analysis could be performed on the difference between actual quantity on hand versus the target amount recorded by the computer, the total value of inventory could be calculated, and so on.

At present, the major disadvantage in data base packages seems to be the sophistication the user needs in order to initially establish the data base. Many data base packages involve a complex set of commands used to define fields and establish records, but an experienced (or patient) user can organize a large amount of information. Once the data base is designed, the main advantage is that the data it contains needs only to be entered and stored once. It can then be accessed by many programs for a variety of purposes. This not only saves storage space, but, more importantly, limits the number of times that data must be updated and ensures that all applications using the data base work with the most current information.

Additional concerns in application software development are program design, file structure, screen formats, and printed formats. Program design deals with the collection of input data, internal manipulation of data, and output routines, while file structure deals with the way data is stored. Although both of these concepts are very important for actually programming software, the typical user need not be expert in either. Users are concerned, however, with ensuring that screen display formats and printed reports are conducive to the ways they will use information. Two additional concepts of importance to users in selecting application software are how "interactive" the programs are and whether they provide "integrated" file structures.

Interactive vs. noninteractive: An interactive program is one in which the system prompts the user to respond to a predetermined sequence of inquiries. As the user responds, the next inquiry in the series is presented. Interactive software is very popular among hospitality operations because it is easier to use and helps ensure that all required information is collected and entered into the computer system. This is important when, for example, a hotel desk clerk is prompted by the computer for information about guests during check-in times. Another advantage of interactive systems is that they can generate reports at any time. This provides an effective means to ensure that data is processed and available to managers in time to be useful in decision making.

Noninteractive systems do not involve a user/system dialogue. Instead, the program reserves specific line numbers for exact data input. Program execution is faster in a noninteractive system since there is no waiting for user response. However, accompanying this gain in execution speed is the loss of on-line editing and the ability to generate reports as needed. Noninteractive programs also demand more sophisticated users, since the data must be entered in the correct order and format without prompting from the computer.

Integrated file structure: Integrated approaches to file storage help achieve data processing objectives because they require a minimum of data handling and operate at high speeds. This is because an integrated software system allows several programs to use the same data base. If the files are integrated, two programs using the identical data only require a single file. For example, data concerning the menu sales mix is essential to calculating both food service revenues and standard food costs. A restaurant employing an electronic cash register (ECR) with the ability to calculate and store menu counts captures this data at the time of a sale. Since menu item prices are also normally stored in an ECR, a revenue report can be generated

without any further data entry by the user. Similarly, an ECR with a recipe costing module can use the identical menu sales mix data to produce food cost reports. However, if the restaurant does not have an ECR, menu sales mix data must be collected from an analysis of guest checks and then entered into an adding machine or nonintegrated computer program to produce revenue information. Similarly, in order to calculate standard or ideal food costs without an ECR, the standard recipe cost for each menu item must first be determined and then menu sales mix data entered for a second time into the adding machine or nonintegrated computer program. The advantages of integrated software over nonintegrated software include speed and data integrity (since data is only stored once, it is possible to update it for ALL applications, not just for one). These make integrated software the preferred approach for hospitality industry applications.

Screen and report formats are important concerns to the users of an application program. While the issues of interactive versus noninteractive, and integrated versus nonintegrated software are important, the true value of a program lies in the comprehensibility and usefulness of its output. Screen displays must allow for easy reading and eye comfort. Cluttered, jumbled, or unclear screens are not as powerful as those possessing good spacing and legible information. In addition, screens which make use of color monitor capabilities are often very helpful to inexperienced users whose eyes can readily follow the color differences.

Similarly, reports should be formatted to take full advantage of the printer's capability. The production of a series of standard sized pages is by far superior to a continuous roll of 2½ wide cash register receipt paper. One of the frequent criticisms of computers is that they produce large volumes of irrelevant information. Streamlining (producing only the reports requested by the user) is becoming the trend for application software developers. It is imperative, therefore, that information needs are determined prior to software selection so that only the information needed by the operation is generated.

Operating System

Hardware describes the equipment within a computer system. Software refers to the instructions that direct the operations of the hardware. How do the hardware and software work together? How are priorities established within the

Exhibit B-4   The Role of the Operating System

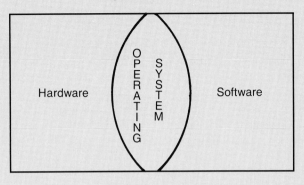

system? The answer to these and related questions lies in the area of the operating system.

The operating system (a portion of which is sometimes called "firmware") is a major component in any computer system application and often differentiates one computer from another. It interfaces hardware and software while maintaining system priorities as shown in Exhibit B-4.

Although it is difficult to imagine how a computer searches for data items, it is similar to the way the human thought process would guide a search for an individual whose address is known. To accomplish this mission, the searcher must evaluate several options about where to go and how to get there, make numerous decisions along the way, and forego alternate activities in the process. Similarly, a computer's operating system directs the computer system's functioning to find the answer to a manager's request for data. The request for the search is made from within an application software program, but it is the computer's operating system that directs the effort and secures the needed data.

Configurations and Networks

When a hospitality operation decides which computer system to purchase, it is important that it match the system with its needs. We have seen that the first consideration is choosing appropriate software to perform the desired tasks and then determining which hardware is needed to run the software. However, the size of the operation and the number of departments needing access to the computer are also significant factors in choosing a computer system. If the business is relatively small, a personal computer which contains a CPU, memory unit, and input/output device may be sufficient. However, if there are a number of distinct groups of people who need to use the computer, more than one CPU and/or input/output device may be required. It is possible to attach these devices to CPUs in various ways so that they meet the user's needs while avoiding spending unnecessary funds on additional hardware.

The design and layout of computer hardware is described as its configuration. How a system is configured affects the communication among its component parts. There are three distinct configuration designs: integrated configuration, distributed configuration, and combined configuration. Each hardware design must address the locations and interactions of the three required pieces of equipment: I/O unit, memory unit, and CPU.

An integrated configuration is characterized by a single central processing unit and a central data base. While the I/O units may be distributed throughout the hospitality establishment, both the CPU used for data processing and the memory unit used for data storage must be in a central location. Since the integrated configuration is dependent on a single CPU and centralized data base, errors there can render the system inoperable and/or result in a permanent loss of stored data. Exhibit B-5 represents one example of an integrated configuration. Note that I/O terminals all communicate with the CPU and that the CPU and memory unit work closely together.

The distributed configuration is very different from the integrated scheme. Instead of one large system, it is a series of smaller systems. Each of the workstation locations possesses a complete computer system, not just an input/output device. The presence of an I/O, memory unit, and CPU at each location provides a multiprocessor environment (many individual computers at different locations) with remote data storage facilities. Since each user group has their own computer there is more specialized application capability (use and storage). The individual stations can be connected—interfaced—to form a local area network (LAN). The LAN facilitates system-wide communication, data sharing, and device sharing. An individual system encountering operational problems would not affect the operation of the other systems in the network. Exhibit B-6 contains a schematic of a distributed configuration.

A combined configuration has some of the characteristics of both integrated and distributed configurations. The interconnection of a personal computer (PC) to an integrated configuration is perhaps the best illustration of the advantages available through combined configurations.

Exhibit B-5   Integrated Configuration

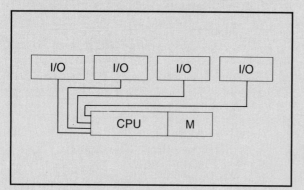

Exhibit B-6   Distributed Configuration

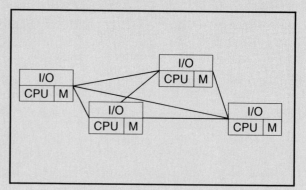

While the PC is distributed in nature (it possesses its own I/O, memory unit, and CPU) its connection to the integrated scheme allows for significant application flexibility not otherwise available. The transfer of data files from the data base of the integrated configuration to the PC enables detailed analysis on that file without affecting the ongoing workings of the integrated design. For example, suppose the integrated configuration depicted in Exhibit B-7 is an electronic cash register system in a hotel with a central data base and a PC in the back office. After transferring the data involving the day's sales, the PC can produce analytical reports without interfering with the ongoing work of the point-of-sale terminals distributed throughout the hotel. The combined configuration is an important arrangement used in the hospitality industry.

The advantages and disadvantages of each system should be considered before purchasing one. The major differences between the different configurations are speed and cost. The CPU is the most expensive component in a computer system; therefore, the more CPUs a configuration requires, the greater its cost. The tradeoff, however, is that the closer the CPU is to the I/O devices, and the fewer I/O devices making demands on it, the faster it will operate. Therefore, the use of different CPU outlets should be studied and evaluated.

The different types of configuration mentioned all make use of links between hardware components. The links, known as networks, allow computers to "talk" to each other. Depending on user needs, the networks can be established to link computers at the same location (in-house), at service bureaus, or at various sites. In-house systems involve the placement of all hardware and software on the user's premises. Service bureaus feature hardware and software at

someone else's premises with the hospitality operation paying for contract applications. For example, some operations use service bureaus to prepare payroll checks. In order to do this, the user inputs the hours worked on the operation's own computer, and "logs on" to the service bureau by making a telephone connection with it. The service bureau then takes the hours worked from the user's computer, combines this with the master payroll file stored at the service bureau, and runs the payroll software. Shared systems support multiple users by distributing portions of the system's hardware and software capability among participant properties. An example of this is a reservation system which allows a reservation for any hotel to be placed at any other hotel in the system.

When computers are located on the same premises, cables can link them together, but when computers are located at different sites, the telephone is used to allow them to communicate with each other. However, computers communicate with one another by relaying digital signals between components, while telephones transmit and receive analog signals. Since computers and telephones communicate using different types of signals, a device called a modem is used to translate analog signals to digital, and vice versa. The word "modem" comes from a combination of the two words *mo*dulate and *dem*odulate. Modulate means to code one type of signal to another; in this case it means to translate the sending computer's digital signals to analog ones. Demodulate refers to the decoding that takes place at the receiving computer which returns the communication to digital signals.

In addition to modems, computers need communication software in order to "talk" to each other. This software regulates the transfer of information by coordinating various factors, such

Exhibit B-7 Combined Configuration

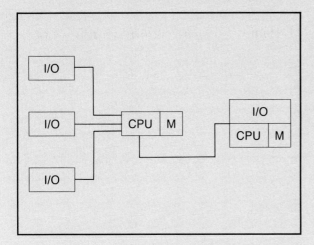

as what type of data will be transferred and how and how quickly the transfer will occur (baud rate). Once both the sending and receiving computers are ready for the transfer to take place, large amounts of information can be easily exchanged using relatively safe and rapid telecommunications techniques.

Data Security

Data security encompasses two major areas of concern for management: energy backup systems and information protection. Although management often focuses on the dangers involved in a power failure, information security can pose a much more serious threat to a hospitality operation. Consider the consequences of payroll information becoming unexpectedly available to employees, the competition gaining access to the guest history files, or the loss of the general ledger files. However, with proper care, both the energy and information problems can be avoided.

The loss or fluctuation of electrical power can lead to problems in computing. Unfortunately, power failures lead to other major problems for a hospitality operation as well; a blackout resulting in a loss of production or storage equipment can be much more traumatic than the temporary absence of a computer. The risks involved in many energy-related computer problems can be significantly reduced by using an uninterruptible power supply (UPS). The UPS is equipped with a battery pack and is placed on the computer's power line so that any fluctuation or degradation in the quality of power coming to

the computer will trigger the battery pack which compensates for any energy deficiencies. This provides the computer with a continually stable energy source. In addition, many systems automatically recharge the batteries whenever the normal power source is in operation. When these preventive measures are taken, concerns about energy supply interruptions can be reduced.

Information security is much more complicated than energy backup procedures and should involve the following strategic considerations:

1. Functional division of duties. In the past, separation of duties involved, for example, ensuring that the person who received cash did not record it. In a computerized environment, this type of separation is often not possible or cost justified. It is important, however, to consider separating programmers from operators so that the system is not easily manipulated by dishonest employees.
2. Recovery. There are procedures to minimize the damage that may result from the loss of data. These will be discussed later in this section.
3. Avoidance. Security is enhanced by protecting assets from potential threats. This includes not only keeping the computer room and data files locked, but also ensuring that important files are kept in fire-proof areas, that the equipment is protected from environmental dangers, and so on.
4. Unauthorized access prevention. Unauthorized use of the computer can be avoided by restricting access to the computer through passwords, locked systems, file access codes, etc.
5. Detection and correction. If a problem is detected early, its impact on operations can be minimized and it will be easier to correct. One method of ensuring the early detection of problems related to data security is the use of error logs. Many computer systems generate error logs every time an unusual request is made to the system; this log may be examined by supervisors who can deal promptly with any potential problem.

If these factors are considered when planning and designing a system, they should protect the operation from unauthorized acquisition, modifi-

Exhibit B-8   Information Backup Strategies

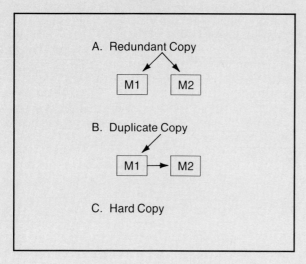

A. Redundant Copy

M1   M2

B. Duplicate Copy

M1 → M2

C. Hard Copy

cation, or destruction of information. They are (notice the first letter of each strategy) set up to prevent FRAUD!

Contingency planning is perhaps one of the most overlooked aspects of computer usage. A preventive maintenance program is essential to ensure against downtime. All components must be kept clean and operational to achieve optimal system productivity. There must also be a predetermined emergency maintenance plan. In case of a crisis, what steps can be taken? For example, in addition to energy backup, there should be plans for hardware backup, spare parts, or loaner equipment.

Backup procedures should not be left to emergency situations. Information backup should be a standard operating procedure to ensure that no data is lost at any time. There are basically three ways to back up information: redundant copy, duplicate copy, and hard copy. Exhibit B-8 illustrates these three strategies. While many computer manufacturers advocate using at least two of the three methods, management must ensure that at least one method is regularly used.

Redundant copy is not a very popular backup technique in the hospitality industry because it requires two memory units working simultaneously. As transactions occur, they are written to both memory devices. Assuming that a food service system employs a disk drive as a base for its secondary memory unit, a second disk drive is required; as data entry takes place, data is

sent to both drives for recording on their respective disks.

This presents an expensive hardware configuration and requires more attention than either of the alternative backup methods. It is analogous to recording a theatrical performance on two tape recorders simultaneously. Many people feel it is more efficient to concentrate on producing one superior recording and duplicating it at a later point in time; two recordings are still obtained, but through duplication, not redundancy.

Duplicate copying is the most popular and efficient means to accomplish information backup. The computer system writes to only one memory unit so a second disk drive is not needed. A copy of the single drive can then be made on any type of secondary storage. Because magnetic tape is comparatively inexpensive, but not as well suited as a main secondary memory medium (due to its sequential access characteristics), some operators use it to back up their disk packs. In other words, at the end of the day, the disk pack is duplicated onto magnetic tape for backup purposes. Since the backup tape is stored and used only in case of a disk error, its sequential access method does not severely reduce the operation's ability to maintain efficient computer operations.

Hard copy backup should only be used in conjunction with redundant or duplicate copy procedures. The operator who relies solely on hard copy (printed) information backup will encounter an avalanche of work should data files need to be reconstructed. All information stored in hard copy must be manually re-entered to recreate the system's data base. By itself, hard copy is not a desirable method. When used to supplement one of the other two approaches, however, it provides a means for troubleshooting missing or incorrect transactional recordings. Should a mishap occur that affects only a small section of the disk, that area of the disk can be compared with the most current hard copy to identify problem areas. The duplicate copy disk could then be used to correct those problematic portions of the system's data base discovered through hard copy comparison.

Human Factors

Although it is the last concept presented in this section, human factors are, perhaps, the most critical in ensuring successful computer use. None of the advantages afforded by computers materialize unless the people using the system are properly trained. In addition to training, there is no substitute for current, accurate system documentation. In effect, the overall performance of the entire computer system hinges on the human engineering aspect of computer use.

Training is an ongoing process which prepares both new and present employees to use the system. Whether during conversion to a new computer system or during new employee orientation, hands-on training is the most successful teaching method. There is no better way to become familiar with computer operations than through experience using the system. Training, however, does not have to take place at the hospitality establishment where it may impede daily operations. Many computer vendors have test sites available where employees can be trained to operate computers. However, they should be avoided when vendor trainers use different equipment from that purchased by the hospitality operation. Training personnel on different equipment from that used in their actual positions could cause them to become confused, disoriented, and less confident in their abilities to use the on-site system. By employing the on-site system (perhaps with the software operating in a training mode) users gain a sense of confidence and competence which is difficult to duplicate elsewhere.

Documentation is a complete record of the software the operation will use. It is an important part of the human factor of computing because it facilitates the training process, explains the operation of the computer, and details the procedures required by application software. Good documentation provides flow charts of how the programs work and interact with each other. If the documentation includes an accurate listing of the program code, the software may be customized to better fit the operation's needs and future modifications may be made more easily. In addition, the documentation should include complete operation instructions to ensure not only that the programs are used correctly, but also that infrequently used options

are not forgotten over time. Finally, the documentation should include users' manuals which highlight all of the features of a specific application software program including input specifications, processing routines, and output format options. These manuals are available from software vendors when requested.

In addition to training and documentation, another important human factor concerns the impact the computer system has on employees. If the employees want to guarantee a system's failure, they certainly can. If, on the other hand, they have a positive attitude, the implementation of a new computer system will be smoother and easier. One strategy for converting to a computerized system is to transfer all applications to the computer simultaneously—to go "cold turkey." However, the most successful approach to implementing a new system appears to be through parallel conversion. In parallel conversion, functions are transferred to the computer system on an application-by-application basis. As new application software is purchased for the system and as employees are trained in its use, more and more operational functions can be computerized. For example, a hotel might convert the accounting functions first. Later, the front desk could be computerized, and finally the food and beverage operations. This allows each department to train its employees, test the software, and verify results independently. Parallel conversions should not be unnecessarily drawn out, but should provide a comfort level for everyone involved.

Finally, perhaps the most important human factor in computerization concerns the ways in which computerized data processing and computer-generated reports are used by managers in their decision-making processes. Remember that the computer is a managerial tool. It cannot do everything. It can only take user-specified input and generate output according to the dictates of its preprogrammed procedures. Its output is only as good as its input, and it cannot make decisions!

Glossary

A

ACCELERATED DEPRECIATION

Methods of depreciation that result in higher depreciation charges in the first year and gradually decline over the life of fixed assets.

ACID-TEST RATIO

Ratio of total cash and near-cash current assets to total current liabilities.

ACCOUNT

Record containing information regarding a particular type of business transaction.

ACCOUNTING

Process of identifying, measuring, and communicating economic information (see accrual and cash basis).

ACCOUNTING CYCLE

Sequence of principal accounting procedures of a fiscal period; analyzing transactions, journal entry, posting to ledger, trial balance, adjustments, preparation of periodic financial statements, account closing, post-closing trial balance.

ACCOUNTING EQUATION

The accounting equation (referred to also as the fundamental accounting equation) is assets = liabilities + proprietorship.

ACCOUNTING PRINCIPLES

The basis for accounting methods and procedures.

ACCOUNTING RATE OF RETURN (ARR)

An approach to evaluating capital budgeting decisions based on the average annual project income (project revenues less project expenses) divided by the average investment.

ACCOUNTING SYSTEM

Subsystem of the information system providing financial reporting for external purposes.

ACCOUNTS PAYABLE

Liabilities incurred for merchandise, equipment, or other goods and services connected with the operation of the property that have been purchased on account.

ACCOUNTS RECEIVABLE

Obligations owed to the organization from sales made on credit.

ACCOUNTS RECEIVABLE TURNOVER

A measure of the rapidity of conversion of accounts receivable into cash; calculated by dividing revenue by average accounts receivable.

ACCRUAL BASIS ACCOUNTING

System of reporting revenues and expenses in the period in which they are considered to have been earned or incurred, regardless of the actual time of collection or payment.

ACCRUED EXPENSE ACCOUNT

Account of expenses that have been incurred but have not yet been paid.

ACCUMULATED DEPRECIATION

A contra-asset account used for accumulating depreciation charges for various fixed assets.

ADJUSTED FORECAST

The preliminary forecast regulated by "other" facts such as conventions, special entertainment events, weather, holidays, and so on.

ADJUSTING ENTRIES

Entries required at the end of an accounting period to record internal transactions.

AGING SCHEDULE

An accounts receivable report reflecting the status of individual accounts and indicating when the charges originated.

ALLOWANCE JOURNAL

Accounting record that serves to reduce or reverse a sale when allowance is given.

AMORTIZATION

The process of writing-off an intangible asset against revenue over its life.

ANNUITY

Refers to the stream of funds provided by a capital investment when the amounts provided are equal at equal intervals (such as the end of each year).

ASSET

Resource available for use by the business, i.e., anything owned by the business that has monetary value.

AUDITING

The process of verifying accounting records and financial reports prepared from accounting records.

AVERAGE COLLECTION PERIOD

The average number of days it takes a hospitality operation to collect all its accounts receivable; calculated by dividing the accounts receivable turnover into 365 (the number of days in a year).

AVOIDABLE COSTS

Costs that are not incurred when a hospitality operation shuts down (e.g., when a resort hotel closes for part of the year).

B

BAD DEBTS

An expense incurred due to failure to collect accounts receivable.

BALANCE SHEET

Statement of the financial position of the hospitality establishment at a given date, giving the account balances for assets, liabilities, and ownership equity.

BANK

Fixed sum of money provided to an employee who handles cash.

BANK STATEMENT

Record of transactions and account balance, prepared by the bank, to be compared with cash balance as shown in accounting records.

BARGAIN PURCHASE

A provision in some capital lease agreements giving the lessee the option to purchase the leased property at the end of the lease at a price substantially lower than the leased property's expected market value at the date the option is to be exercised.

BEGINNING INVENTORY

Goods available for sale on the first day of the accounting period.

BEVERAGE COST PERCENTAGE

A ratio comparing the cost of beverages sold to beverage sales; calculated by dividing the cost of beverages sold by beverage sales.

BILLING CLERK

Person responsible for charging to guests all vouchers representing food, beverages, room service, and merchandise purchases.

BIN CARD

A perpetual inventory record used in the control of food and beverage products.

BOOKKEEPING

The recording, summarizing, and classifying aspects of accounting.

BOOK VALUE

The difference between the cost of a fixed asset and the related accumulated depreciation. This is also referred to as net book value.

BOTTOM-UP PRICING

Methods for establishing retail prices of goods and services that begin with the desired profit and add all incurred expenses (direct and indirect) to determine the selling price.

BREAKEVEN POINT

The level of sales volume at which total revenues equal total costs.

BUSINESS ENTITY

The concept that requires that a business maintain its own set of accounts that are separate from other financial interests of its owners.

BUSINESS TRANSACTION

An event or condition that must be recorded.

C

CAPITAL BUDGET

Management's detailed plan for the acquisition of equipment, land, buildings, and other fixed assets.

CAPITAL LEASE

A classification of lease agreements which are of relatively long duration, generally noncancellable, and in which the lessee assumes responsibility for executory costs. For accounting purposes, capital leases are capitalized in a way similar to the purchase of a fixed asset (i.e., recorded as an asset with recognition of a liability).

CAPITAL RATIONING

An approach to capital budgeting used to evaluate combinations of projects according to their net present value (NPV).

CAPITAL STOCK

Shares of ownership of a corporation.

CASH

A category of current assets consisting of cash in house banks, cash in checking and savings accounts, and certificates of deposit. Cash is shown on the balance sheet at its stated value.

CASH BASIS ACCOUNTING

Reporting of revenues and expenses at the time they are collected or paid.

CASH BUDGET

Management's detailed plan for cash receipts and disbursements.

CASH DISBURSEMENTS AND ACCOUNTS PAYABLE JOURNAL

Accounting record of expense transactions and other cash disbursements.

CASH FLOW

A stream of receipts and disbursements resulting from operational activities or investments.

CASH RECEIPTS AND DISBURSEMENTS JOURNAL

Accounting record of each element of a cash transaction; includes guest identification and room number.

CASHIER

Person responsible for handling all cash transactions made in the front office.

CAUSAL FORECASTS

Forecasts made on the assumption that the future value of one variable is a function of other variables.

CERTIFIED PUBLIC ACCOUNTANTS (CPA)

Public accountants who have been licensed to engage in public practice.

CHART OF ACCOUNTS

Listing of general ledger accounts by type of account including account number and account title.

CITY LEDGER

Subsidiary ledger listing accounts receivable of guests who have checked out—also all other receivables.

CLEARING ACCOUNT

Account used to temporarily store information as part of an accounting procedure.

CLOCK CARDS

Cards used in a time clock to record time spent on the job by employees.

CLOSING ENTRIES

Journal entries prepared at the end of the period (normally yearly) to close the temporary proprietorship accounts.

COEFFICIENT OF CORRELATION

A mathematical measure of the relation between the dependent variable and independent variables used in causal forecasting methods.

COEFFICIENT OF DETERMINATION

The square of the coefficient of correlation.

COLLUSION

Two or more people working together to defraud the hospitality property.

COMMON-SIZE BALANCE SHEETS

Balance sheets used in vertical analysis whose information has been reduced to percentages to facilitate comparisons.

COMMON STOCK

Capital stock of a corporation that generally allows its holders to have voting rights.

COMPARATIVE BALANCE SHEETS

Balance sheets from two or more successive periods used in horizontal analysis.

COMPENSATING BALANCES

A minimum balance for demand deposit accounts required by commercial banks as part of the conditions for a loan agreement.

CONTROLLER

A chief executive position within the organization of a corporation responsible for all accounting functions within the organization. (In some firms, this person is called a comptroller.)

CONSERVATISM

The concept that requires accounting procedures that recognize expenses as soon as possible, but delay the recognition of revenues until they are ensured. For example nonrefundable deposits for future services should be recognized as a liability until the service is actually performed.

CONSISTENCY

The concept that requires that once an accounting method has been adopted, it should be followed from period to period in the future unless a change in accounting methods is warranted and disclosed.

CONTRIBUTION MARGIN

Sales less cost of sales for either an entire operating department or for a given product; represents the amount of sales revenue that is contributed toward fixed costs and/or profits.

CONTROL CYCLE

The never-ending process of planning, assessing results, comparing, correcting, improving, and evaluating.

CONTROLLABLE COSTS

Costs over which a manager is able to exercise judgment and hence be able to keep within predefined boundaries or limits.

CORPORATION

A form of business organization that provides a separate legal entity apart from its owners.

COST

An expense; a reduction of an asset—generally for the purpose of increasing revenues.

COST ACCOUNTING

The branch of accounting dealing with the recording, classification, allocation, and reporting of current and prospective costs.

COST ALLOCATION

The process of distributing expenses among various departments.

COST/BENEFIT ANALYSIS

The process of reviewing an investment proposal; listing the expenses and the perceived returns and using this enumeration as a basis for deciding whether to accept the proposal or not.

COST CENTER

Any segment of the company whose expenses can be accumulated into meaningful classifications of data to provide information to management.

COST JUSTIFICATION

The process of justifying expenditures by providing documentation showing that the expected return on investment exceeds the expense incurred.

COST OF GOODS SOLD

Expense incurred in procuring the goods (rather than the services) that are to be resold in the operation of business.

COST PRINCIPLE

The concept that requires recording the value of transactions for accounting purposes at the actual transaction price (cost).

CREDIT

Decrease in an asset or increase in a liability or capital—entered on the right side of an account; such amounts are said to be credited to the account.

CREDIT MEMORANDUM

A written statement prepared by the purchaser and signed by the purveyor attesting to the fact that the delivered merchandise did not conform with that ordered.

CURRENT ASSETS

Resources of cash and items that will be converted to cash or used in generating income within a year through normal business operations.

CURRENT LIABILITIES

Obligations that are due within a year.

CURRENT RATIO

Ratio of total current assets to total current liabilities expressed as a coverage of so many times; calculated by dividing current assets by current liabilities.

COST-VOLUME-PROFIT ANALYSIS (C-V-P-Analysis)

A set of analytical tools used by managers to examine the relationships among various costs, revenues, and sales volume in either graphic or equation form allowing one to determine the revenue required at any desired profit level.

CYCLICAL PATTERN

A pattern of data (e.g., sales activity) that fluctuates around a trend line according to some regular time period.

D

DEBT-EQUITY RATIO

Compares the debt of a hospitality operation to its net worth (owners' equity) and indicates the operation's ability to withstand adversity and meet its long-term obligations; calculated by dividing total liabilities by total owners' equity.

DEBIT

Increase in an asset or decrease in a liability or capital—entered on the left side of an account; such amounts are said to be debited or charged to the account.

DECLINING BALANCE DEPRECIATION METHOD

Method of distributing depreciation expense based on a declining percentage rate, providing for a larger depreciation expense in the early years.

DEDUCTIONS

Amounts subtracted from gross income to determine taxable income in accordance with prevailing tax laws.

DEFERRED EXPENSE

Postponement of the recognition of an expense already paid.

DELPHI TECHNIQUE

An approach to forecasting future events that involves achieving a consensus of opinion among experts who interact anonymously with each other in the process of exchanging views and information.

DEMAND

The quantity of any amount of goods which consumers will purchase at a particular price.

DEMAND DEPOSIT

A checking account with a commercial bank.

DEPARTMENTAL INCOME

The difference between an operating department's revenue and direct expenses.

DEPARTMENTAL OPERATING INCOME OR LOSS

Revenue less direct operating expenses equals departmental operating income for each profit center in a hospitality establishment.

DEPARTMENTAL STATEMENTS

Supplements to the summary income statement that provide management with detailed financial information by operating department and service centers; also referred to as schedules.

DEPRECIATION

Portion of the cost of a fixed asset recognized as an expense for each accounting period; the asset will be used in generating revenues.

DIFFERENTIAL COSTS

Costs which differ between two alternatives.

DIRECT EXPENSES

Expenses related directly to the department incurring them and consisting of cost of sales, payroll and related expenses, and other expenses.

DIRECTS

Products received by the hospitality operation which go directly to production areas and/or do not enter inventory records.

DISBURSEMENT VOUCHER

Form used as a means of recording the liability and authorization for payment.

DISCRETIONARY COSTS

Costs which managers may (in the short-run) choose to avoid.

DIVIDEND

A distribution of earnings to owners of a corporation's stock.

DIVIDEND PAYOUT RATIO

Indicates the percentage of earnings paid out by the hospitality establishment to stockholders; calculated by dividing dividends paid by earnings.

DOUBLE ENTRY SYSTEM

System of recording any business transaction equally to debits and credits.

DOUBLE TAXATION

Occurs when both corporate profits and dividends paid to stockholders are taxed.

DOUBTFUL ACCOUNTS

Accounts receivable that may not be collected.

DRAWING ACCOUNT

An account in which withdrawals of cash by the owner of a business organized as a sole proprietorship are recorded.

E

EMPLOYEE'S EARNINGS RECORD

A record for each employee to record gross pay, taxes withheld, deductions, and net pay.

ENDING INVENTORY

Goods available for sale on the last day of the accounting period.

EARNINGS PER SHARE (EPS)

A ratio providing a general indicator of the profitability of a hospitality operation by comparing net income to the average common shares outstanding. If preferred stock has been issued for the operation, then preferred dividends are subtracted from net income before calculating EPS.

EXECUTORY COSTS

Obligations for property taxes, insurance, and maintenance of leased property.

EXPENSE

Cost incurred in providing the goods and services offered.

EXPONENTIAL SMOOTHING

A forecasting method that uses a smoothing constant (between 0 and 1), along with recent actual and forecasted data, to reflect the relative stability or growth of the activity being forecasted.

F

FEDERAL INCOME TAX

The income taxes calculated on the firm's taxable income according to the federal tax laws.

FEDERAL INCOME TAX WITHHELD

Taxes withheld from employees' gross pay that must be paid to the federal government.

FINANCIAL ACCOUNTING

A branch of accounting dealing with the recording, classifying, and summarizing of transactions involving revenues, expenses, assets, and liabilities.

FINANCIAL ACCOUNTING STANDARDS BOARD

The private sector group that promulgates accounting standards.

FINANCIAL EXPENSE

Expense associated with owning or renting the property, interest expense, and income taxes.

FINANCIAL POSITION

The position of a firm at the end of the accounting period as shown by the balance sheet.

FINANCIAL STATEMENT

Formal medium for communicating accounting information, e.g., balance sheet, income statement, statement of retained earnings.

FIRST-IN, FIRST-OUT (FIFO) METHOD OF INVENTORY VALUATION

Costs charged against revenue in the order in which they were incurred.

FIXED ASSETS

Long-lived assets of a firm that are tangible, e.g., land, equipment, buildings.

FIXED ASSET TURNOVER

A ratio measuring management's effectiveness in using fixed assets to generate revenue; calculated by dividing average total fixed assets into total revenue generated for the period.

FIXED CHARGES

A category of expense reported on the income statement that relate to decisions outside the area of control of operating management and consisting of rent, property taxes, insurance, interest, management fees, and depreciation and amortization.

FIXED COSTS

Costs which remain constant in the short run even though sales volume varies; examples of fixed costs include salaries, rent expense, insurance expense, and so on.

FLOWCHART

A visual representation of the movement of information and documents within a hospitality operation.

FOOD AND BEVERAGE MANAGER

Person who plans, directs, organizes, and controls all phases of the food and beverage departments of a food service facility.

FOOD COST PERCENTAGE

A ratio comparing the cost of food sold to food sales; calculated by dividing the wholesale dollar amount of total sales by the retail dollar amount of total sales.

FOOD TRANSFERS

The wholesale cost of food that is used in departments other than the kitchen.

FOOTING

Totaling of columns.

FORECAST

A prediction of future events.

FRONT OFFICE

Point of contact between guests and representatives of management; location where accommodations are arranged and guests' accounts are maintained during their stay.

FULL DISCLOSURE

The concept that requires that financial statements must provide information on all the significant facts that have a bearing on their interpretation. Types of disclosures include the accounting methods used, changes in the accounting methods, contingent liabilities, events occurring subsequent to the financial statement date, and unusual and nonrecurring items.

FUNDS

Defined as either cash, working capital, or all financial resources for the purpose of reporting changes on the Statement of Changes in Financial Position.

G

GARDE-MANAGER

Person in charge of cold meat production area in a food service operation.

GENERAL JOURNAL

Record of all accounting transactions.

GENERAL LEDGER

Principal ledger containing all of the balance sheet and income statement accounts.

GOING CONCERN

The concept that requires the preparation of accounting records and reports under the assumption that the business will continue indefinitely and that liquidation is not in prospect; also referred to as continuity of the business unit.

GUEST FOLIO

Form containing current guests' statements.

GUEST LEDGER

Subsidiary ledger listing accounts receivable of current guests.

GUEST SERVICES PERSONNEL

Employees who provide mail, key, message, and information services for guests.

H

HEAT, LIGHT, AND POWER

In the past utility costs of a firm were referred to as heat, light, and power.

HORIZONTAL ANALYSIS

Comparing financial statements for two or more accounting periods in terms of both absolute and relative variances for each line item.

HOUSE PROFIT

Amount left after the common operating expenses have been deducted from revenue; used to cover the fixed capital expenses and provide a net profit.

I

IMPREST BASIS

Method of maintaining funds by replenishing the amount of disbursements since the previous replenishment.

INCOME AND EXPENSE SUMMARY

A temporary account into which revenue and expense accounts are closed at the end of the accounting period.

INCOME EXCLUSION

Income that is reported on federal tax returns but not subject to taxation; exclusions from income shown on tax forms include amounts for dividends and a portion of long-term capital gains.

INCOME STATEMENT

Report on the profitability of operations, including revenues earned and expenses incurred in generating the revenues for the period of time covered by the statement.

INCREMENTAL BORROWING RATE

The rate of interest a lessee would have to pay if financing the purchase of the item to be leased.

INCREMENTAL CASH FLOW

The change in cash flow of an operation that results from an investment.

INFORMATION SYSTEM

All the activities involved in obtaining the information necessary to operate a hotel or motel smoothly and efficiently.

INTEGRATED PRICING

An approach to pricing in a hospitality operation having several revenue producing departments that sets prices for goods and/or services in each profit center so as to optimize the operation's net income.

INTEREST EXPENSE

The charge for borrowing money. It is calculated

by multiplying the principal times the interest rate times the fraction or more of a year the money is borrowed.

INTERIM STATEMENT

Statement prepared in the periods between annual reports.

INTERNAL CONTROL

The organizational plan, methods, and measures adopted by a hospitality operation to safeguard its assets, check the accuracy and reliability of accounting information, promote operational efficiency, and ensure adherence to the operation's policies and procedures.

INTERNAL RATE OF RETURN (IRR)

An approach to evaluating capital budgeting decisions based on the rate of return generated by the investment.

INVENTORY

Food, beverages, and supplies (See Beginning Inventory and Ending Inventory).

INVENTORY TURNOVER

A ratio showing how quickly a hospitality operation's inventory is moving from storage to productive use; calculated by dividing the cost of products (e.g., food or beverages) used by the average product (e.g., food or beverages) inventory.

INVENTORY VALUATION

(See Weighted Average; First-In, First Out; Last-In, First Out).

INVOICE

Statement containing the names and addresses of both the buyer and the seller, the date of the transaction, the terms, the methods of shipment, quantities, descriptions, and prices of the goods.

ISSUING

A distribution of food and beverages from the storeroom to authorized individuals who requisition these items.

ISSUING CLERK

A person who is responsible for the issuing function.

J

JOB DESCRIPTION

A written, detailed list of duties and expectations for each employee position within the hospitality operation.

JOINT COSTS

Costs which, when incurred, simultaneously benefit two or more operating departments.

JOURNAL

Accounting record of business transactions (See Allowance journal, Cash disbursements and accounts payable journal, Cash receipts and disbursements journal, General journal, Payroll journal, Sales journal, and Special journal).

JOURNALIZE

To record a transaction in a journal.

JURY OF OPINION

A consensus of views among knowledgeable individuals used in making decisions or forecasts.

L

LABOR COST

The dollar amount paid to all employees, excluding administrative personnel, during an accounting period which can be daily, weekly, monthly, etc.

LABOR COST PERCENTAGE

A ratio comparing the labor expense for each department by the total revenue generated by the department; total labor cost by department divided by department revenues.

LAST-IN, FIRST-OUT (LIFO) METHOD OF INVENTORY VALUATION

Most recent costs incurred charged against revenue.

LEASE

An agreement conveying the right to use resources (equipment, buildings, and/or land) for specified purposes for limited periods of time. The lessor owns the property and conveys the right of its use to the lessee in exchange for periodic cash payments called rent .

LEASEBACK

A transaction whereby an owner of real estate agrees with an investor to sell the real estate to the investor and simultaneously rent it back for a future period of time, allowing uninterrupted use of the property while providing the operation with capital that was previously tied up in the property.

LEASEHOLD IMPROVEMENTS

Renovations or remodeling performed on leased buildings or space prior to the commencement of operations. For accounting purposes, all leasehold improvements are capitalized (i.e., recorded as an asset with recognition of a liability).

LEDGER

Group of related accounts that comprise a complete unit (See General Ledger, Subsidiary Ledger, Guest Ledger, and City Ledger).

LEVERAGE

The use of debt in place of equity dollars to finance operations and increase the return on the equity dollars already invested.

LIABILITIES

Obligations of a business—largely indebtedness related to the expenses incurred in the process of generating income (See Current and Long-Term Liabilities)

LIMITED PARTNERSHIP

A form of organization consisting of a partnership between two or more individuals having at least one general partner and one limited partner in which the latter's liabilities are limited to investments.

LINE POSITIONS

Positions within the "chain of command" in a hospitality operation that are directly responsible for all decisions involved in using the hospitality operation's resources to generate revenue and attain other goals of their departments.

LIQUIDITY

The ability of a hospitality operation to meet its short-term (current) obligations by maintaining sufficient cash and/or investments easily convertible to cash.

LOCKBOX SYSTEM

A system used to speed the flow of cash from accounts receivable to the hospitality operation's bank accounts consisting of a post office box from which bank personnel collect all incoming mail and deposit any checks directly in the operation's account with the bank.

LONG-LIVED OR LONG-TERM ASSETS (FIXED ASSETS)

Investments or resources of the hotel or motel that will be used to generate income for periods longer than a year.

LONG-TERM LIABILITIES

Obligations at the balance sheet date which are expected to be paid beyond the next 12 months, or if paid in the next year, they will be paid from restricted funds; also called noncurrent liabilities.

M

MANAGERIAL ACCOUNTING

The branch of accounting designed to provide

information to various management levels for the enhancement of controls; includes the preparation of performance reports that compare actual results to budgeted standards.

MANAGEMENT FEES

The cost of using an independent management company to operate the hospitality establishment.

MARKETING RESEARCH

The systematic gathering, recording, and analyzing of data related to the marketing of goods and services.

MARKETABLE SECURITIES

Current assets in the form of investments in stocks and bonds of other corporations.

MARK-UP

An approach to pricing of goods and services which determines retail prices by adding a certain percentage to the cost of goods sold. The mark-up is designed to cover all nonproduct costs (e.g., labor, utilities, supplies, interest expense, taxes, etc.) and also cover the desired profit.

MATERIALITY

The concept that requires that events be recognized and recorded by accounting procedures if "it makes a difference" as determined by some relative standard of comparison. For example, materiality may be established by a rule of thumb which states that an item is recognized if it exceeds X% or more of total assets or income.

MATCHING PRINCIPLE

The concept that requires recording expenses in the same period as the revenues to which they relate.

MENU ENGINEERING

A method of menu analysis and food pricing that considers both the profitability and popularity of competing menu items.

MIXED COSTS

Costs that are a mixture of both fixed and variable costs; (See Fixed Costs and Variable Costs).

MORTGAGE

Security on a loan that gives the creditor a lien on property owned by a debtor.

MOVING AVERAGES

Averaging data from specified time periods in a continually updating manner such that as new results become available, they are used in the average by adding the most recent value and dropping the earliest value.

N

NEGATIVE CASH FLOW

The condition in which cash disbursements exceed cash receipts.

NET BOOK VALUE

The cost of a fixed asset less accumulated depreciation.

NET INCOME

The bottom line on an income statement when revenues exceed expenses.

NET LOSS

The bottom line on an income statement when expenses exceed revenues.

NET PRESENT VALUE (NPV)

An approach to evaluating capital budgeting decisions based on discounting the cash flows relating to the project to their present value; calculated by subtracting the project cost from the present value of the discounted cash flow stream.

NET WORTH

The claims of the owners to assets of a firm. Also, assets less liabilities equal net worth.

NIGHT AUDITOR

Person responsible for posting late charges or credits to guests' accounts; also for checking accounts to see whether or not the day's postings are accurate and in agreement with supporting records.

NONCURRENT RECEIVABLES

Accounts and notes receivable which are not expected to be collected within one year from the balance sheet date.

NOTES PAYABLE

A written promise by a borrower to pay money to a lender on demand or at a definite time.

O

OCCUPANCY PERCENTAGE

A ratio indicating management's success in selling its "product"; for hotels or motels, it is referred to as the occupancy rate and is calculated by dividing the number of rooms sold by the number of rooms available; for food service operations, it is referred to as seat turnover and is calculated by dividing the number of people served by the number of seats available.

OPERATIONS BUDGET

Management's detailed plans for generating revenue and incurring expenses for each department within the hospitality operation; also referred to as the revenue and expense budget.

OPERATING EFFICIENCY RATIO

A measure of management's ability to generate sales and control expenses; calculated by dividing income before fixed charges by total revenue.

OPERATING EXPENSE

Cost incurred in providing the goods and services offered by hotels and motels.

OPERATING LEASE

A classification of lease agreements which are usually of relatively short duration, easily cancelled, and in which the lessor retains responsibility for executory costs. For accounting purposes, operating leases are not capitalized, but simply recognized as an expense when rent is paid.

OPERATING LEVERAGE

The extent to which an operation's expenses are fixed rather than variable; an operation that substitutes fixed costs for variable costs is said to be highly levered.

OPERATING STATEMENTS

Monthly report to management providing detailed financial information reflecting budgeted standards and actual results of the activities of each operating department for the most recent period, the same period a year ago, and year-to-date numbers for both the current and the past year.

OPPORTUNITY COSTS

Costs of the best foregone opportunity in a decision-making situation involving several alternatives.

ORGANIZATIONAL CHART

A visual representation of the hierarchical structure of positions within a hospitality operation showing the different layers of management and the chain of command.

ORGANIZATIONAL COSTS

The costs to incorporate a business.

OVERHEAD COSTS

All expenses other than the direct costs of profit centers; examples include undistributed operating expenses, management fees, fixed charges, and income taxes.

OWNERSHIP EQUITY

Financial interest of the owners of a business—assets minus liabilities.

P

PAID-IN CAPITAL

The capital acquired from stockholders of the corporation.

PAR STOCK

That amount of inventory required to satisfy the normal demand for a certain item during a given period of time.

PARTNERSHIP

A form of business organization involving two or more owners that is not incorporated.

PAYBACK

An approach to evaluating capital budgeting decisions based on the number of years of annual cash flow generated by the fixed asset purchase required to recover the investment.

PAYROLL JOURNAL

Journal providing a means to record checks, total payroll expense, liabilities for amounts deducted, and the net disbursement.

PAYROLL SUMMARY REPORT

Form that can be used in place of a payroll journal to record payroll expense, liabilities for amounts deducted, and net wage and salary disbursements.

PRICE EARNINGS RATIO

A general indicator of the profitability of a hospitality operation that is often used by financial analysts in presenting investment possibilities; calculated by dividing the market price per share by the earnings per share.

PERMANENT OWNERS' EQUITY ACCOUNTS

A classification of owners' equity accounts that are not closed at the end of an accounting period; e.g., accounts for recording capital stock and retained earnings.

PERPETUAL INVENTORY RECORD

Record of inventory kept up-to-date by entering all additions to and subtractions from stock.

PHYSICAL INVENTORY

Detailed listing of the merchandise on hand at a specific time.

PORTION

A standard quantity of food or beverage served for one person.

PORTION COST

The wholesale price associated with all ingredients required to produce one standard portion.

POST

Transfer data entry in the journal to the appropriate account.

PRECHECK REGISTER

A cash register without an operating cash drawer used in revenue control systems to record and transfer sales information.

PREPAID EXPENSES

Expenditures made for expense items prior to the period the expense is incurred.

PREPARATION

The procedure whereby pre-prepared raw food items are processed and made ready for service to the final consumer.

PRICE ELASTICITY OF DEMAND

An expression of the relationship between a change in price and the resulting change in demand.

PRICE QUOTATION SHEET

A standardized sheet that facilitates a competitive buying procedure which remains in conformance with established standard specifications.

PRICING POLICY

A standard procedure that the firm follows in determining the retail sales value of their product(s).

PROCEDURE MANUAL

A written, detailed description of what tasks, jobs, or duties within a hospitality operation are to be performed, including when, by whom, and how they are to be performed.

PROFIT CENTER

A revenue producing department within a hospitality operation.

PROFIT MARGIN

An overall measure of management's ability to generate sales and control expenses; calculated by dividing net income by total revenue.

PROPERTY AND EQUIPMENT

Fixed assets including land, buildings, furniture, equipment, construction in progress, leasehold improvements, and property such as china, glassware, silver, linens, uniforms, etc.

PURCHASE ORDER

Order for material sent by the purchasing department.

PURCHASE REQUISITION

A form used to request the purchasing department to purchase merchandise or other property.

PURCHASING

The acquisition of merchandise by the payment of money or its equivalent.

PURCHASING AGENT

A staff position within a hospitality operation providing assistance in the selection and procurement of products (e.g., food and beverages) by gathering product information, screening potential suppliers, and offering recommendations about products to be used and purchase specifications to be developed.

PURVEYOR

A firm which provides or supplies merchandise to customer firms.

Q

QUICK ASSETS

Current assets consisting of cash or near-cash and excluding inventories and prepaid expenses.

R

RATIO

The mathematical expression of a significant relationship between two related numbers that results from dividing one by the other.

RECEIVING

To accept delivery of merchandise that has been ordered or is expected by the firm and to record such transactions.

RECEIVING CLERK

A person who performs the receiving function.

RECEIVING REPORT

Report on items received, prepared at time of delivery.

REGRESSION ANALYSIS

A mathematical approach to fitting a straight line to data points such that the differences in the distances of the data points from the line is minimized.

RELEVANT COSTS

Costs which must be considered in a decision-making situation; relevant costs must be differential, future, and quantifiable.

RESORT HOTELS

Lodging properties which cater primarily to non-business travelers and tourists.

REQUISITION

Written order to withdraw items from stock.

RETAINED EARNINGS

An account for recording undistributed earnings of a corporation.

RETURN ON ASSETS (ROA)

A ratio providing a general indicator of the profitability of a hospitality operation by comparing net income to total investment; calculated by dividing net income by average total assets.

RETURN ON INVESTMENT (ROI)

The gain associated with the employment of capital.

RETURN ON OWNERS' EQUITY (ROE)

A ratio providing a general indicator of the profitability of a hospitality operation by comparing net income to the owners' investment; calculated by dividing net income by average owners' equity.

REVENUES

Amounts charged to customers in exchange for goods and services.

REVERSING ENTRY

Entry that is the exact reverse of the adjusting entry to which it relates.

S

S CORPORATION

A hybrid form of organization that allows corporations to be taxed in the same manner as a partnership.

SALES HISTORY

The gathering and recording of historical sales data.

SALES JOURNAL

Journal used for posting all sales transactions.

SALES MIX

The combination of products, services, and prices offered by a hospitality operation.

SALVAGE JOURNAL

Estimated market value of an asset at the time it is to be retired from use.

SCATTER DIAGRAM

A graphic approach to determining the fixed and variable elements of a mixed cost.

SEASONAL PATTERN

A pattern of data (e.g. sales activity) that shows regular fluctuations according to some time period (daily, weekly, monthly, yearly).

SEASONALITY

Regular variations in levels of activity experienced by hospitality operations over periods of time that may include fluctuations throughout the day, week, month, or year.

SEGREGATION OF DUTIES

An element of internal control systems in which different personnel are assigned the different functions of accounting, custody of assets, and production; the purpose is to prevent and detect errors and/or theft.

SERVICE BAR

An area that provides beverages exclusively for dining patrons.

SERVICE CENTERS

Departments within a hospitality operation that are not directly involved in generating revenue but that provide supporting services to revenue generating departments within the operation.

SERVING

The task of moving products from production staff to service staff.

SOLE PROPRIETORSHIP

An unincorporated business organized by one person.

SOLVENCY

The extent to which a hospitality operation is financed by debt and is able to meet its long-term obligations. An operation is solvent when its assets exceed its liabilities.

SOLVENCY RATIO

A measure of the extent to which an operation is financed by debt and is able to meet its long-term obligations; calculated by dividing total assets by total liabilities.

SPECIAL INVENTORY

Any counting of stock that is performed at an irregular time for certain extraordinary purposes.

SPECIAL JOURNAL

Journal used to accelerate the recording of specific kinds of accounting transactions.

SPOT CHECK

A random examination of any particular operating procedure.

STAFF ORGANIZATION

A group of assistants to a manager, supervisor, or department head; also, a group of advisors and technical specialists who are charged with aiding the operating departments of a firm.

STAFF POSITIONS

Positions within the organizational structure of a hospitality operation that are responsible for providing expert advice and information to assist management in making decisions. Staff specialists collect information and provide advice, but do not make decisions for line managers.

STAFF SPECIALIST

An advisor or technical expert whose function is to assist operating management.

STAFFING

Selecting and training a body of persons who are then charged with carrying out the work of a firm.

STANDARD COSTS

Forecasts of what actual costs should be under projected conditions; standard costs serve as a standard of comparison for control purposes or for evaluations of productivity.

STANDARD PURCHASE SPECIFICATIONS

Detailed descriptions setting forth the quality, size, and weight factors desired for particular items.

STANDARD RECIPE

A regulated formula for preparing any particular type of retail food or beverage item.

STATEMENT OF CHANGES IN FINANCIAL POSITION

A basic financial statement that shows sources and uses of funds for an accounting period.

STOCKHOLDERS' EQUITY

The difference between assets and liabilities of a corporation.

STORES

Products received by the hospitality operation that are moved into storage areas and entered in inventory records.

STORING

The process of stocking a place with supplies of food, beverage, and other items that are required for future use.

STRAIGHT-LINE DEPRECIATION

Method of distributing depreciation expense evenly throughout the estimated life of the asset.

SUBSIDIARY LEDGER

Special ledger that provides more detailed information about an account; controlled by the general ledger—used when there are several accounts with a common characteristic.

SUM-OF-THE-YEARS'-DIGITS DEPRECIATION METHOD

Method of distributing depreciation expense, with a more rapid depreciation in early years, by estimating the number of years of useful life, adding the digits, and then dividing the sum by the number of years remaining to determine the depreciation rate for the current year.

SUNKEN COSTS

Past costs relating to a past decision; e.g., the net book value of a fixed asset.

T

TAX ACCOUNTING

The branch of accounting dealing with the preparation and filing of tax forms with the various governmental agencies.

TAX AVOIDANCE

Planning transactions to mitigate the impact of taxes or avoid the application of taxes in such a manner as to achieve the lowest possible tax cost within the constraints of other business considerations and the prevailing tax laws and regulations.

TAX CREDITS

Amounts that are subtracted directly from income taxes calculated on taxable income in accordance with prevailing tax laws.

TAX EVASION

The fraudulent denial or concealment of a current or future tax liability such as the underreporting of income and claiming unsubstantiated or excessive income deductions.

TEMPORARY OWNERS' EQUITY ACCOUNTS

A classification of owners' equity accounts that are closed out at the end of each fiscal year; e.g., all revenue and expense accounts.

TIME SERIES FORECASTS

Forecasts made on the assumption that an underlying pattern is recurring over time.

TIME VALUE OF MONEY

The process of placing future years' income on an equal basis with current year expenditures in order to facilitate comparison.

TOLERANCE

An allowable variation between the standard and the actual.

TOTAL CAPITALIZATION

The sum of a hospitality operation's long-term debt and owners' equity.

TRANSACTION ANALYSIS

Process of analyzing a transaction into the appropriate accounts; entering debits and credits equally in the accounting record.

TRANSACTION MOTIVE

The rationale for maintaining adequate balances in checking accounts to meet checks drawn on those accounts.

TRANSIENT HOTELS

Lodging operations that cater primarily to business people; transient hotels tend to be busiest Monday through Thursday.

TREASURY STOCK

Capital stock of a corporation that the corporation has repurchased for future issuance.

TREND

A pattern of data (e.g., sales activity) characterized by a general direction whose long-run estimate is projected into the future.

TRIAL BALANCE

Listing and totaling of all the general ledger accounts on a worksheet.

TRIPLE NET LEASE

A form of lease agreement in which the lessee is obligated to pay property taxes, insurance, and maintenance on the leased property.

U

UNDISTRIBUTED OPERATING EXPENSES

Expenses not directly related to income generating departments and consisting of administrative and general expenses, data processing, human resources, transportation, marketing, property operation and maintenance, and energy expenses.

UNIFORM SYSTEM OF ACCOUNTS

Standardized accounting systems prepared by various segments of the hospitality industry offering detailed information about accounts, classifications, formats, the different kinds, contents, and uses of financial statements and reports, and other useful information.

V

VARIABLE COSTS

Costs which change proportionately with sales volume.

VARIABLE LEASE

A form of leasing agreement in which rental payments are based upon revenues.

VARIANCE ANALYSIS

Process of identifying and investigating causes of significant differences (variances) between budgeted plans and actual results.

VENDOR

A firm that sells wholesale merchandise (See Purveyor).

VERTICAL ANALYSIS

Analyzing individual financial statements reducing financial information to percents by having total assets equal 100% while individual asset categories equal percentages of the 100% and by having total liabilities and owners' equity equal 100% while individual categories of liabilities equal percentages of the 100%.

VOUCHER

Document used for posting a transaction to a guest account.

W

WEIGHTED AVERAGE METHOD OF INVENTORY VALUATION

Total cost of a particular commodity available for sale divided by the total number of units of that commodity, resulting in the unit cost to be charged against revenue earned by sale of that commodity.

WORKING CAPITAL

Current assets minus current liabilities.

WORKSHEET

Working paper used as a preliminary to the preparation of financial statements.

Z

ZERO-BASE BUDGETING

An approach to preparing budgets that requires the justification of all expenses; this approach assumes that each department starts with zero dollars and must justify all budgeted amounts.

The Educational Institute Board of Trustees

The Educational Institute of the American Hotel & Motel Association is fortunate to have both industry and academic leaders, as well as allied members, on its Board of Trustees. Individually and collectively, the following persons play leading roles in supporting the Institute and determining the direction of its programs.

Stevenson W. Fletcher, III, CHA
Department Head/Professor
Hotel, Restaurant & Travel
 Administration
University of Massachusetts
Amherst, Massachusetts

Tom F. Herring, Sr., CHA
President
The Herring Group
Laredo, Texas

Douglass Fontaine, CHA
President & General Manager
La Font Inn
Pascagoula, Mississippi

Creighton Holden, CHA
President
American Leisure Industries,
 Hotel Division
Columbia, South Carolina

Paul R. Handlery, CHA
President
Handlery Hotels, Inc.
San Francisco, California

Howard P. "Bud" James, CHA
Chairman
Global Hospitality Corporation
San Diego, California

Robert C. Hazard, Jr., CHA
President & Chief Executive Officer
Quality Inns International, Inc.
Silver Spring, Maryland

Anthony G. Marshall, CHA, Dean
School of Hospitality Management
Florida International University
Tamiami Campus
Miami, Florida

Kai W. Herbranson, CHA
Senior Vice President, Operations
Renaissance Division of
 Ramada Inc.
Phoenix, Arizona

R. Scott Morrison, CHA
President
Hospitality Division
 of Arvida/Disney Corporation
Boca Raton, Florida

John Norlander, CHA
President
Radisson Hotel Corporation
Minneapolis, Minnesota

Jack J. Vaughn, CHÁ
President
Opryland Hotel
Nashville, Tennessee

Kenneth E. Scripsma, CHA
Coordinator, Hotel Management
 Program
Orange Coast College
Costa Mesa, California

Robert V. Walker, CHA
President
Continental Hospitality
 Advisors, Inc.
Palm Springs, California

Harold J. Serpe, CHA
President
Midway Hospitality Corporation
Brookfield, Wisconsin

Ferdinand Wieland, CHA
General Manager
Hotel du Pont
Wilmington, Delaware

Peter E. Van Kleek, CHA
Dean, School of Hotel/
 Restaurant Management
Northern Arizona University
Flagstaff, Arizona

Index